AFRICANA PHILOSOPHY FROM ANCIENT EGYPT TO THE NINETEENTH CENTURY

PETER ADAMSON AND
CHIKE JEFFERS

AFRICANA PHILOSOPHY FROM ANCIENT EGYPT TO THE NINETEENTH CENTURY

A History of Philosophy Without Any Gaps

VOLUME 7

OXFORD
UNIVERSITY PRESS

OXFORD
UNIVERSITY PRESS

Great Clarendon Street, Oxford, OX2 6DP,
United Kingdom

Oxford University Press is a department of the University of Oxford.
It furthers the University's objective of excellence in research, scholarship,
and education by publishing worldwide. Oxford is a registered trade mark of
Oxford University Press in the UK and in certain other countries

© Peter Adamson and Chike Jeffers 2025

The moral rights of the authors have been asserted

All rights reserved. No part of this publication may be reproduced, stored in a retrieval system, transmitted, used for text and data mining, or used for training artificial intelligence, in any form or by any means, without the prior permission in writing of Oxford University Press, or as expressly permitted by law, by licence or under terms agreed with the appropriate reprographics rights organization. Enquiries concerning reproduction outside the scope of the above should be sent to the Rights Department, Oxford University Press, at the address above.

You must not circulate this work in any other form
and you must impose this same condition on any acquirer

Published in the United States of America by Oxford University Press
198 Madison Avenue, New York, NY 10016, United States of America

British Library Cataloguing in Publication Data
Data available

Library of Congress Control Number: 2024947899

ISBN 9780198927174

DOI: 10.1093/oso/9780198927174.001.0001

Printed and bound in the UK by
Clays Ltd, Elcograf S.p.A.

Links to third party websites are provided by Oxford in good faith and
for information only. Oxford disclaims any responsibility for the materials
contained in any third party website referenced in this work.

The manufacturer's authorised representative in the EU for product safety is
Oxford University Press España S.A. of El Parque Empresarial San Fernando de Henares,
Avenida de Castilla, 2 – 28830 Madrid (www.oup.es/en or product.safety@oup.com).
OUP España S.A. also acts as importer into Spain of products made by the manufacturer.

CONTENTS

Preface ix
Acknowledgments xiii
Dates xv
Map xxii
List of African Peoples Mentioned xxiii

PART I
LOCATING AND DEBATING PRECOLONIAL AFRICAN PHILOSOPHY

1. Something Old, Something New: Introducing Africana Philosophy — 3
2. It's Only Human: Philosophy in Prehistoric Africa — 10
3. Fertile Ground: Philosophy in Ancient Mesopotamia — 16
4. Pyramid Schemes: Philosophy in Ancient Egypt — 24
5. Father Knows Best: Moral and Political Philosophy in the Instructions — 30
6. Heated Exchanges: Philosophy in Egyptian Narratives and Dialogues — 38
7. Solomon, Socrates, and Other Sages: Early Ethiopian Philosophy — 46
8. Only One Truth: Zera Yacob — 56
9. Think for Yourself: Walda Heywat — 63
10. From Here to Timbuktu: Sub-Saharan Islamic Philosophy — 70
11. Renewing the Faith: The Sokoto Caliphate — 78
12. Heard it Through the Grapevine: Oral Philosophy in Africa — 86
13. Event Horizon: African Philosophy of Time — 93
14. One to Rule Them All: God in African Philosophy — 100
15. Behind the Mask: African Philosophy of the Person — 107

16. I Am Because We Are: Communalism in African Ethics and Politics	113
17. The Doctor Will See You Now: Divination, Witchcraft, and Knowledge	120
18. Women Have No Tribe: Gender in African Tradition	127
19. Professionally Speaking: The Reaction Against Ethnophilosophy	135
20. Wise Guys: Sage Philosophy	143
21. Beyond the Reaction: The Continuing Relevance of Precolonial Traditions	150

PART II
SLAVERY AND THE CREATION OF DIASPORIC AFRICANA PHILOSOPHY

22. Out of Africa: Slavery and the Diaspora	161
23. Dualist Personality: Anton Wilhelm Amo	170
24. Talking Book: Early Africana Writing in English	179
25. Young, Gifted, and Black: Phillis Wheatley	188
26. New England Patriot: Lemuel Haynes	196
27. Letters from the Heart: Ignatius Sancho and Benjamin Banneker	205
28. Sons of Africa: Quobna Ottobah Cugoano and Olaudah Equiano	215
29. Liberty, Equality, Humanity: The Haitian Revolution	225
30. My Haitian Pen: Baron de Vastey	233
31. American Africans: Early Black Institutions in the US	241
32. Should I Stay or Should I Go? The Colonization Controversy	249
33. Kill or Be Killed: David Walker's *Appeal*	257
34. Religion and Pure Principles: Maria W. Stewart	266
35. Unnatural Causes: Hosea Easton's *Treatise*	274
36. Written by Himself: The Life of Frederick Douglass	285
37. Happy Holidays: Two Speeches by Frederick Douglass	293

CONTENTS

38. Let Your Motto Be Resistance: Henry Highland Garnet	301
39. Nation Within a Nation: Martin Delany	310
40. I Read Men and Nations: Sojourner Truth and Frances Harper	318
41. Great White North: Emigration to Canada	327
42. Pilgrim's Progress: Alexander Crummell	336
43. Planting the Seeds: James Africanus Beale Horton	344
44. African Personality: Edward Blyden	351
45. Race First, Then Party: T. Thomas Fortune	360
46. A Common Circle: Anténor Firmin	368
47. Frowning at Froudacious Fabrications: J.J. Thomas and F.A. Durham	376
48. Though Late, It Is Liberty: Abolitionism in Brazil	385
49. When and Where I Enter: Anna Julia Cooper	393
50. American Barbarism: Ida B. Wells	401
51. God is a Negro: Henry McNeal Turner	408
52. Separate Fingers, One Hand: Booker T. Washington	416
53. Lifting the Veil: Introducing W.E.B. Du Bois	424
Notes	435
Further Reading	479
Index	493

PREFACE

In many cultures, philosophers and those known for their wisdom have been thought to possess special forms of insight, able, for example, to see into the future. Not something we ourselves believe, even if we will argue for taking beliefs of this type seriously (Chapter 17). Yet it does give us pause to notice that, on April 14, 2013, Chike left a startlingly prescient comment on the website of the History of Philosophy podcast, on which this book series is based. As part of his effort to convince Peter to expand the series to cover philosophy in non-Western cultures, he pointed out that it might be an idea to team up with more knowledgeable co-authors. He even suggested the very co-authors who would, in fact, be lending their expertise in years to come: Jonardon Ganeri for philosophy in India and Karyn Lai for philosophy in China. Chike's foresight is not infallible, though. At the time, he did not so much as suspect that he would wind up being a co-author himself, and for two books' worth of material on Africana philosophy.

That is, in fact, the first thing you need to know about the present volume. It is only the first half of our attempt to tell the story of philosophy in Africa and the African diaspora. Our aim is that, once the second volume is finished, the result will be an unprecedentedly detailed portrayal of the topic. As the further reading suggested at the end of this book shows, we are far from being the first to offer an introduction to these areas of study. But what follows will tackle as never before the full range of themes, figures, and controversies that one can place under the heading of "Africana philosophy." This is in keeping with the "without any gaps" slogan of the series, as is our broad methodological approach. That approach is explained in detail in the opening chapter. For now, we can anticipate the capacious definition given there of Africana philosophy as "any philosophical tradition that is recognizable as somehow special to the continent of Africa or to the African diaspora." It's a definition that takes in everything from ideas about personhood among the Akan to the Baron de Vastey's attack on the slavemasters of Haiti; from the ideas that drove the *jihādīs* of the Sokoto Caliphate to black feminism in the 1970s; from the political and religious reforms of Akhenaten in ancient Egypt to the ideas behind the jazz stylings of Sun Ra (ok, maybe that last one isn't such a big jump).

The breadth of the project may give rise to a worry that our definition is in fact *too* capacious, that we are telling not a single story but many unrelated ones. Here we would say two things. First, as will be clear at many points in the second part of this book, Africana thinkers from the eighteenth century onwards have themselves looked back to ancient Egypt and other African cultures of the past as intellectual points of origin, viewing them as intimately connected to their own projects. The many early African American intellectuals who belonged to the Masonic order, for example, loved to praise the Egyptians as proof of African genius. Figures of the diaspora who went "back" to Africa, like Alexander Crummell and Edward Blyden, were deeply concerned with the nature and value of indigenous African cultures and also with Islam in Africa (with Crummell and Blyden eventually reaching contrasting conclusions on these matters). So, while it would certainly be possible to write a book only about precolonial African philosophy, or only about the first generations of diasporic thinkers, there is a clear benefit to be had from combining them in a single volume. When we come to tell the story of twentieth century Africana thought in the sequel volume, the connections back to these earlier periods will establish even more strongly the interconnection of the various themes and figures that we have chosen to discuss.

Second, we want to warn against a mistake that, in our experience, tends to be made by those skeptical of the idea of Africana philosophy. This is the mistake of supposing that there is just one, correct way to organize the history of philosophy. Thus one might argue, say, that Frederick Douglass is a major figure of American philosophy and should not be shifted over to something called "Africana philosophy"; or that Anton Wilhelm Amo is a figure of Enlightenment Europe and should be treated within that context; or that the ideas that drove the Haitian Revolution echo those that drove the French Revolution, so the two events should be analyzed alongside each other. Indeed, our imaginary objector might say, apart from philosophy in African oral traditions (which raises numerous methodological challenges, as we'll be explaining in the first part of this book), there is no "distinctively Africana" philosophy that could not be classified just as well under some other heading of the history of philosophy.

Our response to this is straightforward. It is indeed a practical necessity—even for those not trying to write a book series like this one—to break up the history of philosophy into some kind of parts, which might be conceptual ("idealism"), geographical ("philosophy in the Americas"), chronological ("medieval philosophy"), cultural ("Confucianism"), or national ("British philosophy"). But there is no reason to suppose that a given text, author, or tradition can belong to only one of these. Just as Hume was a "British philosopher" and an "empiricist," so Frederick Douglass was an American philosopher and an Africana philosopher—and much else besides! Likewise, it would have been perfectly legitimate to cover Ethopian philosophy as part of the story of Christianity in the Near East. Aḥmad Bābā and the Sokoto Caliphate could have been included in the already-published volume of this series on philosophy in the Islamic world. In this very volume, we seek to illuminate ancient Egyptian philosophical literature by presenting it alongside comparable texts from ancient Mesopotamia, which obviously means stepping briefly outside the story of Africana philosophy. Different taxonomies do not need to compete, but may be mutually illuminating.

This is not to say, though, that just any way of dividing intellectual history is equally legitimate. It would be silly to write a whole book about philosophers whose names began with D ("From Democritus to Douglass") or about left-handed philosophers. But Africana philosophy is not like this. It is certainly a sprawling and complex topic, which embraces many sub-topics, but it has sufficient continuity and interconnection between those sub-topics to be the fitting subject for a book. Or in this case, two books. We've already hinted at the reasons for this, but if you are not yet convinced, then we would ask you to do two things: keep an open mind, and keep reading.

ACKNOWLEDGMENTS

This book has benefited from support from many quarters. We'd first like to thank those who were involved with the production of the podcast episodes for the series on Africana philosophy, namely our website designer Julian Rimmer and audio engineer Jim Black. Many experts in the area of Africana philosophy gave us valuable advice and/or kindly agreed to be interviewed on topics up to the end of the nineteenth century; we strongly suggest listening to these interviews as a supplement to the book (go to www.historyofphilosophy.net). They included Britney Cooper, Souleymane Bachir Diagne, Doris Garraway, Samuel Imbo, Teodros Kiros, Kai Kresse, Wilson Moses, Nkiru Nzegwu, Richard Parkinson, Melvin Rogers, James Sidbury, and Justin Smith. We're also grateful for the feedback of Darla Mitchell, Peter Momtchiloff, Adeshina Afolayan, and two anonymous referees on an earlier version of the book manuscript. We must thank Jonathan Egid for his work on the book's index. Above all, of course, we would like to thank our loved ones for their support as we worked on this challenging and time-consuming project!

DATES

		Making of artefacts at Blombos Cave	75000 BC
Imhotep	ca. 27th cent. BC	Early Dynastic period in Egypt	3000–2675 BC
Hardjedef	ca. 26th cent. BC	Old Kingdom in Egypt	2675–2130 BC
Pyramid Texts	ca. 24th–22nd cent. BC		
Nefer-Seshem-Re	ca. 24th cent. BC		
Ptahhotep	ca. 24th cent. BC		
Instruction Addressed to King Merikare	ca. 22nd–21st cent. BC	First Intermediate Period in Egypt	2130–1980 BC
Dispute Between a Man and His Ba	ca. 20th cent. BC		
Tale of the Eloquent Peasant	ca. 19th cent. BC	Middle Kingdom in Egypt	1980–1630 BC
		Egyptian invasion of Nubia (Kush)	1915 BC
Book of the Dead	ca. 17th–7th cent. BC	Reign of Hammurabi in Babylonia	1792–1750 BC
Instruction of Any	ca. 16th cent. BC	Second Intermediate Period in Egypt	1630–1539 BC
		Sack of Babylon by the Hittites	1595 BC
		New Kingdom in Egypt	1539–1075 BC
Akhenaten	d. ca. 1336 BC	Reign of Tutankhamun	1332–1322 BC
Instruction of Amenemope	ca. 13th–11th cent. BC	Third Intermediate Period in Egypt	1075–656 BC
Gilgamesh	8th cent. BC	Late Period in Egypt	664–332 BC
		Babylon conquered by the Persians	539 BC
		Egypt conquered by the Persians	525 BC

		Reign of Persian king Xerxes, destroyer of Babylon	486–465 BC
		Ptolemaic Egypt	305–30 BC
		Rome conquers Carthage	146 BC
		Reign of Cleopatra in Egypt	47–30 BC
Physiologus (Ethiopian version)	ca. 5th cent.	Peak of ancient Aksum	3rd–6th cent. AD
		Conversion of King Ezana of Aksum to Christianity	ca. 330
		Muslim calendar begins with the *hijra* (migration to Medina)	622
		Nubia converts to Christianity	6th cent.
		Muslim conquest of north Africa	7th cent.
		Muslim trading posts established on east African coast	7th–10th cent.
		Muslim rule in Gao on Niger River, present-day Mali	10th cent.
		Rise of Kingdom of Benin	11th cent.
		Rise of Wolof empire in west Africa	ca. 1200
Kebra Negast	completed by 1321	Mali Empire achieves dominance over Ghana empire	13th cent.
Giyorgis of Segla	d. 1425		
		Rise of the Ife empire, present-day Nigeria and Benin	13th cent.

DATES

		Overthrow of Zagwe dynasty in Ethiopia, beginning Solomonic dynasty (which rules until 1974)	1270
Zera Yacob (the Emperor)	1399–1468	Founding of kingdom of Kongo, present-day Angola	1390
Enbaqom	ca. 1470–ca. 1561		
ʿAbd al-Karīm al-Maghīlī	d. 1504	Beginning of Portuguese slave trade	15th cent.
		Reign of emperor Zera Yacob in Ethiopia	1434–68
		Portuguese traders arrive in present-day Ghana	1471
Jalāl al-Dīn al-Suyūṭī	d. ca. 1505	Askia dynasty of Songhai empire, present-day Mali	1493–1591
		Spanish colonies established in Cuba and Hispaniola	ca. 1500
		Invasion of Ethiopia by Islamic forces	1531–43
Book of the Wise Philosophers (Ethiopian)	ca. early 16th cent.	Conversion to Catholicism of Ethiopian emperor Susenyos	1624
Life and Maxims of Secundus (Ethiopian)	ca. early 16th cent.	Founding of the Dutch Cape Colony in south Africa	1652
Juan Latino	ca. 1516–ca. 1597		
Aḥmad Bābā	1556–1627	British capture Jamaica from Spanish	1655
Walatta Petros	1592–1642		
Zera Yacob (the philosopher)	1599–1692		
Muḥammad al-Wālī al-Mālikī	fl. 1688		

Walda Heywat	fl. ca. late 17th cent.–early 18th cent.	Beginning of Asante empire, present-day Ghana	1701
Anton Wilhelm Amo	1703–58	American Revolutionary War	1775–83
James Albert Ukawsaw Gronniosaw	ca. 1710–1775	Peak of the transatlantic slave trade	1780s
Jupiter Hammon	1711–ca. 1806	Haitian Revolution	1791–1804
Jacobus Capitein	ca. 1717–1747		
Ignatius Sancho	ca. 1729–1780		
Benjamin Banneker	1731–1806		
Prince Hall	ca. 1735–1807		
Toussaint Louverture	ca. 1743–1803		
Olaudah Equiano	1745–97	Trinidad captured by British	1797
Absalom Jones	1746–1818		
Shaykh 'Abd Allāh	d. 1829	British abolish slave trade	1807
Lemuel Haynes	1753–1833		
'Uthmān Dan Fodio	1754–1817	Founding of the Sokoto Caliphate	1812
Phillis Wheatley	ca. 1754–1784		
John Marrant	1755–91	Founding of the American Colonization Society	1816
Quobna Ottobah Cugoano	1757–ca. 1791		
Jean-Jacques Dessalines	ca. 1758–1806		
Paul Cuffe	1759–1817	Reign of Shaka Zulu, founder of the Zulu empire	1816–28
Richard Allen	1760–1831		
Thomas Clarkson	1760–1846	Spanish ban on the slave trade	1820
James Forten	1766–1842	Colony of Liberia founded	1821
Daniel Coker	1780–1846		
Peter Williams Jr	ca. 1780–1840	Abolition of slavery in British colonies	1834
Muhammad Bello	1781–1837		
Baron de Vastey	1781–1820	Liberia achieves independence	1847
Jarena Lee	1783–1864		

DATES

Nana Asma'u	1793–1837
Samuel Cornish	1795–1858
David Walker	1796–1830
Sojourner Truth	1797–1883
Hosea Easton	1798–1837
John Russwurm	1799–1851
Maria Stewart	1803–79
William Whipper	1804–76
William Lloyd Garrison	1805–79
Martin Delany	1812–85
James McCune Smith	1813–65
Henry Highland Garnet	1815–81
Samuel Ringgold Ward	1817–66
Frederick Douglass	1818–95
Alexander Crummell	1819–98
Mary Ann Shadd	1823–93
Frances Ellen Watkins Harper	1825–1911
James Theodore Holly	1829–1911
Luiz Gama	1830–82
Demesvar Delorme	1831–1901
Edward Blyden	1832–1912
Henry McNeal Turner	1834–1915
James Africanus Beale Horton	1835–83
Machado de Assis	1839–1908
John Jacob Thomas	1841–89
Richard Theodore Greener	1844–1922

Brazil outlaws importing of slaves	1850
Fugitive Slave Law in US	1850
Peak of emigration of slave fugitives to Canada	1850s
US Civil War	1861–5
Emancipation Proclamation in US	1863
Gold Coast declared a British colony	1874
End of Reconstruction in the US	1877
Gold rush in the Transvaal in southern Africa	1880s
British protectorate proclaimed over Somaliland	1887
Emancipation of slaves in Brazil	1888

Joaquim Nabuco	1849–1910
Antenor Firmin	1850–1911
Fannie Barrier Williams	1855–1944
Louis-Joseph Janvier	1855–1911
Booker T. Washington	1856–1915
T. Thomas Fortune	1856–1928
Anna Julia Cooper	1858–1964
Ida B. Wells	1862–1931
Raul Pompeia	1863–95
Mary Church Terrell	1863–1954
W.E.B. Du Bois	1868–1963

MAP

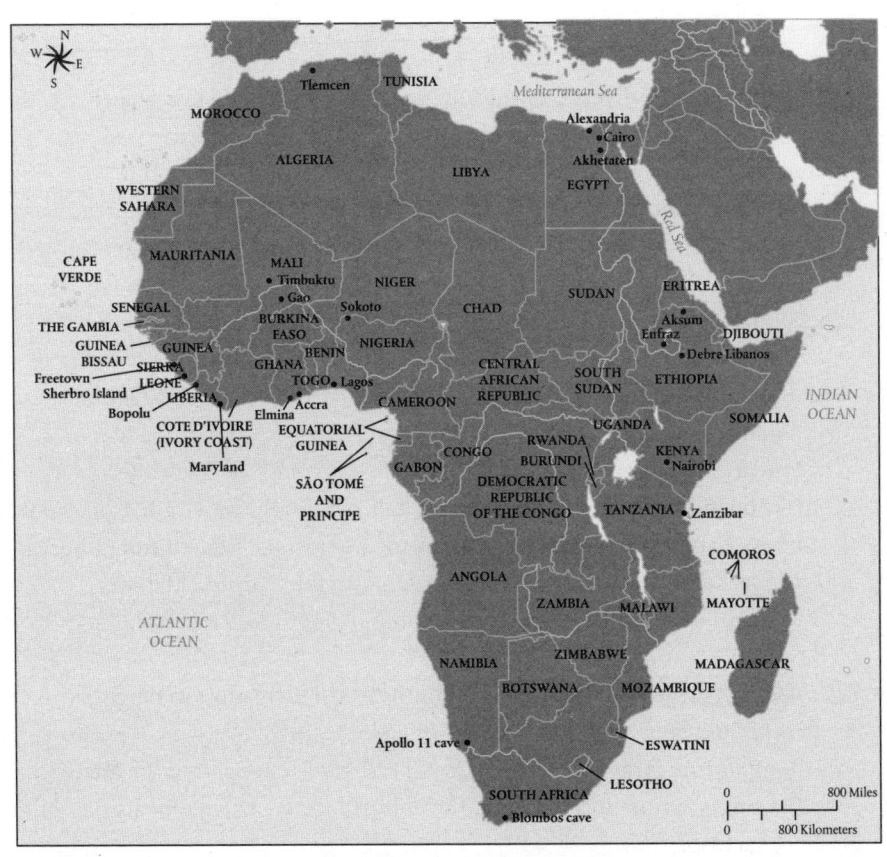

Modern Africa

LIST OF AFRICAN PEOPLES MENTIONED

Africa is famously diverse, ethnically and linguistically. Below is a list of the various peoples (taking "peoples" to mean, roughly, speakers of either a common language or a related group of languages) that we mention in this book, with an indication of where in Africa they are located. The numbers in parentheses are the chapters of the book in which mentions of the people can be found.

- The **Akan** (preface, 13, 14, 15, 16, 17, 18, 20, 21, 23, 32, 43) are located in southern Ghana and southeastern Côte d'Ivoire.
- The **Akwapim** (21) are located in southern Ghana. They are part of the **Akan**.
- The **Ashanti** (16) are located in southern Ghana. They are part of the **Akan**.
- The **Bantu** (12, 13, 19, 20, 21, 42) are located in many countries that collectively make up most of the continent's lower half, including Cameroon, Equatorial Guinea, Gabon, the Republic of Congo, the Democratic Republic of Congo, Uganda, Kenya, Rwanda, Burundi, Tanzania, Angola, Zambia, Malawi, Namibia, Botswana, Zimbabwe, Mozambique, South Africa, Lesotho, and Eswatini.
- The **Bassari** (14) are located mainly in southeastern Senegal and a neighboring part of Guinea.
- The **Beng** (14) are located in eastern Côte d'Ivoire. They are part of the **Mande**.
- The **Dogon** (15, 20) are located in south-central Mali and a neighboring part of Burkina Faso.
- The **Ewe** (43) are located in southeastern Ghana, southern Togo, and southwestern Benin.
- The **Fon** (29) are located in southern Benin and neighboring parts of Togo and Nigeria.
- The **Fulani** (10) are located in many countries across West Africa and stretching into Central Africa, including Mauritania, Senegal, The Gambia, Guinea-Bissau, Guinea, Mali, Sierra Leone, Côte d'Ivoire, Burkina Faso, Ghana, Togo, Benin, Niger, Nigeria, Chad, Cameroon, and the Central African Republic, with a portion as far as eastern Sudan.

LIST OF AFRICAN PEOPLES MENTIONED

The **Ga-Dangme** (13, 15, 43) are located in southern Ghana and a neighboring part of Togo.

The **Gikuyu** (13, 14, 20) are located in central Kenya. They are part of the **Bantu**.

The **Habesha** (7) are located in northern Ethiopia and Eritrea.

The **Hausa** (11) are located in northern Nigeria and southern Niger, along with populations in a number of other West and Central African countries, such as Ghana and Cameroon.

The **Igbo** (15, 18, 20, 28, 43) are located in southeastern Nigeria.

The **Ila** (14) are located in southern Zambia. They are part of the **Bantu**.

The **Kaguru** (13, 14) are located in east-central Tanzania. They are part of the **Bantu**.

The **Kamba** (13, 14) are located in south-central Kenya. They are part of the **Bantu**.

The **Kiga** (13) are located in southwestern Uganda and northern Rwanda. They are part of the **Bantu**.

The **Kongo** (29) are located in the south of the Republic of the Congo, the west of the Democratic Republic of the Congo, and northern Angola. They are part of the **Bantu**.

The **Luba** (12, 16) are located in the south of the Democratic Republic of the Congo. They are part of the **Bantu**.

The **Lugbara** (14, 17) are located in northwestern Uganda and neighboring parts of the Democratic Republic of the Congo and South Sudan.

The **Luo** (20) are located in South Sudan, western Ethiopia, the northeast of the Democratic Republic of the Congo, northern Uganda, western Kenya, and northern Tanzania. At times, the term "Luo" is used to refer more narrowly to the subgroup in western Kenya and northern Tanzania, also known as the Joluo.

The **Maasai** (14, 17) are located in southern Kenya and northern Tanzania.

The **Malagasy** (17) are located in Madagascar.

The **Mande** (10) are located in many countries in West Africa, including Mauritania, Senegal, The Gambia, Mali, Guinea-Bissau, Guinea, Sierra Leone, Liberia, Côte d'Ivoire, Burkina Faso, Ghana, Benin, and Nigeria.

The **Mandinka** (44) are located in The Gambia, southern Senegal, eastern Guinea-Bissau, eastern Guinea, southern Mali, and northwestern Côte d'Ivoire, with further portions in Sierra Leone and Liberia. They are part of the **Mande**.

The **Manjak** (17) are located in western Guinea-Bissau and neighboring parts of Senegal and The Gambia.

LIST OF AFRICAN PEOPLES MENTIONED

The **Mbugwe** (17) are located in north-central Tanzania. They are part of the **Bantu**.

The **Ndau** (15) are located in central Mozambique and a neighboring part of Zimbabwe. They are part of the **Bantu** and sometimes taken to be specifically part of the **Shona**.

The **Ndembu** (17) are located in northwestern Zambia. They are part of the **Bantu**.

The **Nuer** (13, 14) are located in northeastern South Sudan and western Ethiopia.

The **Nupe** (14, 15) are located in west-central Nigeria.

The **Nyole** (17) are located in eastern Uganda. They are part of the **Bantu**.

The **Nzema** (23) are located in southwestern Ghana and a neighboring part of Côte d'Ivoire. They are part of the **Akan**.

The **Ohafia** (18) are located in southeastern Nigeria. They are part of the **Igbo**.

The **Rwandan** people (12) are located in Rwanda and neighboring parts of Burundi, Uganda, and the Democratic Republic of the Congo. They are part of the **Bantu**.

The **San** (2, 18) are located in Botswana, Namibia, South Africa, Angola, and Zimbabwe.

The **Shilluk** (14) are located in northeastern South Sudan. They are part of the **Luo**.

The **Shona** (18) are located in Zimbabwe and some neighboring parts of Mozambique and Zambia. They are part of the **Bantu**.

The **Sisala** (15) are located in northwestern Ghana and a neighboring part of Burkina Faso.

The **Songhay** (10) are located in Mali and Niger, along with portions in Benin, Burkina Faso, Nigeria, Ghana, and Algeria.

The **Swahili** (10, 13, 17) are located along the East African coast, particularly in Kenya, Tanzania, and northern Mozambique, as well as in the Comoros. They are part of the **Bantu** and their language is famously a lingua franca for much of East and Central Africa.

The **Tiv** (13) are located in east-central Nigeria and a neighboring part of Cameroon.

The **Tswana** (18) are located in Botswana, northern South Africa, and a neighboring part of Zimbabwe. They are part of the **Bantu**.

The **Twa** (14) are located in various parts of the Democratic Republic of the Congo, Burundi, Rwanda, and Uganda, among other countries. Unlike most peoples on this list, they are not linguistically unified and speak **Bantu** languages associated with surrounding peoples.

LIST OF AFRICAN PEOPLES MENTIONED

The **Vai** (42) are located in northwestern Liberia and a neighboring part of Sierra Leone. They are part of the **Mande**.

The **Wolof** (43) are located in northwestern Senegal, The Gambia, and southwestern Mauritania.

The **Yaka** (17) are located in the southwest of the Democratic Republic of the Congo and a neighboring part of Angola. They are part of the **Bantu**.

The **Yoruba** (14, 15, 17, 18, 20, 21, 38, 39, 42, 43, 48) are located in southwestern Nigeria, southern Benin, and east-central Togo.

The **Xhosa** (14) are located in southeastern South Africa. They are part of the **Bantu**.

The **Zulu** (12, 16, 25) are located in eastern South Africa. They are part of the **Bantu**.

PART I

LOCATING AND DEBATING PRECOLONIAL AFRICAN PHILOSOPHY

1

SOMETHING OLD, SOMETHING NEW

Introducing Africana Philosophy

Philosophy, in the minds of many people, is something essentially European, but this book series has already revealed that to be a distorted perspective. While it initially set out to tell a continuous story beginning in ancient Greece with the Presocratics and going forward from there, this has already led to the topic of philosophy in the Islamic world. It is true that a whole section of the volume devoted to that topic covered developments in Muslim Andalusia, and Spain and Portugal are indeed part of Europe. For the most part, though, the thinkers of the Islamic world lived well outside of Europe. Several, including the most influential of all Muslim thinkers, Avicenna, hailed from central Asia. With the volume on classical Indian philosophy, the series introduced a philosophical tradition that did not have its origins in ancient Greece. Whatever we decide to believe about the mutual interaction of ancient Indian and classical Greek thought, it's clear that ideas from Greece were not the main spur to philosophical reflection in India.

It is nowadays more or less uncontroversial to speak of "philosophy" in India, and the same goes for China. "Eastern philosophy" is something most of us have at least heard of, if not studied. But what about *African* philosophy? For many people, the phrase will conjure little more than a big blank spot. Some will immediately doubt that there is any such thing, suspecting it to be a case where the word "philosophy" is being applied far too liberally (in every sense of the word). Others may be perfectly willing to grant that there is surely African philosophy too, but unable to name anything that might fit the bill. Even if you have no idea what Confucius or the Bhagavad Gita say, you're likely to have at least heard of them, just as someone may have heard of Plato without being able to name a single dialogue. But who are the familiar figures of African philosophy? What are the major texts? Are we even talking about a tradition in which there *are* known figures and texts?

In this volume, we hope to remove some of the mystery. It is devoted to philosophy in Africa as well as in the African diaspora. That last part is important. This book will introduce you not simply to African philosophy, but to what is known among specialists in the field as *Africana philosophy*. Our topic is, on the one hand, very new and, on the other hand, very, very old. It is new in the sense that the term "Africana philosophy" has only been in common use since the 1990s. The philosopher Lucius Outlaw is generally credited with coining the term.[1] We should also mention another philosopher, Lewis Gordon, who has played a major role in popularizing it.[2] Yet, long before it had a name, there was already Africana philosophy. Indeed, it is arguably the oldest philosophical tradition of them all. As we will discuss in the next chapter, if Africa is where we became what we would now recognize as humans, there is good reason to think that Africa is where we first did philosophy.

Philosophy in Africa, though, is only one component of Africana philosophy. It is an umbrella term that includes African philosophy, Afro-Caribbean philosophy, African American philosophy, African Canadian philosophy, and so on. (Chike, by the way, is from Canada, which means that, while he is passionate in spreading the word about Africana philosophy, he does it very politely.[3]) In other words, the study of Africana philosophy deals with ideas from the African diaspora as well as Africa itself.[4] Perhaps we're explaining the obscure by the obscure here, though, and should say what we mean by "diaspora." It's a word of Greek origin meaning "dispersion," and it was first used in relation to the Jewish people who left Israel. It has since acquired a broader meaning, and refers to the scattering of any people beyond their traditional homeland, with its application to Africans being perhaps the most prominent example. The transatlantic slave trade, which brought Africans to the Americas in large numbers from the sixteenth to the nineteenth centuries, is of course one of the most important instances of the dispersing and scattering of people in the modern world.

Given this broad agenda, Africana philosophy does after all include a number of familiar figures, some of whom are regularly featured in philosophy books that are not devoted specifically to Africana thought. Take Martin Luther King Jr. Some of the most popular introductory anthologies of social and political philosophy in the last few decades have included his "Letter from Birmingham Jail" and his March on Washington Address, also known as the "I Have a Dream" speech.[5] Such collections have therefore encouraged the inclusion of Africana thought in courses on social and political philosophy.

Even the broadest agenda, though, must leave some things out. So let's also say something about the material we will *not* be discussing. According to what we've said so far, "Africana philosophy" would include many thinkers that have already been dealt with in other books of this series, because they lived in Africa for all or part of their lives. Many appeared in the volume on the Islamic world, for instance the Jewish thinkers Saadia Gaon (who worked in Iraq but was born in Egypt) and Maimonides (who worked in Egypt but was born in Andalusia, and is thus also a European philosopher). Also dealt with there were various Muslim thinkers from northern Africa, like Ibn Khaldūn and Muḥammad 'Abduh. But here's something we easily forget: the Roman empire held substantial territory in northern Africa, and there were numerous ancient philosophers of that region. Plotinus was from Egypt, Augustine from Thagaste in modern-day Algeria. That in itself should be enough to satisfy anyone that the term "African philosophy" is not an empty term.

But there's much more to say. This volume will take our story up to the turn of the twentieth century, with a further volume to come on Africana philosophy in that century. We will begin by going all the way back to the Middle Stone Age, to explore the idea that Africa is the first place that anything we could call "philosophy" was ever done. After that, we will begin to look at the history of recorded philosophy in Africa, treating ancient Egypt as one of the two earliest birthplaces in the world of written philosophical thought (we'll also take a detour to consider the other birthplace, Mesopotamia). Then we'll move on to written philosophy in ancient, medieval, and early modern times in other areas of Africa, with a focus on Ethiopia and on Islamic philosophy in sub-Saharan Africa, something that was not covered in the earlier volume on philosophy in the Islamic world.

When focusing on Ethiopia and sub-Saharan Islam, we will be considering traditions of philosophical writing that can be traced back, at least partially, to ancient Greece. Indeed, to our knowledge there exists no currently accessible body of premodern philosophical writing from Africa after the time of ancient Egypt that is completely unconnected to the Greek tradition. As is well known, before the European colonization of Africa in the modern era, the majority of African cultures were oral cultures, that is to say, cultures without writing. Does that mean that the majority of African cultures in the premodern era were cultures without philosophy? This has been a topic of some debate, but we think there is much to be said for answering the question with a firm "no." We'll be devoting numerous chapters to the philosophical ideas that scholars of African philosophy have located in African oral traditions. Together with the treatment of written philosophy in Egypt, Ethiopia, and sub-Saharan Islamic Africa, our look at oral traditions will provide

INTRODUCING AFRICANA PHILOSOPHY

you with a useful and diverse introduction to philosophy in Africa before modern European colonization.

We have titled this first part of the book *Locating and Debating Precolonial African Philosophy*. It is worth pausing here to note that the Nigerian philosopher Olúfẹ́mi Táíwò has recently argued against using the term "precolonial" in the study of Africa.[6] He has pointed out that the term is not often used when telling the history of other continents, and suspects that the reason it is applied to Africa is because "it comes from a not-so-kind genealogy that always takes Africa to be a simple place." How could it be useful and respectful of the long and varied history of Africa's diverse peoples, he wonders, to treat everything from "the beginning of time to the moment when the European, modernity-inflected colonial phenomenon showed up" as a single historical period?

In light of this challenge, we would defend our use of the phrase "precolonial African philosophy" by pointing out that the phrase "African philosophy" itself only comes into existence in the wake of modern European colonization. This was not a meaningful categorization for most African thinkers before the modern era, as most of them had no consciousness of living in a place called "Africa." It is the training of Africans at universities in Europe that brought about the twentieth century phenomenon of African philosophers publishing books and articles about the existence and content of African philosophy. This is why the title of the first part of the present volume evokes the two tasks of locating and debating what existed in precolonial Africa. What developed in the twentieth century under the label of "African philosophy" was indeed a series of debates among self-described African philosophers about precolonial African traditions. A number of scholars sought to retrieve the philosophy that could be found by examining oral cultures in Africa.

In due course, a reaction sprang up against this. Some argued that African philosophy is something new, which Africans must create in the present without pretending that it can be extracted from ethnographic descriptions of traditional life. In the context of this debate, creative compromises were often proposed. For example, one might go beyond mere ethnographic description by interviewing wise people who live in relatively traditional communities; such people might be able to describe and also critically reflect upon their people's traditions. We will be looking in detail at the different positions in this debate, which has been important in the development of the notion of Africana philosophy, and also raises fascinating methodological issues about the nature of philosophy itself.

In the second part of the book, we will broaden our scope to include philosophy in the diaspora. This is not to say that we will have finished talking about philosophy on the African continent. Rather, we will look at how people in both Africa and the African diaspora thought philosophically in the modern era in the wake of the transformative events of slavery and colonialism. This will mean focusing on writings in European languages in the eighteenth and nineteenth centuries.

But let's return now to a question that we seem to have already answered: what is Africana philosophy? We've said that it is philosophy from the African continent and diaspora. That seems clear enough, or at least no more mysterious than the application of the term "philosophy" in a phrase like "Indian philosophy" or "philosophy in the Islamic world." But the definition may have some surprising results, as we can see by considering a celebrated work of philosophy from the late twentieth century that arguably fits the bill: *Mind and World*, by John McDowell, first published in 1994. It is a bold work on the metaphysics and epistemology of experience, according to which our passive experience of the world is not prior to and separate from conceptual thought, but is in itself conceptual. It's one of the most influential monographs in English-language philosophy of the last few decades, and its author was born, raised, and educated in Africa. McDowell was born in Boksburg, South Africa, and received his initial post-secondary education at what was then called the University College of Rhodesia and Nyasaland (known today as the University of Zimbabwe).

So is *Mind and World* a work of Africana philosophy? This is certainly not how people usually think of it. McDowell is a professor at the University of Pittsburgh and if we have to associate his work with any geographical space, it is natural to think of him as a representative of philosophy as it is practiced in the United States. Furthermore, to state the obvious, the fact that McDowell is a white man will make most people hesitant to apply the term "Africana philosophy" here. Indeed, the phrase is often understood to be more or less interchangeable with "philosophy done by black people." Still, it remains the case that, on the very broad understanding of Africana philosophy we sketched so far, *Mind and World* would count. So does this mean that we'll be covering McDowell when we get to the twentieth century, perhaps somewhere between Malcolm X and the black feminist epistemology of Patricia Hill Collins? The answer is no: in fact, *Mind and World* would not be part of our story even if McDowell were a black South African.

In order to count as Africana philosophy, at least for our purposes, the work in question must not only originate from Africa or from the African diaspora. It must, in some sense, be *distinctively Africana*. This may sound vague and even circular. But let us explain. One obvious way in which a philosophical work can be distinctively Africana is if it is concerned to a significant degree with the experiences, problems, and strivings of people in Africa or the African diaspora. A less obvious way was indicated by the Ghanaian philosopher Kwasi Wiredu. He responded at one point to another philosopher who credited him with having produced a fine example of African philosophy, in the shape of an article called "Kant's Synthetic A Priori in Geometry and the Rise of Non-Euclidean Geometries." Wiredu disagreed that his own article could currently be counted as a work of African philosophy, although he noted that he would be happy if it were to *eventually* count as such. But how could the article's categorization as African philosophy be a matter of hope for the future? Wiredu explained: "If an interest in the sort of problems in the philosophy of mathematics that I discussed in that article never develops in African thought, and no tradition emerges on our continent into which my article might naturally fit, then it would not be unjust to exclude it from African philosophy."[7] Notice the flipside of this statement: if many other Africans *do* take up philosophy of mathematics, and especially if they do so in a way that is shaped by the concerns and methods of his article, there will be no good objection to calling it "African philosophy."

The point here is that philosophical work on any topic can be called Africana philosophy, just so long as it is part of a tradition that is recognizable as somehow special to the continent or the diaspora. To label a work of philosophy "Africana philosophy" on these grounds is similar to speaking of British Empiricism, German Idealism, or French Poststructuralism. These European traditions are not distinguished by an explicit focus on the experiences, problems, and strivings of people in Britain, Germany, and France. But they are distinctive approaches to philosophical thought that became associated with those places, through the work of British, German, and French philosophers. Much of the material we will cover in this book will be distinctively Africana in something like this sense. We will be exploring philosophical traditions that can be described as either completely indigenous to Africa or, as in the cases of Ethiopian philosophy and sub-Saharan Islamic philosophy, as cases where people in Africa absorbed and domesticated philosophical thought from elsewhere.

None of this applies to McDowell's *Mind and World*; it is hard to see what justification there might be for describing it as part of a distinctively Africana philosophical tradition. Just like Wiredu's article on the philosophy of mathematics, it is partly structured around an interpretation of the thought of the German philosopher Immanuel Kant. Since Wiredu's article and McDowell's book are connected most clearly to European and Euro-American traditions of thought, it makes sense to classify them as such—or, if that might sound misleading given Wiredu's non-European heritage, then this might be a reason to use the vaguer term "Western philosophy." Of course, something could simultaneously be part of the tradition known as "Western philosophy" and part of Africana philosophy on our definition of the term. King's "Letter from Birmingham Jail" includes a number of references to Socrates as a model in whose footsteps King is attempting to follow. What could be more emblematic of the "Western" tradition than an American thinker modeling himself on Socrates? Yet King is at the same time an African American thinker, whose "Letter" takes up the question of how best to achieve freedom and equality for African Americans. So this is a work of Africana philosophy too. It's important to bear this in mind: to recognize a topic as belonging to Africana philosophy does not exclude the possibility that one could also approach it as part of other stories, like the story of Islamic philosophy, or American philosophy, or for that matter the history of nationalism, or idealism, or socialism. As we said in the preface to this book, there are many legitimate ways to divide up the history of philosophy, and what we are offering here is just one of them.

King's letter also contains a now iconic quotation of Augustine's dictum that "an unjust law is no law at all."[8] The name of Augustine returns us to the issue of thinkers in North Africa who were part of the Hellenistic and Roman worlds of late antiquity. Would they also count as contributing to Africana philosophy on our stricter definition? Would it make sense to see Augustine as part of an African tradition of thought? Since he and other such figures have already been covered in other volumes of this series, we can afford to stay neutral on this question. But we can also point you to someone who has not stayed neutral, the Kenyan philosopher D.A. Masolo. In an intriguing essay entitled "African Philosophers in the Greco-Roman Era," Masolo discusses Augustine, and also Origen and Tertullian, as Church Fathers whose African identities may be relevant to understanding their thought.[9] As this example shows, it is not always easy to decide what is covered by the phrase "Africana philosophy." One should proceed on a case-by-case basis, deciding whether a given author or text is usefully illuminated by applying the term. It seems quite clear that it illuminates little or nothing in McDowell's *Mind and World*, and a great deal in the case of King's letter. As for the works of St. Augustine, we leave it to you to investigate and decide.

2

IT'S ONLY HUMAN

Philosophy in Prehistoric Africa

Is philosophy like ballet, or is it more like dance? This is a question posed by the historian of philosophy Justin E.H. Smith.[1] The point is of course not that philosophy must involve wearing special shoes; after all, Socrates is famous for having gone barefoot. Rather, Smith wants to make us think about what philosophy is and what is involved in studying its history. If philosophy is like ballet, then it is a distinctive cultural tradition whose origin can be traced back to a specific time and place. Ballet was first invented in Italy during the Renaissance, and then developed into the art form we know today in France during the seventeenth century. Perhaps we can tell a similar story about the invention and development of philosophy. On the other hand, what if philosophy is better compared, not with a culturally unique form of dance like ballet, but rather with dance itself? Perhaps it too is a universal activity that is pursued by people of all cultures, varying immensely in its forms, its uses, and its accepted norms. If we take this idea seriously, and suppose that philosophy is truly *universal*, then we must conclude that it has existed whenever and wherever humans have existed. That's the hypothesis we'll be exploring in this chapter.

Of course, it's common to assume that philosophy is more like ballet. Just as we can trace ballet back to Renaissance Italy, we often trace philosophy back to ancient Greece. After all, the word *philosophia* is an ancient Greek one. This is why this book series started with the earliest philosophers who wrote in ancient Greek, namely the first Presocratics who lived on the coast of modern-day Turkey in the sixth century BC. But a further volume has already been devoted to ancient Indian philosophy, which arose independently of ancient Greece. To recognize the existence of ancient Indian philosophy already means denying that philosophy is like ballet. It does not yet imply, though, that philosophy is universal, like dance. Perhaps philosophy emerged twice, in India and in Greece, but only in those places.

PHILOSOPHY IN PREHISTORIC AFRICA

If we want to explore the hypothesis that philosophy is genuinely universal, we'll need to hazard a definition of philosophy broad enough to suit this hypothesis while not being so broad as to treat philosophy as simply interchangeable with thinking in general. We might say that people think philosophically when they raise and seek to answer fundamental questions about the nature of things, about how we know what it is possible to know, or about what we ought to value and how we ought to live our lives. A definition like this manages to capture the major traditional subdivisions of philosophy as an academic discipline, such as metaphysics, epistemology, and ethics. Yet it also captures a thought that has probably struck many a parent: philosophy must belong to the human condition, because even small children ask hard questions about what things are, what is good or bad, and how we know things. Indeed, parents sometimes wish their children could be philosophical a bit less often, and less insistently!

Even if we are reluctant to say that every human is a born "philosopher," we should still take seriously the idea that at least some curious individuals in all societies have raised and sought to answer such questions. If this is so, then historians of philosophy who want to tell the story of the birth and development of philosophy face a truly daunting task. How do we go about tracing the origins of philosophy if it can be found everywhere and has always been with us? No doubt a truly precise genealogy is impossible. But we can at least say this: if philosophy is indeed universal, then it began in Africa, because Africa is the birthplace of humankind. Indeed, not just its birthplace, but its first long-term home, where human ancestors diverging from our closest relatives among the great apes have been evolving for over 6 million years. The only species of humans that still exists, *Homo sapiens*, is thought to have developed in Africa less than half a million years ago.

But it's one thing to find remains of humans who are anatomically recognizable as being the same species as us, another to have evidence that early humans had developed the capacities for thought and language that are necessary for doing philosophy. The fossil and archeological evidence is widely thought to suggest that our species attained the physical characteristics that differentiate us from earlier species of human ancestors significantly earlier than we began to display our distinctive behavior. As it's sometimes put, "anatomical modernity" came long before "behavioral modernity."[2] And until recently (and here we mean really recently, like the last several decades), there was a widespread belief among paleoanthropologists—the people who study the evolutionary development of our species—that while the earliest human remains are found in Africa, it is Europe that boasts the earliest remains of human culture. The great shift would thus be witnessed not in the archeological remains of our African ancestors, but in European cave paintings.

It is beyond doubt that Africa is the place to look for the slow emergence of modern humanity in the anatomical sense. Volcanic ash in Tanzania preserves footprints that are the earliest marks of upright posture, the earliest remains of *Homo ergaster* (the African *Homo erectus*) have been found in Kenya, while Ethiopia is the source of remains showing that we achieved so-called "anatomical modernity" between two and three hundred thousand years ago. East Africa, especially in the Rift Valley, offered favorable conditions for both the emergence of these earliest humans and the preservation of their remains, though discoveries have also been made in West and North Africa.[3] One crucial development in the eventual attainment of behavioral modernity would have been the capacity for language, which required a shift in the anatomy of the larynx. This and other steps in the evolutionary process have been the subject of a good deal of speculation and guesswork. One intriguing thought is that emotional intimacy between the early humans may have been a significant driver in the process.[4]

The oldest artefacts we have are stone tools, such as hand axes. With the power of these tools, humans migrated out of Africa, possibly in successive waves. Speaking of waves, humans rather astonishingly managed to reach Australia by 60,000 years ago, which obviously would have required boat-building technology and fearless sea voyaging.[5] But somehow even these technologies are not consistently counted as "behavioral modernity." When and where do we reach that point? Well, a theory that reached the height of its popularity in the 1980s held that we did not become behaviorally modern until around 40,000 years ago, and that it happened in Europe. You may well have heard of the famous cave paintings in Lascaux in France, and at other sites across southern Europe. These date back to the era of European prehistory known as the Upper Paleolithic, between fifty and ten thousand years ago. The change in behavior in this period is so noticeable in the archeological record that it became known as "the Human Revolution."[6] This revolution was characterized by further technological advances, such as better stone tools, but it was also, as indicated by the renown of the cave paintings, a flowering of symbolic culture. The cave paintings are evidence of human handiwork aimed not simply at survival, but at the creation of decoration and representational art.

To this day, there are some who accept the idea of a human revolution occurring in Europe during the Upper Paleolithic. Excavations and interpretations of archeological evidence from Africa, however, have turned that idea into a minority view. One of the theories that has arisen to displace it holds that, when we pay attention to Africa, the idea of a human revolution simply loses any value. This is the position of Sally McBrearty, a paleoanthropologist at the University of Connecticut. She argues that much of the behavior once thought to be new in the Upper Paleolithic can be found much earlier in Africa, during the period of African prehistory known as the Middle Stone Age, which stretches on her account from around 285,000 to 40,000 years ago. There was, according to McBrearty, no revolution, just a series of gradual developments over a long period and in various places on the African continent.[7] She argues that the idea of a human revolution is a product of Eurocentrism, the privileging of Europe and its particular historical path over objective consideration of the history of Africa and other parts of the world.

If we do retain the notion of a Human Revolution, we might locate it in southern Africa rather than in southern France, and at a much earlier time than the transition to the Upper Paleolithic in Europe. On the coast of South Africa, at a site known as the Blombos Cave, archeologists have discovered remains including sea snail shells, pierced in a way that suggests they were used as beads for necklaces or bracelets, as well as pieces of engraved ochre, that is, blocks of earth, capable of producing colored powder, into which geometrical patterns were scratched. These materials seem to be around 77,000 years old, among the oldest finds of beads anywhere in the world. The beads, stained red by the ochre, indicate concern by those who wore them with how they look to others, which may have been a matter of communicating social status. The abstract engravings in similar patterns on different blocks indicate an understanding of the design itself as meaningful; combined with the beads, this suggests a possibly ritualistic purpose. It seems likely that grammatically complex language of the kind we associate with being human today accompanied and supported these symbolic functions. We can therefore hypothesize that, long before there was philosophy at Athens, Miletus, or other ancient Greek sites, there was philosophy at Blombos.

By the way, if you're unwilling to be impressed by beads and insist on waiting for cave art, Africa offers that too. The Apollo 11 cave, located in present-day Namibia, was excavated in 1969, the year of the space mission after which it is named.[8] It contains stone slabs with paintings of animals on them, executed more than 25,000 years ago. This makes them the oldest paintings yet found in Africa and some of the oldest artworks anywhere in the world (older, for instance, than the cave paintings at Lascaux). The same cave has geometrical paintings done on the walls and, nearby, images of animals are engraved into rock,[9] while the more famous slabs were transported to this rock shelter from elsewhere (hence they have been described with the French expression *art mobilier*, "portable art"). Other finds in the area show that prehistoric peoples lived here at least intermittently over many thousands of years, leaving their traces in the form of decorated eggshells and stone implements, like cutting blades.

The purpose and meaning of these geometrical and animal images, like prehistoric rock art found elsewhere around the world, have been a matter of considerable speculation.[10] One prominent interpretation has been put forward by J.D. Lewis-Williams. He carefully studied more recent rock art produced by the San people, hunter-gatherers of southern Africa, and tried to understand how the paintings might connect to the cultural practices of the San.[11] In particular, he proposes that these can be understood within the context of San shamanism, in which certain people receive a special religious revelation. These manifest as "altered states of consciousness," often involving a vision of an alternative reality populated by spirits. A straightforward inference could be that the rock art is a depiction of what such shamans have been seeing in their visions, and perhaps they have been seeing them for many millennia. Lewis-Williams points to neurological factors that could help to explain the commonalities between such ecstatic experience across space and time.

But he argues for a still more intimate connection between shamanism and the paintings than a mere recording of supernatural experiences. The paintings may actually have been part of the ritual. Lewis-Williams proposes a four-step process, with a vision followed by preparation of paint that is understood to have its own supernatural properties, then the painting, and then use of the resulting pictures in further ritual acts.[12] Obviously, we are not in a position to assess the merits of this interpretation, but we find it worth mentioning here because it would give these artworks a clear philosophical meaning. Complex ideas may have been associated with the paintings by those who originally made them, ideas that had to do with an understanding of the place of humans in a wider, perhaps usually invisible, reality. It must be said, though, that more mundane explanations are also plausible. For example, cave art—especially large images found in larger chambers—might have served as a focal point for social gatherings, perhaps meetings of usually independent smaller groups of hunter-gatherers. Balancing this out, there is art that seems more "personal," like the outline made by blowing pigment over a hand held against the cave wall. Then too, there is no reason to assume that all cave art in Africa, never mind in other places around the world, served the same function.

This is a point we'll be making numerous times: it is important not to underestimate the variation among ideas and practices found in African cultures. We will also find the contrast between individual self-expression and identity, and identity within the context of a community that gathers together, to be a prominent theme throughout the history of Africana philosophy. The case of rock art furthermore gives us a first taste of the methodological issues that arise when discussing philosophy in the context of precolonial Africa. In the absence of written records, scholars have sometimes turned to the empirical methods of anthropology to learn indirectly about the way that earlier (in this case, possibly far, far earlier) peoples have answered questions that were "philosophical" in the broad sense we have suggested.

For a further illustration of this strategy, we may turn to paleoanthropologist Steven Mithen's thoughts on the early origins of art, religion, and science.[13] Mithen argues that our ancestors, while evolving from those that we have in common with other apes, developed specialized intelligences: a social intelligence for interacting with each other; a natural history intelligence for understanding and interacting with the natural world; and a technical intelligence for manipulating things like stone and wood. It is clear that each of these specialized intelligences would have benefited our hunting and gathering ancestors in their fight for survival. Yet the breakthrough to the modern mind only occurred, according to Mithen, once we achieved cognitive fluidity, that is, the ability to integrate knowledge from these three different domains. Art, for example, involves combining the capacity for intentional communication given by social intelligence, the ability to interpret signs of life that comes from natural history intelligence, and, from technical intelligence, the ability to intentionally produce an artefact on the basis of a planned template.

If Mithen is right about this, then we can speculate that philosophy might have first developed among our ancestors in Africa when we began to use knowledge from one domain in order to raise critical questions about what we know in another domain. For example, integrating social intelligence with natural history intelligence may have led our African ancestors to ask whether non-human animals should be seen as fundamentally similar to us. We could then see anthropomorphism—that is, the attribution of human traits to non-human animals, which is a common element of prehistoric art—as one popular response to this philosophical question. By the same token, integrating technical intelligence with natural history intelligence may have led our African ancestors to ask whether the things we see in nature were purposefully created in the same manner in which we create tools and art. Clearly this philosophical question easily leads us in the direction of the idea of a creator god (see Chapter 14).

If we do not assume that philosophy only came to Africa in the form of the tradition born in ancient Greece, and remain open to the possibility that philosophy has existed in all human societies, then reconstructions of this sort are the right way to start telling the story of philosophy in Africa. In doing so, we would be telling the story of the very beginning of philosophy itself. Note, however, that even someone who denies that we can learn about the history of philosophy from prehistoric art and paleoanthropology could potentially end up deeming Africana philosophy the oldest tradition of philosophy there is. For, also long before the Presocratics, there was ancient Egyptian civilization. This culture gives us the first recorded writing of Africa, and for that matter some of the earliest recorded writing known from anywhere on earth. We'll start looking at ancient Egypt in Chapter 4, after we've looked at another ancient culture with which it may usefully be compared.

3

FERTILE GROUND

Philosophy in Ancient Mesopotamia

This book series claims to be presenting the history of philosophy "without any gaps." Yet it arguably started by leaving a huge gap. Rather than beginning in the sixth century BC with Thales and the other earliest Presocratics, who wrote in Greek and lived on the coast of what is now Turkey, it could have started with still more ancient civilizations, which were in part responsible for inspiring those Presocratics. There is no doubt that Greek philosophers were powerfully influenced by Egyptian ideas. For proof, you need only read Plato's dialogue *Phaedrus*, which talks about the invention of writing by the Egyptian god Thoth, or the re-telling of the myth of Iris and Osiris by the later ancient Platonist Plutarch.[1] But, as the Greeks knew full well, Egypt was not the only older civilization with a tradition of writing and science. Mesopotamia, meaning the region "between the two rivers"—namely the Tigris and Euphrates in modern-day Iraq—is often given credit for being the place where writing was invented, Plato's opinion notwithstanding. So if, while bearing in mind the previous chapter's speculations about philosophical thought among Stone Age humans in Africa, we ask when the earliest *recorded* philosophy was written, Mesopotamia looks like a good candidate alongside Egypt.

You presumably won't need to glance at a map to notice that Mesopotamia is not in Africa. But we're still going to devote a chapter to it, not only for the sake of some overdue gap-filling for the book series as a whole but also as context for the next few chapters on Egypt. These two ancient cultures were in contact and even competition with one another. We read of Egyptian scholars present at Mesopotamian courts, and as we'll be seeing, the two cultures sometimes produced literary texts of the same genres. Historians generally place the beginning of writing in both cultures over 5,000 years ago, in the latter half of the fourth millennium BC. Though it has been common to give the prize for innovation to Mesopotamia, or more specifically, to ancient Sumer, it remains within the realm of possibility that writing in Egypt is equally old or even older. Then too, it's not as if writing was invented only once. We know that it was born independently in China and among the Mayans of Mesoamerica. Whatever the case may be, what we can say with certainty is that our earliest examples of writing all come from the area known as the Fertile Crescent, a term that in its broadest usage covers both Mesopotamia and the Nile Valley in Egypt. It makes sense to look within this region for our earliest examples of the writing of philosophy.

A number of different kinds of text survive in cuneiform, the system of writing involving patterns of wedge-shaped impressions, produced not just in Mesopotamia but, given the influence of Mesopotamian powers, in nearby regions as well. These include myths and epics, including most famously the story of Gilgamesh; law codes, notably the law code of Hammurabi; works on various kinds of omens, including dreams and astrological omens; lists of words in Sumerian and Akkadian; poems of lament; and more practical texts which tell us about commerce and things like the use of measurement in these long-ago societies. It's fascinating stuff, enough so that there is a small industry of academics who devote their whole career to studying this culture. But is any of it philosophy? Well, one of those academics, Marc Van de Mieroop, thinks so. He claims that we can look to Mesopotamia for "the only well-documented system of philosophy before the Greeks known to us."[2] Van de Mieroop's "only" seems out of place to us, since as we'll be arguing, much Egyptian thought has just as good a claim to the title "philosophy before the Greeks." But let's leave that aside and evaluate the case he makes for a distinctively Babylonian philosophy.

He considers several of the textual genres we just mentioned, beginning with what seems least promising: lists of words. At first glance—at least, if the person doing the glancing can read cuneiform script—the clay tablets on which these lists are recorded might look like the homework of students who were learning to write or studying for a vocabulary quiz. But this is to underestimate the ambition of the scribes who noted down these words. For one thing, even the preserved number of tablets runs into the thousands—the original number of tablets must have been staggering. For another, Sumerian died out as a living language long before it died as a written language. Beginning in the first half of the second millennium BC, it served a purely literary purpose, like Latin in medieval Europe. Thus the tablets were guides to usage for speakers of Akkadian, not native Sumerian speakers. Finally, there is the comprehensiveness of the word lists. Van de Mieroop notes that they seem to have been trying to record all known Sumerian words, and some more words besides that were simply invented by the scribes. As he puts it, the aim was "to keep together the entirety of Sumerian and Akkadian wisdom, and lexical texts were an integral part of that encyclopedic project."[3]

He next moves on to two other kinds of lists, which record omens and laws. Omens were sometimes based on observations of the heavens, for instance: "if at Venus' rising the Red star enters into it: the king's son will seize the throne."[4] But they could also be, in both senses of the word, mundane: a medical man might infer the likely fate of his client based on objects seen in the street on the way to the sickhouse. Van de Mieroop emphasizes that the entries in these texts always have an "if-then" structure, which is shared by the Babylonian law codes. Thus just as *if* Venus rises and so on *then* the king's son will stage a coup, so Hammurabi writes that "if a man commits murder, then they shall kill that man."[5] This structural similarity is a clue to a deeper parallel. For the Babylonians, gods ruled the universe much as Hammurabi ruled over his people, and the omens they recorded were a record of that divine rule. Indeed, omens were sometimes simply called "decisions," that is, decisions made by the gods.[6]

When you see the rising of a planet at a certain time, note the shape of the liver from a sacrificed sheep, or look to see which way smoke will drift, you are not witnessing the cause of a future event, but a "sign" given to us by the gods. We are told that "the liver is the mirror of heaven," while the heavens themselves were said to be like writing that indicates the gods' will, and in fact to have first been set in order by the gods. The beginning of one of the more important astrological texts, entitled *Enuma Anu Enlil*, reads:

> When Anu, Enlil, and Ea, the great gods, by their firm counsel established the designs of heaven and earth and [also] established that the creation of the day [and] the renewal of the month for humankind to see were in the hands of the great gods: [then] they saw the sun in [his] gate [and] they made [him] appear regularly in the midst of heaven and earth.[7]

All this suggests that the Babylonians saw strong parallels between divine and human justice, even if they also frequently spoke of their gods as willful and unpredictable sources of unprovoked misery in the form of plagues and other natural catastrophes.

Moreover, and this is really Van de Mieroop's driving concern, the lists of words, omens, and laws all operate within the logic of systems of signs. We already mentioned that invented words appear in the vocabulary lists. He argues, similarly, that a law code like Hammurabi's was not really used in concrete legal situations, and that the omens were not based on actually observed events. Rather the scribes were led by the internal logic of language, by intuitive reasoning and wordplay. This interpretation is perhaps strongest when it comes to the question of celestial omens. Here Van de Mieroop's judgment is echoed by Francesca Rochberg.[8] She too points out that the listed omens include signs that cannot possibly have been observed by the Babylonians. We are told, for example, what it means when the sun comes out in the middle of the night. (Though unbeknownst to the scribes, this omen actually is possible: it signifies that you live in Scandinavia, and it's summertime.) Van de Mieroop's conclusion is that the scribes were above all concerned with the play of meanings between linguistic signs, an interpretation which has the Babylonians not so much anticipating Plato and Aristotle by one millennium, as Jacques Derrida by three millennia.[9]

Whatever we make of this, it is worth marking a distinction that Van de Mieroop typically glosses over: the difference between writing that takes an explicit stance on a philosophical issue and writing that only implicitly suggests such a stance. He says at one point that Hammurabi's code "shows that he knew truth, and we should thus read it as a work of epistemology."[10] But this is surely an exaggeration, or to put it more bluntly, a mistake. A work of epistemology is not one that gives the reader to understand that the author has knowledge. A work of epistemology is a text that raises and seeks to answer the question, "what is knowledge?" Van de Mieroop does not do much to help us challenge the claim that Plato was the first to write such works, with dialogues like the *Meno* and *Theaetetus*. He is closer to the mark when he elsewhere writes of the "underlying epistemological principles" of the texts he studies.[11] The scribes do seem to have assumed that homonymy between two Sumerian words reveals a "sympathetic" connection between the things the words signify, and that laws are an expression of justice and wisdom (more even than they are a practical guide to judges). Such assumptions are not stated outright, and certainly not established by argument, but that does not mean they are not at work. As one scholar has observed in relation to such texts, "lack of explicitness in itself is not a method of thinking, but a mode of expression."[12]

We would also contend, however, that Van De Mieroop makes things unnecessarily difficult for himself by passing over products of Babylonian literature that are more obviously philosophical in nature. As with the *Upaniṣads* of ancient India and the works of Plato in ancient Greece, so some of the more intriguing works of the Babylonians come in the form of dialogues. One such work, the so-called *Dialogue of Pessimism*, offers us the first occasion in this book—obviously far from the last—to discuss the condition of slavery. The dialogue in the work is between a rich master and his slave. Each time the master announces an intention to do something, the slave supportively chimes in with a justification for doing that thing. When the master then reconsiders the idea and announces his intention to refrain from the proposed activity, the slave chimes in once again to provide reasons not to do the thing. For example, the master says he is going to love a woman and the slave encouragingly proclaims that "the man who loves a woman forgets sorrow and fear." When the master changes his mind, the slave agrees, saying a woman is "a pitfall" and "a sharp iron dagger that cuts a man's throat."[13]

The dialogue is evidently a satirical reflection on power, as the slave's intellectual prowess generates contradiction after contradiction in service of affirming the master's will. There is more than comedy here, however. The dialogue also raises deeper questions about truth and value, as we are forced to wonder whether the slave's ability to provide justifications both for doing and not doing the proposed actions represents a general lack of ability among humans, when it comes to discerning what we ought to do. At the dialogue's end, the question of who holds power in the relationship between master and slave also comes to the fore in a striking way. The master asks: "What, then, is good?" The slave darkly replies that both of them having their necks broken and being thrown into a river would be good. When the master says the slave will be killed first, the slave warns: "my master would certainly not outlive me by even three days."[14] The implication seems to be that the master is dependent on the slave to survive, which reveals the apparently powerful figure in the relationship as weak in relation to the one he subjugates. The dialogue can therefore be seen as a complex philosophical investigation of truth, value, and social hierarchy. Those familiar with the German philosopher G.W.F. Hegel's famous idea of a master–slave dialectic will also notice that the *Dialogue of Pessimism* is a useful text for comparison and contrast.

Consider, next, *The Instruction of Supe-Ameli*, which is also known by the words that open the text: *Sima Milka*, meaning "Hear the advice."[15] Here a father—the Supe-Ameli of the title—gives advice to his son, much of it quite straightforwardly practical in nature. The son is advised to stay out of taverns, for example, and learns about where to dig a well in a field in order to avoid others mooching off you. If this were a normal instruction text, a standard entry in a genre found in both ancient Mesopotamia and ancient Egypt, the end of the father's advice would be the end of the work. But, in this case, the son talks back, and what he says puts into question the very point of the father's advice.

He speaks of how all his father's riches will mean little when death comes and about how life is short while death is long. "Few are the days in which we eat our bread, but many will be the days in which our teeth will be idle," he says. "Few are the days in which we look at the sun, but many will be the days in which we will sit in the shadows."[16] Where the father offers practical tips for success in life, the son points to life's ephemeral nature. The father presents us with wisdom of old vintage, some of which is similar to that which can be found in still older works like the *Instruction of Shuruppak*. The son contests this age-old wisdom, critically reflecting on whether it actually helps us confront the true nature of mortal existence. *Supe-Ameli* is thus rather explicitly philosophical. It raises fundamental questions about how we ought to live, and indeed what values we should even prioritize as we seek to answer that question.

Yet another work in dialogue format featuring critical reflection on the meaning and value of life is known as the *Babylonian Theodicy*.[17] The word "theodicy" was invented by the early modern German philosopher Gottfried Leibniz, and refers to solutions to the "problem of evil": how can we reconcile the goodness of an all-knowing and all-powerful God with the existence of evil in the world? In the *Babylonian Theodicy*, we have a dialogue between two friends, one of whom is complaining about hardship he has suffered. The sufferer asserts that devotion to the gods has not secured him well-being, bitterly adding that others in society experience great success despite their lack of piety. His friend, on the other hand, defends the justice of the gods and the importance of showing them due respect. The end of the dialogue depicts a narrowing of the gap between the positions, as the friend acknowledges that it is, after all, the gods who chose to create humans with a propensity for wrongdoing. The sufferer meanwhile acknowledges that, at the end of the day, he has no other choice but to continue to seek the mercy of the gods.

The *Babylonian Theodicy* is a rare case where we appear to know the name of the author of an ancient Mesopotamian text. It is written as an acrostic poem, with the initial syllables of the stanzas spelling out the following message: "I, Saggil-kinam-ubbib, an incantation priest, the one who worships the gods and the king." On the strength of this, Saggil-kinam-ubbib can be recognized as one of the earliest philosophers whom we know by name. We should note, though, that, depending on who we count as philosophers, he is preceded by the earliest case in which we know an author's name at all! This was, remarkably, a woman: Enheduanna, daughter of Sargon of Akkad, whose most famous compositions are hymns of devotion to the goddess Inanna. Sophus Helle, a translator of Enheduanna's poetry, points out that she sometimes departs from the standard hierarchy of gods in her elevation of Inanna above all others.[18] It is therefore intriguing to ponder whether this critical revision by Enheduanna of her culture's beliefs might be worth counting as an early instance of feminist philosophy.

In any case, although Saggil-kinam-ubbib's name is probably not familiar to you, the story he tells might well be. There are obvious similarities between the *Babylonian Theodicy* and the biblical Book of Job, in which we also have a sufferer expressing his woes and, in the case of Job, multiple friends responding in ways that affirm the importance of piety even in the face of great misfortune.[19] Another work from ancient Mesopotamia which bears similarities to the Book of Job is the *Poem of the Righteous Sufferer*, again also known by its opening words, in this case *Ludlul Bel Nemeqi*, or "I will praise the Lord of Wisdom." Many suspect that such Mesopotamian texts influenced the Hebrew author of the Book of Job. It is only one of numerous cases where the Bible includes material that resonates with Babylonian literature. Another striking example is a flood myth, including an ark to preserve animals from extinction, in the *Epic of Gilgamesh*.

Speaking of which, we would be remiss if we failed to say something about this epic, by far the most famous work to survive from ancient Mesopotamian culture.[20] The most complete version of the story of Gilgamesh that we have appears to have been written by a scribe and priest by the name of Sin-leqe-unninni, but this Akkadian version evidently draws on earlier Sumerian writings and probably also orally transmitted myths, much as the Homeric epics and the *Mahābhārata* depended respectively on older Greek and Indian oral culture. As with those texts, a sign of its distant origins in oral culture is the repetition of catchphrases and whole passages, which would have made the poem easier to memorize.

The story we are told in Sin-leqe-unninni's version goes like this: Gilgamesh is an unjust ruler who is brought to see sense through divine intervention when a peer and ally is made for him, by the name of Enkidu. Gilgamesh and Enkidu have a series of adventures, with Gilgamesh traveling as far as the underworld after Enkidu dies; as with the story of Noah and the flood, Homer's depiction of Odysseus traveling to Hades seems to be anticipated here by Sin-leqe-unninni and his sources. As this part of the *Epic* suggests, a major theme of the whole narrative is death. Gilgamesh movingly laments the eventual passing of Enkidu, and the story also features a quest in search of the secret of immortality. Another theme of clear philosophical relevance, even if we do not call the epic a work of epistemology, is privileged knowledge: already in its opening lines, Gilgamesh is said to have "gained complete wisdom," "found out what was secret and uncovered what was hidden," and "brought back a tale of times before the Flood."

From the many other themes of philosophical interest that we could pick out from *Gilgamesh*, we'll focus just briefly on the political and anthropological ideas suggested by the material on the first of the clay tablets on which the epic is preserved. As we've said, Gilgamesh is initially presented as an unjust tyrant. He is overdemanding of military service from his subjects' sons, and of sexual service from their daughters. Of course, the behavior of Gilgamesh is itself a cautionary tale for any potentates among the poem's audience, and is implicitly contrasted to the example of the gods, who mercifully respond to pleas for intervention. Then comes the scene in which the goddess Aruru takes a piece of clay and creates from it Enkidu: "his whole body was shaggy with hair, he had a full head of hair like a woman....He knew neither people nor settled living. He ate grasses with the gazelles, and jostled at the watering hole with the animals; as with animals, his thirst was slaked [only] with water."[21] Gilgamesh hears of this wild man and realizes that, in order to be domesticated, Enkidu has to be brought into contact with a woman. Sexual congress will initiate him into the world of human society.

This tells us something about Babylonian gender politics, and also something of how they saw the border between animal and human. Only once he has mated with a woman, groomed himself, and eaten prepared food and drink is Enkidu considered to be properly human.[22] In fact, better than that: he is pronounced to be "like a god." This first tablet ends on a familiar Babylonian note, citing Gilgamesh's prophetic dreams, which along with tales of Gilgamesh's physical prowess persuade Enkidu to become a much-needed friend and adviser, instead of challenging the king in combat. Taking all this together, we can say that socialization and human intercourse—sexual and otherwise—are dominant motifs in this early part of the poem. One might hesitate to call the *Epic of Gilgamesh* a work of political philosophy, but it seems to anticipate Aristotle's famous remark that the human is a "political animal." Human nature is compatible with living like a wild beast, but fully realized only within the fold of human society. Ultimately, humans are the animals capable of receiving wisdom from the gods, and of exercising just political rule, in collaboration with their peers.

4

PYRAMID SCHEMES

Philosophy in Ancient Egypt

Near the beginning of Aristotle's *Metaphysics*, there is an interesting reflection on the development of abstract thought. He thinks that only humans are capable of this, because only we can rise above memory and experience of individual things to reach the level of universals. This allows us to develop the arts and sciences. No doubt, he muses, the very first inventor of the very first art must have been admired as wise and superior above all others (so perhaps Aristotle would have appreciated our own musings about the development of characteristically human behavior in Chapter 2). He then points out that further arts would have been developed for their usefulness or to give pleasure; traditionally Aristotelian examples might be medicine and flute-playing, respectively. But eventually, arts emerged that were pursued for their own sake. He tells us where he believes this first happened: "When all such inventions were already established, the sciences which do not aim at giving pleasure or at the necessities of life were discovered, and first in the places where men first began to have leisure. This is why the mathematical arts were founded in Egypt; for there the priestly caste was allowed to be at leisure" (981b1). So the first completely abstract or theoretical discipline—the first discipline pursued for its own sake rather than for pleasure or usefulness—was, according to Aristotle, born in ancient Egypt.[1]

Later on in the *Metaphysics*, he adds that mathematics is one of only three properly theoretical sciences (1026a1). Natural science is another and the third is theology, which turns out to be the same thing as "first philosophy," or metaphysics. Now, it would be misleading to describe Aristotle as claiming that the disciplines he pursues in the *Physics* or *Metaphysics* were born in Egypt. Indeed, he is generally understood as regarding Thales as the first philosopher (983b1), although this is a fine time to recall that Thales is said to have visited Egypt and learned some mathematics there, specifically geometry. Still, we can say that Aristotle would firmly disagree with those who argue that the Greeks were the first to engage in abstract thought.[2] This has often been treated as a Greek innovation, in contrast with the "mythical" thinking of Egypt, Mesopotamia, and other civilizations. Aristotle instead sees the Egyptians as the forerunners of the Greeks in this respect.[3]

Unlike Aristotle, we are now in the fortunate position of being able to draw on the findings of modern Egyptology. Scholars of this field have unearthed many surviving texts from ancient Egypt, allowing us to evaluate whether some of them may be considered philosophical in a way that Aristotle could not. First, let's consider a set of writings that dates back at least as far as the twenty-fourth century BC, making these writings more than one and a half millennia older than the earliest Greek philosophers. The writings in question are known as the *Pyramid Texts*. They are, or at least appear to be, sets of spells intended to serve the royal owners of the tombs in which they were inscribed during their journey into the afterlife. It is safe to say that they are among the oldest religious texts in the world, and anyone interested in Egyptian mythology will find them to be of interest. Whether they are in any sense "philosophical" is a more difficult question. Here is a quotation from what may be the oldest Pyramid Text, found in the tomb of Unis, the last king of Egypt's Fifth Dynasty:

> Pull back, Baboon's penis! Open, sky's door!
> You sealed door, open a path for Unis on the blast of heat where the gods scoop water.
> Horus' glide path...will Unis glide on, in this blast of heat where the gods scoop
>   water, and they will make a path for Unis that Unis may pass on it: Unis is Horus.[4]

As this quotation suggests, the *Pyramid Texts* are exciting to read but also very difficult to understand. Can we discern any philosophy here? A scholar named Susan Brind Morrow has argued that the answer is yes. According to her, what we have here are not in fact spells but a form of philosophy written in poetic verse, an attempt to answer such perennial questions as: "What is life on earth, how does it relate to time and the interrelationship of all things, what is death, [and] what survives death?"[5] Another scholar and a translator of the *Pyramid Texts*, James P. Allen, is not convinced. He has criticized Morrow's work as a "misrepresentation" of the texts, "a poet's impression of what she *thinks* the texts should say, and not a reflection of what they actually say."[6]

Rather than getting hung up on the question of whether to bestow the name of "philosophy" on these inscriptions, let's step back and consider the cosmological vision that can be pieced together from the *Pyramid Texts* and subsequent, related writings. We mentioned Thales earlier, the Presocratic thinker famous for believing that all things are derived from water. In light of that, it's intriguing that the creator god envisioned in these texts is not described as simply always having been there. Before the existence of anything else he emerged out of Nun, the primordial waters. Given that Thales is said to have visited Egypt, some have wondered whether he may have picked up his water obsession there along with his skill in geometry.[7] If so, this would be an interesting case of mythological representation influencing philosophical doctrine, a reminder that myths can be relevant for the history of philosophy, even if we sharply distinguish mythology from philosophy.

Whatever lines of influence may be found here, it would be a mistake to reduce Egyptian thought and its reflection on the nature of things to mythology. Take Imhotep, who lived during the Third Dynasty of Egypt, somewhere around the twenty-seventh century BC. He has been celebrated as the first great scientific thinker of the ancient world.[8] He was the chief adviser to King Djoser, the first king of Egypt to have ordered the construction of a pyramid. The Step Pyramid of Djoser, which can still be visited today, is a major feat of engineering and Imhotep is credited with being its architect. An inscription at the base of a statue found in the Step Pyramid tells us that Imhotep was also an administrator, a high priest, and a sculptor. As if that weren't enough, later generations of Egyptians remembered him as a master physician. He was eventually deified as a god of medicine and later still identified by the Greeks with their demigod of medicine, Asclepius. There is an ancient Egyptian medical text known as the "Edwin Smith papyrus," which is remarkable for its systematic and relatively magic-free approach to diagnosing and treating injuries. Some Egyptologists have speculated that Imhotep could be its author.[9]

Even if Imhotep did not write the words set down on that papyrus, though, we still have reason to think that he composed works of lasting importance. Two texts, *The Song of the Harper from the Tomb of King Intef* and *The Immortality of Writers*, both of which were evidently written many centuries after Imhotep's time, invoke him as a paradigmatic example of a beloved and oft-read author.[10] Both texts thematize the way that our wise words may live on after we die, so it is a sad irony that no words survive to us that can certainly be ascribed to Imhotep. Still, it is philosophically intriguing that this one individual was associated both with sciences like engineering and medicine, and also—implicitly, through association with the other authors cited in the two texts just mentioned—with the ethical literature that we'll be considering in the next chapter.

Someone whose words can, by contrast, still be read today is Akhenaten, the monumentally important king who is seen by many as the first known proponent of monotheism.[11] His reign in the mid-fourteenth century BC has been called "perhaps the most exhilarating, uncertain, dynamic, and bizarre period in Egyptian history."[12] He inherited the throne from his father, Amenhotep III, and was initially known as Amenhotep IV. Early in his reign, though, he renamed himself Akhenaten, which might be translated as "he who acts effectively on behalf of the Aten." The Aten was a sun-god or perhaps one aspect of the sun-god, specifically its representation as a disk in the sky. Akhenaten elevated the Aten as a god above all other gods, and eventually made it the official religious view of the kingdom that there was no other god but the Aten. To reflect this new belief, he ordered the daunting task of removing the names and images of any other gods from temples, tombs, and monuments. Along with his wife Nefertiti, who held a position of equality with her husband unmatched by most other Egyptian queens, Akhenaten oversaw massive changes in the society he ruled, including the founding of a new capital, Akhetaten, where a roofless temple facilitated very direct worship of the Aten.

There can be no doubt that one effect of Akhenaten's religious revolution, if not its primary motivation, was to concentrate power in Akhenaten's hands. He positioned himself as the son of the Aten and the only one capable of fully knowing and interpreting the will of this solitary divinity. Akhenaten's monotheism was more than a power grab, though. Consider the beginning of a text generally assumed to be composed by him, the *Great Hymn to the Aten*:

> You rise in perfection on the horizon of the sky,
> living Aten, who determines life.
> Whenever you are risen upon the eastern horizon
> you fill every land with your perfection.
> You are appealing, great, sparkling, high over every land;
> your rays embrace the lands as far as everything you have made.[13]

Two themes are especially worth emphasizing here: the universal reach of the Aten and the naturalistic description of this god as the visible shining sun. Aten's illumination of all lands evokes a connection between monotheism and the unity of the world itself, despite the distances and differences between those of us who live in it. According to Akhenaten, the Aten is the ultimate source and the active sustainer of all lands, near or far. When he mentions specific neighboring lands in the Middle East and Africa, like the Levant to the northeast and Nubia to the south, their positioning in relation to the Aten suggests a kind of equality with Egypt: "The lands of Khor and Kush and the land of Egypt: you set every man in his place, you allot their needs, every one of them according to his diet, and his lifetime is counted out."[14] This is a surprising contrast to the way that ancient Egyptians usually insist on the superiority of their own land to all others. While Akhenaten stresses the uniqueness of this divinity, he celebrates the diversity of humanity. Linguistic differences and even the physical difference of skin color are the benevolent doing of the one god who created all of these people: "Tongues are separate in speech, and their characters as well; their skins are different, for you differentiate the foreigners."[15] Here theological innovation appears to have brought about a new understanding of what human beings share and how that relates to what makes us different from one another.

Theological as it may be, though, this is also a highly naturalistic text. It is obvious that the *Great Hymn to the Aten* describes the physical sun as we see it in the sky. This may not sound like a radical break with tradition. After all, one of the few things most of us will know about Egyptian gods is that one of the most important was Ra, a sun-god. Like most Egyptian gods, however, Ra was traditionally represented with human and animal features. By the time Akhenaten's father reigned, Ra was often fused together with the god Amun as Amun-Ra, and depicted with a human body and a falcon's head. Akhenaten vigorously suppressed the cult of Amun-Ra. The *Great Hymn* itself identifies the Aten with Ra, but Akhenaten avoids representing this god as having any human or animal characteristics. The god is just the disk of the sun, a position that has led some to ask whether we should perhaps consider Akhenaten a natural philosopher or perhaps even an atheist who radically rejected the supernatural aspects of his tradition.[16]

Even if we are reluctant to go that far, the philosophical significance of Akhenaten's religious revolution—its transformative power not merely on a social level but at the level of rational thought concerning the nature of things—should by now be clear. As revolutions go, though, this was a short-lived one. Just a few years after Akhenaten's death, efforts to erase his heresy began.[17] His son Tutankhaten took the throne at the age of 9 and changed his name to Tutankhamun, thus indicating the resurrection of the worship of Amun-Ra; you may more readily recognize the modern shortened version of his name, "King Tut." Despite famously dying while still a teen, Tutankhamun had time enough to initiate the return of Egypt to the religious traditions interrupted by the brief embrace of monotheism.

Alongside beliefs about the gods, another religious tradition strongly associated with the ancient Egyptians is of course their elaborate conception of the afterlife, the most celebrated description of which can be found in the text popularly known as the *Egyptian Book of the Dead*.[18] Egyptologists often refer to it as the *Book of Coming* (or *Going*) *Forth By Day*. Individualized versions of it were prepared for burials, in a practice that evokes the earlier *Pyramid Texts*. Like those earlier inscriptions, the *Book of the Dead* touches on cosmological issues. But what is perhaps most intriguing to the philosophical eye is what it has to say about morality. Chapter 125 of the *Book of the Dead* features what have been paradoxically labeled the Negative Confessions—that is, confessions about what one has *not* done. They are also known, less oxymoronically, as the Declarations of Innocence.[19] The person journeying into the afterlife confronts a tribunal of forty-two gods and addresses each of them individually in order to assert innocence of various kinds of wrongdoing. Some of the declarations are: "I have not stolen," "I have not slain people," "I have not destroyed the food offerings," "I have not had intercourse with a married woman," "I have not been hot[-tempered]," "I have not been impatient," and "My voice was not loud."

The declarations take place in the Hall of Two Truths, and in keeping with this one of the declarations is: "I have not told lies." Yet it seems irresistible to suspect that any person undergoing this process will make declarations that are simply untrue. Certainly plenty of people get through life without committing murder or adultery, but it seems rather implausible for someone to claim that they have never once spoken loudly or lost patience. So is this series of declarations more like a spell, meant to guarantee unfettered passage through the afterlife? If so, perhaps the demand for strict adherence to truth would be misplaced, though that would be difficult to square with the prominent emphasis on truth-telling. Either way, aside from the philosophical interest of understanding the paradox involved in making these declarations, this list of wrongdoings serves us at least as an expression of ancient Egyptian ethics, a kind of "not to do list" which offers an implicit guide to how one *should* live. One person who has stressed their importance is Maulana Karenga, the African American intellectual and activist who is most widely known as the inventor of the holiday Kwanzaa. Karenga wrote a doctoral thesis in Social Ethics at the University of Southern California and published that thesis as a book, entitled *Maat: The Moral Ideal in Ancient Egypt*. He identifies the Declarations of Innocence as a "central source of ancient Egyptian moral principles and practice."[20] More generally, the point of his ground-breaking study is that Egyptian thinking about morality is not merely a matter of historical interest, but offers the basis for a living ethical tradition.

Of course, however important a source of ethics they may be, the Declarations do not represent philosophy in an explicitly argumentative mode, and for that matter, neither does Akhenaten's *Great Hymn*. So skeptical readers may be wondering whether any ancient Egyptian texts offered a *reasoned* defense of ethical doctrines, rather than just setting out such doctrines or alluding to them implicitly? Yes, as we'll see in the next chapter, which will focus on the genre of ethical writings known as "instructions" or "teachings." After that, even the most resistant of readers should be like an Egyptian crocodile that has wandered up onto the shore: no longer in denial.

5

FATHER KNOWS BEST

Moral and Political Philosophy in the Instructions

Most fathers find themselves at some point, presumably unwittingly, restaging Act 1, Scene 3 of Shakespeare's *Hamlet*. As you may recall, it features the wily courtier Polonius giving advice to his son Laertes, who is about to embark on a voyage. As with so much of Shakespeare, the scene can be played in a variety of ways. It's not so clear whether the audience is meant to be impressed by Polonius' advice, the fruits of his years and experience, or whether we are supposed to react the way teenaged boys tend to react to unsolicited advice from their own fathers, with impatience and eye-rolling. Either way, Shakespeare was himself unwittingly reprising scenes from much older literature. There are a number of ancient Egyptian writings that characteristically featured an elder figure giving advice to a younger person, usually a father giving advice to his son and often representing in part the preparation of the son by the father to take up the societal role the father had occupied, such as scribe, government official, or king. These texts are known as instructions or teachings, and, as mentioned in Chapter 3, they represent a genre common to the two oldest writing traditions, those of Mesopotamia and Egypt, although it seems fair to say that the tradition was more extensively developed in Egypt.

Another form of writing, known as the funerary autobiography, likely goes back further than the genre of instructions. As the name suggests, these are presentations of a person's life written in the first person and inscribed within that person's tomb. An approach to funerary autobiographies that gains prominence by the time of Egypt's sixth dynasty is the catalogue of virtues.[1] Take this bit of what is inscribed within the tomb of a man named Nefer-Seshem-Re, who served as a government official near the beginning of the sixth dynasty (and so roughly some time in the twenty-fourth century BC):

> I gave bread to the hungry, clothes [to the naked],
> I brought the boatless to land.
> I buried him who had no son,
> I made a boat for him who lacked one.
> I respected my father, I pleased my mother,
> I raised their children.
> So says he whose nickname is Sheshi.[2]

The mention of his nickname is welcome, but otherwise these lines give us little feeling for good old Sheshi as an individual. Instead, they convey the moral values that he and others in his society cherished and strived to uphold. The catalogues of virtues found in funerary autobiographies were thus a vehicle for moral thought. Insofar as they stem from and stimulate reflection on what is fundamentally important to living a good life, these texts provide at the very least an important step in the development of a tradition of moral philosophy.

The genre of instructions continue that tradition and form its most important part. We find in the instructions, as in the funerary autobiographies, a literary form that by its very structure focuses our attention on the question of how to achieve a life well-lived. Which aspects of our conduct are most important, and how should we deal with others? At the outset of an instruction attributed to Prince Hardjedef, the son of King Khufu of the fourth dynasty who commissioned the Great Pyramid of Giza, we read: "Cleanse yourself before your (own) eyes / Lest another cleanse you" (58). This opening exhortation reads like a threat—deal with your own faults before someone else does it—but it also encourages moral reflection. It asks the reader to measure themselves against the ethical standards presupposed by other inscriptions (have you "brought the boatless to land"?) and suggests that to fail to do so and thus end up being corrected by another is a shameful position to inhabit.

The best-known instruction and arguably the masterpiece of the genre is *The Instruction of Ptahhotep*, sometimes called *The Maxims of Ptahhotep*.[3] Ptahhotep was a vizier or chief minister to King Djedkare Isesi during the fifth dynasty, thus living around the twenty-fifth to the twenty-fourth century BC. Egyptologists tend to doubt, though, that the real Hardjedef and Ptahhotep were actually the authors of the instructions attributed to them. Especially in the case of Ptahhotep, the text as we have it is at best a later revision of his original work, if it goes back to him at all. It is written in the variety of the ancient Egyptian language known as Middle Egyptian, which is associated with the period of Egyptian history called the Middle Kingdom, rather than the Old Egyptian of the period known as the Old Kingdom, when Ptahhotep lived.[4] So *The Instruction of Ptahhotep* has often been deemed a product of the literary golden age of Egypt's twelfth dynasty, which would date it somewhere between the twentieth and eighteenth centuries BC.[5]

The work opens with the vizier Ptahhotep complaining about the onset of the infirmities of old age and requesting of the king that his son be appointed as a "staff of old age" for him (63). The king agrees, endorsing the instruction of Ptahhotep's son in the sayings of the past. Ptahhotep then commences offering pieces of advice, usually numbered as thirty-seven maxims, followed by an epilogue on the value of hearing and paying attention to instruction. For some, this framing may provide reason for skepticism that the text is going to be genuinely philosophical. Isn't philosophy about questioning the traditional wisdom of the past, carefully evaluating it rather than dutifully transmitting it? (For more on this criterion, see Chapter 20.) Even if you tend to think so, the very first of Ptahhotep's maxims should persuade you that he is in fact endorsing a self-questioning attitude:

> Don't be proud of your knowledge,
> Consult the ignorant and the wise;
> The limits of art are not reached,
> No artist's skills are perfect;
> Good speech is more hidden than greenstone,
> Yet may be found among maids at the grindstones. (63)

This striking reflection on knowledge invites us to think critically about generally accepted social distinctions and about the nature of education. Seeking knowledge, according to this maxim, is a quest that can never be completed as there is always more to learn. It is easy to slip into a sense of self-satisfaction once we have become advanced learners, worthy of being called wise by the standards of our society. Ptahhotep argues, however, that even the wise ought to strive for further progress, precisely by turning away from the commonly accepted sources of wisdom to those who are widely deemed ignorant, but may also have something to teach. As an example, he points to women of the servant class, in spite of their doubly low status in society. This is certainly not an example of an uncritical acceptance of received wisdom (and, to revisit a concern from Chapter 3, it is plausibly an example of epistemological reflection preceding ancient Greek philosophy).

There is a wide variety of themes in the thirty-six maxims that follow this one, but among the most prominent is an idea that would also find approval with Polonius, who tells his son: "Give every man thy ear, but few thy voice." Often, advises Ptahhotep, the best thing to say is nothing at all. This initially comes to the forefront in maxims 2–4, which give advice concerning what you ought to do when you are party to a dispute that is being judged by officials. The second maxim addresses what you should do if your opponent in the dispute is of a higher social rank than you are, the third what you should do if your opponent is of equal social rank, and the fourth what you should do if the opponent is of lower social rank. In each case, Ptahhotep's advice is the same, and would be echoed by any defense lawyer today: remember that you have the right to remain silent. According to the second maxim, silence in the face of the evil speech of your social superior will communicate a sense of humility and self-control that will help you reach success. The third maxim indicates that silence in the face of evil speech will overturn the equality in social rank between you and your adversary, proving you to be superior in the realm of virtue. Finally the fourth maxim suggests that, by keeping silent, you will allow the opponent of lower social rank to say so much that he winds up refuting himself, while you will also succeed in refraining from wrongdoing, for "wretched is he who injures a poor man" (64).

A number of questions arise out of this treatment of silence as an expressive form of action that is both admirable in itself and effective in helping you to win disputes. Why shouldn't we fear that an eloquent opponent might skillfully sway those judging the dispute with convincing lies, thus making our silence seem as if we have no rebuttal? And isn't there a point at which silence starts to seem less like virtuous self-control, and more like a stubborn refusal to defend oneself? While these pragmatic matters are not resolved by the text, it does go on to connect the theme of virtuous silence to the earlier motif of seeking knowledge in Maxim 24:

> If you are an excellent man,
> who sits in the council of his lord,
> concentrate on excellence!
> You should be quiet! This is better than a potent herb.
> You should speak when you know that you understand:
> only the skilled artist speaks in the council.
> Speaking is harder than any craft:
> only the man who understands it puts it to work for him.

The idea here seems to be that silence is a virtue not just because it demonstrates a capacity for self-control, but also because it helps you to focus your attention on increasing your knowledge and understanding. Again, the point Shakespeare put into the mouth of Polonius is a valid one: when you aren't busy voicing your own views, you can listen to the views of others. When Ptahhotep says that speaking is harder than any craft, his idea is obviously not that any random production of words is difficult. Rather, he wants to say that the wise use of this capacity, speaking from a position of true understanding, is like your grandmother's fruitcake: harder than it looks. Silence provides the best possible means to speaking wisely, which is to say that we ought to be silent precisely so that when we are not silent, there will be no reason to wish we had remained that way.

Perhaps as a direct result of the influence of *The Instruction of Ptahhotep*, the theme of silence as a virtue can be found in other classic instructions, like *The Instruction of Amenemope*, which is thought to have been written during the period of Egyptian history known as the New Kingdom and more specifically during either the nineteenth or twentieth dynasties. These are collectively known as the Ramesside period, because most of the reigning pharaohs were called Ramesses. If *The Instruction of Amenemope* suggests the influence of *Ptahhotep*, it appears to have been influential itself, even beyond Egyptian culture. We mentioned while discussing ancient Mesopotamian literature that some works from that tradition may have shaped the creation of the Bible's Book of Job, and it is natural to suspect that the flood story in the *Epic of Gilgamesh* influenced the story of Noah in Genesis. Similarly, Egyptologists and biblical scholars have long noticed similarities between *The Instruction of Amenemope* and a section of the *Book of Proverbs* known as "Words of the Wise" (from 22:17 to 24:22). In fact, the dominant view among scholars seems to be that the author of the Hebrew text must have drawn upon Amenemope's work.[6] When Jews and Christians read in Proverbs 22:24–5 that you should "not make friends with a hot-tempered person, do not associate with one easily angered, or you may learn their ways and get yourself ensnared," it would seem that they are encountering a Hebrew version of a similar passage in *The Instruction of Amenemope*. This passage yet again contrasts the silent, self-controlled individual with the "heated" or "hot-tempered" person who can't keep his mouth shut.[7]

We have in the instructions, then, a rich and influential tradition of moral philosophy, albeit not one that has been much discussed and analyzed by professional philosophers. One exception is *The Instruction of Ani*. Like *The Instruction of Amenemope*, it appears to be the work of a New Kingdom scribe. In the 1990s, David James and Julie Maybee published articles arguing that this instruction should be counted as a milestone in the history of philosophy.[8] The first thing to note is that, like the Mesopotamian *Instructions of Supe-Ameli*, this Egyptian instruction features an epilogue in which the son who has listened to the foregoing instruction replies to his father. Whereas the Mesopotamian work ends after the son's response, the *Instruction of Ani* builds the scene into a full-blown dialogue, with Ani (the father who gave the instruction) replying to the challenge by Khonshotep (his son), followed by further speeches by Khonshotep and Ani, and then a final, brief, third exchange. Khonshotep's initial challenge to his father in the epilogue involves the idea that the rules laid out in the preceding instruction are too numerous, and that it should be understood that virtue does not come as naturally to him as it does to his father. Ani reacts with a stern rebuke, affirming the possibility of moral education with a series of analogies involving the domestication of animals and the ability of foreigners to learn how to speak Egyptian. Whereas James interprets the further back-and-forth between the two as resulting in a convergence between the father and son's positions, Maybee sees no concession on Ani's part.

This disagreement notwithstanding, James and Maybee both affirm the instruction's historical importance. For James, the fact that *The Instruction of Ani* features "profound philosophical positions, dialectical development, reasoned arguments, and irony" makes it abundantly clear that Socrates was not the first moral philosopher, and that Plato was not the first to compose artful philosophical dialogue.[9] Maybee argues that the transition from the body of the instruction to its epilogue marks a shift from the practical enumeration of virtues, such as we've seen already in the autobiographical tomb inscriptions, to a generalized theoretical account of morality, one which even provides an answer to the question of why we should be moral in the first place. She therefore agrees with James that long before Socrates and Plato, "ancient Egyptians were discussing some of the same, general moral questions that we find being addressed in the ancient Greek texts, and that they were doing so in a manner which anticipates those Greek texts" (150).

To close our discussion of this literary genre, let's turn from instructions mainly exemplifying what we would call moral philosophy to those that contribute most prominently to the development of a tradition of political philosophy. There are a number of texts in this category, including *The Instruction of King Amenemhet*, which does not hide the fictional nature of its attribution to a twelfth dynasty king. It has the king giving advice to his son from beyond the grave after having been assassinated, like the Ghost speaking to Hamlet. Ancient Egyptians therefore attributed it not to the king himself, but to a scribe named Khety. Then there is the so-called *Loyalist Instruction*, the first part of which praises and prescribes loyalty to the king, while the second part includes reflections on how various professions and activities contribute to the success of a society. Perhaps the most famous political instruction, though, is *The Instruction Addressed to King Merikare*. Merikare was a king of either the ninth or tenth dynasty, ruling during the time in between the Old Kingdom and the Middle Kingdom known as the First Intermediate Period. The instruction is, as the title suggests, not ascribed to him but to his father, identified as King Khety. Unfortunately, multiple kings during the ninth and tenth dynasties bore this name, so it is not clear who the author is supposed to be. If it is indeed the work of a king from this period, it dates back to the twenty-second or twenty-first century BC, which has recently led one scholar to proclaim it "the oldest political treatise."[10]

The instruction begins with advice about how to suppress rebellion, which may lead one to expect a manual on how to keep power rather than a reflection on how to create a just society. This suspicion is not well founded, however. It soon becomes clear that *The Instruction Addressed to King Merikare* is, like instructions generally, a meditation on how to uphold *ma'at*. The word *ma'at* is often translated as "truth" or "justice," and can thus be seen as the core of the value system that will later be notably upheld by Superman (minus "the American way"). One central theme related to *ma'at* in *The Instruction Addressed to King Merikare* is punishing justly. Merikare is encouraged to punish in such a way that even in his absence—that is, when he is not there to inspire fear—people will speak well of him. He is also advised to avoid capital punishment, so as not to exact wrongful punishment, the apparent implication being that to be fair we must recognize the limits of our knowledge of innocence and guilt. There is one exception, though. Merikare's father is fine with capital punishment in the case of rebels, which suggests that they represent an intolerable threat to political stability that is categorically distinct from other forms of social deviance.

This instruction also features what is presumably the oldest recorded argument for meritocracy. Merikare's father says:

> Do not prefer the wellborn to the commoner,
> Choose a man on account of his skills,
> Then all crafts are done. (101)

This apparent opposition to entrenching social hierarchy relates to a final point we want to mention. Merikare's father offers an argument for something that might seem quite distasteful from an egalitarian point of view, namely, the importance of a rich bureaucracy. Here is the argument:

> Advance your officials, so that they act by your laws,
> He who has wealth at home will not be partial,
> He is a rich man who lacks nothing.
> The poor man does not speak justly,
> Not righteous is one who says, "I wish I had,"
> He inclines to him who will pay him. (100)

This argument justifies elevating one group within society to a place of economic privilege on the surprising grounds that this is the best way to achieve the equality of all before the law. Officials who judge disputes should be impartial, and officials who lack wealth are more liable to be swayed by bribes. So paradoxically, it is precisely the poor, who are not in a position to offer a bribe, who should want there to be a class of spectacularly rich government officials, since their wealth will make bribery ineffective anyway. We may detect a critical response to this claim in one of the greatest works of moral and political philosophy in ancient Egyptian literature, one which may take some inspiration from the instructions but which is not itself an instruction: *The Tale of the Eloquent Peasant*. Its title character would be a fine example of someone who could crush you in debate if you elected to fall silent.

6

HEATED EXCHANGES

Philosophy in Egyptian Narratives and Dialogues

Have you ever complained about being treated unfairly and gotten short shrift from those who could do something about it? Have you ever found yourself getting into a disagreement, but with yourself? If so, you'll be able to relate to the two classic works of ancient Egyptian philosophy that we will be discussing in what follows, *The Tale of the Eloquent Peasant* and *The Dispute Between a Man and His Ba*. Both have something like a narrative structure, built around speeches or dialogue. The power of the works derives from the content of these speeches, and from the relationship between these speeches and the narrative frame. The fact that these are evidently fictional works makes them of literary interest, to be sure, but the weighty discourses at their center make them the works of ancient Egypt that are perhaps easiest to recognize as philosophical.

Egyptologist Hans Goedicke believed that the two texts in question have more in common than their structure.[1] He hypothesized that they were the creations of a single author, on the basis of linguistic similarities between the two. Goedicke went so far as to identify this person as Khety, whom we mentioned in the last chapter as the acclaimed author of *The Instruction of King Amenemhet* and who also is credited with writing a unique and darkly funny instruction known as *The Satire of the Trades*, in which a scribe impresses upon his son just how much better it is to be a scribe than to have various other jobs. Khety is, in fact, celebrated in *The Immortality of Writers* as perhaps the most important writer of them all. If Goedicke was right to ascribe all these texts to his hand, then he should be ranked among the great literary geniuses of world history. Still, before we get carried away and start petitioning for a very posthumous Nobel Prize, we should remember that these ascriptions to Khety are highly speculative, especially when we get past the cases of *The Satire of the Trades* and *The Instruction of King Amenemhet*. Firm evidence concerning the authorship of ancient Egyptian texts is generally hard to come by.

The Tale of the Eloquent Peasant is set during the First Intermediate Period, a time of disunity and decentralized power falling between periods of political unity known as the Old and Middle Kingdoms.[2] It is only the "First" because there's a later "Second Intermediate Period" between the Middle and New Kingdoms, and even a "Third Intermediate Period" between the New Kingdom and what is known as the Late Period, which comes to an end in 332 BC thanks to Alexander the Great. Some have wondered whether the *Eloquent Peasant* might have been written during the time in which it is set. It is most commonly viewed, though, as a production of the Middle Kingdom and specifically the literary golden age of the twelfth dynasty. Richard Parkinson, the Egyptologist who has done the most to advance our understanding of the *Eloquent Peasant* as a literary work, guesses that it was written during the reign of Senwosret II, which would probably mean somewhere around the mid-nineteenth century BC.[3]

The tale begins with a peasant named Khunanup from Wadi Natrun, an oasis to the northwest of what is now Cairo, telling his wife that he is going to the Nile Valley to get provisions. Stocked with bread and beer to live on and a variety of goods to trade, he heads toward Heracleopolis, at that time the capital of Egypt. Along the way he encounters the tale's villain: Nemtinakht, a scheming aristocrat who devises a plan to steal the peasant's belongings. Nemtinakht sends a servant to lay a sheet on the narrow path between his barley crops and a body of water. When Khunanup tries to travel along the path, Nemtinakht warns him not to trample on the sheet. Trying to obey this command leads Khunanup toward the barley, which he is also warned not to trample, and soon enough one of Khunanup's donkeys can't help but snack on a bit of barley. Nemtinakht seizes upon this justification to confiscate the donkey. When Khunanup protests, Nemtinakht beats him and takes all of his donkeys; you can almost picture him twirling his mustache and cackling as his nefarious plan comes to fruition.

Khunanup spends a week fruitlessly pleading with Nemtinakht to return his belongings, then goes on to Heracleopolis to ask the High Steward Rensi to intervene. Rensi discusses the matter with his fellow officials but they are dismissive, and Rensi himself remains silent, for the moment. Khunanup petitions him again and gives the first of the extended speeches that take up the bulk of the text. Rensi is evidently impressed. He goes to the king, who is called Nebkaure, and tells him of the peasant's eloquence. The king advises Rensi to remain silent so that the peasant will speak more. Rensi should quietly provide for Khunanup's family in the meanwhile. Khunanup petitions Rensi eight more times, thus making a total of nine speeches. Each time Rensi is unresponsive or even hostile: after the third speech, he has poor Khunanup beaten. By the ninth petition, Khunanup despairs that justice will never be done, and appears to be considering suicide. Rensi finally ends his misery and reveals that these petitions have all been recorded in writing. He has them read out and presented to King Nebkaure, who is extremely pleased and tells Rensi to go ahead and judge the case. The wicked Nemtinakht is harshly condemned, and all his property awarded to Khunanup. The end.

There is an irony at the center of the story: though eloquence wins the case for Khunanup in the end, it also postpones the day of justice. As Parkinson puts it: "The eloquence which ensures the peasant's success is also the cause of his prolonged suffering."[4] And there is dramatic irony too, as we sympathize with Khunanup's frustration even while knowing that he has already found favor. These aspects of the text point toward a philosophical question. Is the injustice done to the peasant by Nemtinakht being compounded by a further injustice on the part of Rensi and the king? If so, it is not the one that Khunanup imagines. These powerful men are not rejecting his entreaties, only dragging things out to provoke him to further speechifying. They place aesthetic appreciation above the need for expedient justice. The high-ranking official and the monarch are concerned about the needs of their subjects, but if you display a talent for speaking as well as need, well, it's time to pass the popcorn and your needs are just going to have to wait.

These themes are further deepened by the content of the nine speeches themselves. The Egyptologist Jan Assmann has said that the tale could justifiably be called *A Treatise on Ma'at*.[5] As mentioned in the previous chapter, *ma'at* is an Egyptian concept associated with order and righteousness. It comes up in almost every one of Khunanup's nine petitions, which gives us good reason to view the *Eloquent Peasant* as a work of political philosophy. We might first note some important religious dimensions of the concept, as Ma'at is also a goddess in the Egyptian pantheon, recognizable in iconography by the feather tucked into her headband. In the *Book of the Dead*, we find the memorable image of a scale upon which the heart of the person seeking to reach the afterlife must be weighed against the feather of Ma'at. If one's heart weighs the same as the feather one may pass on; otherwise, a monster sits ready to devour the unfortunate wayfarer.

But in the *Eloquent Peasant* religious connotations remain mostly implicit. Khunanup instead invokes *ma'at* as a moral and social ideal. In the first petition, he says that political authority should be a "destroyer of falsehood" and a "creator of *ma'at*." In the third petition, in the context of demanding that Rensi "deal punishment to the punishable," Khunanup brings up what he identifies as a proverbial saying: "Doing *ma'at* is the breath of the nose." As noted previously, the word's meaning seems to hover between our notions of truth and justice. We can see this in the eighth petition, where Khunanup exhorts Rensi to "speak *ma'at*, do *ma'at*."

The translation "truth" goes better with speaking, whereas "justice" would be more natural for action. Of course, that does not show the Egyptians were philosophically confused. They would no doubt say to speakers of English that we take apart one unified concept, what they called *ma'at*, into two artificially separate ones, obscuring the intimate connection between truth in speaking and justice in action.

Assmann takes the most important passage in the *Eloquent Peasant*, when understood as a kind of philosophical treatise on *ma'at*, to be the part of the ninth and final petition where Khunanup says: "There is no yesterday for the negligent, no friend for him who is deaf to *ma'at*, no holiday for the selfish." Assmann discerns here a tripartite definition of *ma'at* in terms of social solidarity. "There is no yesterday for the negligent": this line opposes *ma'at* to negligence or inactivity, which it associates with forgetfulness of the past. *Ma'at* demands active solidarity, a dedication to reciprocal action that is absent when complaints go unanswered and wicked deeds go unpunished. "No friend for him who is deaf to *ma'at*": whereas the previous line was about a failure to act, this one is about a failure to listen. *Ma'at* is thus communicative solidarity, and Assmann here reminds us of the thematization of the value of hearing in *The Instruction of Ptahhotep*. Finally, "no holiday for the selfish," an aphorism that raises a question of consistency between Madonna's early smash hits, "Holiday" and "Material Girl." As Assmann notes, this line adds the notion of intentional solidarity, an internal commitment to altruism over egoistic self-concern.

The *Eloquent Peasant* stands in an intriguing relationship to the genre of instructions, which standardly ascribe wise words to people in high social positions, like the vizier Ptahhotep, and the king addressing his son Merikare. In this work, by contrast, wisdom is ascribed to a marginal figure, someone of low social status from the fringes of Egypt. This may remind us of Ptahhotep's first maxim that wisdom may be found anywhere. The plot thickens when we note that a number of scholars think Nebkaure from the *Eloquent Peasant* may be the same king who is speaking to his son in *Merikare*.[6] This opens up the possibility that the *Eloquent Peasant* is a critical response to a claim we found in that instruction, that "the poor man does not speak justly." Of course, if Hans Goedicke is right that Khety was so prolific as to have written both the *Eloquent Peasant* and *Merikare*, then this turns out to be a case of an author in dialogue with himself.

Speaking of dialogue with oneself, let's turn to the *Dispute Between a Man and His Ba*.[7] Unfortunately, no manuscript preserves the beginning of the work intact, so the initial setting and narrative framing of the dialogue are now lost. The text as we have it begins with a man in the midst of complaining that he is overwhelmed. His problem is that his *ba* is disagreeing with him. The standard translation of *ba* is "soul," so the work is often called *The Dialogue of a Man and His Soul*, although it is also known as *The Man Who Was Weary of Life*. But as with *ma'at*, we are dealing here with a distinctive ancient Egyptian concept. If the *ba* is a spiritual dimension of the human person not identical with the body, it is not the only such entity.[8] The Egyptians also spoke of a person's *ka*, which is something like vital energy, without which a person could not be alive. While humans appear to have only one *ka*, there are references to gods having multiple *kas*, representing different personifications of different qualities. Some translate *ka* as "spirit." The *ba*, on the other hand, often represented as a bird with a human head, seems to be an aspect of the person that is specifically relevant for the afterlife. So if we use the translation "soul," we should bear in mind especially the connotation of "soul" as a manifestation after death. James Allen describes how, in the *Pyramid Texts*, we get the sense that once the *ka* separates from a person at death, it is the task of the *ba* to reunite with the *ka* in the afterlife, with the resulting union being known as an *akh*, or "effective being."[9]

Understanding all this prepares us for the strangeness of the *Dispute Between a Man and His Ba*. It is a dialogue between a man and an entity that is in some sense his own essence, albeit an essence that is not supposed to be active until after his death, according to other Egyptian cultural evidence. Even more remarkable is the topic of the disagreement. The man is thoroughly dissatisfied with life and enamored by the thought of death. In this, he is opposed by his *ba*, which discourages his morbid obsession and recommends the full embrace of life. This is, therefore, a dispute about the relative value of being alive or being dead, in which the living man upholds the value of death while the version of him that is supposed to be active only after death upholds the value of life.

Actually, though, there is some disagreement among scholars about which side of the debate the man and his *ba* are on, at least initially; the confusion is no doubt partly the result of our missing the beginning of the work. Early on in our surviving text, the man appears to complain that his *ba* is pulling him toward death when he is not ready for it. So here, it seems to be the *ba* who longs for the afterlife, whereas the man is unsure and still clinging to this world. Allen follows this reading, and thus detects later on in the dialogue "a profound reversal in the Soul's attitude" in the wake of which "each party now adopts the other's position, the Soul advocating life and the Man, death."[10] It is possible, though, to read the dialogue in such a way that each party consistently holds the same position. Parkinson explains the man's initial complaint not as a desire to cling to life, but as a lament that he cannot hope for a pleasant afterlife if his *ba* refuses to stand by him in the next world. According to Parkinson, the death toward which the *ba* would drag the man in that case would not be the end of his life in this world, but a more complete destruction of the self: "the second, final, death that was inflicted on the dead who were condemned by the gods."[11]

On either account, it is clear that the debate eventually becomes a conflict between the man's preference for death and the *ba*'s advocacy of life. The two pursue the debate through competing descriptions of death. For the man, it is "sweet relief" and the West, as ancient Egyptians used to call the land of the deceased, is a comforting "harbor" at the end of a voyage (156). His *ba*, on the other hand, describes death as "heartbreak" and as a man's being taken away from his house, rather than as a homecoming. The *ba* furthermore emphasizes how the dead are forgotten, even those buried in magnificent pyramids. Then there are the two parables told by the *ba*, the first of which is clearest in its message. A man's wife and children are killed by crocodiles and the man in the parable mourns most for the children, who lived so briefly. The second parable seems more trivial, as it involves a man who asks for dinner before his wife is prepared to give it to him. The portrayal of the character's impatience seems calculated to reveal how irrational and ignoble it is to wish for something like death before the time for it comes. Thus the two parables seem to encourage us to value life, while not clinging to it, realizing instead that there is an appropriate period of time for each life.

After these parables, the man offers a series of lyrical speeches, the first a lament structured around the memorable refrain: "Look, my name reeks." The second speech is likewise structured around the refrain, "Who can I talk to today?" and goes beyond personal sadness to evoke general societal breakdown, as when the man says: "Who can I talk to today? There are no just men, and the land is left over to the doers of injustice" (159). As you might guess, this phrase involves forms of the word *ma'at* and also the word standardly understood as its antonym, *isfet*. Here we see most clearly why the *Dispute* is often classified as belonging to the genre of texts known as "laments," which includes other works such as *The Prophecies of Neferti*, *The Complaints of Khakheperreseneb*, and *The Admonitions of Ipuwer*, each of which bewail overturned norms and unchecked evil. Both the *Dispute* and the *Eloquent Peasant* feature moments where the personal pain of the protagonist is generalized in this way, allowing for the expression of moral and social ideals through disturbing depictions of what happens when those ideals are abandoned.

In a third speech, the man turns from lamenting life to glorifying death. "Death is to me today like the smell of flowers," he says, and, in a fourth and final speech, he speaks of the afterlife as a place where justice is done, and where one can become truly wise and knowledgeable (160). The work then ends with a reply from his *ba*, which, despite representing no major change in position, nevertheless represents a resolution of the conflict between the two sides. The *ba* urges the man to cease his complaining, saying: "Love me here, having put aside the West, and also still desire to reach the West," and invoking the same image used initially by the man to conclude: "I shall alight when you are weary; so shall we make harbor together" (160). The *ba* therefore ends the argument by once again encouraging the immediate embrace of life while also acknowledging that death is, as the man has been suggesting, something worth looking forward to.

While the *Dispute* may seem to be an uncontroversial example of a philosophical dialogue, Parkinson has pointed out that the two characters do not actually debate, but instead give opposing speeches. Moreover, the resolution at the end arguably fails to make clear any rational basis for the *ba*'s partial agreement with the man.[12] In Parkinson's view, this is therefore a poetic dialogue devoted to a broad theme, rather than an argumentative work. But while it is true that no one speech is presented as a rational argument, such an argument does emerge from the exchange as a whole. The author raises the fundamental question of how the value of life compares to the value of death, and concludes by transforming two seemingly antithetical competing views into complementary attitudes. Life is a limited resource, to be enjoyed fully so long as we can; yet it is also the occasion for many sorrows which will be ended finally only by death. This synthesis of seemingly opposing positions is one major philosophical contribution of the dialogue. Going further, we should recall that this is the dialogue of a man not with another person, but with his own essence. The *Dispute* is therefore an exploration of psychological complexity and fragmentation. It suggests that the sorrows of life may lead to a double alienation, from both the world and from oneself. We need not see the man as having a split personality, necessarily, but he is certainly being pulled in different directions, a feature common to many experiences of depression and other troubled mental states. The resolution of conflict in the *ba*'s final reply thus represents the achievement of psychological wholeness and the related recovery of a sense of agency and direction.

There is, of course, much more that could be said, not only about the *Dispute* or the *Eloquent Peasant*, but about ancient Egyptian literature more generally. We hope, however, to have already demonstrated the range of philosophical themes that can be found in this literature. From here, we might have expected to continue our story by moving south, up the Nile, to ancient Nubia, whose history is deeply influenced by ancient Egypt. The two cultures were most famously intertwined when Nubian kings ruled both Nubia and Egypt during the twenty-fifth dynasty, in the aforementioned Third Intermediate Period. Unfortunately, while there are preserved Nubian inscriptions written in Egyptian, the distinctive body of writing from Nubia in what is called the Meroitic script is currently inaccessible because the language remains very poorly understood. So, in order to continue tracing written philosophical thought in Africa outside the areas colonized by Greeks and Romans, we are forced to move ahead into the Christian era. We will be examining texts that resulted from the spread of Christianity in the eastern part of Africa during antiquity. Nubia, for example, became Christian under the influence of Byzantine missionaries in late antiquity and remained so until the early modern era, by which time Islam became dominant in this area that is now mainly in the modern country of Sudan. Further southward and eastward, in Ethiopia, Christianity gained the status of state religion even earlier than in Nubia and never completely lost its place to Islam, thriving to this day.

7

SOLOMON, SOCRATES, AND OTHER SAGES

Early Ethiopian Philosophy

The 1960s comedian Tom Lehrer devoted one of his songs to the story of Oedipus Rex, the Greek tragic hero who unwittingly killed his own father, married his own mother, and then plucked his eyes out upon discovering what he had done. Lehrer sums up the moral of the story like this: "so be sweet and kind to mother; now and then have a chat. Buy her candy or some flowers or a brand new hat. But maybe you had better let it go at that!" These would have been helpful words of wisdom for another Greek hero, a silent sage named Secundus. According to the story of his life, he was sent away as a child to train as a scholar. At one point during his education, he comes across rather less helpful words of wisdom, stating that "all women are prostitutes."

Shocked by this sweeping statement, Secundus determines to test its truth in the most disturbing way possible. He returns to his home, unrecognizable now that he is an adult with a beard, and through the intermediary of a maid, offers his own mother money to have sex with him. His mother is against the idea at first but is convinced by the maid that sleeping with this handsome stranger is a good idea. Secundus thus spends the night in his mother's bed, resisting her lust and going to sleep with his head on her chest. In the morning, responding to her confusion and dismay at his chastity, he reveals his true identity. His mother, filled with horror and shame at what she has done, goes and hangs herself in the garden. Secundus reacts to this tragic turn of events by vowing to be silent from that point onwards, reflecting that it was his tongue that killed his mother. Even when the Roman emperor Hadrian threatens him with death in order to force him to speak, he remains silent. Only when he is given tools to write is he willing to respond to questions. Most of the book on Secundus' life and thought is taken up not by the sordid story of how he came to be silent but by his written answers to a series of philosophical queries posed to him.

Why, though, are we troubling you with the story of this Greek philosopher and his disastrous use of the experimental method? Shouldn't we be exploring Africa (and, now that we have left ancient Egypt, primarily sub-Saharan Africa) as an alternative home for philosophy, with traditions separate from and not originating with Greek thought? We will indeed be doing that as this book goes on, but things are not that simple. It is common for people to contrast "Western" and "non-Western" philosophy, with the former referring to philosophical traditions that are European in origin, ultimately traceable back to ancient Greece, and the latter to the independent traditions that arose in places like China and India. But this has always been a problematic contrast, and not only because it seems rather rude to define all these other traditions negatively, as *non*-Western or *non*-European. The fact is that Greek philosophy's influence has never been confined to Europe or to territories generally recognized as part of the West. Philosophy in the Islamic world was deeply influenced by Greek philosophy, and some of its greatest authors lived in central Asia while engaging closely with Aristotle.

A similar point can be made in the case of *The Life and Maxims of Secundus* and several other Greek texts that made their way in ancient, medieval, and early modern times to sub-Saharan Africa and, in particular, to Ethiopia. This is just one part of a much larger story of the diffusion of Greek philosophical literature, a diffusion that was much wider and more complex than is usually appreciated. Greek philosophy was rendered into Syriac, Armenian, and Georgian, as well as Arabic.[1] In the case of Ethiopian literature, it may first of all be worth noting that the word "Ethiopia" itself is Greek in origin. It means "burnt face," and was used by the Greeks to refer to the part of Africa that lay beyond Egypt, full of dark-skinned people. Often it specifically referred to Nubia, in what is now the south of Egypt and the country of Sudan. As we'll see later, this ancient Greek usage eventually gave rise to the use of "Ethiopia" as a general term for all of black Africa, something that was still common in the nineteenth century. The story we want to tell in this chapter, though, starts with the spread of Christianity to the Horn of Africa, and in particular to the area that was also called Abyssinia. This was the land of the Habesha people, in what are now the countries of Ethiopia and Eritrea.

The coming of Christianity to Africa is often associated with the colonization of Africa in modern times, but it should not be news that Christianity existed in Africa already in antiquity. Just think of figures like Tertullian, in what is now Tunisia, or Augustine, in what is now Algeria. These thinkers, however, lived in parts of Africa controlled by the Roman empire, in which Christianity started off as a minority religion, often persecuted, and only gradually grew, eventually becoming the sole official faith late in the fourth century. Ethiopia too was Christianized in the fourth century, but through a top-down rather than bottom-up process, beginning with the conversion of King Ezana of Aksum early in the fourth century. The kingdom of Aksum had been flourishing in this area for at least a couple of centuries already, but the conversion of the king by Frumentius, a Syrian Christian who ended up in Aksum by happenstance, made Aksum and thus Ethiopia one of the very first places in the entire world where Christianity held the status of official religion. We have coins and stones inscribed with crosses dating back to this time, with writing on them in various languages, including Greek and Ge'ez. Ge'ez is an Ethiopian language that is Semitic, meaning that it is in the same family of languages as Arabic and Hebrew. The existence of Semitic languages in this region is thought to be a legacy of much more ancient transmissions of culture across the Red Sea from southern Arabia.[2] By the fifth century, we already have the Bible and liturgy being rendered into Ge'ez, once again from Greek.

Coming now to the topic of how Greek philosophical literature was translated into Ge'ez, important to the story is the connection between Ethiopia and a place that is now familiar to us: Egypt. Frumentius travelled to Alexandria to be consecrated as archbishop of Ethiopia by Athanasius.[3] Thereafter it became tradition that the Coptic Church of Egypt would provide Ethiopia with its *abuna* (or archbishop). Only in the twentieth century did they finally take the step of appointing an Ethiopian as head of the Ethiopian Orthodox Church. Before that, it was always an Egyptian. This ecclesiastical connection facilitated the importation of intellectual products, with an interesting early case being a Greek text called the *Physiologus*.[4]

This book introduces the reader to an array of real and mythological animals, which are described in zoological, ethical, and symbolic terms. Some of this material is reminiscent of a text like Aristotle's *History of Animals*, but the symbolism in the text is fervently Christian. For example, the ichneumon or Egyptian mongoose is described as being known to sneak into the open mouth of a sleeping crocodile, eat it from the inside, and then burst through its stomach to freedom. Whereas the modern reader will inevitably note that this mongoose is a cuddly version of the creature from the *Alien* movies, the *Physiologus* instead remarks that it is like Christ himself, who descended into hell to free some souls from death (§25).

The case of the *Physiologus* shows how the dissemination of Greek literature sometimes had little or nothing to do with European connections. Claude Sumner, a Canadian scholar who moved to Ethiopia and became a pioneer in the study of Ethiopian philosophy, tells us that the original Greek version of the *Physiologus* was almost certainly written in Egypt, specifically in Alexandria, probably in the late second or early third century. The Ethiopic translation may have been accomplished as early as the fifth century, quite likely by an Ethiopian monk also living in Egypt.[5] Sumner even argues that certain aspects of the book recall ancient Egyptian thought and culture.[6] Thus with this translation of the text from Greek into Ge'ez, we actually have a text moving from one African culture to another.

The *Physiologus* is one of five works that Sumner has identified as forming the basic texts of Ethiopian philosophy. Three of these are works of translation, deriving ultimately from Greek texts.[7] The *Physiologus*, as we have just said, was translated directly from Greek in late antiquity. *The Life and Maxims of Secundus* was instead translated from an Arabic translation of the original Greek text, possibly as late as the fifteenth or sixteenth century; the same goes for *The Book of the Wise Philosophers*, which we'll discuss below. Finally, in the seventeenth century, we have original compositions in Ge'ez by Zera Yacob and his disciple Walda Heywat, whom we will discuss in the next chapters. Would it be fair to say, then, that before the seventeenth century, there was no original philosophy written in Ge'ez, only translations? J.M. Harden, in his 1926 book, *An Introduction to Ethiopic Christian Literature*, provides what is still a useful overview of literature in Ge'ez but warns the reader early on that this literature is "characterized by a conspicuous defect," namely "its want of originality," as it is "for the most part a literature of translations."[8]

To this, we would say: not so fast. When we discuss Zera Yacob and Walda Heywat, we will begin by exploring the fifteenth and sixteenth centuries leading up to their time as an era of religious controversies. This era produced a number of writings that ought to be re-examined for their philosophical content and implications. For now, just as we looked at the philosophical themes that may be found in the *Epic of Gilgamesh* when discussing ancient Mesopotamian thought, we can look for distinctively Ethiopian philosophical material in what can be called the country's national epic, the *Kebra Nagast* (or "Glory of the Kings").[9] This book is best known for telling the story of the meeting of the Queen of Sheba and King Solomon, a story that can be found in the Hebrew Bible but which is greatly expanded upon in the *Kebra Nagast*. According to the latter, the queen referred to in the Bible was the Queen of Ethiopia, known as Makeda, and her time with King Solomon resulted in a child who became the first King of Ethiopia, traditionally known as Menelik I. Later kings of Ethiopia, in accordance with the account in the *Kebra Nagast*, understood themselves as direct descendants of King Solomon. This understanding certainly goes back at least as far as 1270, when Yekuno Amlak overthrew the Zagwe dynasty that had been ruling prior to that and founded the "Solomonic" dynasty—or, as he saw things, restored that dynasty to power. This dynasty ruled Ethiopia until 1974, when Haile Selassie, the last Emperor of Ethiopia, was deposed by the Communist Derg regime, dying shortly thereafter.

Especially in light of its political significance, the *Kebra Nagast* easily claims the title of most celebrated work in the Ethiopian literary tradition, at least aside from the translation of the Bible. Which brings us to the question: is the *Kebra Nagast* too a work of translation? According to the book itself, the answer is yes. Its colophon or closing statement identifies the book as a translation from Arabic that was in turn based on a Coptic original.[10] (Coptic, by the way, is the liturgical language of the Coptic Church, and can thus be seen as the only surviving variety of the ancient Egyptian language, one written using a variation of the Greek alphabet.) But it is a matter of scholarly debate whether the information in the colophon is accurate. The scholar Richard Pankhurst has stated flatly: "No Coptic or Arabic version has...ever come to light, and it may be assumed that the text was in fact originally written in Ge'ez."[11] Which seems plausible. Bear in mind that this is not merely a national epic, but a thoroughly *nationalistic* epic, one that positions Ethiopians as the chosen people of God who have taken over this role from the Jews. It is natural to think that such a work must originally have been written in an Ethiopian tongue. Some have therefore assumed that the Ge'ez text as we have it is really the original version; we can gather from the colophon that it was completed by 1321, during the rule of the Emperor Amda Seyon.

The truth, though, is almost certainly somewhere between Pankhurst's assumption of complete originality and the colophon's pretense of mere translation. Wendy Belcher observes that some parts of the book dealing with the queen are definitely translated from a pre-existing Arabic text. She suspects that this Arabic text may not have been Egyptian, but Nubian, and written some time in the twelfth century or earlier.[12] Other parts of the *Kebra Nagast*, however, depict real historical events involving the kingdom of Aksum, specifically in the sixth century, when King Kaleb of Aksum conquered a significant portion of southern Arabia, extending Aksumite territory to its largest extent. Interpretation of this material has led one scholar to suppose that there was a version of the *Kebra Nagast* completed already in the sixth century, making it contemporary to the events described.[13] As for the question of what language the work was written in, it has even been proposed that the work may have been first written in Ge'ez, then translated into Coptic, then translated into Arabic, before finally being translated into Ge'ez again (indeed, "geez!" seems like an appropriate reaction).[14] Still, whenever its various parts were first composed, and whatever languages may have been involved in this process, it is clear that the *Kebra Nagast* is a distinctively Ethiopian combination of sources, strikingly original in its own way.

But what, if anything, is philosophical about it? Well, if we recall that the Greek word *philosophia* literally means "love of wisdom," then philosophy is arguably one of the book's central themes. Queen Makeda is praised as having already been a very wise ruler, who nonetheless travels to see King Solomon precisely because she values wisdom above all else. Before departing, she says to her people: "For it is right for us to follow the footprints of wisdom, and for the soles of our feet to stand upon the threshold of the gates of wisdom. Let us seek her, and we shall find her; let us love her, and she will not withdraw herself from us; let us pursue her, and we shall overtake her; let us ask, and we shall receive; and let us turn our hearts to her so that we may never forget her" (§24). It is true that wisdom in this text is defined in a fundamentally religious way, as the most valuable wisdom that Makeda receives from Solomon is knowledge of the one true God of the Jews, causing her to abandon her people's tradition of worshipping the sun and other natural elements or artificial creations. Yet the dialogue between Makeda and Solomon also features general philosophical questions that are not reducible to belief in the Jewish faith, such as: What difference is there in substance or value between a rich monarch like Solomon and a simple laborer? How does the fleeting nature of mortal existence relate to the importance of striving to do good in the world (§27)?

Also worthy of mention are the gender dynamics in the depiction of Makeda and Solomon. Contrary to what Secundus learned about women, it is Makeda who is focused on the pursuit of wisdom, while Solomon is after more (or perhaps we should say "less") than edifying conversation. The story of how he comes to have his way with her is, in its own way, as disturbing as what we find in Secundus, perhaps even more. Makeda asks Solomon to vow that he will not take her by force, and he agrees, but only on the condition that she vow in return not to steal any of his belongings. She laughs at the very idea—after all, she is already wealthy and came seeking only wisdom—but agrees nonetheless. She is offered food that will leave her thirsty and, after a bit of sleep, she wakes up parched. When she tries to drink from a jug of water next to Solomon's bed, he catches her hand, points out that she has broken her vow, and asserts that he is therefore released from his own vow.

Solomon's lust and trickery ultimately result in the glory of Ethiopia, which brings us to another central theme of the *Kebra Nagast*: the providential arrangement of events by God. That very night, after having his way with Makeda, Solomon has a dream in which a bright sun comes down from the heavens to shine over Israel but then flies away, going to shine even more brilliantly over Ethiopia. Makeda, after she returns to Ethiopia, gives birth to Menelik. As an adult, he goes to visit his father, who unsuccessfully seeks to convince him to stay in Israel and inherit the kingdom there. Accepting that he must send his son to go rule over Ethiopia, Solomon makes the fateful decision to send along with Menelik the first-born sons of all the nobles of Israel. It is at this point that the *Kebra Nagast* might earn an alternative title: *The Original Raiders of the Lost Ark*. Azariah, son of the high priest Zadok and one of those appointed to leave for Ethiopia, devises a plan to bring with him and his fellow sons of Israel the Ark of the Covenant, that famous chest containing the Ten Commandments, which is referred to in the *Kebra Nagast* as "the Tabernacle of the Law of God" and also as "Lady Zion."

With angelic support and other forms of divine intervention, the Ark is spirited away and brought to Ethiopia. Its arrival accomplishes the transfer of glory from Israel to Ethiopia. Power is ceremoniously handed over by Makeda to Menelik. Meanwhile, back in Israel, Solomon continues to succumb to lust, as he is tricked by an Egyptian woman into worshipping her pagan gods. By the end of the book, Ethiopia is exalted as the most powerful and blessed kingdom of all, with Rome—that is, the Byzantine empire—in second place. The author writes: "Thus hath God made for the King of Ethiopia more glory, and grace, and majesty than for all the other kings of the earth because of the greatness of Zion, the Tabernacle of the Law of God, the heavenly Zion" (§117).

Given the supernatural trappings and setting in ancient history, this exaltation of Ethiopia may seem to be of little contemporary relevance. Yet the work plays a central role in a recent essay by the Ethiopian philosopher Messay Kebede: "The Ethiopian Conception of Time and Modernity," which was written and published in Amharic, the most widely spoken Ethiopian language today. (Ge'ez apparently died out as a commonly spoken language early in the medieval period and ceased to be the main literary language by the nineteenth century, although it lives on as a liturgical language.) Kebede argues that Ethiopia has failed to flourish in recent times at least in part because of the acceptance, starting in the twentieth century, of Eurocentric models of the trajectory of history and the cultural foundations of modernity. He looks back to the *Kebra Nagast* as a prime example of the fact that, previously, "Ethiopia had her own theory of history," one in which it did not simply follow other countries but stood out as "history's leading force."[15] Kebede says that Ethiopia must once again take ownership of history in order to find direction and attain success.

The *Kebra Nagast*'s vision of the world could, indeed, hardly be less Eurocentric. Yet it also shows how deeply embedded Ethiopian thought has been within a specifically Judeo-Christian framework. How then did Ethiopian thinkers deal with the pagan heritage of the Hellenic world? Here we can turn to *The Book of the Wise Philosophers*.[16] The Ge'ez version of this work dates to somewhere around the second decade of the sixteenth century and is generally attributed to a cleric called

Abba Mikael, an Egyptian. The text is however labeled as coming "by the mouth of Mikael." This might suggest a collaborative process, in which the Egyptian cleric would have recited the text in a form of Arabic understandable to an Ethiopian scribe, who rendered it into Ge'ez. As for the Arabic text, Sumner identifies it as a work of translation by Ḥunayn ibn Isḥāq, a Christian Arab based in Baghdad in the ninth century and one of the greatest figures of the Greek–Arabic translation movement.[17] But it has also been suggested that Ḥunayn's text is one of multiple sources for the immediate Arabic predecessor to the Ge'ez text.[18]

Those coming to *The Book of the Wise Philosophers* expecting recognizable excerpts from Plato's dialogues or Aristotle's treatises will be disappointed. The book is a collection of sayings and anecdotes, the greatest number of which are attributed to anonymous wise men, some to religious figures (including Solomon, as it happens), and some to Greek philosophers, like Socrates, Plato, and Aristotle. But the sayings ascribed to them have little or no basis in the ancient texts through which we know them. Instead, these pagan philosophers are often made to talk of God, sin, and other spiritual matters in a way that is, if not explicitly Christian, at least remarkably congenial to the Christian point of view. A book like this tells us a lot about what the term "philosophy" has meant to people over the ages. Texts of this sort are easy to memorize, easy to appreciate, and also easy to modify, making them likely to acquire and lose material as they are transmitted, especially across language barriers. If we asked a well-educated resident of fifth century Alexandria or tenth century Baghdad or, alternatively, a sixteenth century monk in Ethiopia what they knew about Empedocles or Plato, they likely would not have responded by mentioning cosmology or the theory of Forms. They would probably have quoted from this kind of "wisdom literature," offering up thoughtful sayings or witty remarks that were collected and passed down across the centuries like philosophical baseball cards.[19]

Socrates appears frequently in such literature, and we find some rather amusing gems attributed to him here in *The Book of the Wise Philosophers*. When he asks his wife why she is weeping and she says it is because he is going to be killed unjustly, he replies, "would you be pleased if I were killed justly?" (137). In another manifestation of the historical inaccuracy common to this sort of collection, Socrates is made to say things that were originally associated with other sages, probably because of his more famous name. It is Socrates who is made the protagonist of a famous anecdote told about Diogenes the Cynic and Alexander the Great in antiquity, in which a great king finds the philosopher basking in the sun. When the king offers the philosopher whatever he wants, he is simply told to stop blocking the sunlight (137).

In addition to the historical inaccuracies, the text is a collection of disparate materials, so it is not easy to discern any unified set of ideas within its many sayings.

Sometimes the sayings are outright contradictory: we are told to love and to be merciless to our enemies (108), and that the soul depends on the body for its survival, and that it is immortal (109). Alongside the sort of misogynist remarks familiar from the *Tale of Secundus* (as at 205, 273), we are more convincingly told that "No precious stone is preferable to a good woman" (280) and that a man should respect his wife like an angel (279). Yet despite the apparent lack of any overall philosophical message, *The Book of the Wise Philosophers* is well worth reading, and not only for a sense of how ancient Greek philosophy might have been perceived in sixteenth century Ethiopia. Some of the sayings display such pithiness or insight that we can't resist quoting them: "People are of two types: for and against you" (112); "The rejoicing of the rich adds to the poverty of the poor" (120); "If you want to know the heart of a man, speak nonsense to him. If he accepts it, he is a fool" (180); and perhaps most memorably, "If it were possible to build a house by shouting, a donkey would build two houses a day" (147).

Furthermore, it is not quite right to say that there are no consistent themes in the book. One message any reader will take away is a powerful endorsement of asceticism, which again would fit well with its having been transmitted in monastic contexts.[20] Alongside the pagan philosophers, the heroes of some anecdotes are unnamed monks who, among other things, point to the sky when some travelers ask them for the right way (120-1), or advise us to be "grateful for a handful of food and always ready to die" (138-9). The worst attitude one can have is to love this world, since it distracts us from our true destination during what is in fact only a brief sojourn here in the body. By the same token, one should face hardships with stoicism, knowing that this life will be over soon anyway ("in an hour," 235). Actually, we are dealing here not just with a stoic attitude but real Stoicism. Precepts of Hellenistic thought have found their way into a Christian context, and in the case of this Ethiopian translation are still being put forward a good two millennia after Stoicism first emerged in the fourth century BC.

Devotion to an ascetic moral code, and the use of pagan authority figures in support of Christian belief, can be found in other Ethiopian texts from around the same time as the translations. One example involves an author named Enbaqom.[21] He was originally from Yemen, or perhaps Iraq. He chose to settle in Ethiopia in 1489, and converted from Islam (or possibly Judaism) to Ethiopian Orthodox Christianity, eventually becoming the top-ranking monk at the country's most important monastery, Debre Libanos. Enbaqom is known for having translated a number of texts from Arabic into Ge'ez. One of the them was the story of Barlaam and Josaphat, a Christianized version of the story of the Buddha, which makes for an interesting connection between our story and Indian philosophy. His book *Anqasa Amin*

(*Door of Faith*), on the other hand, is not a translation but an original apologetic work defending Christianity in contrast to Islam.

The *Door of Faith* shows the typical enthusiasm of a convert for his new creed, while also exploiting knowledge of what was most probably his former religion. He refers to numerous passages from the Quran, a book that he says is "full of the mysteries of God." These passages in fact establish the veracity of Christianity, even specific doctrines like the Incarnation and Trinity. The same dogmas are also supported by great sages of the pagan cultures, including Plato and Aristotle. Plato, for example, is quoted as having identified a highest principle of goodness, followed by a creative second principle and a third principle of life. This isn't authentic material from Plato, but does evoke the standard Neoplatonic hierarchy of the Good, Intellect, and Soul. As for asceticism, Enbaqom praises the moral discipline of his new faith: the New Testament encourages us to abandon love of this world, and devote ourselves to prayer and fasting. Such ethical precepts might inspire a man to retreat to a cave, and to contemplate in hopes of receiving wisdom: not, as we'll see next, a merely hypothetical scenario.

8

ONLY ONE TRUTH

Zera Yacob

Once upon a time in Ethiopia, there lived an Italian missionary named Giusto d'Urbino. He communicated regularly with a French scholar named Antoine d'Abbadie, who had made it his mission to collect every work of Ethiopian literature that he could get his hands on. It was in September of 1852 that d'Urbino first wrote to d'Abbadie to tell him of a strange book he had encountered, "a kind of novel or biographical story written by a deist philosopher."[1] About six months later, d'Urbino copied it out in his own hand to send to d'Abbadie. At the very end of the book, there was an addendum by a disciple of the philosopher explaining the circumstances of the philosopher's death and noting that he too (that is, the disciple) had been inspired to write a book. D'Urbino promised d'Abbadie to search for this second work as well. Finally, in 1854, he sent d'Abbadie a full version of the conjoined books by these two seventeenth century Ethiopian philosophers, the master and the student. It was entitled *The Hatata* (or "Inquiry") *of Zera Yacob and Walda Heywat*, and copied out by the hand of an Ethiopian scribe. It is therefore thanks to these efforts by d'Urbino that we have access to two of the most fascinating works in the history of Africana philosophy.

Or might it be the case that we have d'Urbino to thank not merely for finding the texts, but for creating them as well? This, as it turns out, is a matter of ongoing controversy. While scholars of African philosophy working after Claude Sumner's ground-breaking study of the *Hatata* have tended to take it for granted that these are authentic Ethiopian texts, doubts about this have been expressed since early in the twentieth century. The case against them being authentic has recently been made once again, at great length, by the French Ethiopianist, Anaïs Wion. She has revived the suspicion that it was d'Urbino himself who wrote these texts in Ge'ez. For now, we are going to set aside this controversy, but we will return to the question of authenticity later, after giving you a sense of what is at stake through an overview of their complementary explorations of God, reason, knowledge, and human well-being.

To appreciate these texts properly, we need to know something about the intellectual culture from which they (at least supposedly) came. The fifteenth and sixteenth centuries in Ethiopia were a time of intense debate over religious issues. Here we should bear in mind the isolation of Ethiopia as a Christian kingdom during the Middle Ages, especially as Islam was adopted by a number of surrounding peoples. Contact with the Coptic Church in Egypt, which supplied Ethiopia with the head of its church, was at times irregular. According to one scholar, contact became more regular by the time of the Solomonic dynasty and there were attempts by Egyptian metropolitans to update Ethiopian Christianity, but one consequence of such attempts was the opening up of questions of doctrine long settled elsewhere.[2] Old heresies and questions about the nature or natures of Christ and of the Trinity became live issues, the sort of issues dealt with by figures like Giyorgis of Segla. One of the most prolific authors of religious texts in Ge'ez, he wrote a work called the *Book of Mystery*, dated to 1424. Gérard Colin muses that this "voluminous theological opus" has some claim to "be considered the Ethiopian *Summa Theologica*."[3]

Also worth noting is a certain emperor who ruled Ethiopia during the middle third of the fifteenth century and who has been described as the "principal author" of religious nationalism in pre-modern Ethiopia.[4] This emperor's name, as it turns out, was Zera Yacob—the same as the philosopher we will be discussing in what follows. Obviously this is potentially confusing, so we have to be careful to distinguish between Zera Yacob the fifteenth century emperor associated with religious nationalism and the rationalist and arguably non-Christian thinker Zera Yacob of the seventeenth century, whose very existence as a real person has been challenged. There is no doubt that the emperor Zera Yacob was real, and he is credited with writing multiple books. One of the works ascribed to him (but which likely involves a collaborative effort by members of his court) is the *Book of Light*, which reflects the positions that the emperor took on what is and is not heretical.

There was, first of all, the problem what to do about the Ewostathians, or followers of Ewostatewos, who were notable for their belief in keeping two Sabbaths, the Sabbath of the Jews on Saturday and the Sabbath of the Christians on Sunday. So whether you are a fan of an ecumenical approach to religion or just like to keep your weekends free, this is a group you should be able to get behind. Apparently the emperor Zera Yacob felt this way too. Opting in this case for incorporation rather than antagonism, he held a council in 1450 and announced at the end of it that the Ewostathian view was now to be the view of the state: two Sabbaths for all! By contrast, the emperor was not willing to accommodate the Stephanites, followers of Estifanos, who were known to reject the veneration of Mary and the Cross and also prostration before the emperor, arguing that this was respect due only to God Himself.[5]

It is easy to assume that the last part was the worst part in the emperor's eyes, but it may well have been less deplorable to him than their stance on Mary. Some of the most interesting parts in the *Book of Light* involve the central importance he gives to Mary, whom he described as a virgin not only in body but in mind and conscience as well. Virginity of body, the emperor argues, is easy to find among men and women and cannot be what makes Mary special. Only the lack of any intention to sin could have made it possible for God to inhabit her.[6] While traditional Catholics will be familiar with the idea of Mary as lacking sin, they may be surprised by the emperor's subsequent argument that her purity of mind and inhabitance by God meant that Mary was privy to divine knowledge, knowledge to which no other human mind or even angelic mind has ever had access. As a result, she is identified as the ultimate prophet, more powerful than all others.[7] It has been said of the emperor Zera Yacob that he elevates Mary to a status akin to that of a goddess.[8]

If the fifteenth century was marked by questions of doctrine among Christians, the most important conflict of the sixteenth century was with Islam.[9] It was in this century that Ahmad Grañ, the leader of the Adal Sultanate based in what is now Somaliland, declared a *jihād* against Ethiopia, to which it had been paying tribute. The result was the most successful conquest of Ethiopia prior to the Italian occupation of the twentieth century. This conflict provides the relevant context for Enbaqom's *Anqasa Amin*, described at the end of the previous chapter. His defence of Christianity was addressed to none other than Grañ himself. Alongside disputes among Ethiopian Christians and between Christians and Muslims, there was yet another religious controversy that is still more important for understanding Zera Yacob, the philosopher. This is the conflict arising from the influence of Portuguese and Spanish Jesuits on the Ethiopian royal court, an influence that reached its apex in the seventeenth century during Zera Yacob's lifetime. This part of the story goes back to 1543, when Portugal provided aid to combat the invasion by Grañ, who was himself supported by the Ottoman empire. The involvement of international powers in this African war was typical of the increasingly shrinking world of the early modern period.

The ability of Jesuit missionaries to gain an audience with the Ethiopian monarch and operate within Ethiopia ebbed and flowed during the sixteenth century, but they gained new and unprecedented success in the early decades of the seventeenth century.[10] The emperor Za Dengel was converted to Catholicism and, although his rule was short-lived and he was overthrown, a subsequent emperor named Susenyos also converted in 1621. He established Catholicism as the official religion of the realm, replacing the Orthodox Church. This massive change met with much resistance and uprisings and, finally, about a decade later, in 1632, Susenyos declared religious liberty and abdicated power in favor of his son, Fasiladas. Upon taking power, Fasiladas promptly re-established Ethiopian Orthodox Christianity as the state religion and, within a couple of years, he expelled the Jesuits from Ethiopia.

These momentous events directly shaped the life of Zera Yacob, who was born in 1599 in Aksum, the former capital of the empire that first established Christianity as state religion in Ethiopia back in the fourth century. Zera Yacob became a teacher in that city during the rule of the emperor Susenyos, and was well versed in both the Ethiopian Orthodox and Catholic interpretations of the Bible. He tells us that he adopted an ecumenical spirit with regard to the different versions of Christianity that were contending for power in his culture. He wrote, "while teaching and expounding the books [for my students], I said, the foreigners (*frang*) say these things, and the Copts say these other things.' I did not say, 'this interpretation is good' or 'that interpretation is bad.' Rather, I said, 'all of these interpretations are good if we ourselves are good.' They all hated me for this, since to the Copts I seemed like a foreigner, and to the foreigners, I seemed like a Copt" (65).

Let us clarify the two terms he is using here. *Frang*, meaning "foreigner," is derived from Arabic, in which the term originated as the name of the "Franks" who attacked the lands of Islam during the Crusades. Though the application of this term to the Iberian Jesuits might suggest that some sort of racial distinction is being made here, that is clearly not the case in Zera Yacob's usage. He contrasts the term with "Copt," a term that refers neither to race nor even to nationality. Instead, it identifies adherents of the Ethiopian Orthodox Church, making reference to their administrative connection to the Egyptian church. Obviously, when Zera Yacob says that he was mistaken at times for a *Frang*, he is not talking about being mistaken for a European foreigner but rather treating the term as referring to a religious position that anyone can adopt.

Zera Yacob goes on to describe the major turning point in his life. An enemy of his falsely denounced him to the emperor as one of those who promoted rebellion in defence of Ethiopian Orthodoxy after the establishment of Catholicism. To avoid being killed for this, Zera Yacob fled his hometown, taking with him some gold and, even more valuable, his most prized possession: a copy of the Psalms of David. He eventually happened upon a cave that he made into a home for the rest of the time before the abdication and death of Susenyos, which was about two years. It is here that the text shifts from a story of political upheaval to a record of philosophical contemplation. Despite the autobiographical frame he offers us, Zera Yacob devotes most of his book to a report of the philosophical thoughts he had while in this forced seclusion.

He begins his sojourn in the cave by praying to God, but then asks himself whether there truly is a God who hears his prayer. Even in the midst of dark despair, his love for the Psalms shines through, as he expresses his anxiety over the existence of God by quoting Psalm 73: "in vain I have kept my own heart pure" (69). He is then moved to reflect on a rhetorical question, in this case from Psalm 94: "does he who planted the ear not hear?" This leads him to ponder how he himself came to have an ear to hear and, indeed, how he exists at all. He develops a version of what philosophers call the cosmological argument, reasoning that if he traces his existence back to his parents and then asks who created his parents, he must eventually conclude that there is an uncreated thing that created other things out of nothing. Otherwise there would be no end to the chain of causal explanations. He also reasons that this uncreated creator must be intelligent, for only a being with intelligence could bestow intelligence upon beings He created.

Now satisfied that there is an intelligent creator who hears him, he poses to himself a further question: is all that we find in the Holy Scriptures true? This leads him to confront the problem of religious disagreement. Whoever you turn to for advice, you'll simply hear that that person's religious convictions are the right ones, and others false. The Copts and the *Frang*, the Muslims and the Jews, all make exclusive claims for their own faiths, and yet as Zera Yacob puts it, "there is only one truth" (71). The problem, he concludes, is that people find it easier to rely on what they have heard from others, because critical examination of what others say is difficult and we humans are by nature sluggish and weak. It is surprising, then, that he ends the eighth chapter by saying: "To the one who searches, truth will quickly be revealed" (75). If critical examination is so difficult, how can he claim that the revelation of truth is immediate when sought? One way to understand his point is that the difficult part is choosing to let go of preconceived notions inherited from others. Once this has been achieved and one uses the intelligence bestowed by the Creator rather than relying on others, understanding the Creator's intentions is not so difficult. We might make a comparison to changing the channel when the remote control isn't lying on the sofa next to you. Once you have it in hand, changing the channel is easy. It's just that you're lying down here so comfortably and it's all the way over there…

Zera Yacob demonstrates the independent search for truth by considering various imperatives upheld by the Abrahamic religions, and assessing whether they are divine or rather human in origin. All these religions are criticized for encouraging fasting, because eating is necessary for survival. Thus, abstaining from food for significant periods of time is irrational. In fact, abstinence in general, such a central part of Christian tradition in Ethiopia (we just saw it being warmly recommended by Enbaqom), strikes him as irrational. He thus repudiates the glorification of monastic life in comparison with marriage. On the other hand, he finds it equally irrational that Islam countenances polygamy, because when we look around us, we see that there are roughly equal numbers of men and women. We even learn his views on the aforementioned question of which Sabbath to keep, that of the Jews, that of the Christians, or both. His answer is: none of the above. He identifies the rule to keep the Sabbath holy as the one rule of the Ten Commandments that we may know to be of human, not divine, origin, for our reason teaches us nothing about observing a day of rest, while it does teach us to agree with the prohibitions of killing, stealing, lying, and adultery (87).

Aside from criticizing polygamy, another criticism he makes of Islam concerns slavery (79). He writes:

> Also, Muslims say that it is proper to sell and trade human beings like animals. But only through our intelligence do we realise that this Muslim law cannot come from the Creator of human beings, the one who created us equal, as brothers and sisters, meaning that we call the Creator "our father" [as members of his family]. But Mohammed regarded weak human beings as the property of strong human beings and equated rational creation with irrational beasts. Can it be that this violence comes from God?

It strikes us as unfair for him to single out Islam in particular for the evil of slavery. Nonetheless this is a remarkable argument for human equality, one that resonates with the arguments for natural rights that we associate with the European Enlightenment. Zera Yacob can also be said to show a special concern for gender equality. We have already mentioned his arguments in favor of monogamous marriage as the happy compromise between the indefensible extremes of chastity and polygamy. He also criticizes Judaism for treating menstruation as something that makes women unclean, since it is in fact a divinely ordained bodily process involved in reproduction.

Perhaps the most memorable expression of his concern for gender equality, though, is found in Zera Yacob's account of how he came to be married. At this point, the book has returned to autobiography. After leaving his cave, Zera Yacob tells us, he came to live in the home of a rich man named Habtu in the town of Enfraz. He first served Habtu by copying out the Psalms, but then also became a teacher to Habtu's sons. Habtu had a maid named Hirut and, as soon as Zera Yacob expressed interest in marrying her, Habtu cheerfully said: "From today onwards she is not my servant, but your servant." To which Zera Yacob replied: "not my servant, but my wife! Because husband and wife are equals in marriage. We shouldn't call them master and servant, because 'they are one flesh' and one life!" (100). So Zera Yacob instead invited Hirut to marry him of her own free will; she did, and they lived happily ever after.

This work as a whole represents a dramatic turning point in Africana thought. Zera Yacob combines religious piety with relentless rationalism, encouraging us to found our faith upon personal reflection and not unthinking acceptance of what others tell us. He evaluates the practices of religions, including his own, against the same standard. In short, he seems a paradigmatic representative of seventeenth century rationalism, with the significant caveat that he lives and writes in Ethiopia rather than England or France. As we've said, some think that this is quite literally too good to be true and that it is instead a European thinker, namely d'Urbino, who must be credited with all these ideas, and also with the rather different ideas of Zera Yacob's putative disciple, Walda Heywat, the subject of our next chapter.[11]

9

THINK FOR YOURSELF

Walda Heywat

A much-discussed problem in today's philosophy of religion is religious pluralism. Suppose for the sake of argument that you are convinced of God's existence. How do you know which religion to follow, which community to join in worship of this God? Christians, Jews, Muslims, Hindus, and many other religions propose quite different, and often mutually exclusive, beliefs about God and His relation to human affairs. And, of course, the vast majority of religious believers did not adopt their faith after carefully reviewing all the rival candidates. Rather, in the words of Walda Heywat: "Christians' children are Christians, and Muslims' children are Muslims, and Jews' children are Jews; there is no other reason for their faith than this: that they are the children of their ancestors" (112).[1] Like his teacher Zera Yacob, Walda Heywat was much concerned that his beliefs about God not be formed by mere imitation of his parents, or of anyone else; they should instead be grounded in rational inquiry.

Walda Heywat explicitly poses the problem of religious pluralism, and offers a solution to it. He writes: "How can all these different religions be from God? Which of them is true, requiring us to believe in it? Tell me, if you know, because I don't know! I will only believe what God has revealed to me [if it comes] through the light of my intelligence. That way I won't be misled in my religious faith" (118). Effectively, he demands that religious believers start from scratch, divesting themselves of their spiritual upbringing and working out for themselves what can be believed about God. Like Zera Yacob, he thinks it is possible to prove God's existence, though he gives a different proof. Whereas Zera Yacob argued that we need to introduce God to stop an otherwise infinite regress of causal explanation, Walda Heywat argues that everything in our world of experience is subject to creation and destruction. Since such things are incapable of creating things from nothing, there must be a higher principle that creates them (29). By contrast, the specific practices that characterize the various religions, such as dietary laws, cannot be grounded in rational argument and should be dismissed, following Walda Heywat's watchword, "We won't believe it because we don't understand it" (117). If we follow this policy we can never go astray, since we are believing only that which all humans would accept if they devoted sufficient effort to philosophical inquiry.

Walda Heywat and his master knew that theirs was a radically innovative approach to matters of religion. In the final chapter of his book, Zera Yacob calls it an inquiry into things that "have not been explored before" (108). It was an inquiry he undertook at the behest of Walda Heywat himself, who was taught by Zera Yacob from a young age. In the epilogue he appended to his teacher's book, Walda Heywat lets us know that Zera Yacob was 68 when he wrote his book and that he lived another twenty-five years, which would place his death in 1692. Walda Heywat does not inform us as to the date of his own book, saying only that he was well advanced in years at the time of writing. Presumably it was written either in the 1690s, soon after Zera Yacob's death, or otherwise early in the eighteenth century.

Unsurprisingly, it takes up and defends Zera Yacob's views, not least the rationalism that is at the core of both treatises. Walda Heywat writes: "I won't write anything which is inconsistent with our intelligence, but only what is present in the heart of all human beings. Because of this, what I write cannot be false" (119). He even addresses the question of how to defend Zera Yacob's method of rational inquiry from objections that followers of the various established religions are likely to raise. If they ask why you do not believe in what they take to be the true religion, remind them that unbelief is the default. You do need a reason to believe in something, but you don't need a reason *not* to believe in something. If they assert that God revealed the truth to the founders of their faith, remind them this is to rely not on the power of reason bestowed by the very same God they invoke, but on the words of men. Finally, if they threaten that your lack of belief will bring God's judgment upon you, explain that God will not judge us for not believing that which appears to us to be false. For it is God Himself who gave us the rational capacity to distinguish for ourselves between truth and falsehood. Walda Heywat also shows himself a faithful student on such questions as asceticism—criticized forthrightly by both authors—and a benevolent attitude toward people of all faiths. Heywat instructs us not to despise others because they follow a different religion (41), and goes so far as to say, "all human beings are our 'neighbors', whether they are good or evil; whether Christians, Muslims, Jews, or pagans. All of them are our equals and all of them are our siblings because we are all children of one Father, and we are all one creator's creatures" (131). This is reminiscent of the reasoning given by Zera Yacob for opposing the practice of slavery.

On the other hand, Walda Heywat's book is very different in some ways, even in its format and themes. It is not autobiographical at all and most of its thirty-five chapters offer practical guidance on how to live, instead of abstract reflection on foundational matters of knowledge and faith. He concerns himself with such matters as the need to respect your parents, the value of working with your hands, the futility of divorce, and even the importance of personal hygiene. Not that this practical advice is unconnected to the theme of rational inquiry. When Walda Heywat warns his readers to avoid drunkenness, for example, this advice flows directly from the value he and Zera Yacob place on reason: "Drunkenness destroys intelligence, the understanding that makes us superior to the animals" (139). Here we see Walda Heywat outlining the practice that goes with his teacher's theory; the treatise could have been entitled *Applied Zera Yacob*.

In some cases, though, Walda Heywat's practical orientation leads to a difference, at least in emphasis, between him and his master. A major theme in Walda Heywat's book is the importance of working together with others. Reason teaches us this value, he argues, because we see that human beings cannot come into existence, grow, and take care of all their needs on their own. This leads him to argue that it is important to follow the customs of whatever country you happen to be in. Disregarding such customs can lead to quarrels or otherwise impede cooperation. Thus Zera Yacob's sharp irreverence in matters of religious observance is somewhat blunted by Walda Heywat. For instance, he follows Zera Yacob (80–2) in being dismissive of laws on fasting, yet, if confronted by religiously zealous people who insist on this practice, he says one should simply agree "to give the impression that you're like them" (140).

Claude Sumner has relatedly pointed out that Walda Heywat "did not break away from traditional patterns of thought and expression as his master did."[2] A notable difference between the two is that Walda Heywat often makes points using folk tales, some of which are known to have been familiar in Ethiopian tradition. There are also a few occasions where he alludes to or even directly quotes the *Book of the Wise Philosophers*. One unfortunate way in which Walda Heywat seems to have been influenced by older traditions, more so than Zera Yacob was, is in his view of women. Whereas his teacher affirmed the full equality of men and women, Walda Heywat writes: "keep in mind that a woman is a 'weak creature' lacking knowledge. So be strong in the face of her blemished nature and talkativeness" (149). As disturbing as this concession to traditional misogyny is, Walda Heywat does seem to think of himself as writing for women readers as well as male readers, as when he addresses both the husband and wife in giving advice on marriage (146). And it is not to Zera Yacob, but to Walda Heywat, that we may turn for the following, which would not be out of place in a sex therapy manual: "Be intimate sexually with your wife, in wonder and praise for your creator. When you enter her, don't seek the sweetness of sex just for yourself but make it sweet also for your wife. Don't deprive her of her share [of this sweetness] that God gave for her. For her sake, don't perform quickly but wait awhile until she takes her pleasure in it, so that she isn't left behind you, and her pleasure is not lessened" (147). Few in the male-dominated history of philosophy have bothered to defend the pleasure of sexuality in general, never mind validating and inculcating respect for the pleasure enjoyed by a female partner.

It seems then that in Zera Yacob and Walda Heywat, we have two stunningly progressive rationalist thinkers of seventeenth century Ethiopia. Or do we? We mentioned, and then deferred, the question of whether these two treatises are authentic. But we turn to it now, not only because it is important for the history of Africana philosophy, but also because it provides a window onto the philological detective work that quietly goes on in the background of all history of philosophy. As we said, it was the Catholic priest Giusto d'Urbino who claimed to discover both works, which he provided to the manuscript collector Antoine d'Abbadie in the middle of the nineteenth century. Doubts about d'Urbino's apparent discovery seem to have already circulated in his own time: an Ethiopian Catholic priest named Takla Haymanot, who knew d'Urbino, is said to have reported in notes for his memoirs, "Some of those who have seen the book say...that it was written by himself and that it was fictitiously attributed to [Zera Yacob]."[3] Taking his cue from this accusation, an Italian scholar named Carlo Conti Rossini produced a study of the two treatises shortly after World War One.[4] He adduced a number of arguments against their authenticity, which have been followed and expanded upon by several later investigators, such as Eugen Mittwoch in 1932.[5] As we have mentioned, the skeptical view was revived more recently by Anaïs Wion.[6] Thus you can now read d'Urbino's "discovery" being debunked in Italian, German, and French.

Aside from the charge leveled at d'Urbino by his contemporary, several points have been made against the authenticity of the treatises. For starters, d'Urbino is the sole known source for the works, and as an enthusiastic student of Ge'ez literature and language, he would presumably have been able to produce a forgery had he wanted to do so. He was apparently a rather isolated and depressive yet also ambitious personality, which could have given him motive as well as means. There is arguably some overlap between his own ideas, which ran in a rather liberal or rationalist direction, and the bold proclamations we find in Zera Yacob and Walda Heywat. Furthermore, there are linguistic parallels between the treatises and other writings that d'Urbino wrote in Ge'ez. Then, too, it has been proposed that d'Urbino leaves hints of his own deception by having Zera Yacob's life story parallel his own: Zera Yacob's name means "seed of Jacob," and "Jacob" was d'Urbino's baptismal name.

Most of these arguments go back to the studies of the early twentieth century. They are repeated in the recent analysis of Wion, who adds a further point. Giusto d'Urbino claimed to have discovered not just one manuscript of the treatise by Zera Yacob but two, one of which also has the unique treatise by Walda Heywat. This is in itself rather suspicious: here we have a book that is unknown for about 200 years, and a little effort by d'Urbino allowed him to turn up multiple copies in fairly short order. More importantly, Wion compared the different recensions of the treatise by Zera Yacob and found that the differences between them look like active rewriting, and not merely the usual mistakes always made by scribes when copying out texts by hand. In other words, on Wion's analysis, d'Urbino tipped his hand by "improving" the text of Yacob he himself had written when producing the last version that had supposedly come into his possession. This is indeed disquieting, though one can imagine other explanations. For example, perhaps they are different revisions of the text from earlier in the textual transmission, by scribes who wanted to clarify the wording or update the language. Thus the eminent scholar of Ge'ez studies, Getachew Haile, speculates that the manuscripts we have are not "faithfully copied from the original" and thus may not represent the original author's ideas with complete accuracy.[7] Haile's own suspicion is that the original work was indeed written in seventeenth century Ethiopia but that both of the copies we have now show some revision from the mid-nineteenth century, including by d'Urbino.

The other arguments we've mentioned were extensively discussed by Claude Sumner. He and others have dismissed the nineteenth century accusation of forgery as mere hearsay, as it is evident that Takla Haymanot did not himself examine the text. Furthermore, producing such convincing works in Ge'ez would have required a formidable degree of expertise from d'Urbino, and in Sumner's judgment this was well beyond him: his own works in and about the language, including a work on Ge'ez grammar and a dictionary of the language, are said to be riddled with an "appalling" number of errors.[8] The supposed harmony between d'Urbino's thought and the extreme rationalism of the treatises is itself rather persuasively challenged by Sumner. His views were "specifically Christian, Catholic, and clerical" and bringing them together with the perspectives of the two treatises would in fact be a "head on collision."[9] Even the clever point about the choice of Zera Yacob's name is convincingly defused: why would someone allude to their baptismal name if they were writing a heretical work which overturned the Christian faith? Plus, as we saw, "Zera Yacob" is not a name without precedent in earlier Ethiopian society.

Finally, and centrally, Sumner argues that it is hard to believe the two conjoined treatises were written by the same person, which obviously makes it hard to believe that d'Urbino wrote them both. He argues for this on linguistic grounds, pointing out disparities that would have been very difficult or unlikely for d'Urbino to fake: Walda Heywat's sentences are on average a different length than those of Yacob, and his vocabulary is rather different. As we've seen, Walda Heywat has a different assessment of the value of social custom, among other divergences of opinion. So we would have to believe that d'Urbino took the trouble not just to forge these two treatises, but to adopt two different literary and philosophical personas that clash, and yet often in minor ways. That seems rather extraordinary.

Getachew Haile has made a few further points against d'Urbino's authorship. For instance, the controversy about the Sabbath is mentioned in the treatise of Zera Yacob. As we saw this was genuinely a matter of debate in seventeenth century Ethiopia, but would d'Urbino have known this, in order to add it as convincing historical color? Also, there is the use of the Psalms in the texts. It's clear that the version used is that of the Ethiopian church, not the Catholic prayer book that would have been used by d'Urbino. This relates to another disparity between the two treatises: both Zera Yacob and Walda Heywat use the Psalms, but Walda Heywat tends to allude to them implicitly instead of quoting them, as Zera Yacob does.[10] It should be said that if d'Urbino really did invent these two philosophers, he is undoubtedly among the most talented and impressive forgers ever to have lived.[11]

Alongside the preceding details, we would ourselves add the following, rather modest point. The forthright rationality and rejection of uncritically accepting the "faith of one's fathers" has seemed to many readers to be an implausible stance for two thinkers of seventeenth century Ethiopia. It looks more like an idea you'd find in, say, an offbeat nineteenth century intellectual who has been reading a lot of Enlightenment European philosophy—possibly d'Urbino. But this is wrong. In fact, Islamic intellectual culture at that time and for a long time before was profoundly devoted to criticism of what in Arabic is called *taqlīd*: the uncritical acceptance of authority.[12] As we'll be seeing in coming chapters, not a few intellectuals of late medieval and early modern Islam were also proponents of the rationalist idea that in matters of religion one should "think for oneself." Even if we don't appeal to influence from Islamic culture on these Ethiopian thinkers, it is at least clear that Enlightenment Europeans had no monopoly on a critically minded and rationalist approach to religion. Besides, to cite yet another point made by Haile, Zera Yacob and his student could already have been influenced by rationalist currents from Europe, given the presence of Portuguese Jesuits in the Ethiopia of their time.[13]

We hasten to add that the reality of a worthwhile philosophical tradition in Ethiopia does not rise or fall with Zera Yacob and Walda Heywat. Alongside other texts we have looked at already, we would like to mention one final example, one that incidentally gives the lie to Walda Heywat's claim that women are less intelligent than men. We have in mind *The Life and Struggles of Our Mother Walatta Petros*.[14] This is a contribution to an important genre in Ethiopian literature, accounts of the lives of saints, by a monk named Galawdewos.

Walatta Petros was a nun born in 1592 and thus someone whose life was shaped by the disastrous attempt to impose Catholicism on Ethiopia under King Susenyos. She was married with children but left her husband because of his participation as a counsellor to the king and military commander in imposing the foreign faith. Supported by her fellow nun and lifelong companion Eheta Kristos, she became a major voice and leader of resistance against the king and the Jesuits. Among her admirers was King Fasiladas, who re-established the faith and expelled the Jesuits. After the re-establishment of the Ethiopian Orthodox faith, she was celebrated as a hero, and she died famous and beloved in 1642.

As translator Wendy Belcher says, the book by Galawdewos about Walatta Petros' life is the earliest known book length biography of an African woman, and it can be read as an inspiring tale of a successful non-violent movement against European protocolonialism. It is instructive to compare the reactions and experiences of Walatta Petros and Zera Yacob in the time of King Susenyos. There is no doubt that Zera Yacob provides us with a more recognizably philosophical response. On the other hand, the rejection of Catholicism by Ethiopians like Walatta Petros did involve a long-standing metaphysical question posed within Christian theology. When Galawdewos refers to Catholicism as "the filthy faith of the Europeans," he cites the idea that "Christ has two natures" as its distinguishing feature, and says that "the holy faith of Alexandria," by comparison, holds that Christ is "not split or divided in anything" (119–20). At one point, Walatta Petros was subjected to, as Belcher puts it, "thought reform," as the king forced her to spend time with Jesuits endeavoring to convert her. Instead, according to Galawdewos, she "argued with them, defeated them, and embarrassed them" (155). Like Queen Makeda in the *Kebra Nagast*, then, Walatta Petros was an Ethiopian heroine admired for her intellect and leadership. Like all the texts and figures we have discussed, she illustrates that Ethiopian intellectual history deserves to be far better known.

10

FROM HERE TO TIMBUKTU

Sub-Saharan Islamic Philosophy

If you started at the north coast of Africa and started walking south, what would you find? Well, you'd better bring some bottled water because, after passing through the settled regions of northern Africa called the "Maghreb," you will encounter the Sahara desert. Assuming you manage to reach the far side, you will then be in the "Sahel," a zone of transition between the desert and the savannah that stretches from the Atlantic coast across much of Africa. The latter region has historically been known as the "Sudan," though this term covers a much larger area than the modern country of Sudan. Beyond this region lie the forests of equatorial Africa. If you're still hydrated enough to care, you may be interested to know that every region you've passed through has a name derived from the Arabic language, a sign of the impact Islam has had on this part of the world. *Maghrib* means "the west," because this has been the western part of the Islamic world ever since the first Islamic conquests achieved in the first generations of the new faith. *Ṣaḥrā* just means "desert." Thus the "Sahara Desert" is actually the "desert desert," the sort of hidden redundancy you'll find in many other place names around the world. (Quite a few waterways in the United States include Native American words for "river" in their names, like the Ohio River—*Oyo* means "good river" in Iroquois—and "kill" means "creek" in Dutch, as in the case of Fishkill Creek in New York.) *Sāḥil* means "coast" or "border," here referring to the border of the great desert. This is also where the word for the Bantu language Swahili comes from, since that is just the plural form of the same word, *sawāḥil*. As its name suggests, while Bantu in its grammar and most of its vocabulary, this coastal language has been greatly influenced by Arabic.

Finally, there is the Sudan, or to give it its full name *bilād al-sūdān*, meaning "country of the blacks," which is what Arabic speakers called the region to the south of the Sahara. Actually, the Arabic word for "black" was used not only for sub-Saharan

Africans but for a wider range of peoples with darker skin.[1] Muslim intellectuals were torn between two explanations of black skin color: a religious one according to which it is a curse laid on the descendants of Noah's son Ham, and a scientific one that explained black skin as the result of environmental factors. The latter account, inspired by Greek ideas about climate and its influence on the body, was embraced by the North African historian, Ibn Khaldūn.[2] It was also embraced by al-Jāḥiẓ, a great literary figure of ninth century Iraq who is said to have been of African descent. He wrote a book about differences between the races called *The Book of the Glory of the Blacks over the Whites* that has sometimes been assumed to be satirical rather than a serious glorification of black people. Some recent scholars have argued, however, that the book is an earnest defense of black virtue and equality.[3] On this interpretation, we have reason to see it as a truly pioneering text of Africana philosophy, emerging from the Iraqi branch of the diaspora. And on any interpretation, the work forms part of the complicated story of thinking about human difference in the medieval Islamic world, which some scholars take to be the most important precedent for Europe's development of racial thinking in the modern world.[4]

Coming back now to the history of Islam in sub-Saharan Africa itself, the story goes back as far as the story of Islam itself. A small group from among the Prophet Muḥammad's immediate followers, including his wife Umm Salama, retreated across the Red Sea to Ethiopia during the difficult early days of the faith. This occurred even before Muḥammad led his adherents out of Mecca to found the new city of Medina, a key event in Islamic history known as the *hijra*, meaning "emigration." Thus Islamic literary sources call the smaller scale exodus to the safety of Africa the "first emigration." Despite that early event, Islam did not penetrate much into East Africa for quite some time, although the islands of Pemba and Zanzibar off the coast of what is now Tanzania were established as Muslim trading ports early in the medieval period. By the fifteenth century there were Swahili-speaking Muslim communities clustered along much of Africa's eastern coast, and they eventually came into conflict with the Portuguese, who after the voyage of Vasco da Gama in 1498 used the region as a staging post for trade with India. Not far into the interior of East Africa, meanwhile, there were the traditional societies that the Muslims thought of as "pagan."

Further west, the rise of Islam in sub-Saharan Africa likewise meant the gradual and incomplete displacement of "paganism." Given the absence of bottled water in this earlier period, you might expect that the Sahara would have been an insurmountable barrier preventing travel or trade between northern Africa and the Sahel and Sudan. The desert was a more daunting obstacle than a large sea would have been, given that boats were the fastest mode of premodern transport, and the

Maghreb was certainly part of a wider, multi-religious Mediterranean culture during the medieval and early modern periods. Yet it is a mistake to think of northern Africa as unconnected from the rest of the continent. Trans-Saharan caravan routes were established, along which Muslim merchants carried their religion as well as their goods.[5] Often rulers were the first to convert, because of the association between Islam and lucrative trade.

An early case was at the settlement of Gao which lies on the Niger River in present-day Mali, and which is said to have had a Muslim ruler by some time in the tenth century. Then a major incursion of Islam into western Africa occurred in the eleventh century, when the Almoravids swept down from the north to take possession of the Empire of Ghana, which should not be confused with the modern country of Ghana, as it was further north and did not even include any of the territory of that country. (As you can tell, the naming of modern countries after regions or empires that covered a different and often much larger territory is a common occurrence in Africa.) The Almoravids had their power base in the Maghreb and extended north into Spain as well as south into West Africa. But, as in Gao, the presence of Muslim rulers in what was then "Ghana" did not translate into a wholesale abandonment of traditional religion and conversion to Islam. Indeed, as we'll be seeing, Muslim intellectuals in the region routinely complained about the failure of Islam to supplant indigenous belief systems.

Relevant here is a story told about a ruler named Askia Dāwūd, ruler of the Songhay Empire in the latter part of the sixteenth century. He made a show of his piety and studied with a Muslim scholar on a daily basis, yet retained such traditional practices as having his subjects sprinkle dust upon their heads to show him reverence. When his Muslim advisers denounced this as insanity, he said, "I am the head of sinful madmen and I therefore made myself mad."[6] The Songhay Empire in the Niger River region provided a setting for numerous scholars and intellectuals. To give you some idea of how extensive the scholarly community was, a survey led by C.C. Stewart and Bruce Hall has catalogued some 21,000 West African manuscripts.

Of course, those manuscripts aren't all about strictly philosophical topics. The representatives of the learned class, or 'ulamā', who produced them focused above all on the religious sciences, especially Quranic commentary, theology, and Islamic law. But philosophical issues could arise in those contexts, and there was also extensive study of logic. It is unfortunate that the complex history of logic in the post-medieval Islamic world is in general a largely unstudied field,[7] and that goes double for logic as a tradition of sub-Saharan Africa.

The Songhay Empire had as its capital the aforementioned city of Gao. The word "Songhay" refers to the ethnic group who were politically dominant in this state; it is also the name for a group of African languages from the region of the Niger River. The realm included another important city with Timbuktu, first founded as a base for the nomadic Tuaregs at the end of the eleventh century, and destined to be a center for particularly intense scholarly activity. The Songhay Empire was founded in the 1460s by Sunni ʿAlī, who professed adherence to Islam but whose insufficient commitment to the religion was used as a justification for his overthrow by Askia Muḥammad, the father of the aforementioned Askia Dāwūd. Unlike Sunni ʿAlī, Askia Muḥammad made Islam a bulwark of his claims to legitimacy, and did what the religious scholars thought any good ruler should do: ask religious scholars for advice.

Muḥammad turned to two scholars in particular, both from the Maghreb. Their names were Jalāl al-Dīn al-Suyūṭī and ʿAbd al-Karīm al-Maghīlī, and they hailed from Egypt and from Tlemcen in modern-day Algeria, respectively. Both of them died in about 1505. The two were not always in agreement. We are told that al-Maghīlī had to defend the study of logic against the criticism of al-Suyūṭī. Before you leap to the conclusion that al-Maghīlī is therefore the more admirable of the two figures—after all, who doesn't admire logicians?—we should mention that he was also a very enthusiastic persecutor of Jews. At this period, there were a number of prosperous Jewish communities in Africa, and as a biographer of al-Maghīlī puts it, he deemed it licit and even obligatory to "spill their blood and plunder their property."[8] He instigated a massacre of Jews in a city in modern-day Algeria in 1492, a date that in this context may sound darkly familiar. It's the same year that the Christian rulers Ferdinand and Isabella launched a persecution of Jews and Muslims following their "reconquest" of Spain.

Al-Maghīlī's views on this issue were out of step with other scholars. When he argued that a Muslim could fall into unbelief merely through friendly association with Jews, his ruling found no sympathy. Yet he was a respected expert of law and the other sciences, honored by later generations for his heroic role in spreading Islam as he traveled around West Africa. A characteristic anecdote has it that, when he arrived in one community with no books in tow, he simply wrote down the entire Quran from memory for the locals to read.[9] He was also instrumental in bringing Sufism, or Islamic mysticism, to the region. Certainly Askia Muḥammad valued his advice. He posed to al-Maghīlī a set of questions, mostly concerning the legal obligations of a Muslim ruler. In his replies, the north African scholar emphasized that one such obligation is to take council from upright scholars (63). If the ruler is not sure whether they are trustworthy, though, he should err on the side of caution and ignore them. In an observation meant to apply to Islamic law but applicable to ethics in general, al-Maghīlī advises that when we suspect that a certain act is obligatory but are unsure, we should do it just to be on the safe side, and conversely we should avoid things that we think *might* be forbidden. If one is really stuck, the best strategy is to do the opposite of one's instinctive desire, since we all naturally tend toward shirking our duties (68).

Askia Muḥammad's questions and al-Maghīlī's replies betray anxiety over the failure of Islam to win the hearts of the populace. Askia Muḥammad complains about people under his rule that practice idolatry and magic, and of the way that unmarried women go about naked in the traditional fashion (90, 95). Al-Maghīlī is unsparing in his condemnation of such departures from the religious law, and even authorizes the death penalty in some cases, as with the use of magic (91). A related theme is the rules governing warfare within an Islamic framework. It is, according to al-Maghīlī, unlawful for Muslims to live without any ruler commanding them, so autonomous communities of Muslims can rightfully be annexed to the empire. Of course *jihād* can also be launched against non-Muslim rulers, and if necessary one can even risk killing Muslims who may be mixed into a population with a wicked or unbelieving leader, for the sake of the greater good of reforming the society as a whole (82, 88). Al-Maghīlī's legal opinions here are, like his attitude toward the Jews, hardly likely to win our sympathy. But he is far from an unsubtle thinker: his answers show a keen awareness of the dilemmas that arise when we face conflicting moral principles or legal prescriptions.

Something similar might be said for a treatise written by the most famous scholar of Timbuktu during the time of the Songhay Empire, whose name was Aḥmad Bābā. He was perhaps the brightest star in the scholarly firmament of this city, which in the sixteenth century boasted 150 schools of religious education. Already at the start of the fifteenth century a visiting expert reported that the city was "full of Sudanese jurists" who knew even more about Islamic law than he did.[10] Aḥmad Bābā himself wrote dozens of works, especially on Islamic law. One of his most interesting treatises, composed in 1615, concerns the connection between race and slavery. He here hands down a legal judgment concerning the enslavement of black Africans.[11] As a general rule, slavery was seen as acceptable in Islam, with the significant caveat that it was not permitted to enslave other Muslims. Thus a slave who claimed to be a Muslim, at least according to many jurists, should be freed. Indeed al-Maghīlī praised Askia Muḥammad for doing precisely this.

Aḥmad Bābā, however, was worried about how skin color had come to play a role in the way that many North Africans thought about slavery. The trans-Saharan slave trade of his time, it should be noted, was much longer established and was then probably still much larger in volume than the transatlantic trade of the time. Just as in the case of the transatlantic trade, the taking of slaves across the Sahara led to an association between blackness and slavery. This is what led Aḥmad Bābā to investigate whether skin color could play any legitimate role in determining whether someone could legally be enslaved. His answer is an emphatic "no." He rejects the notion that race has any religious significance whatsoever, as it did in some popular versions of that story about the descendants of Ham. Instead, Aḥmad Bābā cites with approval the environmental account of skin color that had been offered by Ibn Khaldūn. It therefore makes no legal or moral difference whether someone is black, only whether someone is a Muslim.

Some scholars have wondered whether this attitude may have had to do with Aḥmad Bābā's own skin color, yet it seems that he did not consider himself to be black, being descended from lighter-skinned Berbers who had lived in this part of West Africa for generations. In fact, he even had some unkind things to say about black people, asserting that they are typically docile and less refined, although it is interesting that he also saw this docility in a positive light, as it could manifest itself in a readiness to convert to Islam. One leading scholar of the Songhay Empire, John Hunwick, nevertheless argues that Aḥmad Bābā's view "was affected by notions of the inferiority and enslavability of black Africans, though his legal mind rejected the simple equivalence of blackness with slavery."[12]

But even if this rejection was not related to Aḥmad Bābā's own identity, we should probably factor in the impact of his mentor, Muḥammad Baghayogo al-Wangarī. We can be quite certain that he was ethnically Mande, and thus a black thinker. The relationship between al-Wangarī and Aḥmad Bābā was characteristic of the intellectual culture of Timbuktu at this time. Thus another scholar, Timothy Cleaveland, argues that we have good reason to think that "Ahmad Baba rejected racial slavery in part because he sympathised with the Black Muslims of West Africa. His beloved hometown, Timbuktu, was a predominantly black town in the predominantly Black kingdom of Songhay, and his *shaykh* was Muhammad Baghayogo al-Wangari."[13]

It must be admitted, though, that his ruling was certainly not intended to put an end to the slave trade in Africa, which was a major part of the economic trade between sub-Saharan Islam and the rest of the Islamic world. Muslims regularly raided the so-called "pagan" areas, seized captives, and put them to work as slaves in their own states or sold them on to North Africa and even such far-flung locales as Italy and Asia Minor. Aḥmad Bābā's point was that the slave trade needed to be regulated by Islamic law, and that in this case the law was colorblind. Ironically, Aḥmad Bābā had earlier experienced his own trauma of captivity at the hands of an invading military force. In 1591, an army from Morocco swept away the Songhay Empire. In the chaos, Aḥmad Bābā lost no fewer than 1,600 books—his vast personal library providing another indication of how scholarship had flourished up to this time[14]—and he was taken captive and brought back to Morocco. After being freed, he returned to Timbuktu, where he wrote the treatise on slavery and many other works.[15] The fall of the Songhay Empire certainly in no way marked the end of Islamic intellectual activity in West Africa. A remarkable example comes from the end of the seventeenth century, with the work of a man named Muḥammad al-Wālī al-Mālikī. Al-Wālī belonged to the (black) ethnic group known as the Fulani, which produced many scholars who spread Islam around sub-Saharan Africa.[16] In keeping with this tradition, he was a self-styled "theologian" or *mutakallim* in the classical mode, who set himself up as a teacher and jurist in the Sultanate of Bagirmi, in what is now the country of Chad. Al-Wālī's most celebrated work is called *The Peerless Method to Knowledge of the Science of Theology*. It is a commentary on a religious creed written by the fifteenth century North African scholar al-Sanūsī, which is still used in religious education in Nigeria in the present day.

There was apparently a long-standing oral tradition in which Fulani religious scholars passed down their understanding of al-Sanūsī's text from one generation to the next. Drawing on that oral tradition, al-Wālī took the decision to set down comments on the work in writing. Dorrit van Dalen, who has written a book about al-Wālī and his commentary, suggests that this was an attempt to assert the authority of the *ʿulamāʾ*, literate scholars who were trained in the Islamic textual tradition.[17] This fits with a particularly prominent theme pursued in his commentary: the condemnation of *taqlīd*. As mentioned in the previous chapter, the Arabic word *taqlīd* means forming one's beliefs through uncritical imitation or acceptance of what others have said, and, when he spoke against it, al-Wālī was taking up a long-running theme of Islamic culture. It was often thought that the *ʿulamāʾ* were distinguished from the common run of Muslim believers precisely by their refusal to engage in *taqlīd*. These were the men who learned to think for themselves (and, as we've already suggested, Zera Yacob and Walda Heywat would have approved). For such scholars, even belief in God was founded in a grasp of argumentative proof (*dalīl*) and not simply acceptance of the religious convictions of their culture.

But al-Wālī went further than this. He argued that not only scholars but *every* Muslim should have good reasons for their beliefs, in order to put their faith on a firm foundation. As van Dalen puts it: "The position of *The Peerless Method* is clear: Muslims had to gather intellectual, as opposed to intuitive, knowledge about their religion, and to use their intellect to understand it." This is why common believers should look to the *ʿulamāʾ* for guidance in understanding the doctrines of their own religion, since it is they who can explain the reasons why the religion deserves credence and thus put any common believer in a position to rationally explain this as well.[18]

Al-Wālī's strictures against uncritical religious belief were, in a sense, a broader application of the values espoused by al-Maghīlī in his advice to Askia Muḥammad.

All Muslims, and especially the rulers, should learn from the intellectuals who have devoted themselves to understanding Islam more fully and who could put its doctrines on a rational foundation. But what should the scholars do when rulers were not ready to listen to them? One option was to help overthrow those rulers. Through the seventeenth and eighteenth centuries, a number of uprisings were launched in an effort to establish more authentically Islamic states.[19] At the turn of the nineteenth century, this movement found its most successful expression in the *jihād* that created the Sokoto Caliphate in what is now Nigeria. Drawing on some of the figures we've just discussed, the scholar and military leader ʿUthmān Dan Fodio deposed rulers he deemed to be insufficiently sincere in their faith and established a new regime. It was intended to put the legal and moral teachings of the *ʿulamāʾ* into practice, and to a greater extent than had ever been managed in West Africa.

11

RENEWING THE FAITH

The Sokoto Caliphate

The idea that political power should be joined to philosophical wisdom goes back at least as far as Plato's *Republic*, with its bold theory that the ideal city should be ruled by philosophers. Or rather, it surely goes back quite a bit further than that. Earlier in the Greek tradition, we know that the Presocratic thinker Anaxagoras was associated with the Athenian statesman Pericles. Further back still, there are the various expressions of the importance of learning to the kings of Egypt, as we have already discussed in this book. One example was *The Instruction Addressed to King Merikare*, and its teaching that the good ruler is one who learns how to uphold the value of *ma'at*. Another was the depiction of the king's interest in the disquisition on *ma'at* given by Khunanup in *The Tale of the Eloquent Peasant*. By contrast, we don't really expect today's leaders to be scholars, or to spend time seeking them out. Deep learning is rarely made a basis for political authority nowadays, and indeed some modern voters might even be leery of a candidate who spends all their free time with books, preferring the effective manager or businessman to the intellectual.

But while the ideal of the scholar king is certainly an antique one, it is not so antiquated as you might think. A number of thinkers, scholars, and political philosophers were among the first generation of leaders of independent nations in Africa, as will be evident in the sequel volume on Africana philosophy in the twentieth century. There was a precedent for this with events that unfolded in what is now northern Nigeria, in the first years of the nineteenth century. The central character of this story is a charismatic preacher named ʿUthmān Dan Fodio, often known as the "Shehu," a version of the Arabic title *shaykh*.[1] Born in 1754, the young ʿUthmān joined his brothers in travels around Hausaland (meaning the area inhabited by the Hausa people) seeking instruction in religion, as well as Sufism and other disciplines like astronomy. Particularly influential upon him was a teacher named Jibrīl ibn 'Umar, who decried the hypocrisy of the nominally Muslim rulers who governed the region, and the fact that many people still pursued traditional African religion. In 1774, the Shehu launched his own missionary work, preaching in favor of Islamic piety and against the traditional practices that he considered to be nothing more than crude paganism.

Ultimately 'Uthmān decided that preaching was not enough. He gathered his followers into an army and launched a military struggle, or *jihād*, against the Hausa rulers. He served as the spiritual leader of this endeavor while military command was taken by his brother 'Abdullāhi and son Muḥammad Bello. The Shehu's forces found themselves victorious in 1812, establishing what has come to be known as the Sokoto Caliphate, after the city of Sokoto which was founded as the capital of this new state. It sounds like a simple story of religious zeal, and certainly 'Uthmān Dan Fodio's leadership was bound up with a reputation for piety and mystical insight, even seemingly magical abilities. But the first family of the Sokoto Caliphate were also scholars and poets. The Shehu, his son Bello, and his daughter Nana Asmā'u were renowned for their learning and composed works in prose and in verse. They wrote either in Arabic or in the local languages of Hausa or Fulani but using Arabic script (this type of text is called *'ajamī*: "non-Arabic").[2]

The family's bookishness was central to their political ideology and their own claims to legitimacy. Again and again, their writings emphasize the importance of gaining understanding, a value epitomized in a saying of the Prophet quoted by Bello: "the most excellent worship is the search for knowledge." Bello himself certainly took this to heart: his sister Asmā'u credits him with having read more than 20,000 books.[3] This sounds like hyperbole, and we are apt to wonder how he could have gotten his hands on so many texts, never mind found time to read them. But as already mentioned, there are thousands of surviving manuscripts in West Africa even today, and more would have existed around 1800. The leaders of the caliphate encouraged the same attitude among their subordinates. Numerous works by 'Uthmān and Bello are addressed to regional governors within their state, and they unfailingly implore these leaders to pay heed to the learned men of the scholarly class, the *'ulamā'* (literally, "those who know"). According to Asmā'u, her father the Shehu laid down four duties of the caliph: "summon scholars, enjoin truth, uphold tradition (*sunna*), and make justice prevail."[4]

You might be surprised that Asmā'u herself was so well educated, being a member of a family that waged Islamic holy war—not something people typically associate with the emancipation of women. But women scholars were not unheard of in West Africa,[5] and the Sokoto Caliphate did not hold the ultra-conservative social and religious values espoused at the same period by Wahhabi Islam, even though the Shehu's teacher Jibrīl may have been influenced by that movement while visiting the Saudi peninsula.[6] In fact the Shehu wrote about the importance of educating women, especially in a work called *The Light of Hearts* (*Nūr al-albāb*), and Bello followed his lead by writing about the virtues of pious women. From their own point of view, they were taking a moderate position on the role of women in society. Women should not have the same freedoms as men and, in particular, should not go out of the house without good reason, but the goal of seeking knowledge counted as a very good reason.[7] There is also an anecdote according to which Asmā'u heard her father apportioning official roles to various men, and spoke up to ask, "what about us, the women?" In response the Shehu appointed her to be the authority over all women in the caliphate, adding, "the women of the caliphate belong to the women and the men belong to the men."[8]

Scholarship was, then, highly valued within this rigorously Islamic society. What did that mean in practice? In the first instance, the learning displayed by the Shehu and other members of the Hausa or Fulani elite was in the area of the so-called "religious sciences," which included Quranic exegesis, knowledge about the life and sayings of the Prophet, and most importantly for us, jurisprudence, Sufism, and rational theology. Quite a lot of philosophy was traditionally involved in these endeavors, and the Sokoto leaders were nothing if not traditional. In matters of law they proclaimed their adherence to scholarly consensus, something else that distinguishes them from the more radical Wahhabis.[9] Following consensus usually meant using tradition to determine rulings on specific legal questions. For instance, like Aḥmad Bābā, the Shehu held that slavery was licit in Islam but that Muslims could not be enslaved. Bello would later specify that anyone under Muslim rulership was thereby ruled out as a potential slave. Similarly, Bello ruled that one can seize booty in war, but only from non-Muslims.[10]

The jurisprudential tradition also involved more general ideas about justice and ethics. When the Shehu identified the upholding of justice as a crucial task for the caliph, he meant in part that the ruler should establish a judiciary with upright and well-trained judges. Indeed, Bello quotes the eleventh century political thinker al-Mawardī to the effect that this is one of a ruler's seven primary duties. The ruler should also be ready to carry out the dictates of justice unflinchingly. Quoting another traditional source, Bello says that "a governor must have strength such that the killing of a man in the cause of truth would be to him like the killing of a sparrow, and he should have such mildness, care, and mercy that he fears to kill a swallow without justice."[11] Elsewhere, he argues that rulership without a basis in justice can never succeed: "there is no rulership without the army, no army without wealth, no wealth without tax, no tax without prosperity, no prosperity without justice. Justice is therefore the base on which the foundation of the state is laid."[12] Thus it is not only individual virtue but the encouragement of virtue in society at large that makes for a good ruler. The Shehu captured this in a description of the ideal ruler who will "strip evil things from religious and temporal affairs and introduce reforms…combat every cause of corruption that occurs in his country and forbid every disapproved thing…and strive to reform the markets, set right the affairs of the poor and the needy, and order the doing of every approved thing."[13]

We should hasten to add, though, that the citizens of the caliphate were not being encouraged to overthrow leaders who failed to measure up to these lofty standards. To the contrary, the Shehu and his children regularly emphasized that good Muslims should accept their subordinate political position, alluding to a passage of the Quran, "obey those who have authority among you" (4:59). Asmā'u explicitly advised her readers to follow this policy even if they should find themselves ruled by the wicked. A poem she wrote on the basis of verses by her father includes the lines, "no matter how pious you are, nor how godly and saintly, nor how profoundly learned, all who refuse to follow the commands of the caliph will be without excuse hereafter."[14] But our obligations to political authority are not unlimited. After all, the Shehu himself did not meekly accept the Hausa rulers, but rose up against them in rebellion. For him they had no legitimacy, since their rule was not based upon Islam.

Legitimate political authority, then, is defined as government in the name of Islam, and any established ruler should be obeyed so long as he does not reject true religion. Yet the ruler has a duty to look to the good of the community and apply principles of justice, paying heed to the scholars who will keep him on the straight and narrow. Hence the production of numerous works of advice for rulers, so-called "mirrors for princes." We saw that the earlier African scholar al-Maghīlī was an influential exponent of this genre, and he was a writer well known to 'Uthmān Dan Fodio. Al-Maghīlī was also a key importer of Sufi thought into the region, and Sufism was a powerful influence on the thought of the Shehu and his family. They were inspired especially by the *qadariyya* Sufi order, named for its founder 'Abd al-Qādir al-Jīlānī.

Asmā'u had particular admiration for the early female ascetic and Sufi Rab'īa, whom she praises for her exceeding piety and learning.[15] Works of other notable Sufis, like Ibn 'Arabī and al-Ghazālī, were also known in Hausaland at this time. 'Uthmān Dan Fodio even wrote a work called *Revival of the Traditions* (*Iḥyā' al-sunan*), evidently in tribute to the title of al-Ghazālī's masterwork, *Revival of the Religious Sciences* (*Iḥyā' 'ulūm al-dīn*). One key idea to come from these Sufi sources was asceticism, a turning away from worldly things and valuing of God alone. It comes out in a passage like the following, written by Nana Asmā'u: "divorce the world, which constantly changes. Fear the world with its endless vacillations and do not take delight in it."[16] We may detect an echo of Platonism in this advice, a rejection of the physical realm on the basis that it lacks stability or constancy. It would be foolish to place our trust and hopes with things in this transitory world, when we could instead direct our attention to the unchanging realm of the divine.[17]

Accordingly, our authors evince a serene faith in divine providence, which often seems to tip over into what philosophers today would call determinism. The Shehu could supposedly foretell future events, like the flourishing of a city that did not yet exist, and Asmā'u reassures her readers that all things unfold according to God's plan. Rather than worrying about potentially problematic implications as regards human freedom, Asmā'u is positively eager to outsource her volition to God. She prays, "God prevail over my will: I cannot control my life by myself and can be guided only by Islamic law."[18] Bello and Asmā'u both wrote works in the genre known as "prophetic medicine," which recommends what we would probably be tempted to call "magical" practices for curing or warding off illness, defeating enemies, and so on. This could include reciting parts of the Quran or even writing it on a scrap of material, like leather, and keeping it upon one's person. But they would certainly have rejected the characterization of this as superstition or magic, something they themselves attacked as a pernicious aspect of pagan society. Prophetic medicine is instead supposed to be a way of asking God to act in the world, something we see still more dramatically with stories of miracles worked by the Shehu and his followers. Asmā'u also got in on the act, reportedly setting an enemy town on fire by pointing a burning stick in its direction.

For a more cerebral aspect of their appropriation of the religious sciences, we can turn to the influence of rational Islamic theology, or *kalām*. The story of *kalām* had been intertwined with the story of philosophy in the Islamic world from the very beginning.[19] While pursuing an uneasy rivalry with the self-styled "philosophers (*falāsifa*)" who took inspiration from Greek texts, Islamic theologians themselves devoted attention to central philosophical issues such as proving the existence of God or the question of human free will. A brief but remarkable example of how *kalām* ideas were received in the Sokoto Caliphate comes in a treatise by Muḥammad Bello called *Infāq al-maysūr* (*Disbursing Prosperity*).[20] Embedded within a history of the region and the *jihād*, Bello offers a paean to the wisdom and virtue of the Shehu, whom Bello honors with the traditional title "renewer of religion (*mujaddid*)" (§10). He explains how the Shehu banished ignorance of religion from Hausaland and brought Sufism, as well as sound learning in the Islamic sciences, writing that his father "filled the countries of West [Africa] with knowledge and with seekers of knowledge" (§11). One of these sciences was theology, the study of God's oneness (*tawḥīd*, §14).

Bello himself was credited with passionate devotion to this branch of learning in a praise poem written by Asmā'u.[21] Reading Bello's summary of the Shehu's own teachings on this subject, we are confronted with arguments and ideas that go right back to the classical period of Islam, about a millennium before the founding of the Sokoto Caliphate. According to 'Uthmān Dan Fodio, we grasp God and His attributes, including His oneness, primarily through the fact that He created the universe (§15). We know that the universe is in fact created because it consists entirely of things that came to be after they did not yet exist, so the world as a whole must likewise go from non-being to being, just like a body of water is wet because every part of it is wet. Here the Shehu is using an argument for God's existence familiar from the earliest days of Islamic theology. Originally invented by the ninth century theologian Abū l-Hudhayl, it has much more recently been influential in contemporary philosophy of religion thanks to its revival by William Lane Craig.[22] It was also used by other intellectuals of West Africa, such as al-Wālī. We saw in the last chapter how he encouraged, even demanded, the use of rational argument to provide religious faith with a solid intellectual basis. It was the proof from creation that he put forward as just such an argument.[23] With his own use of the argument, 'Uthmān Dan Fodio was therefore carrying on the rationalist project of al-Wālī, as inspired by the earlier al-Sanūsī.

Bello's presentation of the teachings of the Shehu goes on to infer a range of divine attributes from the conclusion of the proof from creation. As the cause of the things He creates, God is fundamentally unlike them (§15), securing the truth of the Quranic dictum that "no thing is like to God" (42:11). Furthermore God must be powerful, as the cause of all things, and also knowledgeable because He is able to give them their various characteristics; furthermore He must have free will, since He chose to create. Indeed, Bello tells us that the Shehu emphasized God's untrammeled power for choice, stating that if God's deeds were in any way compelled, then that which is in itself merely possible or contingent would be rendered necessary. Hints toward determinism in other works of the Sokoto Caliphate should not be taken to apply to the case of God Himself. Divine freedom allows for choice between genuinely open alternatives, and God chooses what will happen in our world. This would align the Shehu with the sort of teaching on divine and human action we find in older Sunni theology, as in the Ash'arite school.

Bello's propagation of his father's theology also carries on a theme that will have escaped few readers: the mutually supportive positions of the three family members we've been discussing (that is, the Shehu, Bello, and Asmā'u). In a recent book,

Paul Naylor highlights the more contentious relationships that appear to have existed between the Shehu and his brother ʿAbdullāhi and then, after the Shehu's death, between ʿAbdullāhi and his nephew Bello.[24] For ʿAbdullāhi, the righteous leadership of a political community by a religious authority must not be confused with the practice of kingship, which he associates with unbelief, greed, ostentatious living, and tyranny. The Shehu disagreed—not, of course, with the ideals his brother expressed but with the idea that the title of "king" should be shunned and classified as a failure to uphold those ideals.

This may seem a minor dispute over terminology. The Shehu, for his part, encouraged his readers to treat the writings of his brother with as much respect as the writings of his son and himself. But part of what ʿAbdullāhi found intolerable in the notion of kingship was hereditary rule, which led him to object strenuously to Bello's accession to power after the Shehu's death. This was no minor dispute, and it led to a political divide that lasted a few years until ʿAbdullāhi finally recognized Bello's rule. The crisis played itself out in scholarly writing, with ʿAbdullāhi and Bello both quoting al-Mawardī and other scholars in their arguments against each other's positions. ʿAbdullāhi cited al-Mawardī's view that, in the event of a ruler's death, a community should form an electoral council to choose the most suitable successor. Bello took note of the same passage but argued that might nevertheless makes right. He claimed that a hereditary successor with superior military force on his side should be accepted by all as the lesser evil rather than resisted, as such resistance would result in the greater evil of the loss of Muslim life.

Given that here, as elsewhere, we find the Shehu's family drawing on intellectual traditions tracing right back to the classical period of Islam, it may seem that we have not really been exploring part of the history of Africana philosophy, but instead, part of the history of philosophy in the Islamic world. In fact, though, we have been doing both. The Sokoto Caliphate obviously belongs to African history. It created the conditions that confronted European powers when they extended the reach of colonialism into what is now Nigeria. The creation of a British protectorate in 1903 marked the demise of the state founded by ʿUthmān Dan Fodio. And if we go back to the motive for the establishment of that state, we will recall that the *jihād* was a rejection of the traditional customs of Hausaland, which the Shehu and his fellow warriors and scholars deemed to be pagan. These included such things as celebratory drumming, since these strict Muslims rejected the use of drums in non-military contexts. Other practices they wanted to eliminate included dancing, prostration before kings and other people of honor, and sacrifices to natural things such as rivers, stones, and trees. The lesson to take from the story of the Shehu is not that Islamic thought in Africa was somehow not part of Africana philosophy, but that Africana thought has always been as diverse as Africa itself, and has included intellectual movements that were mutually antagonistic.

Our next major topic is, in fact, traditional African society of the sort uprooted in the rise of the Sokoto Caliphate. In the coming chapters, we will be considering the controversial question of philosophy in African oral culture. Up until now, we have been focusing on written texts, from the writings of ancient Egypt to the treatises of men like al-Wālī and Muḥammad Bello. But oral transmission has played a part: remember how al-Wālī drew on an oral tradition of commentary to write his own exegesis of the religious creed of al-Sanūsī. Indeed, this aspect of intellectual life in Islamic Africa has continued past the time of the Sokoto Caliphate. The modern-day scholar Kai Kresse has devoted himself to what he calls "anthropology of philosophy," doing fieldwork among Swahili speakers on the East African coast to learn about philosophical practices and teachings there.[25] This may take written form, but also finds expression in the *baraza* culture described by Kresse, in which informal gatherings—sometimes at a veranda (*baraza*) in front of someone's home—involve discussion of everything from local gossip to politics, Quranic exegesis, and intellectual debates over morality or the reality of the spirit world. Poetry also continues to play an important role in Swahili intellectual culture, as it did in the Sokoto Caliphate, and of course poetry is a paradigm example of discourse that flourishes in oral settings. Thus, although the spread of Islam brought literacy to many regions of sub-Saharan Africa for the first time, it did not entirely supplant the orality of traditional African cultures.

12

HEARD IT THROUGH THE GRAPEVINE

Oral Philosophy in Africa

Philosophy seems to be found primarily in books. It has its own section in the library and in any good bookstore. Yet some philosophers have had their doubts about writing as a vehicle for philosophical reflection. No less a philosopher, indeed, than Plato. Of course, he did write books, but only in dialogue form, which suggests that, for him, philosophy had its proper home in conversation. That suggestion is strengthened by Plato's comments on writing itself. One of the *Letters* ascribed to him disavows the composition of philosophical treatises, on the grounds that "this knowledge is not something that can be put into words," but is "born in the soul" only after "long continued intercourse between teacher and pupil" (*Letter 7*, 341c).

This epistle is of disputed authenticity, but there is also the definitely authentic Platonic dialogue called the *Phaedrus*. As noted in Chapter 3, it contains a passage relevant in several ways to Africana philosophy, in which Socrates tells the story of how writing was invented by the Egyptian god named Thoth (274c–275c). When this innovation is put before the king of Egypt, the king rejects it on the grounds that whoever uses writing will become weaker at remembering. "You provide your students with the appearance of wisdom," says the king, "not with its reality. Your invention will enable them to hear many things without being properly taught." Classical historians take this passage as symptomatic of the transition from an oral culture to a culture that was increasingly centered around the written word. Think of the epic poems ascribed to Homer, which apparently emerged from a long tradition of recitation before being written down. The same sort of transition happened in other civilizations like India, where the ancient *Vedas* and *Upaniṣads* first existed orally rather than in books. Even in the modern day, academic philosophers are surprisingly conflicted about the writing of philosophy. True, it's become pretty well impossible to get a permanent job in philosophy at any university without publishing your ideas in writing. But nearly all philosophers will wax enthusiastic about the importance of classroom discussion, the give-and-take between teacher and student that Plato already highlighted. This mode of instruction is still called the "Socratic method," in honor of Plato's portrayal of his own teacher.

All of which has an important implication for the study of Africana philosophy. If we were to assume that any philosophy worthy of the name must be written down, then we could probably wrap up our consideration of precolonial philosophy in Africa right now, having covered the textual traditions of ancient Egypt, Ethiopia, and Islamic Africa. But if we take seriously the idea that philosophy can exist without a tradition of writing, we will be open to the idea that philosophy may be found in all of the indigenous cultures of the African continent. These include many cultures that, right up into the twentieth century, transmitted their traditions of wisdom in oral form, just like the ancient Greeks and Indians. Thus Africana philosophy offers an ideal occasion for testing the notion that philosophy can exist without writing.

Intriguing as it may be, this idea runs up against an immediate practical obstacle: namely, the stubborn refusal of time machines to exist. Genuinely "precolonial" indigenous cultures are not directly accessible to the present-day historian of philosophy. But it's not as if we have nothing at all to go on. First of all, there is archeological evidence. We already made use of it in talking about the emergence of philosophical thought in prehistoric Africa, on the basis of cave paintings and other evidence, and archeology will make occasional appearances in the following chapters. But, for the most part, the search for philosophy among the indigenous peoples of Africa has been linked more to anthropology and ethnography. This is true whether we are talking about the work of non-African scholars who have visited Africa or, even more importantly, the auto-ethnographic work of African scholars reflecting on their own cultures. In lieu of a time machine, scholars have drawn on their own memories or on the information they could gather from those most closely in touch with old traditions in order to obtain data of philosophical relevance.

Of course, present-day African communities could never be pristine, untouched replicas of what existed in precolonial times, given the impact of colonialism and even the very presence of anthropologists, something that was itself facilitated by colonialism. Then, too, there is the present dominance of Christianity and Islam; as we explored in the last few chapters, many traditional systems of belief in West Africa and elsewhere had already been partly displaced in the centuries before

European colonialism by the spread of Islam. Still, Christianity and Islam reshaped, rather than completely erasing, older African traditions of thought. The living traditions of present-day communities accessible through the reports of members of those communities, alongside the work of anthropologists, thus remain interesting sources of philosophical material.[1]

Since we are not ourselves field researchers, in what follows we'll be making use of written texts after all. We'll be drawing on reports of ideas that have been passed down orally in cultures that mostly or entirely lack their own traditions of writing. This enterprise is sometimes called "ethnophilosophy," an apt term insofar as it indicates that we are dealing here with an intersection of two fields of research, ethnography and philosophy. Ethnophilosophy is far from an uncontroversial field. The term first gained prominence through its usage by a philosopher from Benin named Paulin Hountondji, who did not intend it as a compliment. He derisively defined ethnophilosophy as "ethnological work with philosophical pretensions."[2] Many have argued that the whole enterprise is itself colonialist, or beset by fatal methodological and conceptual flaws. Ultimately, we're going to let you make up your own mind about that. But to help you do so we are going to introduce the idea of ethnophilosophy in this chapter, and then, in the following chapters, touch on some of the particular themes that have been explored in this sort of research, including time, God, human personhood, communitarian ethics, causation, and gender roles.

At a minimum, you'll be learning a lot about the practices and beliefs of a wide range of indigenous African peoples. More ambitiously, you may be convinced that whole cultures, rather than only texts written by individual thinkers, can indeed be the bearers of philosophical doctrines, teachings, and concepts. Obviously, we'll be tackling the topic only with regard to the communities of Africa. But just as obviously, the questions and problems we'll be exploring would also arise with other still living cultures that look back to oral tradition, like indigenous peoples of the Americas and Oceania. At stake here is, in fact, nothing less than the question whether philosophers should be interested in *all* cultures of the world, or only in traditions of writing that can be traced ultimately to the founding texts of cultures like ancient Greece, India, and China.

Ethnophilosophy is usually reckoned to have a founding text of its own, in the shape of a book written by a Belgian missionary named Placide Tempels. Born in 1906, he spent almost a decade (from 1937 to 1946) working with the Luba people of what is now the Democratic Republic of Congo. His initial motivation was to further the cause of Christian conversion and to understand how this process might be going wrong. As he lived among the Luba, he became increasingly convinced that missionaries and other Westerners were approaching their task in a simplistic and counter-productive fashion. Rather than seeing themselves as teachers of wholly innocent and passive "natives," the Westerners should come to grips with the indigenous beliefs, indeed the "philosophy," of the Africans they encountered. This idea lay at the heart of his 1945 book *Bantu Philosophy*, which was originally written in Dutch, but then swiftly translated into the other major Belgian language, French.[3] He described his own motivation as follows: "Before we set about teaching these Africans our system of philosophical thought, let us try to master theirs" (25).

The humility of this mission statement is balanced by the audacity of Tempels' account of "Bantu philosophy." For him the Bantu worldview centers on the concept of "force" or "life force" (*élan vital*). It provides a key for understanding everything from their political arrangements to certain practices that Westerners tend to call "magic." Thus the chief of a clan has his standing not simply because of family inheritance, but because the "force" of the community and his ancestors has been gathered in his person, which in turn gives him the power to strengthen other forces, both human and natural (42). Humans in general have greater "force" than animals, plants, and minerals. What looks like "magic" is in fact the human's investing of part of his "vital influence" in other non-human objects (46). Behind these cultural phenomena, Tempels discerned a full-blown metaphysical theory, which he contrasted to Western philosophical assumptions. Whereas the Westerner thinks of all being as "static," with individual substances and their properties making up the furniture of the world, for Africans being is "dynamic" because *to be* is to possess a certain kind and degree of force (34). Tempels would presumably be pleased, or simply bemused, to learn that decades later analytic philosophers would be putting forth a not dissimilar idea under the banner of an "ontology of powers."[4] This theory takes dispositional causal powers (or perhaps we could even use Tempels' term, "forces") to be the fundamental building blocks of metaphysical reality. Color, for instance, would be a power for giving rise to a certain visual experience.

It must be said that Tempels' talk of vital force is far less articulate and detailed than what you'd find in such contemporary philosophical discussions. The theory he ascribed to the Bantu is, in fact, rather obscure. What exactly, we may wonder, does it mean to conceive of being "dynamically" and as a force? How would the obvious objections to this way of thinking be answered from the Bantu perspective? Many of his critics, however, were not upset by the vagueness of the theory so much as by the very nature of the project. We can start with the fact that his book, for all its self-conscious openness to African people and their ideas, was written by a non-African with an openly pro-colonialist agenda. He addresses the book to "all who wish to civilize, educate, and raise the Bantu" and thus to "all colonizers with good will...most particularly missionaries" (17).

Then, too, we might question Tempels' grounds for ascribing the metaphysical theory of force to the Bantu. A major source of evidence in the book is traditional sayings. He claims at one point that the "vital force" metaphysics is expressed in standard greetings like "you are strong" or "you have life in you" (32). One could equally imagine a Bantu visitor to Europe concluding that the natives there think that sunshine has moral properties, because the English say "good day," the French "*bonjour*," and the Germans "*guten Tag*." Of course, Tempels' insights rested on a decade of living amongst the people he was studying. As he himself claimed, "one attains the ability to think like the Bantu and to look upon life as they do" (29). He would have vigorously denied foisting his own ideas on the people he studied. Thus, when talking about the Bantu understanding of the human person, he instructed his reader: "We must make a clean sweep of our own psychological concepts and prepare ourselves to finish with a conception of man very different from that which we now accept. The best thing that we can do is to listen, and to analyse what the Bantu say on the subject" (64).

Well and good, but even if we concede that there are genuine Bantu ideas, and not just Tempels' ideas, in this book on Bantu philosophy, it remains the case that the articulation of the conception of vital force in this book is his, and not one produced by the Bantu themselves. Tempels insisted that he was describing a *philosophy* implicitly understood by all members of the community; he called it "wisdom" and even "ontological knowledge" (47). But he did not claim that any member of the Luba community would be able to convey that wisdom in words, as Tempels himself was able to do. To the contrary, he wrote: "We do not claim, of course, that the Bantu are capable of formulating a philosophical treatise, complete with an adequate vocabulary. It is our job to proceed to such systematic development. It is we who will be able to tell them, in precise terms, what their inmost concept of being is" (25). One is reminded of a scene in the movie *Back to the Future*, in which the time traveling white teenager Marty McFly teaches a group of African American musicians how to play rock and roll.[5]

In spite of its condescending aspects, Tempels' work attracted favorable notice from many African readers. His project was positively received, for example, by Alexis Kagamé, whose 1956 work *The Rwandan Bantu Philosophy of Being* displayed Tempels' influence.[6] Kagamé likewise extracted implicit philosophical ideas from widespread cultural features, with the twist that he focused primarily on aspects of African languages, working especially with his mother tongue, Kinyarwanda, as a key example of a Bantu language. He pointed to the use of the same root (*ntu*) behind the words *umuntu*, *ikintu*, and *ahantu*, referring respectively to intelligent beings, unintelligent beings, and the space-time framework within which those beings exist. An implication of Kagamé's approach, much debated in subsequent work on Africana philosophy, is that thinking like a Bantu and talking like a Bantu go together. More generally, we can study the language of any people to discern the underlying philosophical ideas of that people. A further, more discouraging conclusion might be that it is impossible to understand a given system of thought without mastering the language that goes with it. Does this mean that African philosophy, if it is to remain genuinely African, must be practiced in African languages and not in European languages like French or English? This is a question worth asking, even if we are, after all, talking about a continent whose languages number in the thousands.[7] (As many as 3,000, depending how you count. In Cameroon alone, 250 languages are spoken, one for every hundred thousand inhabitants!)

This potential implication of Kagamé's work, that each distinct group in Africa might be expected to have its own local "philosophy," would push against a tendency detectable in Tempels and many other ethnophilosophers. This is the habit of generalizing from findings about one, perhaps very small, group of African people to larger groups, or even *all* Africans. The point was made well by an early critic of Tempels, the Ugandan philosopher and poet Okot p'Bitek. In a damning three-page review of *Bantu Philosophy* published in the early 1960s, p'Bitek complained that Tempels was drawing inferences from his experiences with the Luba to all of the Bantu, without having bothered to go see what other Bantu groups like the Zulus might think about all this "force" business.[8] As p'Bitek put it, "can serious African scholars concerned with a correct appraisal and analysis of African beliefs and philosophies afford this kind of cheap generalization?" We'll see this problem arising again when we move on to look at more specific topics that have been addressed with the tools of ethnophilosophy. As a warning against cheap generalization, we'll frequently be pointing out the diversity of cultural practices and beliefs across the continent.

In his review p'Bitek also complained, predictably and justifiably, about some of Tempels' own language, for instance his constant reference to the Bantu as "primitive." And he fastened on to a point we just made, that the act of rendering the supposed Bantu philosophy explicit was a task for Tempels and not the Bantu themselves. In a longer passage criticizing this aspect of the book and setting out a preferred method, p'Bitek wrote:

> Is it not strange that not even a single Bantu elder should be able to give a rough description of Bantu philosophy?...It is, to say the least, unhelpful pride to start off

> by holding that a people do not know what they believe, or cannot express it; and that it is the student who, after discovering it, will tell them what this belief is. It is the student who is the ignorant person. It is he who learns from a people and he learns only a small part of their philosophy. The role of the student of traditional philosophy, it seems to me, is, as it were, to photograph as much of and in as great detail as possible, the traditional way of life, and then to make comments.

Here p'Bitek is, in a way, insisting on a point Tempels had made himself, but arguably not taken seriously enough. The student of African culture and philosophy is just that: a *student*, not someone preparing to be a *teacher* for people who in the last analysis remain "primitive."

With this, p'Bitek was offering insights that have been embraced in anthropology quite generally. Rather than seeing the people who are being investigated as something like rats in a biologist's laboratory, or substances studied by a chemist, the investigators must realize that they will interact with the people they visit, that their presence will have an impact, and that they themselves may be profoundly changed through their encounters with a foreign culture. As Hountondji put it, ethnophilosophy as exemplified by Tempels appears to treat the "black man [as] a topic, a voiceless face under private investigation, an object to be defined and not the subject of a possible discourse."[9] Anthropology must inevitably be a two-way street, so to speak. This incidentally goes well with the insight that African cultures, as they could be encountered by visitors in the 1930s or now in the twenty-first century, are themselves not static. These are real communities, not mere repositories of ancient cultural notions, and a trip to rural Africa is not tantamount to using a time machine. Rather, these cultures show signs of their own engagement with other peoples and religions, and they have changed to grapple with modernity, not least with colonialism and its after-effects.

13

EVENT HORIZON

African Philosophy of Time

If you were able to visit the distant past, you'd be struck by many obvious differences. There would be the lack of indoor plumbing, the difficulty of traveling long distances, the tragedy of cute things done by pets that are witnessed only by their owners rather than by a global audience of social media users. A more subtle, but even more far-reaching difference would lie in the way that peoples of the past experienced time. Without the technologies that enable exact timekeeping, it would have been impossible to do things like making an appointment for 3:30 pm sharp. The temporal measurements used in everyday life would have been larger: one would think in days rather than minutes. Even where the same measurements were used, these would have different meanings. Many premodern societies divided the time of daylight into a certain number of hours, but with the length of the hours varying through the year, because the sun is up for longer in summer than in winter.

That is something we already see with the ancient Egyptians, who can be credited with devising much of the time system we still use today. They had an annual calendar with 365 days, each of which was split into twenty-four hours, with twelve hours each for daylight and night-time.[1] They were also pioneers in timekeeping technology, devising such things as sundials and water clocks, which were then also used by the Greeks and Romans. Yet the Egyptians seem to have conceptualized time very differently than we do. Nowadays time is often imagined as a kind of indefinitely extending line, with seconds, days, and years marking off smaller and larger sections of the line. For the Egyptians, as for the Indians and some Greek philosophers like the Stoics, it seems instead to have been cyclical.[2]

This despite the fact that time was also believed to be the creation of the gods. A hymn to the goddess Neith praises her in the following terms: "She made the moment, she created the hours, she made the years, she created the months, she gave birth to the season of inundation, to winter, to summer."³ This act of creation comes at the beginning of a cosmic cycle. During each cycle the paramount concern is to preserve order and stability, which is especially threatened at moments of temporal transition like at the start of a new year or passing of day into night. At least going by the texts we have, which were of course produced by the elite of society, priests and rulers had the special task of warding off such chaos. Other humans were simply to carry out lesser roles that had always existed. Thus it has been said that the Egyptians "had very little sense of history or even of past and future…They thought of the world as essentially static and unchanging," and that "the linear character of time scarcely seems to have exceeded the domain of individual existence."⁴ The language used by the Egyptians may reflect this. Their words *djet* and *neneh*, hard if not impossible to translate into English, refer to the temporal aspect of reality as a whole. But whereas *neneh*, associated with the sun god Re and the emergence of the new day, had connotations of change, *djet* was connected with Osiris and the night, and implies that something is already completed. One can thus say that *neneh* "comes" while *djet* "endures."⁵

Once we notice how differently even the Egyptians perceived time, despite their clocks and calendars, we might wonder what time has been like for other peoples who lacked those technologies, and who also had no writing. The written word is after all another technology, which brings with it the power to record what has happened even many years ago. Thus it has been remarked that literacy brings "an awareness of the past as different from the present."⁶ A people with no writing would, we might expect, have even less sense of history than the Egyptians and even less sense of time as an abstract continuum or "vessel" that can be divided into segments, or in which events can be located. That is the hypothesis we want to explore now, as we look at attempts to discover and articulate ideas of time held in traditional African societies.

It's a topic that has been attracting interest for many decades. A pioneering study by the British anthropologist Edward Evans-Pritchard, published in 1939, looked at the "time reckoning" of the Nuer people, who live near one of the Nile's tributaries in what is today South Sudan.⁷ He reported that the Nuer spoke of time in a very concrete fashion, dividing it up in terms of seasonal cycles—especially the wet and dry seasons—and with reference to social events. On a daily basis, this meant speaking of parts of the day in terms of the tasks to be performed, like taking out the cattle. Over longer periods the Nuer were, according to Evans-Pritchard, hardly able to conceive of a past stretching back more than a few generations, basically as far as a given person knows his or her own lineage of ancestors. Furthermore their language has no word for time as such. Thus the

Nuer "cannot, as we can, speak of time as though it were something actual, which passes, can be wasted, can be saved, and so forth."[8]

Similar conclusions were reached by anthropological studies of other groups such as the Tiv of Nigeria and the Kaguru, a Bantu people from Tanzania.[9] In both cases, it was found that time was conceived in the concrete terms of events, and usually only in the context of relating events to one another, as when a pregnancy is measured by full moons. The Kaguru word for "day" is actually the same as their word for "sun (*ijua*)," and like the Nuer, their understanding of years is determined by seasonal rainfall. The anthropologists tried to discover whether these Africans had a largely unspoken concept of more abstract time, and concluded that they did not. One researcher found that the Tiv, despite being well aware of lunar cycles and of seasons, were making no attempt to coordinate the two. (When he says, "I have asked specifically and exhaustively about this point," one can't help wondering whether the Tiv were even more bemused by him than vice versa.[10]) We are told that while the Tiv have folk tales which they tell about the past, they have no real sense of history. Anything further back than the recent past resides in a kind of hazy period called "long ago (*ngise*)," which is how their stories begin, like saying "once upon a time." For the Kaguru, "time is essentially a vague sliding scale focused on the near present in which the past and future are of relatively little concern," so that "they do not reify time in the Western sense in which it sometimes seems to take on the attributes of a substance or a commodity."[11]

Which sounds pretty good, right? Isn't it stressful to believe that time is money, that it is a scarce resource that we must use with maximal efficiency? Arguably, this attitude emerged in Europe precisely along with early modern advancements (if they were really advancements) in keeping track of time, like the ringing of church bells to signal that it was time for mass or to go off to work. Thus, as early as 1399, we have the wife of an Italian merchant admonishing him by letter: "I deem nothing so precious to you, both for body and soul, as time, and think you value it too little."[12]

Of course, we might doubt whether the approach of these anthropologists, whose fieldwork was done in the 1930s and 1950s, was really a foolproof method of discovering African notions of time. But, to some extent, their findings have been borne out by subsequent research on such topics as African proverbs. Thus a much more recent study, from the 1990s, looked at the sayings of the Ga and Dangme, two closely related ethnic groups from Ghana. They do have a word for time, namely *be*, but it has been argued that for them "to talk of time is to talk of some event or activity."[13] They are keenly aware of the way that things arise and then pass, as captured in their saying "no kite has ever remained in the air." The vital thing, though, is to act at the right time. Thus they say "a mother does not wait in the market until the last person leaves" and "you don't haggle of the price of a yam that is still in the ground." It may be that a grasp of time as inextricably linked to concrete events goes together with the idea that events are repeating, or at least that the future will be more or less like the past. Thus we have the entertaining proverb, "when the old woman goes to fetch water, she will return; the issue is when she'll get back,"[14] and among the Yoruba, "if a father has begotten a child, however long it might take, the child may yet beget the father. If a mother gave birth to a child, she can still be reborn by the child."[15]

The most influential attempt to extract a theory of time from this sort of material was put forward by the Kenyan philosopher John Mbiti. His ground-breaking book *African Religions and Philosophy*, first published in 1969, drew on observations concerning many different traditional African societies, including Kenyan peoples like the Kamba (the group to which Mbiti belonged) and the Gikuyu, both of whom speak Bantu languages.[16] An Anglican priest, Mbiti was struck by what he saw as a mismatch between the understanding that Christian missionaries had of their own religion and the worldview of the Africans those missionaries sought to instruct. The Protestant tradition, and Christianity more generally, promise a salvation that may lie in the far-flung future. Africans were bound to find this teaching puzzling, if not meaningless, because for them time has "a long past, a present, and virtually no future."[17]

As evidence for this provocative claim, Mbiti adduced some of the same features of traditional societies highlighted by the anthropological studies we've just mentioned. According to Mbiti, Africans have an exclusively concrete and empirical understanding of time, which is nothing but the sequence of events they have experienced. Their lives are governed by natural phenomena like the seasons, which are expected to continue into the future as they have in the past. Beyond that the future has no meaning: since it "has not been experienced, it does not make sense; it cannot, therefore, constitute part of time."[18] Mbiti introduces a terminological distinction here, using the Swahili words *sasa* and *zamani*. *Sasa* is the immediate present, or at least ongoing events up to a maximum duration of about two years. A larger scale and more abstract, and almost entirely past, kind of time is *zamani*. It swallows up *sasa* as events recede into history, so that *zamani* is, as Mbiti puts it, the "graveyard of time." Speaking of graveyards, when people die, they move from *sasa* into *zamani*, especially once they are forgotten by those still alive. Confronted with something like the eschatology of the Christian missionaries, these Africans can only conclude that salvation is going to occur very imminently. After all, for them there is no real future beyond what is imminent.

Some scholars have found this to be a powerful and convincing analysis of the traditional African conception of time. A few years after Mbiti, one article noted the resonance between his analysis and the earlier findings of anthropologists like Evans-Pritchard. The same author argued that the very division into past, present, and future is "due to an abstract notion of time as an entity which is alien to African thought." For Africans "there are not 'times' but 'events'."[19] More recently, Messay Kebede (in a study already mentioned in Chapter 7) has argued that the Europeanization of Ethiopia displaced the traditional notion of time as cyclical, which had the advantage of rendering social classes fluid. When you were a peasant rather than a king, you knew that your family line just needed to wait its turn.[20] It's worth emphasizing that such inferences were often drawn from the study of African languages. Mbiti observed, regarding the Bantu languages discussed in his book, that they have a verb modifier to indicate the more distant past, but none for the distant future. Similarly, it was pointed out that in the language of the Luba of Katanga (the same people whose views shaped Tempels' *Bantu Philosophy*), there is a distinction between the present and what is further from the present, with the latter being almost always used for the past.[21]

Then came the backlash. Mbiti's account was criticized on a number of grounds, some of which have probably already occurred to you. For one thing, even if we accept his claims concerning the groups he knew best, in Kenya, would that show that his findings apply to *all* Africans prior to their encounter with other cultures? Thus Ernest Beyaraza, in a book published in 2000, allowed that Mbiti might have been right about the Kamba and Gikuyu peoples.[22] But this was only a caveat at the end of a long discussion about conceptions of time among the Kiga of Uganda, which comes to strikingly different conclusions from those of Mbiti. Beyaraza speaks of social conventions that obviously require a conception of the distant future. The Kiga have an arrangement in which a poor man works for years to earn a calf that will be born in coming years, and rituals that look ahead to the prosperity of children once they are grown. Their language includes the sort of indefinite future constructions Mbiti claimed not to find, as well as abstract references to time, which is called *obwire*, days being understood as its parts.

An even more forthright critique was made by Kwame Gyekye, who found expressions for abstract time in another African people, the Akan of Ghana and Côte d'Ivoire. They say that time, *bere*, "is like a bird: if you do not catch it and it flies, you do not see it again."[23] Never mind the future, the Akan even articulate a notion of eternity, by speaking of *beresanten*, meaning "times lined up in a row." Their divination practices show that they have intense interest in future events, as do sayings like: "time has its boundary: we do not traverse it. Everything will end in the hereafter someday." Likewise, a study of time among the Yoruba shows that on closer inspection, their concrete, event-centered, and possibly cyclical approach to time does not rule out the envisioning of long future time.[24]

If these observations suggest that Mbiti was rash in generalizing from one or two groups in Kenya to a pan-African philosophy of time, he can also be accused of not generalizing *enough*. As we have already suggested, any people of the distant past would surely have had a very different experience of time than we do now. To the extent that Mbiti's points do apply to all of Africa, they might well apply to all societies that lack writing, or even more widely than that. Just consider that in Aristotle, the repetition of natural cycles is far more prominent than anything remotely like Christian eschatology. Making this very point, one scholar has remarked that "linear time has as little to do with traditional Africa as it had with Aristotle."[25]

To this, Mbiti would perhaps respond that the linguistic features he has observed among Bantu groups do not necessarily appear in the languages of other premodern societies outside of Africa. But even if his observations are accurate, it is far from obvious that they provide a basis for inferring an implicit philosophy of time.[26] After all, even if you can use English to refer to the remote past and distant future, how often do you talk about anything but the near future, present, and recent past? (Except, that is, when you are talking about the history of philosophy.) There is actually a deep philosophical issue lurking here, as to whether features of a language betray specific conceptual worldviews, or even cause such worldviews to arise. This idea is often called the "Sapir–Whorf hypothesis," after the two linguists who proposed it. Roughly speaking, it posits that language is something like a lens through which people see and think about the world, and shapes the fundamental concepts through which they engage with that world. As it happens a famous, and much criticized, application of the theory was Whorf's own contention that a group of Native Americans, the Hopi, must have a different notion of time, because of the way their language (supposedly) works. And there is more than a whiff of Whorf in Mbiti's approach to the African philosophy of time.

For all these reasons, Mbiti's account is no longer seen with much favor. Yet a number of his critics have agreed that traditional African peoples have something to teach us about time, or at least about the variety of ways that time might be experienced. The Rwandan philosopher Alexis Kagame objected to Mbiti's suggestion that Africans hold no investment in the idea of a distant future by pointing out the importance in Bantu culture of ensuring the success of future generations. Yet he still deemed it possible to generalize from a broader study of Bantu language and culture to a properly "African" idea of time.[27] The evidence he drew on has much in common with those anthropological studies, such as the use of concrete events to name times of day: rather beautifully, it seems that the Tutsi herdsmen of Rwanda call the start of the day "the laughing of dawn (*umuseke*)" and early morning "the song of the little birds (*mu bunyoni*)."[28] Time therefore only becomes meaningful insofar as it belongs to our concrete lives. As Kagame put it, "time is a colorless, neutral entity as long as it is not marked or stamped by some specific event."[29] Intriguingly, though, he also maintained that, while Bantu peoples can and do easily distinguish between time and space in their language, they also have an underlying notion of "localization" that reveals time and space to be part of a single category. It is important that Kagame puts all this forward more as a philosopher than as an anthropologist, albeit one whose proposals are grounded in and inspired by empirical findings. One gets the clear sense that he is not just attempting to describe a traditional African conception of time, but suggesting that this conception might just be the right one.

14

ONE TO RULE THEM ALL

God in African Philosophy

If you read around in older literature about traditional religious beliefs in Africa, there is one word you'll come across repeatedly: "primitive." The epithet conjures up a picture of pre-technological native folk worshipping things like rivers, trees, and stones. As we've seen in the case of the Sokoto Caliphate, this is exactly how Muslims who lived in Africa characterized the practices of the so-called "pagans" with whom they shared the continent. But you don't have to be a nineteenth century jihadi to associate "primitive" religion with polytheism. It's commonly supposed that older religions had many gods, who were closely associated with features and places of the natural world—the superstition of prehistory. Then, as civilization advanced, humans achieved the more abstract and theologically respectable notion of monotheism, as realized most fully in Judaism, Christianity, and then Islam.

Popular conceptions like this are most often oversimplifications, but, in this case, the standard view is even more spectacularly wrong than usual. It's patently obvious, first of all, that sophistication in matters of religion or philosophy is compatible with polytheism: just consider the *Upaniṣads* or the writings of late ancient Platonists, both of them full of references to multiple divinities. Then too, Muslims and Christians in Africa were wrong to suppose that they had brought monotheism there for the first time. Remember the remarkable ancient Egyptian king Akhenaten and his worship of a single god represented as the disk of the sun (Chapter 4). Furthermore, and most relevantly for us now, many scholars of traditional African religion would reject the description of it as "polytheistic." What we find in some cultures is a religious system not unlike late ancient Platonism, with a single first principle that stands over a multitude of lesser divinities. The scholar of African religion E. Bolaji Idowu has called this "diffused monotheism," and rebuked Western scholars for their condescending view that "deity is a philosophical concept which savages are incapable of framing."[1]

Here we are already in danger of replacing one sweeping claim with another. As Idowu himself remarked elsewhere, "It is foolhardy to generalize on Africa."[2] His caution is well placed, given the vast number of peoples and language groups in Africa. So we won't be laying down universal statements like that made by John Mbiti: "Every African people recognizes one God."[3] To place all emphasis on the worship of a single, greatest God is not only to paint with a rather broad brush, but also risks accepting the terms of the standard hierarchy, with sophisticated monotheism (whether "diffused" or not) placed above more simple-minded polytheism. Again, a strident voice of protest against this tendency was that of Okot p'Bitek, who complained about Western scholars who "dress up African deities with Hellenic robes and parade them before the Western world to show that Africans were as civilized as Europeans."[4]

Still, it is a striking fact that many traditional African communities do posit a single God who reigns supreme over other divinities as well as humans. Among the best-studied cases is the belief system of the Yoruba of Nigeria, one of the largest ethnic groups of Africa and one whose cultural influence was spread in the Americas by the slave trade. At first glance, they seem to offer an extreme example of polytheism, with some scholars counting as many as 1,700 Yoruba gods, perhaps the most extensive pantheon in Africa. These divinities, called *oriśa* (pronounced "orisha"), are given responsibility for natural events; thus it is said that the river goddess Yemoja "destroys bridges when she is angry." The *oriśa* are seen as fitting recipients of prayer and sacrifice.[5] However, there is also a supreme God who created the *oriśa* and uses them as emissaries, assistants, or ministers in His dealings with the world. This highest God is called Olodumare. One tale records how the other divinities attempted to challenge His authority, but were forced to submit to Him. Thus a Yoruba poem says, "be there 1400 divinities of the home, be there one thousand two hundred divinities of the marketplace, yet there is not one divinity to compare with Olodumare."[6]

Despite His centrality, Olodumare is strangely absent from everyday religious practice and discourse among the Yoruba. Instead, individual *oriśa* are made the object of cult practices and have their own priests. In stories about the fashioning of the world, Olodumare sends a kind of deputy, Oriśa-nla (or Obatala), to do the actual work of creation. This dynamic is found among other peoples as well, which has prompted some to hypothesize that the African God has somehow "hidden" Himself or "withdrawn" from humans and the world. Or perhaps lesser divinities like the *oriśa* of Yoruba belief are mere intermediaries between the highest God and the world. A particularly radical version of that thesis, which would push African religion towards pure monotheism, would see the lesser divinities as mere manifestations of a single deity.

According to another interpretation, it is deemed overly familiar to pray or sacrifice to a highest God like Olodumare. Just as subjects should not dare to approach the king in a traditional African society, with his regal power being exercised through subordinates, so religious customs would involve dealing directly only with lesser divinities and not the king of heaven.[7] This would fit well with a more general tendency to draw parallels between human political power and divine authority. The Yoruba use the epithet "King" for both Olodumare and the Oriśa-nla, while lesser divinities are sometimes described as ministers in a royal court.[8] A Yoruba prayer to another of the *oriśa* goes as follows: "There is no place where Osun, who is powerful as a king, is not known. The whole world prostrates to the king. There is no limit to his activity on earth."[9] Interestingly, this particular *oriśa* is female, making the ascription of kingship an instance of gender-bending. Meanwhile human kings are invested with religious authority, with the roles of monarch and high priest coinciding in many traditional societies. The dividing line between human and divine rulership is further blurred by the fact that some spiritual entities began their careers as human heroes or monarchs, becoming divinized upon their death.

This brings us to another well-known aspect of African religion, namely the spiritual role of human ancestors. Some would even question whether there is a clear distinction between divinities and ancestors,[10] and not unreasonably so, when you consider that among some peoples even the highest God is termed a "grand ancestor."[11] Still, deceased humans seem most often to occupy a role in the pantheon below the lesser gods, and to serve as intermediaries to the divine realm. A distinction is sometimes drawn between the ancestors whose names are still known, the so-called "living dead," and the ancestors who passed into the spirit world long ago and have been forgotten. That distinction should make us suspicious of an idea sometimes put forward in the debate about the African understanding of time, namely that traditional peoples can look back into history only as far as they can name their ancestors. The issue may be a more pragmatic one: how many names are in fact still known? Thus the Kaguru speak simply of a time "long ago (*katali*)" to refer to the age before living memory.[12]

The picture so far, then, seems to be one in which there is a hierarchy of spiritual beings, from more recently deceased family members who are the closest to those of us who are still living up to lesser divinities and finally the highest God who stands over all things. We might expect that this highest God would possess divine attributes marking his transcendence, like those we find in Judaism, Christianity, and

Islam. Indeed, various peoples describe God not only as "creator" and "king" but also as unknowable, omniscient, and omnipotent. A hymn recited by the Twa people, who live in the forests of central Africa, says, "In the beginning was God, today is God, tomorrow will be God. Who can make an image of God? He has no body, He is as a word which comes out of your mouth. That word! It is no more, it is past, and still it lives! So is God."[13] Notice the interesting implicit point made here about language. The hymn seems to allude to the fact that the meanings of words persist for a long time (perhaps in the understanding of those who hear them?) even though the utterance of a word is a momentary affair. Likewise, God persists unchanging through time. Many other groups likewise insist on God's immutability, or even timelessness. Thus the Nupe say that "God will outlive eternity," the Akan that "No one saw the beginning, none shall see the end, except God," the Gikuyu that "He is the same as He was yesterday," and the Ila that "God has nowhere and nowhen."[14]

Yet the supreme God of African religion is also frequently seen as a more immanent force. There is a widespread association of God with the sky or heaven and with the sending of the rains that sustain life. Indeed, the Akan name for God, *Nyame*, may be connected to their word for rain (*nyankom*).[15] The Lugbara people of the west Nile region call their supreme God *Adroa*, meaning "far away," as contrasted to *adro* or "nearby," a term that can be used for lesser spiritual beings. While this may suggest absolute transcendence for the higher God, it has been suggested that the Lugbara in fact use this terminology to express the way that God is simultaneously transcendent and immanent in the world—*adroa* and *adro* being just two variants of a single name.[16] Certainly many African belief systems do recognize an ongoing relationship between God and the world. Mbiti tells us that the Kamba see God as the maker of all things and also call Him the "cleaver," that is, the principle that causes things to be different from one another.[17] In a trope reminiscent of Plato's cosmological dialogue *Timaeus*, African religions often compare God to a craftsman like a carpenter or potter, who fashions first the world and then individual humans. God and the lesser divinities also reward good and punish evil, especially wicked political rulers.

Here arises an obvious philosophical question: if God and His deputies are at work in the world, how far does their influence reach? Are *all* things brought about by divine decree? In other words, are African religions determinist? This is one of those questions where we need to proceed carefully, without assuming that all traditional religions would give the same answer. Indeed, one can find contrary indications within the oral traditions of a single group. There are plenty of proverbs, prayers, and songs that suggest a form of determinism.[18] The Nupe say, "Should you do anything that is beautiful, Soko has caused it to be beautiful; should you do anything that is evil, Soko has caused it to be evil," the Kongo that "What comes from heaven cannot be resisted." The Kamba end prayers with the phrase "God willing." When someone is ill, the Lugbara predict, "If God wants him to die, then truly he will die. If God wants him to recover, then truly he will recover." Yet it is just as easy to find naturalistic explanations of events. If the crops are poor, this is as likely to be ascribed to inadequate rainfall as to the gods. Rather than assuming that determinism is rife in African belief, it may be safer to suppose that divine agency was invoked for explaining remarkably significant or unusual events. Many African religions give little or no role to chance, especially concerning such notable events.[19] God, not randomness, is thus the explanation of last resort.

Another reason to doubt that divine causation is conceived as being pervasive in the world is that many African peoples seem reluctant to ascribe evil to God. Admittedly, some lesser divinities, like the wicked trickster Esu of Yoruba belief, do inflict punishment and suffering, and in the case of Esu even on other gods as well as humans. But more often evils are blamed not on the gods, but on malign humans who are working magic, something ethnographers often call "witchcraft" (see further Chapter 17). Likewise it is not clear whether God is responsible for the mortality of the human race. Several traditional stories absolve God of responsibility for death, with a nice example being a tale told by the Xhosa of South Africa. God sends Chameleon as a messenger to promise human beings immortal life, but he falls asleep and fails to deliver his message in time. Instead Lizard delivers a corrupted version of the same message, which informs humans that they will die. And so we have, ever since. Similarly the Maasai say that we die because the first human was told to announce the divine command: "Man die and come back again; moon die and stay away." Sadly he got the decree backwards, resulting in both the death of humans and the continuity of the lunar cycle.[20]

Many other religious narratives serve to explain what is otherwise inexplicable or disturbing. Among the most interesting are accounts of human diversity.[21] A story told by the Bassari people of Togo and Ghana has it that when humans were first created, they were given to eat from different bowls, which explains why various communities speak different languages. Another account plays on the aforementioned description of God as being like a potter who shapes individual humans. He is said by the Shilluk to have made different races out of different colors of clay, which explains differentiation of skin color. The Yoruba relate that when their supreme deity Olodumare instructed Oriṣa-Nla to make humans, he fashioned them in all different shapes and colors; yet all humans come originally from Ile-Ife, the fabled city of Yorubaland. The Nuer, finally, have been recorded as saying that white skin color is a punishment from God.

As is clear from these stories about white people, the material we are dealing with is not prehistoric lore completely untouched by contact with groups and traditions from beyond Africa. It is easy to assume that the information ethnographers have gathered tells us about religious beliefs that have existed in Africa since before the dawn of recorded history. But, as no less an observer than Sigmund Freud remarked: "It should not be forgotten that primitive"—(there's that word again)—"races are not young races but are in fact as old as civilized races. There is no reason to suppose that, for the benefit of our information, they have retained their original ideas and institutions undeveloped and undistorted."[22] Or, as a more recent scholar has observed while arguing for likely influence of Christianity on the aforementioned Lugbara idea of God as "far away (*adroa*)," "the present situation of terms and meanings is not the one that existed about a hundred years ago."[23]

Some of the evidence we've presented here looks suspiciously like it may be influenced by Christianity or Islam. The opening line of that Twa hymn, "In the beginning was God," sounds rather familiar, doesn't it? And the Kamba habit of ending prayers with the phrase "God willing" is reminiscent of the pervasive Muslim practice of saying *inshallah*, "if God wills."[24] In many cases influence from other religions is explicit: the Yoruba have divinities that are associated with Islam, for example.[25] Influence can also go the other way too. The name of the aforementioned trickster god "Esu" is sometimes used by Nigerian Muslims to refer to Satan, in place of the traditional Islamic name "Iblis." In short, traditional African beliefs are no more isolated than they are monolithic. They have long been shaped by influence from Mediterranean culture, and also by mutual interaction between African peoples.

We'll conclude with a fascinating illustration of this point: beliefs about newborn children among the Beng of the Ivory Coast.[26] It is not uncommon among African religions to suppose that humans reincarnate, often with a suggestion that individual lives are shaped by a destiny chosen or assigned before birth. Thus the Yoruba say: "That which is affixed to one cannot be rectified with medicine."[27] The Beng too understand humans to have existed before birth, and their picture of the other realm from which the children have come is clearly influenced by contact with Europeans. They apply the name *wrugbe* to the place of the afterlife, or perhaps we should say "beforelife," and describe it as a "space of economic plenty and social harmony." All languages are spoken there, so when it seems to us that a baby is learning to talk, in fact she is in the process of *forgetting* all tongues apart from Beng. For this reason the parents speak to the babies as if they were adults. Newborn babies are strongly tempted to return to the favorable otherworld, which accounts for the frequency of infant mortality. To make sure that babies do not give up on their new lives, they are meticulously washed to remove the traces of the *wrugbe*, and given gifts of money to soften the blow. Significantly, this money comes in two forms: cowrie shells, which were used as currency in precolonial times, and French coins. In a study of this set of beliefs and practices, Alma Gottlieb concluded that it constitutes a reaction to the cultural damage done to the Beng by French colonialism. The otherworld, with its lack of poverty and strife, is a figurative representation of the precolonial time, indirectly remembered as a halcyon age in which Beng culture had not yet been subjected to foreign exploitation and oppression.

Here we see another aspect of the sophistication of African religion: its capacity to adapt in response to changing circumstances. Far from being primitive, the religious beliefs of traditional African peoples raise, and often answer, the full range of philosophical questions we associate with the Abrahamic faiths. How many gods are there? What form does God's causality take, and is that influence pervasive? How does divine authority relate to human political authority? How can evils be accounted for in a world ruled by a benevolent God? Are specific events and features of our experience best explained with reference to nature or in light of divine decree? And as we'll see next, the same goes for the place of the individual human within the universe God and His deputies have made.

15

BEHIND THE MASK

African Philosophy of the Person

You'd think that all philosophers, wherever and whenever they lived, would agree about at least one thing: what it is to be a person. Philosophers are themselves persons, after all, and variations in culture wouldn't seem to make any difference since every culture has persons in it. Besides, it's not like you have to undertake strenuous investigation into the nature of personhood. You are a person and you're right there, ready to think about. On the other hand, persons are pretty complicated. Thoughts interrupt other thoughts, sensations battle with one another for our attention, desires gain and then lose the upper hand over other desires, and actions can both display settled moral character and depart from it. Inner life is not like an a capella performance by a classically trained singer. It's more like a live show by Parliament-Funkadelic, which sometimes might feature as many as thirty musicians who wander unpredictably out to perform for the audience; you get the sense that much of the real action is happening backstage.

Flying in the face of this complexity, philosophers have frequently offered rather simple accounts of personhood. Some, agreeing with Parliament-Funkadelic that "everything is on the one," reduce the person to a single principle. You are nothing but your body. Or you are nothing but an immaterial soul, with a merely incidental relation to a body. A dualist might say that you are both an immaterial soul and a body, though a closer look at some notorious dualists shows them acknowledging a greater degree of multiplicity. Take Plato. In some dialogues, like the *Republic* and *Timaeus*, he gives the soul several parts that can struggle against one another. Or take Īśvarakṛṣṇa, the author of the founding text of the Sāṃkhya tradition in ancient India.[1] He was a dualist who contrasted the material principle called *prakṛti* to a principle of consciousness called *puruṣa*. Yet he took account of our complex mental life by distinguishing in each person an intellect (*buddhi*), a power of self-awareness (*ahaṃkāra*), and a mind (*manas*) for thinking, to say nothing of further sensory powers and powers of the body. A Platonic dualist who came to this treatise in search of a discussion of the "soul" might be unsure whether or not it is there, despite the rich vocabulary used to analyze human psychology.

Likewise, in the case of traditional African belief systems, one should not be too quick to say that a certain word or concept represents what philosophers speaking English might call "soul," or "mind," or "spirit." A better strategy is to look closely at indigenous ideas and understand how they work, even if this means simply leaving their terminology untranslated at first.[2] Admittedly, if we think of "soul" as a "spark of the divine" in each human, the part of the person that makes him or her similar to God, then we do find this notion in numerous African cultures. Thus the Akan say that "all persons are children of God; no one is a child of the earth,"[3] reflecting a conviction that each of us comes from the divine being called Nyame. Similarly, the Igbo people hold that the immortality of human persons is a reflection of the immortality of God.[4] But even if an afterlife of some sort plays a role in all, or nearly all, traditional African religions, this does not mean that these cultures are envisioning a single, immaterial soul for each of us. Among the Dogon, it is believed that there are two parts of the person, which we might be tempted to call two "souls," and which are respectively male and female. The Nupe too are said to postulate two "souls" of which one reincarnates while the other goes back to God. In the literature looking at African ideas about personhood from a philosophical point of view, the most widely discussed belief systems are those of the Akan and Yoruba and, in both cases, we find something more complicated than soul–body or soul–mind dualism.

As Kwame Gyekye and others have shown, the Akan "conceptual scheme" posits two psychological principles within each person over and above the body.[5] These are called *sunsum* and *kra* (alternatively *okra*, but we'll stick to *kra* to keep clear that we are making persons, not Louisiana gumbo). *Kra* is the source of the person's life, and thus closely related to breath (*honhom*). It is given by Nyame, or God, and returns to Him after death. In this life, the *kra* serves to guide the person toward his or her destiny. Thus "his *kra* is good" means "he is lucky." Visiting the Ga people, neighbors of the Akan with a similar psychological scheme, Joyce Engmann likewise found them saying "his *kla* is with him" to mean that someone is lucky, and "his *kla* has left him" to mean that someone has gone mad. She found that they "readily accepted" the idea that this principle corresponds to what Europeans would call a "guardian spirit."[6] This casts some doubt on Gyekye's suggestion of translating *kra* as "soul." It seems rather that the *kra* is a spiritual power that oversees the life of a person and is not exactly identical to that person. If we were going to compare it to something in Platonic philosophy, we might rather see a resonance between the *kra* and the so-called *daimon* who guides the soul to its chosen fate in the myth of the afterlife told at the end of Plato's *Republic*.

A different role again is played by the *sunsum*, which is said to "escort" the *kra* into life and back to God at the point of death. The Akan have a matrilineal kinship system, and see each person's body as linking them to their mother's family through a blood tie. But the spiritual principle that is the *sunsum* links one to one's father. Akan sayings indicate a strong personality or imposing presence by speaking of a "weighty *sunsum*"; one person can have more *sunsum* than another, whereas no one has more or less *kra* than anyone else. Furthermore, the *sunsum* is able to slip away from the body in dreams. It may also linger for some weeks after death before moving on to the world of the dead, during which time it is referred to as a kind of "shadow."[7] It seems that the *sunsum* retains its individuality after death, whereas the *kra* dissolves into the divinity of Nyame.

These points have led to a controversy between scholars of African philosophy over whether the Akan scheme makes the person immaterial.[8] In favor of this, the body is sometimes said to be only a physical "mask" for the true person: each of us is really whatever is behind the mask of our physical shells. Certainly the divine nature of the *kra* makes it tempting to say that it, at least, is indeed incorporeal. As for the *sunsum*, it may seem that this principle must be in some sense physical, since it has location and is capable of motion. It can, after all, wander off during dreams and hang around after death. Spirit mediums are also said to be capable of seeing the *sunsum*, and some have inferred from this that it is physical, since otherwise it could hardly be visible. But this would be a bit like arguing that Americans believe ghosts to be physical, because how else could you dress up as one for Halloween? Clearly the spirit medium is using a special form of insight to be aware of the *sunsum*, so this doesn't seem to require that the *sunsum* is a material being. Insofar as the Akan beliefs commit them one way or another on this question, it seems better to say that the *sunsum* exists on a spiritual plane which is not the same as the body, but nonetheless allows the *sunsum* to interact with bodily things (or vice versa, as when mediums use supernatural abilities to see the *sunsum* of a departed person).

Some of the same issues arise with the views on personhood found among the Yoruba.[9] Here we have a still more complicated story; if Īśvarakṛṣṇa could have traveled from ancient India to visit the Yoruba, even he would have been impressed. For starters we have, of course, the body (*ara*), with a special psychological role being given to the *okan*, which means "heart." As in English and many other languages where "heart" has a more extended, perhaps metaphorical sense (like when a boxer's trainer says "that kid's got a lot of heart"), *okan* is treated as a seat of emotional response. Thus to "strengthen the *okan*" is to increase one's resolve. More rational or cognitive activities are meanwhile placed in the *opolo* or brain. Then on top of all that we have the *emi* and *ori*. The distinctness of these principles is already shown by the fact that different gods of the Yoruba pantheon are responsible for fashioning them. Oriśa-ṅla makes the body and Olodumare the *emi*, while a divinity called Ajala is the so-called "potter of *ori*." The *emi* is therefore what makes us "children of God," as we already saw the Akan putting it. Like the *sunsum* in Akan belief, the Yoruba *emi* can leave the body, especially through the use of witchcraft. In more normal circumstances, it seems to be *emi* that accounts for consciousness and is reincarnated in other bodies. In cases where punishment is called for, a human *emi* can be joined to an animal body after death, and, in general, the Yoruba are happy to speak of animals and plants as possessing *emi*.

Finally, we have the *ori*. Literally this means "head," but, as with "heart," the Yoruba give a more extended range of meaning to the word. It is the *ori* that chooses a destiny before birth. In a fashion reminiscent of the *kra* among the Akan, the *ori* then binds the individual to his or her fate. We might see the unfolding of destiny as an interaction between the *ori* ("head") and the *okan* ("heart"), with the *ori* steering each of us through life while one is emotionally engaged with the resulting events through the *okan*. For this reason, the Yoruba sacrifice to the *ori* for a more favorable lot, in hopes that destiny will smile upon them.[10] The upshot is that the Yoruba understanding of the person resonates with, but does not simply mirror, what we found in the Akan. Here is what one scholar, Segun Gbadegesin, has written in an attempt to line up the two belief systems: "*kra* [in the Akan system] seems the equivalent of *emi* [among the Yoruba], but while *kra* is postulated as the bearer of destiny, *emi* is not. [The Akan] *sunsum* (as that which thinks, feels, etc.) seems the equivalent of Yoruba *okan*, but while *sunsum* is postulated as the determinant of power, success, and wealth, *okan* is not. *Kra* (in Akan) is postulated as responsible for activities for which the Yoruba postulate two parts (*emi and ori*)."[11] This is a good illustration of the point we keep making, that there is not just one philosophical system to be found in African tradition. Rather each culture has its own teachings, without even getting into the issue of disagreements that may arise between members of a single culture.

There are various ways in which this material is philosophically interesting. We've already been seeing that these African cultures recognize a plurality of psychological powers or forces, positing two or even three principles where we might have expected to find them speaking simply of "the soul." But there is another intriguing point in what we've said, namely the way that the Akan *kra* and Yoruba *ori* seem to be simultaneously a part of the individual person and outside that person. Thus the *ori* is, on the one hand, a seat of personality, and represents the life that was chosen before birth; yet, on the other hand, it stands above the person, so that one can appeal to it for favor, be affected by it as if by an outside influence, and either fulfill the destiny it has chosen or fail to do so. As one Yoruba saying has it, "he who is wise, is made so by his *ori*; he who is not wise, it is his *ori* that decrees that he should be stupid."[12] Of course, our point is not that the Yoruba, or the Akan with their notion of *kra*, are confused, running together the incompatible notions of an external guardian angel and an internal soul. Rather they are committed to a genuinely fruitful idea, namely that each person may include a part or principle that is not entirely the same as that person, or at least that person's awareness. To mention Platonism one more time, we find in that ancient Greek tradition the idea that a higher part of the soul could offer guidance to the individual without being part of conscious life. This is what Plotinus understood by the *daimon* often spoken of in Hellenic religious literature and by Plato himself.[13] The Yoruba and Akan seem to have had a similar notion.

In another corner of African tradition, we can find another case of entities being in some sense identical to living persons, and in another sense not. We have in mind the spirits of ancestors. We've already seen how an aspect of a person can linger after death in Akan belief. Similarly, the Sisala of northern Ghana believe that a part of the human called the *dima* remains around the community of the deceased after death as a *nedima* or "ghost."[14] This is considered to be a highly undesirable state, because after losing its body, the *dima* has no kinsmen. It needs help from those still living to go off to the realm of the ancestors (*lelejang*), where it remains until it has been forgotten entirely by those still alive. The deceased may make themselves known in the lives of the living, to remind them of the obligations they owe to their ancestors, for instance by causing illness. When this happens, a diviner may be consulted to learn which ancestor has been angered.

Connected to such beliefs is the phenomenon of "spirit possession," which exists in many African religions and also in African diasporic culture. The basic idea here is that a living person, the "medium," is temporarily taken over by an ancestral spirit. Tony Perman's study of spirit possession among the Ndau of Zimbabwe describes how individual people are linked to specific spirits from birth.[15] During the possession, the medium is passive, apparently being taken over from the outside by the ancestral spirit, and may not even remember what happened once the episode ends. Yet the spirit is in some sense with the medium at all times, beginning from birth. What one witnesses in a possession is the awakening of the ancestor, its use of the medium's body to make itself present in the corporeal world as it cannot usually do. The link between medium and spirit is so strong that the medium's individuality is shaped by that link. As Perman writes, "because the spirit is usually resident from birth and has a tangible impact on that person's personality, skills, or way of knowing, the spirit can actually be considered part of the medium. Consequently, it is an aspect of that person's sense of self." Here then we have another example of what we might call semi-identity. The medium is clearly not just the same person as the spirit. To the contrary, the medium's consciousness and what we would usually think of as his or her "personality" or "personhood" is briefly replaced by that of the spirit. Yet neither is the spirit wholly other than the medium. Much as with the Yoruba *ori*, the ancestor in Ndau belief is outside or above the person, but also within him or her.

So far, we've been considering the nature of personhood from a metaphysical point of view: what is a person, from how many parts is the person made, and to what extent are all those parts entirely within the person? But this is not yet to account for a significant theme connected to personhood in African culture. It's the theme revealed by such sayings as "a person is not a palm tree that he should be self-complete or self-sufficient."[16] This maxim raises the question of whether you get to be a person simply by having the right metaphysical equipment, an *ori* or *kra* or *sunsum* to go with your body. It may be that you *become* a person by taking up your destiny and pursuing it, which above all means growing into a member of the community. As Ifeanyi Menkiti has put it, "personhood is something that has to be achieved."[17] We'll see next that the tendency to define the person in terms of their relation to a larger group has been hailed as one of the most distinctive, and also philosophically appealing, features of traditional African culture.

16

I AM BECAUSE WE ARE

Communalism in African Ethics and Politics

"I think therefore I am." This is one of the most famous phrases in the history of philosophy, crafted by the French philosopher René Descartes. It has inspired t-shirts, mugs, and the pun "I drink, therefore I am," used by everyone from Monty Python to the philosopher Roger Scruton, who made it the title of a guidebook to wine. Perhaps because it can be thought of as a kind of twist on Descartes' phrase, there is a phrase that appears in John Mbiti's book *African Religions and Philosophy* that has been widely quoted and often treated as the best way to summarize a major theme in African thought: "I am because we are." It was in this same book that Mbiti put forward his notorious claim that traditional African societies think of time almost solely in terms of past and present (see above, Chapter 13). Mbiti also argues that, for traditional Africans, it is only through understanding one's place within a community that one understands one's own being, and the duties and privileges that come along with it. One does not suffer or rejoice alone but rather suffers and rejoices communally. As he puts it: "Whatever happens to the individual happens to the whole group, and whatever happens to the whole group happens to the individual. The individual can only say: 'I am because we are, and since we are, therefore I am.'"[1]

What justifies this claim? Mbiti draws our attention to the significance of rituals of incorporation, such as those that mark the transition of a child to the duties of adulthood. According to Mbiti, these are signs that it is the community that, in an important sense, creates the individual. Physical birth is not enough. Rituals of incorporation mark the integration of a child into a society and various other rituals mark transitions from one stage of corporate existence to another, such as marriage rites. Even death is seen as a transition to another community status: the person is now incorporated into the wider communal structure that includes not only the living but also the remembered dead. We just saw how significant these departed members of the community remain: they may make their dissatisfaction known if they are not honored properly, and in some groups there is the possibility of communicating with the ancestors through spirit possession.

The Nigerian philosopher Ifeanyi Menkiti has worked to draw further philosophical implications out of Mbiti's account.[2] Menkiti argues that, on the communalist understanding common to traditional African societies, it is not the case that having a will, or being rational, or having memories is enough to identify one as a person. Personhood is rather an achievement that is attained through certain forms of participation within a community. This also means that personhood is something that one can fail to achieve, and something that one might be better or worse at achieving. Personhood is therefore a condition that is not universally shared among adult humans and it is a condition that admits of degrees. One of the major ways in which we can witness belief in differing degrees of personhood, Menkiti tells us, is through the recognition of elders as being more persons than those who are younger.

As with Mbiti, rituals constitute key evidence for Menkiti's interpretation of the traditional view. He points out that anthropologists have noted the relative lack of ritualized grief when a small child dies, as compared with increasingly elaborate forms of ritualized grief depending on how much older the deceased was. He also notes the significance of linguistic expressions, including one taken from that foundational text of ethno-philosophy, Placide Tempels' *Bantu Philosophy*. The Luba, according to Tempels, differentiate between the levels of force they will attribute to a *muntu*, a term often translated as "human being" (note that the word *bantu* itself can be understood as the plural form of *muntu*, and thus as meaning simply "humans"). Furthermore, the Luba will also say of someone who does not behave properly, *ke muntu po*, or "this is not a *muntu*." Clearly the point is not to correct the fact that people have been mistaking a non-human animal for a human—say, taking a giraffe to be a particularly tall woman in a spotted dress. Rather the point, as Menkiti would have us put it, is that this individual is failing to display "the full complement of excellencies seen as truly definitive of man."[3]

As this remark suggests, the metaphysical question of personhood is tied up with moral questions. One of the most prominent expressions of the moral perspective that comes along with communalism is what is sometimes called the philosophy of *ubuntu*. This term, which can be translated as something like "humanness," evokes both a metaphysical condition and a moral ideal. The term is derived from Zulu and other closely related southern African languages, and is often associated with the phrase *umuntu ngumuntu ngabantu*, meaning "a person is a person through other people." Among those who have promoted the importance of *ubuntu*, perhaps the most famous is Bishop Desmond Tutu, the Nobel Peace Prize winner who played a key role in the struggle against apartheid in South Africa.

According to Tutu, to think in terms of *ubuntu* is to recognize one's own humanity as inextricably bound up with the humanity of others. From this point of view, he has spoken of apartheid as a system that dehumanized both the oppressed black South African and the privileged white South African, especially those white South Africans who played active roles in inflicting suffering and harm upon black people. Given the communal ideal of *ubuntu*, failing to recognize someone else's humanity means losing your own humanity. Tutu likewise saw peaceful reconciliation in the post-apartheid period as the best way to embody the value of *ubuntu*. He has referred to the Truth and Reconciliation Commission hearings of the mid-1990s, at which victims forgave torturers and at which perpetrators of harms confessed and were given amnesty, as "the essence of *ubuntu*."[4] This undoubtedly controversial example shows that serious questions arise when we try to figure out how to bring a traditional value like *ubuntu* to bear upon contemporary affairs.

Professional philosophers have also weighed in on the meaning of *ubuntu*. Notable examples include Mogobe Ramose's book *African Philosophy Through Ubuntu* and Augustine Shutte's *Ubuntu: An Ethic for a New South Africa*. Another striking attempt to bring African communalism, as exemplified in the notion of *ubuntu*, to bear on the contemporary concerns of philosophers would be a series of articles by Thaddeus Metz, an American-born philosopher living and working in South Africa. Metz has attempted to provide a formulation of "African ethics" that could compete with formulations of other common positions in analytic moral philosophy like utilitarianism, Kantian ethics of duty, and Aristotelian virtue ethics. Building especially on Tutu, he gives us as a first approximation the following: "An action is right just insofar as it produces harmony and reduces discord; an act is wrong to the extent that it fails to develop community."[5] He then refines this in order to state more clearly what harmonious communal relationships consist in, ending up with this formulation: "An action is right just insofar as it promotes shared identity among people grounded on good-will; an act is wrong to the extent that it fails to do so and tends to encourage the opposites of division and ill-will."[6] Rather than making healthy communal relationships a kind of welcome result or by-product of good conduct, as utilitarianism or Kantian moral theory would do, Metz makes such relationships definitive of ethical goodness.

Kwasi Wiredu has also taken inspiration from the communalism in traditional African societies in his work on consensus-based democracy.[7] Drawing on historical and anthropological evidence, as well as his own personal knowledge of Ashanti tradition, Wiredu argues that a particularly notable feature of traditional African politics is prolonged discussion aimed at reaching common agreement. In the case of the Ashanti, as Wiredu describes it, decision by consensus took place at a number of levels. Each town or village had a council made up of a chief and the heads of the various matrilineal groupings of the community. Often seniority, with the exception of those who were senile, determined the selection of the head of a lineage, so that it was a mere formality to choose this leading figure. But there were also cases where a choice between several candidates was made through consultations aiming at consensus. Once chosen, council members again operated by means of consensus, and at two levels. First, in order to properly represent their constituency, lineage heads would need to consult with adult members of the lineage. For any matter of significance, consensus was the goal of such consultation. Second, decision by consensus was the mode of operation within the council itself. Furthermore, these councils sent representatives to divisional councils, which in turn sent representatives to the national council of the Ashanti, presided over by the king. At each of these additional levels, councils reached decision by consensus.

Wiredu sees value in this tradition because seeking agreement on how to move forward is a way of affirming the right of everyone involved in a decision-making process to be substantively, and not just formally, represented in that process. Making decisions by simple majority rule means that overruled minorities may find that their wills are not in any way reflected in the final decision. By contrast, decision-making by consensus requires the use of dialogue to arrive at the point where all relevant viewpoints are represented. Wiredu is careful to say that consensus does not mean *total* agreement. The community may strive to reach a compromise consensus without having to agree on all factual and evaluative judgments. Perhaps you think that giraffes are the most noble animal because of their height, while your cousin thinks it is because of their blue tongue; you are able to reach consensus on the overall conclusion even while disagreeing on the reasoning used to reach it. And something similar could of course happen in political contexts.

Wiredu believes that this is not a mere matter of historical interest, but has great practical relevance. He boldly proposes that African countries should consider relinquishing multiparty democracy in favor of no-party democratic systems, in which elected representatives make decisions by consensus. He admits that during the time shortly after independence from colonialism, when one-party rule came to characterize almost all African countries, leaders often justified this rejection of democracy by appealing to the tradition of governance by consensus. Hence one of the most important critical questions to ask about Wiredu's proposal is how to ensure that *no*-party rule differs from *one*-party rule. Nevertheless, especially given the way that ethnic differences in modern African nations can exacerbate problems of majority–minority tensions, and lead to competition rather than cooperation between parties, there are attractions to Wiredu's proposal of reviving the traditional communal ideal of consensus through dialogue.

It is instructive that Wiredu values the ideal of consensus especially for its ability to ensure the representation and consideration of minority viewpoints. It is often feared that communalism runs roughshod over the uniqueness and separateness of individuals, with the result that our rights as individuals may be violated or simply ignored in a society guided by such ideals. Democracy by consensus, as a method that grows out of traditional African communalism, could provide a counterexample. If this strikes you as a trifle idealistic, consider how the multi-layered process of the councils described by Wiredu could make it possible: all parties are directly involved at the level of the local council, and their voices are then passed up the chain. Thus everyone can feel that they contributed to the overall decisions made even at the higher levels.

Kwame Gyekye has also written quite a bit on this topic, and argued that African traditional life does not eliminate the role of the individual by subsuming each person within his or her broader community. In his *Essay on African Philosophical Thought*, he quotes proverbs pointing to the communalistic nature of Akan society, such as: "When a man descends from heaven, he descends into a human society."[8] Then, however, he complicates things by quoting proverbs that point in a more individualistic direction, like: "The clan is like a cluster of trees which, when seen from afar, appear huddled together, but which would be seen to stand individually when closely approached." The point here seems to be that we should not let the connected nature of those who share the close ties of clan life mislead us into forgetting about the ways in which they are simultaneously distinct, separate individuals. As Gyekye puts it, "communality does not obliterate individuality."

In light of this, it is not surprising that, in a later book, we find Gyekye criticizing Mbiti and Menkiti for what he sees as their exaggerations of how overwhelmingly communalistic traditional African life was. He thinks Menkiti succeeded in outlining certain moral dimensions of traditional African conceptions of personhood, and observes that the Akan too use the phrase *onnye onipa* ("he is not a person") as a way of describing someone who consistently behaves in a "cruel, wicked, selfish, or ungenerous" manner.[9] Gyekye clarifies the limitations of this phrasing, however. The person of whom this is said loses no rights whatsoever, and remains as deserving of moral concern as any other human being. Gyekye also rejects the idea that this moral conception of personhood should be seen as closely linked to rituals of social incorporation, and treats the idea that one can become "more a person" as generally bizarre, and especially dubious when connected to becoming an elder. After all, Gyekye writes, "surely there are many elderly people who are known to be wicked, ungenerous, unsympathetic: whose lives, in short, generally do not reflect any moral maturity or excellence."

Beyond the matter of interpretation, it is important to Gyekye as a matter of philosophical truth that even if we are social by nature, we retain other ethically important characteristics as individuals, such as our capacity to make moral judgments. It is this capacity that allows us to distance ourselves from, and critically evaluate, shared values and practices that we may have previously taken for granted as part of our immersion in a communal relationship. As we'll see in Chapter 20, there is an approach to African thought called "sage philosophy" that places great emphasis on this idea of taking critical distance on the beliefs of one's community. Gyekye also argues that membership in a community must not wholly efface individual autonomy. By this, he does not mean to endorse the practical self-sufficiency of individuals, but rather the fundamental fact that individuals have wills of their own. Personhood, according to Gyekye, is not exhaustively defined by the structure of community, even as we recognize that Africans do value community, harmonious relations of cooperation, and a sense of shared fate with each other—and recognize too that such attitudes have value. Thus Gyekye rejects what he calls "radical" or "unrestricted" communalism, and endorses what he calls "moderate" or "restricted" communalism.

In his earlier discussion of Akan tradition, Gyekye draws on a celebrated art motif to express the balance between emphasis on community and recognition of individuality in Akan tradition: the Siamese crocodile, which has two heads joined to a single body. The symbol relates to a proverb that speaks of two heads fighting over food even though they have but one stomach. For Gyekye, the common stomach represents the common good, the identity of interests among members of the community that makes harmonious cooperation so wise. The two heads, though, signify acknowledgment of the basic fact of individuality, with the possible divergences of "will, interests, tastes, and passion" that come with it.[10] These divergences make social conflict possible, and it is the message of this symbol that recognition of the common good can help resolve such conflict.

A final question worth raising is this: if we are not ourselves from communalist societies and find something to admire in that way of life, is it something we could simply adopt? Perhaps not, and especially not if we take seriously the idea put forward in work like that of Menkiti. If communalism involves a radically different attitude toward personhood, to the point that my very identity as a person depends on my place in my community, it may not be something that one can simply decide to embrace just for pragmatic reasons, such as hopes of a more consensual political climate. The scholar of African philosophy Katrin Flikschuh has said that it "would require a radical reorientation in self-conception [for communalism] to become accessible to a Westerner steeped in a rather different metaphysical tradition."[11] This statement raises deep questions about what one can and cannot learn from other philosophical traditions. It seems right to say that real philosophical work might be needed to understand and adopt the ideas of another culture. Yet one should not fall into the trap of approaching African ideas, or the ideas of any society, as so inevitably exotic that one can only appreciate them from an anthropological point of view. It's a trap into which one may easily fall when it comes to our next topic, which has already come up a few times: the place of magic and "witchcraft" in traditional African belief systems.

17

THE DOCTOR WILL SEE YOU NOW

Divination, Witchcraft, and Knowledge

Suppose your child gets sick. She's feverish, unable to sleep, complaining of soreness. What would you do? Presumably go consult a doctor in hopes of getting some medicine to make your daughter well again. You'd expect the doctor to break out some diagnostic equipment, try to discover the cause of the illness, and prescribe a course of treatment. To this extent, your experience would be just like that of someone in the same predicament in a precolonial African culture. Those cultures also had doctors who could determine the cause of sickness and other misfortunes, and who would recommend a remedy. Admittedly, the client experience was not exactly the same. Rather than a stethoscope, the doctor might use a basket full of symbolic objects, like cowrie shells, kola nuts, trays filled with sand, or a divining stick. The underlying cause for the malady might be a dissatisfied ancestor or a malevolent witch, rather than a virus. And the treatment would not be pills collected at a drug store, but perhaps an herbal remedy or the sacrifice of an animal.

Certainly, the details would differ from one culture to another—even from one village to another and one individual healer to another.[1] As always, we need to be wary of making hasty generalizations about African traditions as if they were all just one single belief system. For instance, whereas witchcraft played little or no role in some traditional African societies, it's been described as a central factor in the life of the Mbugwe people of Tanzania. According to an anthropological study from the early 1960s, the Mbugwe feared that as much as half their own population were witches, and had an "essentially pessimistic view of human nature" which led them to avoid dealing with anyone other than a small group of trusted intimates.[2] Many people, and indeed, in the bad old days, many anthropologists, have taken this sort of thing to confirm their prejudices about traditional Africans. Whereas "we" are enlightened, modern, and rational, "they" are primitive, beset by irrational beliefs about magic and imaginary threats, and devoted to superstition rather than anything approximating science. In short, "we" have real doctors, "they" have witch doctors.

Yet a closer look at these aspects of African cultures turns out to be a good way to challenge the condescending opposition between "us" and "them." That view of traditional African peoples frames them—along with other indigenous cultures—as a kind of negative image of everything we admire and consider "modern." You'll notice no group ever thinks of itself as "primitive" or "irrational." The Yoruba, who use cowrie shells to learn about their future welfare, obviously think that what they are doing makes sense.[3] The same goes for the Malagasy, who furnish their houses as a mirror image of the zodiac and do divination with sand-covered boards and seeds.[4] So it's not only out of simple respect, but also in hopes of deeper insight into these cultures and the structure of all human attempts to reach knowledge, that we now want to ask about the philosophical underpinnings of such practices.

To some small extent, we already know the answer. In particular, the ideas we surveyed concerning divinity among the Yoruba are directly relevant to their practices of divination, which have incidentally spread across the world through Yoruba cultural influence on the African diaspora. Also, in the 1960s, the anthropologist William Bascom worked with a Yoruba man named Maranoro Salako, recording him as he recited a staggering number of verses that testify to Salako's hard-earned expertise as a diviner. The *oriśa* play a central role, with one particular divinity called Olufon responsible for Salako's own gift of insight, and Orunmila as the original bestower of divination upon humankind. Another *oriśa*, Osanyin, is the god of medicine and herbalism. Also relevant here are the beliefs about the human person we discussed in Chapter 15, like the seat of personality that the Yoruba call *ori*, which is a carrier or source of the destiny revealed in divination. We can already see that what may at first glance look like mere "superstitions" are, in fact, embedded in a complex web of cultural, religious, and philosophical ideas. The proficient diviner or healer needs to be a master of these ideas and their interconnection. As one Yoruba verse has it: "If we don't have great wisdom, we can't learn strong medicine."[5]

A skeptic might object by returning to that comparison between the diviner and the doctor. Modern medicine has systematic procedures and follows rigorous rules of reasoning. Don't diviners, by contrast, just use their intuition, or wait for a secret to be revealed to them? The answer to this question is not a simple one, in part because of the aforementioned variation across the peoples of Africa. In some divinatory rituals, there is indeed a fairly straightforward "reading" or "vision" of the result. Thus an account of the Yaka in the Democratic Republic of Congo speaks of how the diviner may just "see" the answer to a question in a kind of dreamlike image, or infer it directly from an inanimate object.[6] It is also emphasized in many cultures that the diviner consultant is not really the source of the answer divulged to the client. This comes from the gods, ancestors, or even the divinatory instrument itself.[7] Thus a consultant from the Nyole people of eastern Uganda remarked to one anthropologist, "I don't know anything, I just speak."[8]

In other cases, considerable interpretation and expertise may be needed to determine the result of a given consultation. One widespread technique involves placing many small objects in a basket and then shaking it, looking to see which objects have risen to the top, and then repeating this for further information or confirmation. The diagnosis emerges from the interrelation between the objects seen. Thus, to give an example from Ndembu divination that is atypical in its simplicity but at least easy to explain, if a piece of red clay signifying malign intent turns up next to a small doll representing "elders," this could mean that a misfortune has been caused by a sorcerer who is kin to the chief. As the anthropologist who reported this example remarked, "the dominant unit of divination is not the individual symbol but the symbolic configuration."[9]

It should also be stressed that divination does not always use symbols with simple or obvious meaning. Again, there is variation here, even within a single technique and within a single culture. To return to the example of casting cowrie shells, two shells that land with their "backs" facing one another can be an omen meaning "good marriage,"[10] which is pretty straightforward. But generally the interpretation involves a complicated and not literally symbolic method which revolves around memorizing the meanings of various patterns among the shells. Furthermore, it is not only the diviner who is responsible for determining the outcome of a consultation, because the client too is closely involved. He or she sets the initial terms of the inquiry by posing questions or providing the names of persons, living or dead, who are suspected of causing a misfortune. The client may also work together with the consultant to perform the ritual or interpret its results. This undermines the common conception of divination as involving uncanny or extraordinary individuals who divulge secrets learned through an unexplained access to special, perhaps revelatory, sources of knowledge.[11] Both these points—the complexity of the interpretation and the cooperative nature of the enterprise—have been made concerning a traditional healing technique from South Africa in which various objects are scattered on a grass mat. As a study of this ritual puts it, "the objects land in a configuration that is 'read' through a rhythmic verbal interaction between client and healer."[12]

Another reason to deny that magical rituals involve simplistic naivety is that the clients may be far from credulous.[13] They may "test" diviners to see whether it is worth taking their advice seriously, by posing fake and leading questions or demanding that the consultant work out why the client has come, without being told. Multiple oracles may also be used to answer a single question, thus effectively getting a second or third opinion. The fact that misfortunes may be sent by a client's recent ancestors, or those who live close by, means that it is wise to seek out diviners who live further away and are impartial, having no personal acquaintance with the situation.[14] It's also appreciated that some divinatory techniques are more open to manipulation than others. Among the Lugbara, a standard oracular device is the so-called "rubbing stick," a stalk of sorghum that is rubbed with grass while reciting the names of possible culprits who may be behind a misfortune. When the grass catches upon the mentioning of a given name, this is an indication where guilt lies. Since the diviner could obviously decide when to make the grass seem to catch, other uncontrolled, random rituals are used to confirm the result.[15] By the way, there is a nice story about this same group that illustrates both cultural variation and the skepticism involved in traditional divination. When an anthropologist informed some Lugbara that the Nuer people sometimes offer a vegetable to their ancestors under the pretense that it is an animal sacrifice, the Lugbara "were incredulous and remarked that their own ghosts could see and taste as well as anyone and were not as stupid as those of other peoples."

Finally, we should point out that, even if these practices involve an appeal to "supernatural" explanations and ways of knowing, it's not as if these cultures account for everything by referring to magic, the ancestors, the gods, and so on. As we've said, some cultures lack magical practices where others have them. For example, the Maasai of East Africa do not blame illnesses on supernatural causes.[16] Among those who do offer such explanations, natural accounts are also given when they are available. Natural remedies, like plant-based medicines, should be used for natural problems, while good magic is for fighting evil magic. As a proverb has it, "sword fights a sword."[17] The presence of naturalistic explanation has not always been appreciated by outside observers of these cultures. Though the Swahili word *uchawi* just means "misfortune" in a quite general sense, it is often translated as "witchcraft."[18]

Which is not to deny that something we might legitimately call "witchcraft" is an important part of some African cultures. The idea of witches is, of course, found in many societies around the world, including early modern Europe. Yet again, we find a lot of variation across Africa here, though the variation doesn't extend to worries about ladies with green skin, pointy hats, and flying broomsticks. Admittedly, in some cultures, witches are thought to be predominantly women, and there is talk of witches traveling in unconventional ways or having unusual skin color (for example, ash white). As these points already begin to suggest, witches can perhaps best be understood as an inversion of the properly human. They purposefully do evil instead of good, eat salt to quench thirst, travel at night instead of the day, may go naked or stand on their heads, and can even become non-human animals. They hide among your own local community. It's been remarked that, if the African village is a "moral universe," then witches too must be part of the village, making "their malevolence a distorted funhouse mirror reflection of the communal ideal that binds each group together."[19]

When anthropologists apply the term "witchcraft" in an African context, they have in mind something different from magical healing and divination. They also distinguish between "witches" and "sorcerers." Whereas witches are born with their wicked character and fearsome powers, which are often thought to be inherited through a family line, sorcery can be learned, and in principle can be performed by anyone. Cultural beliefs and practices don't always adhere to such neat boundaries, though. Some witches do both good and bad, so that an effective diviner or healer may more readily be suspected of witchcraft. And diviners, like witches, often find themselves with an unsought "gift," which may first manifest itself as dreams or manic episodes. Still, diviner consultants are an integrated and valued part of society, whereas witches are the ultimate outsiders. As the introduction to a collection of essays on this subject says, "a society composed entirely of witches makes no more sense than a society composed entirely of madmen."[20]

It is perhaps the belief in witchcraft that most inspires accusations of primitiveness and irrationality with regard to traditional African culture. But, as anthropologists and ethnographers have been keen to stress over the last few decades, the understanding of witchcraft and other so-called "magical" phenomena is not frozen in time, a kind of leftover from some benighted past. Just as traditional healing has continued to exist and evolve alongside modern medicine, ideas about traditional medicine, divination, and witchcraft have developed in the postcolonial period, despite extensive efforts at suppression on the part of colonial powers.[21] The Manjak of Guinea-Bissau even have ceremonies at which they discuss how their traditions should be adapted to deal with new situations and influences.[22] The process of cultural adaptation is a long-standing one, as we can see from the fact that many magical practices in Africa have over centuries incorporated material from Islam and Christianity (for example, Arabic book divination or astrology).

This brings us back to our central question about the rationality of such beliefs and practices. The many anthropologists, and small number of philosophers, who have engaged with this question realize that it is ridiculous to label whole cultures as "irrational."[23] Surely these are not, to use the same phrase in service of a different point, societies composed entirely of madmen. Diviners and their clients, and even those who accuse innocent people of being witches, are clearly "rational" in the sense that they have justifications for their beliefs. When the diviner identifies the enemy who has caused your misfortune, the claim comes backed with a well-established rationale. This may be as simple as grass sticking on the rubbing stick at a certain time, or as complicated as an interpretation given for a series of objects turning up in a basket or array of cowrie shells. Those rationales are themselves woven into a rich tapestry of other cultural, religious, and moral convictions. So even a stern critic should go no further than Kwame Anthony Appiah, who wrote, "what's wrong with the theory of witchcraft is not that it doesn't make sense but that it isn't true."[24]

The question, though, is not really whether the diviners are *reasoning*, in the sense of seeking explanations for events, and using their community's standards of what counts as a good explanation. It's obvious they are doing that. The question is whether the whole system within which their beliefs are produced is itself *irrational* because the system lacks features that any acceptable theory should possess.[25] These would be the features we demand of science, like consistency and being open to refutation. We've seen reasons to think that the "divination and witchcraft theory," as we might call it, does satisfy these criteria. Clients are skeptical enough to test consultants and seek confirmation, for example. Yet there is the lingering suspicion that, since the causes invoked in the magical explanations are not real, there must be something epistemologically defective about the whole theory. One worry might be the following. Even if a given consultant can be suspected of lying or incompetence, giving the client reason to do tests and seek confirmation, it doesn't seem that the whole concept of divination or witchcraft is being tested or questioned. The aforementioned Manjak assume that witches use their magic to prevent rain from falling, causing crops to fail. There's a good reason to be suspicious of this, namely, that, in doing so, the witches would be harming themselves along with everyone else. When confronted with this puzzle, group members did not put the theory in question, but shrugged and said: "rain witches are just stupid!"[26]

A second worry might be that there is no empirical confirmation for divination and witchcraft. But this concern is misplaced. Brief reflection shows that there will frequently be such confirmation: diviners will sometimes get predictions right, and sometimes when a witch is "discovered," people will recover from illness. Then, too, witches are secretive and even honest diviners are not infallible, so it would be ridiculous to expect a perfect match between this "theory" and all available evidence. Nor should we overlook the power of the placebo effect. Merely consulting an expert, such as a diviner consultant, may have a powerful salutary effect on the client whether or not genuinely efficacious medicine is involved at any stage. This is exactly why Europeans could believe in Hippocratic and Galenic medicine for about two millennia; and historians of science and philosophy don't go around alleging that all premodern European doctors were irrational.

The most interesting and illuminating way to approach the divination and witchcraft "theory," however, is not to compare it to a scientific hypothesis. Indeed, Kwasi Wiredu complained of scholars unfairly juxtaposing Western science with African superstition, when the latter should really be compared to Western superstition (of which there has always been plenty). The result is to suggest unfairly that "non-scientific" ideas are "a peculiarly African way of thinking" when in fact they are typical for "traditional thought in general."[27] A more fruitful approach might attend to the wider range of functions the theory plays in its own societal context. The theory does involve a search for explanation, just like Western medicine or particle physics does. But it involves much more than that. The intimate and nuanced interaction between diviner and client presupposes, reinforces, and strengthens good relationships within a community. We can see this even in the choice of divinatory instruments, which are sometimes domestic in nature (kitchen tools, for example) so that a community context is inscribed into the very mechanics of the consultation.[28] It has been well said that divination is "a form of social analysis, in the course of which hidden conflicts between persons and factions are brought to light."[29] So if divination and witchcraft is a "theory," it is not only about causation but about ethics and the political community.

Along the same lines, we should remember the wider worldview in which this theory developed. If you have a deep conviction that you are living in a fundamentally good and well-ordered world, perhaps one overseen by divine providence, then it is only sensible to seek out the cause of illnesses, crop failures, injuries that happen by accident, and so on. Kwame Gyekye has drawn attention to sayings of the Akan people: "Nothing just happens (*biribiara nsi kwa*)," and "Everything has its reason (*biribiara wo ne se nti*)." If misfortunes do not occur at random, why not suppose they are happening because of an angry ancestor, a jealous neighbor, or a witch? Thus divination and witchcraft theory also form part of what philosophers call a "theodicy": an explanation of why there is evil and suffering in a world that remains fundamentally good.

18

WOMEN HAVE NO TRIBE

Gender in African Tradition

If you had to choose, would you rather be a woman living in medieval Europe or a woman in Africa around the very same time? Your first reaction is probably that you'd quite like to have a third choice, given that neither prospect would involve reliable internet access. But if forced to choose, you might instead realize that you'd like to hear a bit more about both possibilities. There's a big difference between the life of a female Anglo-Saxon peasant and Eleanor of Aquitaine, after all, so what kind of medieval woman would you be? The same applies, naturally, to traditional African societies. As always, we need to bear in mind the diversity of these societies and of the people who lived in them. Nor should we assume that the most important fact about any person living in precolonial Africa would have been gender. Just as Eleanor of Aquitaine's social position was due to her royal lineage, and not simply her gender, so the experiences of those living in traditional African societies would be determined not just by being a man or woman, but by being as yet unmarried; or by being an elder of the village; or by the fact that the surrounding culture lived from, say, cattle as opposed to hunting or farming.

Is there something more general to say on this topic, something that would help to identify a quintessentially and perhaps uniquely African attitude toward gender? One attempt to do just that was made by the Senegalese polymath Cheikh Anta Diop, who died in 1986. He was, among other things, an anthropologist, Egyptologist, and linguist. In a book written in French in 1963, he marshaled these various skills to put forward a bold account of *The Cultural Unity of Black Africa*, this being the title of his monograph.[1] Actually, the book is not only about Africa. It begins by criticizing earlier theorists, like J.J. Bachofen and Frederick Engels, who saw male-dominated, or "patriarchal," societies as having supplanted more primitive societies that were "matriarchal," dominated by women. According to Bachofen, the rule of men over women simply marks a further stage of human development, in which an "ethereal spirituality" replaces "passive femininity" (6). Diop accepts the basic contrast between two ways of organizing human communities, patriarchal and matriarchal. But he sees the two paradigms being realized in different places, rather than at different times. As he puts it, "humanity has from the beginning been divided into two geographically distinct 'cradles,' one of which was favorable to the flourishing of matriarchy and the other to that of patriarchy" (19).

One cradle lies in the north and encompasses, as chance would have it, lands that have figured prominently in previous volumes of this book series: Europe, of course, and more generally the sphere of Indo-European culture. The other cradle lies in the south and especially in Africa. The contrast may be traced to differences in climate. Whereas in the north, conditions favored the emergence of a physically demanding nomadic lifestyle, the southern environment encouraged early adoption of agriculture and a pastoral way of life. In this sort of setting, Diop writes, woman can "in spite of her physical inferiority, contribute substantially to the economic life" (27). These tendencies were then passed on to later generations. Even after the Indo-European nomads of the northern cradle settled down, they kept their women secluded in domestic spaces. In Africa, by contrast, women had always been a key part of the workforce and retained their cultural authority. Thus we see that in ancient Egypt, the pharaohs' claim to rule was established by appeal to matrilineal descent, hence their practice of marrying their sisters (53). The story of the Queen of Sheba fits nicely with Diop's thesis (48), as do patterns of inheritance and naming in African society. Even supernatural abilities are, in traditional African belief, often supposed to be passed on through the mother's side of the family (33). It is only with the coming of Islam, he argues, with its markers of northern patriarchy, that this unifying feature of culture in Africa started to be undermined (61).

Diop's thesis has much in common with other ambitious theories we've covered, such as Mbiti's claims about the African conception of time or Idowu's argument that African religion should be classified as "diffused monotheism." We have found that such bold proposals point toward genuinely interesting features of traditional African cultures, and raise numerous philosophical questions in the process. But we've also found that such sweeping generalizations need, at the very least, to be qualified and hedged with caveats, in part because of the oft-mentioned diversity of Africa. Much the same verdict should be passed upon Diop's thesis. One might of course challenge his claims about the "northern cradle," but for our purposes, let's focus on his claims about the "southern cradle" of Africa, asking whether we do find there a widespread tendency toward matriarchy, thanks to a generally pastoral way of life.

The answer is, of course, "sort of." In the decades following Diop's work, archeologists have been increasingly interested in the question of gender in the African Stone Age and Iron Age.[2] We can begin by noting that both nomadic and pastoral or sedentary ways of life are indigenous to Africa, with sedentary populations sometimes pushing out nomadic ones but never fully eliminating them. While this obviously casts serious doubt on Diop's idea of a uniformly pastoral "southern cradle," there is some evidence that his basic intuition was right, insofar as the social status of women may be different in these two kinds of social organization, not just in Africa but across the globe. There is some evidence that women can possess more autonomy and outright political power in settled communities, where we are more likely to find female royalty. Yet some anthropologists think it more typical that, for women, status would have *diminished* in the transition from migrant to sedentary cultures. In hunter-gatherer populations, there is a relatively egalitarian situation, where all group members are providing food. Sedentary cultures tend to have somewhat more "complex" societal structures, in the sense that some groups dominate over others, with men often taking the leadership roles for themselves. Thus we see that, in the case of early Iron Age Africa (up to about 1300 AD), there is little evidence for the division of social spaces between the women and men, whereas this does emerge in the late Iron Age, along with practices of male chieftainship. Likewise, sedentary societies in Africa that live off herds of cattle have sometimes designated the area with the cowpens as "male" and the domestic spaces as "female," even burying dead men and women in the two respective parts of the village.

Lying behind such findings could be a basic human tendency to assign certain tasks to women and others to men, with the two sexes having equal or unequal status, depending on how valued these tasks are seen to be. It has been said that the sexual division of labor is "the original and most basic form of economic specialization."[3] But there is room for debate as to whether tasks were divided neatly between men and women in very early African societies. We tend simply to assume that among hunter-gatherers, the men do the hunting and the women the gathering. But that may not be true. Bringing down big game with spears may have required the participation of as many people as possible, of whichever sex, and anthropologists have observed among some modern-day hunter-gatherers that women are involved in the hunting, for instance by chasing animals toward the men who are waiting to pounce with nets. A skeptic might respond to this that such recent evidence is not obviously applicable to peoples of the distant past. Anthropologist Susan Kent has argued that "the fact that modern Bushmen or San behave in a specific way is irrelevant for archaeology, except to expose fallacies of overgeneralization."[4]

So how are we to decide this question given that, as one other anthropologist puts it, "you can't dig up gender"?[5] Actually there are surprisingly many resources on which to draw, alongside the projection of modern ethnographic data back on to much earlier times. We already mentioned the possibility of finding divided spaces in archeological dig sites, though one needs to be cautious to avoid just assuming that, say, the areas with cooking utensils were for women, the areas with weapons for men. Archeology can also join forces with ethnography. A study of Iron Age sites found ritual objects buried under the smelting pits, which seem to bear out what modern-day anthropologists report about ritual beliefs surrounding traditional African ironmaking among various peoples in what is now Tanzania. They conceptualize iron ore as a "maternal" stuff that the male smelter works on and shapes, just as the male seed shapes a child in procreation. More explicit—in every sense of the word—evidence can be found in the form of rock art, which across Africa consistently marks the gender of human figures, for instance by depicting the sexual organs of men and buttocks of women. Rock art also bears out, at least to some extent, the hypothesis that tasks were divided between the sexes, as when showing men with bow and arrow and women with digging sticks. Rock art from the Sahara region has been noted to depict women more often than men, raising the tantalizing possibility that women were dominant among the groups that produced the art.

How does Diop's thesis fare if we advance forward in history to more recent sedentary societies that retain a traditional way of life? Here we must go back to our opening point that sexual difference is only one kind of difference, and that even a culture that values males above females may well exalt *some* females above almost everyone. Consider the report of some Victorian era British nurses living in Zimbabwe in the 1890s. They encountered a socially powerful woman named Nyakuwanikwa who, they reported, "accepted tea, passing her mug, after drinking, to the two men who sat behind her. These were two of her husbands. We were told that she had several, whom she divorced or knocked on the head as seemed most convenient."[6] The story exemplifies the way that women can occupy authoritative positions, but not simply because they are women.

The most common reason for this would be relative seniority. In a group where husbands have authority over their wives, it could still be the case that a senior wife has authority over junior wives and also over younger men. One study has suggested that just this happens among the Akan, with individuals changing their place in the societal power structure as they age.[7] Especially crucial is the transition to adulthood and parenthood, so that men are sometimes mocked for having had no children, and older women take on a role equivalent to that of an adult man. Similarly, we find that among the Shona in Zimbabwe and the Tswana of Botswana,[8] older women outrank all younger people, and that unmarried men have low status; all this is in keeping with the Tswana proverb, "old people are the pillars of this nation." That a woman can step into a relatively "masculine" position is confirmed by another of their sayings that exalts women who are able to take over their husbands' work if needed: "The wife is the man and bull of the family."

African religions offer us another context in which to observe nuanced conceptions of gender and the way that gender interacts with other status markers. In many systems, a central place is given to female deities. To go back to Idowu's notion of "diffused monotheism," in cultures where a supreme god is recognized this god is often male, yet also often has a female partner.[9] Among mere humans, it is often assumed by ethnographers that women play a subordinate role in religion. But this assumption has been challenged in studies of women who perform as spirit mediums.[10] Like being an elder, being a medium can give a woman a special status and power, linked with her ability to heal or to divine the future. Women sometimes dominate the rituals that accompany possession, while the possession itself may be metaphorically described in terms of motherhood or pregnancy. But there is room for doubt as to whether this really amounts to authority or agency for the medium herself. For one thing the possession is temporary, and the medium's subservience may be reinstated as soon as it ends (much as in Europe not all that long ago, servants were served by their masters on Christmas, but kept firmly in their place the rest of the year). For another thing, the medium would typically deny that she is the one bringing about the possession. As that analogy to pregnancy suggests, her role is receptive, or even passive, and it is the spirit who is really the "agent."

Thus far we have been making an assumption so basic that you probably haven't noticed it: that people are unproblematically divided into two genders, male and female. But some scholars have disputed this assumption when it comes to Africa. Particularly notable have been Oyeronke Oyewumi and Ifi Amadiume. In 1997, Oyewumi published a book on the Yoruba called *The Invention of Women*.[11] She noted the absence of gender markers in Yoruba pronouns, another example of something we've seen many times now: the inference of philosophical notions from the features of African languages. She also pointed to something we've already mentioned, the way that social roles depend on factors like seniority or bachelorhood rather than on gender, and also to the existence of Yoruba deities that seem to lack gender entirely. From all this Oyewumi reached the conclusion that women, or females, do not really constitute a single social category in Yoruba culture. The very concept of a female gender was imposed relatively recently from the outside, by colonial powers. To this, critics have responded that even if "seniority can override gender, it usually works as a co-ordinate, rather than as an alternative, to it,"[12] that gender is sometimes projected onto the intrinsically genderless Yoruba deities,[13] and that Yoruba beliefs about witchcraft do seem to be highly gendered. Thus women are thought to have supernatural powers by a natural gift, whereas men acquire it as a learned skill, and men take responsibility for punishing witches.[14]

Another feminist approach to African culture argues not that gender is an imported concept, but that it is to be found there in unstable or fluid form. This is what we have with Ifi Amadiume and her 1987 book *Male Daughters, Female Husbands*, which is based on reportage from the author's hometown of Nnobi in the Igbo region of Nigeria.[15] As the title indicates, Amadiume is among other things interested in the way that women take on apparently male family roles. A "female husband" is a relatively prosperous or senior woman who takes on a younger woman as a "wife" to give her married status; the wife may then have children with men from the female husband's family. This is not unique. A more recent study about the similar practice of *iweto* marriage between women in Kenya mentions that about forty precolonial African societies are known to have had an institution like this.[16] As Betty Wambui has pointed out, the idea that wives could "belong to" other women complicates the more typical pattern of women becoming in some sense the property of men when they are married.[17] As for the "male daughters," these are the women in a household who, because they are on the father's side of the family, outrank senior women who have married in. One of Amadiume's informants explained the practice as follows: "Had they been men, they would have had the same power as lineage men…For this reason, lineage wives will bow down their heads to lineage daughters. If the daughters tell them to leave, they'll pack their things and go" (60).

Conversely, Amadiume also reports that men who are priests of the goddess Idemili dress like women, effectively becoming "female men" (53, 101). Then there are authoritative roles that are not gendered at all, like the title *di-nu-bo* ("master of the household"), which can belong to either a man or a woman (90). These findings tend to confirm an idea fundamental to contemporary feminist philosophy: gender is socially constructed, so much so that people who are women in terms of their biological sex can become men in terms of their gender. More concretely, it is obvious that at least in Nnobi, there are plenty of mechanisms by which women can accrue social standing and power. This is reflected in religious beliefs. The community worships a male god named Aho who is partnered with the aforementioned goddess Idemili, but in stories about their relationship, as Amadiume puts it, "Aho is seen as a man struggling to maintain a male authority over a very wealthy, independent and popular woman" (110). Yet other features of this society look more patriarchal. When a girl is born, she is called a "bag of money," because her main value to the family is to bring in bridewealth (78).

Traditional gender dynamics are fluid in another sense, too, in that they are subject to change over time. In the colonial and postcolonial periods there have been rapid transformations in gender roles and relations. Some observers believe that the coming of Christianity has led to greater oppression of women; but such traditional practices as polygamous marriages and the payment of bridewealth, which might (or might not) be seen as unfavorable to women, are becoming less frequent.[18] Yet change is not only a result of outside influence. African societies have never been static, even in the Stone Age and Iron Age, though change in those periods was no doubt slower in developing. To take just one remarkable example, anthropologists have discovered through analysis of human remains from the coastal region of southern Africa that before about 3000 BC male and female diets were the same. But after that time a contrast emerges with more shellfish being consumed by the men, who were presumably more directly involved in collecting this resource.

A much more recent, and more complicated, case concerns a people who lived not far from Amadiume's town of Nnobi, in southeastern Nigeria.[19] These are the Ohafia, who live on the frontier of the territory dominated by the Igbo people. In the nineteenth century, Ohafia men and women were working at cross-purposes, with different ideals of what their ethnic identity should be. The men tended to understand themselves as part of the Igbo, and formed their identity around warfare and the capture of slaves. The women, though, attempted to build political alliances with non-Igbo groups, especially through intermarriage. At one point in this rather complicated story, all the women of one village decamped to a different location to bring pressure to bear on their menfolk. Part of what was at stake here was a clash between the Igbo patrilineal culture, that is, passing down family identity through the father's side, and the matrilineal customs that had prevailed up to that time among the Ohafia. Those customs help to explain the political power held by the women of the community. In a patrilineal culture, women who marry and leave their family may easily wind up in the position we described before, like guests in another home, and potentially subservient to the so-called "male daughters." As one adage has it: "women have no tribe," meaning that brides may risk losing their kin group when they gain a husband.[20]

The strife within the Ohafia community displays many of the themes we've raised in this chapter: the possibility of change in gender dynamics, the ability of women to exert political and social influence in these traditional societies, and the linking of gender to certain activities or tasks like warfare. But it is only one, highly specific case, and other cases might suggest other conclusions. Unlike Diop, we are skeptical as to whether there is one conception of gender that "unifies" Africa, whether prehistoric, historic, or contemporary. Yet Diop's thesis leads in the right general direction, forcing us to question lazy assumptions about the powerlessness of women in traditional or premodern societies.[21] This is a point of philosophical significance in its own right. Within academic debates over gender identity, and in wider society, it is often assumed that "traditional" and premodern human societies have been marked exclusively by patriarchy and clear gender roles, as if the social mores of 1950s suburban America were simply a manifestation of the human condition. The work of authors like Oyewumi and Amadiume shows that feminists can deny that basic assumption by drawing on a broader range of cultural research.

19

PROFESSIONALLY SPEAKING

The Reaction Against Ethnophilosophy

Imagine, for a second, that you knew nothing at all about philosophy, and that, in this ignorant state, you happen to have the opportunity to visit Harvard or Oxford or some other famous university. Walking the halls and finding yourself by chance in the Philosophy department, you boldly knock on the door of one of the professors and, to your delight, she kindly invites you to enter and sit down. As you take your seat, you explain that you would like very much to know what philosophy is. Not being familiar with the ways of philosophers, you are slightly taken aback when she smiles and says, "ah, now that is itself a difficult philosophical question." You therefore ask what you assume must be an easier question: what would you recommend that I study if I want to learn about what the greatest philosophers in the West have had to say? The professor sits back in her chair, thinks for a while, and finally answers: "I think one of the best bits has to be the thing about, if a black cat crosses your path, that's bad luck. Also, if you break a mirror. Probably one of those two."

Clearly this story went off the rails at the end: it's not merely unlikely but well nigh impossible that a philosophy professor would offer up common superstitions as any part of Western philosophy, never mind the best part. Our tale seeks to dramatize a point that Kwasi Wiredu makes in a classic essay of his, first published in 1976, called "How Not to Compare African Traditional Thought with Western Thought." As we indicated in Chapter 17, Wiredu complains in this essay that belief in various gods and spirits and practices like witchcraft are unfairly seen as characteristic of African thought. After all, beliefs of this kind are common among Westerners as well. As the title of his essay suggests, he implores us to treat traditional African beliefs, which he takes to be most often held superstitiously rather than on the basis of rational support, as comparable with traditional, unscientific beliefs common in the West, also generally based on superstition. What does this mean for the study of philosophy? According to Wiredu, "the least that African philosophers and foreign well-wishers can do in this connection is to refrain, in this day and age, from serving up the usual congeries of unargued conceptions about gods, ghosts, and witches in the name of African philosophy."[1] In other words, if you would refer the person who knows nothing about Western philosophy to Plato or Descartes, and not to beliefs about black cats and broken mirrors bringing bad luck, then why not extend the same courtesy to Africans when talking about African philosophy?

Because of this essay and others he wrote in the 1970s, Wiredu is often classified as a representative of what eventually became known as the "professional school" in African philosophy. The professional school, whether understood as a set of thinkers or as a distinctive approach to doing African philosophy, is distinguished by the way it emerged as a reaction against another school or current within African philosophy, namely, ethnophilosophy. Let us return, then, to the story of breakthrough moments in African philosophy in the twentieth century, so as to see how the professional school came to be and why. As we discussed in Chapter 12, the book *Bantu Philosophy*, by the Belgian missionary Placide Tempels, sparked a great deal of interest. For some Africans it served as an inspiring precedent, encouraging them to look for philosophy in the traditions of their own indigenous cultures; a significant example was Alexis Kagamé's 1956 book *La Philosophie bantu-rwandaise de l'être* (*The Rwandan Bantu Philosophy of Being*). This pioneering work was followed in the rest of the 1950s and during the 1960s by a number of other contributions. Many of these were also in French, notably similar in orientation and very often by thinkers who were, like Tempels and Kagame before them, also Catholic clergymen. In English-speaking Africa, two of the major texts on African philosophy that appeared in the sixties were *The Mind of Africa* by the Ghanaian philosopher William Abraham,[2] and a book we have mentioned a number of times, *African Religions and Philosophy*, by John Mbiti from Kenya. He, for once, was not a Catholic priest, but an Anglican one.

Like a martini about to be served to James Bond, though, this situation was ready to be shaken up. A challenge against the ethnophilosophical approach was launched by another figure we have already mentioned, a philosopher from Benin named Paulin Hountondji. Starting in the late 1960s, he produced numerous lectures and articles on the nature of African philosophy, culminating in a 1976 book.[3] Hountondji called for nothing less than a complete rethinking of what African philosophy is, and a complete reorganization and reorientation of ongoing efforts aimed at developing African philosophy as an academic field of research.

The book begins with a now notorious definition of terms, a definition that is intentionally simple in form yet quite striking in its implications. Hountondji writes: "By 'African philosophy' I mean a set of texts, specifically the set of texts written by Africans and described as philosophical by their authors themselves" (33). At first glance, this definition may sound open-minded, perhaps even excessively broad. What counts as African philosophy? Well, if you are African, have written something, and you would describe it as "philosophical," then congratulations, it counts! Yet in another sense, the definition might seem excessively narrow. We've just devoted several chapters to the idea that philosophy can be located in oral traditions. This definition, though, stipulates that African philosophy can consist only of *written* texts.

What, then, is this definition doing for Hountondji?[4] A number of things, so we will keep count of them as we go. First, he identifies a body of literature that is waiting to be read and critically evaluated, and that can legitimately be called "African philosophy." As radical a rethinking as he is attempting, he does not begin with a question like "Does African philosophy exist?," much less "Is it possible for there to be such a thing as African philosophy?" Instead he begins from the simple observation that some African authors have written works they themselves describe as philosophical in nature. So why not examine these texts and ask whether African philosophy is doing well, or whether it has been afflicted by systematic problems that need diagnosing and fixing?

A second thing Hountondji's definition does is to exclude works like Tempels' *Bantu Philosophy* from its scope, because it was not written by an African. This might come as a surprise, given that *Bantu Philosophy* has often been treated as something like the birth of African philosophy as a distinct genre of writing. Hountondji, however, treats the book as a mere forerunner or precursor to African philosophy, which is embodied in texts written by Africans. *Bantu Philosophy* is therefore revealed to be important as a source for, but not an example of, African philosophy. As we saw, it was in relation to *Bantu Philosophy* that Hountondji first introduced the term "ethnophilosophy," as a way of criticizing Tempels' study as "an ethnological work with philosophical pretensions" (34). He also emphasizes that Tempels' book is explicitly addressed not to Africans but to fellow Europeans, especially those involved in the colonization of Africa, whose people were thus objects of study and not participants in a conversation. By contrast, Hountondji's definition would treat African philosophy as being necessarily a matter of Africans taking up the role of subjects who speak—or rather, subjects who write.

Apart from the problem of his intended audience, there is problem of what Tempels said to that audience. Hountondji alludes to a biting criticism of *Bantu Philosophy* found in the work of Aimé Césaire, an important poet, politician, and philosophical thinker from Martinique.[5] As Hountondji explains, Césaire criticized *Bantu Philosophy* for attempting to create a kind of diversion from the problem of colonial exploitation. Césaire suggested that the message of Tempels in this conversation among Europeans was something like this: you needn't worry so much about Bantus protesting for things like better wages or decent food and housing, if you simply show a little respect for their souls by acknowledging their idea of being as vital force.

Hountondji appreciated that this criticism was itself, well, vitally forceful. Yet for him, it left unnoticed the deepest problem with Tempels' work. Césaire explicitly denied that the target of his criticism was Bantu thought, clarifying that he was attacking only Tempels' use of it. But in Hountondji's eyes, the problem was the very idea of Bantu thought itself. What needs to be attacked and overcome, according to him, is "the idea that there might exist a hidden philosophy to which all Bantus unconsciously and collectively adhered" (37–8). This is the crux of the matter, not just for Hountondji but for all who are classified as part of the professional school. For them, Tempels' work, and the subsequent work of African thinkers who likewise sought to elaborate the philosophy implicit within traditional African cultures, promoted a false idea of what philosophy is. African philosophy cannot be the implicit ideas of a collectivity, according to the members of this school. It can only exist in the form of ideas and arguments worked out by *individual* African thinkers.

To drive this point home, Hountondji considers the differences between Tempels and one of the aforementioned thinkers inspired by him, Alexis Kagamé. Despite what they share, "Kagamé in fact rejects the fundamental thesis of the Belgian missionary, according to which the equivalence of the concepts of being and power is the essential characteristic of Bantu thought" (41). In other words, whereas Tempels claims that being and force are indistinguishable in Bantu thought, so that they have a dynamic conception of being, which is diametrically opposed to the Western conception of being as static, Kagamé argues that all things are alternately static or dynamic according to how you look at them, and that this is the case in both Bantu and Western thought. "Who is right?" Hountondji asks. "Which is the better interpretation?" (42). Under normal circumstances, conflicting interpretations of a philosophical perspective are resolved by returning to the source. If confronted by two opposed readings of Confucius, you would just grab your copy of the *Analects* off your shelf and make up your own mind. In the case of Kagamé's disagreement with Tempels, Hountondji says that there can be no resolution, because there are no written sources to consult. One might object that even if there is not a written text to consult, it nevertheless remains the case that we can interpret oral literature: "proverbs, tales, dynastic poems," and so on (42). Hountondji's reply is that this involves a confusion of categories: the arbitrary projection of the status of philosophical discourse onto products of language evidently not intended as philosophy.

This brings us to a third implication of his definition of African philosophy. It suggests a more general claim, to the effect that philosophical traditions must be tied to traditions of writing. We've already acknowledged that this is a controversial claim; how would he defend it? After all Socrates never wrote anything, yet is recognized as among the greatest philosophers. Hountondji does not find the objection to be a telling one. Certainly one might say something philosophically interesting without writing it down, but it is only through writing that it can become part of a theoretical tradition that can orient future discussion. Thus, according to him: "Thousands of Socrates could never have given birth to Greek philosophy" (106). It is only because associates and disciples like Plato and Xenophon wrote down his thoughts that the historical Socrates could attain his stature in the history of philosophy.

A fourth thing to note is that Hountondji's definition purposefully contrasts the genuinely philosophical nature of written texts by figures like Kagamé and Mbiti to the oral traditions onto which these very same authors imaginatively project the status of philosophy. For Hountondji, Bantu philosophy and all other philosophies ascribed to groups of Africans are nothing but externally imposed, artificial reconstructions. He encourages us to let go of what he calls "the myth of primitive unanimity" or, more famously, "the dogma of unanimism" (60, 62). This is, for him, not merely a rejection of the idea that groups can think but also a call for a renewal of intellectual responsibility. In a move that might be read as either charitable or insulting, Hountondji charges African ethnophilosophers with having misunderstood, of all things, themselves. Even as they were producing the literature that has made up African philosophy as we have it, they took themselves to be not producing but "simply recounting" that which existed before them (38). Hountondji condemns this as "self-denial" and encourages the ethnophilosopher to recognize and accept that it is he or she who is making the theoretical choices, while disguising these choices with the myth of collective philosophy (38).

So what does Hountondji want in place of ethnophilosophy? Here we come to a fifth goal of Hountondji's definition, the last one we will identify: by providing a merely geographical criterion for African philosophy rather than a definition based on subject matter, it is meant to pave the way toward a truly free and mature philosophical conversation among Africans, in place of ethnophilosophy's self-effacing presentation of myths as philosophy. Ethnophilosophy has been a waste of time, he claims, a useless attempt to "codify a supposedly given, ready-constituted thought, instead of wading in, throwing ourselves into the fray and thinking new thoughts on the basis of today's and tomorrow's problems" (50). By today's and tomorrow's problems, he means whatever might be a problem worthy of philosophical attention.

"The first task of African philosophers today," he tells us, "is to promote and sustain constant free discussion about all the problems concerning their discipline" (67). Influenced by his reading of the German philosopher Edmund Husserl and by his teacher, the French philosopher Louis Althusser, Hountondji associates the development of a free and mature philosophical discussion with the development of an appropriately scientific perspective. In fact, he goes so far as to claim that "it is not philosophy but science that Africa needs first" (98).

This is a point of agreement between Hountondji and other members of the professional school, since the group in general placed a high value upon scientific thought. Kwasi Wiredu repeatedly emphasized the importance of science in the transition from traditional to modern life in general and, in particular, in the development of African philosophy as "a matter of individual responsibility" rather than the mere collection of folk traditions.[6] Another philosopher who has emphasized the importance of science is Marcien Towa, from Cameroon. Though Hountondji had already been using "ethnophilosophy" as a term of criticism in the late 1960s, the first critique of the practice to appear in book form was Towa's 1971 "essay" on the "problematic" of philosophy in Africa.[7] He accused ethnophilosophers of wrongfully expanding the concept of philosophy until it becomes "coextensive with that of culture," whereas, properly understood, the doing of "philosophy does not start until the decision to subject a philosophical and cultural heritage to uncompromising critique" (26, 30). Towa argues that ethnophilosophy is doubly a failure, as it is insufficiently neutral to count as good ethnology and insufficiently critical to count as good philosophy (31).

Most strikingly, he argues that, whereas ethnophilosophy involves investment in "the cult of difference and originality," preserving difference is the last thing Africans should be doing if they wish to overcome the legacy of colonial defeat (40). After all, Towa reasons, the secret to the West's victory over Africa must have something to do with the difference between the two. What is necessary for the empowerment of Africa, then, is understanding the competitive advantage of the West and putting its power to African use. That secret, according to Towa, is science and philosophy, and not philosophy in the overly expansive sense used by ethnophilosophers but in the most rigorous and fundamentally modern sense, according to which it is deeply intertwined and in some ways even interchangeable with the concept of science (57). This is the kind of philosophy that Africa needs, according to Towa.

Another name for the professional school is the "universalists." Philosophers like Hountondji, Wiredu, and Towa argued that the word "philosophy" in the term "African philosophy" must not mean something unique and particular to Africa. It must mean the same thing that it does in the term "Western philosophy" and must therefore be recognized as a term of universal significance rather than something that is fundamentally different from place to place. While this ideal of philosophy as a universal practice may seem inspiring and attractive, it can look problematic from another perspective: universalism, as upheld by the professional school, may be not so much an escape from cultural difference as a complete surrender to the cultural dominance of Europe and its notions of philosophy, science, and modernity. Samuel Imbo has summed up this concern by suggesting that, while figures associated with ethnophilosophy may be too invested in affirming African difference, figures like Hountondji offer us instead "a universality that is equally problematic because of its uncritical bowing at the feet of Europe."[8] It may seem a stretch to call Hountondji "uncritical": we're talking about someone who takes inspiration from the critical philosophy of Immanuel Kant. Yet the very fact that he places himself in the tradition of a German philosopher like Kant would seem to be part of Imbo's point. There is something discomfiting in the way he and others of the professional school treat philosophy as so foundationally and comfortably European, and so newly and insecurely African.

Kwame Gyekye has exposed this problem well, pointing out that Wiredu and another English-speaking member of the professional school, Peter Bodunrin, speak of African philosophy as "in the making."[9] At one point, Hountondji too, despite his recognition of African ethnophilosophers as having created a philosophical literature, points African philosophy in the direction he wants it to go by saying that "our philosophy is yet to come." Gyekye claims to catch these critics of ethnophilosophy in an inconsistency, though, for each of them seems to allow that philosophical thinking could not have been completely absent in traditional Africa. Hountondji, for example, when arguing that African philosophy is "before us, not behind us and must be created today by decisive action," nevertheless reassures us that this will not be creation out of nothing: "it will necessarily embrace the heritage of the past and will therefore be a recreation."[10] Gyekye rightfully asks how African philosophy in the present can be a recreation of the heritage of the past, if philosophy played no part in traditional African culture. On this basis, Gyekye strongly rejects the tendency of the professional school to steer African philosophy away from the task of locating philosophical material within oral traditions.

While one may worry that the professional school was too unwilling to challenge European cultural values and conceptions of philosophical practice, the universalism of these authors was compatible with an affirmation of African independence. Even when Towa goes so far as to suggest that Africans should avoid preserving difference and seek instead to attain the secret of the West, his explicit motivation is the achievement of power that will secure African independence, end neocolonialism, and prevent Africa from being vulnerable to colonial exploitation in the future. In this way, he argues, "we are led to adopt...an attitude of openness in relation to European civilization precisely in order to free ourselves from European domination."[11] Hountondji's critique of ethnophilosophy has a significant political dimension as well, even though he has argued that one difference between his and Towa's views is that Towa puts philosophy more completely in the service of politics than he does.[12] Remember that one problem with Tempels and his influence over African philosophy is that he was a European in conversation with other Europeans. Hountondji's firm conviction is that African ethnophilosophy follows Tempels even in this respect. As he puts it: "The quest for originality is always bound up with a desire to show off." In other words, the ethnophilosophical quest to show the distinctiveness of African philosophy is motivated by a desire to be recognized as special from a European perspective. Thus, he argues that "contemporary African philosophy, inasmuch as it remains an ethnophilosophy, has been built up essentially *for a European public*." True independence for Africa would mean putting an end to "this scandalous extraversion." When Africans do philosophy, they should "address it first and foremost to [their] fellow countrymen and offer it for the appreciation and discussion of Africans themselves."

Hountondji's critique and those of the others in the professional school marked a turning point in the history of African philosophy. If you find yourself torn, having been exposed to the philosophical interest of examining African oral traditions, but perhaps also feeling the force of the arguments of the professional school, you might wonder whether perhaps a compromise is possible. One way of providing a compromise here came, ironically, from the very philosopher who first came up with the "professional school" as a label. We are referring to Henry Odera Oruka, a Kenyan philosopher who distinguished between four trends or approaches in African philosophy.[13] First there was ethnophilosophy, and second, the response to it, "professional philosophy." A third was the "nationalist-ideological approach," in which he included the political theories of the first leaders of independent African countries. Then, despite the fact that Oruka identified himself as part of the professional school, he included as the fourth approach something that he himself pioneered: the study of philosophic sagacity.

20

WISE GUYS

Sage Philosophy

Ethnophilosophers are comfortable talking about the ideas of ethnic groups like the Akan, the Yoruba, the Igbo, and even such large and diverse collectivities as the Bantu. According to Henry Odera Oruka, to describe the ideas of African philosophy in this way presents us with the spectacle of "philosophy without philosophers."[1] Oruka, like others in the professional school, was not satisfied with the ethnophilosophical approach. He wrote rather dismissively of the "anthropological fogs" besetting the ethnophilosophical project (xxi), which in some cases was nothing more than "mythology paraded as philosophy."[2] Oruka was highly critical of both Mbiti and Tempels, in particular. The shortcomings he identified in their work are pretty much those we've already discussed: Mbiti's idea that traditional Africans lack an idea of an extended future would, if valid at all, apply to all peasant economies, while Tempels' project was vitiated by his assumption that Africans are incapable of formulating philosophical ideas explicitly for themselves.

Setting out to challenge this condescending view, Oruka sought to answer the following question:

> Would it be possible to identify persons of traditional African culture, capable of the critical, second-order type of thinking about the various problems of human life and nature; persons, that is, who subject beliefs that are traditionally taken for granted to independent rational re-examination, and who are inclined to accept or reject such beliefs on the authority of reason, rather than on the basis of a communal or religious consensus? (5–6)

Oruka's method was to interview selected men and, less frequently, women from his native Kenya who seemed to be particularly wise. These were the "sages" studied in what he came to call "sage philosophy."

Sage philosophy is, thus, the attempt to locate and learn from wise individuals in Africa rather than from groups as a whole. Oruka led efforts to do just this and argued in defense of his method, while also writing on other issues like economic development and the nature of truth, up to his death in 1995. Writing in 1990, he defined the fruits of his research as follows:

> Sage philosophy is the expressed thoughts of wise men and women in any given community, and is a way of thinking and explaining the world that fluctuates between popular wisdom (well-known communal maxims, aphorisms, and general common sense truths) and didactic wisdom (an expounded wisdom and a rational thought of some given individuals within a community).[3]

Here Oruka makes a distinction that is often overlooked in characterizations of his method. He did not understand "sage" to be a synonym for "philosopher." Rather, he distinguished between two kinds of sagacity, contrasting "culture," "popular," or "folk" wisdom to "didactic" or "philosophic" wisdom.

A folk sage is someone who is distinguished for their wisdom but still thinks within their traditional culture. An example of this was provided in an earlier study, often mentioned by Oruka, published by Maurice Griaule. Griaule had been interested in the beliefs of the Dogon people, and to learn about these had done interviews with a sage named Ogotemmeli in 1933.[4] This sounds like an anticipation of Oruka's own method. But Oruka saw limitations in Griaule's work, which simply treated Ogotemmeli as a mouthpiece for ideas assumed to be shared by all Dogon, instead of treating him as a thinker in his own right (45–6). You could say that in this ethnophilosophical study Griaule did, for once, put forward a named individual, but his individuality was irrelevant. As one of Oruka's students put it, "philosophy is a personal enterprise,"[5] and Oruka was duly concerned with Ogotemmeli's own individual wisdom. On the basis of the evidence presented in Griaule's study, Oruka deemed this sage to fall short of true *philosophical* sagacity. He was, as Oruka put it, "not a sage in the second order." In other words, Ogotemmeli did not reflect critically on the ideas of his culture. Indeed the whole point of Griaule's study was that every idea mentioned in the interviews could be ascribed to the Dogon quite generally, so that "most of what he says is known to be common knowledge to the average member of the tribe" (45).

Why was it so important to Oruka that philosophical sages be critically self-reflective? One answer lies in a parallel he liked to draw, between sage philosophy and ancient Greek philosophy. He and his collaborators were able to find illiterate wise men and women who came out with cosmological remarks not unlike those of the Presocratics (37). Take Rose Odhimbo, who may remind us of Heraclitus when she points to the inevitability of both change and stability in all things, and even says that without stability, nothing would be knowable. Or Naftali Ong'alo, who identifies water as a universal principle, much like the first Presocratic Thales.[6] But Oruka's paradigm philosopher seems to have been Socrates, whom we've already mentioned as a famous European thinker who did philosophy in oral conversation, not in writing. Socrates was self-reflective and critical about his own beliefs and the beliefs of his society, a "second-order" sage if ever there was one. He was also passionately committed to the practical relevance of philosophy. He wanted above all to know how to live. For Oruka too a genuinely philosophical outlook should include a strong ethical impulse, and sagacity should be devoted to the improvement of society.[7] (Which seems unduly restrictive: surely we should count as a "philosopher" an African sage whose insights concern only epistemology, metaphysics, or philosophy of language?)

Even if Socrates did not write anything, he was of course literate, whereas most of Oruka's interview subjects were not. In common with the ethnophilosophers he criticized, Oruka believed that philosophy can exist in a purely oral setting: "We should not make a great issue about writing...Writing is not thinking and philosophy is thinking, and one can think even if one is incapable of or has no facilities for writing" (xxii). Yet illiteracy was not an absolute requirement for inclusion in Oruka's project. One of his favorite examples of a philosophical sage, Paul Mbuya Akoko, who died in 1981 at the age of 90, published books in the Luo language (135). But if illiteracy isn't an absolute requirement to qualify as a philosophical sage, it does help. This is because, again like the ethnophilosophers, Oruka was trying to find wisdom in authentically indigenous settings. His subjects had to be, as he put it, "deeply rooted in traditional African culture" (28), rather than, say, philosophers who had trained in Europe or who were professors at African universities. This outlook left Oruka vulnerable to critique. Some of his sages, including Paul Mbuya, who not only wrote books but was Christian and active in politics, were challenged as misleading examples because they were too influenced by the modern world.[8]

The search for distinctively *traditional* wisdom opened Oruka to another charge, which concerned the interviews he and others conducted with candidate sages. Oruka was insistent that the interviewer was only there to "give birth" to the sage's ideas (31), drawing out their teachings by careful questioning. Maybe he was again thinking of Socrates, who in one Platonic dialogue compares himself to a "midwife" for the ideas of younger men (*Theaetetus* 150b–151c). But some readers of Oruka's reported interviews found the questions to be leading ones, which effectively smuggled in certain philosophical concerns or ideas from the Western tradition. This would contaminate the ideas that were supposedly being elicited from the "sages."[9] Actually, a perusal of the interview records suggests that if anything, Oruka's project took its cue from the ethnophilosophical literature Oruka had criticized. Often the sages are asked to remark on the nature of time and the reality of a long future (for example, 101–2, 109, 117, 135–6), a line of questioning that was clearly inspired by the work of Mbiti. Or they are queried about the nature of God or the gods, divination, or communalism, basically the same range of issues we've surveyed in our own look at ethnophilosophy.

Another topic we discussed, and that Oruka frequently stressed in his research, is gender, and in particular the equality between men and women. His interview subjects offered a spectrum of views here, with both folk and philosophical sages commenting on the status of women. Their remarks express everything from fairly blunt misogyny (96, 101, 132) to partially enlightened views (111, 120), and the outright egalitarianism of the aforementioned Paul Mbuya, who said, "given the view that men and woman are inherently equal, we see that woman can be more intelligent than a man just as a man can also be more intelligent than a woman" (140). Oruka took this as a paradigm example of "second-order reflection," since it showed that Mbuya was able to take critical distance on his own culture. Not everyone was convinced. One critic, D.A. Masolo, retorted that this was only a statement "thrown out without much of the usual elaboration that often goes with philosophic exposition."[10] Here we seem to enter into rather murky terrain. How "elaborate" does an exposition need to be before it rises to the level of philosophy?

A more apposite criticism might be that Oruka sometimes seems to conflate the idea of second-order reflection with the idea of offering critical correction to cultural beliefs. In a way, this is natural enough, because anyone who challenges the beliefs of their society thereby shows that they have reflected on those beliefs, and found them wanting. We find clear cases of this in Oruka's interviews, as with Okemba Simuyu Chaungo, who observed that religion had been "used by the white man as a machete to clear the way for colonialism" (114), or Oruka Rang'inya, who argued that medicine men are just people who are skilled at psychologically manipulating their clients (125). But we should bear in mind that someone might engage in second-order reflection on their cultural beliefs, and decide that those beliefs are *correct*.

Some of the figures that Oruka classified as "folk sages" do this. Consider the case of Chege Kamau, a sage of Kikuyuland who was born in 1911. Questioned about the nature of wisdom, he gave the following answer:

> In Kikuyu traditional society, elders are the leaders, the teachers. Children should copy the *good* examples of elders...Education is not found in big books. Education is

out there in the world...when you are walking, sleeping, tilling the land, talking, praying, eating, you are learning. Book education corrupts. It makes man's mind weak...he must run back to his books to check what action to take. (84)

And he later adds that he himself took all his learning "from parents and community" (85). Similarly, Ali Mwitani Masero, also labeled as a "folk sage," stated that "you cannot seek wisdom...it is given at birth" (92). While these discussions may not rise to the level of the "elaboration" that Masolo was hoping to see in Oruka's reports, they are clearly second order. Both folk sages expressed views about the nature of wisdom and what you have to do to get it. Their second-order reflections led them to the conclusion that wisdom is either an inborn gift or precisely something that is passed down from older generations. It may be disappointing to seek out wise members of a community and see them using their wisdom to justify adhering to traditional beliefs, especially if we ourselves think those beliefs are defective, as with sexist attitudes towards women. But as Sophie Oluwole has commented in her reflections on Oruka's project: "Inadequate philosophy is philosophy still."[11]

Our point here is not only that it is difficult to draw a sharp contrast between folk and philosophic sagacity, or that Oruka sometimes drew the line in the wrong place, though others have indeed made these sorts of complaint.[12] It is rather that being reflective can reinforce, rather than undermine, established cultural attitudes and doctrines. Indeed we might go so far as to say that this is what we mostly find in the history of philosophy, not only in Africa but all around the world. True, some of the most famous philosophers, from Socrates and Plato to Marx and Nietzsche, have indeed been highly critical of their societies. But for the most part, philosophers are in the business of vindicating the beliefs of their own social groups. Just think of Thomas Aquinas' proofs for God's existence, Nāgārjuna's ingenious defense of Buddhist ideas of non-dependence, or John Rawls showing his fellow left-wing liberals just how right their political views have been all along. All three distinguished themselves not by overturning the beliefs with which they began, but by putting formidable intelligence at the service of those very beliefs.

Actually, this observation could help, rather than undermine, Oruka's idea of sage philosophy—though it might bring sage philosophy closer to the approach taken in works of ethnophilosophy. Once we recognize that sages can count as philosophers while remaining within traditional worldviews rather than revising them, we will more easily be able to deal with a paradox posed to Oruka by Christian Neugebauer.[13] On the one hand, to earn the name "philosophy," the examples of sagacity put forward by Oruka needed somehow to satisfy the criteria we associate with Greek philosophy and all that came out of it. They needed, among other things, to be critical, argumentative, and reflective. On the other hand, the sage philosophy enterprise seeks to uncover thought that is recognizably "African." After all, the whole point was to offer a new model and method for establishing the reality of something we could plausibly call "African philosophy," while retaining the commonsense idea that philosophy is something done by one person at a time. But how can sagacity simultaneously look so familiar to the Western-minded investigators that they are willing to count it as "philosophy," while also being characteristically, even idiosyncratically, African?

The most straightforward way that this might happen would be to find sages who do reflect on their so-called "folk" culture, but come to the view that that culture is well worth embracing. A good example here would be the Ugandan poet and philosopher Okot p'Bitek, whom we have mentioned as a critic of ethnophilosophy (Chapter 12). Admittedly the well-educated p'Bitek was no one's idea of a traditional African sage. But he did think long and hard about his own African culture and language, and decided that it was valuable, with a kind of value that could only be maintained in a traditional setting. Having studied at several universities in Britain, he returned home and wrote two poems reflecting on the relative merits of Western and African culture. In his *Song of Lawino*, the title character complains of her university-educated husband; a further poem, the *Song of Ocol*, provides the husband's point of view. In these poems p'Bitek acknowledges the seductive appeal of Western education, but suggests that through contact with such foreign influences, Ocol has lost his sense of community, and thus of himself.[14]

Neugebauer's discussion of sage philosophy strikes a more skeptical note concerning the urge to attach African philosophy to African culture. He is especially struck by the tendency, which is arguably shared by both ethnophilosophy and sage philosophy, to want African philosophy to be pure of all Western influence. Think again of how Oruka was sensitive to the charge that a man like Paul Mbuya was too worldly to count as a genuine "African sage." It should be noted that Oruka was not committed to the idea explored with such nuance by p'Bitek, namely that philosophical ideas are permanently linked to the culture, place, or people that gave rise to them. He asked why "the Anglo-Saxon people should be over-flattered to believe that empiricist philosophy is British and that any other person who comes to entertain it would only be swimming in the British *gnosis*."[15] Yet as we've seen, he did want his sages to be "rooted" in traditional culture, and was even convinced that "all philosophical theses are rooted and driven by their cultural origins," so that cultural origins must be made "transparent" in philosophical dialogue.[16]

This takes us back, finally, to the role of the interlocutor or reporter who interviews the sage and tries to get them to divulge their wisdom for the benefit of the rest of us. Critics complained about those leading questions, and also that the whole enterprise involves soliciting philosophical views that would otherwise have remain unexpressed. Wouldn't a real philosopher put forward their views without needing someone else to come along and provoke them into doing so? In the words of one of Oruka's more trenchant opponents, Peter Bodunrin: "It is one thing to show that there are men capable of philosophical dialogue in Africa and another to show that there are African philosophers in the sense of those who have engaged in organized systematic reflections on the thoughts, beliefs and practices of their people" (170).

Though Oruka was at pains to insist on the neutrality of the interview process, he did not deny the active role of the investigator. Remember, he thought that the point of sagacity is to make the world a better place. Accordingly, he did not want to find these sages only to make the point that, as he once put it, "philosophy is not a monopoly of the West."[17] He wanted to find sages in order to *learn* from them. The right response to the transcript of an interview with a sage would not be merely to say, "Gosh, that person is really a philosopher, despite being an uneducated African." It would be to engage with the ideas that are expressed by the sage and take them further. As Oruka said in an interview, "We take the text of one given sage, folk sage or philosophical sage, then we subject that to analysis, to investigation and examination, and so they contribute to positions of our own debate."[18]

21

BEYOND THE REACTION

The Continuing Relevance of Precolonial Traditions

Consider the following remarks: "Arsenal won the league title, going undefeated for the entire season." "Parliament failed to take a position on this critical issue." "The East India Company was guilty of rapacious, colonial practices." "Tottenham disappointed fans yet again." What these statements have in common, apart from their ubiquity in British life, is that they refer to something being done, but not by any one person in particular. The achievements of Arsenal are credited, and the failings of Tottenham Hotspur blamed, on a whole team and not any one player, manager, or owner. An entity like the East India Company or a corporation guilty of polluting the environment may be severely condemned without any single person or persons having to take the blame. Or consider the political example. In the struggle to decide how Britain should leave the EU, it was possible for Parliament as a whole to be "undecided" even though, or rather precisely because, each individual member of Parliament was very much decided, having a strong view on the matter. Philosophers call this phenomenon "group agency," and enjoy thinking about the puzzles that can arise when the subject of an action, or even a belief, is not an individual person but a group working together (or failing to do so). One such puzzle is that a group may reach a decision that no one member of the group actually prefers. Imagine a committee deciding between three options: some members prefer option 1 and reject 3, others prefer 3 and reject 1, but all could just about live with option 2. The committee might take option 2 as a compromise, even though no member of the committee ranked it highest.

Though this is an issue that has only recently received sustained attention from philosophers, perhaps you can already see why it might be relevant to the study of precolonial African philosophy. The debate between the practitioners of ethnophilosophy and the adherents of the professional school was about several things, including the question of whether philosophy must involve writing. But perhaps most fundamentally it was a disagreement about group agency. Could the bearers of philosophical insight, wisdom, or belief be whole communities or cultures, like the Akan, Yoruba, or Bantu? Or must they be individuals like, say, John Mbiti, or one of the sages interviewed by Oruka? A natural way out of the impasse would be to observe that this may be, to some extent, a false dichotomy. Groups are after all made up of individuals. Besides, in the history of philosophy more generally, we freely refer to the doctrines of groups like Cartesians or Platonists, without necessarily implying that the doctrines in question have been held without exception by every Cartesian or Platonist.

Fittingly, then, the debate over the nature of African philosophy eventually moved toward a sort of resolution, as critics of ethnophilosophy gradually expressed more sympathetic views of the study of oral tradition. A case in point would be Kwasi Wiredu. His essay, "How Not to Compare African Thought with Western Thought," which opposed the treatment of folk mythologies as philosophy, was republished in a 1977 book entitled *African Philosophy: An Introduction* alongside essays like "Time in Yoruba Thought," by John Ayoade, and "Causal Theory in Akwapim Akan Philosophy," by Helaine Minkus.[1] So here in the late 1970s ethnophilosophers and their critics were cohabiting between the covers of a book, while maintaining their fundamental disagreement. Then, a series of essays published by Wiredu after 1980 seemed to show a change of heart: "The Akan Concept of Mind," "The Concept of Truth in the Akan Language," "Morality and Religion in Akan Thought," "African Philosophical Tradition: A Case Study of the Akan." Was Wiredu joining the opposing side, like when the defender Sol Campbell quite reasonably left Spurs to play for Arsenal and was decried as a "Judas" by unforgiving Tottenham fans?

If so, Wiredu was not alone. We saw that the arch-enemy of ethnophilosophy, indeed the philosopher who devised this name in the process of attacking the whole enterprise, was Paulin Hountondji. Surely, he would keep the faith! Well, just take a look at the description of a book he edited in 1997 entitled *Endogenous Knowledge: Research Trails*.[2] Promising to uncover "the wealth of traditional African knowledge and techniques," it includes coverage of "a wide variety of topics, from the probability theory of cowry shell diviners, to hydrology and rainmaking, and the links between sorcery and psychosomatic medicine." What is going on here? What seems to have happened is that the polemical critique of ethnophilosophy, so important in the 1970s, gave way to a consensus on the importance of precolonial traditions for the study of African philosophy. Yet this was more complicated than a mere switching of allegiance. The consensus appears to have developed because the critique had served its purpose, making it possible to preserve what was of value in the ethnophilosophical project while being more conscious of its methodology. We can perhaps best understand Wiredu's transition by exploring his essay, "On Defining African Philosophy."[3] Near the essay's beginning, we are not surprised to find him criticizing Mbiti for treating African philosophy as if it were nothing more than a "semianthropological paraphrase of African traditional beliefs" (88). Wiredu also follows Hountondji in rejecting the myth of unanimity as exemplified by Tempels' *Bantu Philosophy*.

But then Wiredu begins to distance himself from Hountondji, especially by opposing the idea that philosophy must be set down in writing. "A philosophical thesis is philosophical whether written or merely spoken," he argues, adding that "it would be inconsistent to suggest that the thesis that every event that happens was bound to happen is philosophical when advanced and argued in, for instance, Richard Taylor's *Metaphysics*, but not philosophical when expressed by my grandfather in an isolated proverb." (94). Furthermore, even though philosophy is a relative newcomer in Africa as an academic discipline, philosophy as a habit of reflection cannot be new to the continent. For, as he says, "any group of human beings will have to have some world outlook, that is, some general conceptions about the world in which they live and about themselves both as individuals and as members of society" (87).

This suggests a distinction between philosophy in a broad sense, which involves having a certain "world outlook," and philosophy in a narrow sense, which is "a technical discipline in which our...world outlook is subjected to systematic scrutiny by rigorous ratiocinative methods" (87). Members of the professional school often drew this sort of distinction, in order then to accuse the ethnophilosophers of ignoring it. The ethnophilosopher, they would argue, pretends to be showing that Africa, like the West, has "philosophy," but equivocates in doing so. Ethnography can show only that Africa has philosophy in the broad sense of the term, but it is of course the narrow sense of the term—ideas presented in writing and backed up with explicit and detailed argument—that is generally at stake when speaking of philosophy in academic contexts in the West. Thus, when Wiredu criticizes Mbiti and Tempels early in the essay for making African philosophy nothing more than a matter of rendering explicit what is supposedly implicit in traditional African folkways, he seems to be making the standard anti-ethnophilosophical argument.

Why then would he go on to admit that a proverb uttered by his grandfather is a "philosophical" thesis? Isn't he guilty of the same equivocation that was seen at the heart of ethnophilosophy? His defense would be, for starters, that the two senses of philosophy do have something in common. Both involve the human habit of reflection. If we see philosophy in the narrow sense as "a second-order enterprise" because it is a reflection on philosophy in the broad sense, then it is, in fact, "doubly second-order, for that on which it reflects—namely, our world outlook—is itself a reflection on the more particularistic, more episodic, judgments of ordinary, day-to-day living" (87). Later in the essay, Wiredu gives us even more reason to see the utterance of a proverb as philosophical. Here his break with the standard position of the professional school is impossible to miss. Taking aim not at Hountondji's definition of African philosophy but at assumptions underlying Oruka's notion of sage philosophy, he writes that "Oruka seems to think that to speak of traditional communal thought as philosophical...is to operate with a 'debased' concept of philosophy" (96). For Oruka, as you may recall, only the critical reflection on communal thought achieved by the individual sage counts as philosophy. Invoking the relation between the broad and narrow usages of the term, though, Wiredu argues that there is an intimate connection between the philosophical thought of the individual sage and "communal philosophy," in the sense of "the communal world outlook" of the sage's people. It is that communal world outlook that provides "the point of departure" for the sage's reflections (96).

Wiredu furthermore encourages us to ask how the communal world outlook came to be in the first place. The natural conclusion would be that "the communal thought itself is the pooling together of these elements of the thought of individual philosophers of the community that remain stuck in the common imagination" (96). The group, in other words, can have a philosophy because it retains views originally proposed by *single members* of the group. In the absence of writing, the names of these individual philosophers, and also any complex arguments and clarifications they were prepared to offer, are most often lost to the communal memory. Still the ideas were products of individual philosophical minds. There is therefore a two-way relationship between the individual sage-philosopher and the communal philosophy, in Wiredu's view: "Not only is it the case that it is this communal thought that provides the sage-philosopher with his philosophical nourishment, but also it is the thought of the sage-philosopher (albeit in the form of highly compressed 'abstracts') that forms and enriches communal thought" (96). One might compare the way that Arsenal wins when its star players perform well, but the club and the rest of the team give them the context and support in which to display their excellence.

There can be no doubt that Wiredu had fruitful conversations about these matters with his colleague at the University of Ghana, Kwame Gyekye, for we find Gyekye making a number of similar points in his own work.[4] Using a different proverb and different Western thinkers, he makes the point that "it would be inconsistent to regard as philosophical the statement 'every event has a cause' found in, say, Aristotle or Leibniz and refuse to regard as philosophical the Akan proverb 'everything has its "because-of"'" (19). He also points out the connection between the philosophy of a group and the contribution of individual members: "A *particular thought or idea* is, as regards its genesis, the product of *an individual mind*... 'Collective' thought, then, is a misnomer. There is, strictly speaking, no such thing as 'collective' thought, if this means that ideas result from the intellectual production of a whole collectivity. What has come to be described as 'collective' thought is nothing but the ideas of individual wise people; individual ideas that, due to the lack of doxographic tradition in Africa, became part of the pool of communal thought" (24). Gyekye and Wiredu seem to be seeking a middle ground between ethnophilosophy and the professional school. Gyekye grants, and Wiredu adheres to, the key claim made by the latter, namely that philosophical ideas in the first instance come from individual thinkers, not groups of people. Traditional thought thus becomes worthy of study precisely because it involves the pooling of the ideas of individual thinkers. So while this may look like an abandonment of the professional school and embrace of ethnophilosophy on Wiredu's part, it is more so an incorporation and harmonizing of viewpoints from both sides of the previous debate.

In Wiredu's "On Defining African Philosophy," we also find him returning to the comparison between traditional thought and modern Western philosophy. He points out that the British, and other European peoples, have their own unwritten communal philosophies. When we speak of British philosophy or whatever other European philosophy, these oral traditions are not what we have in mind (97). But this is simply because in those cases there are also long traditions of written philosophy, so it is generally assumed that whatever is of value in the communal, unwritten tradition has been incorporated into the writings of individuals. Wiredu suggests that the continued growth of written philosophy in Africa will eventually mean that the phrase "African philosophy" too will refer to texts and not oral traditions.

Despite that prediction about the future, Wiredu forthrightly admits that at present, we're nowhere near the point of being ready to forget about communal oral traditions in the African context. On the contrary, "this is the time when there is the maximum need to study African traditional philosophy" (98). The fact of colonialism means that professional African philosophers are trained primarily through foreign sources of philosophical thought, expressed in non-African languages and shaped by cultures from outside of Africa. Wiredu asks: "Why should the African uncritically assimilate the conceptual schemes embedded in foreign languages and cultures?" (98). Not that philosophical truth is impossible to disentangle from cultural contingencies. But the best way to do this is to examine cultural contrasts, such as those between indigenous African languages and the European languages, with respect to what Wiredu calls the "philosophical prepossessions" of these languages (98).

Starting as early as a presentation he gave at a UNESCO conference in Nairobi in 1980, Wiredu began to refer to this comparative mode of doing African philosophy as the project of *conceptual decolonization*. From the 1980s onward, he devoted a number of studies to the traditional ideas of the Akan, and by the time of his 1996 book, *Cultural Universals and Particulars*, it had become a major focus of his work.[5] Take, for example, his reflections in that book on the nature of truth. He argues that if you seek to evaluate what philosophers call the correspondence theory of truth by translating it into Akan, the results will be as underwhelming as Tottenham's trophy cabinet. This is because to express the notion of truth, especially as distinguished from the moral notion of truthfulness, you will use the phrase *nea ete saa*, which might be literally translated as "that which is so" (107). But if you want to express the notion of what we call in English a "fact," you will likewise use *nea ete saa*. The correspondence theory of truth claims that what is true is whatever corresponds to what the facts are. Once translated into Akan this will become an uninformative tautology: the theory would simply state that "what is so" is "what is so."

According to Wiredu, this shows that the relationship between truth and fact may be an issue of philosophical interest in English, but it is what he calls a "tongue-dependent" issue, that is, one that only makes sense in certain languages. To say of a philosophical problem that it is tongue dependent is not to say that it is of no interest whatsoever, but does mean that it is less fundamental as a philosophical problem than those which are not tongue dependent, but universal (103). And there are, according to Wiredu at least, such problems concerning the concept of truth, for he claims that rival theories like the coherence theory of truth or the pragmatic theory of truth "do not suffer any trivialization on being translated into Akan" (112). For him, this illustrates how the exploration of indigenous African languages and cultures can help shed light on the nature of philosophical problems in ways that are instructive both to Africans and non-Africans alike.

So should we say that Wiredu abandoned the professional school? In an interview, Wiredu denied that his turn toward conceptual decolonization involved any fundamental change. It was merely "a shift of emphasis."[6] Even earlier in his career, Wiredu acknowledged the existence of traditional philosophies among African peoples. He credited William Abraham's book *The Mind of Africa* with demonstrating that "in theoretical sweep and practical bearing traditional African philosophies concede nothing to the world views of European philosophies."[7] Thus his notorious remark at that time that African philosophy was "still in the making" was just a particularly forceful way of urging African philosophers not to content themselves with recounting the contents of traditional philosophies. Modern African philosophy should engage with traditional philosophies, but by critically evaluating them and synthesizing them with ideas gleaned from foreign sources.

In that same interview, Wiredu provides an autobiographical explanation for his shift in emphasis. When he was working at the University of Ghana, there were other faculty members, like Gyekye, who could teach African philosophy. Thus his own teaching focused on subjects like logic and epistemology. In this circumstance, he was sensitive to, and reacted against, the way that some viewed such subjects as alien to the tasks of African philosophy, at least when taught with an emphasis on Western accomplishments in the field. But when he began teaching in the United States, where he eventually held a position at the University of South Florida until his retirement in 2007, he had reason to focus on teaching and discussing African philosophy. What seemed to be a change of mind was really more a change of scenery.

Hountondji spent most of his career in Benin, but there were some changes of scenery involved in the evolution of his thought as well. We can see this in a book he published in 1997 that describes his entire intellectual itinerary, from his graduate work on Edmund Husserl, through the critique of ethnophilosophy, to what came after.[8] We learn that his opposition to ethnophilosophy was partly inspired by his experiences teaching in the early 1970s, in the country then still called Zaire (now the Democratic Republic of the Congo), ruled by the infamous dictator Mobutu Sese Seko. Mobutu's official state ideology of "Authenticity" suppressed individuality in a number of ways, all in the name of upholding African tradition. Hountondji reacted against this with his emphasis on the pivotal role of the individual in philosophy. He became accustomed to being quite combative in defending his position, but in 1983 he chose a different path. He tells the poignant story of being in Montreal for a World Congress of Philosophy when he received a phone call from Benin with the terrible news that his father had passed away. Scheduled to give his lecture on the closing day of the conference, Hountondji wrote up something for a colleague to present on his behalf, and flew back home. This was the occasion for what, he reckoned, was "the most conciliatory text" he ever wrote (197), entitled "The Pitfalls of Difference."

He acknowledged the work of the Belgian philosopher A.J. Smet on the political context of Tempels' *Bantu Philosophy* and Tempels' efforts to speak out against the wrongs of the Belgian colonial regime in the Congo. He recognized that many of those who attempted to counter his critiques of ethnophilosophy were understandably attempting to defend "the necessity for any human project, even, and especially if it wants to be innovative, to be rooted in the concrete soil of a tradition" (198).

The time had come to re-read ethnophilosophy, to see how it could offer us, as Hountondji put it, "not some philosophy buried deep down in our collective unconscious" but the opportunity to "re-read our cultures themselves, to study them patiently, methodically, in order to discover, on the one hand, their fertile contradictions, their great alternatives, the historic choices that have made them into what they are today, and on the other hand, their enduring aspects, their material and spiritual constants, all this un-thought that constitutes our common heritage, and with which we must entertain, here and now, a free and critical relationship" (198–9).

In his introduction to the book he went on to edit, *Endogenous Knowledge*, which we mentioned earlier, it's easy to see the continuity between the more polemical and the more conciliatory phases of his career. He remains committed to the goal of African advancement in science and to decrying the problem of intellectual extraversion, complaining that Africa remained "scientifically dependent as it is economically dependent."[9] Just as raw materials leave Africa for Europe while African countries end up importing finished products from European countries, Africa serves as a source of data for European science. African institutions, meanwhile, fail to set research agendas motivated by internal African needs and accept the position of being peripheral and subordinate to the West in the world of science. But now Hountondji takes a further step, arguing that a sign of Africa's problematically outward-facing perspective in science is the neglect of serious research on traditional knowledge and techniques, that is, "ancestral knowledge of plants, animals, health and illness," and so on. At best, there is an awkward juxtaposition where, for example, trained doctors who fail to treat a disease successfully may advise a patient to go back to the village and consult a traditional healer. But this is a highly unsatisfactory coexistence of traditional methods and methods inherited from the West. Instead, Africans should pursue "the possibility of harmonizing them in a more viable composite." Endogenous knowledge should not be neglected but subjected to a process of critical examination, evaluation, and "active reappropriation," in part through the improvement of "accuracy and strictness as a result of contact with exogenous science." In encouraging the study of techniques of divination, rainmaking, traditional healing, and so on, Hountondji is therefore not abandoning his previous position on ethnophilosophy. This call for the advancement of science in Africa through attention to tradition reflects his long-standing desire for Africans to stop serving the interests of the West, and to focus on discovering and meeting their own needs.

By now, it should be abundantly clear why we gave this first half of the book the title *Locating and Debating Precolonial African Philosophy*. We have been considering first-order philosophical issues like the nature of time, the soul, God, and so on, but also second-order or "meta-" philosophical questions. This is one reason that African philosophy is a subject worth studying for everyone with an interest in philosophy itself. It forces us to reflect on fundamental questions about the nature and form of philosophy, in a way that the traditions of, say, ancient Greece or seventeenth century France do not. We've just seen that leading scholars of this field reached a rough consensus concerning the value of oral traditions: as groups are indeed made up of individuals, we should not ignore philosophical teachings that have no identifiable authors and can be located only in broader communities.[10] But it's a deep and difficult question, so whether you accept this consensus and are thus ready to join the communal stance is something for you to ponder.

PART II

SLAVERY AND THE CREATION OF DIASPORIC AFRICANA PHILOSOPHY

22

OUT OF AFRICA

Slavery and the Diaspora

In the year 1770, a 13-year-old boy living in what is now Ghana went to visit his uncle. There were a number of other children in the area, with whom he was able to pass the time playing. Sometimes, though, kids strayed unsafely too far into the forest. One day, the boy was reluctant to go along, but when he was mocked for his cowardice he capitulated to the peer pressure, with disastrous consequences. He and the others were interrupted by rough men, who brought out guns and cutlasses and announced that the kids would be taken to a local ruler to answer for themselves. They were divided into groups. One of the men pretended to be friendly in order to put the kids at ease, telling them that he would clear up everything with the lord as soon as possible. When they stopped to sleep, however, and morning came, the pretended friend was gone. They also began to encounter people who spoke a language unfamiliar to them.

After another half a day's journey, they came upon a town engaging in some sort of a celebration and they were able to join in and enjoy the singing and dancing. But the joy was short-lived. The boy began to suspect that he would not soon be returning home, and indeed, six days later, he was still in the same town. Another man came, claiming to know people in the boy's hometown and promising to bring the boy there, which gave the boy some hope. They went not to his hometown, though, but to the coast. Here the boy saw white people for the first time, which scared him greatly, for he had heard that white people might eat you. He was brought to a slave castle, full of chained prisoners; the man who had brought him there was given a gun, a piece of cloth, and some lead as payment for the boy. After three days, he was brought to a ship and transported to Cape Coast, where another ship was waiting to embark on a voyage across the Atlantic Ocean. After a planned revolt by the captives was foiled, the ship sailed, bringing this boy to the Caribbean island of Grenada and introducing him to his new reality: slavery in the Americas.

SLAVERY AND THE DIASPORA

The boy's name was Quobna Ottobah Cugoano. This heart-rending account of his capture and enslavement comes from the opening pages of his 1787 book, *Thoughts and Sentiments on the Evil and Wicked Traffic of Slavery and Commerce of the Human Species, Humbly Submitted to the Inhabitants of Great-Britain, by Ottobah Cugoano, a Native of Africa*. The autobiographical material we have just recounted takes up but a few pages of the book, which is therefore not primarily a testimony concerning his personal experience of slavery, but rather an exercise in political philosophy, a carefully reasoned yet passionate attack on the transatlantic slave trade and slavery in the West Indies. It thus encapsulates the way that philosophical thought could unfold amidst the trauma of slavery, colonization, and racist oppression inflicted on Africans and their descendants in the eighteenth and nineteenth centuries. That is the story we will be telling in this second part of this volume (Cugoano's own contributions will feature in Chapter 24).

Actually, though, the first thing we need to understand about the enslavement of Africans by Europeans in the modern world is the way in which it is *not* special.[1] For many people today, the word "slavery" automatically conjures up images of black people working cotton plantations in the American South. But the practice of slavery long predates what took place in Britain's American colonies and then the United States. Slavery has played a role of some sort in a great many, perhaps even most, of the social orders devised by human beings, ever since we ceased to be predominantly hunters and gatherers. Slavery arises early in the history of philosophy too, with an infamous example being Aristotle's explanation and defense of the practice in his *Politics*. It is also worth remembering that, etymologically, the word "slave" is commonly thought to be derived through the Latin word *sclavus* from the word "Slav," due to the association in medieval times between slavery and the conquering and selling of Slavic people.

Nor is slavery coming up in this book for the first time, since we already mentioned it in connection with Zera Yacob and Ahmed Baba. Assuming Zera Yacob was a real person, these two thinkers were both alive and active in the early part of the seventeenth century, a time during which the transatlantic slave trade and slavery in the Americas were already under way. But neither of them mentioned this. They thought mainly, and perhaps even exclusively, of slavery in the Islamic world, with Zera Yacob criticizing Islam among the world religions for its tolerance of slavery and Ahmed Baba condoning slavery but upholding the traditional view that Muslims should not be enslaved, regardless of where they come from or how they look. Yet Ahmed Baba also gave us our first example of the association between slavery and black people, as his treatise was provoked by an idea, which had begun circulating in the Islamic world, that black Africans of whatever religion could be justifiably enslaved.

The trans-Saharan slave trade was ultimately dwarfed in its impact, both on human affairs in general and on the development of philosophy in particular, by the transatlantic trade. How did this trade get going, and what made it so incomparably consequential when contrasted with earlier and contemporary forms of slavery? To address the question of its origin, we must look to the history of the cultivation of sugar cane.[2] First domesticated many thousands of years ago by peoples of the South Pacific, the cultivation of sugar gradually made its way westward. By medieval times, it was an important crop in the Middle East. Then the Crusades introduced it to Europeans, which brings us to the central role of sugar production by the Portuguese, the Spanish, and Italians like the Genoese in the story of the slave trade, a story that must be connected to these peoples' more famous roles in European exploration of the so-called New World in the fifteenth and sixteenth centuries. Prior to that, there was a less famous colonization of islands in the Atlantic closer to Europe and Africa, in the earlier half of the fifteenth century. The Spanish, for example, laid claim to the Canary Islands and the Portuguese took the uninhabited islands of Madeira and the Azores.

At the same time, the Portuguese began to sail along the African coast further than they had before. It is in 1441 that we find the first instance of a Portuguese ship taking African captives back to Portugal. There were only twelve of them, and it is unclear whether they were brought as slaves or as exhibits to be shown off, but similar numbers of captives were taken the next year and the year after that. Then, in 1444, 235 people were brought back to be sold. As sugar plantations were created in Madeira and the Canary Islands, Africans were brought there to work those plantations. In the 1480s, the Portuguese began to settle São Tomé, a previously uninhabited island in the Gulf of Guinea, not far from present-day Gabon and today part of the country known as São Tomé and Principe. There too sugar plantations were created and worked by Africans brought from the mainland. The trade that transported people all the way across the Atlantic was thus preceded by a trade bringing people just a short boat ride from the African coast.

How extensive and historically significant the enslavement of Africans by Europeans would have been if Christopher Columbus had not made his voyages, or if the colonization of the Americas had not ensued, is an interesting question. The world we live in, however, is the one in which the various European powers who colonized the Americas ended up using, and in many places completely depending upon, enslaved Africans for the economic growth and development of their colonies. Indeed, even thinking about the life of Columbus—a Genoese merchant who spent time in Madeira, who visited the Portuguese fort of Elmina on the coast of present-day Ghana, and who brought sugar cane with him on his second voyage to the Americas—one is struck by how well he represents the expanding Atlantic world that had been taking shape over the course of the fifteenth century.

Nevertheless, it is well known (or at least it ought to be) that, early on, Columbus saw the enslavement of the indigenous people of the Caribbean as the way forward. The Tainos of Hispaniola were forced to work extracting gold for the Spanish under Columbus' rule. Then in February 1495, the first ship transporting slaves across the Atlantic went not from Africa to the Americas but from Hispaniola to Spain, carrying hundreds of captured Tainos. Reliance on indigenous labor did not last long, however, in large part because of the devastation wrought on these populations by diseases brought by Europeans. This is a good point at which to note the epidemiological dimension of the circumstances that made the slavery of Africans so important to the modern world. The indigenous peoples of the Americas were vulnerable to European diseases at a catastrophic rate. The exact numbers are disputed but this was certainly the largest depopulation of humans in history, with some regions suffering a population decline of 90 percent or more.[3] By contrast, Africans were less vulnerable to disease in the New World than Europeans, as a result of immunities acquired in the coastal African environment. It is possible that there were earlier arrivals unrecorded, but the first certain instance in which an enslaved African went to the New World is a visit to Hispaniola in 1502 by the slave of a rich Spaniard sent to sell goods on his master's behalf. Only eight years later, King Ferdinand—the same Spanish king who had sponsored Columbus' exploration—authorized the shipment of fifty slaves to Hispaniola to work in gold mines. The slave trade to the Americas had begun.

As historian Patrick Manning points out, what distinguishes the slavery of Africans under Europeans is not so much the fact of being enslaved itself. After all, as we have mentioned, peoples of many different backgrounds have been enslaved throughout recorded history. It was more a matter of *when* they were being enslaved. As a global institution, slavery had arguably been on the decline. Certainly, Europeans were being enslaved much less frequently than in the past. Only in the case of Africans did the modern era translate to a sharp and consistent increase in enslavement. Manning includes the situation within Africa itself in making this point, for slavery certainly existed throughout Africa, but "expanded from a somewhat marginal institution to one of central importance during the modern period."[4] Manning also notes that in 1500, even though the Portuguese and the Spanish were already importing African slaves both to the Iberian peninsula and to the islands in the Atlantic they had colonized, Africans still remained a minority among the world's population of slaves. By 1700, though, they made up the overwhelming majority of the slave population of the world. The story of Europe's rise to world dominance in the modern era and especially the story of their colonization of the Americas requires, as a central rather than marginal factor, the story of the draining of a huge portion of Africa's population through the transatlantic slave trade.

Just how many Africans were taken from their home and brought to the Americas in this way? Estimates tend to range between 9 and 12 million, but to this number must be added those taken who did not make it to the Americas.[5] Counting those who perished during the so-called "Middle Passage," the term commonly applied to the voyage across the Atlantic in the squalid and often lethal conditions of slave ships, likely adds a further 1 or 2 million to the total. It is also estimated that another 6 to 7 million enslaved Africans may have been exported through the Sahara and the Indian Ocean to eastern slave markets. We have mentioned the Iberian role in beginning the transatlantic trade, but they were joined by others, particularly the French, British, Dutch, Swedish, Danish, and the German principality of Brandenburg. There was even brief involvement by the Duchy of Courland, a vassal state of the Polish-Lithuanian Commonwealth that is today part of Latvia; that conveys some sense of the pan-European nature of the trade in Africans. Of the non-Iberian powers, the British stand out for the high volume and high profit of their trade, and this is obviously the context for Cugoano's story, with which we began. The trade in slaves to the British colonies of North America and then, once it gained independence, to the United States, makes up a surprisingly small amount of the total trade to the Americas, relative to the attention garnered by slavery in the United States. Probably fewer than half a million Africans ended up being brought there. The country that received the largest numbers of Africans by far was Brazil, where at least 4 million Africans were sent (see further Chapter 48).

The impact of the slave trade on Africans was immense and disastrous. While the lucrative task of meeting the rising demand of European buyers certainly enriched many individual slave traders and various polities active in the trade, the high demand naturally encouraged hostility, war, and raiding between peoples so that captives could be taken and sold. In this respect, the slave trade produced a situation of instability and insecurity on the African continent that could not be conducive to its general economic development, even putting aside matters of human rights. The impact on the Africans who were taken and sold was, of course, as profound as any human experience could possibly be. One sign of it is the fact that European languages now become vehicles for Africana thought. So far in this book, we have been focusing on philosophy as expressed in the precolonial cultures, and thus mainly in the indigenous tongues, of Africa. But henceforth we'll be looking at writings in languages like Latin, English, French, and Portuguese. This reflects one of the most well-known and transformative impacts of slavery in the Americas, namely, the loss of indigenous African languages and of various other aspects of traditional African culture. In part, that was due to active suppression, in part, to the simple fact that the slaves brought together on New World plantations were drawn from different ethnolinguistic backgrounds, making it hard to hold on to languages in subsequent generations.

We should stress, though, that philosophy in Africa will remain part of our story. The presence of Europeans on the western coast of Africa starting as early as the fifteenth century inspired those metaphorically insightful rumors of white cannibalism among inland populations, as mentioned in the story of Cugoano's abduction. This was the beginning of a process of colonization that would ultimately bring almost all of Africa under European power. Philosophical thought produced in European languages by Africans whose intellectual production was shaped by European colonialism will thus also feature in what follows. It's really at this point, however, that the term "Africana philosophy" rather than "African philosophy" becomes most appropriate as a description of our subject matter. While still following the history of philosophy in Africa itself, we will now also be exploring philosophy from the African diaspora, that scattering of peoples created by the triangular trade connecting Africa as source of unpaid labour, the imperial powers of Europe, and the colonized lands of the Americas.

We'd like to forestall a worry you may have, namely that discussions of philosophy written in reaction to slavery and colonization might get rather boring. After all, we're talking about practices that are today recognized as indefensibly, and obviously, wrong. We know that the traffic of the human species is evil and wicked, so what do we really learn by hearing figures like Cugoano say so? Well, for starters, you shouldn't assume that responses to slavery by thinkers of the Africana world were always condemnations of that practice. We'll shortly be meeting Jacobus Capitein, a black thinker of the eighteenth century who, shockingly from our present perspective, defended the compatibility of Christianity and slavery.

Still, as you might expect, Capitein is an exception to the rule. In the more typical case of anti-slavery thinkers, the interest lies in seeing the moral and political principles, the distinctions and arguments, and the broader conceptual frameworks that they offered in what turns out to be a richly varied and complex set of objections to slavery. We'll be asking whether these constituted cogent and effective ways to argue against slavery, and inquiring into the broader implications that follow from their conceptions of humanity, dignity, labor, and the like. Another question with moral and political aspects is how slavery and oppression should be resisted: is violence permissible, and if so under what circumstances? Should black people seek to create separate political spaces and institutions, or attempt to integrate into the majority white population?

Then too, even in a work like Cugoano's *Thoughts and Sentiments*, moral and political matters are not the only matters of philosophical interest that come up. Cugoano responds to interpretations of the Bible as condoning slavery by developing a theory of how God communicates with human beings through symbols, including elements of the natural world. He thus raises important questions of theology, metaphysics, and hermeneutics. To explore philosophy produced in the wake of slavery is not to study only the philosophy of slavery, even in cases like Cugoano's, where the nature of slavery is among his central concerns.

For another hint at how much there is for us to explore, we will spend the rest of this chapter discussing a writer and thinker who came along much earlier than Cugoano. In the Iberian peninsula in the sixteenth century, the time during which the transatlantic slave trade first began to flourish, we find the oldest known book published in a European language by someone of sub-Saharan African descent, a book of poetry by a man known as Juan Latino.[6] He was born in 1516, or perhaps in 1518, and the date of his death is even less certain, as it has been estimated to be either in the last decade of the sixteenth century or in the first decade of the seventeenth. Among the many other things about Latino that we do not know for certain is where he was born. An autobiographical note in his second book of poetry states that he was "taken out of Ethiopia in infancy," which we can take to mean that he was captured in West Africa and brought away as a slave at a young age. (Here the word "Ethiopia" need not refer to the country in the Horn of Africa. It most likely represents appropriation of the classical use of the term to refer to black Africa in general, which is a usage that we'll be encountering regularly.) On the other hand, some sources suggest he was born in Spain.

Whether it was he or his parents who were brought forcibly to Spain, we know that he grew up a slave in the household of the Count of Cabra and his wife, Elvira. Latino was a personal servant and companion to their son, who was, through his mother, the third Duke of Sessa. When the family moved from Baena to Granada after the count's death, the young duke began to study at the Cathedral of Granada. It appears that his servant benefited from attending these lessons as well. He began to show great aptitude in Greek and especially in Latin. The name "Latino" is, in fact, a nickname bestowed as recognition of Juan's consummate skill in Latin (he may not have previously had any surname). Latino's talent led him to achieve multiple degrees from the University of Granada and eventually become a respected Professor of Grammar at the university.

While in this position, he wrote poetry in Latin and, in 1573, published his first book of poetry; we won't bother you with the title because, to the extent that it has one at all, it is a page-length description of the book's contents![7] It is usually simply referred to by the title of the important poem, the *Austrias Carmen*, also known as the *Austriad* or, as Elizabeth Wright translates its title, the *Song of John of Austria*. John of Austria was the illegitimate son of King Charles V, one of the Habsburg rulers of Spain, and while John's half-brother Philip II was on the Spanish throne, John led the naval fleet that defeated the Ottoman empire at the Battle of Lepanto in 1571. Latino's *Austriad* tells the story of the Battle of Lepanto, celebrating Spain's glorious victory over the Turks.

Latino was clearly an exceptional and perhaps unprecedented figure, though ultimately not unique: we'll soon be meeting other black authors who rose from slavery to become noteworthy literary figures. Scholars generally assume that somewhere along the way, Latino was freed from slavery, and he seems to imply as much in the autobiographical note previously mentioned. But we have no clear record of his manumission. In fact, Spanish Golden Age playwright Diego Ximenez de Enciso wrote a play about him early in the seventeenth century, called *The Famous Drama of Juan Latino*, which has as a central plot point the idea that Latino remained a slave even while pursuing knowledge, literary excellence, and love. When his love interest is reluctant to marry him in this subjugated state, the fictionalized Latino asks: "Can soul be slave?"[8]

Latino also reflects on his status as a black author in his own works. In a poem from his book introducing the *Austriad*, addressed to King Philip II, Latino asks permission from the king to sing the praises of the king's brother. He suggests that the uniqueness of John's victory requires the uniqueness of a black poet to celebrate it. To the potential objection that there would be something distasteful about having a black poet play this role, he responds:

> For if our black face, oh king, displeases your emissaries,
>   a white one does not please men of Aethiopia.
> There, a white man who visits the East is considered vile,
>   and there are black leaders, and there is even a dark-skinned king.[9]

Latino here points out the contextual limits of racism: the white part of the world is but one part of the larger whole, and its irrational prejudices are no more indicative of the truth than the prejudices that can be found elsewhere. Furthermore, it makes no sense to associate blackness with slavery given the existence of powerful black rulers.

With intellectual moves like these, Latino was, as we might nowadays say, getting out in front of the problem early, as a contrast between two further responses to black writing in Latin may demonstrate. In 1605, Miguel de Cervantes published the first volume of his famous *Don Quixote*, and in a prefatory poem addressed to the book itself by a character called Urganda the Unknown, he makes reference to the esteemed Professor of Grammar in Granada, saying: "Since it did not please Heaven / That you would turn out as clever / As the black Juan Latino / Avoid speaking Latin."[10] Is there sarcasm here? One imagines that Cervantes sees his own choice to write solely in Spanish, avoiding Latin, as legitimate. Perhaps then Latino is implicitly damned with this praise for his love of a dead language. Nevertheless, Cervantes—who, incidentally, had experienced slavery himself, having been held captive for five years in Algeria—does not appear to have any doubts about Latino's intelligence.

Around a century later, a black man named Francis Williams was born free in Jamaica, spent some time being educated in England, and wrote some poetry in Latin.[11] The famous Scottish philosopher David Hume discusses Williams in a 1753 revision of his essay, "Of National Characters." In a footnote, he writes: "I am apt to suspect the negroes, and in general all the other species of men (for there are four or five different kinds) to be naturally inferior to the whites." Alluding to Williams, he goes on to write: "In Jamaica, indeed, they talk of one negroe as a man of parts and learning; but 'tis likely he is admired for very slender accomplishments, like a parrot, who speaks a few words plainly."[12] This comment from someone generally recognized as one of the most brilliant philosophical minds, not just of his time but of all time, indicates how common and influential the corrosive ideas of natural white superiority and black inferiority had become by the middle of the eighteenth century. As we will see when we discuss Phillis Wheatley, another black African who learned Latin and wrote poetry, albeit poetry in English, Hume's dismissal of Williams as a "parrot" would not be the last time a black poet of the eighteenth century was compared to a caged bird.

23

DUALIST PERSONALITY

Anton Wilhelm Amo

Who, then, was the first white European scholar to admit that black Africans are capable of sophisticated philosophical reflection, to avoid making the sort of mistake committed by Hume? Some might think first of Placide Tempels, pioneer of twentieth century ethnophilosophy. As it turns out, though, even putting aside his doubts about the ability of the Bantu to express their views with sophistication, Tempels came along about 200 years late to claim this particular distinction. Already in the year 1733, Johann Gottfried Kraus, the rector of the University of Wittenberg, hailed the achievements of an African philosopher at his institution.[1] Unlike Tempels, he did not assume that it would take a white European to reveal and articulate the philosophical profundity of African thought. To the contrary, the rector pointed out that the continent had long been a source of eloquent wisdom. He mentioned ancient figures of Roman Africa like Terence, Apuleius, Tertullian, and Augustine. While conceding that Africa has been less fertile in this respect in more recent times, he was pleased to report that his own university hosted living proof that Africans could still be accomplished scholars. The scholar he had in mind was Anton Wilhelm Amo.

Amo's story is remarkable, though he was not the only African to achieve a notable career in early eighteenth century Europe. Indeed it may be that he was raised and educated in imitation of the similar treatment given to Abram Petrovich Gannibal at the Russian court of Peter the Great.[2] Gannibal, named after the great North African general Hannibal, ultimately became a military officer himself after being adopted by the czar; the story is told in a biography written by Gannibal's great-grandson, none other than the famous Russian poet Alexander Pushkin. Probably Amo was, like Gannibal, taken as a slave from his homeland. This was Nzemaland, in modern-day Ghana, meaning that Amo was born into a culture we have often had occasion to mention, that of the Akan. We'll come back to this point below.

Once transported to Europe, Amo evidently received an excellent education while growing up in the household of the Duke of Wolfenbüttel. We know that Amo was baptized there in 1707, but not much else about his early life.[3] It is really with his university career that he arrives in the pages of documented history. He first appears at the University of Halle in 1727, where he studies philosophy and law; then moves to the University of Wittenberg, where he presents his best-known work, an "inaugural dissertation" on the relation of mind and body, in the year 1734. In 1736, he is found back at Halle, and, in 1739, at Jena, where he receives citizenship in 1747. In a document applying for the right to teach at Jena, Amo emphasizes his poverty, giving us the sense of a struggling itinerant academic, rather than a creature of courtly success like his Russian counterpart Gannibal.

Amo's life story takes an unexpected turn when, for reasons that are unclear—one explanation points to a failed love affair, and many suspect an atmosphere of growing racial intolerance[4]—he returns to his native land, the so-called "Gold Coast" (which, as we said, later became the country of Ghana). A contemporary report explains that he was about 50 years old at this time, and that he established himself in his hometown of Axim as a kind of diviner or prophet. This may seem surprising, given that, as we're about to see, Amo's written works show him to be a paradigmatic early eighteenth century thinker, engaging with the thought of philosophers like René Descartes and his fellow Wilhelm, that is, Gottfried Wilhelm Leibniz. But the report on his return to Africa asserts that along with philosophy and an impressive range of languages, both modern and classical, Amo had mastered the study of astrology and astronomy. This is supported by the fact that, in a teaching plan Amo presented for lectures to be delivered in Jena, the topics to be covered included divination and astrology.[5] So perhaps it is, after all, quite natural that Amo was easily able to step into the role of a diviner and sage upon returning to his native homeland.

Whatever the case, the works left to us by Amo reflect his interest in a different set of questions. They are highly technical and rigorous philosophical treatises on human nature, epistemology, logic, and the mind, and follow the conventions of academic dissertations of the period, which lay out a series of claims and supporting arguments, with further defense being offered in a live disputation.[6] It is a form of writing that recalls the procedures of medieval scholastic philosophy. Amo makes a big show of laying down definitions of his key terms and setting up a dialectical dispute with rival thinkers, and the idea that university masters should qualify by performing in a disputation is itself a medieval inheritance. But it's also clear that things have moved on from medieval philosophical discourse. Amo claims to be starting from "clear and distinct ideas," a phrase we readily associate with the paradigmatic early modern philosopher, René Descartes, and Descartes himself is one of the targets Amo selects for refutation.

All three of Amo's extant works were written in the 1730s. Two were dissertations on the relationship between the mind and the body presented at Wittenberg and the third was a treatise on philosophical method published in Halle in 1738. The first dissertation, *On the Impassivity of the Human Mind*, is his most famous work and one that we will discuss in some detail momentarily. The second, entitled the *Philosophical Disputation Containing a Distinct Idea of Those Things That Pertain Either to the Mind or to Our Living and Organic Body*, builds on the first dissertation, working out some of its implications. Scholars have often declined to attribute this second dissertation to Amo, as it was defended as a dissertation by one Johann Theodosius Meiner. It has often been assumed that this is a student of Amo's and the *Philosophical Disputation* was merely supervised rather than written by Amo. This is, as it turns out, a misunderstanding of how defending dissertations in early modern European universities worked. The person defending a dissertation wasn't always the dissertation's author. The content, as well as references in the *Philosophical Disputation* to *On the Impassivity of the Human Mind* and to both previous works in Amo's third and final extant writing, all make it clear that he, not Meiner, is the author of the *Philosophical Disputation*.[7]

The title of that third and final work, the *Treatise on the Art of Philosophizing Soberly and Accurately*, makes clear that it is Amo's summation not merely of his thoughts on the relationship between the mind and the body but of all that is essential for philosophy. He introduces concepts and distinctions of various sorts, concerning the nature of things, differences and relations between aspects of thought, and rules for thinking clearly. His definition of philosophy in this work is one that many today might still find attractive and inspiring: "philosophy is the habit of the intellect and of the will, by which we continually undertake to determinately and adequately know things themselves, with certainty to the extent possible; and by means of the application of this sort of cognition, the perfection of man gains in possible increments" (General Part, chapter II, member II, §1).

Let's return now to his first dissertation, which bears as its full title *On the Impassivity of the Human Mind, or the Absence of Sensation and of the Faculty of Sensing in the Human Mind and their Presence in Our Organic and Living Body*.[8] Actually, that title already provides a useful summary of Amo's philosophical position in the dissertation. He wants to argue that the mind is not, as some philosophers of the period wanted to claim, "affected" when we experience sensation. Suppose that you see a giraffe loping across the African savannah and think: "what a majestic beast!" A natural way to explain this is that your eyes have been affected by the pattern on the giraffe's skin, the lighting conditions, and so on, in order to have a visual experience. Your mind is, in turn, affected by that sensory encounter and moved to think that you are seeing a giraffe.

But Amo rejects this apparently commonsense account, and for good reason: he is a strict dualist, who refuses to believe that mind can be affected by body. For him, the mental and the physical are two very different kinds of thing. Whereas the body can be passively affected, the mind is a "spirit," which means that it is "purely active" and indeed perpetually engaged in understanding (*Impassivity*, ch. 1, member 1, §1). Since sensation is, for Amo, defined as being really affected by the properties of material things in one's environment (ch. 1, member 2), there can be no sensation in the mind. Amo's worry was not a new one. Dualist theories of mind go back to antiquity, and throughout that history, dualism has faced the problem of explaining how the soul or mind can interact with the body. If we take seriously the idea that spirit and body are fundamentally different, then the fact that light affecting the eye can yield a judgment in the mind, or that a choice made by the soul could result in the moving of one's arm, may seem downright inexplicable. It would be as if the number four were to drink a cup of coffee.

Nor is Amo the first dualist who flatly denies that the body can affect the mind. In fact, he isn't even the first African philosopher to deny it. The late ancient Neoplatonist Plotinus, who hailed from Egypt, wrote a treatise which bears a similar (though mercifully briefer) title to that of Amo's dissertation, *On the Impassivity of Incorporeal Things*.[9] But Amo's own points of reference are more recent. He is especially opposed to contemporary thinkers who avoid the problem simply by rejecting strict dualism. Here he would be thinking especially of the vitalist teaching of Georg Ernst Stahl, who believed that the body could interact with the soul in a straightforwardly physical manner, an idea that fit well with medical theories that depicted the human as a psychosomatic unity. Stahl's ideas were dominant at Amo's initial academic environment, the University of Halle. It has been hypothesized that Amo moved from there to Wittenberg in order to find a more congenial intellectual setting, where his dualist anthropology would find support.[10]

Wittenberg was a redoubt of dualist philosophy, and in particular of the ideas of Christian Wolff, who may have helped to inspire Amo's own position. One might assume that Amo would see Descartes too as an ally, given that Descartes is the most famous dualist in early modern philosophy, to the point that nowadays philosophers use the term "Cartesian" as a near synonym for "dualist." Yet as we've mentioned, Amo instead singles him out for criticism. One might say that for Amo, even

Descartes himself was not enough of a Cartesian.[11] He takes exception to a passage in which Descartes admits that the mind "acts and suffers" together with the body (*Impassivity*, ch. 2, "State of the controversy"). Amo thinks that it would have been more consistent for Descartes to adhere rigorously to a dualist position according to which the mind's act of understanding is in no way passive and thus cannot suffer or undergo any bodily caused effects. In other words, you are not caused to think you are seeing a giraffe, or understand anything about giraffes, by seeing a giraffe. Nothing at the bodily level can causally affect the mind.

But of course Amo does not want to deny that the mind somehow registers the presence of a giraffe when one sees a giraffe, or has the idea of giraffes on the basis of encountering them. To the contrary, he adheres to an empiricist theory of knowledge according to which, as he says in the *Treatise*, "Nothing is in the intellect that was not previously in the senses" (*Tractatus*, Special Part, ch. 2, member 1, §2). This makes us humans different from God, or the angels. Whereas those more exalted entities can understand without sensory input, our knowledge is always dependent on the mind's close connection to the body (*Impassivity*, ch. 1, member 1, §1, explanation 2). Once time travel is invented, someone should go back to Amo's defense of his dissertation and push him on this very point. In his writings, he is not very forthcoming about how ideas do appear in the mind thanks to sense-experiences. It seems clear that for him, what happens at the level of sensation is a brute physical or mechanical event, the mere reception of a "sensible quality" (*Tractatus*, General Part, ch. 4, §1). Somehow the mind is then able to form what Amo calls "intentions" concerning the qualities that have been received by sensation.

This is a purely active process, comparable to the mind's choosing to pursue a certain purpose in practical deliberation. Amo thus refers to both the sensible object and the object of a volition as an "end" that the mind consciously intends (*Tractatus*, General Part, ch. 1, member 1, §1). So whether you are identifying a giraffe as the majestic beast you are seeing as it lopes across the savannah, or identifying it as the target of some practical choice—perhaps you've decided to give her a birthday present, like an extremely long scarf—the giraffe is the "end" determined by an intentional, conscious act of the mind. While Amo's view fits into the dualist tradition of Leibniz and Wolff, he is staking out an original position. In particular he makes no use of the Leibnizian idea of "pre-established harmony," whereby events at the level of mind and of body arise independently, yet correspond to one other without any causal influence across the divide.[12] For him the mind does indeed interact with the physical environment, but in a way that is entirely active.

At this point you may be wondering whether it really makes sense to think of Amo as part of the story of Africana philosophy. Sure, he was a black African, but his philosophical concerns, and indeed his philosophical contributions, seem to belong squarely within early modern European thought. Even Paulin Hountondji, who famously defined African philosophy as simply the set of texts written by Africans and described as philosophical by these authors themselves, saw something ill-fitting in the classification of Amo as part of the history of African philosophy. From his universalist, anti-ethnophilosophical point of view, Hountondji does see reason to celebrate what he describes as Amo's "direct and frank dialogue with the great philosophical works of his time and his unaffected and questioning relationship with them."[13] Yet he notes that Amo, as a result of his historical circumstances, could only ever aim his philosophical writings at Europeans. These works were not offered up for the purpose of a conversation among his fellow Africans. This is the sense in which Hountondji views Amo's work as belonging "entirely to a non-African theoretical tradition."[14]

There are a couple of ways to think differently about this question, though. First, we should consider a tentative proposal made by Kwasi Wiredu.[15] As we've seen, Amo came from the Akan people. We learned earlier that the Akan recognize two spiritual powers or principles that help to constitute the human being, the *kra* and *sunsum*, both of which are at least arguably immaterial and thus fundamentally distinct from the body (Chapter 15). Might this have been an influence on Amo's dualist philosophy? Intriguing though this proposal is, it seems rather unlikely given that, as Wiredu himself concedes, Amo was a very young child when transported from his original home. If Amo was ever aware of a resonance between his own philosophy and Akan beliefs, then it could presumably only have been something he discovered upon his return to Africa later in life. It's a nice thought, but probably not relevant for interpreting the academic treatises he wrote while in Germany.

There is a second and much more direct way to connect Amo with the concerns of African peoples. We have not yet mentioned that, in addition to the three rather scholastic treatises we have from his pen, he had earlier defended a very different thesis, concerning the legal status of Africans, or "Moors," living in Europe.[16] Frustratingly, we do not have the written version of this work. In fact, it may be that there never was a written version and that it was only a matter of defending a thesis in a verbal debate. We do however know the gist of his argument, thanks to an academic report from Halle, where the disputation was held. Amo appears to have appealed to the fact that the "Moors" were subjects of the Roman empire via their rulers, who were vassals of emperors like Justinian. Here the word "Moor," if appropriate at all, should apply only to the people of northern Africa who fell into the orbit of Roman power, but Amo was presumably broadening the notion to include all Africans. After all, Amo himself was called a "Moor" by his German contemporaries. On the basis of this historical evidence, Amo went on to investigate the extent of freedom that should be granted to "Moors" enslaved to Christians in Europe. As the Ghanaian philosopher William Abraham has interpreted it, the "kernel of Amo's argument was that Africans were entitled to the same immunities and privileges to precisely the extent that the erstwhile European vassals of Rome enjoyed them, for the African kings had been likewise subject to Rome."[17] Or to quote another modern-day scholar, Justin E.H. Smith, we have here "an argument, made by a slave, against the legitimacy of the institution of slavery, founded in jurisprudence and historical scholarship on Roman law."[18]

Remarkable as this is, we should stress both the limits of our knowledge of what Amo was arguing here and the limits of that argument itself. The report is so sketchy that we are, in fact, making an assumption when supposing that Amo must have concluded that slavery is illegitimate. Even if he did, it is worth noting that Amo did not appeal to a theory of natural rights to justify the freedom and equality of Africans. Instead, he appealed to conventional, legal rights deriving from the imperial reach of classical Rome, and presumably the connection between classical Roman law and the rights available to the inhabitants of the empire's latter-day heir, the Holy Roman Empire. Famously described by the French philosopher Voltaire as neither holy nor Roman nor an empire, this was nevertheless an important political entity for Amo, as it was within this set of mainly German territories that Amo was raised and educated. Basing an attack on slavery on the imagined connection between ancient Rome and the modern Holy Roman Empire may have been a useful strategy for persuading Amo's immediate audience, although it is obviously a rather precarious basis for the rejection of slavery.

Legal convention could be invoked in favor of slavery too, as we can see in a work by a contemporary of Amo's who had a similar life story, involving enslavement in Africa as a child followed by an education in Europe and finally a return to the homeland. His name was Jacobus Elisa Johannes Capitein.[19] After being taken as a slave while still a child and sold at a spot in what is now Côte d'Ivoire, he was given as a present to a merchant of the West India Company stationed at the Gold Coast, by the name of Jacob van Goch. (The name "Capitein" is apparently an allusion to the ship "captain" who gave him to van Goch.) In 1728, the young Capitein was in Holland, meaning that he was automatically manumitted: slavery was illegal in the Netherlands, even though the Dutch were keeping and selling slaves elsewhere in the world. Capitein's mission in life was set early. And we do mean "mission." Inspired by the theologian Hendrik Velse, a young Capitein wrote an essay called *Call of the Heathen* (*De vocatione ethnicorum*) in 1737, arguing for the need to do missionary work in non-Christian lands like his native Africa. This essay is lost, but

Capitein provides us with a summary of its contents, along with a brief autobiography, at the beginning of a lecture on slavery and its compatibility with Christian doctrine, which he delivered at the University of Leiden in 1742.[20]

Capitein's lecture provides us with a glimpse at arguments against slavery, since he dutifully explains the abolitionist position he is refuting. His opponents quote such biblical texts as "the truth will set you free" (John 8:32) to show that Christianity is a religion of liberation, not servitude (ch. 3, §9). Capitein agrees that Christianity is concerned with freedom, but insists that this means only spiritual freedom, that is, the soul's liberation from sin. It has nothing to do with freedom of the body. This is not to say that slavery is a good thing. Capitein ties its existence to the "degradation of the human race" (ch. 2, §4) and concedes that Christianity encourages benevolent treatment of slaves and setting them free (ch. 3, §16).

This gives us, for the second time in this chapter, a parallel between a modern African philosopher and an ancient African philosopher: in this case, Augustine, whose *City of God* condones slavery while identifying its existence as an unfortunate consequence of sin (book 9). Capitein likewise denies that it is obligatory to set slaves free, as slavery is accepted in the law of the Old Testament (ch. 2, §5 and 7, citing Leviticus 25) and, according to Capitein, Roman history provides no legal basis for abolition. Here we see that Capitein was fighting on the same territory chosen by Amo. He also treats slavery as a legal, not moral, issue, and one that calls for us to look back to the practices of antiquity. Capitein's conclusion is that slavery is an institution established "not by nature but the law of nations" (ch. 2, §2). On this basis he explicitly rejects Aristotle's alternative rationalization: that some people are simply born slavish by nature (ch. 2, §1).

Despite this rejection of the idea of natural slavery, it may seem not just disappointing, but inexplicable, that an ex-slave like Capitein should defend the practice of slavery on legal and religious grounds. But it is easier to understand if we consider his intellectual project as a whole. Following the lead of his mentor Velse, Capitein is a theologian whose main aim is to promote missionary work among the "heathens." Accepting that adherence to the Christian faith is incompatible with slavery would mean that missionary work should go hand in hand with abolition. Christians should, in that case, not be enslaving anyone, and certainly not those they are trying to "liberate" by bringing them the news of the gospel. The problem, from Capitein's perspective, is that such a position could undermine enthusiasm for missionary activity in Africa. So he instead pursues what we must recognize as a lamentably modest goal, even if he himself saw it as the most exalted of aspirations: the freeing of souls rather than bodies. Insofar as he pursued it not just in writing but also in life, this project was mostly a failure. He was ordained after graduation from Leiden, thus becoming the first African ordained as a minister by a Protestant church. He then returned to Africa to undertake missionary work, but found this an uphill struggle. Conversions were few and he was beset by financial and personal difficulties before dying at the tender age of 30.[21]

It's ironic that Capitein, like Amo albeit in a far less philosophically sophisticated manner, placed so much emphasis on the difference between body and soul. For Capitein, this contrast could be used to justify slavery of the body, since it is only the soul that counts in Christian theology. For Amo, by contrast, the "impassivity" of the mind may have been bound up with the stance he took *against* slavery. It is clear from his writings that Amo considered human persons to be disembodied minds. He saw them as entirely independent from the influence of body, not only as they experience sensation but as they form the intentions leading to moral action. This radical dualism is a natural fit for an egalitarian view of human nature. To quote Justin E.H. Smith once again, for Amo "humanity is rooted in something metaphysical," namely an immaterial spirit, and "a spirit cannot have a race."[22]

So in opposing the psychosomatic theory of vitalism, Amo had a strong basis to deny that black Africans are slavish because of their supposedly inferior bodies. That would leave only legal and conventional arguments for slavery, and it is especially here that we assume he would have parted ways with Capitein, since his own position seems to have been that the precedent of Roman law should lead to abolition. Nor should we overlook the more direct challenge Amo posed to the ideology of slavery, just by being who he was. When the Rector of Wittenberg held him up as an example of the erudition of which black Africans are capable, he was simply stating what must have been obvious to anyone brought face to face with this formidable scholar. Later on, his name would be mentioned by abolitionists like the French priest and revolutionary Abbé Henri Grégoire, who saw in Amo's works powerful evidence that a so-called "Moor" need not be less than any other human being.

24

TALKING BOOK

Early Africana Writing in English

Sometimes you don't know whether to laugh or cry. You're in that middle ground between comedy and tragedy, the realm of the "tragicomic." It's not an effect that is easy to pull off in a book or movie, to pull on the heartstrings even while tickling the funny bone. And among books, about the last place you'd expect to find tragicomedy is in a slave narrative. Such narratives, autobiographical accounts of the experience of slavery, came to play a very important role in the fight for the abolition of slavery and thus often had an explicitly political purpose.[1] Given that purpose, and their horrific subject matter, these stories are far more apt to provoke tears than laughter. Yet there is a legitimately tragicomic moment in the 1772 book that has some claim to be the very first slave narrative, a claim that warrants its self-confident title, *A Narrative of the Most Remarkable Particulars in the Life of James Albert Ukawsaw Gronniosaw, an African Prince, as Related by Himself*. Gronniosaw's narrative was not so clearly intended as a piece of political activism. A preface to the work by a man named Walter Shirley tells us that a young woman in Leominster, England, whose name we are not given, took down Gronniosaw's words "for her own private satisfaction." The decision to publish was made, first and foremost, as a way of providing relief to Gronniosaw and his family, given their poverty (*UV* 32).[2] Nevertheless, the *Narrative* is pioneering in its first-hand account of Gronniosaw's birth into royalty somewhere in or near what is now northern Nigeria, the journey away from home that ended in him being sold to the captain of a Dutch slave ship, and his various life experiences after that fateful moment.

It is as he describes his voyage across the Atlantic that we get the tragicomic story of Gronniosaw's first encounter with books. Speaking about the Dutch captain who bought him, Gronniosaw relates: "He used to read prayers in public to the ship's crew every Sabbath day; and when first I saw him read, I was never so surprised in my whole life as when I saw the book talk to my master; for I thought it did, as I observed him to look upon it, and move his lips.—I wished it would do so to me.—As soon as my master had done reading I follow'd him to the place where he put the book, being mightily delighted with it, and when nobody saw me, I open'd it and put my ear down close upon it, in great hope that it wou'd say something to me" (*UV* 38). An amusing scene at first, but tragedy is close at hand, as Gronniosaw adds: "I was very sorry and greatly disappointed when I found it would not speak; this thought immediately presented itself to me, that every body and every thing despis'd me because I was black."

As Henry Louis Gates Jr. has observed, Gronniosaw was only the first of numerous black authors in the eighteenth century to describe a first encounter with books marked by misunderstanding.[3] We find such a scene in a book published in 1785 called *A Narrative of the Lord's Wonderful Dealings with John Marrant, A Black*, although in Marrant's autobiography, it is not he but rather a Cherokee princess who tries in vain to listen to his Bible while stopping her father, the king, from taking Marrant's life. In the aforementioned political treatise by Quobna Ottobah Cugoano (which features discussion of Gronniosaw and Marrant's narratives), we find yet another scene in which a royal figure in the Americas listens to a book in hopes of hearing it talk. Here, the royal figure is not someone Cugoano encountered personally, but rather Atahualpa, the last emperor of the Incas. While condemning the injustices of the European colonization of the Americas, Cugoano tells how Atahualpa angered the Spaniards by disdainfully throwing to the ground a liturgical book that refused to speak.

And there's more. A friend and collaborator of Cugoano's, named Olaudah Equiano, was the eighteenth century's most critically and commercially successful black author. If Gronniosaw's narrative was something of a first, then the 1789 publication of *The Interesting Narrative of the Life of Olaudah Equiano* represents a high point, recognized ever since as a particularly masterful and influential instance of the slave narrative genre. Equiano too writes of being a young boy, enslaved and stolen from West Africa, putting his ear to a book to hear it talk and being "very much concerned" when it said nothing (*UV* 211). What can we conclude from these parallel scenes, apart from the fact that eighteenth century people were crying out for the invention of the audiobook?

Well, Gates for one considers what he calls the "trope of the talking book" to be a significant feature of black writing in the eighteenth century. (And he finds it in at least one nineteenth century text, *The Life, History, and Unparalleled Sufferings of John Jea the African Preacher*, published in 1811.) It shows, first, that we have here a literary tradition with authors intentionally repeating and revising each other's imagery, a process Gates calls "signifyin'." But the trope is more than a sign of literary influence. It is a reflection on literature and literacy itself. These works by black authors, most of whom were formerly enslaved, offer us rare glimpses into the inner lives of people of the African diaspora, during a time when most were not merely unable to read and write but forcibly kept in this condition. The image of a book that must have something to say, but refuses to speak, poignantly captures the condition of ignorance systematically enforced upon enslaved Africans. Against this background, the creation of literature by black authors is little short of miraculous. These authors made books talk: telling their own stories, expressing their feelings, and articulating their philosophical thoughts.

We should note, however, that illiteracy in European languages, even when enforced by law, did not always mean complete illiteracy. Having learned something about Islam in Africa earlier in this book, you ought not be surprised that many enslaved Africans were literate in Arabic. It is difficult to say exactly how many Africans brought to the Americas in the transatlantic slave trade were Muslim, though one scholar has suggested that the number could be as high as 3 million.[4] Not all of these enslaved Muslims would have been literate, of course. But estimates of the literacy rate in Muslim West Africa suggest that Muslims enslaved in the Americas would, ironically, have had a higher rate than that found among their white slaveholders.[5] Some of these literate enslaved people produced slave narratives. A forerunner of Gronniosaw's contribution to the genre was an account of the life of a literate Fulani man known as Job Ben Solomon, who came from what is now Senegal and was brought as a slave to Maryland. In 1734, almost forty years before Gronniosaw's narrative was published, Job's life story was published by his friend Thomas Bluett, who had accompanied him to England after Job was freed and who helped to make possible his passage back to Africa. One might thus think of Bluett as the author and biographer, whereas in the case of Gronniosaw we have a first-person narrative (albeit one dictated to someone else). Nonetheless, at least one scholar has been willing to proclaim Job a "father of African American literature."[6]

Looking ahead to the nineteenth century, we have at least two cases in which enslaved Muslim Africans wrote their own autobiographies in Arabic: ʿUmar ibn Saʿīd, who wrote the story of his life while still enslaved in North Carolina in 1831, and Abū Bakr al-Ṣiddīq, who wrote his life story in Jamaica in 1834.[7] Another enslaved Muslim in Jamaica named Muḥammad Kabā, with whom al-Ṣiddīq corresponded, used the pages of a Baptist Missionary Society notebook to write his *Kitāb al-Ṣalāt* (*Book of Prayer*). If we add this to the philosophical material by Muslims that we have discussed earlier, we see that the study of philosophy in the Islamic world takes you not only to places like Cairo and Córdoba, and not just to Timbuktu and Sokoto, but also the Caribbean![8]

But let's not get ahead of ourselves. For now, we want to stay in the eighteenth century, focusing on the philosophical dimensions of black writing in English. While the sixteenth century gave us Juan Latino and while there were important fictional representations of black perspectives in the seventeenth century, such as Aphra Behn's famous *Oroonoko* (1688), it is really in the eighteenth century that we have a critical mass of writing by black authors in European languages. We've seen that some Africana authors from this time, like Francis Williams, Anton Wilhelm Amo, and Jacobus Capitein, set their thoughts down in Latin. But most writing by black authors in a European language in the eighteenth century was in the same language you are reading right now: English.

Not counting more ambiguous cases like that of Job Ben Solomon, the first work of prose to be published in English by a black author was *A Narrative of the Uncommon Sufferings, and Suprizing Deliverance of Briton Hammon, a Negro Man* (1760).[9] It tells the story of a black man from New England who is shipwrecked off the coast of southern Florida, captured by Native Americans, and liberated by a Spanish ship, only to experience a long period of imprisonment in Cuba, and then more adventure after escaping that island. Disconcertingly, the story culminates in his happy reunion in England with a man he refers to as his "master." But was Hammon a slave to this master? Or was he a servant, using the word "master" interchangeably with "employer"? Scholars are divided on this point. Even if he was a slave, though, the narrative is really not about slavery, fitting instead into a popular genre of the time: captivity narratives, amongst which stories of capture by Native Americans were particularly common. Tales in this genre are notorious for mixing fact with fiction, and Hammon's account of his captivity may be at least partially fabricated. The work is perhaps more telling for its depictions of Native Americans as savages than for anything unique to the black experience.[10] Having said that, Hammon closes his narrative by asserting that his adventures must be interpreted as evidence of God's providential care, for he was, as he puts it, "most grievously afflicted, and yet thro' the Divine Goodness, as miraculously preserved" (*UV* 24). As we'll be seeing, this theme of divine providence was characteristic of early Africana literature in English.

Indeed, this invocation of providence brings us back to Gronniosaw, whose narrative is far more philosophical than is typically appreciated. He represents his childhood as unhappy because he had a "curious turn of mind" and sought answers to questions that struck his family members as pointless (*UV* 34). He was especially curious about what "superior power" might lie beyond the sun, moon, and stars, which he says were worshipped by his people (*UV* 34). When he asked his mother how that people came to be, she began to speak of past generations, but Gronniosaw insisted that his question was: "who made the *First Man*"? (*UV* 35). This is puzzling. Gronniosaw seems to be suggesting that the idea of a transcendent deity was foreign to his people, yet he tells us that he comes from Bornu, and the Kanem-Bornu empire in West Africa was predominantly Muslim. Even if he belonged to a non-Muslim people in the area, it seems odd that he should grow up unaware of monotheism. Equally surprising, and for the same reason, is his supposed unfamiliarity with books: even an illiterate person from this area would presumably have known about the Quran.[11] But if the narrative is historically unconvincing, there is a clear philosophical purpose afoot. Gronniosaw's youthful fixation on the idea of a transcendent being is the first step in a process of pursuing divine truth, a process facilitated by God's providential ordering of events.

Later on in the narrative, while a slave in New York to a Dutch preacher, Gronniosaw has a mystical experience that assures him of his soul's salvation. Even in his enslavement, he says, "I would not have changed situations, or been any one but myself for the whole world. I blest God for my poverty, that I had no worldly riches or grandeur to draw my heart from Him" (*UV* 42). Again, we may find this disconcerting. Why does he focus on the glory of conversion instead of the ills of slavery? Especially alarming is the seeming implication that it was, on balance, a good thing that he had been enslaved. As this already begins to show, slave narratives, especially those of the eighteenth century, are more complicated intellectual affairs than one might have thought. These usually Christian authors had to reconcile their brutal experiences of slavery with their understanding of God as a benign sovereign. The classic philosophical question of theodicy—how to justify belief in an all-powerful, all-knowing, and loving God given the existence of evil in the world—is naturally raised again and again by the work of black writers of this era.

One might also be critical of Gronniosaw's attitude towards his African heritage. Gates draws attention to a passage in which Gronniosaw says he was happy that the captain of the slave ship removed the golden rings he wore around his neck, arms, and legs. For Gates this displays a willingness to be rid of his African culture. Together with the lament about being black in the passage on the talking book, Gates infers that the narrative as a whole describes a process of assimilation, a symbolic, if not physical, "passage from black man to white."[12] But it's hard to square this with the way Gronniosaw is repeatedly disappointed by the behavior of white people, many of whom take advantage of him following his emancipation. It is also, at least for the modern reader, rather more comic than tragic that Gronniosaw tells us how his admiration for classic English works on Christianity led him to imagine England as a place full of holy people, so that he was shocked upon arriving there to hear people using—heaven forbid—foul language! The main theme of Gronniosaw's narrative would seem to be that, with all the discomforts, hardships, and iniquities that one can encounter everywhere, from Africa to North America to Europe, we are ultimately homeless pilgrims while on earth, awaiting arrival in our "heavenly home" for true rest and delivery from evil (*UV* 53).

Let us now rewind for a moment to 1760. That year gave us not only Briton Hammon's narrative, but also a poem published on Christmas day called "An Evening Thought," subtitled "Salvation by Christ, with Penitential Cries." The author was identified as "Jupiter Hammon, a Negro belonging to Mr. Lloyd, of Queen's-Village, on Long-Island." We have no reason to think Jupiter was related to Briton, despite the coincidence of two pioneering black authors in English writing in 1760, both named Hammon. Jupiter was already 49 years old when he published his "Evening Thought," in which he gives thanks for salvation and exhorts all nations to come to Jesus. By September of 1786, shortly before his seventy-fifth birthday, he produced the last of his well-known writings, which was not a poem but a kind of speech or open letter entitled "An Address to the Negroes in the State of New-York."

Jupiter wrote this "Address" while still enslaved. Yet again we are liable to be surprised and disconcerted by his frank statement that "for my own part I do not wish to be free" (72).[13] Especially since, just before this, he has acknowledged that "liberty is a great thing, and worth seeking for, if we can get it honestly, and by our good conduct, prevail on our masters to set us free" (72). Nevertheless, according to Jupiter, freedom from the legal status of slave should not be anyone's first priority. As he puts it: "Getting our liberty in this world, is nothing to our having the liberty of the children of God" (72-3). Earlier in the "Address," he relies on the instructions of Paul in Ephesians 6:5-8 to support his claim that "whether it is right, and lawful, in the sight of God, for them to make slave of us or not, I am certain that while we are slaves, it is our duty to obey our masters, in all their lawful commands" (69). What should we make of this apparent capitulation to the power of slavery?

Nothing just yet, because we first must consider a more recently discovered piece of evidence. In October of 2011, a graduate student came across the manuscript of an unpublished poem by Jupiter entitled "An Essay on Slavery, with Submission to Divine Providence, Knowing that God Rules Over All Things." It is dated November 1786 and was thus written very close to the time of his "Address." Whereas Jupiter declines to weigh in on whether slavery is in itself wrong in the "Address," he is much less reticent in the poem, writing: "Dark and dismal was the Day / When slavery began / All humble thoughts were put away / Then slaves were made by Man" (79). This poem makes it crystal clear that, for Jupiter, slavery is in itself an abomination. Yet he sees no contradiction between this condemnation of slavery and the discouragement of preoccupation with obtaining legal freedom in the "Address." Indeed, the very next stanza of "An Essay on Slavery" says: "When God doth please for to permit / That slavery should be / It is our duty to submit / Till Christ shall make us free" (79).

There are nuances here that are difficult to understand, as Jupiter is clear that there is no duty for a slave to obey commands that would contravene God's laws. Why, we might wonder, doesn't slavery itself constitute such a trespass against divine law? Perhaps Jupiter's point is simply that we should patiently suffer the sins committed by others, while being careful never to sin ourselves. Another reason to view Jupiter's "Address" more sympathetically than it often has been is provided in this passage: "Many of us, who are grown up slaves, and have always had masters to take care of us, should hardly know how to take care of ourselves; and it may be more for our own comfort to remain as we are" (72). The sense of helplessness may strike us as distasteful. But an elderly person, like Jupiter was when he wrote these words, could justifiably worry about who and what he would be able to depend upon if liberated. What justice would lie in being left free but at the same time old, frail, and destitute? Jupiter was, then, clear-eyed about the wickedness of slavery, but no less clear-eyed about the real challenges that would still face those who escaped its clutches.

One more work of Jupiter Hammon worth mentioning is his 1778 poem "An Address to Miss Phillis Wheatley." We mentioned that Equiano's 1789 *Interesting Narrative* made him the most critically and commercially successful of black writers of the eighteenth century. But rivaling and perhaps besting him for fame would be Phillis Wheatley, whose collection of poems was published in London in 1773 (and who will be the subject of our next chapter). Jupiter's poem celebrates Wheatley's Christian faith and encourages her to cling to it, presenting us with an early example of African American literature as a communal conversation among African Americans. It's also worth pausing over the fact that Jupiter, living in New York, was reading the work of a fellow black poet who lived in Boston, but who saw her work published in England. This is a reminder, if one were needed, that these authors lived through a time when American history was but one part of the history of the British Empire. The empire provided the political context for most of the works we've discussed in this chapter, whether published in England as with the books of Gronniosaw and Wheatley, or in the American colonies as in the case of the two Hammons.

This political context is vital for understanding the development of black writing in English in the eighteenth century. Our authors were sometimes American patriots. That would apply to Wheatley, for instance, and another important writer of this time, Lemuel Haynes, even fought in the Revolutionary War on the American side (see Chapter 26). But black authors were just as liable to be British loyalists, persuaded by British promises of freedom to slaves who joined their side of the conflict. When the war ended in victory for the Americans, those freed people who had joined the side of the British had to be evacuated. The greatest number were sent to the colony of Nova Scotia, which is today a province of Canada and, incidentally, where Chike lives. Two more authors of autobiographical works from the eighteenth century, David George and Boston King—their names almost too good to be true, given that the British monarch at the time of the American Revolution was King George III—were black loyalists who became leading preachers among black Nova Scotians (*UV* 333–68).

This is also the right time to come back to John Marrant. The full title of his aforementioned 1785 book is *A Narrative of the Lord's Wonderful Dealings with John Marrant, A Black, (Now Going to Preach the Gospel in Nova-Scotia) Born in New-York, in North-America*. The narrative tells of how he was born free in New York, brought up in Florida, Georgia, and South Carolina, and then experienced a religious conversion as a teenager that led to him leaving home and eventually being captured and almost executed by Cherokees. This is therefore, like Briton Hammon's book, a captivity narrative. Less familiar is the twist in the tale: Marrant triumphantly converted his captors and lived for a while among them and other indigenous peoples before returning home. At some point during the Revolutionary War, he was pressed into the service of the Royal Navy. Upon being discharged, he lived in London and was eventually ordained as a minister in the Methodist church organized by Selina Hastings, the Countess of Huntingdon. The countess is central in the story of black writing during this time, as she was also a patron of Gronniosaw, Wheatley, and Equiano.

As the title of Marrant's narrative suggests, by the time it was published, he knew he wanted to answer the call of his brother, who had been evacuated to Nova Scotia, to go there and preach. We know all about how that went, because he published his journal from during his time there. This provides us with a further example of the variety of writing published by black authors of the eighteenth century, and also of how philosophical concerns come across in these works. Marrant adhered to Calvinist Methodism, which meant, among other things, a strong belief in predestination, the doctrine according to which the salvation of some and not others has been predetermined by God. By contrast, the Methodism of John Wesley, followed by Marrant's fellow autobiographer Boston King, was Arminian, which meant rejecting the doctrine of predestination as incompatible with free will. Marrant describes in his journal how Wesleyan Methodists opposed his ministry, inflaming the community against him by saying that he preached that "there was no repentance this side the grave" (104).[14] He writes of his victory over such sabotage, saying: "Some cried one thing and some another; but God over-ruled all things for his glory, and I was permitted to preach in the Arminian meeting (because there was no other in the place) to a very large congregation" (104). Here he boasts that the Arminians failed to stop him precisely because, for all their fervent belief in human free will, they could not change the course of events that God had in fact preordained. In other words, determinists always win in the end...at least, when God wants them to.

25

YOUNG, GIFTED, AND BLACK

Phillis Wheatley

All the world loves a prodigy. The precocious talent immediately fulfilled, the youth who outshines elders in a blaze of early glory. The world envies the prodigy a bit too. It can be hard to take when someone achieves more in their early years than you are likely to do in your whole life. The sentiment was well captured by the musical satirist Tom Lehrer: "It is a sobering thought that, by the time Mozart was my age, he had been dead for two years." How must athletes feel when they contemplate, say, Simone Biles, the American gymnast who was already winning world titles at the tender age of 13? Speaking of Simone, the famous song by singer Nina Simone, "To Be Young, Gifted, and Black," could fittingly have been written in Biles' honor. Except of course that it was recorded in 1969 when Biles was, as Tom Lehrer might have put it, negative 28 years old. Instead the song was dedicated to the playwright and philosophical thinker Lorraine Hansberry, who died at 34, one year younger than Mozart at his death, as it happens.

But perhaps the first woman in America who could have inspired the title "To Be Young, Gifted, and Black" was Phillis Wheatley.[1] Her name is like a concise history of her early life. Upon arriving in Boston in 1761, she was purchased by the Wheatley family, after being brought to America on a slaving ship called the *Phillis*—a voyage during which about one-quarter of the human cargo perished. We don't know much about her life before she was abducted as a young child of about 7. It's not even clear where she was from, exactly, though she herself speaks in one poem of the Gambia River, comparing it to the Garden of Eden in characteristically classical terms: "The various bower, the tuneful flowing stream, / The soft retreats, the lovers golden dream, / Her soil spontaneous, yields exhaustive stores, / For phoebus revels on her verdant shores" (*Works* 144).[2] A memoir written in 1834 by a descendant of the Wheatleys claims that Phillis could remember her own mother pouring out water in a ritual and prostrating to the sun. This may sound to some like the sort of traditional African religious practice that the Americans would have described as "pagan," but others have wondered whether Phillis' mother might have been a Muslim, since Muslims of course face Mecca when they pray, which in this case would have been in the direction of the rising sun.

The Wheatleys had suffered the death of a daughter, and seem to have looked upon young Phillis as a kind of replacement. Though still a slave, she was treated as something like a member of the family and given the sort of education that very few slaves would have received, quickly learning English and then diving into the study of Latin. It's hard to say how good her Latin was, but in English she gained not merely proficiency but virtuosic mastery. At about the same age when Simone Biles started winning world titles, Wheatley was publishing the first of the poems that would make her famous, and also make her only the fifth woman (and first black woman) to have her writing published in America. This was in 1767. But Wheatley really came to prominence in 1770 with a poem in honor of the recently deceased evangelist George Whitefield. Another woman poet took inspiration from her poem about Whitefield, writing, "Shall his due praises be so loudly sung / By a young Afric damsel's virgin tongue? / And I be silent!" (*Essays* 19).

The Wheatleys supported a kind of publicity machine for the precocious poet, trying to raise subscriptions for publishing a collection of her works in Boston already in 1772. This first effort was a failure but the projected book did make its way into print in London one year later, under the title *Poems on Various Subjects, Religious and Moral*. Her youth and race were uppermost in the mind of both her promoters and her readers. In the initial "proposal" for the book, in the front matter of the published volume, and in a later set of proposals for a projected sequel, it was emphasized that Phillis was indeed young, gifted, and black. Her linguistic gift led to the "great astonishment of all who heard her"; she was a "Negro girl" writing "from the strength of her own genius, it being but a few years since she came to this town an uncultivated barbarian from Africa"; and she was promised to be of interest to those who are "always in search of some new thing, that they may obtain a sight of this *rara avis in terra*," Latin for "rare bird in the land."[3] Apparently the good people of Boston were not just astonished but downright incredulous. Thus a so-called "attestation" was published along with Wheatley's poems, in which prominent Bostonians testified that they really were hers. The witnesses included John Hancock, famous for putting his name to a certain other document just a few years later.

Wheatley's book itself was no declaration of independence, though. To the contrary, the attestation says explicitly that she wrote the poems while serving as a slave to the Wheatley family. Happily, Phillis did ultimately win her freedom, securing agreement from the Wheatleys while in London that she would be manumitted upon their return to Boston. Once free, she married a man named John Peters in 1778; unfortunately their life together would be marred by her ill health, the early death of each of her three children, the end of her publishing career, and financial problems that would land Peters in debtor's prison. She died in 1784, when she would have been about 30, even younger than Mozart and Hansberry.

It's unfortunate that Wheatley's second book was never published, because a number of her poems have as a result been lost to posterity. Nonetheless we have more than fifty of her works. It should be said right away that to the modern ear, they inevitably sound rather antiquated in style, and often in the choice of theme. Wheatley's classicizing education frequently shows itself, as in this fairly typical passage which begins a poem inspired by the Latin poetry of Ovid: "Apollo's wrath to man the dreadful spring / Of ills innum'rous, tuneful goddess, sing! / Thou who did'st first th' ideal pencil give, / And taught'st the painter in his works to live" (*Works* 101). Of course, a late eighteenth century audience was more used to this sort of thing, perhaps indeed *too* used to it. Some critics deemed Wheatley's writing derivative, especially of the verses of Alexander Pope (*Essays* 9). And it is true that Pope was a major influence on her poetry, most notably in her use of his style of heroic couplets, which are rhyming pairs of lines in iambic pentameter.[4] This went hand in hand with a further suspicion, that Wheatley was little more than a puppet of her masters. In 1898 one reader complained that "the rare song-bird of Africa was thoroughly tamed in her Boston cage," another, writing in 1913, that "here is no Zulu, but drawing-room English" (*Essays* 58–9).

Her most famous detractor was Thomas Jefferson. Wheatley had a positive encounter with another of America's founding fathers, writing a poem in honor of George Washington which seems to have pleased the general and future president (*Works* 145–6, *Essays* 33–6). But Jefferson had nothing but disdain for her works. While mounting his argument that black people would never be successfully integrated into American society, he wrote: "Religion, indeed, has produced a Phyllis Whately; but it could not produce a poet. The compilations published under her name are below the dignity of criticism" (*Essays* 42). This dismissive remark, complete with misspelling of her name, provoked something of a backlash. Gilbert Imlay wrote in 1797: "I should be glad to be informed what white person upon this continent has written more beautiful lines," and in the early nineteenth century Samuel Stanhope Smith remarked: "I will demand of Mr Jefferson, or any other man, who is acquainted with American planters, how many of these masters could have written poems equal to those of Phillis Whately?" (*Essays* 47, 51).

From this we can see how Wheatley was co-opted into a wider debate over the talents of Africans. Just like Anton Wilhelm Amo, she was held up as an example of the "genius" that could be found among black people, as when the famous abolitionist William Lloyd Garrison wrote that her poems provide "some conception of the amount of genius which slavery is murdering" (*Essays* 54). Still today, the response to her poems tends to revolve around questions concerning her identity as an African. Her detractors express disappointment with passages in which she appears to denigrate Africa, while her champions point to her affirmations of her African identity and her expressions of solidarity with others who were, like her, brought to America as chattel. We'll get on to this debate in due course. First, though, we want to examine some other philosophical ideas in her writing.

We may begin by admitting that Jefferson was right about one thing: it was in no small degree religion that gave us Phillis Wheatley. Her deep piety shines through much of her work, and not infrequently dictates her choice of subject matter. Two early poems, written a mere six years after her arrival in Boston when she was barely even a teenager, are attacks on atheism and deism (*Works* 129-32). These invoke familiar arguments for mainstream Christian belief, as in the line: "If there's no god from whence did all things spring?" A longer poem on divine providence begins with Wheatley exhorting her own soul to praise God like the angels do (*Works* 43). The religious motif reappears throughout her many poems written on the occasion of a death. These "elegies," which make up no fewer than one-third of her published works, sometimes mark the passing of prominent individuals, like that poem in honor of Whitefield. In other cases, she offers consolation to bereaved parents. While frequently admitting the inadequacy of her poems to this and other occasions (*Works* 28, 55, 89, 117), Wheatley encourages her readers to see death as liberation from an inferior realm, a "world of sin, and snares, and pain" (*Works* 26), and as a passage to a better place. In particular we should not fear to lose the pleasures of this world, because when we are called to God, "He welcomes thee to pleasures more refin'd / And better suited to th' immortal mind" (*Works* 30, see also 71, 85, 99).

Before death, poetry offers a foretaste of the afterlife, since the source of poetic inspiration, Wheatley constantly observes, is supernatural. Though Christianity animates her verses, she also talks about the sources of poetic inspiration in terms drawn from classical Greek and Roman myth and literature. Indeed, Jupiter Hammon's poem addressed to Wheatley, mentioned in the last chapter, is thought by some scholars to emphasize the importance of Christianity in critical reaction to Wheatley's investment in classical mythology.[5] Frequently, she invokes the nine Muses, and one of her major poems treats of recollection or Memory, who was mother of the Muses (*Works* 62-4).[6] It begins with the plea: "Inspire, ye sacred nine,

/ Your vent'rous *Afric* in her great design," and goes on to say that Memory "to the high-raptur'd poet gives her aid, / Through the unbounded regions of the mind, / Diffusing light celestial and refin'd." One of her running themes is accordingly that poetry, or at least the kind she hopes to write, has something in common with celestial or angelic, rather than earthly, language (*Works* 25-7, 52). Thus she implores: "Raise my mind to a seraphic strain," and elsewhere laments: "Had I the tongue of a seraphim, how would I exalt thy Praise" (*Works* 43, 133).

This suggestion that poetry puts us in touch with the heavenly realm is reinforced in another of her works, placed in her book just after the poem "On Recollection," and viewed by some critics as her masterpiece. This poem, entitled "On Imagination" (*Works* 65-7), argues that imagination is the soul's greatest faculty, or as she puts it, "leader of the mental train." Its use frees us from the limitations of everyday experience and allows us to grasp other worlds: "From star to star the mental optics rove, / Measure the skies, and range the realms above. / There in one view we grasp the mighty whole, / Or with new worlds amaze th' unbounded soul." John Shields, one of the most prolific interpreters of Wheatley's poetry, has written that Wheatley "enthusiastically embraces liberation as the subject of her writing."[7] It's hard to disagree, as long as it is clear that we are speaking not merely of losing our chains in a physical sense but in the sense that imagination and poetic artistry can free us from all constraint.

Obviously, though, this is a theme that can be related to Wheatley's feelings on slavery, even if that connection often remains tacit. Instead, she presents the unboundedness of the soul and of the imagination in religious, psychological, and aesthetic terms. Dreams, she thinks, are a familiar opportunity for the exercise of imaginative freedom. In lines that wouldn't be out of place in Shakespeare, she writes: "Say, what is sleep? And dreams how passing strange! / When action ceases, and ideas range / Licentious and unbounded o'er the plains, / Where Fancy's queen in giddy triumph reigns" (*Works* 47). Along with poetry, other forms of art offer a path to this dream-like freedom. She draws parallels between the poet and the visual artist in a set of verses dedicated to "a young African painter" (*Works* 114-15). While identified in the poem only by the initials "S.M.," a note she wrote in her own copy of *Poems on Various Subjects, Religious and Moral* names the painter as Scipio Moorhead, who is widely believed to have engraved the most famous portrait of Wheatley. Addressing Moorhead, Wheatley writes: "High to the blissful wonders of the skies / Elate thy soul, and raise thy wishful eyes." Clearly Wheatley is making extravagant claims about the power of art in general. Yet those claims come together with a profound humility, in part because of her Christian awareness of sinfulness and finitude, and in part because for her, artistic inspiration comes from outside the artist, from a heavenly source. Appealing again to the Muses, she asks: "Indulgent muse! My grov'ling mind inspire, / and fill my bosom with celestial fire" (*Works* 78).

In fact, Wheatley's consummate artistry is never more subtle than when she reflects upon her own humility. Here, as promised, we return to the question of her status as an enslaved African, and as a young woman to boot. She is well aware of her socially inferior position, and manipulates this status to create an authorial persona that manages to be ostentatiously modest yet morally authoritative. Often, when she mentions her own origins in the poems, she is doing so in order to shame or otherwise move her more privileged reader. Thus in the diatribe against deism she asks rhetorically: "Must Ethiopians be employed for you?" (*Works* 131). In other words, are these opponents so blind to the truth that even an African has to point it out to them?

It is possible to interpret another passage, one of the most notorious in her poems, in a similar light. It comes in the context of an address to graduates from "the University of Cambridge," later Harvard University (*Works* 15–16). After the usual invocation of the Muses, Wheatley writes: "'Twas not long since I left my native shore / The land of errors, and Egyptian gloom: / Father of mercy, 'twas thy gracious hand / Brought me in safety from those dark abodes." These lines have been deplored, since it sounds as if she is expressing gratitude for her abduction from Africa. When reading this, we should bear in mind her deep belief that God's providence guides all things. For Wheatley, it would have presumably been axiomatic that she was brought to America for a reason. She is suggesting here that she was brought into the light of Christianity and education so that she could serve as a kind of messenger, a bringer of illumination from "gloomy" Africa. On this basis, she goes on to exhort the students to consider Christ's redemptive sacrifice and warns them against sin, writing, "an Ethiop' tells you 'tis your greatest foe."

A similar approach could be taken to another of her poems, only eight lines long, entitled "On Being Brought from Africa to America" (*Works* 18). It's arguably the most famous of all her poems, for better or—some would say—for worse. It's worth quoting in full:

> 'Twas mercy brought me from my pagan land,
> Taught my benighted soul to understand,
> That there's a God, that there's a Saviour too;
> Once I redemption neither sought nor knew.
> Some view of sable race with scornful eye,
> "Their colour is a diabolic die."
> Remember, Christians, Negroes, black as Cain,
> May be refin'd, and join th' angelic train.

Here Wheatley compresses into a shorter space the same kind of reversal seen in the address to the students at Harvard. She expresses what certainly seems like disdain for her "pagan" African homeland, where she was "benighted" by her lack of Christian wisdom, and this disdain she invites the reader to share. She then springs the trap she's laid by telling that same reader *not* to look upon the Africans "scornfully" because, once they are redeemed by accepting the Christian truth, they will be saved just as surely as white believers. In short: what matters is not where you are from or what color your skin is, but whether you believe in God the Father and Christ the Son.

The moral authority Wheatley assumes in these poems, granting herself as an enslaved black girl the right to instruct white male students and to rebuke the hypocrisy of racist white Christians, ought to be noticed and appreciated. Still, one might understandably wish for a clearer statement that slavery is, well, wrong. Those who are only familiar with "On Being Brought from Africa to America" should know, then, that there is a poem of hers that offers a completely different take on the matter. This is "To the Right Honorable William, Earl of Dartmouth," which is perhaps the most important and celebrated of her political poems. Lord Dartmouth served the British government as Secretary of State for the Colonies and was viewed, at the time of Wheatley's poem, as favorable to the cause of the American colonists. After celebrating him for this, Wheatley writes:

> Should you, my lord, while you peruse my song,
> Wonder from whence my love of Freedom sprung,
> Whence flow these wishes for the common good,
> By feeling hearts alone best understood,
> I, young in life, by seeming cruel fate
> Was snatch'd from Afric's fancy'd happy seat;
> What pangs excruciatingly must molest,
> What sorrows labour in my parent's breast?
> Steel'd was that soul and by no misery mov'd
> That from a father seized his babe belov'd;
> Such, such my case. And can I then but pray
> Others may never feel tyrannic sway?

The denunciation of the slave trade in these lines, by one who experienced the horror of the Middle Passage, renders them among Wheatley's most arresting moments as a writer.

Another place we find Wheatley making an explicit connection between America's oppression by the British and the oppression of black Africans by white Americans is in a letter she wrote in 1774. Here she agrees with her correspondent

Samson Occom, a Native American preacher who argued for the "natural rights" of "negroes." Wheatley adds that in her opinion God has "implanted a principle, which we call love of freedom," in all humans. She concludes her letter: "How well the cry for liberty, and the reverse disposition for the exercise of oppressive power over others agree—I humbly think it does not require the penetration of a philosopher to determine" (*Works* 177). Wheatley's critique of slavery here is notably different from the one given by those who held up her poetry, or the sophisticated treatises of Amo, as proof of its wrongs. Such abolitionists sometimes seemed to suggest that it is wrong to enslave Africans simply because the occasional African can write philosophy like Leibniz or poetry like Pope. Think again of Garrison's appeal to the "amount of genius which slavery is murdering"—a well-intentioned point, no doubt, given this passionate abolitionist's commitment to freedom for all. But the phrasing might leave you wondering about slaves who aren't geniuses. Wheatley, in her letter to Occom, makes it absolutely clear that, given the universal desire for freedom, it is not being gifted that justifies liberty. It is being human.

26

NEW ENGLAND PATRIOT

Lemuel Haynes

In Lexington, Massachusetts, not far from where Peter grew up, there is a statue of a minuteman. The minutemen were a militia group in Revolutionary era America, named for their readiness to fight the British with one minute's notice, which is pretty quick (though still one minute longer than it now takes for the British to fight with themselves). The fellow depicted by the statue looks calm and collected, yet resolute; he looks ready to fight in a noble cause; and he looks…white. In fact, the statue is probably intended to represent the group's leader, Captain John Parker. But it could have shown a black man instead. As we have already mentioned, people of African heritage fought in the Revolutionary War, and on both sides. Some of those who fought on the American side were minutemen, among them Lemuel Haynes. Today, we remember Haynes not simply for his service in the war but, above all, for an unfinished essay that was never published during his lifetime. It is thought to have been written in the same year as the Declaration of Independence but it was only rediscovered in the early 1980s. This philosophical work, so long hidden from view, is about the very thing he and the other minutemen were fighting for: liberty, which Haynes argued should be "further extended" to include the emancipation of all slaves.

Though Haynes is not depicted in the minuteman statue at Lexington, or in another minuteman statue at Concord, we do have at least one image of him, the frontispiece from an 1837 biography. It shows a thoughtful man with a gentle, rather round face. He looks more likely to offer you a cuddle than fire a shot in anger. Yet, in his essay, "Liberty Further Extended," Haynes argued passionately that the principles underlying the American uprising against the British would, if consistently applied, also require the elimination of slavery. This essay did not make a name for Haynes in his own time, or even for the following two centuries. But he was well known as black pastor to a number of white churches, at a time when most black people in America were not even allowed to read and write. And his contemporaries did know something of his fiery rhetoric, thanks to a witty and rather savage sermon in which he compared a rival theologian to Satan.

Haynes was born in West Hartford, Connecticut, in 1753 to a white woman, who gave him up because he was mixed race.[1] His father, whose name we do not know, is thought to have been an enslaved African. His mother was, we believe, a Scottish immigrant and servant girl named Alice Fitch. Lemuel inherited his last name from neither of his parents but rather from his mother's employer, John Haynes, in whose house he was born. This namesake, however, had no desire to keep him, so he was indentured as a servant at the age of 5 months to the family of David Rose in Granville, Massachusetts. They appear to have treated him as a valued member of the family. They were very pious and, as he grew older, Haynes himself found Christ while sitting under an apple tree. One might say that, like Isaac Newton, he was suddenly struck by the gravity of his situation: in his case, the state of sin that affects all humans. Wicked as we are, we must recognize that all our desires are motivated by selfish interests, even the desire to be saved from damnation. We can only hope and pray to receive the divine grace that will "regenerate" our souls, allowing us finally to love God and our fellow humans without being motivated by mere self-interest.

With these ideas, Haynes was following the teachings of the "New Divinity" school, also called "consistent Calvinists" for their insistence that every human desire is sinful in the absence of grace.[2] He also had no hesitation in accepting the determinism of the Calvinist tradition, remarking that "fortune" or "chance" is an illusion, and trusting that everything happens according to a divine plan. He therefore accepted the New Divinity idea that the created world is a fundamentally good place, despite the pervasiveness and inevitability of human sin. God "over-rules" evil by turning bad actions to good ends (we already saw this idea of "over-ruling" in Marrant, Chapter 24 above). The central example of this would be the crucifixion of Christ, an evil act that opened a path to salvation for all of humankind.

The New Divinity theologians were followers of the early American philosopher Jonathan Edwards, whose 1754 treatise *Freedom of the Will* argued along traditionally Calvinist lines that God in His omnipotence foreordains all things. Yet Edwards taught that we are still morally blameworthy for our sins, since when we choose them, as we are predestined to do, we make this choice out of selfish desire. Though you might suppose that the enslaving of other people would be a perfect example of acting on such desires, this was not so clear at the beginning of the Edwardsean tradition.[3] Edwards himself owned slaves and never called slaveowning a sin, though he did think that the slave trade should be brought to an end and replaced with missionary work to bring Christianity to Africa. Yet he allowed that slaves already held in America could legitimately be kept. By contrast his son Jonathan Edwards Jr was an abolitionist, as was another leading New Divinity thinker named Samuel Hopkins, who seems to have come to his views after being exposed to the brutality of the slave trade while living in the trading coastal town of Newport, Rhode Island.

Both the younger Edwards and Hopkins made the point that it seemed, to put it mildly, inconsistent for the Americans to be rising up against the tyranny of British rule while condoning the ownership of slaves. Edwards Jr. and a co-author named Ebenezer Baldwin published an essay against slavery in which they wrote: "If it be lawful and right for us to reduce the Africans to a state of slavery, why is it not as right for Great Britain, France, or Spain, not merely to exact duties of us; but to reduce us to the same state of slavery, to which we have reduced them?" In a similar vein, Hopkins asserted that "where liberty is not universal it has no existence," and implored his fellow Americans: "Rouse up then my brethren and assert the Right of universal liberty; you assert your own Right to be free in opposition to the Tyrant of Britain; come be honest men and assert the Right of the Africans to be free in opposition to the Tyrants of America. We cry up Liberty, but know it, the Negros have as good a right as we can pretend to."[4] The point could also be invoked by the British when sneering at the American revolutionaries, as in a famous quote from Samuel Johnson: "How is it we hear the loudest yelps for liberty among the drivers of Negroes?"[5]

There is a third and final example of opposition to slavery by white New Divinity theologians that we must mention before turning back to Haynes. In September of 1774, Levi Hart, a close associate of Hopkins, delivered a noteworthy sermon entitled "Liberty Described and Recommended," which discusses the nature of political freedom, the nature of spiritual freedom, and the connections between these two.[6] According to Hart, civil liberty is the unconstrained ability to act for the public good, which means that one can be justifiably constrained by one's society only if one is acting for private benefit in a way that works against the public good. Slavery, from this vantage point, is clearly not a justifiable constraint on anyone's liberty, but rather a case of acting for private benefit against the public good. Hart therefore attacks slavery as a "palpable" and "flagrant violation of the law of nature" and demands: "When, O when shall the happy day come, that Americans shall be *consistently* engaged in the cause of liberty, and a final end be put to the cruel slavery of our fellow men?"

We know that this sermon made an impact on Haynes, because he quotes that climactic question of Hart's in his own "Liberty Further Extended," the title of which may have been chosen to rhyme with Hart's "Liberty Described and Recommended."

The full title of Haynes' essay is "Liberty Further Extended: Or Free thoughts on the illegality of Slave-keeping; Wherein those Arguments that are used in its vindication Are plainly confuted. Together with an humble address to such as are Concearned in the practice." The previously unknown manuscript was discovered by historian Ruth Bogin along with a poem by Haynes entitled "The Battle of Lexington."[7] While he was not at that famous battle, which kicked off the Revolutionary War, Haynes was already an enlisted minuteman at the time and marched west from Granville the very next day to face the British. He had enlisted the previous year after turning 21, as that birthday had brought an end to his indentured servitude. Bogin suspects that the poem was written in 1775, within a month or so of the Battle of Lexington and thus possibly while the young minuteman was serving at Boston. While Haynes, still 21 at the time, identifies himself in a prefatory inscription as a "young Mollatto," there is nothing in the poem itself that would suggest the author's race. He does speak of being ready to die rather than live as a slave, but this clearly refers to resisting British tyranny over the colonies, not to chattel slavery.

Something changed, then, by the time he wrote "Liberty Further Extended," which focuses squarely on the unjustifiable evil of enslaving Africans. Bogin suspects this essay was first drafted before July of 1776 but revised after the fourth of that month, as it begins with an epigraph from the Declaration of Independence. Surprisingly, at no point in his essay does Haynes use the word "Americans," except when he is quoting from Hart. Haynes instead frames the American Revolution as a matter of Englishmen asserting their right to liberty in the face of oppression by other Englishmen: "To affirm, that an Englishman has a right to his Liberty, is a truth which has Been so clearly Evinced, Especially of Late, that to spend time in illustrating this, would be But Superfluous tautology. But I query, whether Liberty is so contracted a principle as to be Confin'd to any nation under Heaven; nay, I think it not hyperbolical to affirm, that Even an affrican, has Equally as good a right to his Liberty in common with Englishmen" (94).

In this way, Haynes downplayed the difference between the white men on the two sides of this conflict in which he too was fighting, the better to highlight the racial oppression that was going on daily within the newly United States. The point is not that he saw no difference at all between the two sides or was unsure of the patriot cause. Rather, he sought to show that anyone who was truly on the side of liberty must also support the extension of freedom to enslaved Africans. For Haynes, freedom is bestowed upon us by God. It is not for any created power to take away, whether the infringement of freedom is committed by a state regime like the British or by a private slaveholder. Thus he writes: "Liberty is a Jewel which was handed Down to man from the cabinet of heaven, and is Coaeval with his Existance.

And as it proceed from the Supreme Legislature of the univers, so it is he which hath a sole right to take away; therefore, he that would take away a mans Liberty assumes a prerogative that Belongs to another, and acts out of his own domain" (94). To deprive another of liberty, on this view, is blasphemously to consider oneself equal with God.

In another memorable part of the essay, in which he sets out to expose defenses of slavery as "Lame, and Defective," Haynes takes on an argument that one might expect a predestinarian Christian thinker like himself to have trouble rejecting (100). This is the claim that "those Negros that are Emigrated into these colonies are brought out of a Land of Darkness under the meridian Light of the Gospel; and so it is a great Blessing instead of a Curs" (102). We already saw Phillis Wheatley veer in this direction, but Haynes is having none of it. Relying on the Book of Romans, Haynes refutes the idea that one can justifiably choose to do evil so that good may come. While it is true that God can bring good out of evil, even an evil so monstrous as slavery, that is no excuse for humans who take part in it. In any case, those involved in the transatlantic slave trade and slavery in the colonies clearly do not "aim at the Spiritual good of their Slaves" (102). On the coast of Africa, they do not encourage "wholesom conduct" but rather stimulate through their demand for slaves "quarrelings and Blood-Shed," while in the colonies, slaves are "generally kept under the greatest ignorance" (102). So the idea that slavery is a benefit to Africans is, according to Haynes, merely a fraudulent excuse for the greed and laziness that truly motivate those involved in slavery.

Why did Haynes never complete and publish this powerful text? There are signs that he felt it was too radical. We can see in the handwritten text that he twice inserted lines defending violent insurrection against slavery before thinking better of it and crossing the lines out. Whatever his reasons for not publishing "Liberty Further Extended," 1776 also turned out to be the year he moved decisively toward his destiny as a preacher. Still living with the Rose family, he was often asked to read at their Saturday evening devotion. One such evening, he held a book of sermons in his hand, but instead read out a text of his own that he had slipped into the book. Mr. Rose, delighted by the edifying words, wondered whose they were. (He suspected George Whitefield, the preacher eulogized by Wheatley in one of her early poems.) "It's Lemuel's sermon," confessed the young man. From this moment on, Haynes' path to the ministry was supported and encouraged by many. In 1780, a number of respected ministers signed a document certifying that he was qualified to preach.

The first sermon he preached after being licensed used the opening verse from Psalm 97, according to which "the Lord reigneth," to ask whether the supremacy of God counts as a kind of tyranny.[8] God's supremacy may seem incompatible with human freedom, and thus with the possibility of virtue and even the need for human initiative. Haynes responded by arguing that salvation properly understood requires activity and exertion in the form of repentance and faith, so it is contradictory to think salvation is compatible with a failure to strive for virtue. And God is no tyrant: His enemies may be frightened to discover that they are in His hands, but the thought of His omnipotence should provide a sense of security to those who are careful to seek salvation.

In 1785, Haynes became the first black preacher in the United States to be officially ordained. Three years later, he delivered a sermon called "The Influence of Civil Government on Religion." While featuring no mention of slavery, this sermon is an important record of Haynes' views on the purpose of government in a free society. He emphasizes that God, in His omnipotence, could achieve His aims in the world without the intervention of human legislative authority. So the question is not whether we could do without government but rather why government is, if not necessary, then at least helpful. Haynes claims: "When we consider the obvious end for which civil government was instituted, it is easy to see that it was designed as a support to virtue...To oppose the impetuous torrent of iniquity; to humanize the soul, and to conduct men in the way of felicity, are objects to which the laws of God and those which are commonly called the laws of men, do mutually point" (67).[9] Haynes explains that by protecting our lives and interests, human legislative authority enables us to focus on seeking after God.

What then was going on in the government of Haynes' own day? The president at the time was John Adams. Haynes was a strong supporter of Adams' Federalist Party, to which the first president, George Washington, was sympathetic, even if he was officially non-partisan. Haynes was such an advocate for the Federalists that we find him defending one of the most controversial decisions of the Adams administration in this sermon on civil government. Historians tend to look back on the Alien and Sedition Acts, which curtailed immigration and freedom of the press, as shameful constrictions on American freedom. Haynes, however, defended the suppression of sedition by arguing that private individuals have "recourse to the law for satisfaction" when they are the subjects of libel. How much more important, then, is it to protect "the character of a chief magistrate, or of a whole country" from wicked and baseless forms of criticism (72)?

This controversial stance shows that Haynes was willing to see the state impose significant limitations on rights and freedoms. From his Fourth of July address from 1801, "The Nature and Importance of True Republicanism," we can see that he continued to wrestle with such questions as time went on. He attempts in this speech to give a definition of "Republicanism," a word he equates as synonymous with "Independence" and with "Liberty" (79). What all these terms amount to, he claims, is the pursuit of a certain goal, namely, "to defend and secure the natural rights of men," which are "those privileges, whether civil or sacred, that the God of nature hath given us" (79). But how do we know what counts as a natural right or God-given privilege? Haynes tells us: "To know what this charter comprises, we are to view them in their relation to society at large: When they are congenial with this object, we ought most cheerfully to fall in with the design, and view ourselves as breathing the very spirit and life of true liberty" (79). We may here detect a lingering indebtedness to Levi Hart's definition of liberty as the unconstrained ability to act for the public good. Haynes takes the position that the value of individual rights must be justified in relation to the good of the community as a whole, rather than through a focus on the desires of individuals themselves.

This speech is one of two published works of his where we find Haynes returning to the topic of slavery. He contrasts republican government with monarchical government in order to congratulate the United States for leaving behind the various hierarchical distinctions between royalty, nobility, and commoners, which he believes led Europe into conflict and a divide between knowledgeable elites and ignorant masses. But his praise is tempered with criticism: "The propriety of this idea will appear strikingly evident by pointing you to the poor Africans, among us. What has reduced them to their present pitiful, abject state? Is it any distinction that the God of nature hath made in their formation? Nay—but being subjected to slavery, by the cruel hands of oppressors, they have been taught to view themselves as a rank of beings far below others, which has suppressed, in a degree, every principle of manhood, and so they have become despised, ignorant, and licentious. This shews the effect of despotism, and should fill us with the utmost detestation against every attack on the rights of men: while we cherish and diffuse, with a laudable ambition, that heaven-born liberty wherewith Christ hath made us free" (82). After this illustration, however, Haynes goes back to comparing other lands run by tyrants with "the far more peaceful regions of North America" (82). He does not hammer home the point that despotism and tyranny exist within North America too.

There is similar, and perhaps even greater, circumspection in another of his criticisms of slavery, in a sermon called "Dissimulation Illustrated," delivered on the occasion of George Washington's birthday in 1814. In this sermon, he celebrates the fact that Washington, a hero of his, provided for the emancipation of his slaves in his will.[10] Haynes also uses the occasion to harshly criticize President James Madison's administration for its pursuit of what we now know as the War of 1812. He calls it a duty of those called upon to go to war to examine whether the cause is just, and claims that "a *defensive* war only can be vindicated, unless where there is an express command from God, as in the case of Israel's going to war with the nations devoted to destruction" (154). Speaking as a veteran of the Revolutionary War, which he still believes was just in its cause, he condemns the War of 1812 as failing by this standard. That is to say, it is not, in his view, a war of self-defense.

One pretext given for the war was that Britain's Royal Navy would sometimes press American sailors into service. Haynes quotes a Reverend Worcester, who said: "Our president…can talk feelingly on the subject of impressment of our seamen. I am glad to have him feel for them. Yet in his own state, Virginia, there were, in the year 1800, no less than 343,796 human beings [held] in bondage for life!" Haynes then adds: "I ask, would it be the duty of these slaves to rise and massacre their masters? or for us to advise them to such measures? Partial affection, or distress for some of our fellow-creatures, while others, even under our notice, are wholly disregarded, betrays dissimulation" (157). The implicit suggestion here that slave rebellion would be a bad thing recalls his decision to suppress the endorsement of violent resistance by slaves in his unpublished draft of "Liberty Further Extended." Haynes decried hypocrisy, but remained wary of following his own denunciations of tyranny to their logical conclusion.

And indeed Haynes' most popular work, which appeared in no fewer than seventy editions between 1805 and 1860, had nothing to do with slavery but was rather an attack on the concept of "universal salvation" proposed by the Universalist theologian Hosea Ballou. Ballou believed that, given the infinite and perfect goodness of God, all souls would be redeemed, indeed allowed to enter paradise immediately upon death. Haynes responds to this with a satirical sermon that recalls how Satan falsely promised Adam and Eve in the garden of Eden that they would not "die" if they tasted from the tree of good and evil.[11] Haynes wittily concludes: "Universal salvation is no new-fangled scheme, but can boast of great antiquity." In other words, Ballou's misleading doctrine was already put forth by Satan himself. Unfortunately, the notion of universal salvation is still likely to find many adherents, given that Satan remains successful in seducing humans to believe falsehood.

Another memorable instance of Haynes' biting wit returns us to his political views. While his beloved Federalist Party was no longer a political force by the time Andrew Jackson won the presidency in 1828, Haynes remained opposed to the Democratic Party that Jackson represented, just as he had previously opposed its predecessor, the Democratic-Republican party headed by Thomas Jefferson and then James Madison. Right after Jackson's election, Haynes came across a group of supporters in a hotel dining room who asked him to propose a toast to the new president. Haynes obliged, raising his glass and saying: "Andrew Jackson—Psalm 109, verse 8." Only after Haynes had left did someone look up the passage and discover that it read: "Let his days be few, and let another take his office" (xv).

Also worth mentioning is Haynes' account of an extraordinary experience that he had in 1819. Two brothers were imprisoned for a murder which they denied committing. Haynes visited them in jail to offer them spiritual ministry, and became convinced they were indeed innocent. Then, just weeks before a death sentence would be carried out, the supposed murder victim turned up in town, "crazier than ever but unmistakably alive," as one scholar has put it.[12] The miraculous deliverance became the basis for another publication by Haynes, which is both an early entry in the genre of true crime narrative and a powerful assertion of the reality of divine providence. As a Calvinist, Haynes saw God's hand in all events, of course, but with the salvation of the two accused brothers, divine influence and mercy were unusually evident.

Once again, one might wish that Haynes would have drawn out the obvious relevance of the story for the debate over slavery, as he waxes poetic on the pitiable state of the innocents who lost their freedom and celebrates their liberation from bondage. We should not fail to recognize, however, that, until his death in 1833, Haynes lived an extraordinary life in very difficult times for people of African heritage. After serving for thirty years as a pastor in Rutland, Vermont, from 1788 to 1818, he was dismissed from his position. The reason for this, according to one report of what he privately thought of the matter, was that they finally became overly conscious of the disrepute of having a black preacher.[13] He preached afterward in Manchester, Vermont, before finally pastoring a church in Granville, New York (not to be confused with Granville, Massachusetts, where he grew up). His house in South Granville, New York, is today a National Historic Site.

27

LETTERS FROM THE HEART

Ignatius Sancho and Benjamin Banneker

In the British parliamentary election of 1774, a whopping 100 percent of the black vote went to Earl Percy and Lord Thomas Pelham-Clinton, who claimed the two seats in Parliament representing the important constituency of Westminster. We can say this with confidence because, at least as far as we know, there was only one black voter: Ignatius Sancho, who also voted in the next election in 1780, again for the winning candidates.[1] At the time the franchise was extended only to men of sufficient wealth, a test Sancho could meet thanks to his ownership of a thriving grocery store. He is best remembered today, however, not for his pioneering participation in the political process, nor for his business acumen, nor even for what might seem to be his most remarkable accomplishment: he seems also to have been the first black person in history to publish musical compositions. Instead, he is best known as an eloquent writer of letters.[2] Two years after his death in December of 1780, a woman named Frances Crewe edited and published a book entitled *Letters of the Late Ignatius Sancho, An African*, the proceeds of which went to Sancho's widow. It established him as a literary celebrity, comparable in fame to Phillis Wheatley.

Another black exponent of the epistolary art in the eighteenth century was Benjamin Banneker. His name is also remembered, though not so much for writing letters. Every year, especially during Black History Month, children learn about Banneker as an early American scientific genius: an astronomer who published almanacs, an ingenious clockmaker, and a surveyor involved in the creation of his nation's capital, Washington DC. For us, though, Banneker is most important because of a letter he sent in 1791 to Thomas Jefferson, who was at that point Secretary of State. In this letter and some of those written by Sancho, we find philosophical reflections on the role of emotion and imagination in the stimulation of social change and the pursuit of justice.

We will begin by discussing Sancho, whose early life illustrates the horrors of the slave trade.[3] He is said to have been born in 1729, not in Africa, nor in the Americas, nor in his eventual beloved home, Great Britain, but rather on a slave ship crossing the Atlantic Ocean. The ship arrived at Cartagena, in present-day Colombia, where the infant boy's mother died of illness and his father committed suicide. This is where he was baptized and given the name Ignatius. As a 2-year-old orphan, he was brought to England and given to three sisters who apparently wanted him to be nothing more than an ignorant slave. They named him Sancho, after Sancho Panza from *Don Quixote*.

Sancho's fortunes turned when he met John, the Duke of Montagu, who had previously befriended and assisted Job ben Solomon (whom we mentioned in Chapter 24). After the duke's death, Sancho sought to live with his widow, the duchess, but was at first rebuffed. At this low point, he reportedly considered committing suicide like his father before him, but the duchess reconsidered her position and took him on as a butler. He served in this role until her death and she bequeathed him a year's salary as well as a healthy annuity. Unfortunately, Sancho apparently squandered much of his money on womanizing, gambling, and—more admirably, and illustrating his deep love for the arts—the theater. Sancho even aspired to be an actor himself, but was hindered by a speech impediment. In 1758, he married Anne Osborn, a black woman from the Caribbean, and the pressures of a growing family made employment a necessity.

Sancho took up a post as personal valet to the late duke and duchess' son-in-law; his earliest known musical compositions date to this time. By 1773, though, he had to give up this position because of health problems relating to his weight and gout. Fortunately, his ability to handle money had by now improved, and he was able to make the transition from his career in service to the role of entrepreneur, opening the grocery store that kept him busy for the rest of his life. Being a grocer suited Sancho's difficulties with physical mobility, which may also help explain his prolific writing of letters to friends in and around London. He wrote to people like William Stevenson, a printer, bookseller, and banker; Margaret Cocksedge, possibly a governess to Frances Crewe, who edited Sancho's letters; and John Meheux, a visual artist who received patronage from Sancho.[4] His most famous correspondent, however, was the great British novelist Laurence Sterne, author of *The Life and Opinions of Tristram Shandy*.

In a letter of July 21, 1766, Sancho praised Sterne for the brilliance of his fiction and pressed him to work his opposition to slavery into his novels.[5] Sterne wrote back with gratitude and said that he just happened to be working on a tender-hearted tale of a black girl who suffered under slavery. When Sterne's letters were posthumously published in 1775, this gave Sancho his first taste of fame, and put him on display as an articulate champion of the value of sentimentality in art. In his message to Sterne, he begins by identifying himself as black and lamenting his ill fortune, having grown up in a household that enforced his ignorance so as to secure his obedience. Yet he learned to read and write nonetheless; indeed, in adulthood his "chief pleasure has been books" (I, 35). This may remind us of the trope of the "talking book" in slave narratives and other eighteenth century black literature, for Sancho similarly points to the power of the written word. When it was withheld from him, this was a form of oppression, and when he later gained mastery of it, this was a central component and symbol of his freedom.

In the letter, Sancho goes on to say, "Philanthropy I adore," and to confess how much he appreciates the character of Uncle Toby in *Tristram Shandy*, famously portrayed as unwilling to hurt a fly. Sancho declares he would walk ten miles in summer heat just to shake Uncle Toby's hand, which is probably about nine miles more than most of us would walk to shake anyone's hand. This show of devotion to a fictional character sets up Sancho's proposal that Sterne incorporate anti-slavery views into his fictional work. Sancho praises the "affecting" condemnation of slavery found in a book of sermons by Sterne, and claims that if the subject of slavery were to be handled in Sterne's distinctive style of storytelling, this would, as Sancho puts it, "ease the yoke (perhaps) of many—but if only one—Gracious God!—what a feast to a benevolent heart!" In line with this exuberance, Sancho eventually shifts from humble suggestion, to confident assertion, of what Sterne simply must do for black people: "Grief...is eloquent;—figure to yourself their attitudes;—hear their supplicating addresses!—alas!—you cannot refuse.—Humanity must comply." Sancho here draws a tight connection between the production of representational art, the emotional responses of individual readers, and the desired political outcome of broad social change. The fictionalization of harsh realities is a uniquely powerful way to change those very realities, by eliciting strong emotional reactions that can effectively motivate change.

Given that activism against the slave trade was, at best, in its infancy at the time Sancho wrote to Sterne, Sancho was articulating a pioneering strategy when he suggested using popular fiction as a tool of abolitionism. Sancho's collected letters show that he was pioneering in another sense, too: he was the first black literary critic, or at least the first to write in a European language. In a letter of June of 1778 to John Meheux, he compares Sterne to other British authors such as Henry Fielding and Jonathan Swift. Sancho acknowledges Swift, the famous author of *Gulliver's Travels*, as "the first wit of this or any other nation," but differentiates between Swift's "grave-faced irony" and the way Sterne "lashes his whips with jolly laughter" (I, 45).

Again, he here emphasizes literature's humanizing potential, celebrating the emotional impact of Sterne's barbed comedy. Sancho writes: "Swift and Sterne were different in this—Sterne was truly a noble philanthropist—Swift was rather cynical;—what Swift would fret and fume at—such as the petty accidental *sourings* and *bitters* in life's cup—you plainly may see, Sterne would laugh at—and parry off by a larger humanity, and regular good will to man." For Sancho, literature can use both humor and sorrow to improve its readers.

In another letter, written in January of 1778, we find Sancho evaluating a fellow black author: Phillis Wheatley. Her poems, he writes, "do credit to nature—and put art—merely as art—to the blush" (I, 57). Sancho follows Alexander Pope's *Essay on Criticism* by viewing closeness to nature as a standard of good creative writing (I, 65), so this is apt praise for the famously Pope-loving Wheatley. Lest we be tempted to give any of the credit for Wheatley's achievement to her supposedly benevolent owners, Sancho adds: "It reflects nothing either to the glory or generosity of her master—if she is still his slave—except he glories in the *low vanity* of having in his wanton power a mind animated by Heaven—a genius superior to himself."

Two other themes in Sancho's letters worth mentioning are his concern for non-human animals and his religious universalism. Both come up in an August 1777 letter to Meheux, headed with the word "Jack-asses." Sancho describes his disgust upon seeing potato sellers overload and whip a poor donkey. This is "a too common evil—and, for the honor of rationality, calls loudly for redress" (I, 47). Sancho's talk of rationality suggests that he sees a role for reason, as well as sentiment, in reforming human behavior. He is "convinced we feel instinctively the injuries of our fellow creatures": both enslaved humans and beaten donkeys naturally provoke our sympathy, or at least they should. If we fail to intervene, this is because we have been socialized to ignore such natural sentiments. Sancho says he is "convinced that the general inhumanity of mankind proceeds—first, from the cursed false principle of common education." To identify and unlearn these anti-sentimental habits is the job of reason. Rational reflection thus allows us to feel as we *ought* to, and act accordingly.

Sancho believes that a second source of inhumanity is "a total indifference (if not disbelief) of the Christian faith." He points out that Jesus rode a donkey when he triumphantly arrived in Jerusalem and that this has always, for him, "stamped a kind of uncommon value and dignity" upon donkeys. But you shouldn't be an ass in your dealings with other animals either. Rather, "a heart and mind impressed with a firm belief of the Christian tenets must of course exercise itself in a constant uniform general philanthropy." Here Sancho ignores the etymological restriction of the term "philanthropy" to the love of humankind. If we are consistent and maximally rational, we will infer from our own dislike of pain that other sentient creatures too should be freed from suffering, and thus sympathize with non-human animals and not only other humans. Sancho jokes that, if Meheux would write something about the mistreatment of donkeys for the *Morning Post*, he will "bray [his] thanks." Given the racial context, this is more than just an amusing aside. Systems of white supremacy in general and slavery in particular tend to depict black people as comparable to non-human animals. So Sancho's joke involves a provocative embrace of identification with non-human animals—an empathy that was already easy to read into the image of an overburdened creature driven by the whip. Putting this all together, Sancho's implicit message is that it is rational to embrace an emotional reaction of sympathy with both suffering animals and suffering Africans.

After a few more quotidian, yet revealing details—Mrs. Sancho wants to send Meheux some tamarinds, and Sancho just took one of his daughters to see a famous actor friend play Falstaff in Shakespeare's *Henry IV, Part 1*—the letter's final paragraph brings us once again into philosophical territory. Sancho writes, "I am reading a little pamphlet, which I much like: it favours an opinion which I have long indulged—which is the improbability of eternal Damnation—a thought which almost petrifies one—and, in my opinion, derogatory to the fullness, glory, and benefit of the blessed expiation of the Son of the Most High God—who died for the sins of all—all—Jew, Turk, Infidel, and Heretic;—fair—sallow—brown—tawney—black—and you—and I—and every son and daughter of Adam." Here he again connects rational consistency and compassionate sentiment. The damnation of non-Christians is an un-Christian doctrine, given the nature of divine goodness as Sancho understands it. This contrasts vividly with other black writers we have discussed, as so many were wedded to Calvinist forms of Christianity, according to which God saves whomever he chooses to save, with only believing Christians among the elect.

We can link Sancho to the other main character of this chapter, Benjamin Banneker, through the famous person of Thomas Jefferson. Not that Sancho and Jefferson corresponded, or had much in common politically. Sancho did not live to see the outcome of the Revolutionary War, but he celebrated any sign of British victory in his letters and fervently wished for peace in the form of an empire reunited (I, 44; I, 54; II, 77). The connection is rather that Jefferson wrote about Sancho in his book, *Notes on the State of Virginia*, first published in 1785 while Jefferson was Minister to France. For Jefferson, Sancho was the best possible example of a black intellect. This sounds like high praise, but it isn't, because the remark comes in the context of an infamous section that argues for the natural inferiority of black people.

This part of the *Notes* is a digression, brought on by his proposal to emancipate all slaves in Virginia, then send them away from the state. Though he hypocritically owned hundreds of slaves throughout his entire life, Jefferson consistently took the position in his writings that slavery is a wrong that must be ended. Black people should be freed, and then sent away from America, for two main reasons. First, Jefferson expected lasting enmity between the emancipated slaves and their former masters, which could eventually result in a war of extermination. Second, he thought white people had an evident physical and intellectual superiority that would be undermined if proximity caused them regularly to procreate with black people. (If it is true, as significant evidence suggests, that he fathered six children with his slave Sally Hemings, then Jefferson is once again hypocritical here.) It is while arguing for the intellectual inferiority of black people that he makes the disparaging comments about Phillis Wheatley (see Chapter 25).

While unwilling to admit that Wheatley was a true poet, he acknowledges some limited value in Sancho's letters, in a passage that's worth quoting at length:

> Ignatius Sancho has approached nearer to merit in composition; yet his letters do more honour to the heart than the head. They breathe the purest effusions of friendship and general philanthropy, and shew how great a degree of the latter may be compounded with strong religious zeal. He is often happy in the turn of his compliments, and his style is easy and familiar, except when he affects a Shandean fabrication of words. But his imagination is wild and extravagant, escapes incessantly from every restraint of reason and taste, and, in the course of its vagaries, leaves a tract of thought as incoherent and eccentric, as is the course of a meteor through the sky. His subjects should often have led him to a process of sober reasoning: yet we find him always substituting sentiment for demonstration. Upon the whole, though, we admit him to the first place among those of his own colour who have presented themselves to the public judgment, yet when we compare him with the writers of the race among whom he lived, and particularly with the epistolary class, in which he has taken his own stand, we are compelled to enroll him at the bottom of the column. This criticism supposes the letters published under his name to be genuine, and to have received amendment from no other hand; points which would not be of easy investigation. (Query 14)

There is much that is repulsive and grating in the dismissive tone Jefferson adopts here. Sancho proves the rule by being exceptional: the best ever black writer, yet still rather mediocre. Still, Jefferson's remarks are not without insight. He puts his finger directly on the question we too have highlighted, that of the proper relationship between "sentiment" and "sober reasoning." Could it be that, contrary to Jefferson,

Sancho does not so much substitute sentiment for demonstration, as reveal just how essential sentiment is to cogent reasoning about ethics and aesthetics?

The correspondence between Banneker and Jefferson presses this same issue. Banneker initiated this exchange as one between two men of science, yet his letter links scientific reasoning to the experience of tender emotion. Before we get into this, though, let's say something about Banneker's life.[6] He was descended from an indentured servant from England, a white woman who, after becoming independent, bought but eventually freed and married one of her own slaves, a man named Bannaka or Banneky who had been an African prince before being abducted and transported across the Atlantic. Their daughter married another freed slave who had also been born in Africa. The eldest son of this union was Benjamin, who was born in 1731 and grew up helping on the family's tobacco farm. When he was in his early twenties, a budding interest in all things scientific and mathematical led him to an impressive accomplishment. Someone lent him a pocket watch and he took it apart. Once he understood its mechanism, he set himself the task of constructing a clock of his own. He succeeded, building a functioning clock almost completely out of wood, to the astonishment of those living near the family farm.

Significant for Banneker's subsequent development was his relationship with George Ellicott, a wealthy young man who befriended Banneker and supplied him with books about astronomy and instruments such as a telescope. Astronomy became his passion, and he eventually fulfilled his new ambition by producing an almanac. This required calculating the varying positions of celestial bodies over time in order to make predictions for the coming year concerning weather, tides, eclipses and phases of the moon, and so on. Almanacs also regularly featured historical, literary, and philosophical tidbits meant to entertain and edify readers. While at work on his almanac, Banneker was chosen in 1791 by another member of the Ellicott family to help survey the land selected by President Washington for the construction of the new capital of the United States. Banneker's role included the use of a special clock made for making astronomical observations, thus combining his areas of expertise. The *Georgetown Weekly Ledger* reported on Banneker's participation, writing that Ellicott was "attended by *Benjamin Banniker*, an Ethiopian, whose abilities, as a surveyor, and an astronomer, clearly prove that Mr. Jefferson's concluding that race of men were void of mental endowments, was without foundation."[7]

This brings us back to Banneker's letter to Jefferson, sent that same year. As one biographer has written, 1791 was truly his *annus mirabilis*, his year of wonders, when the survey of the federal territory was carried out and his first almanac was published.[8] In August of that year, Banneker sent an advance copy of the almanac to Jefferson, accompanied by his remarkable letter. Unlike that newspaper report, Banneker makes no reference to Jefferson's *Notes on the State of Virginia*. He may even have been unfamiliar with Jefferson's views on black inferiority, because he wrote:

> I suppose it is a truth too well attested to you, to need a proof here, that we are a race of Beings who have long laboured under the abuse and censure of the world, that we have long been looked upon with an eye of contempt, and that we have long been considered rather as brutish than human, and Scarcely capable of mental endowments. Sir I hope I may Safely admit, in consequence of that report which hath reached me, that you are a man far less inflexible in Sentiments of this nature, than many others, that you are measurably friendly and well disposed toward us, and that you are willing and ready to Lend your aid and assistance to our relief from those many distresses and numerous calamities to which we are reduced. (158)

Or perhaps Banneker was familiar with that notorious section in the *Notes*. Jefferson's heinous conclusion there had been framed in the hesitant language of the experimental method: "I advance it therefore as a suspicion only, that the blacks, whether originally a distinct race, or made distinct by time and circumstances, are inferior to the whites in the endowments both of body and mind" (Query 14). Banneker appeals to this Jefferson, the one who likes to think of himself as a man of science, one who is "less inflexible." Such a man can, and should, let the facts overwhelm his prejudice. Banneker also appeals to Jefferson as the author of the Declaration of Independence, which speaks of God-given, inalienable rights (and also to him as the author of those parts of the *Notes on the State of Virginia* that are critical of slavery and its effects: "There must doubtless be an unhappy influence on the manners of our people produced by the existence of slavery among us...Indeed I tremble for my country when I reflect that God is just" (Query 18)). Banneker expects Jefferson to agree that the Creator "hath not only made us all of one flesh, but hath also without partiality afforded us all the Same Sensations, and [endowed] us all with the same faculties" (155).

That allusion to universal human "Sensations" again raises the question of how emotion relates to reason. Prejudice against others, says Banneker, can be overcome by drawing proper inferences from the experience of self-love. He writes: "Sir, I have long been convinced, that if your love for your Selves, and for those inesteemable laws which preserve to you the rights of human nature, was founded on Sincerity, you could not but be Solicitous, that every Individual of whatsoever rank or distinction, might with you equally enjoy the blessings thereof" (161). The argument here may remind us of Lemuel Haynes' essay, "Liberty Further Extended." Banneker encourages Jefferson to think back to the uprising against the British crown as "a time in which [he] clearly saw into the injustice of a State of Slavery, and in which [he] had just apprehensions of the horrors of its condition" (161). Jefferson and other white Americans need only recall the "tender feelings" for themselves they felt at that time. This would allow them to follow the recommendation made by the suffering Job to his friends in the Bible: put their souls in his soul's stead.

In the letter's most audacious moment of all, Banneker attacks Jefferson's hypocrisy: "Sir how pitiable is it to reflect, that altho you were so fully convinced of the benevolence of the Father of mankind, and of his equal and impartial distribution of those rights and privileges which he had conferred upon them, that you should at the Same time counteract his mercies, in detaining by fraud and violence so numerous a part of my brethren under groaning captivity and cruel oppression, that you should at the Same time be found guilty of that most criminal act, which you professedly detested in others, with respect to yourselves" (162). Banneker lays out no plan of political action. Instead, he places his trust in the sympathy Jefferson and others like him will feel, if they would only more vividly imagine what black people experience by reflecting on their own feelings of self-love. Once this form of imaginative sympathy takes root, the same sympathy Sancho thought could be provoked by works of fiction, there will be no need for policy recommendations. As Banneker puts it, "thus shall your hearts be enlarged with kindness and benevolence toward them, and thus shall you need neither the direction of myself or others in what manner to proceed herein" (162). For Banneker, as for Sancho, tender sentiment is the essential first step in securing social progress.

Jefferson sent a gracious reply to Banneker about a week and a half later, complimenting Banneker while depicting himself as virtuously open-minded: "No body wishes more than I do to see such proofs as you exhibit, that nature has given to our black brethren, talents equal to those of the other colours of men, and that the appearance of a want of them is owing merely to the degraded condition of their existence both in Africa and America" (164). He informed Banneker that he was sending the almanac to the Marquis de Condorcet, Secretary of the Academy of Sciences in France, as a testament in favor of black people. His letter to Condorcet, which also survives, describes Banneker as "a very respectable mathematician." Jefferson also indulges in a bit of exaggeration by taking credit for procuring Banneker's services in the surveying of the new capital. Almost two decades later, though, he sang a different tune. Writing to his friend Joel Barlow, Jefferson suggested that he always had a low opinion of Banneker: "We know he had spherical trigonometry enough to make almanacs, but not without the suspicion of aid from Ellicott, who was his neighbor and friend, and never missed an opportunity of puffing him. I have a long letter from Banneker which shows him to have had a mind of very common stature indeed" (297). Ultimately, it seems that Jefferson's belief in black inferiority was harder to shake than the hand of someone ten miles away.

Yet after his death in 1806, Banneker was remembered as a scientific genius, the likes of whom the Africana tradition had not seen since Imhotep. To be fair, his accomplishments are often greatly exaggerated. He has been credited not merely with building a wooden clock from scratch, but with inventing America's first clock; not merely with being a mainly self-taught astronomer but with being the first American astronomer; not merely with publishing the six almanacs he published for the years 1792 to 1797, but with being the first in America to publish an almanac. He didn't just assist in surveying the land that became Washington DC, but supposedly designed the city himself. Such embellishments are, however, quite unnecessary. As Silvio Bedini, author of the most authoritative biography on Banneker, has remarked, "Banneker's attainments, which were impressive and substantial, should be truthfully reported and evaluated, and…his philosophy should be properly understood in order that it may serve as an example to others."[9]

28

SONS OF AFRICA

Quobna Ottobah Cugoano and Olaudah Equiano

Good cop, bad cop. We all know this strategy from movies and television, where a suspect is alternately menaced and offered cups of coffee, in an attempt to secure maximum cooperation. It might seem an uncomfortable analogy for explaining the strategies of black activists, given the history of police brutality and police killings that have disproportionately affected black people in general, and black activists in particular. After all, when Martin Luther King was engaging in protests for civil rights in the southern United States, he met with a whole lot of bad cop and not much good cop. Yet it's an illuminating analogy nonetheless, as we can learn from Coretta Scott King, Martin's wife and in her own right a leading figure of the non-violent Civil Rights Movement. She told the story of a conversation between herself and the fiery black nationalist leader Malcolm X, who famously defended black people's right to violent resistance. Malcolm argued that he was being helpful to the Kings by publicly attacking Martin, saying: "If the white people realize what the alternative is, perhaps they will be more willing to listen to Dr. King."[1]

For a similar contrast, we can look at two authors who were active nearly two centuries earlier: Olaudah Equiano and Quobna Ottobah Cugoano, both of whom have been mentioned already. Cugoano's *Thoughts and Sentiments* burns with the fire of a Malcolm X in its excoriating attack on the slave trade and slavery in the West Indies, complete with repeated attempts to instill fear by warning of the danger of divine retribution, should the British people fail to end this ongoing abomination. Equiano produced something quite different, and arguably much less threatening. *The Interesting Narrative of the Life of Olaudah Equiano, or Gustavus Vassa, the African*, published two years after Cugoano's book, in 1789, is an autobiography unlike anything that came before it in the Africana tradition. Of course, it's not our first autobiographical text: we have already discussed those by Gronniosaw and Marrant

(Chapter 24). But Equiano's work was much longer and more detailed than these and, importantly, written by himself. The title page announces this fact, thus distinguishing Equiano's narrative from those written down, edited, and quite possibly shaped or reshaped in significant ways by a white amanuensis.

Equiano is explicit about the political purpose of his writing. He dedicates the book to the members of the two houses of the British Parliament with these words: "Permit me, with the greatest deference and respect, to lay at your feet the following genuine Narrative; the chief design of which is to excite in your august assemblies a sense of compassion for the miseries which the Slave-Trade has entailed on my unfortunate countrymen" (*Narrative* 7).[2] So even the political target is somewhat more modest than the one at which Cugoano aimed. Cugoano's *Thoughts and Sentiments* attacks with equal vigor the practice of slavery in Britain's colonies and the slave trade itself, whereas Equiano mainly addresses the latter, in cooperation with efforts going on at that time in Parliament. Besides which, there's a difference between fiery warnings of divine retribution and attempting to excite compassion through one man's tale of suffering and overcoming. Does this perhaps make Equiano the good cop to Cugoano's bad cop?

Unlike Martin Luther King and Malcolm X, Cugoano and Equiano were close friends and collaborators, sharing a common cause, if not a common approach. Difference in approach may help explain why Equiano's book was so much more successful than Cugoano's. It's hardly surprising that readers preferred its gentler appeal to compassion.[3] Equiano's greater fame and the more obvious impact and influence of his book eventually put Cugoano in his shadow. But, as historians of philosophy, we're going to give Cugoano pride of place, and not only for chronological reasons. The shadow of Equiano has been so long that Cugoano's *Thoughts and Sentiments*, when remembered at all, has often been categorized as a slave narrative alongside Equiano's, but this is a mistake. True, Cugoano takes a moment early on in the book to tell the story of his life, in the powerful and moving passage we used to introduce the second part of our own book (Chapter 22). But his work as a whole cannot be appropriately described as a narrative; it is rather a treatise of political thought, which includes an autobiographical aside. It is, in fact, arguably the earliest book-length work of Africana philosophy in a European language.

Still, let's not abandon narrative just yet, but instead take up the story of Cugoano's life where we left it. As we noted, he was brought as a slave at the age of 13 from what is now Ghana to the island of Grenada. He spent a little less than a year there before being brought to various other islands that he does not name. Toward the end of 1772, when he would have been 15, he was brought to England by the man who owned him, Alexander Campbell. This just so happened to be the year that the judge Lord Mansfield came to his landmark decision in the case of *Somerset vs Stuart*, which involved the question whether a slave brought to England could be sent back to the colonies against his will. Lord Mansfield said no, a decision generally understood as a ban on slavery in England itself, whatever may be the case in its colonies. We lack details on Cugoano's own emancipation upon arriving in England. We do know that he was baptized, after being advised that doing so might help him avoid a forced return to the colonies, and took the name "John Stuart." While we will continue to use the name he used for the book, judging by the way he signed his own letters and how others have referred to him, he was generally known under this new name in his daily life.

We know little else about Cugoano's life in the 1770s, apart from his successful efforts to gain literacy during this time. By 1784 he was working in the household of Richard and Maria Cosway, both of whom were artists. (Here we have yet another reason to mention Thomas Jefferson, who was deeply in love with Maria Cosway, and corresponded with her until his death in 1826.) Perhaps the only existing likeness of Cugoano is an etching from 1784 that shows Richard and Maria sitting while Cugoano serves them grapes. The polite, obliging servant depicted here is hard to square with the enraged and disgusted tone found in his writing on slavery. That activist side of Cugoano began with a visit he made in July of 1786 to see Granville Sharp, at that time the most prominent anti-slavery activist in Britain. Cugoano and his friend William Green, another black Londoner, informed Sharp that a black man named Harry Demane had been tricked by his employer into getting on to a ship bound for the West Indies, where he was to be enslaved. A writ of habeas corpus was obtained and Demane was saved just in the nick of time, as the ship was about to depart. That same year, 1786, gives us Cugoano's earliest known writing: a letter he sent to the Prince of Wales urging him to "endeavour to release the oppressed and put a stop to that iniquitous traffic of buying and selling men" (*Thoughts* 183).[4]

Cugoano then published his *Thoughts and Sentiments* in July of 1787. At the end of that year, he was among a group of individuals who sent a letter of gratitude to Sharp, thanking him for his many efforts and accomplishments in the struggle against slavery. This letter was signed by Cugoano and ten others, including Equiano, who collectively addressed themselves to Sharp as "the Sons of Africa." This is generally counted as the first of a series of letters sent publicly or privately by this group, whose personnel varied but featured Cugoano and Equiano as core members. The Sons of Africa have been treated by some historians as a pioneering black political organization. Others warn that it was at best a loose network that did little more than write congratulatory letters to leading white figures in the anti-slavery movement. For our purposes, the importance of the Sons of Africa is to frame the philosophical contributions of Cugoano and Equiano, and confirm the shared aims and collaborative spirit underlying their works.

Even as he led efforts within the black community, Cugoano also took inspiration from anti-slavery texts by white authors. Among them was Thomas Clarkson, who eventually attained a stature in the abolitionist movement similar to that of Sharp. In 1786, he published his Cambridge dissertation, originally written in Latin, entitled *An Essay on the Slavery and Commerce of the Human Species, Particularly the African*. It is no coincidence that Cugoano echoes Clarkson in the full title of his book: *Thoughts and Sentiments on the Evil and Wicked Traffic of the Slavery and Commerce of the Human Species, Humbly Submitted to the Inhabitants of Great-Britain, by Ottobah Cugoano, a Native of Africa*. This marks it as a sort of sequel to Clarkson's treatise, written by an African who had first-hand experience of the slave trade and slavery in the colonies. Cugoano even quotes and paraphrases Clarkson during his reflections on the divine retribution Europeans invite upon themselves through the evil practice of slavery.

Another admired precursor of Cugoano's was James Ramsay, an Anglican priest who spent time in St. Kitts, witnessing and protesting against the brutality of slavery there. After returning to Britain, he wrote a book called *An Essay on the Treatment and Conversion of African Slaves in the British Sugar Colonies*, published in 1784. This eye-opening attack on colonial slavery provoked a response by a plantation owner named James Tobin, published anonymously under the title *Cursory Remarks upon the Reverend Mr. Ramsay's Essay on the Treatment and Conversion of African Slaves in the British Sugar Colonies*. (For all their other disagreements, authors of this time were united in their preference for a nice long title.) Cugoano's first order of business, after bringing to a close the autobiographical portion of his book, is to refute Tobin, whom he calls the "Cursory Remarker."

One of Tobin's strategies was to argue that West Indian slaves are better off than the poor in England, who must fend for themselves while slaves are provided for by their masters. In response, Cugoano argues that we must distinguish between hardship and losing status as a human being. Even if some dogs would refuse crumbs that a person in dire poverty would be glad to eat, this does not mean the person would be willing to trade places with the dog. Here we can already see that Cugoano is operating at the level of political philosophy, as well as polemic: his point is that freedom has an absolute value that is incommensurable with material welfare. But let's grant for the sake of argument, Cugoano tells us, that the situation of slaves is superior to that of the English poor. Would this justify slavery, as Tobin suggests? Why should it not instead spur us to fight against all suffering and oppression, whether in the form of poverty or slavery? If anything, Tobin's comparison leads us toward greater appreciation of the purpose of political community itself. Cugoano writes: "And this seems to be pointed out by the circumstances he describes; that it is the great duty, and ought to be the highest ambition of all governors, to order and establish such policy, and in such a wise manner, that every thing should be so managed, as to be conducive to the moral, temporal and eternal welfare of every individual from the lowest degree to the highest; and the consequence of this would be, the harmony, happiness and good prosperity of the whole community" (*Thoughts* 20).

Thoughts and Sentiments also has interesting things to say about the origins, and value, of racial difference. Proponents of slavery like Tobin seemed to think that being black was enough to justify oppression. Cugoano resists this with a mix of religious and rational argumentation. He draws first on Paul's claim in Acts 17:26 that God has made all nations "of one blood"; the context, as it happens, is Paul's visit to Athens and controversy with Epicurean and Stoic philosophers. For Cugoano, this verse establishes that all people, whatever their color, share a common origin. In fact, it suggests that at one time, we were all the *same* color. How is it then that we are now so diverse in complexion? Not by choice, obviously, so God Himself must be the source of this variety.

When we observe the globe, Cugoano claims, we may further notice a purposeful pattern in this variety: "As the bodies of men are tempered with a different degree to enable them to endure the respective climates of their habitations, so their colors vary, in some degree, in a regular gradation from the equator towards either of the poles" (*Thoughts* 29-30). The implication is that diversity in color is actually a product of divine benevolence. He concludes that "it may be reasonably, as well as religiously inferred, that He who placed them in their various situations, hath extended equally his care and protection to all; and from thence, that it becometh unlawful to counteract his benignity, by reducing others of different complexions to undeserved bondage" (*Thoughts* 30). So the systematic subjugation of others who are different in color is not merely unjustified but also irrational. It perversely treats a sign of God's special concern for the flourishing of His creatures as a reason to interfere with, and undermine, that very flourishing.

Understanding God and His divine plan is, more generally, a central theme in the book. Nowhere is it more thoughtfully and audaciously pursued than in what we may call Cugoano's "emblem theory" of divine communication. Apologists for slavery routinely made the point that bondage was practiced by the Israelites under the law of Moses. Cugoano contends that this was not slavery, but vassalage, which requires the consent of the person kept in servitude. In truth, this is a very questionable interpretation of Old Testament labor practices, but Cugoano could shrug off that objection, because his more important point is that the Old Testament is no model for social practices in the present. We are meant rather to understand it as metaphorically significant for our individual struggles to attain salvation. He follows this point to its logical conclusion by claiming that God may intend any natural phenomenon or historical event to teach us how we may be saved. He sees a "sacred language" operating in "all the variety of things in nature," with the result that we should see all things as "figures, types and emblems, and other symbolical representations, to bring forward, usher in, hold forth, and illustrate that most amazing transaction," namely, our salvation and redemption through Jesus Christ (*Thoughts* 38–9). The whole world, we might say, is the ultimate "talking book," and the story it tells is a Christian one.

This is inspiring stuff, but it leads Cugoano to a line of thought we're apt to find uncomfortable. He illustrates the emblem theory by referring to Jeremiah 13:23: "Can the Ethiopian change his skin, or the leopard his spots? Then may ye also do good, that are accustomed to do evil." Which sounds like just a simple analogy, but Cugoano's theory implies that the very purpose and function of the leopard's and black person's skin is, at least in part, to teach all humans that they cannot rid themselves of their sinful nature by their own efforts. Earlier, he proclaimed that dark skin is evidence of God's beneficence; here, it is, disturbingly, connected to the tenacious grip of sinfulness on our soul. Cugoano appears to recognize that he is in danger of self-contradiction, as he emphasizes the need to remember that "the external blackness of the Ethiopians, is as innocent and natural, as spots in the leopards" (*Thoughts* 41). No one blames the leopard for having spots and, similarly, black people should not be thought of as evil on account of their color. Still, it is hard not to feel that this application of the emblem theory brings evil uncomfortably close to blackness.

Let's return from what Cugoano calls "the sublime science of metaphysics" (*Thoughts* 39) to more straightforwardly moral and political matters. We saw Lemuel Haynes draw back from defending the right of the enslaved to resist violently, but Cugoano was not so reticent. Just as Malcolm X would later speak of attaining black freedom "by any means necessary," Cugoano claims in *Thoughts and Sentiments* that we have a duty to seek to escape enslavement. Thus "if there was no other way to deliver a man from slavery, but by enslaving his master, it would be lawful for him to do so if he was able, for this would be doing justice to himself, and be justice as the law requires, to chastise his master for enslaving…him wrongfully" (*Thoughts* 59). We shouldn't push the comparisons with Malcolm too far, however. In an earlier passage, Cugoano sounds more like the non-violent King. Having just invoked the Golden Rule to say that slaveowners ought to treat others as they wish to be treated, he cautions his enslaved brethren: "But our Divine Lord and Master Christ also teacheth men to forgive one another their trespasses, and that we are not to do evil because others do so, and to revenge injuries done unto us, wherefore it is better, and more our duty, to suffer ourselves to be lashed and cruelly treated, than to take up the task of their barbarity" (*Thoughts* 52). So which is it: bad cop or good cop?

Actually, Cugoano is not being inconsistent. Cugoano tells slaves to avoid vengeful brutality, not any and all violence. He can still approve the use of force so long as it is necessary for the sake of deliverance, rather than revenge. But when Cugoano wants most to strike fear into the heart of those defending slavery, he concentrates on the threat from above. "Nothing else," he says, "can be expected for such violations of taking away the natural rights and liberties of men, but that those who are the doers of it will meet with some awful visitation of the righteous judgment of God, and in such a manner as it cannot be thought that his just vengeance for their iniquity will be the less tremendous because his judgments are long delayed" (*Thoughts* 61). And it is not only those who own or defend slaves who should be frightened. Cugoano goes so far as to say that "while ever such a horrible business as the slavery and oppression of the Africans is carried on, there is not one man in all Great-Britain and her colonies, that knoweth any thing of it, can be innocent and safe, unless he speedily riseth up with abhorrence of it in his own judgment, and, to avert evil, declare himself against it, and all such notorious wickedness" (*Thoughts* 79). Invoking the most fearsome bad cop of all, the one we know from the Old Testament, Cugoano exhorts all his countrymen to erupt in protest, lest they bring divine punishment down upon themselves.

Sadly, we have no contemporary reviews of *Thoughts and Sentiments* to tell us how white readers reacted to this heavy indictment of all those who had not yet spoken out against slavery. By contrast, we have a number of responses to Equiano's *Interesting Narrative*, including one by a figure of great importance in the history of feminist philosophy: Mary Wollstonecraft.[5] She found the book's depiction of the slave trade and Equiano's quest for freedom compelling, but less so Equiano's focus on his spiritual journey to the Christian faith.

Equiano's first chapter gives us a nice connection between this stage of Africana philosophy and our discussion of precolonial Africa. He tells us he was born in 1745 in Igboland, in what is now Nigeria, and then launches into a detailed description of as many of the customs of his people as he can recall, covering political structure, law, marriage rites, music, dance, clothing, food, drink, architecture, commerce, agriculture, war, religion, measurement of time, hygiene, burial rites, and more. All this ethnographic detail conveys a sense of cultural pride. Indeed, Equiano justifies this digression as a product of the principle of "love of one's country" (*Narrative* 46). Yet there is some doubt as to whether Igboland really was his country. His modern biographer Vincent Carretta points to evidence that he may in fact have been born in South Carolina.[6] Still, many of the ethnographic details of that opening chapter, such as transliterated Igbo words, remain credible. If the claim of an African birthplace is indeed fictional license, that would, in fact, all the more highlight Equiano's pride in being a son of Africa. This pride is expressed in another way when he compares Igbo customs with those of the ancient Hebrews as recorded in the Bible. These similarities suggest to him that his people were directly descended from the Jewish people. (Even today, a distinct minority among the Igbo take themselves to be descended from a lost tribe of Israel and practice Judaism.)

According to Equiano's account, he was 11 years old when he and his sister were abducted. He speaks in heart-breaking terms of being separated from her, then briefly reunited, before a second, permanent separation. Eventually, he endured the horrible trip across the Atlantic and was brought via Barbados to Virginia, where he was purchased by a Mr. Campbell. Amazingly, this may be the same Alexander Campbell who later purchased Cugoano and then brought him to England, which would mean that Equiano and Cugoano, later activists and friends, may have both been enslaved by the same man in different places and at different times.

Equiano's time with Campbell was brief. A lieutenant in the Royal Navy named Michael Henry Pascal bought him, initially planning to give him as a present to friends in England. During the trip to England, Pascal gave him the name Gustavus Vassa, after the first king of modern Sweden. (Like his friend Cugoano, Equiano generally used this European name throughout his life, but chose to use his African name when publishing his book.) Equiano accompanied Lt. Pascal on various voyages, and saw action during the Seven Years War against the French. As he gained in experience and education, the teenaged Equiano began to look forward to eventually gaining his freedom, but he was unexpectedly sold and brought to the Caribbean island of Montserrat. There he was purchased by a Quaker merchant, Robert King, who clearly did not follow the prohibition on involvement with slavery that we often associate with Quakers. Nevertheless, he did allow Equiano to purchase his freedom after building up sufficient funds by working on ships, and so, in 1766, Equiano was emancipated. Once free, he kept to the sea, traveling all the way to Turkey, where he was "surprised to see how the Greeks are, in some measure, kept under by the Turks, as the negroes are in the West Indies by the white people" (*Narrative* 167–8). He also took part in a failed attempt to find the Northwest Passage to Asia through the Arctic Circle; when his ship got stuck in the ice, the ordeal focused Equiano's mind on his eternal salvation. Although at one point he found himself more attracted to Islam than Christianity, he had a transformative religious experience in 1774 that confirmed him as a Christian (specifically, like a number of other black writers of the time, a Calvinist Methodist).

Next comes a shocking turn in the *Interesting Narrative*: Equiano chooses to accompany his friend Dr. Charles Irving to the Mosquito Coast of Central America in order to develop a sugar plantation. Equiano says he even helped purchase slaves for the plantation: "I chose them all my own countrymen" (*Narrative* 178). Carretta explains Equiano's decision by saying that he "was convinced that his own experiences and observations as a slave enabled him to be a humane overseer of slaves"; only later would he recognize "humane slavery" as a contradiction in terms.[7] Yet by this point, in 1776, Equiano was already familiar with Granville Sharp. He had called on Sharp to help him in 1774 when a friend of his named John Annis was captured in order to be sent back to the Caribbean. Unfortunately, Annis was not saved.

Once the 1780s came along, Equiano too turned to anti-slavery activism. At the end of his *Interesting Narrative*, Equiano traces his role as public abolitionist to an address of gratitude to the Quakers written by himself and others in 1785. He does not give specifics, but this is almost certainly an action by the Sons of Africa, including Cugoano, that predates their letter to Sharp. Equiano was also the one who got Sharp involved with what is now known as the Zong massacre: after 133 Africans were thrown off a slave ship to drown, a dispute resulted from the shipowners' attempt to collect insurance money for their loss. Sharp unsuccessfully tried to have the ship's crew charged with murder.[8] Connection with Sharp also played a role in Equiano's involvement with the Sierra Leone project. This was a government-sponsored plan by Sharp and others to provide for the resettlement in West Africa of the so-called "Black Poor" of London, who included many Loyalist veterans of the Revolutionary War in America, and even some people from India who had worked for the East India Company.

Equiano was selected by the Committee for the Relief of the Black Poor to help oversee the project, but conflict with a colleague led to his dismissal. A letter from Equiano to Cugoano about the messy affair was published in the *Public Advertiser*. In *Thoughts and Sentiments*, published mere months after ships left England for Sierra Leone, Cugoano brought his characteristic insight to the matter. On the one hand, he deemed the plan for resettlement "a more honorable way of colonization, than any Christian nation have ever done before" (*Thoughts* 104). On the other hand, he pointed out the fundamental flaw and hypocrisy of the British government seeking to establish a free colony not far from where it continued to "support its forts and garrisons, to ensnare, merchandize, and to carry others into captivity and slavery" (*Thoughts* 106). The initial Sierra Leone colony failed, but five years later a new infusion of Black Loyalists from Nova Scotia gave it new impetus. The revived colony has grown into the modern nation of Sierra Leone.

Equiano ends his *Interesting Narrative* by arguing that the abolition of the slave trade will facilitate mutually beneficial trade between the British and Africa: "It is trading upon safe grounds. A commercial intercourse with Africa opens an inexhaustible source of wealth to the manufacturing interests of Great Britain, and to all which the slave trade is an objection" (*Narrative* 250-1). Thinking along the same lines, Cugoano outlines three steps toward achieving this goal. First, national days of mourning and fasting to seek forgiveness from God. Second, total abolition of slavery. Third, "that a fleet of some ships of war should be immediately sent to the coast of Africa, and particularly where the slave trade is carried on, with faithful men to direct that none should be brought from the coast of Africa without their own consent and the approbation of their friends, and to intercept all merchant ships that were bringing them away, until such a scrutiny was made, whatever nation they belonged to" (*Thoughts* 100).

Equiano died in 1797, by which time Cugoano was probably also dead, though his activities are unknown after 1791, when he published a shorter, lightly revised version of *Thoughts and Sentiments*. So probably neither man lived to see the British outlaw the slave trade in 1807 and slavery in the colonies in 1834. Surely they would have been gratified that, following abolition, Britain adopted the third policy proposed by Cugoano. The same Royal Navy with whom Equiano had often sailed established the West Africa Squadron to patrol the West African coast. It is estimated that 1,600 slave ships were seized and 150,000 captured Africans were freed through this effort. Many of these "recaptives," as they were called, chose to settle in Sierra Leone, greatly growing the colony's population: sons and daughters of Africa who could live free in the motherland.

29

LIBERTY, EQUALITY, HUMANITY

The Haitian Revolution

Some revolutions are violent, others not. The French Revolution was famously bloody, as was the American Revolution. On the non-violent side, you might think of such events as the fall of the Berlin Wall or the 2004 Orange Revolution in Ukraine. Plus the earth performs a revolution around the sun once a year rather peacefully, and the Beatles' "Revolution Number 9," while pretty weird, does not involve any actual bloodshed. The Haitian Revolution, though, belongs in the violent category. It began with a slave insurrection in 1791 and culminated with Haiti's independence at the start of 1804. Over a decade and more of warfare there was tremendous loss of life, numbering in the hundreds of thousands. The revolution exemplifies the old adage that violence begets violence. In the late eighteenth century, what is now the independent nation of Haiti was the colony of Saint Domingue. It was a hugely lucrative colony for the French, producing about half the supply of both sugar and coffee for the entire world, alongside cotton and indigo.[1] But the enormous profits were extracted with enormous brutality. Every year, 30,000 slaves were imported from Africa, with about one-third of them dying within one year of their arrival, from disease and the harsh working conditions. To maintain the submission of their supposedly subhuman chattel, the slavemasters and overseers displayed a creative sadism that was itself inhuman.

In his pioneering account of the Haitian revolution, the Trinidadian historian and political theorist C.L.R. James enumerated some of the tortures and execution methods used by the French: pouring boiling sugar on the skin, stuffing the slaves with gunpowder and then igniting it, burying them up to their necks in the earth and smearing their heads with sugar, so that insects would devour them. Even in the course of normal working days, as James put it, "the slaves received the whip with more certainty and regularity than they received their food" (*Black Jacobins* 12).[2] After the revolution and the final grand victory of defeating Napoleon's army in 1803, the tables turned. In 1804, the revolutionary leader Jean-Jacques Dessalines undertook a campaign of extermination against white residents of the island. He justified his own violence by referring to what had been done by the slavedrivers: "We have given these true cannibals war for war, crimes for crimes, outrages for outrages. Yes, I have saved my country, I have avenged America."[3]

The Haitian Revolution was the largest modern slave revolt, the only one that succeeded in eliminating slavery within the territory where it occurred, and the only one that resulted in the establishment of a continuously existing independent state. Obviously it was, in large part, a matter of enslaved Africans being fed up with their horrific treatment. Scholars have debated the question of whether another important influence on this singular uprising was the French Enlightenment. The aforementioned C.L.R. James already suggested its relevance with the title of his book on the Revolution: *The Black Jacobins*.[4] For James it was no coincidence that the black population of Saint Domingue erupted in revolt in 1791, just two years after the Declaration of the Rights of Man in France, then in the early stages of its own revolution. James pointed out that the rebel leaders, especially Toussaint L'Ouverture, made frequent reference to the Enlightenment values of liberty and equality. On this telling, the Haitian revolutionaries were accepting an invitation extended by French intellectuals like Denis Diderot, who had spoken out against slavery and even predicted uprisings. One work in particular, called *Philosophical History of the Two Indies*, published by the Abbé Raynal in 1779, was definitely known to Toussaint. Raynal had written, "a courageous chief only is wanted," and as Toussaint explicitly said, it was he who became that chief (*Black Jacobins* 25; *Toussaint* 41).[5]

Writing in 1938, C.L.R. James saw these historical events as urgently relevant to his own time. He saw a kinship between the slaveholders of the Caribbean and the racist colonizers of his day (*Black Jacobins* 43). The rebellious slaves meanwhile provided a positive example: James looked forward to similar uprisings in twentieth century Africa (*Black Jacobins* 141, 376). This was Marxist history, pointing to the revolutionary potential of all oppressed masses by exploring a unique case, one in which the most oppressed masses of all quite literally realized that they had nothing to lose but their chains, and managed to seize power from their tormentors. James' own political agenda is clear from the fierce aphorisms sprinkled throughout his historical narrative, such as "the rich are only defeated when running for their lives" and "when did property ever listen to reason except when cowed by violence?" (*Black Jacobins* 78, 70).

James saw the plantation workers as the closest thing that the late eighteenth century had to a "proletariat" (*Black Jacobins* 86) and also understood the revolution back in France in terms of bottom-up, rather than top-down, social forces.[6] His hopes for the Africa of his own time were expressed in the same terms: "From the people heaving in action will come the leaders; not the isolated blacks at Guys' Hospital or the Sorbonne, the dabblers in surrealisme or the lawyers" (*Black Jacobins* 377). And elsewhere: "Let the blacks but hear from Europe the slogans of Revolution, and the Internationale, in the same concrete manner that the slaves of San Domingo heard Liberty and Equality and the Marseillaise, and from the mass uprising will emerge the Toussaints, the Christophes, and the Dessalines."[7]

Following a Marxist analysis in terms of class, which took the Haitian Revolution to be an inevitable manifestation of economic forces, James sometimes de-emphasized the factor of race. If this was a war of black against white, that was because black skin was correlated with being a victim of economic oppression. Thus James was capable of writing, of the parallel developments back in France, "had the monarchists been white, the bourgeoisie brown, and the masses of France black, the French Revolution would have gone down in history as a race war" (*Black Jacobins* 128). On the other hand, James did not intend to suggest that race could be ignored or treated as completely inconsequential: "To neglect the racial factor as merely incidental is an error only less grave than to make it fundamental" (283). This was, after all, a story of complex racial and economic divisions, in which slaves, free people of color, poor whites, and rich colonists all pursued separate agendas and variously worked with or against one another at different stages, not to mention the involvement of three European powers—France, Britain, and Spain—with whom different factions had shifting allegiances.

Some historians have doubted whether the ideas of the French Enlightenment really helped to motivate the wider black population.[8] As historians of philosophy, we will leave that question to the historians of events and focus instead on James' valuable observation that leaders of the Revolution did indeed cite Enlightenment values and work them into the fabric of the new state that they founded. A letter supposedly written by three of the initial leaders of the revolt addressed white slaveowners in the following terms: "We are your equals by natural right, and if nature pleases itself to diversify colors within the human race, it is not a crime to be born black nor an advantage to be white...Have you forgotten that you have formally vowed the Declaration of the Rights of Man, which says that men are born free, equal in their rights, that their natural rights include liberty, property, security and resistance to oppression?" (*Toussaint* 6–7).

There is some doubt about the authenticity of that letter, but the public pronouncements and letters of Toussaint L'Ouverture himself are full of the same sentiments.[9] When he first announced himself as a rebel leader, he said, "I have undertaken this vengeance, and I want liberty and equality to reign in St-Domingue" (*Toussaint* 1). He never tired of repeating his commitment to anti-monarchist, republican values, stating for example that "anyone who is a subject or vassal of kings is no more than a vile slave, and a republican alone is truly a man" (*Toussaint* 16). This helps us to make sense of the fact that, after forcing the French grudgingly to emancipate the slaves of Saint Domingue, Toussaint fought under the banner of the republican French government against the Spanish, with whom he was previously allied, and against a British invasion of the island.

Some have questioned Toussaint's sincerity, or at least the depth of his conviction, as a proponent of freedom and equality, charging that, upon assuming unchallenged leadership over his people, he all but reinstated the slave system.[10] He required workers to return to the fields and forbade them to leave their plantations, stopping them from heading to the towns in search of more lucrative and less backbreaking occupations. Children were to start laboring "as soon as they can walk," and identification cards were introduced to make it easier to monitor the workers' movements (*Toussaint* 67, 70). But for Toussaint, there was no contradiction between his idealistic promises and rigorous demands.[11] Pre-revolutionary Saint Domingue had been a slave state, not a republic, with no legitimate relations of justice whatsoever. When plantation workers threw off their yoke, they were not defying the rule of law, because the law of slavery, as enshrined in the infamous "Black Code (*Code Noir*)" of the French colonies, was in fact no law at all. Now that the island's inhabitants were free, they needed to contribute to the prosperity and happiness of the society as a whole. Thus Toussaint justified his draconian measures as follows: "To ensure freedom, without which man cannot be happy, it is necessary for all to occupy themselves usefully in order to contribute to the public good and general tranquility" (*Toussaint* 28). Later on, looking back on these decisions after being captured by the French, he was still prepared to defend them: "It was for the general happiness of the island, for the interest of the Republic" (*Toussaint* 95).

What we see in the political thinking of Toussaint L'Ouverture, then, is a particular blend of republican values of liberty and equality with more authoritarian ideas of compulsory social solidarity. A similar blend was, of course, also espoused by some revolutionary thinkers back in France, notably and most infamously by the best-known Jacobin of them all, Maximilien Robespierre. Toussaint, we might say, held a certain sort of "communitarian" political ideal. His Constitution of 1801, which established him as "governor for life" (*Toussaint* 51, Article 28), sets out a vision of social harmony in terms of a close-knit family, describing the head of each plantation as the symbolic "father" of those who work there (*Toussaint* 48, Article 15). This echoed Toussaint's earlier aspiration of making the residents of Saint Domingue "a single, unified family of friends and brothers" (*Toussaint* 30). It's an idea he also applied to the issue of race, talking fondly of the notion that the black and white man might see each other as "brothers from the same mother" (*Toussaint* 28).

We know already that "communal" political structures were common in precolonial Africa (Chapter 16). It does not seem far-fetched to see Toussaint as deliberately invoking this cultural tendency. His idea of making each plantation, and Saint Domingue as a whole, "one happy family" might have purposely appealed to transported Africans who had grown up with communalist values. More generally, we should not assume that the ideas and ideologies that helped inspire the Haitian Revolution must have been European. Before Toussaint assumed center stage, there had been other rebel leaders who spoke not, or not only, in terms of Enlightenment ideals but also in the religious language of Vodou.

A first, unsuccessful case was that of Makandal, who already in 1758 planned a mass poisoning attack on slaveholders but was betrayed before he could carry through his plot. This charismatic figure was said to possess magical abilities, such as knowledge of the future (which apparently failed him at the crucial hour) and shapeshifting, as in the legend that he transformed into an insect to escape when he was captured and burnt to death. More decisive was the rebel leader Boukman Dutty, who came to Haiti from Jamaica. He was among those that triggered the initial uprising in 1791. Famously, Boukman and a Vodou priestess named Cécile Fatiman led a ceremony in which a pig was sacrificed, and its blood drunk. Boukman then reportedly gave a short speech ending with the sort of language also found in the proclamations of Toussaint L'Ouverture: "Listen to the voice of liberty, which speaks in the hearts of us all" (*Black Jacobins* 87).

In assessing this event, we can benefit from what we learned about traditional religious practices in Africa. As we saw when looking at topics like God and divination, spiritual beliefs across Africa are many and varied, and that variety was transported to Saint Domingue and other colonies along with the unfortunate victims of the slave trade. Modern historians have tried to identify the specific cultural context of the pig sacrifice as described in several historical documents, and proposed either a Kongo or Fon background.[12] As in other colonies, the enslaved population would have been diverse. So we might wonder whether, already at this early period, there was a standardized and widely shared system of Vodou beliefs or ritual practices that could unify all those who rose up in revolt. What we do know, at least, is that, in many African cultures, political power was regularly linked to religious authority.

This gives us a useful context for understanding how figures like Makandal and Boukman were able to galvanize and mobilize members of the slave population.

One reason to prefer explanations of the Haitian Revolution that focus on African cultural factors rather than the European Enlightenment would be the proponents of that Enlightenment were often remarkably racist in their thinking and inadequate in their opposition to slavery. True, there were critics of slavery in France in the generation or two leading up to the time of the Revolution, like Diderot and Raynal. But even the self-styled "Friends of the Blacks (*Amis des Noirs*)," a French abolitionist group, argued only for gradual emancipation. A number of apparently progressive Enlightenment thinkers had hands that were well stained by the blood of Africans. Modern-day scholar Louis Sala-Molins has called out various heroes from the history of philosophy for making only half-hearted protests, or no protests at all, against the slave trade, and for investing their own money in that trade.[13] He condemns such famous names as Condorcet, Montesquieu, and Rousseau, and even the aforementioned critics of slavery Raynal and Diderot.

In fact, argues Sala-Molins, the Enlightenment and the French Revolution it helped spawn were only possible in the first place because of the French colonial empire. The wealth it generated gave a class of intellectuals enough autonomy and ambition that they were able to envision overthrowing their own masters. As C.L.R. James already noted, "the slave-trade and slavery were the economic basis of the French Revolution" (*Black Jacobins* 47). Another of James' nice aphorisms captures the way that self-interest limited the French intelligentsia's willingness to act against slavery: the bourgeois "put the Rights of Man in their pockets whenever the colonial question came up" (*Black Jacobins* 68–9). Then too, there is the fact that the right to *property* was itself a fundamental Enlightenment value. That right was, of course, constantly emphasized by the slaveowners. They met every attempt to curtail their brutality by insisting upon their sacred right to dispose of their possessions as they wished, the possessions in this case being other humans.

But perhaps this is no reason to dismiss the importance of the Enlightenment for the uprising in Saint Domingue. To the contrary, the hypocrisy of European thinkers might lead us to conclude that it was only in the Haitian Revolution that the values at stake in the French Revolution were truly embraced. As Sala-Molins memorably puts it, "Louverture settled the question, not the Enlightenment; Dessalines, not Napoleon."[14] We can perhaps go even further, if we accept with some scholars that the events in Haiti influenced the development of European thought, and not just the other way around. It seems clear at least that the revolutionaries in France were pushed towards applying their own ideas to the topic of race precisely by seeing what happened in the Caribbean. Officially opposed as they were to all tyranny and aristocracy, they found it increasingly uncomfortable to support an "aristocracy of the skin."[15]

A case along these lines has been made for the writings of G.W.F. Hegel. A study by Susan Buck-Morss published in 2000 showed that Hegel was a regular reader of a number of periodicals that informed Europeans about events in the Atlantic.[16] So he knew exactly what had happened in Haiti, and it seems scarcely credible that this is irrelevant to his famous theory of the master–slave dialectic. Without getting into too much detail, Hegel argued that the relation between slave and master is predicated on the master's self-interested independence, while the slave is seen—even by himself—as a mere thing to be used to fulfill the master's needs. This dynamic is transcended when the slave, by performing labor and seeing his ability to affect his environment, comes to a realization of his own agency. At the same time, the master recognizes that he is in fact dependent on the slave, compromising his earlier assumptions about his own autonomy. Hegel does not explicitly refer to Haiti in this context, but when we consider that his *Phenomenology of Spirit* was written in 1807, just a few years after Haiti declared independence, and that he sees mutual recognition between humans as a key engine of political progress, it is indeed tempting to suppose that the famous passage may have been written with Haiti at least in the back of his mind.

Finally, what can be said about the wider political and ideological impact of the Haitian Revolution? It would be nice to report that it sparked a chain of uprisings that led to the quick collapse of the Atlantic slave trade. As you presumably know, this is not the case. On the contrary, the slave population in the New World as a whole increased in size after the Revolution. Furthermore, it seems to have provoked a backlash in other slaveholding territories, including the United States.[17] Several southern states passed draconian laws to prevent history from repeating itself, for example by forbidding freed slaves from staying in the state for more than a short time after manumission. Perhaps they were aware of the crucial role played in Haiti by free blacks who were former slaves, Toussaint L'Ouverture himself being the most obvious example.

Or consider, yet again, Thomas Jefferson, whose half-hearted and ineffectual handwringing over slavery would have fit right in among the French intellectuals we just discussed. Dessalines wrote to President Jefferson in 1803, asking for an opening of trade between the new nation of Haiti and the United States, a natural alliance, one might think, since the Americans had also recently freed themselves from tyrannical rule. President John Adams, who preceded Jefferson, had negotiated collaboratively with the L'Ouverture regime, but, at this point, Jefferson once again acted inconsistently with his proclaimed belief in the need to end slavery. After staying neutral during the Revolution, Jefferson protected the pro-slavery interests of the southern states by embargoing trade with Haiti and refusing to recognize it as an independent nation.[18]

Still, it would be unfair to say that Haiti had no wider impact, or that the impact it did have was only to encourage slaveowners to keep a tighter grip on their supposed property. Just ask Frederick Douglass. Speaking in 1893 at the Haitian Pavilion at the Chicago World's Fair, he said of the Haitian people: "When they struck for freedom, they struck for the freedom of every black man in the world."[19] We'll see shortly that free black intellectuals in the United States were thrilled by the independence of Haiti. Some even chose it as the best destination for emigration from the United States, a land much closer than Africa where black men and women could be truly free. Haiti did not have the economic or military power to export its revolution beyond its own shores. But it had shown that freedom could be more than an idea praised in books of philosophy. At the cost of great sacrifice, it could be a reality. As Toussaint L'Ouverture put it when addressing his soldiers in 1797 (*Toussaint* 28): "Let us go forth to plant the tree of liberty, breaking the chains of those of our brothers still held captive under the shameful yoke of slavery. Let us bring them under the compass of our rights, the imprescriptible and inalienable rights of free men. Let us overcome the barriers that separate nations, and unite the human species into a single brotherhood."

30

MY HAITIAN PEN

Baron de Vastey

Great achievements are often followed by great uncertainty. You come home from your high school or college graduation ceremony, from the hospital where you've just given birth, from running your fastest ever race, or climbing your highest ever mountain, and you think: okay, now what? The same rule holds in political life, as we can see from the history of revolutions. Overthrowing the old regime is not the last step, but the first. In the case of the Haitian Revolution, the first step was already a giant leap for humankind. Whatever else happened in the aftermath of the country's independence in 1804, at least the population could take pride in staging the world's greatest and most successful slave revolt. But much else remained unclear.

First of all, there was the matter of the mode of government. Jean-Jacques Dessalines had himself crowned the Emperor of Haiti in October of 1804, taking the title Jacques I. The constitution of 1805 confirmed this establishment of Haiti as an empire and gave Dessalines the power to appoint his own successor. He didn't get the chance, though. Dessalines was assassinated in 1806, and disagreement over the way forward left the country divided between two rulers. Alexandre Pétion, who was of mixed ancestry and born free before the Revolution, ruled the southern part as an ostensibly democratic republic, though it wasn't very democratic in practice. By 1816, a new constitution named Pétion president for life, again with the power to select his successor, though as a nod to republican principles the Senate had the job of confirming this choice. Meanwhile, the north was under the rule of Henri Christophe, brought to Saint Domingue from Grenada as a slave before the Revolution. Christophe believed that a weak presidency was inadequate for the purposes of leadership and so, in 1811, he had himself crowned as the king of a hereditary monarchy.

Then there was the small matter of the rest of the world. France refused to recognize Haiti's independence, and other European powers and the United States followed suit. Under these circumstances, could the country manage to retain its autonomy, whether as a republic or a monarchy, even as the French schemed to retake it and reimpose colonial control and possibly slavery? Alongside all these uncertainties were more abstract questions about the meaning of the Revolution itself. Apologists for slavery were predictably appalled at the Revolution's success. They wrote retrospective justifications of the French policies in Haiti and argued that the violence of the uprising just showed that slavery was indeed necessary to keep black populations docile. It's a preposterous argument from today's perspective, but, at the time, it put white abolitionists on the defensive. As early as 1792, the French poet and feminist philosopher Olympe de Gouges criticized Haitians for the excesses of their rebellion, writing: "by imitating the tyrants so cruelly, you justify them...Men were not made for chains, but you prove that they are necessary."[1]

But here's another change brought by the Revolution: now black Haitians could speak from a position of (relative) power, refuting arguments in favor of slavery and presenting justifications of the Revolution and the political regimes that grew from it. Among the most important, and most philosophically interesting, of the authors to do so in the post-revolutionary generation was Jean Louis Vastey, who became the Baron de Vastey under the monarchical rule of King Christophe. Given the division of the country between Christophe and Pétion, Vastey actually had a dual political goal: arguing on behalf of Haiti as a whole, and arguing on behalf of King Christophe in particular. While this much is clear from Vastey's own writings, his life story keeps us solidly with our theme of uncertainty, because there is much that is disputed about his biography. We do know that his given name was Jean Louis and that he had a white father from Normandy and a free black mother. He may have traveled to France as a young man, and should perhaps be identified with a poet who published there under the name of Pompée Valentin Vastey.[2] But he was back in Haiti for the Revolution and left the French army to join the forces led by Dessalines in 1803. Later in life he described his decision thusly: "I threw myself into the arms of my brothers...I uttered an oath never to separate my cause from that of my fellow men."[3] In the second decade of the nineteenth century, we find him at the side of Christophe.

Vastey was happy to describe himself as the king's "publiciste." In this capacity, he published a number of treatises, including the first full-length history of the Revolution written from the Haitian point of view, and two shorter works which will be occupying our attention in what follows. The first, which appeared in 1814, is entitled *The Colonial System Unveiled,* and is an unprecedented attack on the slave system and its depredations.[4] The second, published in 1816 and translated into English by a British botanist and abolitionist named William Hamilton only a year later, is his *Reflections on Blacks and Whites*.[5] Both works are refutations aimed at slavery apologists. In *Colonial System Unveiled*, Vastey is responding to Pierre Victor Malouet.[6] Even the title is an ironic appropriation of the words of Malouet, who had written: "Experience teaches us that the doctrine and principle of liberty and equality, transplanted to the Antilles, can produce nothing there except devastation, massacres, and conflagrations...That principle being the fundamental base of what I call the colonial system, I insist on it, as an obvious fact" (*System* 47). Similarly, in *Reflections on Blacks and Whites* the target is an ex-colonist named Mazères, who had tried to justify slavery by saying that black people are naturally inferior, having a different origin than whites.[7] Against this, Vastey argues for the unity of the human race and mounts a complex argument against the charge of black inferiority. Just as *Colonial System Unveiled* was path-breaking in its detailed account of the cruelties of colonialism and slavery as an organized system, so *Reflections* was a pioneering work in the philosophy of race.

Vastey's brilliance was recognized early on. Abolitionists in Europe and America eagerly touted the works of this learned and rhetorically gifted polemicist. A review of the *Reflections* called him "the Alpha and Omega of Haytian intellect and literature," and another was pleasantly surprised by Vastey's "degree of learning and classical knowledge, which we could not by any means have expected in a country which Europeans are in the habit of considering as in a very uncivilized state."[8] The English version of the *Reflections* begins with a prologue which observes that the writings of Ignatius Sancho and Phillis Wheatley "are alone sufficient to shew, that neither good sense nor true taste are irreconcileable strangers to the African breast." Still, Vastey is praised as a unique thinker. The *Reflections*, says the prologue, "is perhaps the first work by a Negro, in which the energies of the mind have been powerfully excited and have found a proper scope for action...and where in fact this long oppressed race have been suffered to say a word in their own defence" (*Reflections* 9–10).

Modern-day readers have likewise recognized Vastey as something new in the history of Africana thought, yet at the same time fretted over the political context in which he wrote. Writing in the 1970s, an expert on Haitian literature, David Nicholls, described Vastey as "the official ideologist and apologist" of his king, and more recently Chris Bongie has spoken of Vastey as a "scribe" for the Christophe regime.[9] The first of these descriptions, taken without any immediate value judgment, is hard to deny. In a letter to the British abolitionist Thomas Clarkson,[10] this is how Vastey explains the purpose of his pioneering work of history, entitled

Essay on the Causes of Haiti's Revolution and Civil Wars: "Exasperated at seeing in the journals of the South and in those of France, their faithful echoes, the calumnies which the enemies of Haiti and the King endlessly repeat concerning his government and his person, I decided to refute them" (quoted at *System* 37). Clearly, then, defending the king and the government of which he was a part was a primary source of motivation for Vastey. To refer to him as a "scribe," however, seriously underplays his originality, a point that has been made forcefully by Marlene Daut.[11]

From a contemporary perspective, Vastey's sense of dedication to an authoritarian monarchy may seem problematic, especially given the existence of a republican alternative to the south at that very time. Vastey, however, devised a series of arguments to show that the freedom for which the revolutionaries fought would not be best maintained by a republic. For one thing, he argued that republican opposition to the system of nobility that made him a baron, and others under Christophe's rule into dukes, counts, and chevaliers, rested on a misunderstanding of the idea of equality. "Equality of rights before the law" is, according to Vastey, the "only equality that can exist on earth" and he claims that this is both what Haitians fought for during the Revolution and what citizens in Christophe's kingdom enjoy. By contrast, it would be the height of folly to seek to establish absolute equality, the loss of all differences in rank and relative standing: "The rich and the poor, the strong and the weak, the brave and the cowardly, the enlightened and the ignorant, can they be equal? Do not the simple deliverances of common sense forbid this imaginary equality in an organized society?"[12]

And as he pointed out, the track record of France's own revolutionary government hardly suggested that republican values and slavery are antithetical. In fact, Haitians more generally had great hopes that the restoration of the monarchy in France after the fall of Napoleon would be followed by normalization of relations between the two nations, though these hopes were dashed. Furthermore, Vastey accused Pétion's republican government in southern Haiti of willingness to collaborate with the French. Against the backdrop of these political considerations, he dismissed objections to Christophe's monarchy as plain racism: "One would say to hear them, that a black king is a phenomenon that has never been seen in the world! Of all the prejudices that afflict and dishonor the human species, there is not one that is more odious, more absurd, and more fatal in all its consequences than colour prejudice. Who will therefore reign over the blacks, if the blacks cannot be kings. Is royalty such a privilege that it belongs exclusively to the white?"[13]

For Vastey, King Christophe, whom he calls "one of the best men in the new world," was the benevolent overseer of a safe haven for black people, their "sole asylum of liberty" (*Reflections* 69 and 64). Vastey sees monarchy, the strongest possible form of centralized power, as one natural result of a struggle for liberation. If this sounds surprising, consider his favorite example: Britain, a country in which the free population are subjects of the crown. In fact, Vastey often had nice things to say about the British, since one of his goals was to persuade them to offer recognition to Haiti. The Christophe regime even toyed with the idea of making English the national language of Haiti, in order to make a clean break with the French oppressors and entice the British to adopt a more friendly policy.[14] Vastey also wanted the British to expand their efforts to "civilize" Africa, which had already begun in Sierra Leone (*System* 95–6). On Vastey's telling, Britain and other European powers at this time were defenders of freedom and promoters of enlightened culture, with France the lamentable odd man out (*System* 83). He saw hypocrisy as endemic to the French governing and intellectual classes, about whom he presciently remarked: "Posterity will never credit the fact that, in an enlightened century like ours, some men who call themselves scholars and philosophers have endeavored to reduce other men to the condition of brute beast, by denying there is but one original type of the human race, and that they have done so solely for the sake of maintaining the abominable privilege of oppressing one portion of humankind" (*System* 103). True philosophers will stand up against tyrants, he says, giving the obvious example of Socrates and the rather dubious example of Seneca (*Reflections* 62–3; Seneca is often considered to have compromised himself through services to Emperor Nero).

The thesis that humans have more than one origin is the target of the *Reflections*. As we've already mentioned, Vastey was prompted to write this work in opposition to the ex-colonist Mazères. This work begins by accusing Mazères and his family of cruelty towards their Haitian slaves: his opponent "disgraced humanity by his crimes" even before he undertook to justify slavery (*Reflections* 13). For Mazères, the relation between blacks and whites is like that between two different animal species, like asses and horses or different breeds of dog. Vastey's response to this illustrates his biting and sarcastic style: "Mazères may draw parallels between himself and asses and dogs, I will not prevent him" (23). Besides, since we are interested in skin color, wouldn't a better comparison be black horses and white horses? In fact, of course, Mazères's idea, and pseudo-scientific arguments that support it, are bunk. Instead—now sounding not unlike Socrates voicing Plato's theory of Forms—Vastey claims that there is a single "prototype" of humanity which secures the unity of the whole race (17–18).

Even if it were true that blacks were fundamentally different from whites, it would still be wrong to say that black skin is a sign of inferiority. Both here in the *Reflections* (23) and in *Colonial System Unveiled*, Vastey points out that there are plenty of barbaric and uncivilized white people. "Why not buy some?" he asks the colonists.

"Your markets will be abundantly provided for" (*System* 98). Indeed, the French themselves were, back in late antiquity, much less civilized than modern Africans (*Reflections* 60). That's a point typical of Vastey's *Reflections*, which draws heavily on his reading in history. One of his trump arguments against African inferiority is that Europeans, and specifically the Greeks, were raised to a higher standard of civilization by the Egyptians, who taught them the sciences (*Reflections* 34, *System* 96). He admits that Africa has fallen to a lower level in more recent centuries, something he blames partly on the coming of Islam (*Reflections* 37). But this is just an example of the rise and fall that affects all cultures. Perhaps in the future, he muses, Europe will slump to a lower level and Africa will wake from "her long slumber" to emerge as the world's leading civilization (*Reflections* 61).

The *Reflections* includes a striking passage describing the horrors that French colonists inflicted upon their human chattel: burning slaves alive and having them attacked by dogs, those "quadruped brethren" of the colonists who are "a thousand times less savage than [the colonists] themselves" (75). But these remarks are merely a brief interlude compared to what we find in the *Colonial System Unveiled*. This earlier text falls into two parts, the second consisting largely of a catalogue of tortures and cruelties from the history of slavery in Haiti. The latter is certainly the more memorable part of the treatise, but it's worth noting how the first section prepares the way for the second. Vastey puts the Haitian experience in context by describing the exploitation of the new world more generally. Mostly he is here drawing on other authors, whom he cites at length to demonstrate the oppression suffered by indigenous Americans at the hands of colonizers. Despite the abundant use of quotation, the idea of this section is a bold and original one. Vastey is proposing that slavery is continuous and logically integrated with the colonial project as a cohesive whole, a coherent system. In a proof of the truism that "one crime leads to another," African slaves were imported as a substitute labor force for indigenous Americans (*System* 92).

As in his other works, Vastey writes here for a broad readership, seeking to stiffen the resolve of his fellow Haitians and win the support of potentially friendly readers abroad. But *Colonial System Unveiled* is above all a thunderous accusation aimed at the French colonists whose sadism provoked the well-justified uprising of the Haitian people. Vastey explains his motivation as follows: "The time has finally arrived when the truth must come to light. I, who am neither a white man nor a colonist, may not possess the same erudition, but I will not be lacking when it comes to citing examples. My Haitian pen will be lacking in eloquence, no doubt, but it will be truthful…I will be heard and understood by the feeling and impartial European, and the brutal colonist will shake and tremble upon seeing his foul deeds brought to light" (*System* 108). The false modesty cannot obscure the fury and power of Vastey's words, as he launches into an extraordinary litany of the crimes committed on Haitian soil by the colonists. For page after page, he lists the stomach-churning torments endured by the slave population.

There are several noteworthy features of this catalogue of horrors. For one thing, the guilty slaveowners are mentioned by name, and so, often, are the slave victims. The point seems to be identifying as many perpetrators as possible. In some cases, we get a longer anecdote, but often a given atrocity will be sketched in just one sentence, like "Michau, settler, resident of Ennery, had blacks of his placed in a bread oven while still alive" (114). Sometimes the culprits are named with hardly any detail concerning their crimes, as when he writes, "Mistress le Roi had them clubbed to death. Mistress Lamestière acted likewise" (121). Obviously the sheer quantity of reports is meant to have an impact, by conveying the scale of the horror and also increasing the credibility of Vastey's case. The specific names and the itemization of many specific crimes also indicates that he is, indeed, building a case. It's like an extended charge sheet or indictment of the colonists, a speech for the prosecution submitted to the court of public opinion.[15]

Vastey's approach is a new one in anti-slavery literature. Obviously, other texts had offered examples of cruelty against blacks, often within the first-person testimony of a slave narrative. It was such a standard feature of abolitionist texts that Olaudah Equiano excused himself from producing such stories: "The punishments of the slaves, on every trifling occasion, are so frequent, and so well known, together with the different instruments with which they are tortured, that it cannot any longer afford novelty to recite them."[16] But Vastey does not try to present us with a heart-rending narrative, first person or otherwise.[17] Instead he has gathered evidence at second hand, and presented it in an ostentatiously factual, almost detached way. His strategy is precisely the opposite of the one proposed by Ignatius Sancho. As you will recall, Sancho wanted Laurence Sterne to write a piece of fiction that would appeal to the readers' "benevolent hearts" (see Chapter 27). The whole point of Vastey's account is that it is *not* fictional. With a tone of seething rage instead of lachrymose pity, he reports events that should induce any fair-minded reader to recoil from the wicked deeds of the colonists. As Vastey himself says: "This is not a novel I am writing. It is an exposé of the ordeals, the protracted suffering, and unparalleled acts of torture that an ill-fated people have experienced for centuries" (109).

Which is not to deny that Vastey appeals to his readers' emotions, or "sentiment": he even says at one point that he is writing for "people of sensitivity (*hommes sensibles*)."[18] This accounts for some other striking features of the text, like his emphasis on the sexual liaisons between masters and slaves, which leads to fathers tormenting and murdering their own children. He also dwells on spectacular acts of abuse by jealous wives. One makes her husband shoot the slave she thinks he has been raping. When the slave survives, the wife cuts off her ears with scissors and has the woman branded with a red-hot iron, so disfiguring her that she becomes worthless and impossible to sell on (111). Vastey seems particularly concerned to convey the sadism of colonist women. He concludes his evidence with a chilling story in which one Mistress Langlois is told that one of her slaves has lost an arm, which needed to be cut off to stop her from being pulled into a vat of boiling sugar. Mistress Langlois replies: "Gracious me, that wouldn't have been such a disaster when all's said and done, if it weren't that the body might have spoiled my cane-juice" (123).

As these examples show—and we could have quoted many, many more—Vastey's *Colonial System Unveiled* is unsparing in its descriptions of violence. Yet because of its tone and mode of presentation, it avoids the voyeurism and sentimentality that was arguably a weakness of earlier and contemporary abolitionist literature. Was this new strategy effective? Well, as we've already seen, Vastey was held up alongside figures like Sancho and Wheatley as proof of the intellectual potential of black people, and abolitionists did frequently refer to his work and especially his documentation of colonial cruelty. The ideas of Vastey, and the Revolution more generally, had an impact on a European and American readership. Some free African Americans were encouraged to consider emigrating to Haiti, in order to escape the endemic racism of American society.[19] Officially, though, Christophe's government was not in the business of fomenting slave revolt abroad. Speaking on his king's behalf, Vastey said: "we are not revolutionaries, no one is more devoted than we are to the stability of empires."[20] Nevertheless, if the Haitian regime was unwilling or unable to turn its fire physically on neighboring slave states, Vastey's fiery writing in the *Colonial System Unveiled* clearly served the cause of abolition. The result was, as Doris Garraway has put it, "a radicalization of the contemporary antislavery tract and a transformation of the slave narrative into a form of public diplomacy defending the agency of an abolitionist state."[21]

31

AMERICAN AFRICANS

Early Black Institutions in the US

You choose some identities, while others are thrust upon you. It seems to be an accident of birth whether you come into the world as male or female, black or white, American or Canadian. But you can choose your religion, your sports team, your political party. Actually, we live in a day and age when identity is more subject to self-definition than ever before. Even gender, which until recently was widely assumed to be given by nature, is now often acknowledged as a complex matter of social construction and personal decision, with some of us identifying in terms of previously unrecognized genders or no gender at all. We also live in a time when people are increasingly aware of having more than one identity at a time. The word "intersectionality," introduced in the 1980s by the black feminist legal scholar Kimberlé Crenshaw, has become widely used in the current century for this phenomenon, for the way your experiences as, say, a black woman will differ from those of a black man or a white woman.

The concept of intersectionality would have seemed familiar to African Americans of the late eighteenth and early nineteenth centuries, even when not thinking about gender. They often saw themselves as Africans and as Americans and explored ways to embrace both of these identities, while confronting a society that was not going to allow them much personal discretion in defining those identities. Here's a story from 1792 that illustrates the dilemma.[1] A group of black Methodists, whose leaders were Richard Allen and his friend Absalom Jones, had been attending services at St. George's Church in Philadelphia, but the white parishioners segregated the church space, putting the black worshippers up in a separate balcony. When some of the black Methodists instead knelt on the main floor of the church, the whites tried to pull them away. Absalom Jones pleaded that they should at least wait until the prayer was ended, but to no avail. The black Methodists had had enough: they walked out in disgust, never to return. Richard Allen set up his own church, known as "Mother Bethel," and went on to become the nation's first black bishop as the head of the African Methodist Episcopal Church, the first fully independent black denomination in the African diaspora. His importance in the community was later recognized by the fiery abolitionist David Walker, who stated that Allen had "done more in a spiritual sense for his ignorant and wretched brethren than any other man of colour has, since the world began."[2] Absalom Jones, meanwhile, set up an Episcopalian church and became the first black priest ordained by that denomination.

As this sequence of events illustrates, free black people in this period often sought to join in the wider American society and its institutions, but also found it desirable and indeed necessary to found their own institutions. We might now call these "safe spaces," another twenty-first century phrase that perfectly captures an eighteenth and nineteenth century reality. Reflecting on the need for such spaces, the poet and abolitionist author Sarah Forten wrote in a letter to her fellow abolitionist Angelina Grimke, "we never travel far from home and seldom go to public places unless quite sure that admission is free to all."[3] Yet her own father, James Forten—who was another Philadelphia community leader and colleague of Bishop Richard Allen—had made quite literally heroic efforts to embrace his identity as a member of wider American society. He signed up to fight for the American Revolution at the tender age of 15, and when captured by the British refused to join them, proclaiming: "I am here a prisoner for the liberties of my country; I never, never, shall prove a traitor to her interests."[4] Many other black Americans saw this conflict differently. A white minister wrote in his diary that nearly the whole black population of Philadelphia was hoping for British victory, thanks to a 1775 proclamation that offered freedom to Africans who helped to put down the Revolution.[5] So James Forten was already not representative of all in his enthusiasm for the young American nation and even he would conclude, later in life, that America would never offer a true home to those of African descent, saying, "they will never become a people until they come out from amongst the white people."[6]

Forten was far from alone in experiencing a slide from patriotism to disenchantment. In this chapter, we'll see black Americans trying to persuade white Americans to accept them, while simultaneously founding their own churches and other organizations, and ultimately wondering whether the project of being both African and American is a lost cause. We will focus on developments in the northern states, for the obvious reason that it was in these parts of America that black people had the most opportunity to organize and to publish their ideas in writing. There were some parallel developments in southern states, such as the African Baptist Church in Savannah, Georgia.[7] But it's telling that Richard Allen himself once turned down an opportunity to travel to the deep south, after being warned it would not be safe for him to associate with other blacks there or even to sleep anywhere other than in his carriage.[8] The main centers of black activism and community building in early America were Philadelphia (thanks to figures like Allen, Jones, and Forten) and Boston.

The tellingly named African Society, formed in Boston in 1796, gives us a window into the ideas and concerns of black Bostonians at the turn of the nineteenth century. A pamphlet published by this society in 1808, entitled "The Sons of Africans: An Essay on Freedom,"[9] praises Massachusetts and the town of Salem in particular as a haven for free black people at this time (*ENW* 22). The authors argue that freedom ought to be recognized as the birthright of all Africans in America, as of all humans everywhere upon the globe. In part, this is on religious grounds. They mention that in the Bible, slavery is strongly associated with sin, identifying Pharaoh's oppression of Moses and his people as a paradigm case of slaveholding (*ENW* 15). They also point out hypocrisy of the kind that Lemuel Haynes deplored in "Liberty Further Extended." Taking for granted that the cause of American freedom was a just one, they ask: "If desirable to America under such circumstances, why not to any or all the nations of the earth?" (*ENW* 18).

Perhaps most philosophically interesting, though, is their point that slavery is only one, particularly brutal form of bondage (*ENW* 23). One may also be constrained by unhappy marriage, vicious neighbors, or even one's own personal moral failings. In each case, bondage is an evil and something no one would desire. How then can it be right to inflict it on other humans? Anticipating the objection that Africans, being inferior, need masters to guide them, they admit that some humans do need the guidance of others. This is true of the insane, the simple-minded, and children. But no one would infer from this that we should enslave and brutalize these groups; instead it is obvious that they should be treated with benevolence (*ENW* 25).

Another important institution founded in Boston around this time, and one that would go on to exercise immense influence among African Americans over the following generations, was the Masonic Lodge led by a man named Prince Hall. The Masons were a secret society whose initiates could identify one another through coded gestures and words. They were very successful at this point in American history, counting among their number such figures as George Washington and Benjamin Franklin. White Masons excluded blacks from their meetings, and Prince Hall was not even able to win recognition of his separate black Lodge from his American "brethren." It was instead chartered with the support of the British Masons in 1787. Under Hall's leadership, the Boston Lodge became a forum for social work, political pressure, and outspoken protest. Many other luminaries of nineteenth century Africana thought, such as David Walker, Henry Highland Garnet, Martin Delany, and W.E.B. Du Bois, were Masons—as, by the way, were Richard Allen and Absalom Jones down in Philadelphia.

Masonic ideology is fused with the concerns of the black community in two speeches, or "Charges," delivered at the Lodge by Prince Hall and published in 1792 and 1797, and also, prior to those, in a 1789 sermon given at the Lodge by none other than John Marrant.[10] When last we saw Marrant (in Chapter 24), he was preaching to the black people of Nova Scotia on behalf of the Methodists associated with the Countess of Huntingdon. He left Nova Scotia in 1787 and moved to Boston. From his 1789 sermon and Hall's speeches, we can come to understand some of the attraction of Masonry for early black Americans.[11] Marrant and Hall would have been very glad to see that we began this book by looking at ancient Egypt and Ethiopia, because they looked back to these civilizations as their forerunners. Masonic lore included Egyptian elements and had at its center the temple built by King Solomon, giving Prince Hall a chance to allude to the Queen of Sheba in his second speech (*ENW* 73). Marrant went so far as to make the following claim about the location of the Garden of Eden: "Paradise did as it were border upon Egypt, which is the principal part of the African Ethiopia" (8). Capitalizing on this broad understanding of the word "Ethiopia," which is by now familiar to us, Prince Hall referred in both his speeches to the biblical line: "Ethiopia shall soon stretch out her hands unto God" (*ENW* 67, 74). Found in Psalm 68, verse 31, this verse would prove to be a favorite of black thinkers in the century to come. When Hall invokes this aspirational phrase in his 1797 "Charge," he connects it to the glory of the Haitian Revolution.

Marrant and Hall also valued the Masonic project as an instrument of racial uplift, as when Hall petitioned the Massachusetts government to support the education of black children. Yet, even as they were forced by the rejection of white Masons to strike out on their own and create what they called an "African Lodge," they continued to insist that the whole organization stood for an ethic of universal brotherhood. For Marrant, this was indeed a main advantage of the Masonic Society, which was "a society founded upon such friendly and comprehensive principles, that men of all nations and languages, or sects of religion, are and may be admitted and received as members" (22). Likewise, Hall implored his listeners to show benevolence toward all, including non-Masons and even non-Christians (*ENW* 65). In Hall's two "Charges," the universalist moral code of the Masons is linked to the ideal of racial harmony. He reminded his listeners about the black soldiers who fought for

America in the Revolution marching "shoulder to shoulder" with white soldiers (*ENW* 68). On the other hand, he condemned post-revolutionary uprisings like that led by the white farmer Daniel Shays, which Hall offered to help put down with a militia of black Bostonians. For Hall, even slavery should be opposed with pious virtue, not with violence. "We must be good subjects to the laws of the land in which we dwell," he wrote. "However just [uprising] may be on the side of the opprest, yet it doth not in the least, or rather ought not, abate that love and fellow-feeling which we ought to have for our brother fellow men" (*ENW* 64).

In Philadelphia, a similar message could be heard from the pulpit of Richard Allen's church.[12] He had plenty of opportunities to despair of acceptance by white America, even—or rather especially—by his fellow Methodists. After the exodus of the blacks from St. George's Church, white church leaders tried to stop Allen from operating autonomously. They sent white preachers to give sermons there against the black parishioners' will and even forced Allen to raise money for buying the church he had built with his own hands, in order to secure its independence. Yet he spared no effort to show the white community that black folk could play a strong, positive role in Philadelphia. He for one was going to do his part to help it earn its nickname, "the city of brotherly love."

The most famous example came when he and Absalom Jones led an effort to nurse victims of a yellow fever epidemic. When white publisher Mathew Carey praised their efforts, but criticized other black residents of the city for engaging in theft and other misdeeds during the outbreak, Allen and Jones responded with a powerful statement of black solidarity.[13] In their pamphlet describing the whole episode, called *A Narrative of the Proceedings of the Black People, During the Awful Late Calamity in Philadelphia*, they refused to allow Carey to drive a wedge between the elite community leaders and poorer, more easily demonized African Americans. In fact, almost all of those who had committed crimes during the epidemic had been white (13–14), while humble black people had performed in exemplary fashion, risking their lives by tending to the sick. In one typical vignette, they tell how a sick man was ignored by callous white Philadelphians, got a sympathetic hearing but no actual help from a visiting foreigner, and was then finally aided by a "poor black man" who proudly refused to accept any reward (10–11).

Jones and Allen appended to their *Narrative* several short texts on the plight of black Americans in general. In an "Address to those who keep Slaves, and approve the practice," they asked white people to imagine how they would feel if they were enslaved, and demolished the argument that black people need to be enslaved because of their natural inferiority. If black people seem inferior, it is because they have been deprived of education and other forms of social integration and support.

"Will you," they asked, "because you have reduced us to the unhappy condition our colour is in, plead our incapacity for freedom?" (25). Contrasting with this focus on white responsibility, a further text spoke to "People of Colour," and reminded them that their moral failings could be used as an excuse for further oppression: "Much depends upon us for the help of our colour more than many are aware; if we are lazy and idle, the enemies of freedom plead it as a cause why we ought not to be free, and say we are better in a state of servitude, and that giving us our liberty would be an injury to us, and by such conduct we strengthen the bands of oppression, and keep many in bondage who are more worthy than ourselves" (27).

This moralizing message was enthusiastically received by women involved in the black religious movement. Allen's wife Sarah, known to all as "Mother Allen," was a bulwark of the black community in Philadelphia and Richard Allen—rather grudgingly, it must be said—came to accept that religious leadership could be displayed by women too, not only men like himself. He did turn down the request of a woman named Dorothy Ripley to speak at his church,[14] and at first also rebuffed the charismatic preacher Jarena Lee. But when Lee dared to interrupt a meeting and speak extemporaneously, Allen was so impressed that he gave in, and even supported her further activities as an itinerant spiritualist. Her autobiography, *The Life and Religious Experience of Jarena Lee*, is a valuable document for understanding the role of women in the early American black church.[15] She speaks of her intense awareness of her own sinfulness but also of the presence of a divine force within her, "a living principle, an immortal spirit, which cannot die, and must forever either enjoy the smiles of its Creator, or feel the pangs of ceaseless damnation." She felt compelled by this to challenge the restrictions placed on her because of her color and her gender, in order to "preach the Gospel" and call others to the path of God. As she herself demanded, "If a man may preach, because the Saviour died for him, why not the woman? Seeing he died for her also." Jarena Lee, it seems safe to say, already knew all about intersectionality.

Preachers like Allen and Lee spoke above all to their fellow African Americans, offering them inspiration, encouragement, and comfort. But, as we have seen, Allen also wanted to deliver messages to white America. An eloquent example was his eulogy delivered on the occasion of George Washington's death in 1799.[16] Notoriously, Washington owned slaves, and made a concerted effort to apprehend and recover two of them who fled from his home at Mount Vernon. Showing the usual lack of empathy of slaveholders toward their human chattel, he complained that one of them, Ona Judge, had run away "without the least provocation."[17] Yet Allen did not hesitate to extol Washington as a role model of emancipation, because he arranged for his slaves to be manumitted upon his death (something

Lemuel Haynes also celebrated, as we saw). It's possible that Allen even met the nation's first president, because one of the ways he made his living was as a chimney sweep, and he worked in this capacity at the Washingtons' home in Philadelphia. Screenwriters, take note: we have here the makings of a *Mary Poppins* sequel about American race relations. Allen's eulogy would make a fitting climax to such a film, as he stated on behalf of the black Philadelphia community: "We participate in common with the feelings of a grateful people," and encouraged that community to love the nation in imitation of Washington. White readers of the published sermon were presumably intended to take the point that they should imitate him too, by freeing their slaves.

In word and in deed, Allen and his allies could hardly have done more to demonstrate their value to the nation. During the War of 1812, James Forten and Absalom Jones raised a so-called "black brigade" to defend Philadelphia against possible attack. We've already spoken of the service they rendered during the yellow fever epidemic, and seen how black soldiers like Haynes and Forten helped to free America from British rule. Richard Allen made the point as follows: "This land which we have watered with our tears and our blood, is now our mother country."[18] But to write these words as he did late in life, Allen had to go through multiple changes of heart. His early optimism for integration with white America, as typified by his eulogy of Washington, was battered by the interference and hostility of the white church, and by political setbacks. A petition organized by Allen and Jones was submitted to the US Congress, asking that full citizenship be given to free blacks, but it was rejected by a vote of 84 to 1. On this occasion, a congressman from Georgia offered the most revealing seven-word summary of American racism you'll ever see: "'We the people' does not mean them."

In the face of such animosity, black leaders began to wonder whether the roots of black community could ever thrive in the inhospitable soil of the United States. The various figures we've been discussing started to support the project of emigration. Prince Hall, as early as 1787, thought this a splendid idea. That year, he joined seventy-three other petitioners in requesting that Massachusetts fund transport to Africa, arguing that it remained "our native country, which warm climate is more natural and agreeable to us; and where we shall live among our equals and be more comfortable and happy, than we can be in our present situation."[19] Hall and other black leaders regularly encountered the problem that once you have chosen your identity, you need society as a whole to acknowledge that choice. For all their pious words about brotherhood, for all their efforts in the cause of national liberty, evidence showed time and again that their white "compatriots" would only ever see them as Africans, not as Americans.

This same lesson resulted in the late pessimism of James Forten. We saw him refusing to abandon the American cause when captured by the British, and he later optimistically wrote that the architects of the Revolution "adopted the glorious fabrick of our liberties, and, declaring 'all men' free, they did not particularize white and black, because they never supposed it would be made a question whether we were men or not."[20] Yet Forten too came to support emigration to Africa, joining forces with Allen in an attempt to persuade the parishioners at Bethel to support the project. The two men were stunned when the congregation, as with a single voice, shouted down the proposal; as Forten put it, "There was not a soul that was in favor of going to Africa." Dutifully accepting direction from their own flock, Allen and Forten wrote up a declaration that said in part: "Whereas our ancestors (not of choice) were the first successful cultivators of the wilds of America, we their descendants feel ourselves entitled to participate in the blessings of her luxuriant soil which their blood and sweat manured." But Allen would not erase thoughts of emigration, later exploring the question of going to Haiti, the site of a revolution that was fought to destroy slavery, whereas the American Revolution had preserved it.[21]

32

SHOULD I STAY OR SHOULD I GO?

The Colonization Controversy

A Quaker man is in bed, and hears a noise downstairs. Grabbing his hunting rifle, he creeps down the stairs and finds that a thief has broken into his house. Aiming his gun at the thief, he says: "friend, I mean thee no harm, but thou art standing where I'm about to shoot." Not a great joke, perhaps, but it does illustrate one of the moral and religious convictions for which the Quakers are known: their rejection of violence. In hard-drinking early American society, they also stood out for their teetotaling ways—hence the pithier joke: "two Quakers walk into a bar…then realize their error." More relevantly to our present concerns, the Quakers were distinguished by their fierce, though of course pacifist, objection to slavery. A leading voice among them was John Woolman. His 1748 pamphlet *Some Considerations on the Keeping of Negroes* is remarkable for its early expression of the abolitionist position and its affirmation of equality between the races, founded in what Woolman called "an idea of general brotherhood" which is too often undermined by attention to "outward circumstances" like skin color. Quakers were ahead of the rest of white America when it came to banning trade in, and then ownership of, slaves. In 1775, they founded the Philadelphia Abolition Society, the country's first anti-slavery organization.

Quakers were also willing to put money where their mouths were, as Daniel Coker was glad to discover in 1802. Coker had been born into slavery in Maryland, but he escaped and was eventually able to purchase his freedom with the financial support of the Quakers. Like Richard Allen, he became a preacher and leader of the African Methodist movement, and also like Allen, he appealed to Christian principles as a basis for freedom and equality. In 1810, he published a remarkable pamphlet of his own, entitled *A Dialogue Between a Virginian and an African Minister*.[1] The Minister of the title may be seen as a mouthpiece for Coker, although, as this Minister engages in polite discussion with a slaveowning Virginian, the Minister asks a friend called Mr. C—presumably short for Coker—to write down the conversation. This makes the work reminiscent of one of Plato's later dialogues, in which we take Socrates to be serving as a mouthpiece for Plato, even though we know that Plato was, historically, a student of Socrates.

In any case, it must be said that if real pro-slavery southerners had been as reasonable and easy to convince as the character of the Virginian, the course of American history would have been very different. More pliable than most interlocutors in Plato's dialogues, he immediately concedes every point made by the Minister before trying in vain to come up with a counter-argument. For example, admitting that his knowledge of the Bible is rather sketchy (57), he gladly takes instruction on the true meaning of the scriptural passages that the white minister whose church he attends has scurrilously used to justify slavery.

Coker also uses his *Dialogue* to refute pragmatic and legalistic, rather than straightforwardly ethical or religious, justifications of slavery. Of particular philosophical interest is the issue of property rights. Coker has the "Virginian" argue that, whether it is right or wrong in moral terms, slaves are the legal property of their masters. To this, the Minister offers a double response. On the one hand, laws allowing slavery have no force, because no legislature has the standing to grant one person ownership over another. To think otherwise would be like supposing that the government could allow the Minister to buy another man's head. "Have I," asks the Minister, "in consequence of this law and this purchase, a better claim to this man's head than himself?" (54). In keeping with this analogy, the Minister claims that to free a slave is "not wronging the master, but doing justice to the slave, restoring him to himself" (54). Yet, right after this, the Minister concedes that the slaveowner may suffer because of his loss, and indeed, may suffer greatly. The Minister is even willing to call this suffering a kind of injustice. But "this is his own fault, and the fault of the enslaving law, and not of the law that does justice to the oppressed" (54). The master is therefore victimized by his loss, but this is partly a self-inflicted wrong and partly the fault of the legislature that failed to forbid slavery in the first place. The Minister concludes that since injustice in this situation is unavoidable, it is obvious that we must maximize justice by forcing slaveowners to free their slaves, rather than forcing the enslaved to remain the property of their masters.

Less appealing to the modern eye, at least at first, is Coker's response to the pragmatic argument against emancipation that it would lead to mixing of the races. His Minister grants without hesitation that the proliferation of mixed-race children would be a "very alarming circumstance." He then points out, however, that, under slavery, masters are already fathering children with slave women, meaning that "the matter is already gone beyond recovery; for it may be proved with mathematical certainty, that if things go on in the present course, the future inhabitants of America will be much checkered" (60-1). Coker suggests that emancipation is in fact more likely to preserve racial purity. Even if it doesn't, the "evil" at stake here is already happening anyway, and in a manner that is more "truly disgraceful" to both races (61). Miscegenation under slavery means fathers owning their children as slaves, brothers or sisters inheriting their siblings as property, and passing them down so that people eventually end up owning their own uncles and aunts.

The Minister's concession that miscegenation is an evil is especially striking because Coker himself was the son of a white mother. In fact, he may have declined to serve as bishop of the African Methodist Episcopal Church because of concerns over his light skin.[2] After Allen took the position instead, Coker was for a time excluded from the church, for reasons that remain unclear. Facing financial hardship, he made a momentous decision: he would go back to Africa. Or rather, we might say, not *back*, as Coker was born in Maryland. He was, nevertheless, one of numerous Americans of African heritage who, seeing dim prospects for themselves and their families even in the free northern states, decided to settle in one of the colonies being established in West Africa. Coker was a member of the first group of settlers sent by the American Colonization Society, which was formed in 1816 and which went on to found the colony of Liberia.[3] For Coker, the Colonization project offered the chance for a new start, as he explained in a journal he kept during his trip that was then published under the auspices of the ACS.[4]

Coker knew he had chosen a difficult road. Imagining himself as a latter-day Moses leading his people to a new promised land, he wrote: "I expect to give my life to bleeding, groaning, dark, benighted Africa...It is a good land; it is a rich land, and I do believe it will be a great nation, and a powerful and worthy nation: but those who break the way will suffer much." Coker was right to expect trials and tribulations. The initial colony, which was established on Sherbro Island, was a failure, so he abandoned it and the ACS to go settle in the British colony of Sierra Leone, of which Sherbro Island eventually became a part. This mention of Sierra Leone brings us back to the Quakers, and to one Quaker in particular: Paul Cuffe.[5]

Cuffe was born in 1759 in Massachusetts to parents who were not official "Friends," as those in the Quaker movement are known, but who did follow its principles. His father was an Akan taken as a slave and then freed by his Quaker master; the surname Cuffe was a version of his father's original African name, Kofi. His mother, Ruth Moses, was Native American, specifically a Wampanoag. From rather modest beginnings, Paul Cuffe would rise to make his fortune in the shipping trade, becoming arguably the most prominent black man of early nineteenth century America and almost certainly the richest. Cuffe was even invited to meet with President James Madison, who favored the idea of ending slavery by transporting the black population of America to Africa. In this endeavor, Cuffe was a promising ally.

He first became interested in the emigrationist cause in 1787, when he heard about developments in Sierra Leone. Tellingly, this was the same year that Prince Hall and others submitted a petition in Boston to request support for transportation to Africa. As a successful merchant, Cuffe had means and opportunity to move people between the United States and Africa. He was also frequently in Great Britain, where he was enthusiastically received by philanthropists who hoped that Sierra Leone could be a successful homeland for free black people. In 1807, the Royal African Institution in Britain even published a biography of Cuffe. In a pattern that has already become familiar to us, his success as a trader was held up as a proof of the talent to be found among Africans.[6]

Cuffe is central to the story of the African emigrationist project. He transported settlers on his own ships and took a keen interest in their fortunes, as we learn from his extensive writings in the form of preserved letters and captain's logs.[7] He aimed to keep open what he called a "channel" between America and Africa (119-20, 139, 257, 435), and though he was aware of the challenges facing settlers in Africa, he trusted that the colonies established there would benefit generations to come (330). Cuffe's motivations in this undertaking were complex. Most obviously, he acted out of his sense of solidarity with fellow African Americans. This had long been clear from the way he conducted business: he employed all-black crews on his ships, which caused consternation when they docked in places like Maryland.[8] And it's clear from his writings, as shown by an anecdote about meeting two Methodists in the street who asked whether Cuffe spoke English. Understandably offended, Cuffe replied yes, but that "There Was a Part I did not understand (Viz) that of one Brother professor makeing merchandize of and holding in Bondage their Brother professor. This parte I should be glad they Would Clear up to me" (216).

But Cuffe was not only trying to help African Americans escape slavery and racism. He also hoped to transform Africa itself. This motive drove his initial interest in Sierra Leone. He wrote of "feeling a real desire that the inhabitants of Africa might become an enlightened people...As I am of the African race I feel myself interested for them and if I am favored with a talent I think I am willing that they should be benefited thereby" (80). Or take this later, briefer remark: "My mind is to render all the aid to Africa in my power" (246). He spoke freely of wanting to promote "civilization" in Africa (253, 255), and saw this as a kind of recompense for the ravaging of the continent by the slave trade. Religion and Quaker values were central to this undertaking, and were captured eloquently by the list of gifts he presented to a native king upon arriving in West Africa: a bible, a Quaker history, and an essay on pacifism.[9]

Cuffe was also a deeply practical man, who penned a "watchword" summing up his ethical outlook that began: "By Experence I have Ever found when I Attended to my business I Seldom Suffered loss," and finished, "The Surest way to Conquer Strong Drink is to make no use of it. We are born and must die" (467). His thinking about African emigration was likewise practical in nature. He knew colonies there would succeed only if they made money. So he linked the cause of "civilizing" Africa to the creation of wealth, writing: "Now if we could return into the countery of our ancestors and carry the seeds of civilization in return for this great ingery that she has so long groaned under and thus for her to injoy a peaceable prevelige of agriculture and Commeras as the other historyen Nations do injoy it doth feel to me that this would be the greatest blessing that that countery could be favoured with" (342). He harped constantly on the need for settlers in Sierra Leone to be of good character (as at 227, 327, 467), not merely because Cuffe was a moralist, but because he thought the colony would otherwise fail.

Cuffe lived long enough to see the founding, and initial forays, of the American Colonization Society before he died in 1817. Like Daniel Coker, Cuffe saw the ACS more as an ally than a competitor. But as Richard Allen and James Forten realized when their community unanimously rejected proposals for removing blacks to Africa, the ACS was ultimately counter-productive for the cause to which Cuffe devoted so much time, money, and effort. This is because the motives of the Society were highly suspect. While some of its members and leaders were sincere abolitionists, the ACS also included such figures as Henry Clay, Speaker of the House of Representatives, a slaveowner who said frankly that he wanted to remove free blacks in order "to rid our country of a useless and pernicious, if not dangerous part of our population."[10] Another well-known member who owned slaves was Francis Scott Key, who wrote the lyrics of the national anthem of the United States, "The Star-Spangled Banner."

Many African American leaders in the North therefore turned against the ACS.[11] The fiery abolitionist David Walker, whom we will meet in the next chapter, called it a "cunningly devised plot of Satan." Even some who had originally been in favor of emigration, like Allen and Forten, adopted a more critical stance, with Allen writing that it was clearly "for the interest of the slave holder" that black people still in chains should be prevented from seeing free brethren in the same nation.

An excellent example of this shift in attitude is provided by Peter Williams Jr. of New York. At first, he was a supporter of emigration and close collaborator of his "dear friend" Cuffe (385). But, by 1830, he was giving an impassioned sermon on the Fourth of July in which he attacked the ACS and its perverse proposal that black Americans could be improved by "being sent far from civilized society."[12] This was not necessary for the improvement of Africa, which could be achieved without exiling free black Americans there. In fact, that might well backfire, given that, as Williams alertly observed, European colonization had "caused ruin" among Native Americans. The following passage sums up the gist of Williams' sermon nicely:

> We are natives of this country, we ask only to be treated as well as foreigners. Not a few of our fathers suffered and bled to purchase its independence; we ask only to be treated as well as those who fought against it. We have toiled to cultivate it, and to raise it to its present prosperous condition; we ask only to share equal privileges with those who come from distant lands, to enjoy the fruits of our labour. Let these moderate requests be granted, and we need not go to Africa nor anywhere else to be improved and happy.

Amidst this turn of black opinion against the ACS, it was bound to cause controversy when one African American leader suddenly came to support its policies. This happened with John Russwurm, whose change of mind went in the reverse direction to what we've just seen with Williams. In New York City, together with Samuel Cornish, the Jamaican-born Russwurm had founded *Freedom's Journal*, the first black newspaper in the United States. At first, he took a strong stand against colonization, proclaiming dedication to the cause of emancipating all "brethren who are in bondage" and promising: "never shall we consent to emigrate from America, until the prior removal from this land of their degradation and suffering."[13] But in an about-face that shocked contemporaries, Russwurm declared his support for the ACS in 1829 and then went to Liberia himself. He was accused of selling out, in the most literal sense: many asserted that he only switched his allegiance to the ACS because he had fallen on hard times. Among those who made this charge was the abolitionist William Lloyd Garrison, despite the fact that Garrison himself was initially a supporter of the ACS.[14] The controversy over Russwurm continues to the present day, with two recent monographs on him taking respectively a highly critical and highly laudatory view of Russwurm's change of mind and subsequent career in Africa.[15]

Much of the disagreement concerns the question of Russwurm's attitudes toward the indigenous peoples of Africa he ruled over as governor of the colony called Maryland in Liberia, which was founded by the Maryland State Colonization

Society. Some argue that his good intentions came together with a disdainful attitude towards the existing culture among the local population, resulting in a rather high-handed approach to his office. Russwurm's choice to emigrate, though, was not primarily a matter of negative or positive attitudes towards Africa. It was inspired above all by his pessimism concerning the United States. Having concluded that it was "impossible to rise" in America because "the mere name of colour, blocks up every avenue," he saw the so-called "land of the free" as a place where freedom would forever remain out of reach. Provocatively, he wrote in an editorial in the *Liberia Herald*: "Before God, we know of no other home for the man of color, of republican principles, than Africa. Has he no ambition? Is he dead to every thing noble? Is he contented with his condition? Let him remain in America: Let him who might here be an honor to society—remain a sojourner in a land where it is impossible to be otherwise. His spirit is extinct, and his friends may as well bury him *now*."[16]

Here we arrive at the philosophical heart of the dispute over colonization. From the practically minded captain's logs of Paul Cuffe, detailing how much African wood had been loaded onto his trading ships, to the bitter recriminations and justifications that have surrounded John Russwurm for nearly two centuries now, the documents concerning emigration all circle around a central question: if individuals belonging to a group that has been subject to discrimination are to have rights, does the group to which they belong need to have political autonomy? Cuffe zeroed in on this issue when he wrote of Sierra Leone, "I am convinced that that is the Countery in which this Peopel Might rise to be a Peopel, if they could be prepared for Self Gouvernment" (436). Implicit in this optimistic remark is the assumption that being "a people" requires escaping from the constraints imposed by *other* people. The same view was put forward in a more pessimistic tone by Russwurm, who came to the conclusion that it was impossible to attain success in America as an African. When a society is sufficiently hostile, you must disengage from it, rather than trying fruitlessly to reform it. Of course, to a large extent, this question was simply a practical one—what were the real prospects of full citizenship for free blacks in early nineteenth century America? But, at a more abstract level, it is a question that still lies at the heart of many of today's political disputes, and not only those concerning race. When separatist movements around the world seek independence, or when some feminists insist upon the need for "women only" spaces, they too are asserting an intimate connection between individual freedom and institutional self-determination.

These same political movements were then, and still are, also expressions of group identity. Indeed, if you consider the figures we've covered in our tour of early American history, you'll realize that they were—along with figures we've covered in

England, like Sancho, Cugoano, and Equiano—among the earliest thinkers to define an identity or "people" that spans Africa and the African diaspora. They were articulating an idea that is also embodied by this book as a whole. We have labeled our topic as "Africana" philosophy, and our coverage has reached as far back as ancient Egypt and considered everything from the intellectual traditions of precolonial Africa up to recent thought in Africa and the African diaspora. While reading the book, even some sympathetic readers may have mistakenly assumed that this approach must be a recent one, traceable perhaps to race-conscious movements in the 1960s or so. But, by now, it should be evident that for diasporic Africans, identity has always been political, and also that our guiding idea of "Africana" culture has been embraced under various labels by intellectuals and leaders for several centuries. Thus we saw Prince Hall identifying Egyptian antiquity as part of his Masonic heritage, an ideal foundation upon which to build a new African American identity.

We find something similar in John Russwurm. Writing in *Freedom's Journal* about the experience of seeing an exhibited Egyptian mummy, he mused: "My thoughts were insensibly carried back to former times, when Egypt was in her splendor, and the only seat of chivalry, science, arts and civilization. As a descendant of Cush, I could not but mourn over her present degradation, while reflecting upon the mutability of human affairs, and upon the present condition of a people, who, for more than one thousand years, were the most civilized and enlightened."[17] It's clear that even if Russwurm, Cuffe, and other emigrationists saw the people of Africa in their time as "uncivilized," in need of both commercial and religious uplift, they also saw these Africans as their brethren. Cuffe referred at one point to the "great family of Africa,"[18] while Peter Williams expressed the hope and conviction that Cuffe's work would promote "the spiritual and temporal welfare of our unhappy race" (357). Who was it that Williams intended to refer to here as unhappy and in need of uplifting—black Americans? The indigenous peoples of Africa? The obvious answer is both.

33

KILL OR BE KILLED

David Walker's Appeal

To indicate emphasis in writing, you can use underlining or boldface characters. To really lay it on thick, though, there's nothing like an exclamation point! Depending on how strongly you feel, you might even decide that one exclamation point is not enough. Judging from social media, three of them would seem to be a popular choice. For David Walker, though, three exclamation points counted as understatement. This pioneering figure in the African American philosophical tradition regularly used up to eight of them in his classic work, first published in 1829 under another of those lengthy titles: *Walker's Appeal, in Four Articles; Together with a Preamble, to the Coloured Citizens of the World, but in Particular, and Very Expressly, to Those of the United States of America.*

A radical and uncompromising indictment of American racial oppression, Walker's *Appeal* uses punctuation to express rage, frustration, and disbelief at how African Americans are treated. Consider this statement of purpose from the Preamble: "I appeal to Heaven for my motive in writing—who knows that my object is, if possible, to awaken in the breasts of my afflicted, degraded and slumbering brethren, a spirit of inquiry and investigation respecting our miseries and wretchedness in this *Republican Land of Liberty!!!!!!*" (4–5).[1] Points don't get much more exclamatory than that. For Walker the very idea that the United States is a land of freedom and civic equality is a mockery, a sham, in light of the experiences of African Americans. As one scholar who has studied the typography of the *Appeal* has pointed out, Walker did not live in an age when writing such a string of exclamation points would be a simple matter of holding down two keys for a while.[2] Whether through a manuscript or perhaps even in person, Walker had to direct the printer to set the precise number of exclamation points through the manual arrangement of individual pieces of type. Just imagine what he could have done with emojis!!!!!!!!

But let's come to the point: who was this passionate writer and thinker, and how was his radical denunciation of American racism received? What we know of Walker's place of birth and parentage comes from a biographical sketch written by Henry Highland Garnet, who was influenced by Walker and will be discussed later in this book (Chapter 38). Walker was born in the port city of Wilmington, North Carolina, probably in 1796 or 1797, the son of an enslaved father and a free mother. As one inherited the status of one's mother, this meant Walker was born free. Wilmington at this time was majority-black, with all but a tiny few of this majority enslaved. While still a young man, Walker left Wilmington for Charleston, South Carolina, where there was a much larger free black population. While we don't know for sure when he lived in Charleston, it is quite possible that he was there for the momentous events of 1822, when the apparent discovery and foiling of a plot for a massive rebellion against slavery, allegedly organized by a man named Denmark Vesey, led to the execution of Vesey and thirty-four others.

Recent historical scholarship on the Vesey plot is divided. Many believe that Vesey was not so much a conspiratorial leader as the victim of a conspiracy by the white authorities who executed him, supported by testimony from witnesses who were tortured and threatened with death.[3] So we should not necessarily assume that the surviving testimony of these witnesses gives us access to Vesey's thought. Still, there are striking similarities between the ideas those witnesses attributed to Vesey and what we find in Walker's *Appeal*. This point has been made by Peter Hinks, author of the most thorough study of Walker's life and times. He notes parallels between Vesey and Walker on such matters as the religious foundation for resistance, the need for black ambition and self-exertion, the necessity of violence, the treachery of informants, the importance of unity, and the role of Haiti as a paradigm of solidarity.[4] Perhaps then the Charleston of 1822 was the very time and place in which Walker's political philosophy first took shape.

Within the next couple of years Walker left Charleston, apparently to various points further south and further west. This period of travel is not of merely biographical significance, for his observations of the slaveholding South and other parts of the country serve as the empirical foundation of Walker's analysis of the African American condition in his *Appeal*. He probably made his way to Philadelphia, because he was a great admirer of Richard Allen and writes of him in terms that suggest personal acquaintance. By late 1824, Walker arrived in Boston and established a business there, a second-hand clothing store. From here to his death in 1830, we have much better documentation for his life story. These six years saw Walker establish himself as a business owner, leading activist, public speaker, and, most importantly for our purposes, author. He also married and started a family before his untimely death. While in Boston, he became a Mason. He was initiated in the summer of 1826 into the same African Lodge founded by Prince Hall some four decades prior. The following year, the Boston lodge declared its independence from the English and established itself as the Grand Lodge for all Prince Hall freemasons, as they now called themselves. Walker's membership connected him with other significant members of Boston's black community.

In another link to figures we've already discussed, Walker was one of the most enthusiastic supporters and promoters of *Freedom's Journal*, the black newspaper edited by Cornish and Russwurm. Even before the newspaper's first issue was published in March of 1827, Walker held a gathering at his home to drum up interest and support. He was the New York-based newspaper's subscription agent in Boston, and multiple speeches of his were reported or recorded in *Freedom's Journal*. Most prominent among these was a December 1828 speech, which brings us to his involvement in the founding of the Massachusetts General Colored Association, a pioneering civil rights organization. It lasted as a distinct group only from 1828 to 1833, when it became an auxiliary of William Lloyd Garrison's New England Anti-Slavery Society. But, at its founding, Walker believed it could play a major role in bringing about change not just in Massachusetts but nationwide. Speaking at the first of its semi-annual meetings, he announced that "the primary object of this institution is, to unite the colored population, so far, through the United States of America, as may be practicable and expedient."[5] He complained that disunity was a major factor in the failure of African Americans to achieve progress.

Once they were unified, he proposed that the community should go on to explore all possible avenues toward change. As he put it, "it is indispensably our duty to try every scheme that we think will have a tendency to facilitate our salvation, and leave the final result to that God, who holds the destinies of people in the hollow of his hand, and who ever has, and will, repay every nation according to its works." How many listening to Walker on that day knew that when he said *every* scheme must be tried, he was in deadly earnest? He left implicit in this speech what would become explosively explicit in his *Appeal*: his belief that African Americans must be prepared to engage in violence, whenever necessary, in order to secure their liberation. His book, first published in September of 1829, was revolutionary in this non-metaphorical sense.

In fact, 1829 was a year that saw several important publications in Africana literature and political thought. In Walker's home state of North Carolina, there lived an enslaved man named George Moses Horton, who, like Jupiter Hammon and Phillis Wheatley before him, gained recognition for his poetry.[6] In 1829, he was able to publish a collection of his poems called *The Hope of Liberty*. The book's title was earnest and literal, because Horton hoped to raise money enough through its publication to purchase his freedom. Walker knew of Horton and joined with other subscribers to *Freedom's Journal* in raising money to secure his freedom, but to no avail. Horton continued to write and publish poetry but remained enslaved until the Civil War and the emancipation of all slaves.

More similar to Walker's *Appeal*, but also frustratingly mysterious, is a pamphlet published in February of 1829 called *The Ethiopian Manifesto: Issued in Defence of the Black Man's Rights in the Scale of Universal Freedom*. The author identified himself as "Rednaxela," which is "Alexander" backwards. We know because of his registration of the pamphlet that his name was Robert Alexander Young. Decrying the lack of rights for black people around the globe, and issuing a prophetic call for change, it is thematically comparable to Walker's *Appeal*, but we have no evidence concerning whether Walker read it. Most philosophically interesting in the *Manifesto* is its introspective description of an inner "voice of intuitive justice" that demands recognition of human equality.[7] Most bizarre, on the other hand, is its messianic revelation that a liberator who will bring an end to slavery has already been born, a savior in relation to whom Young considers himself a sort of John the Baptist. This man, according to Young, is white in appearance but born of a black mother on the island of Grenada, and has webbed toes on both of his feet. That Young is speaking of a particular person seems likely from the details given, but it is unknown who he was and why Young believed him to be so special.

There is actually a messianic moment in Walker's *Appeal*, too, where he writes: "Beloved brethren—here let me tell you, and believe it, that the Lord our God, as true as he sits on his throne in heaven, and as true our Saviour died to redeem the world, will give you a Hannibal...The person whom God shall give you, give him your support and let him go his length, and behold in him the salvation of your God" (23). Unlike Young, though, Walker spends little time encouraging this kind of faith in a coming liberator and much more time preaching the necessity of unity, self-reliance, and bravery on the part of all black people, including bravery to commit violence where appropriate. Like Thomas Paine's *Common Sense* before it and Marx and Engels' *Communist Manifesto* after it, this is a philosophical work but also an impassioned plea for collective action. In a note placed before the Preamble in the third and final edition, Walker writes: "It is expected that all coloured men, women and children of every nation, language and tongue under heaven, will try to procure a copy of this *Appeal* and read it, or get some one to read it to them, for it is designed more particularly for them" (2).

This was no idle wish. Walker did his best to put his book into the hands of those who needed to read it. Within a few months of the publication of the first edition, the police department of Savannah, Georgia, seized sixty copies of it that had been delivered to a local black preacher. Once alerted to its contents, the state of Georgia banned the book and made new laws quarantining all black sailors entering Georgia ports. The mayor of Savannah wrote to the mayor of Boston demanding that Walker be arrested, but received the unwelcome reply that despite the "bad and inflammatory tendency" of the work, no Massachusetts law had been broken. We also know of copies sent to Virginia, North Carolina, South Carolina, and Louisiana, because in all these places, arrests were made and further legal action was taken to contain it. The laws passed were harsh. For example, a law against literature that might incite black unrest in Louisiana made distribution of Walker's book punishable by death. It is unknown how many incidents of slave rebellion, planned or executed, can be connected to the circulation of the *Appeal*, but at the time some certainly believed Walker to have been the inspiration for an attempt in North Carolina in 1830. Sixty slaves gathered in a swamp and armed themselves, but a local militia got to them and all were killed. The most famous slave revolt in US history occurred in 1831 in Virginia, led by a Baptist preacher named Nat Turner. It has been irresistible for scholars to speculate on the possible influence of Walker on Turner's uprising, but there is no hard evidence allowing us to draw that connection.

Let's turn now from the hysteria surrounding the book's publication to what the book itself has to say. Perhaps the best way to understand its structure and organizing theme is to put aside its most controversial element—its advocacy of violent resistance—and focus instead on Walker's engagement with Thomas Jefferson, whom he praises in extravagant terms: "a much greater philosopher the world never afforded" (31).[8] There is characteristic bombast here, no doubt, but not sarcasm. His criticism of Jefferson is, in fact, all the more poignant given his recognition of Jefferson as brilliant, a vast repository of knowledge, and a political thinker capable of writing such a document as the Declaration of Independence. Yet this same man was responsible for the repugnant remarks on the natural inferiority of black people in Query XIV of his *Notes on the State of Virginia*, remarks that we discussed in some detail already (Chapter 27).

It's a telling instance of the mind-warping power of American racism that the otherwise brilliant Jefferson's thoughts on black people are so ridiculous. Walker writes: "Has Mr. Jefferson declared to the world, that we are inferior to the whites, both in the endowments of our bodies and of minds? It is indeed surprising, that a man of such great learning, combined with such excellent natural parts, should speak so of a set of men in chains. I do not know what to compare it to, unless, like putting one wild deer in an iron cage, where it will be secured, and hold another by the side of the same, then let it go, and expect the one in the cage to run as fast as the one at liberty" (12–13). The obvious inadequacy of Jefferson's analysis illustrates how white Americans resort to the flimsiest of reasonings to justify the domination of black Americans.

In one memorable passage, though, Walker states that his aim is to "solicit each of my brethren, who has the spirit of a man, to buy a copy of Mr. Jefferson's *Notes on Virginia*, and put it in the hand of his son" (17). Why? He explains that some white writers have opposed Jefferson's comments about black people, but this is insufficient. "For let no one of us suppose that the refutations which have been written by our white friends are enough—they are *whites*—we are *blacks*. We, and the world wish to see the charges of Mr. Jefferson refuted by the blacks *themselves,* according to their chance; for we must remember that what the whites have written respecting this subject, is other men's labours, and did not emanate from the blacks" (17–18). Later, he puts the point even more forcefully: "Unless we try to refute Mr. Jefferson's arguments respecting us, we will only establish them." Walker here exploits Jefferson's racism as a challenge to African Americans, a means of goading them toward outstanding accomplishments that will disprove Jefferson's claims about natural inferiority.

But why is this necessary, if the flimsiness of Jefferson's argument is so obvious? Why take time disproving claims that are ridiculous on their face? Is Walker trying to have it both ways? One way to resolve the contradiction is to see Walker as encouraging simultaneous awareness of two different perspectives. On the one hand, there is an impartial perspective from which it is obvious that black people are not inferior in the way that Jefferson suggests. This perspective is useful to buttress a sense of self-worth among blacks. On the other hand, one should not underestimate how widespread and entrenched are derogatory perspectives on black people. Even the brilliant Jefferson took their natural inferiority as a completely reasonable hypothesis worth investigating, rather than seeing it for the preposterous bigotry it is.

The culminating point of Jefferson's discussion of black inferiority is his claim that the study of slavery in ancient times helps prove that it is not the social condition of slavery, but something more inherent, that makes black people inferior. We know, he says, "that among the Romans, about the Augustan age especially, the condition of their slaves was much more deplorable than that of the blacks on the continent of America." After compiling evidence for this claim, Jefferson draws a conclusion: "notwithstanding these and other discouraging circumstances among the Romans, their slaves were often their rarest artists. They excelled too in science, insomuch as to be usually employed as tutors to their master's children. Epictetus, Terence, and Phædrus, were slaves. But they were of the race of whites. It is not their condition then, but nature, which has produced the distinction."

Once one has noticed the various functions Jefferson serves in Walker's argument, it becomes more obvious that the book is structured around this very point: Walker needs to prove that it is indeed the vicious treatment of slaves in America that explains their condition. The Preamble begins with a sort of thesis statement for the book as a whole: "Having travelled over a considerable portion of these United States, and having, in the course of my travels, taken the most accurate observations of things as they exist—the result of my observations has warranted the full and unshaken conviction, that we, (coloured people of these United States,) are the most degraded, wretched, and abject set of beings that ever lived since the world began; and I pray God that none like us ever may live again until time shall be no more" (3). After the Preamble, the *Appeal* is divided into four sections or chapters that Walker calls, in imitation of the Constitution, "articles."

Each article reinforces the thesis by exploring a different dimension of the unprecedented degradation of African Americans. Article 1 is entitled "Our Wretchedness in Consequence of Slavery." It is here that Walker responds most directly to Jefferson's comparative argument, making his own comparisons between African Americans and ancient peoples who were enslaved, such as the Hebrews in Egypt, the helots of Sparta, and of course the slaves of the Romans. Article 2, "Our Wretchedness in Consequence of Ignorance," does address ignorance in the sense of a lack of knowledge, as when Walker complains of widespread ignorance of English grammar. More central though is the notion of *moral* ignorance, which he associates with servility and a failure to value the humanity of one's fellow black people. Article 3 is "Our Wretchedness in Consequence of the Preachers of the Religion of Jesus Christ." As one might imagine, it discusses white Christian hypocrisy. Finally, in Article 4, "Our Wretchedness in Consequence of the Colonizing Plan," Walker rails against the American Colonization Society and strongly opposes the emigration of African Americans to Liberia. The fact that this Article is by far the longest of the four reminds us what a central concern and matter of controversy this was at the time.

Articles 1 and 2 are where we find Walker's thoughts on another controversial subject: violence. From the first to the third edition of the *Appeal*, he became more and more outspoken on this topic. In the first edition, we find him saying: "Remember that unless you are united, keeping your tongues within your teeth, you will be afraid to trust your secrets to each other, and thus perpetuate our miseries under the *Christians!!!!!*" (13). The casual reader might find this claim a bit vague—what are these secrets, and what does keeping them have to do with the perpetuation of miseries? The second edition clarifies that he has in mind secret plans for violent resistance. He endorses this form of resistance without reservation, proclaiming it to be divinely sanctioned, though he is also careful to warn that it must only be used when the time is right. "Remember," he writes, "also to lay humble at the feet of our Lord and Master Jesus Christ, with prayers and fastings. Let our enemies go on with their butcheries, and at once fill up their cup. Never make an attempt to gain our freedom of *natural right,* from under our cruel oppressors and murderers, until you see your way clear—when that hour arrives and you move, be not afraid or dismayed; for be you assured that Jesus Christ the King of heaven and of earth who is the God of justice and of armies, will surely go before you" (14).

Walker defends violence as not merely permissible but, in certain circumstances, obligatory. In a striking section of Article 2, he conversely criticizes mercy as being strictly impermissible in some cases. He quotes a newspaper report of an incident in Kentucky. Sixty slaves were being transported through the state when some managed to get loose. They attacked the three white men transporting them, killing two and leaving a third for dead, a man named Gordon. An enslaved woman helped Gordon to mount his horse and he managed to rally the neighborhood, thus enabling the capture of all the escaped slaves and the execution of eight of them. Walker minces no words in expressing his utter disgust at the behavior of the woman who helped Gordon. To the excuse that it was her "natural *fine feelings*" that motivated her to help him, Walker replies: "But I declare, the actions of this black woman are really insupportable. For my own part, I cannot think it was any thing but servile deceit, combined with the most gross ignorance: for we must remember that *humanity, kindness* and the *fear of the Lord,* does not consist in protecting *devils*" (28). In this case, mercy towards Gordon ultimately led to the most unmerciful of results, an observation that justifies this steely-eyed advice: "If you commence, make sure work—do not trifle, for they will not trifle with you—they want us for their slaves, and think nothing of murdering us in order to subject us to that wretched condition—therefore, if there is an *attempt* made by us, kill or be killed" (29-30).

In a particularly harsh and even shocking passage found in the aforementioned addition to Article 1, he asserts the obligatory nature of violent resistance in this way: "The man who would not fight under our Lord and Master Jesus Christ, in the glorious and heavenly cause of freedom and of God—to be delivered from the most wretched, abject and servile slavery, that ever a people was afflicted with since the foundation of the world, to the present day—ought to be kept with all of his children or family, in slavery, or in chains, to be butchered by his *cruel enemies*" (15). Can he really mean this? Or is it just heavy-handed rhetoric, intended to motivate resistance? Certainly, one need not be a pacifist to worry that Walker has gone too far.

It would be a mistake, though, to fasten on to these passages as if they contained Walker's entire moral and political thought. In fact, his impassioned writing was capable of inspiring readers who were not attracted by the justification of violence.

We can see this by turning to a subsequent thinker who was inspired by Walker, but who chose to downplay the threat of violence, almost to the point of eliminating it entirely. We are speaking of Maria W. Stewart, who became the first American woman to give public lectures—not just black woman, but, to keep with our punctuation theme, the first American woman to give public lectures, full stop.

34

RELIGION AND PURE PRINCIPLES

Maria W. Stewart

If you ask people who the first feminist philosopher was, the name you're most likely to hear is Mary Wollstonecraft, thanks to her pioneering *Vindication of the Rights of Woman*, published in 1790. There are much earlier claimants for that title, though, like Christine de Pizan. Her *Book of the City of Ladies*, a defense of the virtues of womankind, was published almost four centuries earlier, in 1405, and in her wake followed several female Renaissance humanists like Moderata Fonte and Lucrezia Marinella, who argued stridently for the moral and intellectual equality of women. From these humanists to Wollstonecraft, a constant refrain is the value of education for girls. Fonte wrote that if this were offered from a young age, "we'd outstrip men's performance in any science or art you care to name."[1] Many hundreds of years later, Wollstonecraft was still making the same plea. Education is one of the main themes of her *Vindication*. She recommends teaching the two sexes together outside the home in "day schools," and emphasizes that this will in due course prepare women to be better wives, with husbands benefiting from having more equal, learned, and virtuous spouses.

It makes sense that all these authors would put a high value on education, since they themselves had an unusually high level of schooling for women of their times. But this was not only a matter of the intelligentsia praising its own intelligence. Whether in the fifteenth, the eighteenth, or the twenty-first century, education is a crucial step towards equality, an obvious route of escape for oppressed social groups. Oppressors know this too, which is why in nineteenth century America, slaves were often violently prevented from obtaining even basic literacy. The point did not escape David Walker. He observed that the American slaveowners' "greatest object and glory is centered in keeping us sunk in the most profound ignorance and stupidity...If they catch a colored person...with a book in his hand, [they] will beat him nearly to death."[2]

If learning seemed a great and necessary goal to women authors, and to African American authors, then how much would it be valued by an author who was an African American woman? Lots, as we can see from the life and writings of Maria W. Stewart, a great admirer of Walker who followed him in lending her rhetorical skill to the cause of racial liberation and uplift. We know a good deal about her life story, thanks to autobiographical remarks in her own writings and surviving documents, including her pension claim as the widow of a veteran of the War of 1812.[3] Born Maria Miller in 1803 in Connecticut, she was orphaned as a child and grew up as an indentured servant. Even after being released from this status, she continued doing domestic work in order to support herself, but also began to seek education by attending Sabbath school classes. At some point, she moved to Boston, where she met the man she married, James W. Stewart. Somewhat unusually, and apparently at his request, she took not only his last name but his middle initial as well, becoming Maria W. Stewart.

It is impossible to know what sort of public profile, if any, Stewart would have achieved if she had been able to continue living as James' wife. What happened instead is that James died in December of 1829. This tragic event was further compounded by race-based injustice, as white executors managed to cheat Stewart out of the inheritance left to her by her husband. Thus Stewart lived through precisely what Walker described in his *Appeal*: "But I must, really, observe that in this very city [Boston], when a man of colour dies, if he owned any real estate it most generally falls into the hands of some white person. The wife and children of the deceased may weep and lament if they please, but the estate will be kept snug enough by its white possessor" (12). Stewart and her husband would have known Walker as members of Boston's black community. In fact, when Walker and his wife Eliza moved out of their home at 81 Joy Street in 1829, the Stewarts moved in, and Maria continued to live there after James' death. So it was a further emotional blow to Maria when, while still dealing with her grief over the loss of her husband, Walker suddenly died in August of 1830. There has been controversy ever since concerning what caused Walker's death. There is relatively strong evidence that he died of tuberculosis, but at the time and ever since, many have suspected that he was poisoned, and thus have seen his death as a form of martyrdom in light of the audacious publication of his *Appeal*.

In the wake of these events, Stewart experienced a religious transformation, a sort of new conversion to the truth of Christianity in spite of the fact that she had already had ties to the church before then. Along with this newfound piety came a burning desire to speak out for the cause of black freedom. Near the beginning of her first publication, a pamphlet entitled *Religion and the Pure Principles of Morality, the Sure Foundation On Which We Must Build*, she announces: "Many will suffer for pleading the cause of oppressed Africa, and I shall glory in being one of her martyrs; for I am firmly persuaded, that the God in whom I trust is able to protect me from the rage and malice of mine enemies, and from them that will rise up against me; and if there is no other way for me to escape, he is able to take me to himself, as he did the most noble, fearless, and undaunted David Walker" (30).

This passage exemplifies the way Stewart treats Walker as an icon of resistance, sometimes invoking him in this way without even saying his name. In one speech, she asks: "But where is the man that has distinguished himself in these modern days by acting wholly in the defense of African rights and liberty? There was one; although he sleeps, his memory lives" (57). There can be no doubt that she means Walker, especially because she is echoing what she wrote in *Religion and the Pure Principles of Morality*: "God hath raised you up a Walker and a Garrison. Though Walker sleeps, yet he lives, and his name shall be held in everlasting remembrance" (40). The "Garrison" mentioned here is of course William Lloyd Garrison, the radical white abolitionist. It was Garrison who printed *Religion and the Pure Principles of Morality* for Stewart in 1831 and, once she started giving path-breaking public speeches the following year, he advertised and printed them in his newspaper, the *Liberator*.

Decades later, Garrison wrote to Stewart recalling how impressed he had been when they first met, and adding: "your whole adult life has been devoted to the noble task of educating and elevating your people" (90). He was not exaggerating: in the wake of the Civil War, she opened a Sunday school near the Freedman's hospital where she served as matron (85, 95). Both Garrison and Stewart died in 1879. Stewart's funeral was overseen by Alexander Crummell. In a testimony attached to a collection of her writings, Crummell wrote somewhat patronizingly of his "great surprise" at the "literary aspiration and ambitious authorship" of Stewart, given that these were traits otherwise seen "almost exclusively" among the men of the black community at the time he met her (93-4). Garrison, by contrast, allowed only that he had felt "satisfaction," not necessarily "surprise" on meeting Stewart—though he did print her pieces in the section of his paper called the "Ladies' Department."

When she devoted her later years to educating the black community, Stewart was quite literally practicing what she had preached back in the 1830s. In the public lectures that she gave in Boston—something unprecedented for an American woman of any color—a constant refrain is the need for her black audience to establish schools and seek knowledge. Through these means, they may avoid wasting their talents, which go unencouraged and unexploited by American society as a whole (34). "Many bright and intelligent ones are in the midst of us; but because they are not calculated to display a classical education, they hide their talents behind a napkin" (44). Education, she observes, is not foreign to the African soul: "History informs us that we sprung from one of the most learned nations of the whole earth, from the seat, if not the parent, of science. Yes, poor despised Africa was once the resort of sages and legislators of other nations, was esteemed the school for learning, and the most illustrious men of Greece flocked thither for instruction" (58).

Stewart often addresses herself to women hearers, and, speaking especially to the mothers among them, she recommends that they look to the educating of their children. Even if proper schools are inaccessible to them as blacks, they can at least "have them taught in the first rudiments of useful knowledge" and then hire private tutors for more advanced topics (36). She stresses that this goes for girls, as well as boys. "How long," she asks, "shall the fair daughters of Africa be compelled to bury their minds and talents beneath a load of iron pots and kettles?" She then answers her own question: "Until union, knowledge and love begin to flow among us...We have never had an opportunity of displaying our talents; therefore the world thinks we know nothing" (38). She endorses the old adage that "knowledge is power" and sees wisdom and understanding, alongside trust in God, as the tools to overcome the fears that grip the African American population, inhibiting them from striving for greater things (41).

As the talk of private tutors indicates, Stewart is not speaking primarily to slaves here, but to "free blacks" whose legal and financial condition gives them at least some measure of control over their own lives. She laments that this modest opportunity for self-determination is often squandered. She certainly recognizes the oppression faced by free blacks, who are usually allowed only to work as servants so that their status is in fact little better than that of slaves (45-7). But more often, Stewart turns her oratorical fire on the black community itself. It is they who fail to invest in schools as they should: "We ought to follow the example of the whites in this respect. Nothing would raise our respectability, add to our peace and happiness, and reflect so much honor upon us, as to be ourselves the promoters of temperance, and the supporters, as far as we are able, of useful and scientific knowledge" (60).

Given the stern and earnest tone of her writings, it's pretty easy to picture what Stewart herself must have been like as a teacher. You can bet no one was whispering at the back or passing notes in her class. This is a woman who, at an older age, pronounced herself "horrified" at the suggestion that a celebration of Christmas might include music and dancing (103). She was above all a moralist and a religious crusader, fired by an early religious experience and motivated in all her writing by a deep faith. She imagines critics complaining of the way she harps on religion as an abiding theme (32, 71-2), but invokes divine guidance for the very fact that she is daring to make her ideas public: "I believe that God has fired my soul with a holy zeal for His cause. It was God alone who inspired my heart to publish the meditations thereof" (52). On this score, Stewart is comparable to Walker, who also put what he called "pure and undefiled religion" at the core of his teaching.[4] Using the same language, Stewart says that America was "founded on religion and pure principles" and promises her listeners and readers, "pure religion will burst your fetters" (43, 72).

Stewart, like Wollstonecraft, also sees a close connection between education and virtue. Again, she emphasizes this connection especially for her female audience: "O woman, woman, would thou only strive to excel in merit and virtue; would thou only store thy mind with useful knowledge, great would be thine influence" (31). With what may look like undue optimism, she even predicts that, were "the American free people of color to turn their attention more assiduously to moral worth and intellectual improvement," the result would be that "prejudice would gradually diminish, and the whites would be compelled to say, unloose those fetters!" (46). This is not to say that she sees the white population through rose-tinted spectacles. Again, she is all too aware of the limits that white racism places on blacks and their moral and intellectual development. But her default tone is one of moral exhortation and even chastisement of her own community, a strategy she at one point explicitly defends: "Let us no longer talk of prejudice, till prejudice becomes extinct at home. Let us no longer talk of opposition, till we cease to oppose our own. For while these evils exist, to talk is like giving breath to the air, and labor to the wind" (70-1).

Here we may return to the comparison between Stewart and her hero, David Walker. On most points that were being debated by black leaders of the time, Walker and Stewart were in full agreement. For example, she wholeheartedly echoed his opposition to the idea that black Americans should settle in Africa, as proposed by the American Colonization Society. She dwelt on this topic in an address she gave at the African Masonic Hall in 1833, not long before leaving Boston. We saw that Prince Hall, founder of the Masonic Lodge in this city, had tried to raise funds for transportation of free blacks to Africa. But Stewart has nothing but disdain for the scheme of the ACS. Showing again her concern with education, she tartly remarks in her speech at the Masonic Hall: "If the colonizers are the real friends to Africa, let them expend the money which they collect in erecting a college to educate her injured sons in this land of gospel, light, and liberty" (61).

Demonstrating how seriously she takes white racism, she depicts the colonization scheme as the latest turn of a cycle in which non-white people are displaced in order to avoid treating them equally. In a single passage she encapsulates a whole history of American injustice, writing: "The unfriendly whites first drove the native American from his much loved home. Then they stole our fathers from their peaceful and quiet dwellings, and brought them hither, and made bond-men and bond-women of them and their little ones. They have obliged our brethren to labor; kept them in utter ignorance; nourished them in vice, and raised them in degradation; and now that we have enriched their soil, and filled their coffers, they say that we are not capable of becoming like white men, and that we never can rise to respectability in this country. They would drive us to a strange land." Her repudiation of this dynamic of displacement would not be out of place in Walker's writings: "Before I go, the bayonet shall pierce me through."

Yet there appears to be at least one major difference between the two. Without ever acknowledging disagreement with Walker, Stewart explicitly declines to encourage violent resistance, and at one point expresses a decided preference for moral and pedagogical exhortation: "Far be it from me to recommend to you either to kill, burn, or destroy. But I would strongly recommend to you to improve your talents; let not one lie buried in the earth. Show forth your powers of mind" (29). One can easily imagine Walker responding with characteristic passion: "Far be it from me to discourage killing, burning, and destroying when it may result in our freedom," and adding a string of exclamation points for good measure! Despite the broad agreement between the two thinkers, this difference over the issue of violent resistance seems a weighty one.

But scholars are not of one mind about this matter. Christina Henderson has argued that Stewart does, in fact, advocate violent resistance, and in a unique and surprising way. According to Henderson, "by grounding violent resistance in an ethic of Christian sympathy and kindness, Stewart complicates the discourse of both movements, offering a unique model of love-inspired violence."[5] Henderson points to a variety of sentiments in Stewart's speeches to defend this interpretation. Prominent among them are those that involve the embrace of martyrdom, something we have mentioned above. Henderson cites this declaration from the second of Stewart's four speeches: "I can but die for expressing my sentiments; and I am as willing to die by the sword as by the pestilence" (46).

But is this a matter of taking up swords, or simply of being prepared to be cut down by one if it comes to that? At times she even seems almost ready to recommend violence, only to pull back at the last moment. In *Religion and the Pure Principles of Morality*, she uncharacteristically addresses white Americans and warns:

"We claim our rights. We will tell you that we are not afraid of them that kill the body, and after that can do no more; but we will tell you whom we do fear. We fear Him who is able, after he hath killed, to destroy both soul and body in hell forever" (40). If this were Walker, these remarks would be followed by a reflection on the obligatory nature of violent resistance in certain circumstances. Stewart, though, goes on by returning to her African American audience: "Then, my brethren, sheath your swords, and calm your angry passions. Stand still, and know that the Lord he is God. Vengeance is his, and he will repay" (40).

Should we see this as a repudiation of Walker? Certainly not of his thought as a whole. Though Walker did endorse violent resistance, he put just as much emphasis on the need for self-improvement through learning and ambition. Stewart takes up this dimension of Walker's thought and makes it her central theme. "Have the sons of Africa no souls? Feel they no ambitious desires? Shall the chains of ignorance forever confine them?...Where can we find among ourselves the man of science, or a philosopher, or an able statesman, or a counsellor at law? Show me our fearless and brave, our noble and gallant ones. Where are our lecturers on natural history and our critics in useful knowledge?" (57).

But if Stewart in this sense carries on Walker's legacy, she also adds a distinctive twist. She is, unsurprisingly, more interested than Walker in the specific predicament faced by black women, who form a distinct group with its own challenges and responsibilities. She thus speaks of the need to achieve unity specifically among women, not only among African Americans more generally (37). Her idea is that such unity could express itself in founding schools, as well as a common determination to live prudently and economically: her usual recommendations. She does not, however, call for women to step forward and speak in public, as she is doing. She is keenly aware that religious crusading and political polemic is hardly something her contemporaries will expect from her gender. You may remember the resistance that Jarena Lee had to overcome to become a public preacher (Chapter 31).

She tackles this issue head on in her "Farewell Address" in Boston, the last of her public speeches, in which she complains of the opposition that met her from within her own community (70–1).[6] Stewart asks "What if I am a woman?" and then justifies her political oratory with reference to female figures from the Bible as an authorizing precedent. Perhaps because she's expecting potential critics to cite it against her, she mentions St. Paul's infamous ban on women speaking in public. Just as quickly, though, she dismisses the relevance of this for her own situation. St. Paul himself would surely approve, "did he but know of our wrongs and deprivations" (68). She also takes inspiration from earlier women authors, even referring to those same Renaissance humanists we mentioned above. Since there were learned women already in the fifteenth century, she says: "why cannot we become divines and scholars?" (69). For this information, she is drawing on a work called *Sketches of the Fair Sex*, written in 1790 by John Adams (not the famous one). As with her allusion to the scientific heritage of Africa in ancient times, Stewart draws on historical research to buttress her case for the dignity of both black and white people, of both women and men.

It is here that we should locate Stewart's most important and distinctive contribution to Africana thought in the first half of the nineteenth century. We've seen a number of male authors speaking eloquently and explicitly about racial equality, but we haven't seen those authors making a parallel case for equality between the sexes. Stewart does precisely that. She strikes a fairly familiar note by arguing that "it is not the color of the skin that makes the man, but it is the principles formed within the soul" (29, see also 70). But it's less familiar when she argues that black *women* have just as much talent as anyone else. We've already seen her complaining of the servitude of "the fair daughters of Africa," their talents squandered among the pots and kettles, and we've heard of her involvement with educational societies devised specifically for black women. And consider this remarkable passage, addressed to white women on behalf of black women: "Had we had the opportunity that you have had, to improve our moral and mental faculties, what would have hindered our intellects from being as bright, and our manners from being as dignified as yours? Had it been our lot to have been nursed in the lap of affluence and ease, and to have basked beneath the smiles and sunshine of fortune, should we not have naturally supposed that we were never made to toil?" (48). Even if Mary Wollstonecraft had committed herself to extending her educational campaign to black women as well as white women, we doubt that she could have said it better herself.

35

UNNATURAL CAUSES

Hosea Easton's Treatise

Thus far we've considered some underappreciated and relatively unknown figures. Take David Walker. Experts in African American history certainly do appreciate and know about him, to the point that one encyclopedia entry on Walker begins by describing him as "perhaps the most influential African American author in the 19th century."[1] Closer to his own time, no less a figure than Frederick Douglass said that Walker's "appeal against slavery startled the land like a trump of coming judgment."[2] Yet today, most people are much, much more likely to know about Douglass than Walker. That goes double for Maria W. Stewart. She may have been, as noted in the aforementioned encyclopedia, "one of the first African American women to consciously write…about political matters," but Stewart is far from being well known today. And, unlike Walker, her significance was underrated even back in the nineteenth century. After her farewell speech in Boston and departure for New York in 1833, her bold efforts soon became mostly forgotten. In 1878, almost four decades after the death of her husband, a change in the law finally allowed her to collect her widow's pension. With the proceeds, she published her collected speeches and older writings along with more recent autobiographical reflections. That was in 1879, the same year as her death: she went to the next world still seeking to make her mark on this one.

Like Walker and Stewart, the subject of this chapter, Hosea Easton, was active in the black community of Boston around the year 1830. If Walker and Stewart are not well remembered, however, they are positively household names compared to Easton. Indeed, the same encyclopedia to which we have turned for evidence of expert opinions gives him no entry at all. Nevertheless, Bruce Dain, one of the few scholars to pay serious attention to Easton, confidently asserts that "with his 1837 *Treatise*, Hosea Easton…became the first African American to articulate a systematic theory of race."[3] Dain is referring here to Easton's most important work, his *Treatise on the Intellectual Character, and Civil and Political Condition of the Colored People of the United States; and the Prejudice Exercised Toward Them*. Dain's claim is a bold one, given how much Walker, Stewart, and others before them had concerned themselves with the topic of racial difference. Indeed, we're not sure we would go along with Dain on this, but we certainly agree that Easton was an uncommonly systematic thinker, one who opposed slavery and discrimination with creative and challenging ideas and arguments about the nature of race and racial prejudice.

For example, Easton asks whether prejudice against his people is caused by the physical difference of color, as he thinks most people suppose. If so, we might pessimistically conclude that there is an "insurmountable barrier" to functional social and political relations between white and black Americans. After all, black people can hardly change the color of their skins. Easton argues against this common assumption in two steps, invoking abstract laws concerning the nature of things. The first law states that "effects…partake of their parent cause in nature and quantity" (101).[4] In other words, more intense causes produce stronger effects. In the case of skin color, if it were the cause of racial prejudice, we should see a tight correspondence between darker skin and more intense prejudice. Easton denies, however, that this is how American racism works. Even being as white in appearance as someone of European ancestry, or whiter still, is no protection from prejudice as intense as that suffered by those with the darkest skin: all that matters is recent African ancestry.

His second law is that "that which cannot be contemplated as a principle, abstractly, cannot be an efficient cause of any thing" (102). Easton's idea here is that there are active principles, which are real causes, and passive principles, which depend on active principles for their existence and thus are only imagined to be causes. Active principles, Easton argues, must possess a power of activity independent of bodies that live, die, and decompose. Skin color is not independent in this way and thus can only be an imaginary cause of prejudice. We may usefully recognize it as, in his words, "a trait by which a principle is identified," but we must go beyond this surface-level identification—this literally skin-deep veneer—in order to recognize the true principle of which it is but a mere sign (102). Having thus objected in these two ways to the idea of skin color as the cause of prejudice, he clarifies that slavery is the real cause. Slavery "efficiently causes" prejudice that can equally victimize people regardless of how dark their skin is; and slavery acts in a manner independent of the body.

It's easy to think of objections to Easton's argument. Starting with his empirical claim about skin color, is it really true that darker skin does not provoke greater prejudice? It may seem to do so today, though, of course, in Easton's time, lighter skin was no shield against being enslaved. Then also, why exactly can't that which dies and decomposes be an active principle? Perhaps he has in mind something like this: if you punch a wall, it's not the wall that causes the punching, and not even your fist, but your soul, which commanded your fist to move. Not all would endorse this claim, but plenty of philosophers throughout history have done so. In any case, Easton's effort here toward systematic argument shows how he founded a plausible sociocultural claim—that slavery rather than skin color is the ultimate foundation of racial prejudice against African Americans—on philosophical principles. As this suggests, historians of Africana philosophy can find in Easton a rich and barely touched resource.

Easton was born in 1798 in what is today Brockton, Massachusetts, south of Boston. He was the seventh and last child of James and Sarah Easton, both of whom were, like their children, born free. Indeed, Easton mentions in his *Treatise* that he is "of the third generation from slave parents," possibly suggesting that not only both of his parents but all of his grandparents were born free (89). Historians take his father James Easton to have been descended from slaves emancipated by Quakers in the late seventeenth century. Like the similarly named James Forten (see Chapter 31), James Easton served the colonial cause during the Revolutionary War and managed afterward to achieve a measure of financial success. The elder Easton worked as a blacksmith but grew his business to the point where he would be more appropriately called a general contractor for a construction company. He was well respected and friendly with other important people of the time and place, like Paul Cuffe. From his parents, young Hosea Easton learned powerful lessons about challenging racism and uplifting the black community.

The Easton family engaged in the first recorded sit-ins of American history.[5] Some time before Hosea was born, the church they attended installed a porch for the seating of black attendants, thus segregating the congregation. The Eastons refused to sit there and had to be physically removed from their seating in the white section of the church. Later, when Hosea was a child, the family purchased a pew in a different church. When racist parishioners poured tar on it, the Eastons responded by bringing their own seats. Prevented from setting these up, they sat in the aisle. They kept this up until they were formally expelled from the church. One can only imagine the deep impact of this dramatic protest on the young Hosea.

We don't have to imagine the impact of another event on Hosea, as it is discussed in his *Treatise*. The elder Easton decided some time around the end of the first decade of the nineteenth century to turn his factory for ironworking into a school focused on manual labor. In addition to smithing, student-laborers attending the school learned farming, shoemaking, reading, writing, and arithmetic. It was a visionary approach to black education, coming long before similar efforts later on in the century. James poured time and money into the school while Hosea and his brothers were among those who learned there. Over the two decades that it existed, however, this effort was actively opposed by many white community members. It closed for good not long before James Easton's death in 1830.

Here is how his son writes about it in the *Treatise*: "By reason of the repeated surges of the tide of prejudice, the establishment, like a ship in a boisterous hurricane at sea, went beneath its waves, richly laden, well manned, and well managed, and all sunk to rise no more" (110–11). Embittered by this experience, Easton gradually turned his attention from manual labor to ministry and social activism over the course of the 1820s. With his wife Louisa, he moved to Boston and, while preparing for ministry, became a prominent community member. He was, for example, involved in the Massachusetts General Colored Association, one of multiple ways he came into contact with Walker. As another example of their connection, in March of 1828, Easton chaired a meeting in support of the newspaper *Freedom's Journal* at which Walker spoke.

Easton himself soon proved to be a public speaker in demand. In November of 1828, he traveled to Providence, Rhode Island, to deliver a Thanksgiving Day address to the black community of that city. He had not intended to publish the speech but was prevailed upon to do so; aside from the *Treatise*, it is the main document preserving his thought. The speech contributes to our sense that something special was happening in the intellectual world of black Boston in the late 1820s, as it is remarkably easy to connect parts of the speech to the works of Walker and Stewart. In structure, though, it foreshadows a later speech, one of the most famous given by a black American of the nineteenth century: Frederick Douglass' "The Meaning of July Fourth for the Negro," which we will soon explore in depth (Chapter 37). As Douglass would later do, Easton began by evoking, with apparent sympathy, the patriotism many Americans feel on the occasion of the holiday being celebrated. In this case, the holiday is Thanksgiving, a time for Americans to be grateful to God for "rearing us from nothing, to a great and mighty nation" (51). But he then switches to a passionate denunciation of slavery and discrimination, which make it impossible for African Americans to feel the same gratefulness for the "expanded wings of Liberty" (52).

Easton dwells on the unfreedom of African Americans in a manner reminiscent of Walker's argument against Thomas Jefferson, claiming that African Americans have been rendered the most wretched beings in human history through the closure of every door of opportunity and the added indignity of being blamed as the cause of this exclusion. Speaking of free black people striving to better themselves through entrepreneurship, Easton complains that even in the northern states, a "man of business" will "not pass ten miles without meeting with insults almost sufficient to enrage a saint." Oblivious to this, "the question is asked by the whites: Why is it that Negroes cannot do business like other people?" When Easton moves to conclude his speech, though, there is yet another switch. He suggests to his black audience that they should after all be thankful for "rays of rational intelligence and literary acquirements" that are beginning to break through the "darkness, which has so long pervaded the minds" of this population (59).

He does not recommend simply taking comfort in these positive signs, however, advocating instead precisely the kind of exertion central to Stewart's message in her speeches: "It is evident that we ought to turn our attention to moral improvement. A principle of jealousy one towards another, has become almost hereditary; which prevents any combined operation among us. The first thing necessary, is, to cultivate the principles of concord and unanimity among ourselves, that we may become aids to each other" (60). Like Stewart, Easton declines to advocate violent resistance and suggests instead that the way forward lies in the unification of the black community, as they strive to improve their minds and behavior. Despite the similarities, and despite the fact that we know Easton was in contact with Walker and probably with Stewart, it's doubtful that they influenced Easton's 1828 speech. It precedes the publication of Walker's *Appeal* in 1829 and Stewart's writings and speeches of the early 1830s. So, if anything, the influence may have gone the other way around. It is perhaps safest to speak vaguely of ideas that were in the air at the time.

When we turn to his *Treatise*, which did come after Walker's *Appeal* and Stewart's productions, we see a sharp contrast between Easton and these two. This may be a sign of his philosophical mind working out tensions that arise from the lines of thought we have associated with Walker and Stewart, and which are also present in his Thanksgiving Day speech. He spends much of that speech depicting American oppression as an almost inescapably soul-crushing system, much as Walker does. But he ends on a surprisingly optimistic note by suggesting, like Stewart, that black people should trust in the power of self-improvement. As we noted, Stewart's thoughts on self-improvement certainly built on Walker's strategy of disproving white racism through black accomplishment. But her focus on what black people can achieve, if they just put their minds to it, at times leads her to relegate systematic prejudice to the background. This tension between identifying the barriers to black progress and recognizing black people as masters of their own fate runs through the works of all three thinkers, but it may be most palpable in Easton's Thanksgiving speech.

Before we address the resolution of this tension in the *Treatise*, let's catch up with Easton during the decade or so leading up to his 1837 masterwork. In 1831, he traveled to Philadelphia as one of four delegates from Massachusetts to attend a meeting that was billed as the first annual convention of free people of color. At the risk of being pedantic, there had actually been another such meeting already, in the previous year. It was presided over by Richard Allen, who died just months later. But this second meeting in 1831 did initiate a series of so-called "Colored Conventions." Throughout the antebellum period and even afterward, these events would serve as feats of organized activism and offer important spaces for the expression of ideas. Easton served as chaplain at subsequent conventions and is recorded as proposing and seconding motions, attending each year until 1834. The movement temporarily died out after 1835 but, as we will see when we discuss Henry Highland Garnet, dramatically re-ignited in 1843.

In 1833, Easton and his family moved to Hartford, Connecticut, where he pastored two churches in succession before his untimely death in July of 1837, only a few months after publishing his *Treatise*. His experience in Hartford was a trying one. White racists harassed black people in the city and Easton's own parishioners were sometimes physically attacked. As if that weren't enough, after Easton founded and began to pastor his second church, it burned to the ground. It was during this time of hardship that Easton wrote his *Treatise* and seemingly other works as well, as the final page of the *Treatise* promises the coming publication of Easton's *Lectures on Civil, Social, and Moral Economy*. That work, if it was completed, is unfortunately lost, but its title is indicative of Easton's aim of developing a comprehensive moral and political philosophy. His view seems to have been that when the going gets tough, the tough get theoretical.

The opening of the *Treatise* gives little clue of the originality of what is to come. Central to the Introduction is an attempt to investigate "national difference of intellect" by "comparing the history of Europe and Africa" (70). In making the comparison, Easton turns to ancient Egypt and glorifies not only its accomplishments but the way its advances were shared with others, such as the Greeks. So far, so familiar, from thinkers like Walker and Stewart. Walker, for example, spoke of the importance of taking "a retrospective view of the arts and sciences—the wise legislators—the Pyramids, and other magnificent buildings—the turning of the channel of the river Nile, by the sons of Africa or of Ham, among whom learning originated, and was carried thence into Greece."[6] It is notable, though, that Easton goes into the subject in greater depth. He constructs, to the best of his ability, a chronology of Egypt from its foundation all the way to the period of Muslim rule, and contrasts its history to that of Europe from ancient times to the age of exploration and colonization.

He depicts Europe's history as one of war and brutality. If it is widely supposed that Europeans advanced arts and sciences more than Africans, he suggests, this is due partly to the erasure of African history through imperialistic destruction.

Powerful, anti-Eurocentric stuff. One would naturally assume that his point is to encourage pride in African Americans as modern-day sons and daughters of Africa. That certainly seems to be the intent of Walker and Stewart. It is striking, in fact, that Walker and Stewart generally use the term "Americans" to refer to the white people of the United States, while they refer to their own people simply as "Africans." The irony of this is strongest when they are attacking the American Colonization Society and the idea of going to Liberia. Right after vowing that she will be pierced by the bayonet rather than be driven to "a strange land," Stewart closes her speech at the African Masonic Hall with the same sentence she used to open it: "African rights and liberty is a subject that ought to fire the breast of every free man of color in these United States, and excite in his bosom a lively, deep, decided, and heartfelt interest."[7] Thus Stewart can speak of Africa as a strange land while accepting in the next breath that the most sensible way to refer to her own people in the United States is as "Africans."

Easton sharply breaks with this pattern. The first chapter of the *Treatise* repudiates any close connection between ancient Egypt, or Africa in general, and the people in the United States with which he identifies: "In this country we behold the remnant of a once noble, but now heathenish people. In calling the attention of my readers to the subject which I here present them, I would have them lose sight of the African character, about which I have made some remarks in my introduction. For at this time, circumstances have established as much difference between them and their ancestry, as exists between them and any other race or nation. In the first place the colored people who are born in this country, are Americans in every sense of the word. Americans by birth, genius, habits, language, &c." (83). This difference between Easton and his fellow Bostonian thinkers is not trivial. He here relinquishes any share for African Americans in the glory he attributed to Egypt, and thus rejects a key component of the strategy for encouraging self-improvement we find in Walker and Stewart. Why then has he bothered with an Afrocentric account of ancient Egypt's greatness, if this is irrelevant to the character and potential of African Americans?

The reason is that his goal in the Introduction is to clear away the myth of inherent white superiority. He opens it by assuming as given the biblical claim that "God hath made of one blood all nations of men for to dwell on all the face of the earth" (67). Just as flowers come in varying colors, so do human beings. This is the result of the desire for variety that impels nature, which is a principle of activity that Easton treats as created and empowered by God, not as identical to Him. But while nature has the power to produce such physical variation, Easton says he "cannot believe that nature has any thing to do in variegating intellect," for "mind can act on matter, but matter cannot act upon mind" (68); remember again his insistence that only things independent from bodies are active causes. Nature, whose domain of activity is matter, therefore does not produce variation in intellect. Nor can we attribute this variation to God, because all God's works are perfect, and do not admit of better and worse. This means that human intellect, as initially created by God, admitted of no variation in quality. It is the fall from grace that produced intellectual variation.

Easton's glorification of ancient Egypt illustrates this point. It proves that the myth of white superiority is just that, a myth, as Africans can achieve and display intellectual attainments matching and exceeding those attained by Europeans. In the first chapter, though, he admits that, among present-day African Americans, there is instead inferiority, which, he believes, results from the evil of slavery. This is, undoubtedly, the most controversial aspect of the *Treatise* and possibly an aspect of the book that was so unappealing to readers that it helps to explain its obscurity. Easton affirms "the intellectual and physical inferiority of the slave population" (85). With respect to physical features, he recapitulates descriptions by white authors of "contracted and sloped foreheads; prominent eyeballs; projecting underjaw; certain distended muscles about the mouth, or lower parts of the face; thick lips and flat nose; hips and rump projecting; crooked shins; flat feet, with large projecting heels" (85). While accepting such descriptions unchallenged, he calls it "bad grace" on the part of white people to speak so derisively of deformities that originate in their own acts of oppression. It is not Easton's intention to disparage black people as a race. Indeed, his point is that the intellectual and physical inferiority of the slave population "can be accounted for without imputing it to an original hereditary cause," as white racists do (85).

He turns to the biology of pregnancy to reveal just how powerful the ill effects of slavery are. Easton compares the emotional support and nutritious food required for healthy pregnancy with the sights, sounds, and sufferings experienced by an enslaved pregnant woman, concluding that it is impossible to avoid the consequence of deficiencies in the children born from such pregnancies. Once again raising his argument to the level of metaphysical generality, he writes: "If we are permitted to decide that natural causes produce natural effects, then it must be equally true that unnatural causes produce unnatural effects. The slave system is an unnatural cause, and has produced its unnatural effects, as displayed in the deformity of two and a half millions of beings, who have been under its soul-and-body-destroying influence, lineally, for near three hundred years" (87).

Over the course of the book's remaining three chapters, Easton elaborates a theory of the relationship between legal and political structures, on the one hand, and what he calls "public sentiment," on the other hand. Public sentiment, as he explains in the Introduction, is "founded on the real or imaginary interests of parties, whose individual interests are identified one with another" (69). When these individuals identifying with each other's interests have high ideals, societies are improved. When public sentiment is corrupted by greed and malice, on the other hand, no legal and political structure can withstand the pernicious effects. As he puts it, "good laws, and a good form of government, are of but very little use to a wicked people" (90). In fact, he holds that "the perversion of infinite good is infinite evil," and thus that the better the form of government, the worse the results when public sentiment is corrupted (91). The republicanism of the United States is therefore no blessing while slavery rules through public sentiment.

We have already explored his argument for slavery as the root of prejudice, but we should add a further point, namely, his distinction between malignant prejudice and forms of prejudice that are either harmless or harmful but more or less easily dispelled, since they derive from mistaken belief or ignorance rather than ill will. Anti-Irish prejudice, for instance, is rooted in "different manners and religion" and is thus not malignant, because it easily fades in the wake of Irish assimilation. Prejudice against Native Americans, by contrast, is malignant, although Easton claims that it only rears its ugly head when they "show signs of national life" and thus threaten to "recover their rightful possessions" (100–1). Anti-black prejudice is something worse: a persistent attitude targeting a people who have lost their homeland beyond possible recovery, and are not allowed to become American through assimilation.

There is much of philosophical interest throughout these discussions, from the philosophy of language involved in Easton's analysis of how "nigger" operates as a slur, to the way he views mind as acting on matter when prejudice leads bright young people toward an early grave. But where does all this lead him in terms of a practical solution? His Thanksgiving Day speech optimistically preached self-improvement in the face of systematic oppression and exclusion. In the *Treatise*, however, Easton radically departs from Walker and Stewart by refusing to lay any responsibility on African Americans themselves. He advocates neither violent resistance nor uplift through increasing knowledge and better behavior. The inferiority inculcated through the practice of slavery can and must be reversed, and there is only one way to do it: the onus is on white Americans to pursue immediate emancipation and subsequently commit to ongoing efforts at repair.

All the elements of his view as expressed in what has come before join together in this proposal of the concluding fourth chapter. He emphasizes once again that black

Americans are Americans, not Africans. In fact, he even claims that "there is not a drop of African blood...flowing in the veins of an American born child, though black as jet" (113). His argument is that, even for the slave born in Africa, exposure to the food, climate, and surroundings of America has an effect that changes the body. By the time we are speaking of children born in America, it is meaningless, in his view, to say they are African by blood. As Americans in every sense of the term, these people clearly merit every right and opportunity available to other Americans.

Easton also tackles the argument that the slaves are not immediately fit for freedom, thus requiring a gradual process that will prepare them for that higher state. This is nonsense, he says, even though he has admitted the debilitating effects of slavery on the minds and bodies of the enslaved. In fact, he tells the story of visiting New York and hearing of how those set free by the more recent emancipation of slaves in that state are terribly lazy and self-indulgent. This is to be expected, according to Easton, because "a slave is metamorphosed into a machine, adapted to a specific operation, and propelled by the despotic power of the slave system," which means that "when the principles of slavery ceases to act upon him, to the end for which he is a slave, he is left a mere out-of-use wreck of machinery" (118). This debilitation nevertheless cannot serve as justification for gradual emancipation, because continued slavery means further debilitation.

Easton therefore takes a stance that is unique in abolitionist literature: emancipation is insufficient for bringing about the end of slavery. For him, "emancipation embraces the idea that the emancipated must be placed back where slavery found them, and restore to them all that slavery has taken away from them" (119). Given Easton's views on the Americanness of African Americans, this obviously does not mean that the emancipated must be returned to Africa, but rather that the emancipated must be helped toward that fullness of humanity that slavery systematically destroyed. Easton is not very specific about the measures that are needed, but we can imagine that support for projects like his father's school would qualify. Philanthropic efforts of this kind will have physical effects: "The countenance which has been cast down, hitherto, would brighten up with joy. Their narrow foreheads which have hitherto been contracted for the want of mental exercise, would begin to broaden. Their eye balls, hitherto strained out to prominence by a frenzy excited by the flourish of the whip, would fall back under a thick foliage of curly eyebrows, indicative of deep penetrating thought" (119–20).

One reason Easton's unique vision was generally overlooked is that he had little opportunity to promote the book and revise it for further editions, owing to his death just a few months after its publication. George R. Price and James Brewer Stewart, who have done the most to bring Easton to current scholarly attention, speculate that another reason for the fate of the *Treatise* was a change in leadership.[8] A majority of the leaders we have described in the past few chapters were born free, but as the nineteenth century wore on, leaders like Frederick Douglass, Harriet Tubman, and Sojourner Truth emerged, all of them former slaves. It is likely, Price and Stewart suggest, that Easton's acceptance of descriptions of the enslaved as inferior won little sympathy in light of this development. Yet at least one abolitionist leader of the middle of the nineteenth century remembered Easton fondly. William Cooper Nell was the son of William G. Cooper, yet another figure from Boston, who participated in the Massachusetts General Colored Association alongside Easton and Walker. In an 1855 book called *The Colored Patriots of the American Revolution*, a pioneering work of history by a black author, Nell mentioned James Easton as a veteran of the Revolutionary War. In this context, he made a well-justified remark about James' son: by writing the *Treatise*, Nell claimed, Hosea Easton displayed "the heart of a philanthropist and the head of a philosopher."[9]

36

WRITTEN BY HIMSELF

The Life of Frederick Douglass

On the speaking tours that established Frederick Douglass' reputation, one of his favorite topics was "self-made men." This quintessentially American theme could not have been more appropriate, because America has produced no greater self-made man than Douglass. Born into slavery in Maryland in the year 1818, he seized at scraps of opportunity to become literate, earn money on the side as a ship caulker, and then escape his master Thomas Auld in 1838. Within a decade, he would be world famous. He first came to prominence as a public orator excoriating the evils of slavery. Then, in 1845, he published his autobiography, *The Narrative of the Life of Frederick Douglass, an American Slave, Written by Himself*, which became a sensation. It would sell 11,000 copies in the US and go through nine editions in the UK.[1] Douglass traveled to Ireland and Britain and, while there, purchased his freedom with the financial support of friends. With further support, he launched an anti-slavery newspaper, the *North Star*. Ultimately, he would befriend Abraham Lincoln, who said to Douglass: "there is no man in the country whose opinion I value more than yours." After the end of the Civil War, he received political appointments, becoming Marshal of the District of Columbia and later Consul General to Haiti. He died in 1895, having made himself into the foremost black intellectual of the nineteenth century.

That's just a sketch of Douglass' staggeringly eventful and impressive life. It's a story that has been told numerous times, starting with Douglass himself. He followed up his bestselling *Narrative* with two more autobiographies, *My Bondage and My Freedom* in 1855, and, finally, the *Life and Times of Frederick Douglass* in 1881. Or rather, not finally, because he extended the book in a second edition in 1892.[2] Then quite a few later authors have also written biographies of him.[3] The allure is obvious: his experiences as a child and young man formed an unanswerable rebuke to the evils of slavery, while his escape and rise to prominence were an irresistible story of redemption. Yet Douglass himself said, in his preface to *My Bondage and My Freedom:* "I have never placed my opposition to slavery on a basis as narrow as my own enslavement."[4] That work is much longer than the first autobiography, despite covering not much more of his life story, in part because it goes into more detail but also in part because Douglass reflects at greater length on the nature of slavery, and what it does to both the slave and the slaveholder.

Having said that, we already hear in the *Narrative* Douglass' distinctive voice, which also made him such an effective speaker. As a contemporary newspaper report remarked: "He was a living, speaking, startling proof of the folly, absurdity and inconsistency (to say nothing worse) of slavery. Fluent, graceful, eloquent, shrewd, sarcastic, he was, without making any allowance, a fine specimen of an orator."[5] As we've seen, questions of authorship could be raised about many earlier slave narratives. Intermediaries and well-meaning supporters might record, shape, and otherwise frame the experiences of those who actually endured slavery, a phenomenon that has been compared to putting black messages in white envelopes.[6] As with Equiano before him, there is none of this with Douglass. Hence that final phrase, *Written by Himself*, at the end of the title of his first autobiography. Those three words promise that, in what follows, Douglass will be speaking for himself.

To get a real sense of his authorial voice you will need to read his autobiographies and other writings, which survive in considerable quantity despite many of his papers and journalistic efforts being destroyed in a fire in 1872. Douglass presents himself as a paradigm of self-reliance, a characteristically American value most famously theorized by that characteristically American philosopher, Ralph Waldo Emerson. He is an acute and impassioned critic of injustice, with enough imagination to see into the mind of the slaveholder, and enough outrage to fuel vigorous condemnations laced with religious rhetoric. The autobiographies are powerful, suspenseful, touching, and sometimes surprisingly funny. Humor was an important weapon in Douglass' arsenal, both as author and as public speaker.[7] One of his standard early performances was a parody of a racist preacher, who Douglass imagined giving a speech full of obviously absurd religious justifications for slavery. In another case, he mocked racism by telling the anecdote of a white girl who dreamed of going to heaven. Asked whether there were any black people there, she replied: "oh, I didn't go into the kitchen!"[8]

This sort of thing was not to everyone's taste. A letter from one audience member, written in 1843, complained that "he was more in the narrative and familiar vein & kept the audience laughing all the time."[9] She would probably not have liked the more sarcastic passages in Douglass' autobiographies, either, like the part of

My Bondage and My Freedom that explains how wonderful it is to be a young slave: such a child can't ruin his clothes while playing because he doesn't have any, and "he is never reprimanded for soiling the tablecloth, for he takes his meals on the clay floor" (144). But Douglass was offering more than irony and parody. Not much later, we have a section describing his early struggles to understand the slave system. Looking back on his 7- or 8-year-old self, Douglass says: "I could not reconcile the relation of slavery with my crude notions of goodness." Finally light dawned: "It was not color, but crime, not God, but man, that afforded the true explanation of the existence of slavery...The appalling darkness faded away, and I was master of the subject" (178–9). The reference to his enslaved child self as "master" itself looks like barbed wordplay, but used to make the most serious of points. The point is in part a philosophical one, as Douglass suggests the reliability of inborn and unspoiled moral intuition.

Indeed, one of the reasons slavery is so wicked is that it undermines that natural tendency to see what is good. This critique is implicit in Douglass' description of his relationship to his first owner, Captain Aaron Anthony, who he also at times suspected was his father. In awe of the "absolute power of this distant 'old master'," the young Douglass was aware of his own "entire dependence on the will of somebody I had never seen" (144, 147). His unjust relationship to this owner is a perversion of man's relation to a distant and absolutely powerful, but perfectly just God. This idea that slavery perverts morality and Christian religion is a leitmotif in Douglass' writing. Speaking of another master's wife, Sophia Auld, he remarks that her natural kindness and generosity was undermined by the need to oppress her human chattel, so that "slavery proved as injurious to her as it did to me" (40). Or, as he elsewhere puts it, there is some truth to the saying that "slavery is a greater evil to the master than the slave" (189). Douglass observes that slaveholders, as much as slaves, have their very status as rational beings undermined by the tyrannical power they wield. Whereas the slaves are reduced to the level of a mere beast to be bought and sold, the masters' license to wield arbitrary violence means that they simply follow their irrational passions, rather than having to give reasons for their actions—even to themselves.[10]

In the autobiographies, Douglass gives many concrete examples of the immorality of the slaveowners. There are scenes of murder and beating, and intimations of systematic rape, and he also speaks of the way masters encourage drinking and other bad behavior among slaves to keep them passive and weak. He notes that it is worse to be the slave of a master who aspires to religious piety than a more secular-minded one (67–8). An appendix to his first autobiography discusses the vast gulf between real Christianity and Christianity as it actually exists in the slaveholding

United States (97). But amidst all this hypocrisy Douglass was able to maintain his own ethical compass. This feat ratifies his theory of innate moral intuition, and also fits with his repeated claims that he has been guided throughout his life by divine providence (36, 213).

One of Douglass' most famous quotes, "knowledge makes a man unfit to be a slave," expresses another idea that echoes throughout the autobiographies. It is in the interest of the slaveholder to turn their human chattel, who are in fact "moral and intellectual beings," into ignorant creatures on a level with animals (237). The slightest glimpse of a more fully human life will make them restless and disobedient. This was Douglass' own experience: every slight improvement in his condition made him chafe more at his unfreedom (83), this being an inevitable feature of human nature (297). One of the most powerful roads to self-mastery is education, something else that Douglass intuited at an early age. He thinks he may have inherited the ambition from his mother. He was not allowed to know her well, but proudly reports that she was unusual in being literate (155–6).

This was an instinct Douglass' masters needed to suppress. For, as he observes, "to make a contented slave, you must make a thoughtless one. It is necessary to darken his moral and mental vision, and, as far as possible, to annihilate his power of reason" (337). We are given a particularly sickening glimpse into life among the slaveholding class when Sophia Auld is berated by her husband for teaching Douglass how to read. Auld tells her: "Learning would spoil the best nigger in the world. Now if you teach that nigger how to read, there would be no keeping him. It would forever unfit him to be slave" (37). Douglass elsewhere comments that this logic is, in its own terms, impeccable, even when it again leads to an undermining of Christian piety: "If slavery be right, Sabbath schools for teaching slaves to read the bible are wrong, and ought to be put down" (299). But he was not to be dissuaded from his goal, and got white boys in the street to teach him how to read (41, 257). He would go on to teach other slaves in turn.

The fact that slavery seeks to turn its victims into illiterate beasts comes to the fore in the most famous incident of Douglass' enslavement, his conflict with the sadistic, bullying, and cowardly Edward Covey. This was a man to whom Douglass was loaned out who had a reputation as a "slave-breaker," that is, someone who could turn an unruly slave into an obedient one. It was in standing up to Covey that the self-made man first began to make himself: "I was nothing before; I was a man now" (286). The story begins when the teenaged Douglass is beaten mercilessly by Covey for losing control of a pair of oxen. He goes to his master to complain, saying that he fears for his life if Covey continues to have power over him, but is summarily dismissed. At this point, Douglass' Christian instinct to turn the other cheek is literally beaten out of him, in another illustration of the way that slavery defeats piety: "My hands were no longer tied by my religion" (282). He confronts Covey and the two get into a protracted and brutal fistfight, which cows Covey to the extent that he never lays a hand on Douglass again. There's a lot to say about this tale, which is treated as central in all three autobiographies, but given different emphasis and detail in each case. For starters, Douglass is able to inflict a final defeat on Covey by casting him as a minor character in his own story. Like the Baron de Vastey before him, Douglass identifies victimizers, exposing them to the judgment of posterity. As he says when introducing a particularly egregious religious hypocrite named Rigby Hopkins, "I might as well immortalize another of my neighbors, by calling him by name, and putting him in print" (294).

As for the aforementioned theme of humans and animals, when describing his rough treatment at Covey's hands, Douglass explicitly compares himself to the poor beasts of burden: "They were to be broken, so was I" (263). Yet he goes on to compare Covey to another animal, namely, the sneaky and dangerous snake: it is the slave-driver, not the slave, who is truly bestial. By defying the animalistic Covey, Douglass lays claim to his own humanity. This fits pretty well with a philosophical approach to the story, first put forward by Angela Davis, that interprets it in terms of existentialism.[11] The insight here is that Douglass was desperate enough to risk death in order to stake a claim to freedom. His assertion of dignity and self-worth shows that he, and he alone, is responsible for that freedom. This is a powerful reading and makes especially good sense of the version in the *Narrative*, Douglass' first autobiography, which does seem to put the individual struggle at the center of the tale. To extrapolate, the message of the Covey incident would be that black Americans should rise up as free individual subjects, violently if necessary, to defy the constraints placed upon them.

As several other commentators have pointed out, though, the version of the story we get in *My Bondage and My Freedom* is rather different. It puts more emphasis on black solidarity, telling how two other slaves courageously refused to help Covey restrain Douglass. Thus, in this version, we don't have the irreducible individual faced by an existential struggle for his own freedom, but a politically united group that works together to win space for at least a limited degree of practical autonomy. On this interpretation, the story of Covey would go together with Douglass' account of how he joined forces with several other slaves, who were "true as steel" and like a "band of brothers," to plot an escape from bondage (301). Extrapolating now from this second reading, we would get the idea that black Americans should join together to carry out politically engaged action. As we'll be seeing in more detail below, Douglass' views on political action were complex and evolved over time.

For now, we can say that as his career developed, he became increasingly open to the idea of working within America's political system to achieve emancipation and uplift for African Americans. He thereby moved away from the ideas of his initial backer William Lloyd Garrison, whose group of abolitionist public speakers Douglass joined after he escaped from slavery.

Douglass first became aware of Garrison through the latter's newspaper, the *Liberator*; upon reading it, Douglass says, his "soul was set all on fire" (96). Once he got in touch with Garrison's group and joined his roster of speakers, Douglass for a time followed Garrison's lead on tactical and philosophical matters. This meant staying out of conventional politics. Garrison was convinced that America's system was rotten to the core, and that the Constitution itself was a pro-slavery document. He thus followed a policy of defiant non-involvement in the country's political institutions. At first, Douglass was inclined to agree. Upon arriving in Ireland, he experienced what life could be like without the daily humiliations of American racism; according to him, he "was not treated as a color, but as a man."[12] Douglass also wrote at one point to Garrison to say that patriotism had been "whipped out of me long since, by the lash of the American soul-drivers" (372). But he would eventually become deeply involved in national politics.

His nuanced attitude toward the United States is something else that we will discuss in the next chapter, but we should note right now that his break with Garrison was not only over political principles. It was also because of the way Garrison and his associates saw Douglass, or perhaps we might say "used" him. Certainly they showed him more respect than many Americans would have. Garrison was a tireless opponent of slavery. In the first issue of the *Liberator*, he had written, "I will not equivocate—I will not excuse—I will not retreat a single inch." And when he first brought Douglass onto a stage in Nantucket, in 1841, he thundered, "Have we been listening to a thing, a piece of property, or to a man?"[13] Douglass presumably liked the sound of that, but would have been less enthused at the way Garrison tried to make the same point on a different occasion: "It is recorded in holy writ that a beast once spoke. A greater miracle is here tonight. A chattel becomes a man!"[14] This suggests how little the Garrisonians wanted from Douglass: to be living proof that black people are indeed people, and to win sympathy by recounting his moving life story. As one of the group told him, "give us the facts, we will take care of the philosophy." But Douglass wanted more: "It did not entirely satisfy me to *narrate* wrongs, I felt like *denouncing* them" (367).

The measure of his dissatisfaction is told by the distance between his first and second autobiographies. For all its rhetorical brilliance, the *Narrative* adheres to the usual conventions of a slave narrative. *My Bondage and My Freedom*, by contrast, offers many passages of moral reflection and editorial commentary. Douglass says modestly that "it is not within the scope of the design of my simple story, to comment upon every phase of slavery not within my experience as a slave" (257). But you can tell he doesn't mean it. His involvement with white abolitionists allowed him to travel, to buy his freedom, and to make a name for himself, but he found the role they had assigned to him confining, and was deliberately going beyond it in the second autobiography. David Blight has summed up the situation well: "He was trapped in a deal that both offered him the world and stifled the kind of freedom he perhaps cherished most—the freedom of mind and of the words he would choose to express himself."[15] Douglass finally broke away from Garrison in 1847, when he founded his own newspaper, the *North Star*, edited together with Martin Delany (see Chapter 39). Garrison didn't appreciate the competition and saw it as a betrayal, the beginning of a long deterioration in their relationship which would end with Garrison calling Douglass one of his "malignant enemies."[16]

The masthead on the first issue of Douglass' new paper proclaimed: "Right is of no Sex—Truth is of no Color—God is the Father of us all, and we are all Brethren." As that first phrase indicates, slavery was not the only injustice against which Douglass fought. He was an early proponent of women's suffrage, having been converted by the arguments of Elizabeth Cady Stanton. He spoke at the first convention for women's rights at Seneca Falls in 1848, where he was the only black participant. This is an especially admirable aspect of Douglass' already more than admirable career, and he knew it. "When I ran away from slavery," he said, "it was for myself; when I advocated emancipation, it was for my people; but when I stood up for the rights of woman, self was out of the question, and I found a little nobility in the act."[17] He recognized the crusade against sexism as continuous with the fight against racism, saying after abolition that the women's suffrage campaign was a "continuance of the old anti-slavery movement" and involved much the same arguments.[18] Some sense of the parallel is conveyed by the similarity of the following two quotations from his pen: "I deny that the black man's degradation is essential to the white man's elevation"; "woman cannot be elevated without elevating man, and man cannot be depressed without depressing woman also."

As with Garrison, though, Douglass would experience tensions with his allies in the women's movement. Though he did see gender equality as an urgent issue, he didn't think it was quite as urgent as racial equality, because blacks were subject to levels of violence and oppression that simply didn't affect white women. He rejected equivalences drawn between slavery and the plight of females in a male-dominated society, and had no objection to the enfranchisement of black male voters before women received the vote. On the other side of this debate, the priorities were the other way around, and some proponents of women's suffrage indulged in racist arguments. Stanton, Douglass' erstwhile tutor in the subject of gender oppression, complained that under American law, women were "classed with idiots, lunatics, and Negroes."[19]

Though Douglass' rise from slavery to national spokesman is the most famous and gripping part of his life, we should touch at least briefly on a few points from Douglass' later career, which is covered in his third and final autobiography, the *Life and Times*.[20] He here discusses his steadfast adherence to the Republican Party, which survived moments of frustration at Lincoln's caution with abolition, and then the measures he proposed to take toward a defeated South. At one point, he even complained that Lincoln's tendency was to "do evil by choice, right from necessity." Yet he mourned Lincoln's death, which he said united the people of his city, Rochester, to the extent that it "made us more than countrymen, it made us kin." Given the racism of the Democratic Party of his day, he continued to support the Republican Party after the Civil War. Douglass was, unsurprisingly, disappointed at the failure of Reconstruction in the south and the resulting suppression of voting rights, along with the increasing occurrence of lynching. As he remarked at the 1876 Republican National Convention: "What does it all amount to, if the black man, after having been made free by the letter of your law, is unable to exercise that freedom, and, having been freed from the slaveholder's lash, he is to be subject to the slaveholder's shotgun?"

In the third autobiography, Douglass is also at pains to defend his conduct as envoy to Haiti, where he was torn between his sympathy for the black population of the island and his assigned task of pursuing American interests, notably by securing dominion over a port there. In 1891, he resigned, his position undermined by the impression that he sided with the Haitians, but this is probably unfair. Douglass was willing to criticize the Haitian government of the day for its repressive policies, just as he was willing to admonish his own government for trying to bully this poor country into making disadvantageous agreements. Still, if he regretted his involvement with Haiti, that doesn't show in the final autobiography, which concludes by calling his invitation to represent the island at the World Exposition in 1893 "a fitting and happy close to my whole public life" (1045).

37

HAPPY HOLIDAYS

Two Speeches by Frederick Douglass

Mark Twain once said to an interviewer, while reflecting on his life of traveling and speaking: "they say lecturers and burglars never reform. I don't know how it is with burglars—it is so long since I had intimate relations with those people—but it is quite true of lecturers. They never reform. Lecturers…say they are going to leave the lecture platform never to return. They mean it, they mean it. But there comes in time an overpowering temptation to come out on the platform and give truth and morality one more lift. You can't resist it." In his prize-winning biography of Frederick Douglass, David Blight speculates that Mark Twain is probably the only competitor Douglass has for the title of most widely traveled American of the nineteenth century. In fact, Blight deems it "likely that more Americans heard Douglass speak than any other public figure of his times."[1] Clearly, Douglass found it hard to resist giving "truth and morality one more lift." Alongside Douglass' autobiographies, his many speeches offer a further rich source for understanding his thought. We're going to focus here on two addresses delivered to mark holidays. They are among his most famous; if you come across someone quoting from a Douglass speech, it would be a safe bet that it is from one of these two.[2]

Oft-quoted though they may be, they are rarely systematically compared to each other. In one speech, delivered in 1852, Douglass speaks as an American to his fellow Americans about the most American holiday of them all: Independence Day, which of course commemorates July 4, 1776, the day that thirteen American colonies declared themselves free from the British empire. In the other speech, delivered in 1857, Douglass also speaks as an American to fellow Americans, but this time about Emancipation Day, which celebrates freedom not from the British empire but within it. This holiday, still recognized as one of the most important of the year in many countries of the Caribbean and now also officially celebrated in Canada, commemorates August 1, 1834, when the law abolishing slavery in the British empire first came into effect. So we have a certain irony here: when speaking of the American holiday, Douglass says that he and other Americans like him are unable to celebrate this day of national freedom. By contrast, Douglass sees the holiday that commemorates a law that applied only to British subjects, and not Americans, as an occasion for joyous celebration. Together the speeches raise the questions of what holidays are for, what they might accomplish in drawing us together, and how, by marking them, we represent and understand ourselves as part of a people.

It would be easy to explain the irony away by noting that the Independence Day speech was delivered to an audience primarily made up of white Americans, while the Emancipation Day speech was delivered to a black audience. We might naturally suppose that the difference between the speeches has to do simply with Douglass' membership of a particular group, namely, black people. Slavery prevents them from relating to the freedom celebrated on Independence Day, and gives them a reason to celebrate Emancipation Day in solidarity with the liberated black people of places like the Caribbean. But this is, at best, only part of the story. A central theme in both speeches is the importance of seeing oneself as a citizen of the world, as belonging not merely to this or that nation or particular people but, first and foremost, to the *human* race.

Let us now delve into the details of the speeches, beginning with "The Meaning of July Fourth for the Negro."[3] Douglass had been invited to give an Independence Day speech by the Rochester Ladies' Anti-Slavery Sewing Society. Rochester, New York, was where Douglass lived at the time and this society had been founded not long before, by (among others) his close friend Julia Griffiths, a British abolitionist who had moved to the United States of America to work with him. She helped him with his newspaper, the *North Star*, and its successor, called *Frederick Douglass' Paper*—not the most imaginative of titles, perhaps, but it does underscore that his name was by this time one to conjure with. Griffiths also supported his move away from William Lloyd Garrison and the Garrisonians, a major source of conflict for Douglass at this time. In this setting, the audience would have been friendly and like-minded. Yet the speech reads at points like an impassioned cry to white Americans who have never yet considered opposing slavery. The mismatch between audience and message may take a bit of magic away from the speech as a historical occasion, especially when we add that it was actually delivered on July 5 because the Fourth was a Sunday. But Douglass' approach was fitting nonetheless, because he intended to speak to the nation as a whole. He had the address printed and sold copies of it through his newspaper and on the lecture circuit. From the beginning, then, this was not merely an oratorical feat, but an important moment for the development of African American and abolitionist literature.

Douglass begins by meditating on the relative youth of the United States, only seventy-six years removed from independence. He then begins to evoke the circumstances of the American Revolution, bringing to life the drama of that period. To celebrate the revolt against English tyranny in 1852 is, he notes, quite a different thing from joining that side of the conflict in 1776. As he puts it: "To say now that America was right, and England wrong, is exceedingly easy. Everybody can say it; the dastard, not less than the noble brave, can flippantly discant on the tyranny of England towards the American Colonies. It is fashionable to do so; but there was a time when, to pronounce against England, and in favor of the cause of the colonies, tried men's souls. They who did so were accounted in their day plotters of mischief, agitators and rebels, dangerous men" (183-4). The implication is that Americans of his own day who feel threatened by trouble-making abolitionists betray the legacy of trouble-making that gave birth to the nation.

And he does seem happy to praise the extraordinary accomplishment of the Revolution, transporting his audience back to that remarkable era by saying: "The whole scene, as I look back to it, was simple, dignified and sublime. The population of the country, at the time, stood at the insignificant number of three millions. The country was poor in the munitions of war. The population was weak and scattered, and the country a wilderness unsubdued. There were then no means of concert and combination, such as exist now. Neither steam nor lightning had then been reduced to order and discipline. From the Potomac to the Delaware was a journey of many days. Under these, and innumerable other disadvantages, your fathers declared for liberty and independence and triumphed" (186). This is the kind of celebration of American glory you might expect from an Independence Day speech. But Douglass is setting up a dramatic reversal, in which the hollowness of the celebration is revealed. The patriotic bent of his description of the revolution is not necessarily insincere, but he urges that American patriotism should be rooted in the recognition of certain moral principles that are foundational to the country's identity. He tells his audience that the Declaration of Independence is "the ringbolt to the chain of your nation's destiny," and includes within it "saving principles" to be defended constantly: "Stand by those principles, be true to them on all occasions, in all places, against all foes, and at whatever cost" (185). He means to do more than inspire pride when he says "your fathers, the fathers of this republic, did, most deliberately, under the inspiration of a glorious patriotism, and with a sublime faith in the great principles of justice and freedom, lay deep, the corner-stone of the national super-structure, which has risen and still rises in grandeur around you" (187). For Douglass, it was their commitment to justice and freedom that made their patriotism glorious; only such commitment could make a patriotic celebration of a nation's founding worthwhile.

So the famous twist in the speech does not contradict its earlier invocations of revolutionary glory. It is precisely the distance between the America of his time and its original principles of justice and freedom that leads him to ask: "Fellow-citizens, pardon me, allow me to ask, why am I called upon to speak here to-day? What have I, or those I represent, to do with your national independence? Are the great principles of political freedom and of natural justice, embodied in that Declaration of Independence, extended to us? and am I, therefore, called upon to bring our humble offering to the national altar, and to confess the benefits and express devout gratitude for the blessings resulting from your independence to us?" (188–9). Not long after this, he utters the simple words at the heart of the speech: "This Fourth July is *yours*, not *mine*. You may rejoice, I must mourn" (189). Further on, he puts it in the form of a question that has given the speech one of its commonly known titles: "What, to the American slave, is your 4th of July? I answer: a day that reveals to him, more than all other days in the year, the gross injustice and cruelty to which he is the constant victim" (192).

Here the speech transforms into a harsh confrontation, an excoriation of the evil of slavery. In what follows, we meet a passage that is of particular interest for us, since we are concerned with what it means to view Douglass as a philosopher. It suggests that he may have seen philosophy as unnecessary, or impotent, in relation to slavery. Responding to an imagined critic who objects to his severe language, he replies: "I fancy I hear some one of my audience say, 'It is just in this circumstance that you and your brother abolitionists fail to make a favorable impression on the public mind. Would you argue more, and denounce less; would you persuade more, and rebuke less; your cause would be much more likely to succeed'" (190). Douglass responds that argument and persuasion by logical means are not needed; what is called for is the rhetorical force of fierce scolding. But as we know from thinkers of other places and times—whether al-Ghazālī in the Islamic world, Nāgārjuna the ancient Indian Buddhist, or Wittgenstein in twentieth century European philosophy—it can be profoundly philosophical to point to the limitations of rational argument, and of philosophy itself. Douglass is in fact offering a careful and powerful philosophical case for using denunciation and rebuke instead of argument, at least in this particular context of confronting the problem of slavery in his time.

"Where all is plain there is nothing to be argued," he says (190). So which anti-slavery principle would be in need of demonstration? Must he prove that slaves are human beings? This point is conceded already by the existence of laws that slaves are expected to obey, often under threat of punishment by death. "What is this, but the acknowledgment that the slave is a moral, intellectual, and responsible being?" (190–1). If it is admitted that slaves are human, could the question be whether humans are entitled to liberty? But that was of course "already declared" in the Declaration of Independence (191). Douglass continues in this vein before concluding: "At a time like this, scorching irony, not convincing argument, is needed. O! had I the ability, and could reach the nation's ear, I would, to-day, pour out a fiery stream of biting ridicule, blasting reproach, withering sarcasm, and stern rebuke" (192). Since no argument is needed when all the points to be argued are conceded, either implicitly or explicitly, in the nation's legislation and founding documents, the goal must instead be to shake the nation out of its complacent hypocrisy through effective appeals to the conscience.

Douglass therefore goes on to depict the horror of slavery vividly, as only he can. He also tackles topics like the evil of the Fugitive Slave Law, which was passed in 1850 as part of a compromise with the South and which made the North far less secure for both escaped slaves and free black people. He attacks the hypocrisy of leaders of the church who defend slavery, saying boldly: "For my part, I would say, welcome infidelity! welcome atheism! welcome anything! in preference to the gospel, as preached by those Divines!" (197). He addresses too the question of whether the Constitution is a pro-slavery document, something he denies, emphasizing that slavery is nowhere explicitly mentioned in the Constitution. Here he disagrees with other abolitionists, including William Lloyd Garrison, and also with his former self. As recently as March of 1849, Douglass had published a reflection on the Constitution and slavery in the *North Star*, detailing how its implicit references to slavery should lead any reasonable person to see it as "radically and essentially proslavery."[4] But, partially due to the influence of abolitionist Gerrit Smith, Douglass changed his mind and left behind this position, part of a painful and dramatic break with Garrison and the Garrisonians that led to vicious criticism on both sides in the early 1850s. Controversy over this aspect of Douglass' thought has continued long after his death. In the 1990s, Charles Mills, a leading philosopher of race, criticized this reversal by Douglass as part of his larger criticism that the Fourth of July speech is "simultaneously inspiring and naive."[5]

Naively or not, this speech of denunciation ends on an optimistic note. Douglass thinks slavery may meet its end in the not too distant future. He speaks of the "tendencies of the age," given the shrinking of the world that was already under way in the nineteenth century (203). As usual, his words on this point are eloquent: "A change has now come over the affairs of mankind. Walled cities and empires have become unfashionable. The arm of commerce has borne away the gates of the strong city. Intelligence is penetrating the darkest corners of the globe. It makes its pathway over and under the sea, as well as on the earth. Wind, steam, and lightning are its chartered agents. Oceans no longer divide, but link nations together. From Boston to London is now a holiday excursion. Space is comparatively annihilated. Thoughts expressed on one side of the Atlantic are distinctly heard on the other" (203). As an example of a practice put under pressure by these developments, Douglass mentions the shaming of China over the custom of foot binding. Slavery in America cannot long survive the glare of a world looking on with an increasing sense of disgust. Notice, by the way, that over the course of the speech, he has gone from talking about the daunting distance between the Potomac and Delaware Rivers in the eighteenth century, to speaking of the closeness of Boston to London in his own day. He ends the speech by leaving aside patriotic celebration of the American past in order to celebrate the increasing interconnections rendering the whole world into a single community.

This theme of global unity is also central to his Emancipation Day speech.[6] African American celebrations of the end of slavery in the British empire were a common occurrence in the North in the decades before the Civil War. The event helped people envision a time of abolition in America. Sometimes the holiday was called "West India Day" and Douglass' speech, delivered on August 4, 1857, in Canandaigua, New York, is known under the title "West India Emancipation." As he gets under way, Douglass again invokes the changes brought by the nineteenth century: "I wish you to look at West India emancipation as one complex transaction of vast and sublime significance, surpassing all power of exaggeration. We hear and read much of the achievements of this nineteenth century, and much can be said, and truthfully said of them. The world has literally shot forward with the speed of steam and lightning. It has probably made more progress during the last fifty years, than in any five hundred years to which we can refer in the history of the race. Knowledge has been greatly increased, and its blessing widely diffused. Locomotion has been marvelously improved, so that the very ends of the earth are being rapidly brought together. Time to the traveler has been annihilated" (428–9). Note that, in the Fourth of July speech, we encountered the annihilation of space; here, it is time. Douglass sure knows how to make the destruction of the universe sound exciting!

But these technological advances, remarkable though they are, pale in comparison to British emancipation, which he calls "the most interesting and sublime event of the nineteenth century," and "the triumph of a great moral principle" (430). The continuity with his earlier speech is even clearer here. Douglass consistently locates the point of celebrating holidays in the cherishing of moral principles. This helps him wave away the objection that Americans should not be marking this British festivity. He laments even having to address this point: "From the inmost core of my soul I pity the mean spirits, who can see in these celebrations nothing but British feeling" (433). But he addresses it nevertheless, and in a way that may surprise us. It is natural to assume that African Americans would want to mark Emancipation Day in order to express their sense of connection to other people in the black world. It seems obvious that they would take special pleasure in the attainment of black freedom elsewhere, in spite of—or perhaps even because of—the enduring lack of freedom in America. This, however, is not how Douglass thinks about the matter. Instead, he argues that "the man who limits his admiration of good actions to the country in which he happens to be born...or to the nation or community of which he forms a small part, is a most pitiable object" (433). For him, Emancipation Day is not an international *black* holiday; rather, the accomplishment it celebrates "belongs not exclusively to England and the English people, but to the lovers of Liberty and of mankind the world over" (433-4).

In light of this thoroughly cosmopolitan outlook, it is interesting how Douglass deals with a second worry about celebrating Emancipation Day, one that comes not from an enemy but a friend. Indeed, a personal friend, one who is unjustly overlooked as a figure of nineteenth century African American thought: James McCune Smith, who was born a slave in New York City but who rose from this condition to become the first African American to hold a medical degree. According to Douglass, McCune Smith expressed the following concern: "It is said that we, the colored people, should do something ourselves worthy of celebration, and not be everlastingly celebrating the deeds of a race by which we are despised" (434). What troubled McCune Smith, then, was not the spectacle of Americans being disloyal, but of African Americans being passive. Douglass' response has multiple layers and takes up the entire remainder of the speech, giving us some classic quotations along the way. The two most famous lines are: "If there is no struggle there is no progress" and "Power concedes nothing without demand" (437). With these lines Douglass acknowledges, in accord with McCune Smith, the need for activity on the part of African Americans. This belongs to what he calls "the philosophy of reform" (437). The activity in question—struggle and demand for change—may, according to Douglass, "be a moral one, or it may be a physical one, and it may be both moral and physical" (437). Where Garrison and the Garrisonians promoted pacifism, Douglass at this point felt ready to endorse both the moral force of skillful rhetoric and the alternative force of physical violence.

This leads to one of the boldest moments in all of his work. He speaks of the use of violence against slavery but begins, unexpectedly, with examples where the violence is turned inward, so to speak. His shocking first example is that of Margaret Garner, who killed her 2-year-old daughter when she was caught while escaping. Douglass says, solemnly: "My friends, every mother who, like Margaret Garner, plunges a knife into the bosom of her infant to save it from the hell of our Christian Slavery, should be held and honored as a benefactress" (437). After another example involving suicide, he turns to cases in which violence was turned against slave catchers. The spirit of David Walker comes through strongly in this part of the speech. All this defense of resistance has not yet answered McCune Smith's question, but it has prepared the way toward an answer. Douglass thinks that McCune Smith, by implying that Emancipation Day celebrates only the actions of the British government, misses the role of violent resistance by slaves in the West Indies in the achievement of emancipation. There was, in his view, a division of labor, with British abolitionists like William Wilberforce and rebellious slaves both having their roles to play: "What Wilberforce was endeavoring to win from the British Senate by his magic eloquence, the Slaves themselves were endeavoring to gain by outbreaks and violence. The combined action of one and the other wrought out the final result. While one showed that slavery was wrong, the other showed that it was dangerous as well as wrong" (438). McCune Smith's objection was thus misplaced: in fact, to celebrate Emancipation Day is precisely to celebrate and promote active black resistance. And, in spite of his broader theme of celebrating the holiday as a citizen of the world, Douglass here embraces the connection between black Americans and black West Indians, with the latter offered up as a model for the former.

These speeches by Douglass are but two of a truly impressive set of orations stretching from the 1840s to the 1890s. Philosophers have begun to explore their profundity, though much work remains to be done. Not in this book, though. We'll instead be continuing our journey through nineteenth century Africana thought with a man who was present at the Emancipation Day celebration at which Douglass gave his "West India Emancipation" speech. Douglass mentions him by name: "As to what has been the effect of West India freedom upon the material condition of the people of those Islands, I am happy that there is one on this platform, who can speak with authority of positive knowledge. Henry Highland Garnet has lived and labored among those emancipated people" (432). More irony lurks here: Garnet, too, was a public speaker, and when he sought to encourage slave uprisings in his most famous speech, Douglass strongly objected. One wonders what Garnet thought and felt as he sat there, listening to Douglass praise violent resistance in the West Indies.

38

LET YOUR MOTTO BE RESISTANCE

Henry Highland Garnet

"To hear [him] in his prime was a rare privilege and a high delight. He had a voice of vast compass and of the sweetest tones. His presence, his scrupulous neatness, his gentlemanly address, his deferential attitude, his fine enthusiasm always won his audience from the start. And then, when he thoroughly warmed up to his subject and brought his hearers into full accord with himself, he carried them whithersoever he pleased. Now he convulsed them with laughter and filled them with delight; and then by a sudden turn his entire audience would be bathed in tears."[1] These words describe a prominent African American leader of the nineteenth century, and it would be a fine guess to venture that they are about Frederick Douglass. But, in fact, they come from Alexander Crummell's eulogy for his friend Henry Highland Garnet, whose fame and influence challenged Douglass' at the time, but who is much less well remembered today. Garnet and Douglass clashed intellectually multiple times, sometimes in print but also in person. One can only imagine what it was like to witness their duelling eloquence in the flesh.

As we will see later (Chapter 42), a significant portion of Crummell's story unfolded in Liberia, as he spent two decades there, from 1853 to 1873. By the time of his eulogy for Garnet in May of 1882, though, Crummell was living and working in Washington DC. Less than a year earlier, he had beseeched Garnet to turn down an appointment from President James Garfield to serve as minister and consul general to Liberia. It was the highest diplomatic post ever given to an African American at the time, preceding Douglass' similar appointment to Haiti by eight years. Notwithstanding how great an honor this undoubtedly was, Crummell felt that Garnet's age and physical condition made it unwise for him to journey to

Liberia. Sadly, these worries were well founded. Garnet died within a few months of arriving in Liberia. Delivering the eulogy, Crummell could see in his mind's eye the very spot where Garnet was laid to rest, a cemetery called Palm Grove: "There he lies; the deep Atlantic but a few steps beyond; its perpetual surges beating at his feet, chanting evermore the choral anthems of the ocean, the solemn requiem of the dead" (*AA* 305).

The eulogy naturally provided an occasion to reflect on Garnet's life in America. Few were better placed than Crummell to do so, because he had known Garnet ever since the two of them were children. As Crummell recounts: "Our distinguished friend was born in slavery, in Kent County, Md., December 23, 1815, on the plantation of Colonel William Spencer" (*AA* 272). His grandfather was a Mandinka chieftain, brought from Africa after being captured in war. When Henry was just 9 years old, his father, George, led eleven family members in a daring escape from slavery. The family's new surname "Garnet" may have been chosen as a variation on "Garrett," the name of a Quaker who aided them during their journey to freedom.

The family, or rather the part of it that included Henry, eventually ended up in New York City, where they lived next door to Crummell's family. Crummell reminisces: "Here, as little boys, Garnet and myself became school-mates and life-long friends" (*AA* 274). If it is already remarkable that two major African American thinkers of the nineteenth century were next-door neighbors, then the concentration of greatness at the school they attended is simply astounding. They were students at the African Free School, first founded in 1787 by the New York Manumission Society. Other students at this same time were James McCune Smith, whom we've just mentioned in the previous chapter as the first African American to hold a medical degree; Ira Aldridge, the most famous black actor of the nineteenth century and the first to perform in Shakespeare's plays; Patrick Reason, a pioneering engraver and lithographer; Patrick's younger brother, Charles Reason, who became a mathematician and linguist and the first African American hired as a college professor; George Thomas Downing, a prominent abolitionist and business owner; and, finally, Samuel Ringgold Ward, a second cousin of Garnet's who gained fame as a journalist and abolitionist speaker (on him, see Chapter 41).

Incidents during Garnet's youth foreshadowed the significance of the theme of violent resistance in his later thought. At the age of 14, having left school, Garnet was working as a cabin boy on a ship that sometimes made trips to Cuba. Upon returning from one such trip, Garnet found his home empty, his family having fled from slave catchers. His reaction to this news was to use what money he had to buy a knife, which he held as he walked along Broadway, waiting and apparently hoping for a confrontation. Friends had to convince him to get out of the city in order to stay safe. A second incident involves his continued pursuit of education. After further schooling in New York City once it was safe to come back, Garnet headed in 1835 to Canaan, New Hampshire, along with Crummell and another alumnus of the African Free School, Thomas Sidney. They went to attend the newly founded Noyes Academy, a school founded by abolitionists for both black and white students. Many white people in the surrounding area strongly objected to this experiment in racial integration. One summer day, around ninety-five oxen were used to pull the school from its foundations.

When night came, the students in their quarters feared being the victims of mob violence. Garnet, despite suffering from a long-standing disease that in coming years would result in the amputation of his right leg, was the hero of the moment. As Crummell thrillingly relates: "under Garnet, as our leader, the boys in the boarding-house were molding bullets, expecting an attack on our dwelling. About eleven o'clock at night the tramp of horses was heard approaching, and as one rapid rider passed the house and fired at it, Garnet quickly replied by a discharge from a double-barrelled shotgun which blazed away through the window…that musket shot by Garnet doubtless saved our lives. The cowardly ruffians dared not attack us" (AA 280–1). Having defended himself and the others, Garnet and his two friends left New Hampshire and went home to New York City, venturing out once again after only a few months when they learned of another integrated school in Utica, New York, called the Oneida Institute. Their studies there were, thankfully, more peaceful.

As these incidents show, violent resistance was a reality in Garnet's life, not just a matter for philosophical debate. Another important factor in his life was religion. Before his time at Noyes Academy, he came under the influence of a black Presbyterian pastor named Theodore Wright, who baptized him and encouraged him to consider going into ministry. After his time at Oneida, Garnet settled in the city of Troy, New York, where he immediately became involved in a local church. He was eventually licensed to preach and then ordained as the pastor of Liberty Street Presbyterian Church. He held this position for most of the 1840s, the decade in which he came to prominence as a radical abolitionist. In 1843, he brought together the themes of religion and violent resistance in a radical speech that remains his principal claim to fame. He had helped to organize a National Convention of Colored Citizens in Buffalo, New York. As we mentioned in Chapter 35, this revitalized a tradition that had started at the beginning of the 1830s but which had petered out by the middle of that decade. On the second day of the Convention, Garnet delivered his famous "Address to the Slaves of the United States of America," which he proposed for adoption as an official statement of the Convention.[2]

The title already suggests why the speech was controversial. It was not aimed at slaveowners, or non-slaveowning white people who might be persuaded to oppose slavery, or even the free black people who made up its immediate audience at the Convention. Instead, the real audience was the presently enslaved. Garnet's message to these people was, to put it simply: stop being enslaved. The speech begins by acknowledging how novel it was to address the enslaved, rather than to lament and critique the institution of slavery itself. "We have never until this time," he says, "sent a word of consolation and advice to you" (AS 90).[3] By doing so, he acknowledges the need for solidarity and recognition of shared interest. Troubling the distinction between free and unfree, he notes: "While you have been oppressed, we have also been partakers with you; nor can we be free while you are enslaved. We therefore write to you as being bound with you" (AS 90).

Garnet gestures at the sad history of slavery in America, including the disappointment that it was not abolished even after a revolution whose popular cry was "liberty or death!" He notes that slavery aims to distance people from their humanity and dim their mental capacities, then moves to his key claim: "TO SUCH DEGRADATION IT IS SINFUL IN THE EXTREME FOR YOU TO MAKE VOLUNTARY SUBMISSION" (AS 92). This was how Garnet had come to understand his Christian faith. Obviously, slavery is sinful for the slaveowner, but submitting to it is also sinful for the enslaved. "You are not certain of Heaven," he claims, "because you suffer yourselves to remain in a state of slavery, where you cannot obey the commandments of the Sovereign of the universe" (AS 93). He also puts the point more abstractly: "Your condition does not absolve you from your moral obligation" (AS 93).

Thus he claims that freeing oneself is a duty and, adding further fuel to the fire, a duty to make use of every means—"moral, intellectual, and physical"—that seems promising for the success of this effort (AS 93). The enslaved must act for themselves, because they can plead their cause and thus "do the work of emancipation" better than any others (AS 93). Implicitly speaking directly to adult male slaves, he implores them to consider the sufferings of their wives and children. A further source of motivation can be found in the hybrid identity to which all African Americans can lay claim: "Think of the undying glory that hangs around the ancient name of Africa:—and forget not that you are native-born American citizens, and as such, you are justly entitled to all the rights that are granted to the freest" (AS 94). Reason enough to demand freedom and, in case freedom is not granted, he unflinchingly states: "You had far better all die—*die immediately*, than live slaves, and entail your wretchedness upon your posterity" (AS 94). He points out that the heroes of the American Revolution never had it as hard as slaves, so how much more should slaves be ready to demand liberty or death? As he draws to a close, he delivers a phrase that has become the most famous part of the speech: "Let your motto be resistance! resistance! resistance!" (*AS* 96). He asks the enslaved to "trust in the living God" and to "remember that you are three millions" (*AS* 96).

It's probably obvious to you that Garnet is building here on the approach to religion and resistance in David Walker's *Appeal*. By way of confirmation, we can add that, in 1848, Garnet published his speech as an appendix to a reprinting of the *Appeal*, for which he also wrote "A Brief Sketch of the Life of David Walker." He is said to have been assisted in publishing this volume by none other than John Brown, the white abolitionist who would go on to lead his famous raid on the federal armory at Harper's Ferry in an effort to spark a general slave insurrection.[4] By publishing this volume, Garnet, like Maria W. Stewart before him, positioned himself philosophically as a Walkerite (to coin a phrase), developing and advancing ideas found in the *Appeal*. But, of course, scholars love nothing so much as making the seemingly straightforward and obvious more complicated. Just as we considered the suggestion that Stewart, contrary to appearances, may have been an advocate for violent resistance, we must note that multiple scholars have suggested that Garnet actually rejects rather than recommends violent resistance in his "Address."

Most recently, James Jasinski has argued that Garnet calls for the enslaved to carry out a non-violent general strike, despite knowing that violent retaliation by their masters would likely greet any such refusal to work. Jasinski claims: "Garnet never called upon slaves to arm themselves even in self-defense, let alone encouraged slaves to attack white southerners."[5] He goes so far as to compare Garnet to the greatest icon of non-violence, Martin Luther King, Jr. Given Garnet's reputation, this seems a bit like calling the winner of a hot dog eating contest a champion of vegetarianism. To be fair to Jasinski and others who hold this interpretation, though, there is a passage in Garnet's speech that appears to directly repudiate violence and argue for something like a general strike. Sounding a good deal like Stewart, Garnet says: "We do not advise you to attempt a revolution with the sword, because it would be inexpedient. Your numbers are too small, and moreover the rising spirit of the age, and the spirit of the gospel, are opposed to war and bloodshed. But from this moment cease to labor for tyrants who will not remunerate you. Let every slave throughout the land do this, and the days of slavery are numbered" (*AS* 96).

In response to this apparent smoking gun—or rather, encouragement to avoid smoking guns—we should note the context. It comes right after Garnet lists heroes who are role models for slave resistance, each of whom either violently resisted or planned to do so. Specifically, he mentions Denmark Vesey and Nat Turner, who we introduced in the chapter on Walker, as well as Joseph Cinque, leader of the revolt on the *Amistad*, and Madison Washington, who led a revolt on a ship called the

Creole. The latter two incidents would have been especially fresh in the memories of his listeners, having taken place just a couple of years prior. Given Garnet's glorification of these heroes, the passage that sounds puzzlingly non-violent is likely best understood as an admission that one big violent revolution is unlikely to work in the United States. This wouldn't imply rejection of violence in more specific cases. This reading fits with a remark in the closing paragraph of the speech: "What kind of resistance you had better make, you must decide by the circumstances that surround you, and according to the suggestion of expediency" (*AS* 96).

It is also telling that, in James McCune Smith's introduction to a speech Garnet delivered in 1865 before the House of Representatives in Washington DC, the "Address to the Slaves" is reproduced in full, but with some revision. Most notably, the passage discouraging "revolution with the sword" is gone, replaced by: "Brethren, arise, arise! Strike for your lives and liberties. Now is the day and the hour. Let every slave throughout the land do this, and the days of slavery are numbered."[6] Let's assume, though, that it is the 1848 version, rather than this later text, that faithfully reproduces what Garnet said at the Convention, and move on to the debate that erupted between Douglass and Garnet over the speech. The Minutes of the Convention tell us that Douglass objected that "there was too much physical force" in the speech and that he "was for trying the moral means a little longer." Douglass thus seems to have understood Garnet to endorse the use of violence. On the other hand, Garnet was rather more nuanced in his response to Douglass. He replied, "the most the address said...was, that it advised the slaves to go to their masters and tell them that they wanted liberty, and had come to ask for it; and if the master refused it, to tell them, then we shall take it, let the consequence be what it may."[7] Douglass replied that this would obviously lead to insurrection.

Thus began a debate that carried on from Wednesday, when Garnet gave the speech, until Saturday, the last day of the Convention, when a final vote was taken on whether to adopt the speech as an official statement by the Convention. Douglass' side prevailed, but this was only a single battle in an ideological war, one that would ultimately go Garnet's way. At the time, Douglass was still a faithful Garrisonian. Garnet too had been an early admirer of William Lloyd Garrison. As a teenager in New York City in 1834, he co-founded a literary society called the Garrison Literary and Benevolent Association. Later, in May of 1840, he delivered a speech at a meeting of the American Anti-Slavery Society and had the honor of being introduced by Garrison himself. That same month, however, a rift among the Garrisonians resulted in the founding of a rival organization, which Garnet supported. He quickly got on board with the position that participation in the US political system was a viable way of fighting slavery, breaking with the Garrisonian position that such participation meant being in league with slaveholders. Garnet became a fervent supporter of the Liberty Party, which emerged from this abolitionist split as a third party seeking to challenge the acceptance of slavery by the two major political parties of the time.

As we have seen, Douglass too eventually broke with Garrison. Gradually, he came to explore the paths of political participation and violent resistance that Garnet had traveled earlier and more readily. Douglass' greater fame, however, would come to obscure Garnet's early prominence, something we might explain with reference to, among other things, the success of Douglass' *Narrative* and the platform provided by Douglass' newspaper, the *North Star*. Garnet made attempts at journalism too, but they were comparatively unsuccessful. In fact, the debate between Douglass and Garnet played itself out in the pages of the *North Star*. In 1849, knowing that Garnet was planning a trip to England, Douglass published an editorial criticizing him as an unworthy representative of the abolitionist cause, writing: "Mr. Garnet has again and again declared that he had no faith in moral means for the overthrow of American Slavery. That his hope for success was in the sword."[8]

Garnet's response in a letter Douglass published in his paper does much to clarify how Garnet conceptualized the nature of resistance: "You publish that I have no faith in the use of moral means for the extinction of American Slavery. *I believe with all my heart in such means—and I believe that political power ought to be used for that end, and that when rightly used, it is strictly moral.* I also believe that the slave has a moral right to use his physical power to obtain his liberty—my motto is, give me liberty, or give me death. Dare you, Frederick Douglass, say otherwise?"[9] We've seen how Douglass later endorsed violent resistance, as in the West India Emancipation speech, and it is hard not to suspect that Garnet may have influenced his development. Yet, even in that later speech, Douglass speaks of moral and physical resistance as distinct, if equally justified, forms of resistance. Garnet's point in this 1849 letter seems to have been that *all* justified resistance necessarily counts as *moral* resistance, precisely by virtue of being justified.

Though Douglass more or less came around to Garnet's point of view on these issues, he remained opposed to another tendency in Garnet's thought that emerged in the late 1840s: greater openness to emigration. In a letter published in the *North Star* in 1849, Garnet wrote of his shifting views on Liberia, which had declared its independence from the American Colonization Society and established itself as a republic just two years before: "I hesitate not to say, that my mind, of late, has greatly changed in regard to the American Colonization scheme. So far as it benefits the land of my fathers, I bid it God-speed; but so far as it denies the possibility of our elevation here, I oppose it. I would rather see a man free in Liberia, than a slave in the United States."[10] The caveat—that emigration must not undermine uplift in the United States—shows he had not changed his mind as fully as John Russwurm did before him. He repeatedly denied calling for all African Americans to leave America. But this did not stop Douglass and others, including former schoolmate George T. Downing, from vigorously opposing him on anti-colonizationist grounds.

Garnet arrived in England in August of 1850 and lectured successfully in the British Isles for about two and a half years, after which he did not return to the United States but took up a position as a Presbyterian missionary in Jamaica. He was joined there by his wife Julia Garnet, born Julia Williams, whom he first met back at the ill-fated Noyes Academy and, who like him, had then gone to the Oneida Institute. He once suggested that the only influence upon his "Address to the Slaves" outside his own mind was Julia's.[11] In Jamaica, she organized a Female Industrial School while her husband carried on his ministry. They left to go back to the United States in 1855 because of illness, and Garnet soon took up a pastorship in New York City. This is what he was doing by the time he attended the Emancipation Day celebration where Douglass gave his speech. The two were on better terms by that point.

By the late 1850s, however, Garnet once again became fascinated with ideas of emigration. He founded the African Civilization Society; critics of emigration predictably pointed out its familiar-sounding acronym. He became excited about possibilities of emigration to West Africa, particularly Yorubaland, and later also Haiti. Like most leaders of the time, though, he eventually became caught up in the drama of the Civil War. He recruited for the Union Army and created posters with slogans characteristic of his thought: "Rather Die Free Men than Live as Slaves…Rise Now and Fly to Arms."[12] It is a testament to the enduring respect many had for him as an abolitionist that, after the ratification of the Thirteenth Amendment in January of 1865, Garnet was invited to preach before the House of Representatives, becoming the first black person invited to speak to Congress. The introduction to the publication of the speech by James McCune Smith is the most thorough recounting and appreciation of Garnet's life before Crummell's eulogy.

Much less attention has been paid by scholars to the story of Garnet's life after 1865, but it is worth noting that, more than many American contemporaries, he devoted himself to opposing slavery in other parts of the world. In 1872, he was elected secretary of the Cuban Anti-Slavery Society and campaigned for emancipation on that island, which would not be secured until 1886, after his death. Unfortunately, his last years were also characterized by isolation and lack of influence. As Crummell puts it: "Sorrow and discouragement fell upon his soul, and at times the wounded spirit sighed for release; and the strong desire arose to escape to some foreign land, where, oblivious of the ingratitude and forgetfulness of his people, he might have a few final days of peace and comfort, and at last sink quietly to his grave" (*AA* 302). Crummell reports him saying, after getting the appointment from President Garfield as minister to Liberia: "Would you have me linger here in an old age of neglect and want?...No...I go gladly to Africa! Please the Lord I can only safely cross the ocean, land on the coast of Africa, look around upon its green fields, tread the soil of my ancestors, live if but a few weeks; then I shall be glad to lie down and be buried beneath its sod!" (*AA* 303). Garnet got his wish.

39

NATION WITHIN A NATION

Martin Delany

A commonly heard lament these days is that people have ever shorter attention spans. Thanks to a combination of social media, sound bites, and speed of access to information and services, we've reached the stage where we have a standard abbreviation for the expression: "too long; didn't read."[1] Such complaints inevitably make one sound like an old fogey. But perhaps there is something to this one, when you consider the length of public speeches that were more or less cheerfully endured by nineteenth century Americans. Admittedly the most famous of these, the Gettysburg Address, was a tidy 272 words long. The audience still had to be patient to hear Lincoln give it, as the previous speaker took about two hours to get through his own speech. That was not a prodigiously long performance by the standards of the time, as we can see from the record of Martin Delany. Like his colleague and sometime adversary Frederick Douglass, Delany was an accomplished orator. In Cleveland in August 1854, he put his skills to work in a nearly four-hour speech called "Political Destiny of the Colored Race on the American Continent." In the same year, it's claimed that his address as chairman of the business committee for the National Emigration Convention clocked in at a scarcely credible seven hours!

His theme in both speeches was the need for free black Americans to abandon their country.[2] They should leave behind the unremitting repression of the United States for a better future. At this time, he argued for remaining on the same side of the Atlantic, in the Caribbean or in Central or South America. He was dismissive of Liberia, the colony created in Africa by the American Colonization Society, through a scheme he called "degrading, insolent, and slaveholding" (143, cf. 205). Later, though, he would involve himself in other schemes for colonizing Africa, at one point even accepting financial support from the ACS. Delany himself made his way to Africa in 1859, traveling to Liberia before moving on to Lagos and sizing up the prospects for a settlement in Yorubaland.[3] Here, he was impressed by some of the same cultural features we discussed in the first part of this book, such as an apparent commitment to monotheism. He returned to the US in 1860, visiting the United Kingdom en route and causing a sensation when appearing at the International Statistical Congress in London. There, he had the pleasure of publicly stating to no less a personage than Prince Albert: "I assure your royal highness that *I am a man*" (360).

It is especially, but not only, on the basis of this active emigrationist phase of Delany's career that he is hailed—or blamed—as a "father of black nationalism" in the United States.[4] He had an abiding pessimism about the situation of American blacks, still involving himself in emigrationist projects in 1878, after the Civil War and the abolition of slavery. More than that, he vehemently voiced pride in his African heritage, glorying in his "pure blood" and dark complexion, and arguing repeatedly that black people needed to form their own communities and govern themselves. "Africa for the African race," he implored, "and black men to rule them" (356). You can probably guess who Delany judged to be "the *most* African of all the black men" in the United States: himself (463). In public, he sometimes wore a dashiki, a very uncommon move for a nineteenth century figure born in the diaspora, and at other times he donned what he claimed to be the wedding dress of an African chief. In a document reporting on his tour of Africa, he stated: "I have outgrown, long since, the boundaries of North America" (350). Delany seems to have been many decades ahead of his time, the Pan-Africanist leader in waiting of a separate black nation.

This is the Delany that people love to contrast with the aforementioned Frederick Douglass.[5] The two were both newspapermen as well as public speakers. Delany put out a paper called the *Mystery* for several years before joining Douglass in 1847 to help put out a paper with a larger circulation, the *North Star*. But they would clash in the coming years. One disagreement concerned the famous book by Harriet Beecher Stowe, *Uncle Tom's Cabin*. While Douglass welcomed Stowe's support of the abolitionist cause, Delany decried reliance by black people on a white woman who "knows nothing about us," adding, "neither does any other white person" (224). Though he thereafter allowed that this was partly ironic exaggeration, he stood by his criticism of Stowe, especially in light of her low opinion of Haiti (232). At a more abstract level, it can be argued that Douglass focused more on encouraging individual reliance, while Delany's stress was more on solidarity and political autonomy among black people.[6] In this respect, it's telling that Douglass' chief writings were autobiographies, whereas Delany's were mostly political commentary and histories, on such topics as the origins of race, economic theory, and the differing situations in various regions of the United States.

Yet Delany's most famous phrase already hints at the deeper ambiguities and complexities of his thought. This phrase comes in the best known of his treatises, *The Condition, Elevation, Emigration and Destiny of the Colored People of the United States*, published in 1852, in a passage where he observes that world history is full of oppressed classes, each of them a "nation within a nation." The Israelites in Egypt, the gladiators in Rome, the Welsh and Irish in Britain, all of them suffered from "deprivation of political equality" (190). Echoing David Walker's claim about unsurpassed wretchedness in his *Appeal*, Delany concluded that the most unfavorable condition of all these disadvantaged classes was that of "the colored people of the United States" (191). This makes clear the reasons for his support of emigration, and calling the black population a "nation" emphasizes the potential, even the need, for separate governance and perhaps a land for black people to call their own.[7] On the other hand, if black Americans also find themselves *within* a nation, is it not possible that the most suitable outcome of political struggle would be their accommodation and integration within that larger nation?

This brings us to the other side of Delany's thought. From early on, he was a zealous advocate of advancement for black Americans within American society. Delany was born in Charleston, Virginia, but his family moved to Pennsylvania when he was still a child, and his intellectual formation took place in Pittsburgh. Here he studied medicine—in fact, the newspaper he later founded had the additional function of advertising his services as a doctor—and came under the influence of his teacher the Reverend Lewis Woodson.[8] Woodson and another mentor, William Whipper, were optimists when it came to the plight of black people in America. Calling to mind the moralizing approach of Maria Stewart rather than the militancy of David Walker, Woodson and Whipper believed in moral suasion through self-improvement. If African Americans could display industriousness and virtue, then racism would gradually recede.

Throughout his career, Delany laid particular stress on one aspect of this approach: economic uplift. As he put it, "give us wealth, and we can obtain all the rest" (156). Like most people of the time, Delany was a Christian and he saw human history in biblical terms. Nevertheless, he had little faith in religion as an engine of equality, especially if religious formation was not joined to more practical efforts like vocational training. In fact, Delany often lamented that Christianity was used as a tool for keeping slaves docile, and persuading even free black people to endure patiently the injustices meted out to them by the white majority. "Our masters," he wrote, "have been so accustomed to teach us how to live in the world to come, that they have forgotten to teach us how to live in this world; but are always very careful to teach their own children and themselves, however religious they may be, how to make a living here, while in this world" (155). The slavers exercised earthly oppression, and needed to be fought with earthly, not heavenly, resistance.

Even political liberty would not be enough without increased prosperity, as Delany wrote in the *North Star* when encouraging the learning of practical trades (88). This was a striking anticipation of the later ideas of Booker T. Washington, as was Delany's scornful dismissal of idealists who sought to give African Americans a classical education. For them to learn Latin or Greek, as if the goal was to turn black people into scholars and professors, was a matter of "taking a leap from the deepest abyss to the highest summit, rising from the ridiculous to the sublime, without a medium."[9] He was also strongly in favor of educating girls, though the rationale he emphasized, which was also articulated by women thinkers like Stewart before him and Anna Julia Cooper after him, was the questionably feminist point that educated women will make better homes: "Our females must be qualified, because they are to be the mothers of our children…Raise the mothers above the level of degradation, and the offspring is elevated with them" (212).[10]

He duly lavished praise on earlier luminaries like Benjamin Banneker, whom he calls a "scientist and philosopher," as well as Phillis Wheatley and Paul Cuffe (140, 195–7). Such figures showed the great potential that could be realized by African Americans. Looking further back, Delany trumpeted the achievements of ancient Africans, especially in Egypt. He praised what he understood as the early emergence of monotheism there, identifying "the great god of Egypt and Ethiopia" as "Jupiter Ammon," a name for Egyptian god Amun that shines new light on the name of the poet and thinker we discussed in Chapter 24, Jupiter Hammon (53, 363; on Akhenaten's monotheism, see Chapter 4 above). Delany even suggested that Egyptian religious thought anticipated the Christian doctrine of the Trinity (55). Some of these remarks were made in a context that will be familiar to us: the Masonic movement.[11] Delany was elected Master of a Lodge in Pittsburgh in 1852 and was the first to write a history of Prince Hall Masonry. He joined the long line of authors who pointed to the African origins of this tradition, asking: "From whence sprung Masonry but from Ethiopia, Egypt, and Assyria—all settled and peopled by the children of Ham?" (65).

The history of black Masonry was marked by the same tensions that characterized Delany's career. In theory, these organizations should have helped African Americans to establish themselves amongst their white neighbors. Here was a chance to join a club that counted even George Washington among its members! In practice, the white Freemasons tried to exclude them; recall Prince Hall's struggle to get official recognition for his Lodge in the 1780s. In 1853, Delany was still having to insist that "our rights are equal to those of other American Masons, if not better than some; and it comes not with the best grace for *them* to *deny* us" (51). Such rejections were of course a small-scale reflection of what was happening in wider American society. The 1850s were a time of great disappointment for activists like Delany. The decade began with the passage of the Fugitive Slave Law in 1850, which made it easier to catch escaped slaves—or supposed escaped slaves—in the north and bring them back to the slave states. As Delany and others pointed out, this meant that even legally free black people were permanently in danger of being seized, wherever they lived. They were, as Delany put it, "slaves in the midst of freedom, waiting patiently, and unconcernedly—indifferently, and stupidly, for masters to come and lay claim to us" (201). Then, in 1857, came the infamous *Dred Scott* case, in which the Supreme Court ruled that black people had no right to citizenship.

Alongside these political setbacks came personal ones. Precisely on the grounds that he was not a citizen, Delany saw an application for a patent turned down in 1852 (his idea had to do with transporting locomotives across the Allegheny Mountains, bringing a whole new meaning to the idea of uplift through industrial training).[12] One year earlier, he had been dismissed from Harvard Medical School along with two other black students, after protests from white students over their admission. It's no wonder that Delany was led to pose the question, "shall we fly, or shall we resist?" (201), and to think that the right answer was to fly: away from the United States, to a better life elsewhere. He moved to Canada in 1856, to the town of Chatham in what is now Ontario, and by the end of the decade was exploring the west coast of Africa and planning settlements. Yet later in life we find him running for statewide political office in South Carolina and serving as a judge in Charleston. When he died in 1885, it was in Ohio, not Cuba, Canada, or Yorubaland.

One way to explain his shifting political and personal goals, and also the central tension between separation and integration that seems to run through his works, is to appeal to chronology. A book on Delany by the Nigerian scholar Tunde Adeleke argues that the standard view of Delany as a pioneering black nationalist and Pan-Africanist depends mostly on his writings and activities from a relatively brief part of his career, spanning from the early 1850s to 1862.[13] This phase culminated with Delany's novel *Blake, or the Huts of America*, which appeared serialized in newspapers from 1859 to 1862 and remained unfinished.[14] A kind of militant answer to Harriet Beecher Stowe and *Dred Scott*,[15] it tells the story of an escaped slave who aims to foment an uprising in Mississippi, and then goes on to plan a further uprising in Cuba.

This novel gives us a portrait of Delany's ideals around 1860. In many respects, it is consistent with themes he had been sounding his whole life, for instance, concerning the inefficacy of religion alone as a means of fighting injustice. At one point, the lead character is told to "stand still" and wait for salvation, to which he responds, "I've been standing still long enough," and admits, "I have altogether lost my faith in the religion of my oppressors."[16] The novel also articulates the value of solidarity and self-reliance. One of Blake's co-conspirators observes that "people never entertain proper opinions of themselves until they begin to act for themselves."[17] Delany furthermore follows Walker in arguing that black resistance requires disciplined secrecy. The point is dramatized when Blake inspires revolt by whispering a message in slaves' ears that is never divulged to the reader.[18] Secrecy stands for solidarity, which can strike fear into the hearts of the white masters, who are motivated solely by greed. That point too is made dramatically, through the portrayal of a cynical slaveowner who admits: "I would just as readily hold a white as a black in slavery, were it the custom and policy of the country to do so. It is all a matter of self-interest with me."[19] This is a case Delany made elsewhere in non-fictional settings, as when he observed that white Americans started by oppressing Native Americans before finding it more expedient to victimize Africans. It's always in the interest of a ruling class to have a dominated class who are as weak as possible, and racism is merely a retrospective justification (192–3).

Then, with the Emancipation Proclamation, issued on January 1, 1863, everything changed. Having so recently turned his back on his country, Delany now literally fought to preserve it, joining the Union Army and receiving the rank of Major. He also petitioned Lincoln to create an all-black force to fight in the Civil War (386). Once the war was won, he was full of ideas for improving the lot of the freed slaves. Characteristically, these proposals focused on economic uplift. He pointed out the large potential market constituted by black people, and envisioned a "triple alliance" between black labor, southern land, and northern capital (399–401). As Reconstruction wore on, Delany was not just integrationist but downright conservative, at least in comparison to more radical voices who insisted on quick and dramatic reform. He was worried that these radicals, who formed a faction of the Republican Party, would sow racial discord with their demands. As he memorably put it, "we must not in finding room for ourselves undertake to elbow the white people out of their own places."[20] This led to further tensions with Douglass, who said that, if anyone other than Delany was making these arguments, he would suppose him to be an ally of the "old planters."[21] In 1868, Delany went so far as to argue against insisting that black politicians be put in office. Yet, in 1871, we find him writing in a letter to Douglass: "Colored people must have intelligent leaders of their own race, and white people intelligent leaders of theirs" (439).

Adeleke is surely right to point out that Delany's views changed along with the political situation in the US. As this last example shows, though, the tension between integrationism and separatism seems to run throughout his whole career, including during Reconstruction. Later, after the end of Reconstruction, we find writings that fit with Delany's reputation as a black nationalist, like *Principia of Ethnology: The Origin of Races and Color*. He here argues that there are three pure races, descended from the sons of Noah. Black people are, as he has long held, the "sons of Ham." They should take pride in their color, given the stunning achievements of their forebears. As in his address to the Masons, he refers to the Ethiopians and Egyptians as the first to be advanced in "morals, religion, arts, science and literature" (479). His extreme investment in racial difference is underscored by his perplexing notion that the mixing of races is, in the longer term, impossible. After a few generations, pure blood and pure white, black, or yellow skin will re-emerge, so that eventually the three "original sterling races" (482) will make up the entire population of the world.

This sort of material was evidently designed to justify and encourage an embrace of black identity and nationhood. One way to reconcile that with his more conservative political statements and actions is to say that Delany's nationalism was pragmatic in nature. This is the line taken by Tommie Shelby, who argues that Delany "vacillated between (and perhaps even confused)" two conceptions of black nationalism, one in which separate nationhood would be an end in itself, another in which it is just an instrumental means to achieving a better lot for people of African heritage.[22] It would make sense to shift from endorsing emigration to encouraging political integration, if facts on the ground made it more reasonable to suppose that African Americans had a chance to achieve equality, or even just work toward it. Where the Fugitive Slave Law and *Dred Scott* seemed to make this impossible, the Emancipation Proclamation and opportunities afforded by Reconstruction put it back on the table.

Shelby's interpretation has been forcefully rejected by Tommy Curry, who defends the traditional assessment of Delany as a black nationalist (or as he prefers to say "nationist") who "champions racial solidarity" and embraces a distinctive culture not shared by white Europeans and Americans.[23] No less than Shelby, Curry is able to cite strong evidence, especially the race theory of Delany's *Principia*, which is indeed difficult to read the way Shelby does, as the work of a man who was "at most halfhearted" in his commitment to black separatism. Nor was this a commitment he developed late in life. Earlier in his career, Delany had written that "the elevation of the colored man can only be completed by the elevation of the pure descendants of Africa" (194).

Without pretending we can resolve this dispute here, we would like to propose a different way of finding consistency across Delany's works and throughout his evolving political thought. He clearly had different views at different times about the best way to attain political self-determination for African Americans. Nevertheless, he remained consistent in his philosophical view about why self-determination is important in the first place. He puts forth, in the long speech we mentioned at the beginning of this chapter, "a great principle of political economy, that no people can be free who themselves do not constitute an essential part of the ruling element of the country in which they live" (247, cf. 371). Or, as he says elsewhere: "A people to be free must be their own rulers; each individual must in himself be an essential element of the sovereign power which composes the true basis of his liberty" (417).

Mere "suffrage," the right to vote, is not enough. The "nation within the nation" that is black America must have its political fortunes in its own hands, which Delany calls "enfranchisement."[24] Without this, not even personal safety is assured, never mind a chance at prosperity, as was vividly shown by the case of the Fugitive Slave Law. Whatever caution or prudence might dictate, this is the ultimate goal that must be pursued. As Delany puts it in a passage that maintains an exquisite balance between nationalism and integrationism: "I am not in favor of caste, nor a separation of the brotherhood of mankind, and would as willingly live among white men as black, if I had an equal possession and enjoyment of privileges; but shall never be reconciled to live among them, subservient to their will—existing by mere sufferance, as we, the colored people, do in this country" (200).

40

I READ MEN AND NATIONS

Sojourner Truth and Frances Harper

Some years ago, Peter was on the radio to talk about the ancient Greek philosopher Heraclitus. Having been asked to discuss his most famous saying, which states that "different waters flow over those who step into the same rivers," he read out the Greek text, to make the point that, in the original, the saying is onomatopoetic, since it actually sounds like flowing water. The host of the show was so taken with this that he asked to hear the Greek again. This led to a great regret on Peter's part. Only later that day did he realize he should have recited the text again and added: "there, I've just shown it's possible to read out the same river fragment twice!" That's something we've all experienced, coming up with the perfect comment or retort only once it's too late. It happens even to people with much greater rhetorical gifts, like, of all people, Frederick Douglass. Speaking at a public meeting, in 1852, he gave vent to his frustration at the obstacles put in the way of black progress, and thundered that violence rather than moral suasion might be needed if black people were to secure their rights. A voice came from the front row, saying simply, "Frederick, is God dead?" The entire audience was stunned, as if by an electric shock, and Douglass himself was reduced to silence by this moralizing rebuke. It came from Sojourner Truth, who alongside Douglass is now the most famous of the African American abolitionists.

This anecdote was included in the *Book of Life* (at 148), a collection of anecdotes and documents appended to the much-read *Narrative* of her life.[1] It was also related by Douglass himself. Decades later, he admitted that Sojourner's intervention brought the event "to a standstill" as if someone had thrown a brick through the window. This is also confirmed by a contemporary report in the abolitionist press. In the third and last of his autobiographies, though, Douglass took the liberty of giving himself a snappy comeback: when Truth asked whether God was dead, he supposedly answered: "No, and because God is not dead slavery can only end in blood."[2] Whatever the truth of this confrontation between Douglass and, well, Truth, it invites us to consider these two figures alongside one another. Both former slaves, both active as public speakers in the campaign against slavery and then for decades after its abolition, both made famous by narratives setting down their life stories, both torn over time as to the necessity of violence. Truth occasionally wielded the fiery rhetoric we have seen in David Walker, as when she said: "I do not want any man to be killed, but I am sorry to see them so short-minded. But we'll have our rights; see if we don't; and you can't stop us from them; see if you can."[3]

This remark, like everything else Sojourner Truth is known to have said, was preserved by other witnesses, in this case of a lecture she gave in New York City in 1853. She was not literate, having grown up in rural New York as the uneducated slave of a Dutch-speaking family. English was therefore her second language. Truth said herself that, when she first came to New York City, her English was still poor and she was "ignorant as a horse."[4] She had literally walked to freedom, after her master John Dumont reneged on a promise to free her after a certain period of time, on the grounds that a hand injury had prevented her from doing her full work (62–3). When Dumont caught up with her, he grudgingly agreed to sell her to a family with whom she had found shelter, the Van Wageners. But Dumont sold Truth's son Peter to another family, who then broke New York law by selling Peter into the South. Truth contested this in court, insisting with terse determination: "I'll have my child again." Incredibly, she was successful in stopping the sale and her son was returned to her. She had been rewarded twice for her courage and perceptive grasp of what was possible, even for a slave with no resources apart from a profound sense of justice and faith in God. As she once put it, "I don't read such small stuff as letters, I read men and nations."[5]

All this happened in 1826, early in Truth's long and eventful life, which stretched from her birth some time around the end of the eighteenth century to her death in 1883. We have a detailed account of her early experiences in the aforementioned *Narrative* which was, of course, not set down by Truth herself but by a white abolitionist named Olive Gilbert. A friend of William Lloyd Garrison, Gilbert met Truth through the Northampton Association of Education and Industry, a utopian community in Massachusetts which, it has been said, was treated by Garrison and Frederick Douglass "as a sort of progressive summer camp."[6] The fact that it was Gilbert who wrote the *Narrative* makes this biography of Truth unlike those of Douglass, which, as we saw, were very emphatically "written by himself." Throughout, it speaks of Truth in the third person, and Gilbert editorializes and comments on the story as she goes along. Still, it's clear that Truth had a strong hand in shaping the story of her life. Already before telling that story to Gilbert, she had decided to call herself "Sojourner Truth," having originally been called Isabella—the new name, she said, was given to her by God. Her involvement in the composition of the *Narrative* is clear at certain points, as when Gilbert remarks of one anecdote that it is a "comparatively trifling incident she wishes related" (56). There follows one of the more famous passages in the *Narrative*, in which Truth was scolded for serving up greyish potatoes, and it turned out that another servant had been spilling ash into the cooking water.

Her insistence on including this anecdote shows Truth's eye for the telling detail and humble parable. Her homespun and disarmingly direct rhetorical style made it easy for reporters, even admiring ones, to diminish her with rather patronizing descriptions. Douglass wrote of her: "She was a genuine specimen of the uncultured negro. She cared very little for elegance of speech or refinement of manners. She seemed to please herself and others best when she put her ideas in the oddest forms...Her quaint speeches easily gave her an audience."[7] Here Douglass subtly puts Truth in her place, implicitly contrasting his own more polished style to that of a woman who was both a cherished ally and a potential rival for attention and acclaim. Like Douglass, Truth spent much of her life as an itinerant lecturer, appearing in cities all over America to decry slavery and, after abolition, to exhort audiences both white and black, both male and female, to assist the population of freed slaves. She especially focused on the cause of free land grants in the western United States, submitting an official petition for this cause to the US Congress (167). This was, to her mind, a far preferable solution to black poverty than emigration to Liberia (194).

In the many press reports of her speeches and public appearances, Truth was reliably presented as a kind of naive sage, and sometimes explicitly called a "philosopher" to mark this status (169, 180). This is clear from the representation of her persona, and her speech, in Gilbert's *Narrative* and in other contemporary documents, many of which were collected by a Quaker woman named Frances Gage in the aforementioned *Book of Life* that she added to the *Narrative*. That title, *Book of Life*, had been used by Truth for a keepsake volume of signatures from people she had met, including Abraham Lincoln. In these documents and contemporary newspapers, we have a reminder of the contrast between the oral and the written, which was one of our abiding themes earlier in this book: Oruka might well have called her a "philosophical sage." Many stories about Truth show her in conversational settings or responding to others in a witty or penetrating fashion, like her comment at Douglass' speech or on the occasion when she met Lincoln. When the president showed her a bible sent him by the black population of Baltimore, she praised its beauty and then added: "The colored people have given this to the head of the government, and that government once sanctioned laws that would not permit its people to learn enough to enable them to read this Book. And for what? Let them answer who can" (154).

In this case, the report of her remark is written out in standard English, but frequently reports about her employ irregular spelling, seemingly for the purpose of capturing her dialect. In a report on her public lecturing taken from a Boston newspaper and included in the *Book of Life*, it's related how she got a laugh with the following reminiscence: "I said, O God, my mother tole me ef I asked you to make my marster an' misteress good, you'd do it, an' dey didn't get good. [Laughter.] Why, says I, God, mebbe you can't do it. Kill 'em." The supposedly phonetic transcription may distract us from the deep significance of the anecdote. Like Douglass looking back on his growing understanding of slavery as a youth, she here recalls a precocious concern with the problem of evil—why does God allow the tyranny of slavery?—and, with somewhat morbid humor, alludes to the question of whether this tyranny should be met with violence.

The typographical markers of Truth's uneducated speaking style were mirrored in explicit descriptions of her as a lecturer, as with the example we just saw in Douglass or this account from a Rochester paper: "she is unable to read or write, and in her manner and style is perfectly natural and original. She acts and speaks with the simplicity and innocence of a child, and seems to have nothing to conceal" (186). Another press report is somewhat more nuanced: "Her matter and manner were simply indescribable, often straying far away from the starting point; but each digression was fraught with telling logic, rough humor, or effective sarcasm" (195). More insightful still, an English journalist named Gilbert Vale who interviewed Truth said that she "is not exactly what she seems. She had her own or private opinion on every thing, and these opinions of her own we have frequently found very correct."[8]

These issues of representation are vividly on display in the two most famous accounts of Sojourner Truth, which come to us from the Ohio activist Frances Gage and Harriet Beecher Stowe, author of *Uncle Tom's Cabin*. Stowe wrote a piece about Truth which appeared in the *Atlantic Monthly* in 1863, the year of the Emancipation Proclamation. It styles Sojourner as a "Lybian Sybil" (136) and consists in part of an interview in which Stowe's questions are in standard English and Truth's in extravagantly marked dialect ("you's heerd o' me, I reckon?"). It repeats the story of Truth's escape from slavery and dwells on her conversion to a deeply felt Christianity. A key insight came after God inspired her to set out for freedom, when she came to realization of His omnipresence, saying, "O God, I didn't know as you was so great!" (140).

This same story appears in the *Narrative* (79), in which Olive Gilbert emphasizes that Truth herself looks back on her earlier religious beliefs as ignorant and simplistic, like "the dark imagery of a fitful dream" (61).

Stowe's presentation is fond but rather condescending, and makes for a vivid contrast with the personality depicted by Frances Gage in her report of Truth's most renowned speech, which was given in Akron, Ohio in 1851. As one modern-day scholar has commented, "while Stowe drew Truth as a quaint, minstrel-like, nineteenth-century Negro, Gage made her into a tough-minded, feminist emblem by stressing Truth's strength and the clash of conventions of race and gender and by the riveting refrain, 'and ar'n't I a woman?'"[9] This is indeed the most famous line in the speech, and it is worth quoting the passage in full:

> "I tink dat 'twixt de niggers of de Souf and de women at de Norf all a talkin' 'bout rights, de white men will be in a fix pretty soon. But what's all dis here talkin' 'bout? Dat man ober dar say dat women needs to be helped into carriages, and lifted ober ditches, and to have de best place every whar. Nobody eber help me into carriages, or ober mud puddles, or gives me any best place and ar'n't I a woman? Look at me! Look at my arm!"

Here Gage adds, "and she bared her right arm to the shoulder, showing her tremendous muscular power." The speech continues:

> "I have plowed, and planted, and gathered into barns, and no man could head me—and ar'n't I a woman? I could work as much and eat as much as a man (when I could get it), and bear de lash as well—and ar'n't I a woman? I have borne thirteen chilern and seen 'em mos' all sold off into slavery, and when I cried out with a mother's grief, none but Jesus heard—and ar'n't I a woman? Den dey talks 'bout dis ting in de head—what dis dey call it?' 'Intellect,' whispered some one near. 'Dat's it honey. What's dat got to do with women's rights or niggers' rights? If my cup won't hold but a pint and yourn holds a quart, wouldn't ye be mean not to let me have my little half-measure full?'"(125)

As in Stowe, Truth's words are written out in unconventional spelling to mark her dialect. Great emphasis is placed upon her physical forcefulness, her "almost Amazon form" and a voice "like rolling thunder." Here one may have the uncomfortable feeling that Gage reduces Truth to a kind of simple-minded figure whose power comes from the strength of her black body rather than her mind.

Yet Truth herself seems to be undermining that construal in the speech, as she emphasizes the importance of her mind in her claim to rights. And, by the way, contemporary reports of this speech found in newspapers write out the "pint and quart" remark in conventional English and do not have her needing help to come up with the word "intellect."[10] In fact, Truth's strategy seems to have been more complicated and self-knowing. She understood that her audience would see her in terms of her body and what it had endured, and she manipulated those attitudes for rhetorical effect. On another famous occasion, while speaking in Indiana, she was suspected of being a man, because of her deep voice. She informed her white male accusers that, as a slave, she had been required to nurse white baby boys. Then baring her breasts, she asked them if they wished to suckle from them. It's hard to imagine a more dramatic reversal of the prevailing power dynamics, reminding members of the dominant race and gender that they have sometimes been vulnerable and dependent for their very survival on a black woman.

As the speech in Akron and this anecdote reveal, Truth was extraordinary in her insight into the plight of black women and the parallel between the repression of black people and of women. She saw the campaign for women's rights as a kind of extension of the struggle against slavery. In another example of her rather ambiguous views on violence—never to be welcomed, but perhaps to be acknowledged as necessary—she said after emancipation that freedom for black people had come "through blood," adding "I am sorry it came in that way. We are now trying for liberty that requires no blood—that women shall have their rights." Of course, we know already that Truth was not the only woman to speak out on these issues. It is true that she herself said, "I suppose that I am about the only colored woman that goes about to speak for the rights of the colored woman."[11] But her famous refrain "aren't I a woman" is reminiscent of Maria Stewart's earlier rhetorical question, "what if I am a woman?" And she was not the only African American woman in this period to make public lectures or to link the causes of racial and sexual equality.

One of the more prominent of her fellow activists was Frances Ellen Watkins Harper. Her biography makes for a sharp contrast with that of Truth. Born free in 1825 and orphaned at a young age, she grew up with her uncle William Watkins in Baltimore. Watkins was himself a significant figure in African American letters. He founded an Academy of Negro Youth and was himself highly educated, having proficiency in classical languages and medicine. He published essays in Garrison's *Liberator* and sometimes wrote under the pen-name of the "colored Baltimorean." Under this name, he is acknowledged in no less a work than David Walker's *Appeal* as a "judicious" opponent of the colonization scheme. Thanks to Watkins, his niece

Frances got an excellent education and put it to good use. Like Phillis Wheatley before her, she wrote publishable poetry from a fairly young age, and, like her contemporary Martin Delany, she gave public lectures and wrote novels. Her poetry is more overtly political than Wheatley's. It often focuses on the perspective of black women, for instance, describing a runaway slave: "She is a mother—her child is a slave— / And she'll give him his freedom, or find him a grave!"[12] In another poem about a slave auction, she writes: "And mothers stood with streaming eyes / And saw their dearest daughters sold / Unheeded rose their bitter cries / While tyrants bartered them for gold."

The plight of women is thematized in one of her more famous speeches, "We Are All Bound Up Together," given in 1866 in New York at the National Women's Rights Convention. She speaks of the devastating consequences for her family when her husband died, leaving her with four children to care for. Had she been a man, she could simply have remarried, but instead she was left in precarious circumstances, losing all her property but a looking glass. This passage is typical of her writing. The detail about the mirror metaphorically suggests that, even in such dire straits, she is left with a kind of self-knowledge that escapes her oppressors. Alongside such literary flourishes, she makes frank emotional appeals to her audience, in this case pointing to the sort of vulnerability that also affected Maria Stewart when her own husband died. As Michael Stancliff has written in a book-length study of Harper, her speech showed that when "husbands and other male guardians die, black women are forced into a realization of their status as property."[13]

As we can see from the fact that she was speaking at a convention for women's rights, Harper was active in this movement as well as advocating for abolition and, after the Civil War, "radical reconstruction" in the South. Like Frederick Douglass, she was willing to prioritize black voting rights above those of women. She said: "When it was a question of race, I let the lesser question of sex go. But the white women all go for sex." As for her own view, she "would not have the black woman put a single straw in the way, if only the men of the race could obtain what they wanted."[14] To white suffragists who were insufficiently alive to the plight of African Americans, she said: "You white women speak here of rights. I speak of wrongs. I, as a colored woman, have had in this country an education which has made me feel as if I were in the situation of Ishmael, my hand against every man, and every man's hand against me."[15]

In keeping with this, Harper was aware that voting rights were only a step toward genuine liberation. She used her eloquence to promote domestic stability in the black community: "The colored man needs something more than a vote in his hand: he needs to know the value of home life; to rightly appreciate the value of the marriage relation; to know how and to be incited to leave behind him the old shards and shells of slavery and to rise in the scale of character, wealth, and influence."[16] She was a prominent supporter of temperance, writing such poems as "The Drunkard's Child" to call attention to the dangers of alcohol. Note again her focus on the way that societal evils manifest themselves in the domestic sphere, a constant refrain of her remarks on racial injustice, as when she said that failure in reconstruction would lead to "trouble in every parlor and every kitchen."[17] All this may suggest that, like Maria Stewart, she focused mostly on moral exhortation. But she also had an eye on economic policy. She was a determined proponent of the "free produce" movement, a campaign to boycott goods made with slave labor. In this context, she perceptively asked: "Could slavery exist long if it did not sit on a commercial throne?"[18]

Frances Harper and Sojourner Truth make for an interesting comparison. They had similar political aims, moved in the same circles, and both appeared at women's rights events. But we've seen how reports about Truth constantly called attention to her humble origins and unpolished speech. By contrast, a newspaper account of a lecture by Harper said that she "has a splendid articulation, uses chaste, pure language, has a pleasant voice, and allows no one to tire of hearing her."[19] Where Sojourner Truth was known for her performance of folksy, if politically pointed, songs, Harper was known for her artful poetry. It's hard to imagine Truth alluding, as Harper did, to the dying words of Goethe, or the political situation in contemporary Russia. Most obviously, where Truth was famously illiterate, Harper was above all a literary figure, an author of such productions as a book-length poem about Moses, whom she considers the "first disunionist" for his leadership of the slave population in Egypt.

Interestingly, whereas Truth was regularly quoted by others in "dialect," represented by unorthodox spellings and grammar, Harper used this device herself as an author in works like *Sketches of Southern Life*, a collection of poetry and a short story published in 1872, and her novel, *Iola Leroy*, which appeared in 1892.[20] Harper was, in fact, long thought of as the first African American woman to write a novel, until the rediscovery in the 1980s of Harriet Wilson's *Our Nig*, from 1859. Scholars have credited Harper with employing in her narrative writings a relatively naturalistic way of using spelling to convey real black speech, and with varying this technique from one character to another. She also shows characters doing what we would nowadays call "code switching," that is, varying between dialect and Standard English.[21]

Ultimately, then, while Truth and Harper can both be thought of as (among other things) "philosophers," this is true in rather different senses. We saw that contemporaries did call Truth a "philosopher," meaning by this that she fell into a long tradition of figures who critique hypocrisy and moral and political failings by the example of their own life and through barbed wit. A striking parallel from the ancient world would be Socrates, whom Oruka, to mention him again, singled out as a major philosopher who did not write anything. Or, even better, we might think of Diogenes the Cynic, who called his society to account through face-to-face confrontation rather than writing. Actually, at one point, the resonances with Diogenes are almost uncanny. A report about Truth says of her that, "cosmopolitan in her nature, she calls the world her home" (203), just as Diogenes famously proclaimed that he was a "citizen of the world."

Harper was far more didactic and systematic in her approach, and thus more the sort of figure we usually associate with philosophy. She frequently articulated the fundamental principles underlying the causes for which she campaigned. She explained the need to educate and liberate women by saying: "It is one of women's most sacred rights to have the privilege of forming the symmetry and adjusting the mental balance of an immortal mind."[22] Her remarks on political philosophy include such observations as this one: "A government that can protect its citizens and will not, is a vicious government; a government that would protect its citizens and cannot, is a weak government." In her 1891 speech, "Duty to Dependent Races," she sounds very much like a modern-day liberal theorist when she argues that "the strongest nation on earth cannot afford to deal unjustly towards its weakest and feeblest members."

It was precisely these contrasting styles that made both women such formidable figures in the struggle against oppression. We've seen how Frederick Douglass seems to have been uneasy in the face of Sojourner Truth, because of what another contemporary called her "humorous, commonsense style" (173). Another activist was more explicit in admitting her reluctance to appear alongside Harper, conceding that "wisdom obliges me to keep out of the way, as with her prepared lectures there would be no chance of a favorable comparison."[23] But the woman who said that was no slouch herself. Her name was Mary Ann Shadd and she published her newspaper, the *Provincial Freeman*, in Canada, where she emigrated and to which she encouraged other African Americans to go as well. Alongside Harper, the example of Shadd will make it clear that the contributions of black women in this period were not just Truth and nothing but the Truth.

41

GREAT WHITE NORTH

Emigration to Canada

Oh Canada! For many Americans, it's a place of shivering cold, but also the metaphorical warmth of polite people, clean streets, pristine wilderness, and universal health care. Every four years, right after each presidential election, there are Americans who threaten to emigrate to Canada. Most don't actually do it, though some Americans do move there every year and there were modest but noticeable spikes in these numbers following victories by George W. Bush and Donald Trump. The Vietnam War also saw large numbers of Americans escaping to Canada, evading the draft or deserting the US Army. Some of those emigrants were African American and they were, in a sense, carrying on an important tradition. In the nineteenth century, the Underground Railroad famously brought escaped slaves to Canada. Even further back, there was the arrival in Nova Scotia of the Black Loyalists following the Revolutionary War. A similar influx followed the War of 1812, when, once again, the British promised freedom to those who would join their side of the conflict. Those who came to Nova Scotia at that time became known as the Black Refugees. At the times of these previous migrations to Nova Scotia, slavery was actually legal in Canada. But, as in the northern states and in contrast to the American South, the Caribbean, and certain parts of Latin America, slavery was never that significant to the economic development of the French and British colonies that became Canada. From the 1790s onward, gradual abolition through statutes and judicial decisions limited slavery. By the time it was abolished throughout the British empire in 1834, there were very few slaves still left in Canada.[1]

So Canada was attractive for those seeking freedom, even before 1834. Peter Williams Jr. raised money to help a large group of African Americans who left Cincinnati, Ohio, after a major riot attacking black residents there in 1829. This group established the Wilberforce colony in what was then the colony of Upper

Canada, now the province of Ontario. We previously discussed Williams' repudiation of the American Colonization Society, despite his earlier support for his friend Paul Cuffe's plans for bringing people to Africa (Chapter 32). As it turns out, he expressed that opposition to the ACS at a meeting for the benefit of the Wilberforce colony. Thus, while an important theme of his speech was that African Americans should not have to leave the United States, he also argued that "God, in his good providence, has opened for such of us as may choose to leave these States an asylum in the neighboring British province of Canada."[2] Emigration to Canada reached its zenith in the 1850s, in the wake of the passage of the Fugitive Slave Law. With northern states thereby becoming less safe for escaped slaves and even for those born free, thousands of fugitives and emigrants poured into Canada during the time between the law's passage in 1850 and the sparking of the Civil War in 1861.

One of the most famous was Mary Ann Shadd, also known by her married name, Mary Ann Shadd Cary. This remarkably accomplished woman had interesting ideas on securing freedom through emigration, as did another figure who spent time in Canada in the 1850s. He was Samuel Ringgold Ward, already mentioned as a classmate and cousin of Henry Highland Garnet at the African Free School. The two of them will be our main characters in what follows, but we'll also revisit the work of Martin Delany. As we noted, he too spent time living in Canada in the 1850s. Because he saw relocation to Canada, and what African Americans ought to do once they were there, quite differently than Shadd and Ward, Delany will offer us an illuminating contrast.

Shadd remains a figure often commemorated in Canada, especially during Black History Month, and is best remembered today for editing her own newspaper, the *Provincial Freeman*. When it first appeared, though, and for the first year or so of its existence, its editor was identified as Ward, who had previous experience editing newspapers in the United States. From the beginning, this attribution masked the fact that Shadd was the true editor. Eventually the charade was dropped and she was acknowledged as the sole force behind the paper. Later, she would again claim to be handing over the reins to another male editor. Rather ironically, it was in an editorial written to mark this supposed change in leadership that she reflected on her own pioneering role: "To colored women, we have a word—we have 'broken the editorial ice,' whether willingly or not, for your class in America; so go to Editing, as many of you as are willing, and able, and as soon as you may if you think you are ready."[3] Even after this apparent farewell, Shadd continued to preside over the *Provincial Freeman*.

But it will not be her tireless journalistic efforts that occupy our attention here. Instead we'll be focusing on her most famous piece of writing, a pamphlet she published less than a year after arriving in Canada. Its title is so long that in northern Canada, you could start reading it before sunrise on a winter's day and not finish until after sunset: *A Plea for Emigration; or Notes of Canada West, in Its Moral, Social, and Political Aspect: with Suggestions Respecting Mexico, West Indies, and Vancouver's Island, for the Information of Colored Emigrants*. We'll shorten this to *A Plea for Emigration*, although scholars sometimes use *Notes of Canada West* as the short title.[4] Where, you may ask, is "Canada West"? It is what we now call Ontario,[5] while "Canada East" was the name of modern-day Quebec. In keeping with the usage of the time Shadd refers to them together as "the Canadas."

Shadd herself had only just recently chosen to become one of the "colored emigrants" of her title. She was born free in Delaware in 1823 and had been working as a teacher when she journeyed to Toronto to attend a black-organized anti-slavery convention in September of 1851. She was so impressed that she decided not to return. She moved to Windsor and opened a school, receiving support from the American Missionary Association. It was while living and teaching in Windsor that she had her *Plea for Emigration* published in Detroit, in June of 1852. The little book's primary aim is to acquaint the reader with all possibly relevant facts about Canada as a destination for African Americans who seek to escape the United States: climate, soil, crops, the price of land, opportunities for employment, places of worship, education, political rights, and so on. If Tim Hortons donuts had existed at the time, you can be sure she would have mentioned them. Shadd also evaluates Mexico, the British colonies of the Caribbean, and other alternatives (including Vancouver Island, which would, of course, eventually become part of Canada). She concludes that Canada West offers the most suitable home for black emigrants. In the book's final paragraph, she declares that extensive emigration by free black Americans will do more to fight slavery than staying in the United States. She depicts it as a form of peaceful protest that is more dignified than what she derides as "a miserable scampering from state to state," seeking "crumbs of freedom" that pro-slavery forces may sweep away at any moment (44).

We find a similar, but in some ways less optimistic assessment in Samuel Ringgold Ward's *Autobiography of a Fugitive Negro*, published in London in 1855. Ward was born enslaved in Maryland in 1817 but was only 2 years old when his parents escaped north to freedom. A licensed preacher, he gained fame as an abolitionist lecturer before the event that resulted in his leaving the United States for Canada: the Jerry rescue. A man named William "Jerry" Henry had been arrested in Syracuse, New York, and was in danger of being sent back to slavery in accordance with the Fugitive Slave Law. A mob, encouraged by Ward and others, stormed the building where he was being held and liberated him. Ward had already been planning to move to Canada anyway, but, thanks to his participation in the Jerry rescue, it was indeed as a "fugitive" from the law that he settled in Toronto in October of 1851.

Ward quickly got involved with the Anti-Slavery Society of Canada, lecturing and organizing branches of the organization in various places in Canada West. Then, in the spring of 1853, the Society sent Ward to lecture and raise money in England. His stay there lengthened well beyond what was initially projected. It lasted about two years and it is during this time that he wrote his autobiography. He never returned to Canada, moving instead to Jamaica, where he spent the remainder of his life. The fact that Ward wrote in England, possibly aware that he would not return to Canada, is pertinent in contrasting his discussion of the black Canadian experience with Shadd's. Given their collaboration, it's no surprise that they agreed on many things. Both viewed Canada as a land of legal equality ennobled by the values of British aristocratic culture. Both called for black emigrants in Canada to integrate with white Canadians, rather than build separate communities. They were on the same side of certain intellectual and practical controversies among black leadership in Canada. But where Shadd treats coming to Canada as an escape not just from slavery but from anti-black racism itself, Ward identifies such racism as a common and systemic problem in Canada.

Shadd first addresses the question of Canadian racism in the section of her *Plea for Emigration* dealing with labor and trades. She claims that in Canada all trades are "patronized by whomsoever carries on—no man's complexion affecting his business." Then in the same paragraph, she provides an explanation of Canada's superiority: "There is no degraded class to identify him with, therefore every man's work stands or falls according to merit, not as is his color" (16). This comment reveals much about Shadd's understanding of the nature of racism and how it operates in the United States. The very existence in the United States of chattel slavery as a legally condoned, institutionalized practice results in the general stigmatizing of black people, no matter their status as free or slave. For Shadd, then, racism is truly systemic, a matter of interlocking parts in which one part—specifically, slavery in the South—affects other parts, creating a society in which African Americans cannot expect to be judged fairly.

By contrast, she considers the situation in Canada to be completely free of racism. She tells us, for example, that her aim is to "set forth the advantage of a residence in a country, in which chattel slavery is not tolerated, and prejudice of color has no existence whatever" (16–17). When she does acknowledge that differential and negative treatment of black people may be encountered in Canada, she treats it as non-systemic in character. Thus she writes: "Colored persons have been refused entertainment in taverns, (invariably of an inferior class), and on some boats distinction is made; but in all cases, it is that kind of distinction that is made between poor foreigners and other passengers, on the cars and steamboats of the Northern States" (35). So if you're a black person being discriminated against in Canada, you can at least comfort yourself that it's because you're poor, or from another country, not because you're black. Shadd claims that Canadian social relations are structured by an aristocratic, class-based differentiation derived from "the old country," as opposed to racism: "There is no approach to Southern chivalry, nor the sensitive democracy prevalent at the North; but there is an aristocracy of birth, not of skin, as with Americans" (35).

Jane Rhodes writes in her biography of Shadd that *A Plea for Emigration* is "an unabashed propaganda tract that exaggerated the benefits of the Canadian haven while ignoring many endemic problems."[6] There is, in fact, a tricky challenge of interpretation here. It is hard to avoid concluding that Shadd downplayed difficulties faced by black emigrants on the basis of race, but should we see this as a conscious strategy or the more innocent flaw of naivety? Is it better to accuse her of knowingly deceiving readers by painting a pretty picture that does not match what she saw? Or is it better to scale down our appreciation of her intellect by deeming her insufficiently aware of what was going on? In any case, even if we must be wary of Shadd's tendency to anticipate Tim Hortons, by sugar-coating things quite a bit, she makes some philosophical observations about race and racism that are worth considering.

Commenting on how black emigrants should prepare themselves mentally for what they will encounter in Canada, she writes: "It is an easy matter to make out a case of prejudice in any country. We naturally look for it, and the conduct of many is calculated to cause unpleasant treatment, and to make it difficult for well-mannered persons to get comfortable accommodations. There is a medium between servility and presumption, that recommends itself to all persons of common sense, of whatever ranks or complexion; and if colored people would avoid the two extremes, there would be but few cases of prejudices to complain of in Canada" (35). Shadd's prediction about the rarity of prejudice is overly optimistic, to be sure, but it's not so easy to dismiss her point that we can make mistakes about how we are being treated. Not every perceived case of race-based unfairness is genuinely unfair, or race based. Just as a servile disposition renders one shamefully willing to put up with racist incidents, a tendency toward presumption can result in unnecessary confrontations over wholly imagined slights. Shadd insightfully suggests that we need to aim for an Aristotelian golden mean between the excess of presumption and the deficiency of servility.

Ward, by contrast, thinks that Canadian racism is far from rare. He discusses this in the context of explaining the usefulness of anti-slavery activism in Canada.

Having discussed factors related to Canada's shared border with the United States (such as how often pro-slavery Yankees come into Canada to visit or even settle), Ward turns to "some more unwelcome facts." There is, first, "pro-slavery feeling" on the part of "British-born subjects," and second, the more general problem of Canadian "Negro-hate" (99).[7] (His use of this phrase calls to our attention that the term "racism" would not enter common usage until the 1930s.) Some of those who openly supported slavery in Canada were, he says, "heretofore planters in the West Indies," still bitter about abolition in the British empire (99). He also speaks of Canadians who have familial or economic ties to the slaveholding American South, or even just fond memories of travel to the South. Both of these points place Canada in a larger global context. If Shadd was right to define racism in purely systemic terms, she should not have overlooked the systemic ties binding Canada to the broader social context of the English-speaking world.

Ward begins the second part of his discussion with a surprising claim: "Canadian Negro-haters are the very worst of their class" (101). He proceeds to describe a number of cases of discrimination in public accommodations, including his own humiliating experiences in Hamilton in December of 1851. He was denied a seat on a horse-drawn bus, and when he nonetheless managed to reach his hotel, he was refused a room. "Two cases like these," claims Ward, "I have not known in the States for twenty years" (103). Ward's frankness about racism in Canada seems to make him the polar opposite of Shadd. Like her, though, he picks up on the importance of class relations in Canada. For him, social hierarchy provides a context for understanding Canadian racism. "Negro-hate" abounds, he tells us, among "the lowest, the least educated, of all the white population" (101). Their racism, according to Ward, is directly related to their ignorance: they "know but little, next to nothing, of what are liberal enlightened views and genteel behaviour" (101). For all the discrimination he's seen north of the border, none of it involved a perpetrator who could claim the title of "gentleman": "Either that class do not participate in the feeling, or their good sense and good taste and good breeding forbid its appearance" (106). Perhaps the elite do internally harbor racist sentiments, but they are also endowed with enough self-restraint not to let those sentiments undermine their good manners.

This might look like the nineteenth-century version of Americans marveling at how polite Canadians are: the kind of people who apologize when you walk into them on the street even though they were standing still, and then offer you a donut. But, in fact, Ward epitomizes another phenomenon, sometimes called African American Anglophilia. Ward writes: "I do not expect any one to understand how great is my pleasure in saying that, so far as my experience goes (and that is considerable), the British gentleman is a gentleman everywhere, and under all circumstances. Therefore, in every town of Canada, and especially in Toronto, I see what I saw in but extremely few and exceptional cases in the States—viz., that among gentlemen, the black takes just the place for which he is qualified, as if his color were similar to that of other gentlemen—as if there were no Negro-crushing country hard by—as if there were no Negro-hating lower classes in their midst" (106). Modern-day scholar Elisa Tamarkin has written on the love of all things British among African American abolitionists. She argues that Ward puts Anglophilia as it exists among white Americans to "novel social use," because he "offers the allure of social difference as what whites have to gain by assuming a 'British' liberality on matters of race."[8]

Tamarkin is certainly on to something here, but probably draws her point too narrowly by suggesting that white Americans constitute the primary audience for Ward's remarks. He's certainly encouraging white Americans to be more British, but also calling for white Canadians to multiply the power of their Britishness in light of the real problem of Canadian "Negro-hate." And remember, his book was published in London. So he is also calling for the British themselves to continue, and further extend, the moral leadership he ascribes to them. Ward confronts the harsh reality of racism in Canada in a way that Shadd does not, but his solution is to affirm the very aristocracy she pointed out as the only true source of discrimination in Canada.

Shadd and Ward also agree that it would be counter-productive to build specifically black institutions in Canada. In a section of *A Plea for Emigration* on religion, Shadd reports: "I was forcibly struck, when at Toronto, with the contrast the religious community there presented, to our own large body of American Christians. In the churches, originally built by the white Canadians, the presence of colored persons, promiscuously seated, elicited no comment whatever" (17). Toronto seemed to her a beautiful vision of how things could be, with racial division transcended in the context of religious worship. She is saddened by the fact that a majority of black parishioners in Canada attend predominantly or exclusively black churches. The effect of this fact on the black population, she says, is "to perpetuate ignorance, both of their true position as British subjects, and of the Christian religion in its purity" (18). A hatred of white people, born of American oppression, is nurtured within the black church when this feeling ought to have been left behind in the US.

Ward also criticizes separate black churches in Canada in his autobiography, allowing that these have been a necessity in the United States but complaining that, even there, the result was that "we were shut up to such poor ignorant teachings as our own preachers alone could give us, and our ignorance was greatly perpetuated thereby" (143). In Canada, he sees no reason to maintain such institutions. Nor are churches the only form of self-imposed segregation opposed by Ward. His point is instead a general one: "I do not agree with the policy of colored people settling themselves together, in a particular part of a town or village" (142). Surprisingly, Ward defends this point not by saying that white people can help black neighbors to improve, but rather the reverse: "Some of their white neighbors need to be taught even the first ideas of civilization, by being near to enlightened progressive colored people, such as are not few in Canada" (142). Integration is facilitated by the greater freedom for social interaction across racial lines in Canada, and is a powerful tool for defeating "Negro-hate": "After all, you can better teach by intermingling than isolation, to those who deny the Negro's capacity, what he can do" (151).

This aspect of the writings of Shadd and Ward shows us how complex were the issues surrounding what we might call black "separatism" in this period. Here we have two figures arguing explicitly for emigration from the United States, but also for integration within another white society. This suggests that we should avoid hastily equating the emigrationist movement with what would later be called "black nationalism." But for an unmistakably nationalist perspective on emigration to Canada, we can turn back to Martin Delany. In his famous 1854 speech, "Political Destiny of the Colored Race on the American Continent," he sees Canada as a kind of second best option for emigration, after the Caribbean or Central and South America.[9] For one thing, he has a foreboding that, "according to political tendency, the Canadas—as all British America—at no very distant day, are destined to come into the United States" (249). He recognizes that his prediction might be wrong, and good thing too, as it obviously was. More decisive, though, is his reflection on Canadian demographics: "The odds are against us, because the ruling element there, as in the United States, is, and ever must be white—the population now standing, in all British America, two and a half millions of whites, to but forty thousand of the black race...the difference being eleven times greater than in the United States—so that colored people might never hope for anything more than to exist politically by mere sufferance—occupying a secondary position to the whites of the Canadas" (249–50).

Near the end of his speech, Delany admits that Canada could be a good choice if moving to the Americas proves unworkable:

> should anything occur to prevent a successful emigration to the South—Central, South America and the West Indies—we have no hesitancy, rather than remain in the United States, the merest subordinates and serviles of the whites, should the Canadas still continue separate in their political relations from this country, to

recommend to the great body of our people, to remove to Canada West, where being politically equal to the whites, physically united with each other by a concentration of strength; when worse comes to worse, we may be found, not as a scattered, weak and impotent people, as we now are separated from each other throughout the Union, but a united and powerful body of freemen, mighty in politics, and terrible in any conflict which might ensue, in the event of an attempt at the disturbance of our political relations, domestic repose, and peaceful firesides. (279)

Here, as promised, we see the distinctively nationalist take on the goal of emigration that was absent in Shadd and Ward. For Delany, Canada did not offer the chance to construct a post-racial utopia. Rather, political equality there would open space for building up black strength and organization.

As we know, Delany did indeed move to Canada but then came back to the United States at the time of the Civil War. So too did Shadd, who worked as a recruitment agent for the Union Army. After the war, she moved to Washington DC, again working as a teacher and then pursuing a law degree, becoming only the second black woman to attain such a degree. But not all of the Shadds returned to the United States. Some stayed in Ontario and, among those living today, the Canadian historian Adrienne Shadd has spoken with pride about being descended from one of Mary Ann Shadd's brothers.[10] So the story of this family has continued to be bound up with that of Canada, just as, thanks to figures like Shadd and Ward, Canada will always have a place in accounts of the history of nineteenth century Africana thought.[11]

42

PILGRIM'S PROGRESS

Alexander Crummell

If you hang around with mathematicians, you may have heard the phrase "Erdős number." It refers to Paul Erdős, a prolific and brilliant Hungarian mathematician who wrote many collaborative papers. If you published something with Erdős, your Erdős number is 1; if you published something with one of his collaborators, your number is 2, and so on. Then of course there's the "Bacon number," which grew out of the game "seven degrees of Kevin Bacon." For instance, the silent movie star Buster Keaton's "Bacon number" is, rather incredibly, a mere 2. He was in a movie version of Mark Twain's *Huckleberry Finn* with Patty McCormack, who in turn was in the movie *Frost-Nixon* with, yes, Kevin Bacon. If you ask us, this is more an honor for Kevin than for Buster. In any case, the reason we bring all this up is so that we can introduce the concept of a "Crummell number," which would measure the links between black activists of the nineteenth century and Alexander Crummell.

It turns out that pretty much all those activists have a Crummell number of 1. You already know that he was a childhood friend of Henry Highland Garnet, whose life Crummell described in a touching eulogy. We also mentioned that the two of them were classmates of Samuel Ringgold Ward at the African Free School. Moving beyond what we have already mentioned, though, the abolitionist periodical *Freedom's Journal*, published by John Russwurm and Samuel Cornish, was launched in the Crummell household, thanks to the fact that Alexander's father, Boston Crummell, himself moved in activist circles. Later on, Alexander Crummell moved to Liberia, where he lived for about twenty years; there, he was visited by Martin Delany, and served as commissioner alongside Edward Blyden, whom we'll discuss in a coming chapter. Once he was back in the US, Crummell debated Frederick Douglass in person and had Maria W. Stewart as one of the parishioners in his church. In the context of the American Negro Academy, which began under Crummell's leadership in 1897, he was a mentor to W.E.B. Du Bois, a figure of immense importance whom we will introduce by the end of this book and then discuss much more in the sequel volume. If we bend the rules a bit, we can even link Crummell to an eighteenth century figure, as it seems like a young Crummell probably wrote a piece using the name "Ignatius Sancho" as a pseudonym.[1]

So who was this astoundingly well-connected man? Well, he was born free in 1819.[2] His father had been a slave, after being kidnapped as a young teenager in the region that became Sierra Leone.[3] He was ordained as an Episcopalian priest but fell afoul of his local bishop, who treated him with racist disdain, leading to years of conflict between the two. Then in 1848, he traveled to England. This trip may initially have been for the sake of church fund-raising but he stayed on to study at Cambridge, before moving to Liberia in 1853. Here he continued his work as a preacher, seeing his life's work as bringing Christian "civilization" to the native Africans, whom he frequently called "pagans" and "heathens."[4] Depending on his mood and audience, he could be cheerfully optimistic or deeply pessimistic about this project, and about the whole experience of living in Africa. He and his wife suffered from poor health and the death of a young child, and Crummell was frustrated by his inability to inspire audiences as well as by conflict with church and government authorities.

He seems not to have been an easy man to get on with, something admitted in Du Bois' moving posthumous portrait of Crummell in his famous book, *The Souls of Black Folk*. Du Bois spoke of his "unbending righteousness," something that Crummell would probably have taken as a compliment. He once said that he was pleased to be called "a little too rigid": "it is in evidence that I tolerated no iniquity, and that I rebuked depravity" (*Destiny* 41). But Du Bois portrayed him as a rather tragic figure, an isolated man who "worked alone, with so little human sympathy." The ambiguity here may be intentional, a suggestion that Crummell both received little sympathy and had little for others.[5] On one well-known reading of his portrait of Crummell, Du Bois critically exposes the way that, estranged and disappointed by racist treatment, Crummell turned this feeling against his own people. When his high-flown and classicizing preaching failed to inspire religious devotion, Du Bois suggested, Crummell could not help thinking, "what do you expect?" (*Destiny* 25). "In another age," wrote Du Bois, "he might have sat among the elders of the land in purple-bordered toga" (*Destiny* 28), but his intellectual refinement did not make him a celebrated figure. Similar remarks were made in his own lifetime. Frederick Douglass ruefully remarked that the homespun approach of Sojourner Truth meant she was "more readily quoted" than a learned man such as Crummell. The bishop of Liberia, who sparred with Crummell almost as much as his counterpart back in New York, remarked with dry understatement that he was no "popular preacher."[6]

Like Kevin Bacon's movie career, then, Crummell's career as a religious leader provoked mixed reviews. He was admired for his learning. But his Cambridge education, which gave him a mastery of classical languages, and his constant harping on the value of "civilization," could also make him seem an elitist who was out of touch with the real needs of both Africans and African Americans. He would have vigorously rejected this charge. For one thing, that same education gave him special insight into the problems faced by the victims of slavery and colonialism. Already as a youngster, while being educated at the Oneida Institute along with Garnet, he fell under the influence of Beriah Green.[7] Green communicated to Crummell the ideals of European Romanticism as found in the writings of figures like Johann Wolfgang von Goethe, Thomas Carlyle, and Samuel Taylor Coleridge. Then during his time in England, he came into contact with the still-living tradition of Cambridge Platonism, and learned moral philosophy from the works of figures like Joseph Butler and William Paley. He would soon recommend these works to students in Liberia, along with those of John Locke, Francis Bacon, and other philosophical luminaries (*Future* 42). All this gave him the basis for a metaphysical objection to racial injustice: to enslave a human is to treat an immortal, immaterial, and free soul as if it were a mere physical object to be owned.

In keeping with this, Crummell thought it an eminently practical and indeed urgent undertaking to bring black people to a higher level of moral, intellectual, and, above all, religious development. He said that under slavery, "our natures have been dwarfed and our souls shrivelled" (*Future* 75). Like David Walker and Martin Delany, Crummell believed that African Americans were unique in the level of the oppression they suffered, asserting that they were the "most forlorn and degraded race of human beings on the face of the globe" (*Destiny* 150–1). Though he insisted on the potential and innate talent of black people, he despaired over their "benighted" condition: "It seems manifest to me that, as a race in this land, we have no art; we have no science; we have no philosophy; we have no scholarship…Until we attain the role of civilization, we cannot stand up and hold our place in the world of culture and enlightenment" (*Destiny* 285).

Once in Liberia, he had a similarly bleak assessment of the situation there. "I found there great crudities, and sad anomalies. How could it have been otherwise? Was not Liberia the fruit, the product of slavery? Did not its illiteracy and its immorality spring directly from the plantation?" (*Destiny* 40). From his correspondence, we know that he often struggled with his family life, church politics, and recalcitrant parishioners in Africa. But such evidence is balanced by far sunnier passages in his writing. He assures us that he is "never disappointed" by the Liberians (*Destiny* 246), admires the natural thriftiness and sexual restraint of the people there, as well as their talent for economic trade (*Future* 227), and is amazed by their beauty. Unlike the "physical inferiority, at times repulsiveness" he claims to have seen among African Americans, the African "natives" had beautifully pure complexions, each of them "an erect, finely proportioned, well developed, symmetrical and a noble being" (*Destiny* 62-5). In a single passage that encapsulates his own mixed reviews of the African locals, he goes within a few sentences from calling the Vey people "industrious, highly intelligent, polite, and spirited" to lamenting "the deep degradation of heathenism" among them (*Destiny* 78).

But this was no contradiction. What Crummell admired in Africans, and optimistically believed was still preserved among African Americans, was immense *potential* for becoming truly "civilized" and "cultivated." What did he mean by this? That's an easy question to answer, because civilization is one of his favorite themes. At one point, he simply equates civilization with "schools and religion" (*Destiny* 168), and elsewhere defines it in part as follows: "I mean by it the clarity of the mind from the dominion of false heathen ideas. I mean by it the conscious impress of individualism and personal responsibility" (*Destiny* 272). As you'll notice, he closely associates moral and intellectual progress with religion, whose cultivation he sees as a primary duty of the state, alongside "the maintenance of justice, the progress of education, the upholding of law and order, and national growth" (*Future* 66). He thus finds little or no value in indigenous African practices and beliefs. Native religions are, he says, entirely barren of true ideas about the divine, unless these are "expressed in an obscure and distorted manner" (*Future* 20).

Even here, though, he finds grounds for optimism, since black people in general have a strong impulse toward piety: "Religious susceptibility and moral dispositions are the more marked characteristics of the Negro family, and the main point in which they differ from other races" (*Future* 302). Samuel Ajayi Crowther, a Yoruba missionary from around the same time, said that, when confronted with Christianity, the so-called "heathens" offered the defense that "their gods were inferior deities commissioned by the great God to superintend inferior matters on earth. Having received the same from their forefathers, they insisted upon continuing their worship as they found it was good for them."[8] This should ring familiar bells, since it shows these nineteenth century missionaries already wrestling with the coherence of "diffused monotheism," which we discussed in Chapter 14. For Crummell, though, such polytheistic sentiments rang only alarm bells. Complaining of "devil worship" and the use of "fetiches" among the natives, he said simply: "They have not the Gospel. They are living without God" (*Future* 220).

He was determined that the Africans should take on Christian principles and build their whole society upon them. In doing so, Liberia could become a beacon of truth for the rest of the world, an example for others to live up to instead of an example of what can go wrong. As he puts it: "The world *needs* a higher type of true nationality than it now has: why should not we furnish it?" (*Future* 90). In his most hopeful moments, he sees this as not merely a possibility but a destiny, even a "manifest destiny" (*Future* 100), toward which Africa is tending. In another manifestation of his debt to Romanticism, he has a fundamentally progressive understanding of history, although it is important that for him, it is God's providence that is actively steering humankind toward a glorious future.[9]

Obviously, all this may strike the modern-day reader as more than a little problematic. Crummell was far from underestimating the devastation that Europeans had visited upon Africa. He writes of how, in order for European culture to exert influence upon Africa, "a whole continent has been brought to ruin," and "nations on the threshold of civilization reduced to barbarism" (*Future* 29–30, cf. *Destiny* 174). Still, he hopes, indeed demands, that Africans adopt the religion that Europeans brought them and believes that, in doing so, they will be ennobled. If there is a distinctive contribution of Africans to make in the long march of history toward progress, it is not in the production of original ideas or values. It is, rather, the ability of black people to take on good ideas and values brought to them by others. He thus extols the "flexibility of the negro character," saying that "the race is possessed of a nature more easily moulded than any other class of men."

His classically trained mind is irresistibly brought to compare black people to the ancient Greeks and Romans, who also took over the best ideas of the cultures they contacted. Like them, "the Negro, with a mobile and plastic nature, with a strong receptive faculty, seizes upon and makes over to himself, by imitation, the better qualities of others" (*Destiny* 201–2). This is in contrast to an alternative attitude articulated by Martin Delany, who once pointedly asked: "The English, French, Irish, German, Italian, Turk, Persian, Greek, Jew, and all other races, have their native or inherent peculiarities, and why not our race?" (251). Later thinkers will develop this idea of black uniqueness as something to be preserved: as we'll be seeing, noteworthy examples include Du Bois and Anna Julia Cooper, both of whom admired Crummell. For him, though, being unique held no value. What mattered was recognizing, receiving, and embodying the best that humanity had to offer.

The ability of Africans to play a cultural imitation game was shown by the speed with which the English language spread in Liberia. The significance of English to

Liberia is a topic to which Crummell devoted a whole essay. Taking stock of the language's progress, he marveled at the fact that natives who still went about naked were literate, and spoke of a man who was "a leader in Devil-dances, and yet can read and write like a scholar" (*Future* 14). Facility with English was more than useful, in his eyes. Mastering it was a crucial step toward enlightenment, because Crummell saw English as quite simply far superior to native African tongues.[10] He quotes with approval another writer who calls these languages "harsh, abrupt, energetic, indistinct in enunciation, meagre in point of words" with little grammar and difficult to learn. For good measure, Crummell adds that they are "characterized by lowness of ideas," "the speech of rude barbarians," lacking "those ideas of virtue, of moral truth, and those distinctions of right and wrong with which we, all our life long have been familiar" (*Future* 19–20). Again, Crummell is not totally unaware of the appalling implications of what he's saying here. He concedes that languages spread from one culture to another through "conquest," and that English in particular "is indicative of sorrowful history" (*Future* 18). But he sees this as fitting with his overall point, since he assumes that African languages as he encounters them are only "dregs" of original, more noble ones that have been ruined through societal collapse (*Future* 50).

Now, it would be easy to get the wrong idea here and to suppose that Crummell has the rather implausible theory that some languages are, in their very grammatical structure, morally superior to others. That would go pretty well with his acceptance of the widespread but false notion that some natural languages have "less grammar" than others. (By the way, if they are grammatically so rudimentary, why are they harder to learn?) His view, however, seems to be the more plausible one that languages preserve within them the history and values of the people who speak them. Thus English is full of expressions that have to do with morality and liberty, which he takes to be deeply ingrained in British culture. It is, he says at one point, "the language of freedom" (*Future* 23). Even slaves in the American South have imbibed the value of freedom as they matured, simply by growing up as native speakers (*Future* 51). No less important for Crummell is, of course, the intimate connection of English with (Protestant) Christianity. He speaks of the importance of the English Bible and says that there is a kind of "identity" between this language and religion itself (*Future* 28). So here Crummell signals his agreement with other nineteenth century theorists of language who were convinced that language shapes thought. One could even say that, despite his disdain for native African tongues, he is not that far from the approach of some of the ethnophilosophers we discussed earlier. Compare, for example, Alexis Kagame's attempt to extract philosophical commitments from the very vocabulary and syntax of Bantu languages (Chapter 12).

To better understand Crummell's ideas about race, we can turn to another essay, published in 1889, called "The Race-Problem in America."[11] Crummell begins by seeking in the past for what he calls "laws of population" in order to predict what may come of America's problems of racial conflict and domination.[12] He concludes that history, from the relations of peoples in ancient Mesopotamia to the encounter between Europeans and indigenous peoples in the Americas, displays not one clear pattern but rather a range of possible outcomes. The races may mingle together and the difference between them will disappear, or there may be conflict resulting in the expulsion or eradication of one of the races, or they may remain in the same place and achieve peace while nevertheless remaining separate. The first option of mingling together he rejects as a possibility for the black and white races in the United States, which may remind us of Martin Delany's claim that pure races can never be eliminated through interbreeding. Crummell's argument is less perplexing: he claims that intermixing has almost always been the result of white men raping black women, and that the free black population will never willingly undergo "amalgamation" with the majority race.

Still, he is, as much as Delany, committed to the notion that differences between races are of divine origin. He defines a race as "a compact, homogeneous population of one blood, ancestry, and lineage," and as this suggests, he thinks that races can be compared to families, and even *identified* as large families (*Problem* 10–11). They have every right to hold on to their unique identity, just as smaller families perpetuate themselves. Since America is going to continue to have the two separate races, then, the "problem" becomes the distinctively "moral" one of how they will live together in "amity" (*Problem* 12). To his mind, there can be only one answer: "the complete and entire civil and political equality of all the peoples of this land." The fulfillment of this goal through the democratic participation of all, instead of the oligarchic domination of one race over the other, will demonstrate "God's hand in history" (*Problem* 14).

Here we can see Crummell, now late in his career, adapting ideas he developed in his years in Liberia for use in an American context. His faith in moral and religious progress manifests as the expectation that African Americans will form an increasingly enlightened group of citizens within the wider culture. Crummell's theological understanding of history remains broadly the same, but his political objective is now very different: no longer an independent nation of native and émigré Africans on African soil, but a "nation within a nation" that is the United States (he uses this phrase at *Destiny* 257). Because he remains a fundamentally future-oriented thinker, he encourages the emancipated African Americans to stop lamenting the wrongs of slavery, to look ahead and not back.

It was this that brought him into conflict with Frederick Douglass in a debate at Harper's Ferry in 1885. Douglass thought it was important to continue reflecting on the history of slavery, so as to understand and remedy its lingering effects, in order to achieve the ultimate goal of integrating into white society. Crummell's advice was instead, in effect: let's get over the sufferings of the past and strive toward a better tomorrow. Wilson Moses phrases the dispute nicely in his intellectual biography of Crummell: "Douglass's program was for black people to remember slavery and to forget that they were black. Crummell's was for them to remember that they were black and forget slavery."[13]

Douglass was also impatient with Crummell's rather disdainful attitude toward uneducated African Americans. But it is questionable whether Crummell really deserves his reputation for elitist snobbery. Both in Liberia and in the United States, he emphasized that it would be foolish to promote advanced learning at the cost of practical skills which might lead to commercial prosperity. It would be pointless to teach the "heathens" of Africa to read Latin and Greek and leave them too "delicate" for manual labor. And we should remember that the great European scholars were always men of action, as well as men of letters (*Future* 79–80). As he elsewhere remarks, "a people may have learning and yet be poor, degraded and vicious" (*Destiny* 207). So the focus should not be on, for instance, getting universities to admit more black students, but on vocational skills and of course the moral character Crummell likes to call "manhood" (for the contrast with mere book learning, see *Destiny* 251). He was, of course, the last person to disdain higher learning, having benefited from it himself. He thought that his much vaunted "civilization" would be instilled in the black population above all by "scholars and thinkers" (*Destiny* 287). One of the more vituperative passages in his writings (though there is plenty of competition for that title) attacks an author who dared to suggest that "the kind of education the Negro should receive should not be very refined nor classical, but adapted to his present condition." Crummell's response: "As though there is to be no future for the Negro!" (*Destiny* 294).

43

PLANTING THE SEEDS

James Africanus Beale Horton

As no one who lived through the early 2020s will need to be told, there are few factors that shape human history as much as disease. Many an army has suffered more deaths from sickness than from the enemy, and many a leader has died or been incapacitated at a crucial moment. This particular horseman of the apocalypse is fond of riding out when populations come together, as they constantly do in today's globalized world, and as happened more suddenly in earlier times. We have made mention of the mass deaths caused by infection when the Europeans invaded what they called the New World, and the horrific mortality rate of enslaved Africans in places like Haiti were due to disease as well as to overwork and sadistic punishment by the masters. Of course, Europeans were affected too. The soldiers of French armies sent to subdue Haiti considered the assignment to be tantamount to a death sentence, and colonizers sent to Africa itself frequently fell ill. Nor were newcomers to Africa rendered immune by an African lineage. We just saw, for instance, how Alexander Crummell and his family suffered from sicknesses after coming to Liberia.

Hence the subtitle of a work called *Physical and Medical Climate and Meteorology of the West Coast of Africa*, published in 1867 by James Africanus Beale Horton. After the already lengthy title, the book's cover adds the promise: *with Valuable Hints to Europeans for the Preservation of Health in the Tropics*. This is also the title of the final chapter of the work, which suggests a range of "rules" and "precautions" to be taken by European colonizers. There are recommendations about clothing, food and drink, sleeping arrangements—here Horton suggests using mosquito netting, a better idea than he could have suspected—and also ethical conduct. "The passions" must be regulated, because "a strict moral principle" such as observed by Christians is liable to keep one healthy in body as well as soul.[1] Horton knew whereof he spoke, being both a doctor and, frequently, a patient who contracted many ailments in the time of his service with the British Army thanks to poor sanitation in the military camps.[2] Eventually he was promoted to the rank of Surgeon General. He studied at King's College London and then Edinburgh, where he wrote a thesis for his medical degree on the *Medical Topography of the West Coast of Africa with Sketches of its Botany*.

But Horton was not a European. He was African, and proudly so, as we can see from his decision to include "Africanus" as part of his name on the title page of his Edinburgh thesis and subsequent publications. He was born in 1835 in Sierra Leone to parents who were recaptives. As we explained in Chapter 28, after the end of the British slave trade, British ships patrolled the West African coast and liberated captured Africans, with many of these so-called recaptives settling in Sierra Leone. Horton first studied at Fourah Bay College in Freetown, and was one of three outstanding students from there who were sent to study medicine in Britain. It was hoped that these students would be resistant, if not impervious, to the diseases rampant among British soldiers serving in the African tropics. The regiments in which Horton served were averaging something like a 15 percent attrition rate. But as shown by the publication of his study on *Physical and Medical Climate*, Horton was not satisfied simply to dispense quinine and sound advice to his military colleagues. He was a scientist, who made careful observations of the plant life, soil, epidemiology, and climate of West Africa. In keeping with the theories current in his day, he assumed that such diseases as malaria were caused by poisonous vapors emitted, for example, by moldering vegetation.[3]

He also seems to have applied his interest in environmental factors to a topic that has been of more central concern to us in this book: race. For this we need to turn to his most famous work, *West African Countries and Peoples, British and Native*, which was published only a year after the treatise on climate and adopts the same empirical frame of mind.[4] Again, the subtitle is telling. Or actually subtitles, because there are two of them. The first promises a discussion of the *Requirements Necessary for Establishing That Self Government Recommended by the Committee of the House of Commons, 1865*. We'll come back to this shortly. The second subtitle is more pithy: *and a Vindication of the African Race*. This vindication avoids to a great extent the essentializing approach that we've seen in other nineteenth century thinkers. Horton is notable for his emphasis on the malleability of races, the way that they are affected by the environment and can change over generations, just like animals do (35, 51).

Admittedly, Horton does make comments about race that may strike us as strange and, indeed, just empirically false. When it comes to mixed-race people, his views are themselves mixed. He pronounces them "less healthy and less energetic" (29) but also rises to their defense by refuting claims that they are never upstanding members of society (54). Weighing in on a topic also broached by Martin Delany and Alexander Crummell, he assumes that mixed-race people will inevitably "either merge into one or other races (black or white), or gradually die out" (271). But aside from this dubious claim, he generally insists on what he calls the "unity of the races," with factors like climate explaining apparently deep-seated differences (56). As for skin color, he discards it as basically irrelevant, since black skin is just caused by the same pigment that explains freckles and tanned skin in white people who have been in the sun (47). With respect to features such as moral tendencies and intellectual capacity, humans do not differ much if at all in these respects, and it is only their upbringing that leads to the wide variation we see in peoples of the globe.

That's the good news. The bad news is that many factors have conspired to make the environment in Africa a disastrous one for its inhabitants. Having emphasized the unhealthiness of the tropics in his work on physical climate, he now adds that the cultural climate of Africa has led to all manner of spiritual maladies. He is particularly horrified by the practice of domestic slavery, that is, the enslaving of Africans by other Africans, which he sees as antithetical to "civilization." "Where the one exists," he says, "it is impossible for the other to thrive" (117), and he identifies domestic slavery as "in every way the most destructive element in the Gold Coast politics" (259). Another problem is traditional African religion, which for Horton is nothing but "heathenism." Between these factors, the effects of constant warfare, and exploitation by European powers, the Africans are in Horton's judgment "rude and barbarous," in a "primitive state of ignorance and poverty."

Even this is an improvement, though, as the indigenous people were in "a state of utter barbarism" until the British came along (2, 5, 28). In Horton's estimation, the benevolent influence of the British has brought many Africans to a condition of "semi-civilization." He is particularly impressed by the progress in his native Sierra Leone: "it cannot be shown in the world's history that any people with so limited advantages has shown such results within fifty years" (26). This of course supports his more abstract philosophical point, namely that human nature is the same everywhere, so that even a few years of benevolent oversight and education can work wonders. Sure, the African natives may be backward and brutish, but this was no less true of the British themselves in ancient history, before the Romans brought civilization (28, 30). This allows him to reach the conclusion: "I claim the existence of the attribute of a common humanity in the African or negro race...the amount of moral and intellectual endowments exhibited him, as originally conferred by nature, is the same, or nearly so, as that found amongst the European nations, and it is an incontrovertible logical inference that the difference arises entirely from the influences of external circumstances. Truly *natura una et communis omnium est*" (29).

Since this was written in the nineteenth century, he doesn't bother to translate the Latin, so we will: "nature is one and common to all."

In developing this thesis, Horton was engaging in a polemic against racist pseudoscientists, men like Carl Vogt, who described the typical African as having a short neck and "pendulous belly," "which affords a glimmer of the ape beneath the human envelope" (43). Horton laughs this out of court, saying that of the thousands of Africans he's met, not one of them fit the grotesque description offered by Vogt. Another sparring partner was the travel writer Richard Burton, whom Horton termed "the most determined African hater" on the basis of his luridly racist book *Wanderings in West Africa*.[5] Indeed, we can think of Horton's own book on West Africa as a response to Burton's, Horton offering careful observation where Burton aimed at entertaining a white audience who shared his own "fiendish hatred against the negro" (iii).

Despite this, Horton has plenty of negative things to say about the specific groups who populate West Africa. He announces at the outset that he will restrict himself to the British colonies of Sierra Leone, Lagos, and Gambia, as well as the American settlement of Liberia. He is impressed by the industry and restraint of some of the communities in these regions, but others, he deems lazy and corrupt. So, for instance, he draws a stark contrast between the Wolof in the Gambia, who he says are "spendthrift" and hedonistic, and the Yoruba and Igbo receptives, who are the reverse (75–6). It is perhaps not a coincidence that both of Horton's parents were Igbo. Still, the fact that Horton is so sensitive to variation and diversity among the native population itself distinguishes him from racist authors like Vogt and Burton, and also from more sympathetic writers who painted all West Africans with a broad brush. A case in point would be Alexander Crummell. As we saw, Crummell ascribed a "mobile and plastic nature" to "the Negro" in general. Horton approvingly quotes Crummell on this very topic, and agrees that among Africans we can find a "passion" for imitating others. But tellingly, he ascribes this trait not to *all* Africans, or even all West Africans, but to the Igbo people specifically (176).

So we can give Horton credit for grasping a point we made frequently in the first part of this book, namely, that it is questionable to generalize about African cultures. In fact, Horton sees that this is true for some of the same topics we discussed regarding precolonial African thought, making remarks that seem startlingly prescient in light of those discussions. For instance, he notes the variation between African religions and credits the Igbo, again, with the "monotheism" that so many later authors detected in African tradition. Like Equiano before him, Horton hypothesizes that the similarity between Igbo and Abrahamic religious beliefs may be no coincidence, since it is possible that a lost tribe of Israel found its way to West Africa, so that Igbo beliefs are thus effectively a form of Judaism (183).

Other ideas mentioned by Horton will ring further bells for us.[6] Like John Mbiti, he discusses limitations on the conception of time. Lacking literacy, the peoples he describes depend on orally transmitted tales and thus "have no history," so that "successive events once out of sight are for ever lost" (4). He reports on theories of personhood, describing ideas of reincarnation in which a person's self can go into a human or animal body (186). Horton is also sensitive to the differences between African languages spoken in close proximity to each other. While discussing the Gold Coast, or present-day Ghana, he distinguishes between the Twi spoken by the Akan and the languages of the Ga and the Ewe peoples, noting that these are "distinct languages, about as different as German, English, and French, if not more so, and each is again subdivided into different dialects" (112). He furthermore hypothesizes that while the Akan tongue has influenced the other two, they are actually more closely related to Yoruba.

Here Horton touches on a topic that was being researched around this same time by Samuel Ajayi Crowther, whom we mentioned briefly in the last chapter. At a young age, Crowther was taken in the domestic slave trade decried by Horton and sold to Portuguese buyers, but he was liberated by the British and educated in Sierra Leone at the Fourah Bay College, where Horton also studied. Crowther became a pioneering linguist and helped to produce the first Bible in the Yoruba language, which may very well have been the first translation of the whole Bible into a sub-Saharan African language by a native speaker. He also published a text on the vocabulary of this language and the first book ever published on the Igbo tongue.

Balancing out Horton's openness to the diversity of West African cultures, there is the undeniable fact that he saw much good in the colonial enterprise that we nowadays take to have been inimical to those cultures. When the British annexed Lagos, he said, "we must unhesitatingly state that it was the greatest blessing that could have happened."[7] As a member of the British armed forces, he did not shrink from defending violence in the cause of colonial power, stating that "a little despotism is absolutely necessary" for governing a "semi-barbarous race," as long as "the aim is to bring up the governed rapidly in industrial pursuits, education, and general social condition." Ultimately, he thought the British had done far more good than harm. While they had sometimes committed excessive violence, this was because they understood that fear was needed to keep control over a restless native population riven by internal divisions (159).

This brings us back to the first of the two subtitles of Horton's study of West Africa, which promises a treatment of the prospects for self-governance in this region of the world. He praises the British government for its stated aim of gradually withdrawing from its colonies, with the exception of Sierra Leone, and quotes from the minutes of a House of Commons committee on African affairs. In this testimony, it's admitted that it might be fifty years or even a full century until the Africans are capable of political independence (70), but Horton is more optimistic. Radical reforms of the kind he proposes could make it possible in "less than a quarter of a century" to install in a place like the Gambia "an enlightened native king, chosen by universal suffrage" (86). He envisions a gradual transition in which monarchs are put in overall command over the lesser potentates who currently style themselves "kings," something Horton finds somewhat ridiculous since some of them reign over nothing more than a single village (131, 150). In another resonance with topics we discussed earlier, Horton is aware that African peoples often conduct politics in a communitarian fashion. "In matters of great interest," he reports, "in many cases a whole nation assemble together for deliberation" (2–3). So he sees native governance as being a mix of monarchical and republican tendencies. Nonetheless, he insists on the need for a single ruler in the decolonized state of the future in order to keep different factions in line (97). Note however that, as just mentioned, this king is to be chosen by "universal suffrage," that is, elected and not simply put in post by the departing colonial power.

Horton's plan for the British colonies may be usefully compared to that of Crummell for Liberia. The two agreed about the fundamental value of what they called "civilization," and about the need to import it into Africa from the outside. Horton says so quite explicitly: "It is impossible for a nation to civilize itself; civilization must come from abroad" (196). This side of Horton leads him to condemn indigenous cultural practices. Even the carrying of swaddled infants comes in for his harsh criticism since it supposedly deforms their bodies (57). At times, Horton can be almost comically blind to the appeal of traditional African life. He complains about the way that the men of the Gold Coast are able to spend most of their time sitting about telling stories, since they subsist on a simple diet and have no grand ambition for economic advancement. Which, of course, doesn't sound half bad, but it moves Horton to grumble, "this shows a very low scale of civilization" (107). To be fair, though, his critical attitude in this passage is in part based on the unequal distribution of labor between men and women, with more falling on the latter.

Horton also saw that a brighter future demanded more than the establishment of European habits and institutions on African soil. To flourish, the colonies needed to stop being colonies at some point. Horton provides detailed proposals for a constitution of an independent nation in West Africa, and though this is clearly based on the British model,[8] it would be put in place by the votes of Africans. Under his system, the "African element" would be free to express itself. For the same reason, he complains that under colonial rule, the involvement of natives in the Legislative

Council has been trivial, mere window dressing to disguise a British monopoly on power (200).

Paying tribute to his expertise in botany, then, we might say that Horton wanted to plant the seeds of a strong and independent West Africa. Toward this end he made numerous practical proposals, including the creation of banks and a post office, the use of vaccines, and the planting of well-chosen crops like tobacco. Along the same lines, he envisioned several projects for improving education in the colonies. He wanted to see a medical school established in Sierra Leone, and his old school, the Fourah Bay College, transformed into a full-blown university for West Africa.[9] These ideas came to nothing, as did a high school he endowed in his will, which unfortunately never materialized after his death in 1883.[10] But at least Horton died still dreaming of a better future. According to the Nigerian philosopher Olúfẹ́mi Táíwò, who has celebrated Horton, Crowther, and others as "apostles of modernity": "simply put, when we shall have devoted to his political philosophical writings the attention they deserve, we would have to conclude that Horton was also one of the pioneer political philosophers of the modern age in Africa."[11]

Which is not to say that his program for West Africa is beyond criticism. The kind of education Horton wanted to see was modeled closely on what he himself experienced in England and Scotland. Western-style education and acculturation was the only way for Africa to be lifted out of "utter darkness" and "barbarism" (ii–iii). Writing in 2000, the Kenyan author Ngũgĩ wa Thiong'o judged this a failing on Horton's part, and contrasted Horton with one of his contemporaries, who was more open-minded, able not just to catalogue and describe the languages, beliefs, and practices of indigenous Africans as Horton did, but actually to value them. This was Edward Blyden, a colleague of Crummell's in Liberia, quoted with approval by Horton concerning the great strides made by the Liberians in the most challenging of circumstances (15–16). For Ngũgĩ wa Thiong'o, Blyden represented a fundamentally different approach than that taken by Horton, especially through placing greater value on African languages. Blyden, writes Ngũgĩ, "rejects the assumptions underlying the relationship of Africa to the world which equates knowledge, modernity, modernization, civilization, progress, development—whatever the name—to an acquisition of European tongues. There are hundreds of languages in Africa and the world, each of which is a unique store of memories and thoughts and experiences which are of benefit to human life."[12] Let us turn, then, to Blyden's own career and ideas.

44

AFRICAN PERSONALITY

Edward Blyden

Eid Mubarak! This phrase, which can be translated as "blessed feast," is used by Muslims to greet each other at the end of Ramadan, a month-long time of fasting, self-reflection, and communal gathering. Edward Blyden once wrote of a trip he made to the Mandinka-dominated town of Bopolu, today part of Liberia, where he stayed for three weeks from December of 1868 to January of the following year, and during which he witnessed the observance of Ramadan. Blyden found himself enchanted by the call to prayer, which he described as a "simple and solemn melody...which, after it had ceased, still lingered pleasantly on the ear, and often, despite ourselves, drew us out to the mosque" (*CINR* 211–12).[1] He found the worship at the mosque beautiful as well, noting that the chanting of the *shahāda*, that is, the testimony that there is but one God and the Prophet Muhammad is his messenger, was not in a sad and mournful minor key, as he had found to be the case among Arabs, but a more joyful diatonic scale.

He deemed the Mandinka people he encountered "exceedingly polite and hospitable," and credited their good manners to the "restraints of their religion" (*CINR* 212). Those who could speak Arabic impressed him by how they preserved all the vowels of the classical language, as compared with the colloquial forms of Arabic he had encountered when visiting Egypt and Syria. In addition to the infinite value placed upon the Quran, Blyden found that other works of literature were appreciated in Bopolu as well, such as the *Maqāmāt* of al-Ḥarīrī, a collection of poetic stories first set down in Basra in the twelfth century. While he does not speak of encountering traditionally philosophical texts in Bopolu, he notes that others traveling through Africa have apparently met with translations of Aristotle, Plato, and the Hippocratic corpus.

We're returning to the subject of Islamic West Africa because of Blyden's interest in the Muslim faith, as expressed in his most famous book, *Christianity, Islam and the Negro Race*, first published in 1887. Two other important books by Blyden are *Liberia's Offering*, an earlier book published in 1862, and *African Life and Customs*, a later book published in 1908.[2] There is quite a noticeable change between the Blyden of 1862 and the Blyden of 1908. To draw the contrast rather simply, the Blyden of 1862 is a political nationalist, concerned with achieving the political independence of black people, and not much concerned with their cultural independence. In this sense, the early Blyden is much like Crummell or Horton. The Blyden of 1908 is a strong believer in the value of African culture and the need to preserve its distinct character, yet no longer much concerned with political independence from European rule. *Christianity, Islam and the Negro Race* is thus one of the most interesting reflections on religion in the history of Africana philosophy, and also the key text from the middle of Blyden's career, through which we can gain some understanding of how and why his perspective on political and cultural matters shifted so dramatically.[3]

We should begin, though, by saying how Blyden ended up in West Africa in the first place. He was born in 1832 to free and literate parents on the Caribbean island of St. Thomas, which is today part of the US Virgin Islands but was at that time part of the Danish West Indies. At the age of 18, with the encouragement of a mentor, he came to the United States in 1850, with the hope of attending a theological college. Finding the institutions of higher education closed to men of his race, he considered returning to St. Thomas, but instead accepted the aid of the New York Colonization Society, a subsidiary of the American Colonization Society, and went to Liberia, which was then in its third year of existence as an independent nation. There he resumed his education, quickly distinguishing himself as a student and even taking over for the principal of his high school when necessary. He also spent some time editing a newspaper, the *Liberia Herald*, and was ordained as a Presbyterian minister.

Aside from some letters in periodicals, his first publication was a pamphlet entitled *A Voice from Bleeding Africa, on Behalf of Her Exiled Children*, from 1856. It is an abolitionist text in which Blyden carefully demolishes arguments defending slavery, considering every objection he can anticipate. It also defends the Republic of Liberia as an aid rather than hindrance to the anti-slavery movement, in light of the lingering concern of many that Liberia's creation by the American Colonization Society was intended to strengthen the power of slavery. Blyden does not seek to prove that the motives involved in the colonization project were pure, but argues that these initial intentions do not matter in the long run. What matters is the result, namely, a republic where black freedom and development are possible. Liberia thus represents a political project worthy of all black people's support.

A pivotal year in Blyden's intellectual development was 1862. First came the founding of Liberia College, arguably the first secular institution of higher learning in sub-Saharan Africa. Blyden was appointed Professor of Classics while Crummell was chosen as Professor of Philosophy and English. At the ceremony opening the college, Blyden delivered an inaugural address that focused on the value of learning Greek and Latin. His appreciation of classical European culture was accompanied by a bleak assessment of modern-day Africa. He lamented, rather bluntly, that "as a race we have been quite unfortunate. We have no pleasing antecedents—nothing in the past to inspire us. All behind us is dark, and gloomy, and repulsive. All our agreeable associations are connected with the future" (*LO* 120). Even Crummell and Horton rarely expressed such a dim view of traditional African culture. This inaugural address was published as one of the chapters in Blyden's book, *Liberia's Offering*, which also features his essay "The Call of Providence to the Descendants of Africa in America." As the title suggests, this piece is directed squarely at African Americans. He delivered it as a speech in a number of American cities during the summer of 1862, when Blyden and Crummell visited as official commissioners of emigration working on behalf of the Liberian government. Blyden also visited the Caribbean and Canada as part of his efforts to promote emigration.

Like Cugoano before him, Blyden reflects in "The Call of Providence" on the question of how God communicates with human beings. He argues that just as God speaks through revelation, so too does He speak to us about what we ought to do through His providential ordering of the world. Playing the role of interpreter, Blyden argues that God is telling African Americans to go home and build a powerful nation in Africa. He claims that God has made this duty clear in four ways:

> First; By suffering them to be brought here and placed in circumstances where they could receive a training fitting them for the work of civilizing and evangelizing the land from whence they were torn, and by preserving them under the severest trials and afflictions. Secondly; By allowing them, notwithstanding all the services they have rendered to this country, to be treated as strangers and aliens, so as to cause them to have anguish of spirit, as was the case with the Jews in Egypt, and to make them long for some refuge from their social and civil deprivations. Thirdly; By bearing a portion of them across the tempestuous seas back to Africa, by preserving them through the process of acclimation, and by establishing them in the land, despite the attempts of misguided men to drive them away. Fourthly; By keeping their fatherland in reserve for them in their absence. (*LO* 71–2)

When he claims that the fatherland has been kept in reserve, Blyden is referring to the fact that Europeans had as yet made few incursions into Africa. He treats slavery in the United States as a sort of training camp—a civilization-and-Christianity school, if you will—which Africans have attended in a land that has been definitively claimed by Europeans (that is, America), in preparation for their return to the land that Europeans have not managed to claim (that is, Africa). The successful founding of Liberia proves that benefits acquired abroad can be returned to Africa. Meanwhile, the wisdom of this return is certified by the second-class treatment experienced in the land of sojourn, even by those in the North who are no longer enslaved.

Blyden articulates the goal of black political nationalism with an eloquence seldom paralleled in "The Call of Providence": "We must build up negro states; we must establish and maintain the various institutions; we must make and administer laws, erect and preserve churches, and support the worship of God; we must have governments; we must have legislation of our own; we must build ships and navigate them; we must ply the trades, instruct the schools, control the press, and thus aid in shaping the opinions and guiding the destinies of mankind" (*LO* 75–6).[4] Later on in the essay, we see a hint of his coming shift toward valuing cultural uniqueness. He claims that "Africa will furnish a development of civilization which the world has never yet witnessed. Its great peculiarity will be its moral element" (*LO* 82–3). He goes on to interpret that most beloved of biblical quotations for nineteenth century Africana thinkers, "Ethiopia shall soon stretch out her hands unto God," as suggesting that Africa is destined "not to foreign conquests, not to wide-spread domination, but to the possession of spiritual qualities, to the elevation of the soul heavenward, to spiritual aspirations and divine communications." His hope for Africa lies in the future, which is consistent with his stinging devaluation of Africa's past and present. Still, he does here anticipate his later view that Africa needs not only, or even primarily, a separate political existence, but rather distinct cultural development.

This shift becomes more visible in Blyden's writings of the 1870s. His fascination with Islam as practiced in West Africa plays a central role in this transformation, even as he continues to show a low regard for many, perhaps even most indigenous African customs. His essay "Mohammedanism and the Negro Race," which was published in 1875 and later became the first chapter of *Christianity, Islam and the Negro Race*, draws the following contrast: "When we left a Pagan and entered a Mohammedan community, we at once noticed that we had entered a moral atmosphere widely separated from, and far loftier than, the one we had left" (*CINR* 7). Blyden celebrates the fact that those who would have, in other communities, amused themselves with drumming and dancing instead go to the mosque five times a day to pray.

Nonetheless, he begins to show appreciation for African cultural uniqueness, not with his contrast between Muslims and so-called "pagans" but through a different contrast between West African Islam and the experiences of black people with Christianity. Blyden argues that "wherever the Negro is found in Christian lands, his leading trait is not docility, as has often been alleged, but servility" (*CINR* 12). By contrast, he claims: "There are numerous Negro Mohammedan communities and states in Africa which are self-reliant, productive, independent and dominant, supporting, without the countenance or patronage of the parent country, Arabia, whence they derived them, their political, literary and ecclesiastical institutions" (*CINR* 12). The reason for this disparity is that the two religions were introduced in very different circumstances. Blyden claims that Islam "found its Negro converts at home in a state of freedom and independence of the teachers who brought it to them" while "Christianity, on the other hand, came to the Negro as a slave" (*CINR* 12, 14).

Given his original political nationalist goals of freedom and independence for all black people, it is not surprising that he would perceive the circumstances in which West African Islam flourished as more conducive to the needs of the race than Christianity. Yet he also begins to perceive that Islam flourished by preserving and complementing what was already there. "While it brought them a great deal that was absolutely new," Blyden writes, "and inspired them with spiritual feelings to which they before had been utter strangers, it strengthened and hastened certain tendencies to independence and self-reliance which were already at work. Their local institutions were not destroyed by the Arab influence. They only assumed new forms, and adapted themselves to the new teachings. In all thriving Mohammedan communities, in West and Central Africa, it may be noticed that the Arab superstructure has been superimposed on a permanent indigenous substructure; so that what took place, when the Arab met the Negro in his own home, was a healthy amalgamation, and not an absorption or an undue repression" (*CINR* 13–14).

The arrival of Christianity was very different. When Europeans brought this faith, they also brought subjugation, and so "owing to the physical, mental, and social pressure under which the Africans received these influences of Christianity, their development was necessarily partial and one-sided, cramped and abnormal. All tendencies to independent individuality were repressed and destroyed. Their ideas and aspirations could be expressed only in conformity with the views and tastes of those who held rule over them" (*CINR* 15). Blyden's very emphasis on political independence seems to have led him to connect the admirable features of West African Islam to a valuable culture which Islam enhanced rather than replaced.

This change in perspective must have begun before Blyden's time in Sierra Leone, from 1871 to 1873. Blyden fled there from Liberia after an attempt on his life amidst a constitutional crisis that eventually led to a coup that deposed a president with whom he was friendly. While in Sierra Leone, he edited a newspaper titled *The Negro*, and advised the colony's government. Most importantly for our purposes, he engaged in correspondence with William Grant, a black member of the Legislative Council, and John Pope Hennessy, the colony's white governor, about the idea of founding what he envisioned as a true West African university.[5] Blyden argued that parents ought not to have to send their children away to Europe to be educated. Not because of the considerable expense, but because a foreign education attained among white people could only produce the "unnatural and artificial condition of a *Europeanized* African" (*BS* 224). Putting his point especially starkly in a letter to Governor Hennessy, Blyden claimed that black people with Western education "suffer from a kind of slavery in many ways far more subversive of the real welfare of the race than the ancient physical fetters" because "slavery of the mind is far more destructive than that of the body" (*BS* 228).

There is thus a stark contrast between the aforementioned 1862 speech at the founding of Liberia College, and Blyden's inaugural speech as the President of Liberia College in 1881, delivered some eight years after his return to Liberia from Sierra Leone. In the 1862 speech, indigenous Africans had been treated as a kind of contaminating force of ignorance and the embodiment of Liberia's isolation from the West: "No country in the world needs, more than Liberia, to have mind properly directed. We are here isolated from the civilized world, and surrounded by a benighted people, with whom we are closely identified" (*LO* 98). In the 1881 speech, the relationship has reversed. It is the settlers who seem to be contaminated, while indigenous Africans beyond the borders of Liberia are no longer a threat but a purifying, rectifying destiny: "Every thinking man will allow that all we have been doing in this country so far, whether in church, in state, or in school—our forms of religion, our politics, our literature, such as it is—is only temporary and transitional. When we advance further into Africa, and become one with the great tribes on the continent, these things will take the form which the genius of the race shall prescribe. The civilization of that vast population, untouched by foreign influence, not yet affected by European habits, is not to be organised according to foreign patterns, but will organise itself according to the nature of the people and the country" (*CINR* 82).

In other writings of the 1880s, we get a still deeper sense of what Blyden thinks Africa's unique cultural contribution will be. Already in "The Call of Providence" he had suggested that Africa has a particular contribution to make, which is spiritual in nature. Now he gradually comes to envision a kind of division of labor: while Europe achieves material progress, Africa will handle spiritual development, with the two mutually benefiting from their interaction. He imagines that "Africa may yet prove to be the spiritual conservatory of the world" and that "when the civilised nations, in consequence of their wonderful material development, shall have had their spiritual perceptions darkened and their spiritual susceptibilities blunted through the agency of a captivating and absorbing materialism, it may be, that they may have to resort to Africa to recover some of the simple elements of faith" (*CINR* 143).

There are climatic factors that shape this vision. Temperate regions, in his view, force humans to grapple with recurring problems of survival and sustenance in a way that tropical regions do not. So it is the pressures of the temperate zone that have produced "the scientific intellect and the thoughtfulness of the European" (*CINR* 126). If Africans can leave to the Europeans the problem of how to achieve material progress, then they will be able to live rural but comfortable lives, giving them "leisure and taste for the metaphysical and spiritual" (*CINR* 127). This is obviously a far more optimistic assessment of the effects of African climate than we found in Horton. Far from warning against the illnesses provoked by a tropical environment, Blyden thinks Africans should live in harmony with their natural surroundings, and avoid the development of large, crowded cities. It's not hard to imagine the dismay Blyden would feel upon seeing modern day Lagos in Nigeria, one of the densest and busiest cities in the entire world.

Blyden's transformation into a cultural nationalist had a lasting effect on Africana thought. For example, in an 1893 lecture entitled "Study and Race" he criticized those Africans whose Western education caused them to desire to "do away with our African personality and be lost, if possible, in another Race" (*BS* 201). This phrase, "African personality," was later taken up in the work of Kwame Nkrumah, the first President of Ghana after its independence in 1957 and one of the most celebrated leaders of Pan-Africanist thought. Ironically enough, the political independence fought for and won by Nkrumah and other African leaders of the 1950s and 1960s was not something that Blyden in 1893 much valued. As he aged, he increasingly put his emphasis on cultural rather than political autonomy.

This is evident in his last book, *African Life and Customs*, published in 1908. Blyden has now completely transcended his early low regard for traditional African culture. He concerns himself with, and more than ever before glorifies, what he calls "the African pure and simple—the so-called Pagan African—the man untouched either by European or Asiatic influence" (*ALC* 10). Having left behind his early valorization of Christianization, and his middle-period contrast between the virtue of Islam and the backwardness of traditional customs, he now even moves past simplistic generalities about the spiritual nature of the African character. Instead, he undertakes a more nuanced examination of African culture from an anthropological perspective. His discussion of various aspects of traditional African society—most prominently, marriage, the production and distribution of wealth, punishment, and religion—are united by his claim that the African "has developed and organised a system useful to him for all the needs of life" (*ALC* 10).

But in a move more likely to disturb modern-day readers, Blyden joins his emphasis on African cultural strength to an embrace of European imperialism. As his focus shifts from black political independence to the importance of being rooted in African culture, he encourages more than engagement or interaction between Africa and Europe: he openly welcomes European political and economic rulership, which he had come to see as beneficial and compatible with black cultural independence. Thus in *African Life and Customs*, after denying that Africa needs the "theological interference of Europe" because European theology is made to suit the European mind and tendencies, Blyden remarks: "What Africa does need from Europe is its Imperial and scientific help, ruling from the 'top of things'...and directing in the material development of the country" (*ALC* 63).

Again, the seeds of this idea were planted in his earlier writing. We saw that for Blyden, God's providential design can be discerned in worldly events. At the time of "The Call of Providence," he thought it evident that Africa had been preserved from European control and that emigration by black people from the United States and elsewhere would be essential to African development. When there was no grand exodus back to Africa, Blyden instead placed his hopes in indigenous African culture. Meanwhile, he was deeply affected by the infamous "Scramble for Africa," the rush by European powers to acquire African colonies leading up to and following the 1884–5 conference in Berlin at which the rules for annexing territory in Africa were decided. By the time he published an essay in 1895 called "The African Problem," he was admitting that the question was not *whether* such nations as Britain, France, Germany, and Belgium would rule the continent, but rather *how* they would rule. As he put it, "the 'scramble' is over, and now the question is how to utilize the plunder in the interests of civilization and progress."[6] As usual, Blyden was hoping for the best, optimistically assuming that if African culture could be preserved and cultivated, if the African personality could continue to express itself, a colonized Africa might be just fine.

Another, and no less controversial, element of his views was his understanding of race. The political situation in Liberia involved tensions between so-called mulattoes, or mixed-race Americo-Liberians, and those of unmixed or not obviously mixed African ancestry. Blyden came to think that "mulattoes" were a separate people with distinct inclinations, who were apt to slow down rather than aid the progress of true Africans. He discouraged the ACS from accepting mixed-race applicants for emigration. On visits to the United States, his prickliness around this subject got in the way of respectful exchange with some African Americans. When he could not help but be impressed by a so-called "mulatto," he found ways to explain away the discrepancy. Having met Frederick Douglass in the spring of 1880, he wrote: "He is strongly Negro, though of mixed blood. His genius and power come evidently from the African side of his nature. He reminds me in his manner and bearing more of some aristocratic African chief such as I have seen in the distant interior, rather than any cultivated European I have ever seen."[7] And he made similar allowance for Henry McNeal Turner, whom we will discuss in a coming chapter. He was less impressed by T. Thomas Fortune, another light-skinned African American, who made his name particularly in journalism. When Fortune initiated a civil rights organization called the Afro-American League, Blyden dismissed it as a way for lazy but ambitious people of mixed background to obtain positions of influence. That's a very reductive view of Fortune, but as luck would have it, we're just about to give him the more appreciative treatment he so richly deserves.

45

RACE FIRST, THEN PARTY

T. Thomas Fortune

Imagine, if you can, a version of the United States in which black people vote almost unanimously for the Republican Party, and newspapers are the most powerful force shaping public opinion. Actually, you don't have to imagine it, but only look back into history, because both were the case in late nineteenth century America. We've had plenty of reason to mention newspapers already. The fight for abolition was waged by such organs as William Lloyd Garrison's *Liberator* and Frederick Douglass' *North Star*. They built on the foundation laid by John Russwurm and Samuel Cornish with *Freedom's Journal*, and we cannot forget the breakthrough of Mary Ann Shadd's editorship of the *Provincial Freeman* up in Canada. Even those who were not involved in the newspaper business had their remarks and ideas disseminated by newspapers, with Sojourner Truth being the most obvious example.

Like so many other things in nineteenth century America, the press was divided by a color line. There was a "Negro press" which spoke to the concerns of African Americans. Already by 1880, there were about thirty black newspapers in the country, and they had plenty of injustices to report, even if slavery had been ended by the Civil War. These included the rise of lynching, the lack of economic opportunity for the formerly enslaved, and legal setbacks such as the Supreme Court decision that declared it unconstitutional to legislate against segregation. The Civil Rights Act of 1875 had forbidden racial discrimination in hotels, public transport, theaters, and so on, but the Court struck this down. They ruled that, even if the thirteenth amendment to the Constitution had abolished slavery, "mere discriminations on account of race or color were not regarded as badges of slavery." As one observer trenchantly remarked, this was effectively a reassertion of the implication of the infamous *Dred Scott* case, that "the black man has no rights that a white man is bound to respect."[1]

That observer's name was T. Thomas Fortune, writing in a newspaper he edited, called the *New York Globe*. Under a variety of names—including the *Freeman* and the *New York Age* under Fortune's editorship—this paper would survive until 1960. In recognition of his work on this and other periodicals, another newspaper said that Fortune was "without peer or superior as a colored journalist," and after his death he was hailed as "the best developed journalist that the Negro race has produced in the Western World."[2] But the word "journalist" may be misleading. He was not in the business of getting inside sources to spill secrets, interviewing politicians, or exposing scandals. In his hands, a newspaper, especially its editorial page, was the tool of a polemicist, or to use his favorite term, "agitator." There were scandals enough in open view, inequities that Fortune was determined to defeat by using his pen, with occasional suggestions that the sword might also be appropriate. His writings were designed to provoke outrage and determination in his readers, snapping them out of their lethargy or fatalism. This is what he had in mind when he wrote, "we believe in dissatisfaction; we believe in the manifold virtues of agitation" (*TTF* 115).[3] If, as they say, politics is war by other means, then Fortune pursued journalism as politics by other means.

Which brings us back to that other exotic feature of nineteenth century America: the popularity of the Republican Party among black voters. In the 2022 Congressional elections, the Republicans got only a 5 percent share of this demographic. In the wake of the Civil War the situation was the reverse. Black voters gave massive support to the Republicans, who were the "party of Lincoln," and despised Democrats as a party of racists who wanted to maintain white power in the southern states. Thus we find other black activists, not least Douglass, saying things like, "the Republican Party is the ship, all else is the sea."[4] Fortune was different. He mocked such devotion as "this 'eternal gratitude' business,"[5] arguing that political support should not be offered in recognition of past achievements, but in expectation of support in the future.

Not that the Republicans' past performance impressed Fortune overmuch. Even Lincoln, he observed, freed the slaves more out of political calculation than anything else, whatever his private feelings about emancipation might have been. And no wonder, because "politicians are simply the servants of public opinion" (*TTF* 36). Since the war, the party had done little for black people, whom it treated like "babies" (*TTF* 76). Fortune was so disappointed by this that he at one point proposed forming a third party that would actually take an interest in race rights. This was no act of disloyalty, as far as he was concerned. "We have not deserted any party," he wrote, "the party deserted us" (*TTF* 80). Fortune was taking a financial risk with this unpopular stance. He kept his newspaper, the *Globe*, independent of party affiliation despite knowing it could harm its circulation. A bold and principled move, especially for a man who, in spite of his name, was constantly strapped for cash. You might say that Fortune was putting his lack of money where his mouth was.

Fortune laid out a lengthy defense of his stance in an 1886 pamphlet called *The Negro in Politics* (*TTF* 27–69). It presents Republican politicians as having cynically exploited the reliable support of black voters. They "used our votes and flattered self-esteem just so long as our votes held out," but this "political vassalage" has won African Americans little real assistance. In fact "neither party cares a snap of the finger for race rights," and Republican partisans like Douglass are convicted of naivety. Partly Fortune's polemic here was driven by tactics: black people should make the Republicans earn their votes, and could exercise more influence by voting for both parties, if only to demonstrate that they are prepared to do so (*BW* 78).[6]

But another factor was his understanding of what politics is all about in the first place. He ends his pamphlet with these words: "Parties are nothing but the instruments of tyranny when they degenerate into machines, when they cease to represent progressive justice. It is for the people to see to it that parties conserve the public interest, or submit to defeat and humiliation" (*TTF* 69). Four years later, he would make a similar point, saying: "Parties are not things sacred to me. They are brought into existence by men to serve certain ends…When they have fulfilled the objects for which they were created or when they prove false to the great purpose for their creation, what further use are they?" (*TTF* 142–3). Fortune teaches us that we should support political organizations only when we can convince them to represent our beliefs and objectives, and never because we simply identify with them as "our side," like fans of a sports team.

If no political party could claim Fortune's allegiance, then what could? In a word, race. This pamphlet offers the motto "Race first, then party" (*TTF* 51), and throughout his career Fortune consistently argued for unified action on behalf of African American interests. In the 1880s, he proposed and then helped to found the National Afro-American League, which soon fell apart but was reborn in 1898 as the National Afro-American Council.[7] Fortune had noted that other demographic groups in America had organizations for promoting unity and to serve as a platform for political action. He was particularly inspired by the example of the Irish, whom he mentions often in his writings as another group that had suffered from oppression. "Like the Irish subjects of Great Britain," he remarked, "we have received everything from our country but justice" (*TTF* 6–7, cf. 31, 97, 125, 213).

In a related move with similarly enduring resonance, Fortune argued against using the term "Negroes," a term favored by many colleagues in activist circles.

He preferred "Afro-Americans," on analogy to Irish Americans and other groups (*TTF* 215–18). He defined the Afro-American people as a mixed-race group, including not just "black" but also "colored" people, where the color in question could even be white (*TTF* 251). The fact that Afro-Americans can often, though not always, be identified visually by their skin color is actually irrelevant to their forming a subgroup of the population. What unites them is the same as what unites Irish or Italian Americans: ancestry. Thus he says, "we are African in origin and American in birth, therefore, by the logic of it, Afro-Americans."[8] Consistently with this, Fortune (who himself had an Irish grandfather, by the way) had no patience for discrimination against lighter skinned Afro-Americans by darker skinned ones. He had harsh words against Edward Blyden on this score (*TTF* 230), and was one of the few prominent activists publicly to support Frederick Douglass' decision to marry a white woman, Helen Pitts. That decision provoked negative reactions, like this one from the *Pittsburgh Weekly News*: "We have no further use for him. His picture hangs in our parlor, we will hang it in the stables." But as far as Fortune was concerned, censuring this kind of relationship was a violation of rights, just as much as segregation laws were: "When a law prohibits a black man from marrying a white woman, because of his color, it strikes at the root of natural liberty."[9]

Notice that Fortune's political thought revolves exclusively around the interests of his race. Apart from occasional passing remarks, he makes little or no use of Christianity in his arguments. This is in sharp contrast to most of the other nineteenth century figures we've looked at so far, including Blyden and Douglass. Fortune actually complained about the religious education, or perhaps he would say indoctrination, to which he was subjected when he studied at Howard University in Washington DC in the 1870s (*TTF* 175). He argued against rallying around religion, instead of race, as a unifying factor in politics (*TTF* 214). The exception that proves this rule came with the most tragic episode of Fortune's life story. In 1907, shattered by overwork, money problems, alcohol abuse, and separation from his wife, he had a mental breakdown from which it would take him years to recover. During this time he became intensely and uncharacteristically religious, commenting: "When a man has been sick in heart and head for four long months he must get very close to his Maker."[10]

His usually more irreverent attitude toward Christianity helped Fortune promote openness to violent resistance. We've seen how Douglass, in his more aggressive moments, was opposed by pious activists like Truth (remember her show-stopping question, "Frederick, is God dead?"). Fortune, by contrast, openly believed in using force against injustice, whatever the Bible might say. He put forward this rather breathtaking inversion of the Golden Rule: "In theory 'do unto others as you would have them do unto you' is splendid, but in practice the philosophy of conduct is 'do unto others as they do unto you,' the sooner to make them understand that a dagger of the right sort has two edges" (*TTF* 210–11). So, while he encouraged the defense of justice through democratic means, he was always ready to entertain the use of other, more radical means if this failed. "I believe in law and order," he said, "but I believe, as a condition precedent, that law and order should be predicated upon right and justice, pure and simple" (*BW* 97). Likewise, while allowing that it was a good idea to use the instruments of "ballot box and the courts," he stated that "if others use the weapons of violence to combat our peaceful arguments it is not for us to run away from violence."[11]

Fortune's free talk of violence, which became still freer when he took the stage while drunk, ultimately led his colleagues in the Afro-American League to see him as a liability.[12] This is a shame, because when it came to the "ballot box and the courts," Fortune was a subtle thinker who anticipated the political struggles that were to come. He had studied the law while at Howard University, and took forward the ideas of one of his professors, John Mercer Langston.[13] Langston had distinguished between legal and social rights; Fortune would likewise contrast "civil rights" to "social privileges" (*TTF* 129, 217) Whereas civil rights are enshrined in law, social privileges are extended to citizens only by custom and are not the business of the law or the government. An example might be that we have a civil or legal right to free speech, but not a civil or legal right that anyone will pay attention to us when we speak. It's rude to ignore people when they talk to you, but it's not a crime.

Fortune furthermore pointed out that civil rights by their very nature belong equally to every citizen, while social privilege is distributed unequally. Try walking into a fancy restaurant: if you look like a rich white person, you'll likely get a very different reception than if you look like a poor black person. This is just a fact of life, thought Fortune, and cannot be legislated away. As he put it: "Every citizen has a co-equal right in all benefits of government; but every citizen has not on this account, a legal right to demand or expect the concession of any social privilege. The one he can force by legal process; the other he must win by conduct, position, superior abilities, affluence" (*TTF* 132). The urgent question, then, was which forms of equal treatment are guaranteed by right, and which have to be secured as a matter of social privilege? According to the Supreme Court, access to non-segregated public transport or education was (in Fortune's terms) a matter of social privilege, not legal right. This is why they set aside the 1875 Civil Rights Act. Fortune argued that they were wrong to do so, because the government's whole purpose was to protect the enjoyment of life, liberty, and the pursuit of happiness (*TTF* 21). As a matter of law, the waiters at the fancy restaurant cannot be made to smile and ingratiate themselves with the poor black customer, but they do have to offer him a table.

Fortune thought, however, that justice called for more than just desegregating street cars, hotels, and schools. He believed that the whole economic system of the United States, especially in the South, needed to be overhauled in order to give the laboring class a chance at prosperity. Notice, not only black laborers, but *all* laborers. This is the argument of his remarkable 1884 book, *Black and White: Land, Labor, and Politics in the South*, a pioneering critique of American capitalism.[14] As he says in the preface, he aims to show that "poverty and misfortune make no invidious distinctions of 'race, color, or previous condition,' but that wealth unduly centralized oppresses all alike." He takes his departure from the aforementioned conception of government and its purpose, asking: "What shall we say of that government which has not power or inclination to insure the exercise of those solemn rights and immunities which it guarantees?" (*BW* 16). The American government has failed its people in this respect, because it has allowed one class of citizens to exploit another for its own enrichment (*BW* 34). This was most obvious under slavery, but has continued to be the case afterward. White and black laborers need to understand that they are jointly victimized by the way that the "hereditary landlords of the south" keep a "grip upon the throat of Southern labor" (*BW* 128), and thus that "their cause is common; that they should unite under the one banner and work upon the same platform of principles for the uplifting of labor" (*BW* 106, cf. 150).

In terms of practical remedies, beyond the proper protection of civil rights, Fortune recommends an ambitious program of land redistribution. Actually, he considers land to be a "common right," like water or air, and thus to be "the property of the whole people" (*BW* 133–4). So it should be shared out among the laboring class equally, instead of concentrated in the hands of a wealthy few. If this seems rather utopian, Fortune would say that it is still less realistic to suppose that monopolization of land can continue indefinitely without a violent reaction, an "explosion" of the kind that led to the French Revolution and, if that isn't frightening enough, the fall of the Roman Empire (*BW* 135, 149). Again, we see here his conviction that violence is an appropriate reaction to injustice; indeed, it is an inevitable result of severe exploitation.

In the meantime, though, Fortune also had some ideas about what black people should be doing to improve their own situation. He was rather scornful of the high-minded, "civilizing" projects envisioned by men like Alexander Crummell. The beneficiaries of such "higher learning," Fortune couldn't help noticing, often became "social parasites" (*TTF* 90). Instead the race would advance through the learning of practical, economically valuable skills, which means not "theology and the classics" but education suitable for "the mechanic and the farmer" (*TTF* 47). These proposals resonate powerfully with those of a far more celebrated contemporary of Fortune's, Booker T. Washington. And in fact the two were close colleagues and friends, at times writing letters to one another on a daily basis. Washington was often uncomfortable with the more fiery and irascible Fortune, while Fortune bristled when critics of Washington assumed that he was just a spokesman for the famous "wizard of Tuskegee." One such critic was fellow journalist William Monroe Trotter, who used his newspaper the *Guardian* to inveigh against Washington, whom he dubbed "the Great Traitor" and the "Benedict Arnold of the Negro race" because he thought Washington was too willing to accommodate white power and black subjugation.[15]

Trotter also mocked Fortune, as being "only a 'me too' to whatever Washington aspires to do" and as "furnishing whatever brains the combination needs."[16] But this was an inaccurate assessment of their relationship. Out in the open, Fortune hailed Washington as the "Negro Moses" and only suitable successor to Douglass. Though he admitted in one public performance that Washington was "a decided conservative," he hastened to add that "he loves Professor Washington and places unbounded confidence in him."[17] Behind the scenes, the two had an increasingly fractious relationship. Washington would eventually be glad to see the unpredictable Fortune step away from his work as editor and activist within the Afro-American League. The result of this sidelining, and of the psychologically and financially parlous state of his later years, was that Fortune remains something of a forgotten man in the history of American race relations. He deserves more credit, not only for the ideas we've presented above, but also for his promotion of fellow activists like Ida B. Wells, whom he praised for her crusade against lynching (*TTF* 158, 226). Of her, he admiringly wrote in his own paper, "She has become famous as one of the few women what handles a goose quill with diamond point as handily as any of us men in newspaper work...She is smart as a steel trap and she has no sympathy for humbug."[18] More generally he supported the idea of women joining activist groups like his League, saying: "In the League a woman is just as good as a man. Out of it she is usually much better."

Happily, there was at least one leading intellectual of the time who was willing to give Fortune his due: Fortune himself. Writing in 1916 upon the death of Booker T. Washington, and taking stock of the history of black activism in his own lifetime, Fortune discerned three phases in that history (*TTF* 192–7). The leading figure was initially Frederick Douglass, but his prominence came to a sudden end in 1884 because of his interracial marriage. More than thirty years later, Fortune still rankles at the absurdity of the hostility this provoked. Next came what Fortune calls the "Afro-American period of leadership," in which he himself played a central role through his journalism and his founding of the National Afro-American League. This highpoint of agitation gave way to widespread resignation and acceptance around 1900 (*TTF* 189). It was only in 1904—"when I got out of the way," says Fortune—that Booker T. Washington came to preeminence. Fortune claims he was willing to help Washington, despite having had "nothing in common with the policies" that Washington endorsed, being rather the intellectual and political heir of the great Douglass. This telling of events is of course open to challenge at numerous points. But it is closer to being right than the more popular version of American history, which edits Fortune and his achievements out of the story completely.

46

A COMMON CIRCLE

Anténor Firmin

Ask anyone who has taught courses at a university, and they will tell you that education is a two-way street: the teachers learn from the students, just as much as the other way around. Sometimes students even say things that lead their professors to take on major research projects. This is what happened in 1988, when an anthropologist named Carolyn Fluehr-Lobban was teaching a class about Count Joseph Arthur de Gobineau, who in the 1850s wrote a book on "the inequality of the human races." Happily, one of her students was from Haiti, and asked if she had ever heard of the Haitian scholar Anténor Firmin, who had responded with a book of his own intended to combat the pseudo-science of Gobineau and other French anthropologists. Fluehr-Lobban had to admit that the name was new to her, but she looked into this intriguing figure, and eventually wound up writing the introduction to an English translation of Firmin's treatise.[1] This translation, published only in 2000, brought Firmin unprecedented attention, and now he is increasingly acknowledged as a major figure in the history of anthropology and the philosophy of race.

A glance at the repugnant ideas of Gobineau shows us what Firmin was up against.[2] Gobineau divided humanity into three races, with whites at the top of the hierarchy, followed by the "yellow" Asian races and then black people at the bottom. His message was a deeply pessimistic one, since he thought that the mating of whites with other races would degrade their biological stock, and that this process was already well under way. Ideally, there would never have been mixing of the races, in which case, as he put it, "the supremacy would no doubt have always been in the hands of the finest of the white race, and the yellow and black varieties would have crawled forever at the feet of the lowest of the whites."[3] But now, non-white blood was in the genetic pool, so to speak. Gobineau called this "an evil that nothing can balance or repair." Pretty extreme stuff, you might think. But none of this was far from the mainstream of nineteenth century anthropology, which largely took for granted that black people are biologically inferior and can never attain equality with whites.

Still, the anthropologists allowed that there might be exceptions to the rule. In 1884, while in Paris as a political refugee from his native Haiti, Firmin was allowed to join the Paris Anthropological Society. His presence, indeed his mere existence, was an anomaly from the point of view of his new colleagues. At a later meeting in 1892, he was pointedly asked whether he had any white ancestors, which would help to explain his evident intelligence and eloquence.[4] And of course he encountered many who thought like Gobineau, even if the latter was not a particularly influential figure. Firmin's experiences convinced him that he needed to write a refutation of the dominant theories of race, taking inspiration from a like-minded Haitian anthropologist who was also in Paris, Louis-Joseph Janvier.[5] Janvier had already written a pamphlet arguing for the equality of the races, and Firmin would follow this up with an ambitious treatise drawing on history, literature, ethnography, and biology to make the same point.

One thing he and his opponents did agree on was that race is, at least in the present, central to anthropology. Early in his *On the Equality of the Races*, Firmin defines this science as "the study of man in his physical, intellectual, and moral dimensions, as he is found among the different races which constitute the human species" (10). Yet at the conclusion of the book, he envisions future scientists being able to dispense with the concept of race altogether, once the basic unity and equality of the human species has become appreciated and practically acknowledged. The differentiation of nations according to their level of civilization will still be possible as a sociological enterprise, but, as he puts it, "there will be no question of race, for the word implies a biological and natural fatality which has no correlation with the degree of ability observable among the different human communities spread around the globe" (449). Firmin's goal is thus to establish that the study of racial inequality is a *social* science, not a *biological* one. But it remains vitally important to him that his project, and anthropology in general, are indeed empirical in approach. His charge against the inequality thesis is not merely that it is false, but that it is unscientific, with "no natural law to support it" (89).

Firmin's devotion to empiricism was inspired by the writings of August Comte, whose positivist philosophy Firmin discovered as a student in Haiti.[6] A fellow classmate recalled that after reading Comte, Firmin was inspired to explore every scientific discipline under the sun: "He refused to specialize in any of them; he boldly sought them all."[7] In *On the Equality of the Races*, Firmin states openly that positivism is "a school of thought which I embrace totally" (166). As he explains, this school downgrades purely abstract disciplines like mathematics, though they do have their place (170). Real science takes its lead from empirical observations, which must be the basis of all sound theory. Firmin celebrates the collapse of older "spiritualist" approaches, which identified the true human with the immaterial soul (38). Now, in a more enlightened time, we realize that the human is just another animal, which "differs from the other animals only by a few degrees of superiority" (9). This leaves it as an entirely empirical question whether black people are in fact biologically inferior to whites.

And Firmin was in a strong position here, since the biological theories he attacked as utter nonsense were, of course, utter nonsense. A notorious example is the study of the human skull, and how its shape and size varies amongst peoples of the globe and is correlated to degrees of intelligence. For Firmin, anthropologists who take this seriously are just repeating a folk belief with a pretense of scientific exactness (148). He gleefully points out the inconsistencies between published measurements, and observes that these findings are just being used to justify assumptions of racial inequality that were made in advance: "Any researcher with a large number of skulls at his disposal can easily find a way to make them say whatever he wants" (105). These researchers have not really submitted the inequality thesis to serious inquiry, instead taking it as a kind of "dogmatic revelation" or just as "common sense" (328). It is, to use a phrase that for a positivist like Firmin is something close to an obscenity, *a priori*, in other words taken for granted without empirical evidence. These "scientists concluded, without any study, that what they saw, or what they were told must be, was consistent with the natural order" (333). Janvier had made the same complaint, pointing to the practice of chattel slavery and its violent collapse in the United States as "decisive proof of the danger of *a priori* affirmations in matters of ethnography."[8]

Firmin places the racist anthropologists of his own day within a long tradition, which goes back to antiquity. Already Aristotle, when he set out a theory of "natural slavery" in his *Politics*, was guilty of seeking a kind of retrospective justification for an entrenched social practice (143). The pseudo-science of the nineteenth century is similar, insofar as it seeks to "assuage the conscience" of white people who might otherwise have misgivings about having oppressed, slaughtered, and enslaved non-white people all over the globe (383). But there is a telling difference between ancient and modern rationalizations of slavery, a difference that exposes the artificiality of the inequality thesis. A glance at the historical record shows that slavery was thought to be "natural" long before it was associated with race. The very word "slave," Firmin rightly points out, is connected to "Slav," and Slavs are not black

(335). From antiquity too, there is abundant textual evidence to show that the Greeks and Romans subjected others of their *own* race to enslavement (144, 420).

At a more theoretical level, Firmin also engaged critically with then-current ideas about what "race" might mean in the first place. As with the case of skull measurements, he was able to produce numerous, mutually inconsistent attempts to divide up the human species into distinct groups (18). There's a connection here to a controversy that had been raging in the Paris Anthropological Society, which Firmin also mentions in his book (32). Back in 1858, the scientist Paul Broca had triggered this controversy by announcing the successful cross-breeding of a rabbit and a hare. This undermined one convenient way of demarcating species from one another, namely that two animals belong to the same species if they can mate together.[9] But it also re-opened the door for those who believed that humans are not one, but several distinct species, who can reproduce across the divisions like the rabbit and hare. This hare-brained position was called polygenesis, as opposed to monogenesis, which is of course the doctrine that the human species is one. Polygenesis had been defended by various thinkers since the seventeenth century, including the famous French philosopher Voltaire.

You might expect Firmin to resist polygenesis at all costs, but in fact he shows himself relaxed about the entire debate. After all, even if different human races have different origins, they might still be equal (35). He also thinks that the main evidence so far produced for monogenesis is scriptural, since the Book of Genesis tells us that we are all descended from Adam and Eve (78). As a good positivist, Firmin dismisses this out of hand, in one of several rather irreverent passages that would have had the pious Alexander Crummell spinning in his grave, if Crummell had not been alive and well at the time. (Firmin's book was published in 1885, the same year that Crummell debated Frederick Douglass at Harper's Ferry.) In the end, Firmin cautiously adopts a kind of compromise view, according to which humans arose separately in several different places of the globe, but still as one species and according to a "single blueprint (*unité de plan*)."

As for racial intermixing, which Gobineau thought so disastrous, Firmin welcomes it as a dramatic confirmation of his equality thesis. Mixed-race people are as intelligent as white people, and their difference from pure blacks or pure whites "is a purely physiological phenomenon, nothing more" (207). He takes pride in pointing to Haiti, where numerous men of mixed race have shown great talent in poetry and other fields (74). Haiti is in fact crucial to Firmin's argument, and not only for patriotic reasons. Again, in this he is following Janvier, who called the island a "sociological field of experimentation," though Firmin would prefer the term "observation" (312, 359). The value of Haiti is that, following independence in 1804, people of African ancestry have been able to improve themselves in a way that Firmin thinks all but impossible in Africa itself (358).[10]

Here we have another fundamental flaw in the method of those who propound the inequality of the races: they do not compare like with like. Instead, they consider a highly educated intellectual from Paris, contrast him with an uneducated African, and conclude that the former must be biologically superior to the latter. Firmin does not take the route we might expect, or at least prefer, by arguing that inhabitants of traditional African society are every bit the equals of urban Parisians. Instead he concedes the inferiority of Africans as an uncontroversial point. Occasionally we get a caveat, as when he says that African culture is rather more civilized than Europeans usually assume (401). At one point he even quotes African ideas about God as being too transcendent to be concerned with human affairs, which Firmin welcomes as a sign of rationality (342). So this is another case of a nineteenth century thinker picking up on a theme we discussed when looking at traditional African conceptions of the divine (Chapter 14). Generally, though, he agrees without protest that white people are indeed currently superior to black people (36). He is even prepared to admit that whites are on average more physically attractive (186), and also that they have produced the best scientists and scholars.

But there is, he insists, no evidence that this is a matter of biology. To the contrary, it is a matter of environment, upbringing, and education. It is only once black and white people have been equally educated that the potential of both groups can be compared (150). Given what he sees as the undeveloped state of Africa, which is partly due to climate, partly to the lingering effects of the slave trade, opportunities to make such a fair comparison are limited. Hence the importance of Haiti. Through their exposure to the values of the Enlightenment, French literature, and so on, Haitians have already made huge strides in catching up with the white race, which Firmin takes already to have "journeyed along a progressive path which all the other human groups must follow" (354). Talented Haitians have been able to rise to the level of whites, to the point that they can hardly be distinguished from whites. Thus in a preface Firmin wrote to the poetry of a black poet named Paul Lochard, he asked, "Can one ever notice the strong dose of African blood that flows in his veins?"[11] This is apt to strike us as a more unattractive side of Firmin's thought. He may have been less religious than Crummell, but he echoed Crummell's notion that black people must advance by adopting the values and knowledge of white culture: "Backward peoples need to come into contact with more advanced peoples in order to progress" (296).

Firmin is consistent enough about this that he also applies the idea to the difference between the two sexes. This isn't a topic that comes up often in his book, which is of course about racial inequality, not gender inequality. In fact, during his discussion of brain size, he dismisses female brains as irrelevant (164). But later on, he asks, in a striking passage: "Does not civilization always tend to cause men and women to become equal and achieve the same qualities?" (195). And of course his whole argument could easily be adapted to show that claims of female inferiority are as poorly founded as claims of racial inferiority. Disappointingly, Firmin doesn't seem to have drawn that conclusion himself. This emerges from a passage where he is attacking Clémence Royer, who produced the French translation of Darwin's *Origin of Species*. He says that she is "a learned woman, but a woman nonetheless (*une femme savant, mais une femme*). There are problems of such complexity that they can be properly studied only by men" (271). But Firmin does add, in explanation of this obnoxious remark: "Only men, because of their particular education and their temperament as males, can see [these problems] from every angle." If the reference to "temperament (*tempérament*)" suggests natural inferiority on the part of women, the mention of "particular education (*éducation particulière*)" holds out the prospect that equal education might put women on a par with men.

The reason Firmin lashed out at Royer is that, in her preface to the translation of Darwin, she claimed that the new evolutionary theory supported the thesis of inequality between the races. She even looked forward to the prospect that, through biological competition, the superior human race would win out against and ultimately extinguish the lesser ones—no prizes for guessing which race she took to be superior.[12] But Firmin disagrees about whether this is an implication of Darwinism. To the contrary, he cites the theory of evolution as proving his own thesis that it is environment that makes the difference between the races (272). He goes remarkably far here, assuming that changes in social and physical surroundings can even lead to changes in the physical features that make people more or less beautiful.

Apart from Haiti, Firmin's favorite way to demonstrate the centrality of environment is one that will be very familiar to us: ancient Egypt. He devotes an entire chapter of *Equality of the Races* to this topic, attempting to refute those who claimed that the Egyptians must have been white, given their astounding achievements in science and architecture (228). Nonsense, says Firmin. You can see that Egyptians were black just by examining the statues they made. He also invokes Ethiopia, which had impressive achievements of its own, and concludes that "the population of Egypt was black like the Ethiopians, and the inhabitants of Ethiopia were as civilized as the Egyptians" (250). Like many other nineteenth-century Africana thinkers, he furthermore stresses the debt owed to Egypt by Greek and Roman philosophy and science (394–5). So you might say that for Firmin, white people are further along the path of progress than any other group, but only because they were given an initial push by black people. Yet along with these arguments about African sources of wisdom and the great potential of all who have African ancestry, Firmin in the very same context repeats his negative assessment of the Africans of his own day, taking recourse to (of all things) the measurement of skulls. Though he has discredited this method elsewhere in the book, he here notes that comparison of ancient Egyptian skulls to those of modern-day Africans reflects the fact that the latter have "now fallen into barbarism" (287).

As we've already seen, Haiti is Firmin's example of a society where black people have once again progressed beyond such barbarism. Given the value he places upon his countrymen's ability to participate in French intellectual and artistic culture, Firmin clearly represents an elitist form of Haitian nationalism. In this respect, we might compare him to other figures of the contemporary Haitian scene, like Demesvar Delorme. Delorme's magnum opus *The Theoreticians in Power* (*Les theoriciens au pouvoir*) takes up the question famously raised by Plato's *Republic*: whether any social order can be successful without empowering intellectuals. The question is pursued through the depiction of a dialogue between two Haitians concerning the thoughts of luminaries from ancient Greece, ancient Rome, and Enlightenment France.[13]

Like Delorme, who was a government minister, Firmin was no armchair philosopher. He acted on his ideas about progress in Haiti by getting involved in the political life of the island. After his years in Paris refuting racist anthropological theories, we find him back in Haiti as of 1887. In 1891 he was serving as minister of finance and foreign affairs when none other than Frederick Douglass turned up, in his role as American ambassador. Firmin must have been thrilled: he had cited Douglass in *Equality of the Races* as an outstanding mind, and quoted at length from the famous scene in which Douglass described the vicious slavedriver Covey (331–2; we discussed the story in Chapter 36). The two got on well, perhaps too well, since they were accused of making secret agreements rather than looking after their respective national interests. Both wound up losing their positions.[14] But Firmin tried again. In 1902 he led a political movement in Haiti that sparked a full-blown civil war. His side lost and he fled the island never to return, though another "Firminist" insurgency flared up in 1910 before being put down again.

He spent his later years in exile on the island of St. Thomas, the same island where Edward Blyden was born and raised. There Firmin wrote another major work, the *Letters of Saint Thomas*, arguing for a Caribbean-wide coalition that would unite the interests of the region.[15] He wrote: "By joining together their national destinies and attracting all the other Antillean islands, which live today under colonial rule, they would ultimately form a substantial State, capable of maintaining itself on its own and establishing such a name for itself as could be held in high esteem by other nations."[16] An important plank in his platform was the encouragement of foreign investment in Haiti and the rest of the Caribbean. Here we see his continued commitment to the idea that black societies would benefit from exchange and connection to white ones, as long as the relationship was no longer exploitative.

Indeed, if we look back to his earlier treatise on the equality of races, we can see that Firmin always had his eye on the wider political implications of the anthropological disputes. Consistently with his premise that it is environment and not biology that causes inequality, Firmin was attentive to disparities within a single race or society (66). Uncovering the incoherence of racist arguments was thus a step toward a more egalitarian future, in terms of economic class as well as race. As he wrote: "Recognition of the equality of the races entails a definitive recognition of the equality of all social classes in every nation of the world...Wherever social inequality is still a cause of conflict, the doctrine of the equality of the races will be a remedy" (438). Admittedly, this is not a major theme of the work; Firmin was no Marxist. But he did believe in what he called "human solidarity" (448). Whereas Marx told people that they had nothing to lose but their chains, Firmin chose to end his treatise by proclaiming that "an invisible chain links all the members of humanity in a common circle (*c'est qu'une chaîne invisible réunit tous les membres de l'humanité dans un cercle commun*)" (662).

47

FROWNING AT FROUDACIOUS FABRICATIONS

J.J. Thomas and F.A. Durham

Much as Carolyn Fluehr-Lobban came to know Firmin's work by chance after a Haitian student brought him up in her classroom, Chike was actually looking for something else on the internet when he stumbled across a book entitled *The Lone-Star of Liberia: Being the Outcome of Reflections on Our Own People*.[1] The book's cover page identifies its author, Frederick Alexander Durham, as a law student and a member of Lincoln's Inn, a barrister association in London. As he began to skim the book's contents, Chike discovered that Durham was from Trinidad. Beyond this, and the fact that Durham studied law in London in 1892—the same year that saw the publication of his book—very little is known about him. Both he and his book have been almost completely forgotten. Even most scholars of Caribbean thought are unaware of his existence.

By making Durham one of the two figures we will discuss in this chapter, we are, even more than usual, mining the unexplored riches of Africana philosophy. And as Chike realized when he read *The Lone-Star of Liberia* more carefully, Durham is indeed a priceless find. Among proponents of a return of diasporic Africans to their homeland, he was the only writer to focus particularly on racial oppression in the Caribbean as a rationale. While unique in this respect, he was also a man of his time and place. His writing in the early 1890s self-consciously builds upon the contributions of two other Afro-Caribbean thinkers who had written in the previous decades, especially in the late 1880s: Edward Blyden, whom we have previously discussed (Chapter 44), and Durham's fellow Trinidadian John Jacob Thomas.

We identified *Christianity, Islam and the Negro Race*, published in 1887, as Blyden's most famous work and the one that marked his transformation into a pioneering cultural nationalist. It clearly made an impression on Durham. In the preface to *Lone-Star of Liberia*, he writes that a black reader who has read Blyden's book should already have "more than a fair knowledge of the History of his Race and Fatherland," and expresses the hope that his own book "will be found a not unsuitable appendix or supplement to that work" (*LSL* xii). Though Durham presents both Blyden's book and his own as historical works, they are in fact wide-ranging reflections on Africa and its diaspora, looking at the history of black people, the present-day state of affairs, and the future development of the race. If there is one theme that ties together Blyden's various concerns, from the differential impacts of the Abrahamic faiths on Africans to the prospects for progress in Liberia as a republic born of diasporic return, it is his emphasis on the potential for achieving black unity and autonomy in Africa. Durham takes over this theme. It makes sense, then, that he should see his book and Blyden's as forming a kind of unified text, and modestly describe his own contribution as a mere supplement to what Blyden had already achieved.

As for Durham's other inspiration, J.J. Thomas, he was arguably the most prominent black intellectual based in the English-speaking Caribbean in the nineteenth century. Born in 1841, very shortly after the end of slavery in the British Empire, he became first a schoolteacher and then a member of the civil service. It was while holding the latter position that he completed his first book, *The Theory and Practice of Creole Grammar*.[2] This linguistic study reflected the history of Trinidad's colonization. After three centuries as a somewhat neglected possession of Spain, Trinidad was opened up to French settlers from elsewhere in the Caribbean beginning in the 1770s. This jump-started the island's development while also swelling its enslaved population. Then in 1797, Trinidad was captured by the British and remained a British colony until gaining independence as part of the twin island nation of Trinidad and Tobago in 1962. As a result of this history, during Thomas' lifetime, English was the official language of Trinidad but French Creole of the kind that one associates with Haiti and the French islands of Martinique and Guadeloupe was very commonly spoken. Its influence can still be noticed today, though the use of French Creole as a primary language of communication began to die out by the early twentieth century and is now exceedingly rare. This makes Thomas' study of the language in his *Theory and Practice of Creole Grammar* a fascinating time capsule, and makes Thomas himself a pioneering black linguist, like Samuel Ajayi Crowther.

Thomas makes philosophically interesting points about the value of such linguistic investigation. He argues that the social forces of law and religion were both hampered by insufficient understanding of *patois*, as French Creole was commonly called. Less than competent translations from Creole to English were an impediment to the administration of justice, and with regard to religion, Catholic sermons were often delivered in standard French, only vaguely intelligible to the Creole speaker. In both cases, the root of the problem was a prejudice that Creole is nothing but badly pronounced French. Thomas aims to combat this dismissive oversimplification: "Spoken as it is by thousands upon thousands of human beings, to most of whom all other language is unknown, the Creole would have been a singular dialect indeed, if, from its formation up to the present time, it had continued to be a mere jumble of French words, uncouthly pronounced, and, at best, pervertedly understood. A language spoken and yet inert is an impossibility" (*TPCG* 72–3). Thomas goes on to discuss, in connection with this point, the dynamic formation of new words, a process characterizing Creole as much as any living language.

Another service Thomas provided in this book was the collection and translation of proverbs that circulated in Creole. On this point, he arguably anticipated the philosophical approach to oral traditions in Africa we discussed above (Chapters 12–18). Thomas too recognizes the special place of proverbs, referring to them as "the beautiful sayings which form the ornament of African discourse" and claiming that this fund of wisdom "has been the instruction and delight of the Negro race in all ages and stages of its existence." As Kwame Gyekye would later do, he identifies them as a useful resource for studying "the mental habits and capabilities of the people who invent them." He connects the role of proverbs as a form of seeking and disseminating knowledge in his own time to their use in the non-Christian setting of traditional African life: "We prize them as beautiful no less than intelligent deductions from the teachings of Nature, that free, infallible, and sublime volume, which Providence has displayed to all men, but more distinctly to those who have no other revelation and guidance" (*TPGC* 120).

The Theory and Practice of Creole Grammar brought Thomas significant recognition. On a visit to England in 1873, he was elected a member of the Philological Society of Britain. Back in Trinidad, he continued to hold various positions of importance in the civil service and frequently contributed opinions to newspapers. From the late 1870s onward, however, he was beset by illness that disrupted his career and his literary efforts. He left to spend time in Grenada and hoped to return to England for further research and writing in England, but had to cancel his plans on account of "rheumatic paralysis." So he was living in St. George's, the capital of Grenada, at the fateful moment when an Englishman by the name of James Anthony Froude published a book that would inspire, or rather provoke, Thomas' most famous literary effort.

Froude was a prominent intellectual who made his name as a historian of sixteenth century England. During the 1870s and 1880s, he traveled through the British empire, visiting South Africa, Australia, New Zealand, and the islands of the

Caribbean. This led to two books, *Oceana or England and Her Colonies*, published in 1886, and *The English in the West Indies or The Bow of Ulysses*, published in 1888. Part travelogue, part political theory, these books place great value on the unity of the British Empire. But Froude thinks the empire will be preserved by respecting and empowering those who are British in an ancestral sense. Self-government in places like Australia and Canada seems to him useful for keeping the empire together on a happy and voluntary basis, but is inappropriate for the Caribbean, where it will inevitably result in the unacceptable consequence of black rule. Envisioning a time when "an English governor-general will be found presiding over a black council, delivering the speeches made for him by a black prime minister," Froude says with a shudder that "no English gentleman would consent to occupy so absurd a situation."[3]

Thomas was among those angered by such passages. In response he published a series of articles in a newspaper called *The St. George's Chronicle and Grenada Gazette*. These became the first draft of his charmingly titled book, *Froudacity*.[4] Thomas completed and published the book in England, which he finally reached in the summer of 1888. By the time *Froudacity* was published a year later, illness was again getting the better of him and he died in London in September of 1889, mere weeks after the book's publication. Thomas saw the refutation of Froude and defense of Caribbean self-government as a "patriotic duty" (*Fr.* 16). Speaking on behalf of black West Indians, and indeed West Indians of all racial backgrounds, he asserts the following principle: "We, the said Colonies, being an integral portion of the British Empire, and having, in intelligence and every form of civilized progress, outgrown the stage of political tutelage, should be accorded some measure of emancipation therefrom" (*Fr.* 148). The time had come for West Indians of all colors, as British subjects, to display their political maturity.

Froude's diatribe was therefore not only out of order, but out of date. His views showed no awareness of the passage of time, which Thomas likes to personify with a capital T. Early on Thomas argues that, from the perspective of black West Indians, racial hatred based on the slavery of the past has become irrelevant: "Death, with undiscriminating hand, had gathered in the human harvest of masters and slaves alike, according to the normal laws of nature; while Time had been letting down on the stage of our existence drop-scene after drop-scene of years, to the number of something like fifty, which had been curtaining off the tragic incidents of the past from the peaceful activities of the present. Being thus circumstanced, we thought, what rational elements of mutual hatred should *now* continue to exist in the bosoms of the races?" (*Fr.* 9–10). This optimistic perspective on historical memory and race relations underlies many of Thomas' criticisms of Froude.

Froude had summed up the history of the West Indies as follows: "We have been a ruling power there for two hundred and fifty years; the whites whom we planted as our representatives are drifting into ruin, and they regard England and England's policy as the principal cause of it. The blacks who, in a fit of virtuous benevolence, we emancipated, do not feel that they are particularly obliged to us. They think, if they think at all, that they were ill treated originally and have received no more than was due to them."[5] Thomas ably reveals the problems with this picture (*Fr.* 115). He notes that those who experienced emancipation, far from being ungrateful, exhibit a remarkable attachment to the Queen, precisely out of gratitude for their freedom. As for those born free, it's absurd to think anyone should be grateful simply for never having been enslaved. The ideals of those born after emancipation are more ambitious: to look after their own affairs and pursue their highest aspirations, which is precisely what Froude seeks to deny them. Froude's inability to see this shows that his sympathies lie not with these striving black subjects, but with the white planters. Thomas diagnoses in Froude an "impotent grudge" against the black population, whose activities nevertheless provide "a living refutation of the sinister predictions ventured upon generally against their race, with frantic recklessness...by affrighted slave-holders, of whose ravings Mr. Froude's book is only a diluted echo, out of season and outrageous to the conscience of modern civilization" (*Fr.* 127–8).

Among the many who were inspired by Thomas' response to Froude's racism was Frederick Alexander Durham. Durham himself highlights a similarity between *Froudacity* and his own *Lone-Star of Liberia*: like Thomas, Durham is responding to a book by an English writer, William Laird Clowes. While working as a journalist for the *London Times*, Clowes spent time in the American South and published a series of letters in the *Times* describing and analyzing the social and political situation there. These were collected and published in 1891 as a book entitled *Black America: A Study of the Ex-Slave and His Late Master*. Like Froude, Clowes opposed the political empowerment of black people. For him, the mere presence of such people in the United States was an almost insoluble challenge to its democratic system of governance. He expressed the paradox this way: "Equality between the races is a hopeless dream; yet the whole fabric of American institutions rests upon the assumed equality of its citizens."[6] He mentioned proposals to solve the problem by surrendering some or all of the so-called Black Belt of the southern US to the black population. But this would presuppose what Clowes termed "the unjustifiable premiss that the negro is fit for self-government." And whom did he cite as an authority when rejecting this premise? None other than his countryman, James Anthony Froude, and specifically Froude's arguments in *The English in the West Indies* that Haiti had been a horrific failure, a warning against the granting of self-government to black West Indians.

Sounding much like Thomas, Durham explains in the preface to *The Lone-Star of Liberia* that "the aspersions and libels cast on the African Race by Mr. W. Laird Clowes in his 'Black America'...impose on me the duty of repelling and refuting the same" (*LSL* xi). Durham does just this over the course of the book, including a whirlwind discussion of the intellectual giants of Africa, going all the way back to such figures as Augustine, Tertullian, and Origen. When he gets to the modern period, he touches on practically every figure we have covered, or even mentioned in passing, in the second part of this book, from Juan Latino all the way up to J.J. Thomas, of whom he writes: "The late Mr. John Jacob Thomas, whom we knew personally, was a grammarian and author. It was his pen that supplied a long-felt want of those who were ignorant of the French Creole *patois*" (*LSL* 40).

Thus Durham enters Thomas into the list of intellectual giants, and celebrates *The Theory and Practice of Creole Grammar* as the latter's most significant contribution. But Thomas comes up again at the end of chapter 5, which Durham closes with a poem that appeared in *Froudacity*. Thomas treated the poem as a quotation and ascribed it to an anonymous "West Indian Negro," but, at least according to Durham, the poem is by Thomas himself. Durham writes: "The above quoted lines were written by our late esteemed and distinguished countryman, John Jacob Thomas, author of 'The Creole Grammar,' and 'Froudacity-Froudacity,' in a reply to Mr. James Anthony Froude's 'The English in the West Indies.' Mr. Thomas coined it from the historian of Henry the Eighth's cognomen, Froudacity being synonymous with mendacity. Hence, an Africo-American, a West Indo-African, or other African would term the assertions made by W. Laird Clowes and other calumniators of the mighty and wonderful Ethiopian race, *froudacious*" (*LSL* 221).

Which is all good fun. But, even putting aside the mistaken repetition in the title of Thomas' book, Durham's etymology of "froudacity" may be wrong. The word is often understood to be a portmanteau of Froude's name and "audacity," not "mendacity." Furthermore, the term "froudacious" was used before Thomas' book appeared, in a critique of Froude by a white Guyanese writer named Nicholas Darnell Davis, and reportedly prior to that by Australian critics of Froude. For our purposes, though, the main point is that Durham is consciously building upon Thomas' work. In fact, one might have the impression that Durham's relationship with Thomas was similar to the bond of influence and inspiration between Durham and Blyden, or perhaps even closer, given that Durham tells us he knew Thomas personally. But that impression would be wrong. While Durham nowhere openly criticizes Thomas in *The Lone-Star of Liberia*, the book is nevertheless a radical rejection of Thomas' political vision. Durham's approach to Blyden is the reverse: he openly criticizes Blyden, but in a way that shows just how ideologically in tune with Blyden he really is.

Durham's critique of Blyden is found in the final chapter of *The Lone-Star of Liberia*, entitled "Repatriation and Liberia." Here, Durham lays out his ideas about how people of African descent in the Americas can overcome their oppression. For all his sharp criticisms of Clowes, he agrees with Clowes that the only way to solve the problem of racial strife in the United States is for African Americans to be supported in emigrating to Africa. Of course, given his skepticism as to whether black people are capable of self-government, Clowes could only picture African Americans flourishing in Africa if they were under British rule. They would be happy subjects there, as he imagined black people in the Caribbean to be happy under British colonial dominion. For Durham, by contrast, the whole point of going to Africa is the attainment of true and complete independence. Thus he arrives at his radical position: "We propose to send all Africans who are living out of Africa, and who are willing to go, to the Independent Republic of Liberia. This is *the* country all Africans except the Haytians should go to" (*LSL* 245). The title of Durham's book evokes Liberia's flag, which resembles the flag of the United States but with only one star. At a more metaphorical level, the title indicates that Liberia is a beacon that should attract all black people back toward Africa. The only exception is the Haitians, who can already boast of living in an independent black republic.

It is in this context that Durham muses, "Honest and well-meaning men like…Liberian Professor Blyden will sometimes say things which on second thoughts they would not say" (*LSL* 251). He refers here to a lecture delivered by Blyden in Lagos in 1891, the same year that Clowes' book was published. Blyden encouraged his audience to "imagine the result of one hundred thousand Negroes from America settled in the Yoruba country, with their knowledge of, and practice in, the use not only of implements of peace, but of the instruments of war." Durham quotes the passage and then admonishes: "What we think a distinguished and talented man like Liberian Blyden 'should imagine,' or rather work for, is the unity and concentration of the Ethiopian race—at least, the English-speaking portion of it…We do not want a man who will *scatter*, but one who will *unite*, the already scattered race. Let a talented man like Liberian Blyden unite the Ethiopian race in Liberia" (*LSL* 252).

Here Durham aims, we might say, to out-Blyden Blyden himself. He seeks to push Blyden's emigrationism to its logical conclusion, which means single-minded dedication to the growth of Liberia. To say that his vision for Liberia is an expansionist one would be a gross understatement. Because Haiti is geographically bounded, being just part of an island, it cannot offer an adequate home for all black emigrants. The situation in West Africa is different. Durham thinks it is not only possible but absolutely essential that "Liberia should be reinforced, consolidated, and extended" (*LSL* 301). Given Durham's adamant opposition to division among Africans, one gets the impression that he would find it quite satisfactory if the borders of Liberia were to expand until they contained within them all of Africa, or at least all of what we might call black Africa.

If this vision of independence through emigration to Liberia and the subsequent expansion of that country was even more ambitious than the one envisioned by Blyden, it puts Durham completely at odds with Thomas. Durham, unlike Thomas, sees no value in black West Indians remaining and being acknowledged as an "integral portion of the British Empire." In response to the kind of aspiration toward self-government defended in *Froudacity*, Durham responds: "Does the African subject of the British Empire desire Home Rule? There is Liberia; she enjoys *Independence*" (*LSL* 290). At one point, he speaks directly to Afro-Trinidadians, naming towns and villages in various parts of the island, and imploring their inhabitants to seek a better life in Liberia instead (*LSL* 300). Thomas and Durham thus adopt very different agendas for black people in Trinidad and the rest of the Caribbean. Yet Durham avoids making this deep disagreement explicit when he speaks of Thomas. Perhaps because, with Thomas already dead and gone, there could be no fruitful debate between them.

But what happened to Durham? When did he die? Or more pertinently, *where* did he die? We know he hailed from Trinidad and spent time in England, where he wrote his book. But did he follow his own advice and end up in Liberia? To our knowledge, the only published work with information about Durham's life is Marika Sherwood's biography of Henry Sylvester Williams, another important Afro-Trinidadian. Williams is often cited as a founder of Pan-Africanism, despite following in the footsteps of others with a strong claim to this title, like Paul Cuffe and Martin Delany. This is because he organized the first ever Pan-African conference in London in 1900, thereby giving the movement its name. A few years before this, he created an organization called the African Association, and Sherwood's book reveals that Durham was involved, along with two brothers of his. Durham, both of these brothers, and Williams were all Trinidadians who studied law in London. But unlike his brothers and other figures we will discuss in chapters to come, such as Anna Julia Cooper and W.E.B. Du Bois, Durham does not appear on Sherwood's list of attendees at the Pan-African conference.[7] So where was he? We can't say for sure, but a scholar named Peter Fraser has found a record of Durham in the Gold Coast, or present-day

Ghana, in 1915.[8] So Durham was indeed true to his principles: he did go to Africa. Perhaps he even spent time in Liberia before ending up in the Gold Coast. It's nice that we haven't completely lost track of him in his final years, and even nicer that this mostly lost voice of nineteenth century Africana thought should finally get the attention he deserves.

48

THOUGH LATE, IT IS LIBERTY

Abolitionism in Brazil

If you're from North America or Europe, chances are that when you think of the transatlantic slave trade, what comes to mind is the cotton plantations of the southern United States. Beyond that, you're likely to think of the sugar plantations of the Caribbean islands. But, in fact, the colony in the Americas with the largest number of African slaves was Brazil, with more than 3 million arriving there over the hundreds of years the slave trade was in business.[1] The Portuguese began taking people from Africa already in the fifteenth century, at first mostly bringing their captives to Europe to serve as domestic slaves but eventually transporting them to the so-called "New World" as manpower for an empire funded by agriculture. As in Haiti, sugar and later on coffee were the major crops, though, in Brazil, slaves also labored in mines and in cotton fields—indeed, in every sector of the economy. The Portuguese did also enslave the indigenous population, but came to prefer slaves from Africa, in part because they were more likely already to have acquired immunity to European diseases.

The result, demographically speaking, was a population where black and mixed-race people collectively constituted (and still constitute) the majority. By the nineteenth century, the so-called "free colored" greatly outnumbered those still enslaved, with the two groups together numbering about 5.8 million in 1872 (about 1.5 million more than the black population of the United States at the same time). The result appalled observers like Count Joseph Arthur de Gobineau, who lamented that the Brazilians were "a completely mulatto population, of polluted blood and spirit," with "not a single Brazilian of pure blood."[2] Brazil's pattern of racial diversity resulted in people not being classified as simply white or black. One survey has counted forty different terms to describe skin color, literal shades of meaning across a spectrum that could not be reduced to the three basic terms—*branco, pardo*, and *preto*—meaning "white, mulatto, and black."[3] With measures like dress codes and the exclusion of non-whites from holding public office, Brazilian society made skin color the key determinant of social mobility.[4] Every bit of melanin made a difference: all else being equal, the whiter you were, the better your prospects.

You might hope that the sizeable non-white population, even among free citizens, would have led to a relatively early date for abolition. But the reverse was the case. The slaves were finally emancipated only in 1888, making Brazil the last country in the Americas to abolish slavery. Even this was achieved only after several, more faltering steps in this direction.[5] Importation of slaves ended in 1850, and in 1871 the "Law of the Free Womb" declared that, henceforth, no one would be born into slavery. The idea was that slavery would be phased out slowly, giving the agricultural system that depended on it time to adapt. But as critics pointed out, it would mean delaying abolition by decades, in addition to which children born to slaves were still going to grow up within the same oppressive system, even if they were legally free.

Thanks to this stuttering and contradictory approach to emancipation, in the middle of the nineteenth century many were being held as slaves illegally, for instance because they had been smuggled into the country in violation of the ban on the slave trade. Activists sought to use the legal system to free such people. One such activist was Luiz Gama. His mother, Luisa Mahin, was Nago, a term that in the Brazilian context refers to being of Yoruba background. She secured her freedom some time before Gama was born in 1830. What became of her is shrouded in mystery but, as one scholar reports, "according to popular tradition, she became an outstanding leader of several slave uprisings which rocked [the Brazilian state of] Bahia during the early part of the nineteenth century."[6] She is sometimes said to have been deported to Angola as a result of this leadership role. Apparently Gama's father was a white man, though Gama declined to say so explicitly, making the telling remark, "in this country, such assertions regarding the delicate subject of human color are quite risky in face of the truth."[7] When he was 10, his father sold him into slavery to cover gambling bets. He fled from this illegal captivity at the age of 18 and became a crusader in the courts for others, eventually winning freedom for more than 500 people, and for himself the honorary title, "advocate of the wretched."[8]

Gama's career echoes developments we've seen in the United States. He became master of a Masonic Lodge and used it as an instrument to fight for abolition. He wrote for newspapers and gave prominent speeches, including an 1873 address to the First Republican Congress in Rio de Janeiro, in which he attacked the halfway-house compromise that was the Law of the Free Womb. But he is also remembered as a literary figure, especially for poems like *Who Am I?* (*Quem sou eu?*), in which he satirically compared human skin tones to the color of goats, because "goat" was a term of abuse used for blacks. Yes, he said, there are white goats and black ones, and poor goats and rich ones too, just as he could claim common ancestry with the mixed-race aristocrats of Brazilian society. In another poem, he ironically showed off his flair as a writer even while lamenting his exclusion from the world of letters: "Sciences and letters / Are not for you / Black from the coast / You are no one here...I don't want them to say / That I was too bold / And that I intruded / Upon science / Sorry, my dear friend / There is nothing I can give you / In the land ruled by the white / We're deprived even of thinking!"[9]

He also inspired others, for instance the journalist and political cartoonist Raúl Pompeia, who met Gama in 1881 and idolized him, calling him "friend to the whole world." With Pompeia we come to a distinctive theme of the abolitionist movement in Brazil, namely a feeling of shame at the nation's failure to end slavery.[10] Pompeia was himself the son of plantation owners. Nonetheless, he joined Gama and other abolitionist writers like André Pinto Rebouças and José Carlos do Patrocínio in their campaign against slavery, trying to mobilize popular opinion in Brazil to support total abolition. Yet Pompeia was sensitive about appealing to popular opinion *outside* Brazil. He attacked those who aired the nation's dirty moral laundry in the international press. For him, national pride was a reason to end slavery, but it was also a reason not to admit to the world that the cruel slave system still defined Brazilian society.

On this issue he was at odds with the man who remains the most famous representative of Brazilian abolitionism, Joaquim Nabuco. Together with Rebouças he founded the Brazilian Anti-Slavery Society in 1880; three years later he published his most important work, called simply *Abolitionism*.[11] More international in outlook than Pompeia, Nabuco was inspired by the example of the United States, which had managed to abolish slavery before Brazil did. In his book he alludes to admired names like William Lloyd Garrison, Harriet Beecher Stowe, and Frederick Douglass (24, 33). Elsewhere he even used "Garrison" as a pen-name. He also speaks of the national disgrace of being condemned by the British, and invokes the French declaration of the Rights of Man (70, 89). You can imagine him flushing with embarrassment as he recounts how Charles Darwin ended a visit to Brazil by remarking, "I thank God, I shall never again visit a slave-country" (162).

Despite Nabuco's disagreement with Pompeia over the question of whether critiques of slavery should be aimed at a global audience, the two certainly agreed that being a good Brazilian patriot was a sound basis for abolitionism. Indeed, as he freely admitted, he spoke not from "the point of view of the slave" but "the standpoint of the patriot" (141). Nabuco was himself a member of the white elite, whose father had also been an important national politician. He was thus motivated more by a feeling of national honor than by any sense of identification with slaves, or with the free citizens classified as "colored." Indeed he took racial inequality to be more or less a given fact, something that comes out in a few passages of his *Abolitionism*, as when he complains that instead of elevating the Africans who have come to Brazil, the country has seen "the bastardization of the more advanced race by the more backward" (102). At one point he says that he wishes to see the liberation of both slaves *and masters* from this wicked practice (107); some modern-day readers think it was the liberation of the masters that concerned him most.[12] Still, his *Abolitionism* does express concern over the plight of those currently enslaved and emphasizes the need to work toward their economic uplift after emancipation, which will be only the first step in true abolition (3, 9–10). He saw the integration of former slaves into a thriving, democratic Brazil as a long-term project. In the shorter term he supported the Brazilian monarchy, not least because the royal family might be enlisted as allies in the struggle against slavery, but also because he had a low opinion of the Brazilian people, who seemed to him insufficiently educated and civilized to govern themselves.[13]

Despite his elitist and at times racist outlook, Nabuco can also take credit for refusing to minimize the tyranny of slaveholding in Brazil. Proponents of slavery liked to tell themselves that masters in Brazil were gentler than those in, say, the United States. Brazil was less racist, less violent, and offered greater opportunity for slaves to win freedom and integrate into wider society. This reassuring story didn't fit very well with the long history of slave uprisings in Brazil, some of which led to the establishment of *quilombos*, communities of former slaves who had escaped to freedom. Luiz Gama told of how, when his father sold him, it was difficult to find a buyer because he was from Bahia, where, as we noted in relation to his mother, several rebellions had occurred.[14] Nonetheless, the narrative of "mild" slavemasters was still being put forward in the twentieth century. A prominent case was Gilberto Freyre, whose influential 1933 book *The Masters and the Slaves* argued for the relative benevolence of slavery in Brazil, which he depicted as a socially mobile, multi-ethnic, and multi-racial society. Freyre gave credit to the cultural values of the Portuguese and their approach to colonization, which was free of the "race hatred" that characterized slavery in the United States.[15] This made possible a more integrated society after abolition, which Freyre optimistically called "one of the most harmonious unions of culture with nature and of one culture with another that the lands of this hemisphere have ever known."

Freyre's positive portrait of Brazilian culture remains appealing, insofar as he identified its diverse population as a strength. We're a long way here from

Gobineau's laments about "polluted blood." But the notion of more or less gentle or harmonious slaveholding, which of course echoes elements of American nostalgia for the antebellum South, had already been refuted quite effectively decades before, by Nabuco. In principle "all slavery is the same," he said, because it is an "attack on all humanity" and a violation of the natural law (81, 95). If a master can get away with treating his victims gently, Nabuco observed, this is simply because those victims have had their spirits crushed to the point of resignation. As he nicely put it, "The limit of the master's cruelty is to be found in the meekness of the slave. When meekness ceases cruelty begins" (96). He also argued persuasively that slavery was a corrupting force for Brazilian society as a whole. He would have agreed with Freyre that nineteenth century Brazilian discrimination was less vicious than could be found in the United States at the same time, especially as concerning free blacks (22). But slavery still divided the nation along race lines. Again, his paramount concern was what this did to the Brazilian national character: "With slavery there is no national patriotism, only the patriotism of caste or of race" (133).

A far more subtle portrait of the corruption caused by slavery can be found in the writings of the most famous Brazilian author of this period, Machado de Assis. He is not known as a political campaigner or activist, but as a novelist and poet, indeed in the judgment of literary critic Harold Bloom, the "greatest black writer in the history of universal literature."[16] He was mixed race, on which point there's a story that illustrates the aforementioned Brazilian sensitivity to terms denoting skin color: when an admirer of Machado referred to him as a "mulatto" after he died, none other than Nabuco protested that this was a derogatory designation.[17] What about Machado himself? Would he have appreciated being identified as a "mulatto"? Well, while there is no doubting Machado's importance in the history of Brazilian literature, people have doubted whether he identified at all with people of color, or was interested in their legal and social condition.

Against this, two lines of interpretation have been offered to highlight the relevance of race in his writings. One is straightforward: he did in fact write in favor of abolition, albeit sometimes under pseudonyms,[18] and there are passages in his fiction and poetry that engage directly with slavery and race. In a story from 1872, a house slave is taken aback by a visitor's refusal to accept being turned away at the door. Machado writes, "the young man's resolute tone shocked the slave, whose spirit, accustomed to obedience, almost didn't know how to distinguish it from duty." The psychological point here couldn't have come from someone who gave no thought to the nature of slavery. It plays a more central role in a poem called *Sabina*, from 1875, which tells the story of a slave who is seduced and then abandoned by her master's son, leaving her with an illegitimate child. Later on, in a novel that appeared in 1908, Machado has a character reflect back on abolition in the following terms: "I still recall what I read in the foreign press about us on the occasion of Lincoln's famous proclamation. More than one newspaper made a nominal allusion to Brazil, saying there remained only one Christian population to imitate them and end slavery. I hope that today they praise us. Even though late, it is liberty."

If you detect a note of irony mixed in there, along with a patriotic sentiment that would be at home in Nabuco or Pompeia, then you've got a good ear. Which brings us to the second, more subtle, interpretation. It has been put forward especially by the literature scholar Roberto Schwarz in a magisterial analysis of Machado's great novel *The Posthumous Memoirs of Brás Cubas*.[19] This novel is not about slavery, at least not at the level of plot. Instead it tells the story of an intellectual and politician, the Brás Cubas of the title, his love affairs, family relations, and so on. But at a deeper level, at least on Schwarz's reading, the novel is a reaction to slavery and the other exploitative class dynamics that corrupt Brazilian society.

We find this pretty convincing. For one thing, even a cursory skimming will tell you that whatever the book is about, it isn't the plot. It's a novel full of literary gamesmanship and amusing, layered ironies. One chapter is made up entirely of a redacted conversation; another chapter tells us it that it should be inserted into the previous one; another remarks on its own pointlessness; yet another begins "Now watch the skill, the art with which I make the greatest transition in this book. Watch!" (ch. 9). Naturally, the book concludes with a list of things that *didn't* happen to the narrator (ch. 160). As for how it starts, the narrator decides to begin his story with his death, rather than his birth: "I was accompanied to the cemetery by eleven friends. Eleven friends! The fact is, there hadn't been any cards or announcements. On top of that, it was raining" (ch. 1). Along with the joke, there's an allusion here to Laurence Sterne's novel *The Life and Opinions of Tristram Shandy*, which by contrast does begin by having the title character relate the story of his own conception and birth. Sterne (who unexpectedly has managed to appear twice in this book, as we mentioned him in the chapter on Ignatius Sancho) is famous for his digressive, meandering style. That style is echoed by Brás Cubas, who at one point compares his own story to the staggerings of a drunk (ch. 71).

This is all quite entertaining, but also has the effect of underscoring the narrator's fundamental unseriousness. Which is where Schwarz's reading gets its purchase. For him, Machado is trying to unmask the hollowness and triviality of the values held by the Brazilian elite, as represented by the main character and narrator Brás Cubas. At several points, Cubas and other characters put forth grand philosophies of life that depict superficiality as the deepest of insights and narcissism as the highest ethical principle. One chapter is dedicated to the "philosophy of the nose," inspired by a practice of Indian ascetics where one focuses on the tip of one's own nose to the exclusion of all other things (ch. 49). Brás Cubas explains: "Such contemplation, whose effect is subordination to just one nose, constitutes the equilibrium of societies." So this "philosophy" is an explicit justification of self-obsession, which we're told is needed to balance out "love" for other people. In another chapter, we meet an exponent of Humanitism, a philosophy that revolves around concern with one's own worldly existence and pleasures (ch. 117). This philosopher illustrates Humanitism by saying that he has just had chicken for lunch, which was fed on grain planted by slaves who were abducted from Africa. From which he draws the following lesson: "This chicken, which I've just had for lunch, is the result of a multitude of exertions and struggles, carried out with the single aim of satisfying my appetite."

Such monstrous self-regard makes it impossible to give things their correct moral weight. This is echoed more concretely in the person of the narrator's brother-in-law. He is a slave trader, who has committed terrible violence against his victims. The narrator blandly remarks: "Having been long involved in the smuggling of slaves, he'd become accustomed to a certain way of dealing that was a bit harsher than the business required, and one can't honestly attribute to the original nature of a man what is simply the effect of his social relations" (ch. 123). Admittedly, his brother-in-law isn't perfect, adds the narrator: he does have an annoying tendency to boast about his charity work. Long before Hannah Arendt, Machado was already depicting the banality of evil in a fictional setting. He also explores the way violence begets violence. While reminiscing about his childhood, the narrator tells us of how, as a boy, he would make a young slave named Prudêncio pretend to be his horse and whip him as part of the "game." When Prudêncio dared to complain, the narrator would shout at him "shut your mouth, beast (*cala a boca, besta*)!" (ch. 11). Later in the novel, the now adult narrator comes upon a black man beating his own slave and saying exactly the same thing (ch. 68). The one wielding the whip is none other than Prudêncio, who has gained his freedom and is now using it to "rid himself of the beatings he'd received by transmitting them to someone else."

For Schwarz, Machado's satire responds to the hypocrisy and shameful exploitation of Brazilian society, no less than the more direct political response of Nabuco. As Schwarz puts it, "from the practical perspective, slavery was a contemporary necessity; from the emotional perspective, a traditional presence; and from the ideological perspective, an archaic disgrace."[20] The appearance of philosophy itself as a mere affectation, and the narrator's failure to respond adequately to the sufferings of others, help to create what Schwarz calls an "intimate combination of social satisfaction and moral dead end," which for him is definitive of Machado's writing.[21] It all results from the psychological conflict felt by the Brazilian ruling class. On the one hand, this elite knew and admired the liberal values of the European Enlightenment; on the other hand, their dominant position was secured through illiberal tyranny and oppression. Compared to the strident rhetoric of an author like Nabuco, a comedic and ironic novel may seem an insufficiently outraged reaction to the horror of slavery. But if you want to learn about the insidious psychology and moral evasion of a slaveowning elite, you can do no better than to read Machado de Assis.

49

WHEN AND WHERE I ENTER

Anna Julia Cooper

On March 23, 1925, a Martinican student by the name of Jane Nardal attended a dissertation defence at the prestigious Sorbonne in Paris. The event left an indelible mark on Nardal, who was then 23 years old. She wrote of its impact a few years later in a letter to Alain Locke, the African American professional philosopher best known as the premier theorist of the cultural movement we now call the Harlem Renaissance. In her letter to Locke, Nardal writes of going to congratulate the impressive scholar who had just defended her doctoral dissertation, a 66-year-old black woman from the United States whose thesis explored attitudes toward slavery during the time of the French and Haitian Revolutions. Reflecting on the effect that this experience had on her burgeoning racial consciousness, Nardal explains that "my curiosity, my interest, already captured by other [Negro things], began to awaken."[1] Who was this remarkable older woman, who took an unapproved leave of absence from her job as a high school teacher in Washington DC to go to France and become the first black woman to earn a PhD from the Sorbonne? Nardal identifies her in the letter as "Mrs. J.J. Cooper," but clearly misheard or incorrectly remembered the first initial, for her name was Anna Julia Cooper. She lived a very long and intellectually productive life. Well before her achievement in Paris, she sealed her place in the annals of Africana thought with her 1892 book, *A Voice from the South*, which is now widely acknowledged as one of the philosophical masterpieces of black writing in the nineteenth century.[2]

Cooper was born into slavery as Annie Hayward in 1858 in Raleigh, North Carolina. Her mother was an enslaved black woman and it is generally assumed that her father was her mother's master.[3] At the age of 9, just a couple of years after the end of slavery, she began studying at Saint Augustine Normal School, which would eventually become Saint Augustine's University, a black college. Her studies there would stretch over fourteen years and she served as a tutor and teacher for the school. It was also at Saint Augustine's that she met George Cooper, whom she married in 1877. Unfortunately, he died after just two years of marriage. Such tragedy is necessarily saddening, although, as in the case of Maria Stewart, being widowed arguably allowed Cooper to forge a path as a public intellectual. She earned a bachelor's and then a master's degree in Mathematics from Oberlin College in Ohio, and eventually ended up in Washington DC, which is where she lived most of her life from the late 1880s all the way until her death at the age of 105 (yes, you read that right) in 1964. For much of this time, she taught at the M Street High School, later renamed after the poet Paul Laurence Dunbar, and for some of the early years of the twentieth century, she was the school's principal.

It was during the early years of her time as a teacher that Cooper gave us *A Voice from the South*. Its uniqueness is evident from the book's preface, entitled "Our Raison d'Être." Here Cooper uses both musical and legal analogies to explain the significance of her intervention. Within "the Silent South," as the white writer George Washington Cable had critically called the region, there is what Cooper calls "the muffled strain," a "jarring chord and a vague and uncomprehended cadenza" that is "the Negro" (*VS* i). "Of that muffled chord," she adds, "the one mute and voiceless note has been the sadly expectant Black Woman" (*VS* i). This description of the black woman as a voiceless note can be connected to Cooper's choice to label the first of the book's two parts, which is the part that focuses most on women in general and on black women in particular, "Soprano Obligato." The voice from the South heard in this book is the voice of a black woman, making a long-ignored yet indispensable contribution to the mix of voices speaking out on America's present and future.

Switching to the metaphor of a courtroom in which attorneys dispute "the colored man's inheritance," while barely paying attention to what this black client has to say, Cooper writes: "One important witness has not yet been heard from. The summing up of the evidence deposed, and the charge to the jury have been made—but no word from the Black Woman" (*VS* i–ii). After describing the black woman yet again as "open-eyed but hitherto voiceless," Cooper makes a key point that demonstrates why this book has been so cherished by subsequent generations of black feminists (*VS* ii). Ending the black woman's muteness is necessary, because "as our Caucasian barristers are not to blame if they cannot *quite* put themselves in the dark man's place, neither should the dark man be wholly expected fully and adequately to reproduce the exact Voice of the Black Woman" (*VS* iii). In other words, the black woman is not merely a part of a genderless black collective that can be represented sufficiently by black male authors. Neither can the white woman stand in and speak up for her. The black woman's voice is unique, and it must be heard.

The first chapter of *A Voice from the South* is called "Womanhood a Vital Element in the Regeneration and Progress of a Race." The earliest of Cooper's major writings, it was initially delivered as an address to a gathering of black Episcopalian clergy in 1886. One especially noteworthy and much-quoted sentence from this chapter is considered to be among the most insightful statements of black feminism ever articulated. We'll leave you in suspense for a bit, and lay out the context of the remark before quoting it. The chapter begins with an extended reflection on the relationship between social progress and the treatment of women. Taking a breathtakingly broad perspective, Cooper pursues this topic through a comparative global history spanning millennia. This starting point is also troubling, as she posits a divide between East and West that homogenizes the East in order to criticize it and glorify the West. She subsumes cultures from China to Turkey under her sweeping judgment that "in Oriental countries woman has been uniformly devoted to a life of ignorance, infamy, and complete stagnation" (*VS* 9). The general stasis that results in the East is, she thinks, in sharp contrast with the "progressive, elevating and inspiring" character of what she calls "the European bud and the American flower of modern civilization" (*VS* 10). Cooper's metaphor seems to suggest that America is the culmination of all the world's progress, and thus beyond reproach. Culmination it may be, but America is far from perfect in her view. To the contrary, she is careful to note that "our satisfaction in American institutions rests not on the fruition we now enjoy, but springs rather from the possibilities and promise that are inherent in the system, though as yet, perhaps, far in the future" (*VS* 12).

Cooper argues that European civilization has reached its greatest point thus far in American life, because a high regard for women was built into two of its sources, namely Christianity and feudalism. A tender regard for women among the Germanic barbarians informed the value of chivalry that was central to feudalism, a value that magnified and elevated the position of women. You might wonder if appreciating feudalism in this way means ignoring or condoning its rigid hierarchy, but for Cooper, this is precisely where Christianity comes in. She celebrates this religion's leveling ideals, and portrays Jesus as a brilliant feminist who upheld a single standard of purity for both women and men, and who stood against the judgmental tendencies through which men hypocritically place themselves above women. After the fall of Rome, Christianity adapted itself sufficiently to the tastes and prejudices of barbarian culture that the ennobling forces within both traditions could be preserved. This, for Cooper, laid the groundwork for the greatness of Western civilization.

So far this has been a broadly empirical, historical account. But now Cooper shifts to an *a priori* argument that there must be a close relationship between progress in general and the advancement of women in society. In other words, she sees this as a matter of pure reasoning, which is in no need of empirical evidence. This should presumably not be understood to render her historical account superfluous; rather, she seeks better to explain the mechanisms of progress that her account sought to capture. Her *a priori* argument is, nevertheless, among the more controversial points of the essay and her thought in general. The position of women determines the progressive and regenerative character of society "not because woman is better or stronger or wiser than man, but from the nature of the case, because it is she who must first form the man by directing the earliest impulses of his character" (*VS* 21). In other words, the child-rearing role of mothers is what makes women crucial to social progress, or its lack.

This has some common sense plausibility, but might be criticized on the grounds that Cooper ties womanhood so closely to motherhood and home-making that she undercuts the feminist ideal of empowering women—the very ideal that she is clearly trying to promote. A similar, though more nuanced, impression may be taken from her book's second chapter, "The Higher Education of Women." She extols the nineteenth century as a time of spectacular progress, as witnessed by the numbers of women accessing higher education, and thereby gaining greater influence on the ideas and actions of the world. She feels the need, though, to consider the objection that higher learning unfits women for marriage. Cooper is unapologetic in celebrating the way education gives women greater self-reliance and expands their sense of what is possible. Yet she also relies on Mary Frances Armstrong's argument that education can make women better homemakers: "Their knowledge of physiology makes them better mothers and housekeepers; their knowledge of chemistry makes them better cooks; while from their training in other natural sciences and in mathematics, they obtain an accuracy and fair-mindedness which is of great value to them in dealing with their children or employees" (*VS* 71–2).

These passages may suggest that Cooper felt unable to challenge the essential domestic duties of women—not surprising, you might think, since as we've said this book came out in 1892. But when we turn to the fourth chapter, "The Status of Women in America," we find her discussing the fact that domesticity was far *less* inevitable in 1892 than it had been in former times. Half a century before the time of writing, women's activities were far more confined to "the kitchen" and "the nursery" (*VS* 142). Now in the 1890s, Cooper sees no sphere as completely closed off to women: "Not one of the issues of this plodding, toiling, sinning, repenting, falling, aspiring humanity can afford to shut her out, or can deny the reality of her influence. No plan for renovating society, no scheme for purifying politics, no reform in church or in state, no moral, social, or economic question, no movement upward or downward in the human plane is lost on her" (*VS* 142-3). While Cooper does not disavow the important role of mother and homemaker highlighted in the first chapter, she here affirms more clearly than ever that women can and should be involved in affairs outside the home, on an equal footing with men.

Returning to that first chapter, we now arrive at Cooper's transition from discussing the social progress of women in general to the case of black women in particular. Here she acknowledges the contribution of Alexander Crummell, while also challenging his views. She proclaims woman's influence on social progress to be as obvious as the sun's influence on the world as the source of light and heat, and suggests it is equally unnecessary for her to spend time applying this principle to the question of black social progress. Paraphrasing *Ecclesiastes*, she explains: "For is it not written, 'Cursed is he that cometh after the king?' and has not the King already preceded me in 'The Black Woman of the South'?" (*VS* 24). The "King" here is Crummell, "The Black Woman of the South" being the title of an address he delivered in 1883. There is indeed much in that address that anticipates Cooper's essay. For example, Crummell expresses the importance of women to social progress in the following terms: "I am anxious for a permanent and uplifting civilization to be engrafted on the Negro race in this land. And this can only be secured through the womanhood of the race. If you want the civilization of a people to reach the very best elements of their being, and then, having reached them, there to abide, as an indigenous principle, you must imbue the *womanhood* of that people with all its elements and qualities" (*AA* 79).[4]

To this Cooper adds what she modestly suggests is a simple amendment, though on closer inspection it may plausibly be regarded as more of a rebuke—a complaint to the king disguised as a mere extension of his royal proclamation, if you will. Crummell's essay insisted on distinguishing the racial terms "black" and "colored," saying: "In speaking to-day of the 'black woman', I must needs make a very clear distinction. The African race in this country is divided into two classes, that is—the *colored people* and the *negro population*" (*AA* 62). Whereas "black" and "negro" are interchangeable for Crummell, neither has the same meaning as "colored," which he uses to refer to those who are of mixed ancestry. The distinction is important, he thinks, because of how differently situated the two groups are, especially with regard to literacy and material prosperity. The much smaller "colored" group outstrips the much larger "black" group with respect to both criteria. Crummell thinks the reason is obvious: "The colored population received, in numerous cases, the kindness and generosity of their white kindred—white fathers and relatives" (*AA* 62). By contrast, the black population—and, most importantly for his purposes, the black woman—has been left comparatively uneducated and destitute.

This is the context for Cooper's remark: "I would beg, however, with the Doctor's permission, to add my plea for the *Colored Girls* of the South:—that large, bright, promising fatally beautiful class that stand shivering like a delicate plantlet before the fury of tempestuous elements, so full of promise and possibilities, yet so sure of destruction" (*VS* 24-5). Cooper, herself a "colored girl" (or rather "colored woman") in this sense of the phrase, is not just adding what was left out by Crummell but rather rejecting his treatment of those in this category as straightforwardly privileged. Against his emphasis on the kindness of white progenitors and kin, she describes the "colored girl" as being "often without a father to whom they dare apply the loving term, often without a stronger brother to espouse their cause and defend their honor with his life's blood; in the midst of pitfalls and snares, waylaid by the lower classes of white men, with no shelter, no protection nearer than the great blue vault above, which half conceals and half reveals the one Care-Taker they know so little of" (*VS* 25).

It should be noted that Cooper does not consistently adhere to Crummell's terminological distinction. The very title page of *A Voice from the South* describes its author as "a Black Woman of the South," not a "colored" one. And Cooper includes Crummell, who was definitely and proudly on the black side of the distinction, in a list of "colored men" in the book's sixth chapter (*VS* 200). The very fact that "black" and "colored" are usually roughly synonymous for Cooper underscores that her point in this passage is indeed to engage critically with "the Doctor," as she calls him. And Cooper is not done taking on great black thinkers of the recent past. Having expressed her dissatisfaction with Crummell, she next turns her attention to Martin Delany.

As Kathryn Sophia Belle has pointed out, Cooper echoes Delany no less than Crummell with her main thesis. Much earlier than Crummell, Delany already wrote: "No people are ever elevated above the condition of their *females*; hence, the condition of the *mother* determines the condition of the child. To know the position of a people, it is only necessary to know the *condition* of their *females*; and despite themselves, they cannot rise above their level."[5] We cannot be certain whether Cooper knew of this passage from Delany's 1852 book, *The Condition, Elevation, Emigration, and Destiny of the Colored People of the United States*. Even if she did, this is not why she brings him up. Rather, Delany is for her the perfect example of a black male leader who regularly presents himself as representative of the race in its entirety. This is the Delany targeted by a memorable comment attributed to Frederick Douglass: "I thank God for making me a man simply; but Delany always thanks him for making him a *black man*."[6]

Writing in 1886—so, shortly after Delany's death in 1885—Cooper gives us an example of this tendency on his part while once again bringing up the matter of mixed or unmixed racial identity: "The late Martin R. Delany, who was an unadulterated black man, used to say when honors of state fell upon him, that when he entered the council of kings the black race entered with him; meaning, I suppose, that there was no discounting his race identity and attributing his achievements to some admixture of Saxon blood" (VS 30). Cooper shows herself charitable in explaining why Delany might have been drawn to count himself as an embodiment of his people. Yet she thinks it is a sheer confusion to treat any one leader as a representative of that whole race. This is a distraction from the real mechanisms of progress. She argues that "a stream cannot rise higher than its source," that "a race is but a total of families," and that "the atmosphere of homes is no rarer and purer and sweeter than are the mothers in those homes" (VS 29).

All of this leads, finally, to the phrase we promised to quote, the one for which she is now most famous: "Only the BLACK WOMAN can say 'when and where I enter, in the quiet, undisputed dignity of my womanhood, without violence and without suing or special patronage, then and there the whole *Negro race enters with me*'" (VS 31). As early as 1920, W.E.B. Du Bois quoted this comment in his feminist essay, "The Damnation of Women."[7] Much later, in 1984, Paula Giddings titled a book on black women's activism, *When and Where I Enter: The Impact of Black Women on Race and Sex in America*. At that time Cooper was still a little-known figure, but by the second decade of the twenty-first century, Cooper had become the only woman to be quoted on the pages of the official United States passport. The quotation comes from chapter 3 of *A Voice from the South*, "Woman vs. the Indian." In context, it is a reflection on the compatibility of the struggles against the oppression of women and against the oppression of Native Americans, indeed against all forms of oppression. So if you acquired a US passport some time between 2007 and the writing of this book, you've carried around these words of Cooper's in your pocket: "The cause of freedom is not the cause of a race or a sect, a party or a class,—it is the cause of humankind, the very birthright of humanity" (VS 120–1).

This is pretty good evidence that Cooper is now well on her way to being an iconic American thinker, but she has only just begun to receive her due as a philosopher. On this point, it's worth mentioning the final chapter of *A Voice from the South*, "The Gain from a Belief." It leaves behind the tight focus on matters of gender and race so prominent in the rest of the book, and turns to the classic philosophical question of what justifies religious belief. She traces a skeptical position, which for her is a threatening problem, back to Voltaire through David Hume, and then in the nineteenth century to Auguste Comte. Unlike Antenor Firmin, who as we saw was a devoted follower of Comte, Cooper harshly criticizes Comte's positivist philosophy as absurd. Given the *a priori* argumentation we found her using in the book's first chapter, it is perhaps unsurprising to find her rejecting a system of thought that, as she describes it, "scoffs at as presumptuous and unwarrantable all facts that cannot be discerned through the senses" (*VS* 293).

She furthermore takes as her chief antagonist in the essay Robert Ingersoll, who was known as the Great Agnostic. Against agnosticism, she champions faith, but not by defending faith within the realm of ideas. Instead she argues for a close connection between faith and activism: "The great, the fundamental need of any nation, any race, is for heroism, devotion, sacrifice; and there cannot be heroism, devotion, or sacrifice in a primarily skeptical spirit" (*VS* 297). This is no simplistic form of religious fundamentalism. If anything, one might detect here a tendency toward relativism: whatever belief system can best inspire activism in the name of justice deserves our allegiance. But that may not be the best "-ism" to capture what Cooper is saying. In a brilliant essay focused on this chapter, V. Denise James compares Cooper with the pragmatist philosopher William James and argues that Cooper articulates what we may call a "black feminist visionary pragmatism."[8] Religious fervor proves itself not through ironclad arguments, but by what it can accomplish.

50

AMERICAN BARBARISM

Ida B. Wells

Most political thinkers would be gratified to learn of their ideas remaining vitally relevant over many decades. Ida B. Wells, though, would be horrified to know that her writings speak so directly to the concerns of America some ninety years after her death. The murder of George Floyd in May of 2020 galvanized a new wave of protests under the banner of the Black Lives Matter movement, which has, since 2013, aimed to end police violence and all racially motivated violence against African Americans. This movement responds to what is clearly a systemic problem: the *Guardian* reported that police killed 1,134 people in America in 2015, with young black men nine times more likely to be killed than anyone else.[1] In providing these statistics, the *Guardian* was reprising the journalistic efforts of Wells, who likewise gathered information about extra-judicial violence against black men, and put it before the public. But Wells did something more. She offered an explanation of the system of brutality she catalogued, an explanation that was based on her observations of the American South in the decades following the Civil War, but remains startlingly, and depressingly, applicable to modern-day race relations.

As she explains in an *Autobiography* that remained unfinished at her death in 1931, Wells was born during the Civil War, in Mississippi in 1862.[2] Her parents were enslaved, with her father James Wells being the offspring of a white plantation owner and Peggy, one of this owner's slaves. In another resonance with our current era, Ida was orphaned as a teenager due to an epidemic, in this case of yellow fever, with the result that she had to take over the care of her younger siblings at the tender age of 16. From these inauspicious beginnings, she would rise to be a star in the firmament of African American activism. Her career began when she twice sued railroad companies for ejecting her from first-class cars. She described her experiences, which included biting the hand of the conductor who tried to remove her, in articles published by a newspaper in Memphis, where Wells was working as a teacher. Her story was picked up by the *New York Globe*, edited by none other than T. Thomas Fortune. Soon the name of Wells, or rather "Iola," the pen-name she used for her articles, was known around the country to readers of the black press. In 1888, she even became the first woman officer of the National Colored Press Association.

But it was an event in March of 1892 that brought her to true prominence. After three black men accused of causing unrest were arrested in Memphis, a white mob broke into the jail in the middle of the night, dragged them away, and shot them. Outraged, Wells wrote an editorial recommending that black people abandon Memphis, which she called "a town which will neither protect our lives and property, nor give us a fair trial in the courts, but takes us out and murders us in cold blood when accused by white persons" (*Autobiography* 52). In a flash of the sardonic wit that would become familiar to her readers, she remarked in another article that African Americans were comparing Memphis to hell, "without stopping to think they were doing the real hell an injustice." Wells had found her calling, as a crusader against lynching. She traveled to Philadelphia, where she stayed with another character familiar to us, Frances Ellen Watkins Harper, and to New York, to join forces with Fortune. In that same year of 1892 and in New York, she gave the first of many public addresses on the topic of lynching. The following year saw her campaigning abroad, in England and Scotland. In another case of the admiration that black activists felt for Britain in this period, she said that "America cannot and will not ignore the voice of a nation that is her superior in civilization" (100–1).[3] Like Frederick Douglass, she contrasted the openness of British society to the racism of the United States, saying that visiting England was like "being born into another world" (135).

This strategy of provoking international condemnation against the racist violence of her homeland infuriated white racists in America. Through threats of violence, they had already closed her newspaper back in Memphis and made her afraid to return to the city. Now, an Atlanta paper called her a "negro adventuress who has so deftly gulled a number of credulous persons in England."[4] But Wells did not back down; she doubled down. Over the coming decade she published a series of works on the topic of lynching, including *Southern Horrors: Lynch Law in All Its Phases*, *A Red Record*, and *Mob Rule in New Orleans*.[5] Her project had the explicit backing of Frederick Douglass, who noted that the power of these works lay in their wealth of hard information about the prevalence of lynching, facts laid out "plain" and "unvarnished," as she herself put it (*Mob Rule*, Introduction).[6] In *A Red Record*, especially, she included statistics on lynchings by state, and also names of victims along with the putative crimes for which they were executed. This list of offenses features items like "self defense," "insulting whites," "asking white woman to marry him," and "no offense" at all (*Red Record* ch. 2). As she says later in this book, black people at this time could be "lynched for anything or nothing" (ch. 5). To preempt charges of inaccuracy, Wells quotes reports from the white press to document all this information, saying, "out of their own mouths shall the murderers be condemned" (ch. 1).

All of this did have some effect, as shown by a gradual decline in the number of lynchings and by legal moves made by some states in the south to put a stop to the practice. As Wells saw clearly, moral condemnation had its place, but what really did the trick was economic threat. She wryly remarked that "the appeal to the white man's pocket has ever been more effectual than all the appeals ever made to his conscience" (*Southern Horrors* ch. 6). The real cost of lynchings was paid in blood by their victims, of course, but they also hurt southern economies by discouraging investment and causing a flight of African American labor to the North. Thus in 1893 the governor of Alabama said that these murders were not only dishonorable, but also "a great obstacle to our healthy progress and prosperity." For similar reasons Georgia introduced anti-lynching legislation, though this was of dubious value, at least in the short term. As Wells recorded, Georgia was the state with the most lynchings in 1894, with nineteen in that year alone, out of 197 nationwide (*Red Record* ch. 9). Over a longer period, it's been calculated that between 1889 and 1932, almost 4,000 people were lynched in the United States: that's three people every week for more than thirty years.[7]

Wells' campaign was obviously important and admirable. But why would it be of interest to philosophers? It hardly takes subtle moral reasoning to disapprove of gangs of private citizens torturing people to death, without even being sure whether they are guilty of a crime. (Actually, as Wells pointed out, sometimes the mob knew for sure the victim *wasn't* guilty: she relates an episode where a boy was killed in his stepfather's stead, simply because the stepfather couldn't be found: *Red Record* ch. 4.) Yet Wells' achievement is indeed of lasting philosophical importance, because of her incisive analysis of the role that gender and systematic oppression played in lynch law.

Taking gender first, it is of course not irrelevant that Wells was herself a woman. She faced a tension between her career as an activist and her role as a wife and mother. Her husband, Ferdinand Barnett, was also an activist and had even written against lynching. So their marriage was a political alliance as well as a chance for Wells to gain financial stability. That was perhaps underappreciated by her friend, the white women's rights campaigner Susan B. Anthony, who told Wells that the decision to wed had left her with "divided duty" (*Autobiography* 255). Wells, or Wells-Barnett as she was known after having married, promoted the importance of family life for women, writing that those who "shirk their duties in that respect…have robbed themselves of one of the most glorious advantages in the development of their own womanhood" (251). But this may have been in part because she knew her readers might object to the efforts she continued to devote to activism, when she could instead have been focusing on her children. Always canny in her self-presentation, she made sure to include a scene in the *Autobiography* where she hesitated whether to travel away from her family to confront yet another injustice, and was encouraged by her young son to do so: "Mother, if you don't go nobody else will" (311).

She faced such problems even before marrying, since it seemed to some inappropriate for a single woman to be speaking so prominently, and on the issue of lynching in particular. Bear in mind we are literally dealing with the Victorian Age here, when single women were supposed to be sexually innocent, at least if they were virtuous. But here was Wells talking about lynching, and this inevitably involved talking about sex. The primary justification offered for lynch law was that without it, black men could not be stopped from assaulting and raping white women. Thus for instance, and to the eternal shame of our favorite discipline, Collins Denny, who was Professor of Mental and Moral Philosophy at Vanderbilt University, argued, "Rape must cease, and then lynching will cease. Have you thought about studying 'rape' as well as 'lynching'?"[8] If this was not used as an outright justification for lynchings, it was invoked to make the outbursts of violence seem at least understandable, a case of chivalrous white southern men rising to the defense of their womenfolk. This was a message one could hear from the highest levels of society. Theodore Roosevelt did want the lynchings to stop, but assumed they were caused by black men raping white women. The governor of Georgia who passed the aforementioned laws against lynching also said that the state had "had no lynching at first except for rape."[9]

The result was that, in order to condemn lynching, Wells had to explore the intimate connections between racial violence and violence against women. She asked how white racists could pretend to be horrified by interracial sexual relations, given the huge number of mixed-race people fathered by slavemasters with captive women. Indeed, as we saw, Wells' own father had issued from such a union. From a modern-day point of view, we would presumably consider any sexual encounter between a master and slave to be non-consensual, but Wells did not need to insist on this point to make the case that black women were routinely being raped by white men, both during and after slavery. None of which assaults, of course, were punished by lynching; indeed very few were punished at all. Apparently the famous southern chivalry stopped at the color line (*Red Record* chs 1, 6). Wells also pointed to the fact that, although it was tacitly acceptable for white men to rape black women, it was unthinkable for white men to marry them: "You can not deny that the white man is continually mixing his blood with black; it is only when he seeks to do it honorably that it becomes a crime."[10] Here it is worth noting that, like T. Thomas Fortune, Wells refused to condemn Frederick Douglass for marrying a white woman. To the contrary, she visited their home and was told by Douglass that she was the first black visitor ever to show civility and politeness to his wife (*Autobiography* 71).

Wells made a still more provocative point when she argued that the vast majority of supposed rapes of white women by black men were actually cases of consensual sex. This was a central claim in her writing from the very beginning. One of her first editorials caused huge uproar with the following passage: "Nobody believes the old thread-bare lie that Negro men assault white women. If Southern white men are not careful they will over-reach themselves and a conclusion will be reached which will be very damaging to the moral reputation of their women."[11] A white newspaper spluttered in response that "there are some things that the Southern white man will not tolerate," in this case the outrageous suggestion that white women might actually *want* to have affairs with black men.

Much of Wells' campaign was devoted to rendering this proposition a plausible one. As usual she did so by offering documentary evidence, for instance of white women who had long-standing relationships with black men and then accused them of rape, perhaps out of fear they may have a mixed-race baby (*Red Record* ch. 6). In light of this sort of evidence, she said, it was clear that lynching was only a means by which "the Southern white men in insatiate fury wreak their vengeance without intervention of law upon the Afro-Americans who consort with their women" (*Southern Horrors* ch. 2). Then too, Wells had more than evidence on her side; there was also common sense. Racist propaganda pretended that the abolition of slavery had unleashed the propensities of black men to commit sexual violence. As one article from a white newspaper put it, "there is no longer a restraint upon the brute passion of the Negro."[12] Wells exposed the absurdity of this: "The thinking public will not easily believe freedom and education more brutalizing than slavery, and the world knows that the crime of rape was unknown during four years of civil war, when the white women of the South were at the mercy of the race which is all at once charged with being a bestial one" (*Southern Horrors* ch. 1). Finally, if even all these arguments were ignored, she could point to the fact that most lynchings were not even supposedly in retribution for rape. Fewer than one-third of them involved even a charge, never mind proof, of this crime.

This aspect of Wells' critique remains relevant for modern-day race relations. She would have been wholly unsurprised by Donald Trump's warnings about rapists coming across the Mexican border. But of still deeper significance is her analysis of violence against black men as a tool of racial oppression. As with the police killings in today's America, the sheer number of lynchings across the American South in the late nineteenth century showed that something systematic was happening, something that was, at some level, deliberate. Occasionally defenders of lynch law would come out and say as much. As one of them explained, the difference between the races was so great that black people should not be governed by "Anglo-Saxon law" but by "lynch law": it was necessary to have "one standard of right for the white citizen and another law, and another standard of right for the black citizen."[13] At a more crass level, we find such documents as a horrifying photograph commemorating a multiple hanging, which has a doggerel poem printed below it: "This is a land of white man's rule. The Red Man once in an early day, was told by the White's, to mend his way. The negro, now, by eternal grace, must learn to stay in the negro's place."[14]

Wells was the African American activist who understood this best. She saw that lynchings were not a response to a supposed decline of black men into criminal brutality. To the contrary, they were a response to the gradual *rise* of African Americans within American society. That triple murder in Memphis, she said, "opened my eyes to what lynching really was. An excuse to get rid of Negroes who were acquiring wealth and property and thus keep the race terrorized" (*Autobiography* 64). The removal of the restraints of slavery was indeed relevant, but not for the reason given by the apologists of lynching. Rather, it was because the white population needed to find a way to hold on to their supremacy. "The more I studied the situation," she wrote, "the more I was convinced that the Southerner had never gotten over his resentment that the Negro was no longer his plaything, his servant, and his source of income" (70).

Lynching was thus intended to convey a message to all black people, not only or even primarily its direct victims. "The real purpose of these savage demonstrations," said Wells, "is to teach the Negro that in the South he has no rights that the law will enforce."[15] Or more pithily, while discussing the motivation of the lynchers: "They say, 'we must teach them a lesson.' What lesson? The lesson of subordination" (*Southern Horrors* ch. 4). Nor did Wells confine her critique to the lynchers and their apologists. All white America was complicit in lynch law, if only by failing to end it. In a typically rhetorical passage, she wrote: "Men and women of America, are you proud of this record which the Anglo-Saxon race has made for itself? Your silence seems to say that you are. Your silence encourages a continuance of this sort of horror. Only by earnest, active, united endeavor to arouse public sentiment can we hope to put a stop to these demonstrations of American barbarism."[16]

And Wells was indeed optimistic that racial violence could be eliminated from American society. In a chapter at the end of her book *A Red Record* called "The Remedy," she put her faith—ironically enough—in the American legal system. She wrote, "We do ask that the law shall punish all alike," and juxtaposed the "anarchy" of lynch law with the "success of self government" (ch. 10). Consistently with this, Wells spent much of her later life engaging in more conventional political activism. She was involved in the suffrage movement, though she saw that the enfranchisement of white women would likely be of no help in ending racial oppression, the way her friend Susan B. Anthony hoped.[17] This was only one of many disagreements with fellow activists. She was occasionally critical even of early sponsors like Fortune, finding his rhetoric too divisive, though she wholeheartedly endorsed his principle of party neutrality.[18] She knew both Booker T. Washington and W.E.B. Du Bois, and sided with the latter in being critical of Washington's focus on vocational education for blacks, accusing Washington of "the sophistry of the reasoning that any one system of education could fit the needs of an entire race" (*Autobiography* 280–1).

With the turn of the twentieth century, her influence began to wane. In 1895 Wells had been hailed in one newspaper as "the proper person to succeed Frederick Douglass as leader of the Afro-American race."[19] But an organization she helped found in 1909, the Negro Fellowship League, was overtaken by the NAACP, from which she was alienated after a dispute over whether she would be given a leadership position (*Autobiography* 326–8). Through it all, though, she never stopped decrying violence and false accusations against African Americans. Near the end of her *Autobiography*, she tells the story of what happened when she distributed buttons in support of a group of black soldiers who had been court-martialed and executed by the US military. When policemen came to tell her to desist, on the grounds that her actions were treasonous, she thundered at them: "I'd rather go down in history as one lone Negro who dared to tell the government that it had done a dastardly thing than to save my skin by taking back what I have said" (370). Then she quoted Shakespeare at them. The police were utterly flummoxed, says Wells, "and looked at me as if they didn't know what to do." Which is one problem she never had.

51

GOD IS A NEGRO

Henry McNeal Turner

There's a saying that goes: if you aren't a liberal when you are young, then you have no heart, and if you're not a conservative when you get older, then you have no head. And it's true that this is a well-beaten political path. That icon of modern American conservativism, Ronald Reagan, for instance, was once upon a time a liberal who supported the New Deal. It seems that the explanation for such changes of heart, or as the saying would have it, abandonments of the heart for the head, is not far to seek. People start out with optimistic ideals and the conviction that the world may be changed to fit those ideals. When the world stubbornly refuses to do so, they abandon their idealism and adopt pragmatic caution instead. Thus Irving Kristol, another left-winger who became right-wing, said that a conservative is "a liberal who has been mugged by reality."[1]

But the world can teach the opposite lesson too: that caution and modest demands for incremental improvement achieve very little, so that a more radical approach is needed. This was the lesson learned by Henry McNeal Turner, a leading figure of the African American church in the late nineteenth century, who made his mark as a preacher, theologian, journalist, and politician.[2] The versatility of his pursuits matched the diversity of the positions he adopted. He was first an apostle of economic integration, then a stubborn advocate of emigration; first a valued colleague of white politicians, then a firebrand who assured his readers that the devil is white, not black; a man devoted to organizing and growing his church, who nonetheless seemed almost to delight in adopting unpopular opinions; a great enthusiast for the promise of Africa, who was convinced that that promise could be fulfilled only if Africa became more like America. His more radical final position is the one that inspired this remark, by an early biographer of Turner: "No man of our race has ever said so many harsh, unvarnished and biting things about the white American and lived to repeat it."[3]

Turner was born in 1834 in South Carolina, but not into slavery: his family's story had it that this was because his grandfather was of royal African blood. He first learned to read at a law firm where he had a job doing menial labor. From this humble beginning, he became an itinerant preacher criss-crossing the antebellum South. He himself would later claim to have traveled more than 15,000 miles in the service of the church, and say that he "had to pass through blood and fire," which sounds melodramatic until you hear him tell of hiding in hollow logs from the Ku Klux Klan, who repeatedly threatened violence against him. He joined the Union Army as a chaplain, now a recruiter of soldiers as well as souls, but left this post to focus on building up the African Methodist Episcopal Church in Georgia.[4] It was here that his political career would reach its greatest heights. Following the Civil War, he was a representative at the Georgia constitutional convention in 1867, then elected to the state's House of Representatives in 1868. It was at this point that Turner got mugged by reality.

His policy had been to work together with white politicians, even former rebels of the Confederacy, whose right to sit in the Georgia House was supported by Turner. "Let us love the whites," he said, "and let bygones be bygones, neither taunt nor insult them for past grievances, respect them; honor them; work for them; but still let us be men."[5] So his white peers valued him as a man they could work with, until they decided that they didn't have to. The House voted to expel all the black members, with the measure being carried by a whopping 83-23 vote. Republican lawmakers actually gave up their own majority by supporting the expulsion, in a sinister, white supremacist version of T. Thomas Fortune's advice to put race above party. Turner was not pleased. Before the vote, but knowing what the outcome would be, he delivered a speech condemning the white representatives. "So far as I am personally concerned," he admitted, "no man in Georgia has been more conservative than I. 'Anything to please the white folks' has been my motto." Now things were different: "I am here to demand my rights, and to hurl thunderbolts at the men who would dare to cross the threshold of my manhood." Turner called on the tropes of religious preaching, telling his opponents that by expelling him and his black colleagues from the legislature, they were in effect expelling themselves from God's community.[6]

This event was arguably the moment that Turner, true to his name, reached a turning point. Tunde Adeleke has commented that, from here on out, "Turner's alienation was total and unequivocal."[7] Increasingly, he became known as a supporter of emigration to Africa. His rationale for this was laid out in numerous writings, for instance a speech "On the Present Duties and Future Destiny of the Negro Race," from 1872. Here he touches on the familiar theme of black uplift, saying that "the prospectus of the Negro lies in his own intellectual cabinet...the Negro must climb his own ladder, if he ever scales the mount of distinction." For the most part in fact, this speech seems to be describing progress within American culture, as Turner extols the value of agricultural innovation and even jury duty. But he then comes to defend the desirability of emigration. Black Americans are outnumbered by white ones, who show every sign of continuing to oppress them. Even the open spaces out west will soon enough by dominated by the white population, and the best option is to leave the country entirely.

Turner was criticized for this stance by, among others, Frederick Douglass. In response, he denied that he was entirely giving up on America. A piece from the following year, "The Negro in All Ages," addressed Douglass directly: "I do not wish it understood that I am advocating African emigration, but I believe it is our duty to civilize our fatherland, and the only way to civilize a people is to move into their midst and live among them." His idea was not to have the whole black population move across the sea, but to engage in a "slow and gradual operation," the strategy that had always been pursued by the American Colonization Society. Turner did not hesitate to praise this controversial organization, which he admired as the sole means by which African Americans were connected back to the "Fatherland." This line of argument was pursued in greater depth in his 1879 essay, "Emigration of the Colored People of the United States." Here Turner loses the reticence to embrace the term "emigration" that he had earlier shown while responding to Douglass. The essay opens by stressing that emigration or colonization is a *voluntary* movement of peoples—the tacit contrast being, of course, the slave trade—and that this sort of movement has gone on through history, going back to antiquity. This shows, argues Turner, that emigration "has the sanction of heaven" and is "an indispensable prerequisite to the material, social, and intellectual growth of a people."

Here we come to the core philosophical and theological justification of Turner's emigrationism: it is divinely ordained, in part because travel to Africa offered a way for African Americans to escape oppression. As Turner said, "we must either rebel at home or seek fortunes elsewhere. We can never acquire power sitting here quietly as menials." Or, on another occasion, "Don't you see it's a white man's Government? And don't you see they mean at all hazards to keep the Negro down? And don't you see the Negro does not intend to stay down, without a fuss and an interminable broil? Then why waste our time in trying to stay here?"[8] But there was another important purpose to the emigrationist project, namely that the emigrants would bring moral and religious instruction to Africa. Indeed these two goals, liberation for African Americans and enlightenment for native Africans, were closely linked in Turner's mind. In an essay called "To Colored People," written quite a bit later, in

1895, he said, "I believe that two or three millions of us ought to go to Africa and build up a civilized nation and show the world that we can be statesmen, generals, bankers, merchants, philosophers, inventors and everything that anybody else is." That aspiration stayed with Turner throughout his career. He mounted (often unsuccessful) emigrationist projects, beginning as early as 1862, when he targeted Panama as a possible site of settlement, and as late as 1903, now an elderly statesman who continued to think that leaving the States was a fine idea.

For Turner, the building of "civilization" in Africa would retrospectively justify the evils that made emigration necessary in the first place. A small example of this kind of thinking can be found in his discussion of the ACS in "The Negro in All Ages." Many critics of this organization had argued that its founders did not have the welfare of the emigrants or the African continent at heart. As we've seen, the ACS was often suspected of wanting to deport free blacks so as to ensure greater control over those who were still enslaved. To which Turner said, in effect, so what? Many a racist soldier had fought for the North in the Civil War and helped to end slavery. In the same way, the nefarious motives of some white members of the ACS were simply "another evidence that Providence over-rules evil for good."

A more significant, and more startling, application of his theodicy comes in Turner's attempt to reconcile slavery itself with the universality of divine providence. He was convinced that the suffering of African Americans must have had some purpose. This purpose he located in the fact that enslaved Africans were exposed to European religion and culture, which would not have happened otherwise. He called slavery "the most rapid transit from barbarism to Christian civilization for the Negro."[9] When Turner called slavery "providential," he gave this term a rather technical sense. He drew a distinction between two kinds of thing ordained by God, those that are "providential" and those that are "divine."[10] Divine things are permanent features of God's creation, whereas providential things are temporary, decreed by God with a view to some specific end. In this case, the end in view was the enlightenment of Africa by its returning children, a great good made possible by the great suffering of the slave trade.

This goes hand in hand with his idea that only a part of the African American population might need to go to Africa. These should be among the best and brightest, those well equipped for shedding the light of truth, knowledge, and morality upon a still dark continent. Turner put it like this: "As soon as we are educated sufficiently to assume control of our vast ancestral domain, we will hear the voice of a mysterious Providence, saying 'Return to the land of your fathers.'"[11] And it must be said that Turner practiced what he preached. In fact, he did so precisely by preaching. In 1891 he traveled to Sierra Leone and Liberia to spread the gospel. While there he failed to develop the same cultural openness that marked his contemporary Edward Blyden, as Turner thought little of Islam and no more of traditional African beliefs, which he characterized as "heathen darkness." West Africans were not that impressed with Turner either, but he had more success proselytizing for the church in South Africa.

Turner's reconciliation of slavery with God's providence is open to criticism, and not only because of his disdain for indigenous African culture. The aforementioned Tunde Adeleke critiques Turner for setting himself up "as someone with the superior and civilized values to transform Africans culturally." Adekele also thinks Turner was effectively letting white slaveholders off the hook by making them instruments of God's plan.[12] Of course the white Americans of Turner's day, especially those who had owned slaves or otherwise been involved in what was euphemistically called the "peculiar institution," might have been glad to think of themselves as such instruments. The Christianization of Africans had indeed long been invoked as a justification for slavery (we may here cast our minds all the way back to Jacobus Capitein; see Chapter 23). But Turner himself was not offering them absolution. To the contrary, he was clear that even if their wickedness was turned to good ends, this justified God, not them. While he admitted that slavery was "a historical necessity," he charged the white man with defaulting on "his obligation to God and the Black man by forbidding 'blacks' to improve themselves."[13]

So when Turner remarked that emigration would fulfill a plan in which "infinite wisdom intended to evolve ultimate good out of a temporary evil," both the temporary evil and ultimate good were real. His theodicy was designed to explain how good is providentially brought forth from evil, not to show that evil does not exist. Which makes it puzzling that Turner can also be found rejecting what he called the "placid logic" that makes all events contribute to "some great good," since evil is never "used by infinite Wisdom, as an indispensable requisite for political or moral good."[14] At first glance this statement looks to be in flat contradiction to his own theodicy. We might explain the discrepancy by noticing that the passage was written in 1864, years before his disappointment with the Georgia legislature and fervent support of emigration to Africa. But that's unlikely, since only two years later he was saying that God "winked" at slavery because it was an effective means to bring "moral and intellectual culture" to Africa.[15] Evidently, this was an idea that Turner held throughout his career. So instead, we might lay stress on the word "indispensable" in that problematic passage. Confronted by evil freely committed by humans, God is able to turn it to good ends, but this does not mean He could never bring about those ends without using evil as an instrument.

It's characteristic of Turner, who was after all a preacher and bishop, that he approached philosophical questions through the prism of religion. This applies to his treatment of race in his lecture, "The Negro in All Ages," which promises to refute "abominable, anti-scriptural, and pseudo-philosophical theories" about the inferiority of black people. Turner does indeed meet pseudo-science on its own ground, for example by noting that he has seen cadavers with the skin removed, and learned that the differences between black and white bodies are quite literally only skin-deep. Differences in color are, he says, simply the result of climate. Yet his overall approach is in sharp contrast to the sort of anthropological and empirical argumentation we found in Anténor Firmin. Attacking the same racist pseudo-science that Firmin demolished with real science, Turner for the most part depends on biblical proof to establish what he calls the "great doctrine of race unity," namely that all humans have "one original source." His approach to scripture is not naively literalist, and he makes clear that one cannot simply take the Bible at face value when calculating things like the age of humankind. But the central Christian doctrine of original sin does require that all humans share common descent. Humans have not evolved from monkeys, as Darwin would claim—Turner pours scorn on this theory—but from the humans who committed that original sin. As he said on a later occasion, "I wish I could trace my race to some other source, than the fallen and unfortunate Adam; I wish I could give both him and mother Eve to our white friends if they desire it, but I can't; he is my daddy too."[16]

In what may seem another paradox of Turner's thought, his insistence on the superficiality of racial difference did not stop him from finding his identity, including his religious identity, in blackness. Like many other nineteenth century African American intellectuals, he pointed to the long history of achievement among Africans, going back to Egypt and Ethiopia, with the brilliance of the race shown more recently by such figures as Ignatius Sancho, Benjamin Banneker, and Frederick Douglass. Turner also pointed out that Jesus was not white, and proposed retranslating the Bible with an eye to the concerns of black people, here taking inspiration from feminists who had the idea of producing a version of the Bible translated from a female point of view. More provocative still was his notorious remark, made in an 1895 sermon at Atlanta, that "God is a Negro." It's not quite clear how seriously we should take this; or rather, it's clear it was meant seriously, but perhaps not literally. Turner's point was that black people should not hesitate to do as humans always have done, and imagine a deity who looks more or less like them.

In this respect, his claim that "God is a Negro" was fundamentally an expression of racial pride. He explained himself by saying, "We do not believe that there is any hope for a race of people who do not believe that they look like God."[17] Yet just one year earlier he had said: "There is no such being as a white God; God is neither white nor black." Perhaps it's the first part of that statement that captures his point best. White people needed to stop thinking that they alone were created in God's image; and for sure black people needed to stop following suit, for instance by hoping that in the afterlife they may rise with white bodies. So in another variation on the theme he said: "We are no stickler as to God's color...but we certainly protest against God being a white man."[18] His musings on God's color were intended to bring his audience to a self-respect, and a sense of their own dignity, that he thought was sorely lacking. In a formulation that sounds strikingly like more famous slogans that have emerged closer to our own day, Turner argued: "A man must believe he is somebody before he is acknowledged as somebody...Respect black."

While he was consistent in promoting that central message, it must be said that Turner was given to making bold, even inflammatory, declarations and then backing away from them when challenged. It was a habit he kept in later life, like in 1906 when he said: "To the Negro in the country, the American flag is a dirty and contemptible rag. Not a star in it can the colored man claim, for it is no longer the symbol of our manhood, rights, and liberty." This statement, with its echoes of Douglass' strident speech about the Fourth of July, could have gotten Turner indicted for treason, and he hastened to insist that his remarks had been taken out of context. But we're not really buying that story, given that back in 1883, Turner had already said, in response to the Supreme Court's overturning of the Civil Rights Law, that this decision "absolves the negro's allegiance to the general government, makes the American flag to him a rag of contempt instead of a symbol of liberty."

A philosophically-minded reader may wish that Turner had stuck to his guns and been more consistent. (Speaking of guns, the black socialist thinker A. Philip Randolph recalled an episode that nicely illustrates Turner's more militant side: while preaching, he "pulled two revolvers out of his pocket and placed them on the pulpit."[19]) But it's actually philosophically illuminating that he was so often pulled in different directions, both politically and ideologically. Indeed it is striking that many of the figures we've been discussing in this part of the book changed their views over time, or seemed hard to pin down throughout their career. Examples would include Douglass' views on the acceptability of violence, Blyden's movement from political to cultural nationalism, and the changes of heart found in Russwurm and Delany, both of whom came to support emigration after they too were mugged by the reality of American racism.

We can take a broader lesson from this, about how valid moral and political principles can clash with one another. We may feel allegiance to our whole community or nation, and want to find our place in it; but equally, we may have a sense of belonging to a smaller group, defined for instance along racial or gender lines. We may rage against injustice, but have moral compunctions about using violence or other extreme measures to fight that injustice. We may hold that one set of moral, scientific, or religious principles is the truth, while also seeing that other cultural perspectives should not be dismissed as worthless. Such tensions were felt keenly and in a distinctive way by a range of nineteenth-century thinkers in the face of the monstrous oppression of slavery. But they didn't go away with emancipation.

52

SEPARATE FINGERS, ONE HAND

Booker T. Washington

Stop us if this sounds familiar, but in the early 1950s the United States was gripped by fear of a terrible pandemic and desperate for a vaccine. Tragically, it especially struck children, who were often quarantined at home to keep them from catching the illness. That illness was polio, and the man who provided the vaccine in the end was Dr. Jonas Salk. Less well known is the story of how the Tuskegee Institute helped bring the disease to heel. Led by the black doctors Russell Brown and James Henderson, and with the involvement of many female technicians, the Tuskegee research center played a crucial role in providing cells that could be used to test the vaccine, and in the process developed new protocols for growing cell cultures.[1] It's a story that would have delighted the Institute's first president Booker T. Washington, whose fondest hope was that the school would teach its students to "conquer the forces of nature" and prove the usefulness, reliability, and worth of his race.[2]

The school at Tuskegee, Alabama opened in 1881. Once he was appointed to run it, Washington applied lessons he had learned at the Hampton Institute in Virginia, lessons he then tried to impart to the students of Tuskegee and, by extension, all African Americans. He articulated this vision in a work called *The Future of the American Negro*, published in 1900.[3] At this point he was already having to challenge a belief that remains widespread even today, that Tuskegee education was all about embracing the drudgery of mindless, manual labor. Now, Washington fervently believed that there was nothing ignoble or unworthy about manual labor. The Tuskegee ethos was meant to undo one pernicious effect of slavery, namely that labor had become associated with unfreedom (*Fut.* ch. 4). The hard-won "industrial" skills, of use in such occupations as carpentry and agriculture, were taken for granted by slaves—"it was natural, like breathing" (*Fut.* ch. 3)—and forgotten as soon as possible once emancipation came. But for Washington, this sort of work should never be mindless. "The constant aim," he said, "is to show the student how to put brains into every process of labor" (*Fut.* ch. 5). At Tuskegee the black man was to "be taught to put so much intelligence into his labor that he will see dignity and beauty in the occupation, and love it for its own sake" (*Fut.* ch. 8).

This message made for a striking contrast with those being advanced by other black leaders of the Reconstruction and Jim Crow era. Where figures like Douglass, Turner, Wells, and Fortune issued fiery demands for political equality and better treatment from whites, Washington demanded a better work ethic from his own race. In fact he was rather skeptical about allowing poor, uneducated black men across the South to vote. He did mention equality in this context, but only to argue that the literacy and education tests that eliminated these people from the voter registry should also strike off poor, uneducated whites. The happy result would be to get rid of "the large mass of ignorant voters of both races" (*Fut.* ch. 6). Simply letting everyone vote without qualifications actually took away an important incentive for them to seek education (*Fut.* ch. 8). As for other manifestations of southern white racism, Washington preferred not to dwell on them. He instead emphasized the common benefit that both races would enjoy from improved relations, and claimed that most whites were friendly to their African American fellows and wished them well. Writing about the "future of the Negro," he foresaw good things ahead: "With the best white people and the best black people standing together, in favor of law and order and justice, I believe that the safety and happiness of both races will be made secure" (*Fut.* ch. 7).

Views like this led Washington's contemporaries to see him as an "accommodationist" and a "conservative," labels still applied to him today. How, many have wondered, could he be so naive? There's a story about the Russian anarchist Peter Kropotkin being told that one of the leading black figures in America was a conservative, bursting into laughter, and asking what the American blacks had to conserve.[4] Closer to home, William Monroe Trotter got himself arrested for causing outrage at a public event in Boston, in 1903, after shouting at Washington, "Are the rope and the torch all the race is to get under your leadership?"[5] He disdainfully said that if Washington was recognized as a leader of the black race, this was simply because he was "chosen for that position by the white American race." Trotter had a point. Washington got funding for Tuskegee from wealthy white donors, including Andrew Carnegie, and consorted with presidents. One of them, Teddy Roosevelt, called him "one of the most useful, as well as one of the most distinguished, of American citizens of any race."[6]

What exactly did Washington do, or say, to become so enamored of white Americans and so loathed by more radical black colleagues? The key event was a speech he gave at an International Exposition in Atlanta in September, 1895. As he himself noted, it was remarkable that he was speaking at a major event together on a platform with southern whites. No less remarkable was the artfulness with which Washington managed to be both conciliatory and inspiring. He encouraged black people to cultivate "friendly relations with the Southern white man, who is their next-door neighbor." As for white listeners, he reminded them of how often black people had cared for them when sick or nursed them as children. (Here we might recall the far more provocative way that Sojourner Truth reminded whites of this same fact: by baring her breasts at them.) Right after that came the most famous, or perhaps notorious, part of the speech. Washington said: "We shall stand by you with a devotion that no foreigner can approach, ready to lay down our lives, if need be, in defence of yours, interlacing our industrial, commercial, civil, and religious life with yours in a way that shall make the interests of both races one. In all things that are purely social we can be as separate as the fingers, yet one as the hand in all things essential to mutual progress."

This was pure Washington, and the mixed-race crowd went wild. The white press commended Washington's tact, with the *New Orleans Picayune* calling him "a prominent and sensible man [who] had given a most temperate address."[7] The *Atlanta Constitution* was more enthusiastic still, calling the speech "a turning point in the progress of the Negro race."[8] Looking back on the event, Washington could rightly argue that many black people who read the speech found it excellent, even if some felt it was insufficiently militant. He himself was proud of the address, and included it in his autobiography *Up from Slavery*, published in 1901 and still his most widely read work.[9] Much like Douglass, who died in February of the year that Washington delivered his address, Washington sought to weave his philosophy of race relations into the story of his own life. He too was born into slavery, but there is nothing in his autobiography to remind us of Douglass' confrontation with the slavedriver Covey. Instead Washington mildly remarks that his masters were not especially cruel. More generally he allows that "the black man got nearly as much out of slavery as the white man did." While not denying the vicious injustice of slavery, he tends to agree with those who saw a kind of providence in the way that it had brought Africans to America. The result was "ten million Negroes…[who are] in a stronger and more hopeful condition, materially, intellectually, morally, and religiously, than is true of an equal number of black people in any other portion of the globe" (*Up* ch. 1).

Of course Washington also takes the opportunity to preach the gospel of hard work in his autobiography. He deplores the way that, in the heady days after the

Civil War, black southerners prioritized higher learning and political office over maintaining and developing "industrial" skills. At Tuskegee, he is proud to say, new students have to put in a full day's labor at the laundry or brickyard before enjoying the "privilege of studying academic branches for two hours in the evening" (*Up* ch. 13). By way of contrast, he tells the story of a dirt poor black man he once found sitting in a miserable shack, focused on studying a French grammar book (*Up* ch. 8). While often critical of his people, he rarely has a harsh word for whites. He does describe being turned away from a hotel for his skin color, but hastens to add that he felt no bitterness about it (*Up* ch. 3), and claims that he has never once been insulted by any southern white man (*Up* ch. 11). As for those whites who do try to restrain black progress, he has only pity for them, since their "mistake" stems from their "own lack of opportunity for the highest kind of growth." In any case they are only fighting the inevitable, like people trying to stop a train by throwing themselves on the track (*Up* ch. 13). A minor, but telling contrast between this narrative and the autobiographical writings of Frederick Douglass comes with the way both talk about traveling in Europe. We saw that Douglass, and Ida B. Wells likewise, pointedly contrasted the viciousness of American racism to the welcome they received in Britain and Ireland. Washington by contrast makes no such comparison, instead waxing enthusiastic about the wonderful herds of Holstein cattle he saw in Holland (*Up* ch. 16).

With the benefit of hindsight, Washington's excessive optimism can often seem downright painful, as when he airily remarks at the very beginning of the twentieth century that the racist terrorism of the Ku Klux Klan has already faded into historical irrelevance (*Up* ch. 4). Actually, hindsight was not really necessary in order to object to his rosy assessment of race relations in the American South. Apart from the aforementioned attacks by Trotter, there was John Hope, the President of Atlanta University. He said already in 1896, following on Washington's speech in Atlanta, that it was "cowardly and dishonest" not to demand full equality for African Americans. Years later he was somewhat more balanced in his judgment, but still critical: Washington had "helped to produce tolerance for the Negro, but at too great a price."[10] Ida B. Wells complained, as we mentioned while discussing her, that Washington's one-size-fits-all approach to black education was simplistic. She also criticized his habit of complaining about poor moral standards among African Americans, charging that he was willing "to injure his race for the benefit of his school."[11]

Still today, Washington has plenty of detractors, especially when he is compared to his younger rival W.E.B. Du Bois, the most famous critic of his approach to black uplift. Du Bois was at first guardedly admiring of Washington, saying after the famous Atlanta speech that the compromise it offered "might be the basis of a real settlement between whites and blacks in the South, if the South opened up to the Negroes the doors of economic opportunity."[12] But he would change his mind, convicting Washington of effectively conceding "the alleged inferiority of the Negro race," and withdrawing "many of the high demands of Negroes as men and American citizens."[13] Much later, as an old man looking back from the perspective of 1954, Du Bois was more moderate in his assessment, though hardly congratulatory: "Oh, Washington was a politician. He was a man who believed that we should get what we could get."[14]

Not too long after that, though, Washington and his legacy started to be reassessed.[15] The historian Emma Lou Thornborough, writing in the 1960s, pointed out that while progressive white contemporaries loved Washington, many white supremacists despised him, precisely because he offered such a plausible route to interracial harmony. Later still, Louis R. Harlan began to study the collected papers of Washington and offered a far more nuanced picture than the one presented by his most famous text, *Up from Slavery*. We now know that Washington's peace-loving public persona went together with behind-the-scenes lobbying and legal activity, for instance by quietly supporting court cases against segregation. This more textured and detailed portrait of Washington has opened up new avenues for criticism too, especially as regards his ruthless use of the tools of political patronage.

If we want to evaluate Washington from a more theoretical perspective, the obvious place to start is with his theory of education. This involved more than just the exhortation to roll up your sleeves and get to work. As we've already intimated, Washington was all for the application of science and intelligence to labor. A hidden cost of slavery was that, with an abundance of manpower, labor-saving devices were not in demand, and therefore not developed. Tuskegee would not make the same mistake. Those 1950s scientists who helped cure polio could have taken inspiration from their own school at the turn of the century, since at that time the famous agricultural scientist George Washington Carver worked at the Institute. In keeping with this, Washington did not, contrary to popular conception, simply scorn higher book learning. True, he did mock that poor fellow in the shack trying to learn French, and likewise told the story of an African who could read Cicero, but was wearing no trousers. On a larger political scale, he criticized Haiti for its ambitious educational schemes, modeled on those in France, which left it having to import skilled workers like engineers (*Fut.* ch. 4). But Washington's considered opinion was that advanced learning would be appropriate as a further step, following after more basic material and economic achievements.

Thus he said that the girls at Tuskegee could well be offered such learning, so long as they also acquired practical skills: "I favor any kind of training, whether in the languages or mathematics, that gives strength and culture to the mind—but at the same time to give them the most thorough training in the latest and best methods of laundrying and other kindred occupations" (*Up* ch. 5). He also outright denied that practical economic success was a goal to be pursued in its own right: "Material possession is not the chief end of life, but should be a means of aiding us in securing our rightful place as citizens."[16] Industrial education was only ever a means to a further end, the end being full equality and freedom for the black race: "I plead for industrial education and development for the Negro not because I want to cramp him, but because I want to free him."[17] Washington's "first things first" approach to racial progress can, in fact, be seen as fitting into a larger pattern of American moral and political thought, one that is also reflected in the works of Frederick Douglass, as we observed when discussing him. Both embraced the ideal of self-reliance, which Washington explicitly extended from the personal to the political level: "The crucial test for a race, as for an individual, is its ability to stand upon its own feet."[18]

Another thing worth bearing in mind as one reads Washington's public pronouncements is that they are just that: pronouncements meant for public consumption, and aimed at manipulating his audience in various ways. Both his allies and his enemies realized that Washington's long-term goals were more ambitious than he let on. A colleague allowed that the goal was to "bring the wooden horse inside the walls of Troy," while one hardline racist warned that the Tuskegee program was not really intended to produce humble, cooperative workers. Rather, Washington was "training them all to be masters of men, to be independent."[19] In *Up from Slavery* Washington himself talks of crafting his message for each audience (ch. 13). If, as other African American activists complained, he was more harsh in criticism of his own race than of the white race, this is because he thought attacking white listeners would do less good than appealing to their better nature. This he did constantly, often by calling upon their Christian sense of morality.[20] A favorite tactic was to emphasize the friendliness of most southern whites toward their black neighbors. As we've admitted, this can seem overoptimistic and naive, but it can also be read as an aspiration disguised as a statement of fact. When, in *The Future of the American Negro*, he says that in general the white man wants the black man to "improve his present condition," he is implicitly inviting his white audience to identify with that goal.

This brings us to what we see as a fundamental, though often underappreciated, aspect of Washington's thought: his emphasis on moral character. His ideas on this topic can be gleaned from a collection of short addresses, or one might call them "homilies," that Washington gave to his students at Tuskegee.[21] At first glance they seem like mere pep-talks, laced with avuncular humor and tough love. But upon more careful reading, they show that ethical virtue is what Washington most wanted to impart to his students, even more than skills in carpentry or agriculture (though he does find time to praise once again those wonderful cows in Holland, *Char.* 74). He tells his young charges that they are being trained as leaders of the race (*Char.* 69), and that they will achieve this through self-discipline and high ideals. He could be talking about his own tactics for coaxing white people toward benevolence, when he tells them, "Grow into the habit of talking about the bright side of life…Just in proportion as you do this, you will find that you will not only influence yourself in the right direction, but that you will also influence others that way" (*Char.* 8). He was an inveterate optimist all right, but for him optimism didn't mean making things out to be better than they are now. It meant imagining how they might get better in the future, and getting others to imagine this too.

One of the most revealing passages of the book comes when Washington preaches, "Character is a power. If you want to be powerful in the world, if you want to be strong, influential and useful, you can be so in no better way than by having strong character" (*Char.* 91). This is itself a very optimistic remark: Washington thinks that the world just has a way of cooperating with virtue. It's been said that Washington "deliberately confuses the personal and the political,"[22] but it might be more accurate to say that he *replaces* the political with the personal. He has little faith in the efficacy of purely political movements, since in the end racial oppression will be ended only if both black and white Americans improve morally. In the Atlanta address and again in *Up from Slavery*, he uses the phrase "artificial forcing" to describe attempts to end southern racism through agitation or pressure from the North (*Up* ch. 14). This, he says, will never work. Rights will only ever "be accorded to the Negro by the Southern white people themselves."

How will they be induced to do this? By being confronted with black people who are obviously good citizens. Not just because they will see the benefit of this in material terms, but also because character is contagious. Virtue on the part of blacks will hold up a standard for whites to imitate. Conversely, like Plato's Socrates, he believes that wickedness hurts the perpetrator more than the victim: whites who defraud blacks become dishonest more generally, and those who start by lynching members of another race end by lynching their own (*Up* ch. 11). Evil breeds evil, just as goodness breeds goodness. This is why, according to Washington, the two races must inevitably "rise or fall together."[23] Yoked together in a single nation, black and white people can learn to live together, but only if they learn how to live.

As you might expect, given the bright outlook he foresaw for black people in America, he was dismissive about the project of emigration. The notion that African Americans should move *en masse* across the ocean to their homeland was, to his mind, "out of the question" and "chimerical" on practical grounds alone (*Fut.* chs 7, 8). But this did not stop him from taking an interest in Africa, even if he passed up chances to visit there in person.[24] Washington's views on Africa evolved over his life. He admitted that as a youngster, he absorbed the usual clichés about the continent: "people who roamed naked through the forest like wild beasts." This attitude toward African culture is incidentally expressed in his provocative observation: "We went into slavery without a language; we came out speaking the proud Anglo-Saxon tongue."[25] But Washington was impressed by the glories of ancient Egypt when he heard about them from a specialist on this subject at the University of Chicago, and he also cherished hopes of exporting the Tuskegee philosophy to Africa. A group of the school's graduates attempted to apply its agricultural methods in Togo, albeit without much success.

More fruitfully, Tuskegee was also visited by the Zulu leader John Dube, who would later become the first president of the political party that rules South Africa today, the African National Congress. Dube was impressed by Washington's methods and established a school along similar lines near Durban in 1901. Dube himself was sometimes called the "Booker T. Washington of South Africa." Later, up in West Africa, J.E.K. Aggrey of the Gold Coast, present-day Ghana, worked with the Phelps Stokes Fund to advance education in various parts of the continent. The philanthropist behind this fund had previously contributed to Tuskegee. Aggrey too became known as a "Booker T. Washington," in his case, of Africa as a whole. The reception of Washington's ideas in Africa also provides us with a striking connection to the oral traditions we covered in the first part of this book. When a report of the famous Atlanta Compromise speech reached Edward Blyden, Blyden was favorably impressed by the line about one hand and separate fingers. He observed that the image was "a common one among the aborigines of Africa."[26]

53

LIFTING THE VEIL

Introducing W.E.B. Du Bois

Once upon a time in Berlin, on a presumably cold February evening in 1893, an American student celebrated his twenty-fifth birthday. Alone in his room, he conducted an idiosyncratic little ritual involving Greek wine, candles, and oil. Later on, reflecting on the mysteries of existence, he wrote in his notebook: "O I wonder what I am—I wonder what the world is—I wonder if life is worth the striving. I do not know—perhaps I shall never know; but this I do know: be the Truth what it may I shall seek it on the pure assumption that it is worth seeking—and Heaven nor Hell, God nor Devil shall turn me from my purpose till I die" (*AR* 28–9).[1] It's an admirable profession of faith in truth-seeking as a vocation, fitting for a man who is widely considered one of the great philosophical minds of American history. That he would eventually be perceived this way, acclaimed as a major figure not just in philosophy but in all of the humanities and the social sciences, would have pleased the young William Edward Burghardt Du Bois, best known as W.E.B. Du Bois. On that same February night back in 1893, he also wrote in his diary: "These are my plans: to make a name in science, to make a name in literature and thus to raise my race" (*AR* 29). He was nothing if not ambitious, from his youth through the rest of his life. And he made good on that ambition. Arguably, Du Bois did more to "raise his race" over the course of his life than any other black public intellectual active at the same time as him.

We've mentioned Du Bois numerous times, but now we come finally to his early life and thought; we will take up the story of his later achievements in our second volume on Africana philosophy in the twentieth century.[2] In fact Du Bois is typically viewed as a twentieth century figure, and with good reason, as he had been active as a leader and thinker for almost two-thirds of that century when he died in 1963. But he was born in 1868, and so came of age in the nineteenth century. Some of his most lasting contributions actually date back to the 1890s. He was born in Great Barrington, in western Massachusetts, and raised by a single mother. From early on, his aptitude for learning and academic achievement was evident. During his teen years, while excelling in school, he also pursued an interest in journalism, becoming a local correspondent for a couple of newspapers, including T. Thomas Fortune's *New York Globe*. From high school he moved on to Fisk University, a black college in Nashville, Tennessee. This was a magical time for Du Bois, coming as he did from a small, predominantly white town in the North. Fisk placed him within a much larger black world. It is here that he first developed a love for philosophy, which he would take with him to Harvard after completing his first degree at Fisk. During his time at Harvard, some of the biggest names in the history of American philosophy taught there, people like William James, Josiah Royce, and George Santayana.

Du Bois took James, in particular, as a mentor. Yet James suggested to Du Bois that he should refrain from pursuing professional philosophy as a career option. It's tempting to assume that this was a case of racist gatekeeping. Yet Du Bois, who could be very sensitive to perceived slights, never once indicated that he saw anything malicious in James advising him that "if you can turn aside into something else, do so" for it is "hard to earn a living with philosophy."[3] To the contrary, we get the sense that Du Bois appreciated James' advice and that he never regretted diverting his path from "the lovely but sterile land of philosophic speculation," in order to take up instead "the social sciences for gathering and interpreting that body of fact which would apply to my program for the Negro" (*Auto*. 93).[4] Does this mean that Du Bois should not be categorized as a philosopher? No, as we can see from another comment he made on his change of path: "I conceived the idea of applying philosophy to an historical interpretation of race relations" (*Auto*. 93). Even without this clarification that his aim was to combine philosophy with social science, we would still have his body of writing, so philosophically rich that it banishes any doubt.

After graduating and receiving his second bachelor's degree, Du Bois did a master's degree in history at Harvard. During this time, he heard about an opportunity being offered by the John F. Slater Fund for the Education of Negroes, pledging support for study in Europe to a worthy candidate. Presiding over the fund at the time was Rutherford B. Hayes, former President of the United States and, incidentally, the one whose controversial election had led to the end of Reconstruction. Hayes expressed doubt that anyone suitable for the fellowship could be found. When Du Bois applied and was told that the plan had been given up, he wrote back in anger, calling the withdrawal of the opportunity an "almost irreparable" injury to "the race I represent, and am not ashamed of" (*Auto*. 95). His boldness paid off. Hayes told Du Bois to re-apply the following year, which he did; he sailed for Europe in the summer of 1892.

Du Bois' time in Europe was life-changing in a way similar to his time at Fisk, as it broadened him and made him feel part of a larger world—in this case, actually the whole world. He studied at the University of Berlin, or the Friedrich-Wilhelms-Universität, as it was officially called at that time. Gustav Schmoller, a leading economist of the time, supervised Du Bois' thesis on agriculture in the American South. The young American who celebrated his twenty-fifth birthday with those ambitious notebook writings was as prepared as he could be to attain the prestige of a PhD from the foremost German university, and at a time when German higher education was the most respected in the world. Unfortunately, the Slater Fund denied him the financial support he needed for an additional semester of study before he could be allowed to defend his thesis. So Du Bois had to come home and settle for becoming the first black person to obtain a PhD from Harvard.

His doctoral dissertation expanded on work he had done for his master's thesis. In 1896, the year after he finished, the dissertation was published as a book.[5] It was the first volume in the Harvard Historical Studies book series, a new venture in the early days of university-sponsored publishing. Here Du Bois' skill as a historian was on display, as he traced the evolving role of the slave trade in American political and economic life, and the successes and failures of attempts at abolition. In a connection to topics we have covered in this book, it featured a chapter called "Toussaint L'Ouverture and Anti-Slavery Effort, 1787–1806." Du Bois argued that the Haitian Revolution played a significant role in shaping the legal suppression of the slave trade to the United States, and the American debate over the abolition of slavery. Recall also that Anna Julia Cooper later made the Haitian Revolution central to her own historical dissertation, which made her the first black woman to gain a PhD from the Sorbonne. This underscores something we've seen several times: the importance of the revolution as an inspiring event for African American thinkers.

Du Bois got his first job at Wilberforce University, a black college in southwestern Ohio affiliated with the AME Church. His appointment was in Classics but he taught not just Greek and Latin but also German, English, and History. An anecdote from his time there is indicative of Du Bois' complicated relationship with religion. He wandered into a prayer meeting and the student leading it announced that "Professor Du Bois will lead us in prayer," to which Du Bois quickly responded: "No, he won't." The quip nearly lost him his job, for it apparently "took a great deal of explaining to the board of bishops why a professor in Wilberforce should be not able at all times and sundry to address God in extemporaneous prayer" (*Auto.* 117). During his time at Wilberforce he also met Nina Gomer, a student at the university, who became his wife.

In 1896, the same year they were married, the couple left Wilberforce for Philadelphia. The reason for the departure is that Du Bois accepted an offer of temporary employment by the University of Pennsylvania, not to teach but to carry out a study of Philadelphia's Seventh Ward, an impoverished area of the city in which a large portion of its black population lived. Excited to focus his energies on sociology, which he could not do while at Wilberforce, Du Bois literally went door to door, personally interviewing thousands of people in order to obtain as clear and as comprehensive a picture as possible of the conditions and characteristics of the area's inhabitants. The resulting book, *The Philadelphia Negro*, was published in 1899.[6] It has increasingly been recognized as part of the pioneering work that made Du Bois an early founder of the field of sociology as we know it.

As 1899 brings us to the end of the century, we will now step back a bit from there to focus on what Du Bois accomplished in 1897, truly an *annus mirabilis*. In March of that year, Du Bois visited Washington DC, to attend the first meeting of the American Negro Academy, which was organized by Alexander Crummell. Du Bois first met Crummell when he gave a commencement address a few years prior at Wilberforce. He would later write of that first encounter: "Instinctively I bowed before this man, as one bows before the prophets of the world."[7] At the meeting of the American Negro Academy, Du Bois delivered a paper entitled "The Conservation of Races," which has since become his single most influential writing within the field of philosophy.[8]

While in DC, he also met with the federal government's Bureau of Labor Statistics to discuss producing studies of African American economic progress. As a result of this successful interview, Du Bois left Philadelphia to spend July and August doing sociological research in Farmville, Virginia. The result was a sort of counterpart to *The Philadelphia Negro*, complementing the study of African Americans in the urban North in that book with a study of the rural South and pointing out connections between the two. For example, he claims that children and the elderly make up a larger proportion of the population in a place like Farmville, in part because of the migration to the North of married couples without their children. As a result the "family in Farmville is the complement of the Negro family in a city like Philadelphia, and these two families are very often but parts of one family."[9]

August of 1897 was also the month in which Du Bois first reached a wider, nonacademic reading public with his writing, through an article published in *The Atlantic Monthly*, entitled "Strivings of the Negro People." This was later revised to become the first chapter of his 1903 book, *The Souls of Black Folk*. In that form, it would ultimately become his most influential, most often quoted, and most widely discussed piece of writing. He would certainly have been entitled to call it a year and have a rest during autumn, but he still had one more seminal contribution in him. In November, he presented a paper entitled "The Study of the Negro Problems" at the annual meeting of the American Academy of Political and Social Science, which took place in Philadelphia.[10] This too has come to be recognized as one of his classic works. And the year was momentous in other ways too. He became a father in October to a son named Burghardt. In December, he, Nina, and Burghardt moved to Atlanta, where he would begin employment in the new year at a black college called Atlanta University, today known as Clark Atlanta University. This would be his institutional home for the rest of his career as a college professor, even as he also remained very active outside the university.

Having surveyed his wondrous productivity in 1897, we can now look more closely at the three most important philosophical writings of that year: "The Conservation of Races," "Strivings of the Negro People," and "The Study of the Negro Problems." We take the last first, given that the other two essays are both more famous, and closely linked to one another. "The Study of the Negro Problems" can be understood as a kind of sociological manifesto, in which Du Bois argues that this discipline, still in its infancy, will grow toward being a real science by attending to the problems involved in the presence of black people in America. He defines a social problem as "the failure of an organized social group to realize its group ideals, through the inability to adapt a certain desired line of action to given conditions of life" (*TSNP* 2). He discusses the role of slavery in the origin of the social problems involving African Americans, and makes recommendations for the study of these problems.

An aspect of the essay that has gained attention in recent years is Du Bois' philosophy of science. He writes: "Students must be careful to insist that science as such—be it physics, chemistry, psychology, sociology—has but one simple aim: the discovery of truth. Its results lie open for the use of all men—merchants, physicians, men of letters, and philanthropists, but the aim of science itself is simple truth. Any attempt to give it a double aim, to make social reform the immediate instead of the mediate object of a search for truth, will inevitably tend to defeat both objects" (*TSNP* 16). At first glance, it seems paradoxical that Du Bois should also claim: "The sole aim of any society is to settle its problems in accordance with its highest ideals, and the only rational method of accomplishing this is to study those problems in the light of the best scientific research" (*TSNP* 10). So which is it: should scientists aim solely at the truth for its own sake, or take social improvement as their goal? In a study of Du Bois' philosophy of science, Liam Kofi Bright has explained that for Du Bois, public trust in scientists is essential if their research is to aid social reform within a democracy.[11] This public trust, he suggests, is best secured if scientists are *perceived* as having no other goal than seeking the truth, and no investment in particular forms of social reform. And that has consequences for the scientists' everyday practice: for example, even if the ultimate motivation of studying economic conditions in Philadelphia is to improve the situation of the residents of that city, the scientist must be scrupulous in collecting and reporting data accurately and without bias.

If "The Study of the Negro Problems" has just recently come to be seen as relevant to debates in the philosophy of science, "The Conservation of Races" has long been recognized as centrally important to debates in the philosophy of race. In the 1980s, Kwame Anthony Appiah's critical interpretation of Du Bois' essay sparked an ongoing debate about whether Du Bois helps us understand racial difference as a social, rather than biological, reality.[12] Du Bois argues that physical differences cannot be used to consistently sort human beings into discrete, non-arbitrary groupings that we can call races. Still he claims that races, "while they perhaps transcend scientific definition, nevertheless, are clearly defined to the eye of the Historian and Sociologist" (*Cons.* 40). In other words, races are not natural but socio-historical in origin. Du Bois defines a race as "a vast family of human beings, generally of common blood and language, always of common history, traditions and impulses, who are both voluntarily and involuntarily striving together for the accomplishment of certain more or less vividly conceived ideals of life" (*Cons.* 40). This definition makes race a fundamentally social phenomenon—note that "common blood" is only *generally* involved, whereas "common history" is *always* at stake. The passage also reveals that race, in Du Bois' eyes, is a matter of cultural continuity, as implied by his talk of "traditions" and "ideals of life."

Du Bois goes on to argue that races, by striving for ideals of life, advance civilization. There are, according to him, eight major races in the world in the socio-historical sense of the term: "the Slavs of Eastern Europe, the Teutons of middle Europe, the English of Great Britain and America, the Romance nations of Southern and Western Europe, the Negroes of Africa and America, the Semitic people of Western Asia and Northern Africa, the Hindoos of Central Asia and the Mongolians of Eastern Asia" (*Cons.* 40). In his broad retelling of the history of races, some of these groups have distinctive contributions for which they can be recognized: "The English nation stood for constitutional liberty and commercial freedom; the German nation for science and philosophy; the Romance nations stood for literature and art" (*Cons.* 42). By contrast, the black race has clearly not yet finished giving to modern civilization its "full spiritual message" (*Cons.* 42). He begins the essay by acknowledging that African Americans are sometimes tempted to downplay racial difference in reaction to racist denigration. In light of the task of bringing the black gift to the world's table, though, African Americans have a duty to embrace their distinctive character as members of the global black race: hence the value of "Conserving" the race, as mentioned in the title of the essay.

Du Bois seems to have been directly influenced by Anna Julia Cooper in articulating this ideal. In the chapter of *A Voice from the South* entitled "Has America a Race Problem; If So, How Can It Best Be Solved?" Cooper claims that different races specialize in different forms of life in order to bring about a divinely ordered perfection. As she puts it: "Each race has its badge, its exponent, its message, branded in its forehead by the great Master's hand which is its own peculiar keynote, and its contribution to the harmony of the world."[13] Still earlier thinkers likely influenced them both, such as the German philosopher Johann Gottfried von Herder and the Africana thinkers Martin Delany and Edward Blyden, but enough recognizable words and themes are echoed in Du Bois that direct influence from Cooper is a safe bet.

Another important part of "The Conservation of Races" is Du Bois' articulation of a dilemma faced by African Americans: is racial difference something to be embraced or downplayed? "No Negro who has given earnest thought to the situation of his people in America has failed, at some time in life, to find himself at these cross-roads; has failed to ask himself at some time: What, after all, am I? Am I an American or am I a Negro? Can I be both? Or is it my duty to cease to be a Negro as soon as possible and be an American? If I strive as a Negro, am I not perpetuating the very cleft that threatens and separates Black and White America?" (*Cons.* 11) If you already knew just one thing about Du Bois, it's likely the fact that he drew attention to this psychological phenomenon. His name is today strongly associated with a phrase that he uses to label it in "Strivings of the Negro People": "double consciousness."[14] We do not find that exact phrase here in "The Conservation of Races," but we do find the concept, or to be more accurate, the closely related concept of "twoness."

As Robert Gooding-Williams has pointed out, the three seminal essays of 1897 ask a series of related philosophical questions.[15] "The Conservation of Races" asks what it is to be part of the Negro race, while "The Study of the Negro Problems" asks about the nature of the social problems involving that race. At the beginning of "Strivings of the Negro People," Du Bois claims that for black people, interactions with white interlocutors often involve the unasked question, how does it feel to be a problem? This observation provides a different way into the subject matter of the two other essays. "Strivings of the Negro People" shifts focus away from an external anthropological or sociological point of view, and toward the psychological issue of what it feels like to be a part of this race, under the social conditions of being a problem.[16]

Du Bois famously reveals in the essay when he first realized that he was a problem. Back in Great Barrington, he and his classmates were playing a game involving the exchange of visiting cards when a tall newcomer to the class refused his card—"refused it peremptorily, with a glance" (*SNP* 194). Recounting his experience of this moment, Du Bois introduces a metaphor he would use often in upcoming work, the metaphor of the veil: "Then it dawned upon me with a certain suddenness that I was different from the others; or like, mayhap, in heart and life and longing, but shut out from their world by a vast veil" (*SNP* 194). This way of evoking invidious racial distinction captures how, as an American among Americans, the African American is not separate from America, but is nevertheless kept apart. Notice that he does not speak of a *wall*: the thinness of a veil or curtain captures the subtlety of his point, and of the experience.

Soon after this in the text comes the "double consciousness" passage. It begins by placing the Negro in a list of peoples different from the list of eight races in "The Conservation of Races." He appears to be referring to the phases of world history in the German philosopher G.W.F. Hegel's lectures on the philosophy of history. Whereas Hegel claimed in these lectures that black Africans exist outside of history, Du Bois argues that, in America, the race is stepping on to the world stage in a new and powerful way. Here then is the famous passage:

> After the Egyptian and Indian, the Greek and Roman, the Teuton and Mongolian, the Negro is a sort of seventh son, born with a veil, and gifted with second-sight in this American world,—a world which yields him no self-consciousness, but only lets him see himself through the revelation of the other world. It is a peculiar sensation, this double-consciousness, this sense of always looking at one's self through the eyes of others, of measuring one's soul by the tape of a world that looks on in amused contempt and pity. One ever feels his two-ness,—an American, a Negro; two souls, two thoughts, two unreconciled strivings; two warring ideals in one dark body, whose dogged strength alone keeps it from being torn asunder. (*SNP* 194)

Du Bois introduces three related, but distinct concepts here: second sight, double consciousness, and twoness. When he says the African American is gifted with second sight, he indicates the ability to see from a perspective different from one's own. In some circumstances, this could indeed be a gift. Unfortunately, in the context of a racist America, it is a capacity that leads to the problem of double consciousness. This is the problem of seeing one's self from another perspective that is demeaning, and having this "second sight" so often that it dominates and to some extent overpowers healthy self-consciousness. An example of double consciousness would be a black person hearing on the news that a violent assault has been committed, and immediately hoping the culprit will not turn out to be black. This is because, even though the person who committed the crime is a complete stranger whose actions should not be taken to reflect on other black people, the black person in a majority-white society may worry that media coverage of crime committed by black people will nevertheless serve to reinforce stereotypes that make life harder for all black people.

As for "twoness," this is not simply double consciousness under another name, but rather the conflict that results from double consciousness in light of the fact that one's self-consciousness is dominated but not totally erased by this outside view. From this inside view, black people are full human beings with distinctive ideals, precisely what they are not when seen from the external viewpoint. Thus there is a clash of perspectives and a clash of ideals. How can this be resolved, in favor of a single and adequate perspective? Must the external viewpoint be eliminated by rejecting America itself, perhaps through emigration? Or should there be a hope of getting rid of racial difference and becoming simply, and proudly, American? Du Bois rejects both options: "The history of the American Negro is the history of this strife,—this longing to attain self-conscious manhood, to merge his double self into a better and truer self. In this merging he wishes neither of the older selves to be lost. He would not Africanize America, for America has too much to teach the world and Africa. He would not bleach his Negro soul in a flood of white Americanism, for he knows that Negro blood has a message for the world. He simply wishes to make it possible for a man to be both a Negro and an American, without being cursed and spit upon by his fellows, without having the doors of Opportunity closed roughly in his face" (*SNP* 194).

We can explain this by saying, with a bit of anachronism, that Du Bois was defending the coherence of the very term "African American." Twoness is the feeling that the two parts of this term conflict with one another. Du Bois argues that there is no solution in trying to avoid conflict by cutting off one part or the other. To attempt to cut the "American" part off is misguided and ill-advised. After all, black people have been present in the United States from the very beginning of the country's development. They are familiar with the best and the worst that America has to offer, and are arguably better placed than anyone else to appreciate what is of value in the American experiment. To attempt to cut off the "African" part would be equally wrong, though. It would be a tragic case of suppressing difference, when it is precisely that difference that ought to be appreciated as a fruitful contribution, both to America and to the world as a whole.

In this book, we have considered various fruitful contributions to the world of philosophy by Africana thinkers and traditions of thought. We will continue this journey in our second volume, which will cover Africana philosophy in the twentieth century. Du Bois will be a prominent figure, but we will also meet many other important thinkers, such as Marcus Garvey, Alain Locke, Zora Neale Hurston, Leopold Senghor, C.L.R. James, Frantz Fanon, Angela Davis, and Cornel West. We will encounter philosophy in the artistic and intellectual movements of the Harlem Renaissance and Negritude. We will find philosophy in the music of artists like Sun Ra, Bob Marley, and Fela Kuti. We will explore the philosophical dimensions of political movements like Black Power and the new black feminism of the late twentieth century. All these topics, and many more besides, await us as we turn to a bountiful century in the history of Africana philosophy.

NOTES

Chapter 1

1. L.T. Outlaw, "African, African American, Africana Philosophy," *Philosophical Forum* 24 (1992), 63–93.
2. L.R. Gordon, *Existentia Africana: Understanding Africana Existential Thought* (New York: 2000); L.R. Gordon, *An Introduction to Africana Philosophy* (Cambridge: 2008).
3. C. Jeffers, "Do We Need African Canadian Philosophy?" *Dialogue* 51 (2012), 643–66.
4. We know from the comments of some anonymous referees that some do not take African philosophy to be a component of Africana philosophy, because they identify "Africana" philosophy in its entirety with the philosophy of the African diaspora alone. This is, however, a clear misunderstanding. Here is Outlaw's definition: "'Africana philosophy' is the phrase I use as a 'gathering' notion under which to situate the articulations (writings, speeches, etc.), and traditions of Africans and peoples of African descent collectively, as well as the subdiscipline- or field-forming, tradition-defining or tradition-organizing reconstructive efforts, which are (to be) regarded as philosophy" (at Outlaw, "African, African American, Africana Philosophy," 64).
5. See e.g. S. Cahn (ed.), *Political Philosophy: The Essential Texts*, 3rd ed. (New York: 2014).
6. In a blog post on the online journal *Aeon*: <aeon.co/essays/the-idea-of-precolonial-africa-is-vacuous-and-wrong>.
7. K. Wiredu, "On Defining African Philosophy," in T. Serequeberhan (ed.), *African Philosophy: The Essential Readings* (New York: 1991), 87–110, at 92.
8. King is here quoting from Augustine's *On Free Choice of the Will*.
9. D.A. Masolo, "African Philosophers in the Greco-Roman Era," in K. Wiredu (ed.), *A Companion to African Philosophy* (Malden: 2004), 50–65.

Chapter 2

1. J.E.H. Smith, *The Philosopher: A History in Six Types* (Princeton: 2014), ch. 2.
2. K. Sterelny, "From Hominins to Humans: How *Sapiens* Became Behaviourally Modern," *Philosophical Transactions of the Royal Society B* 366 (2011), 809–22.
3. J. Iliffo, *Africans: The History of a Continent* (Cambridge: 1995), 6; J.D. Clark (ed.), *The Cambridge History of Africa, vol.1: From the Earliest Times to c.500 BC* (Cambridge: 1982), 189.
4. For this see S.I. Greenspan and S.G. Shanker, *The First Idea: How Symbols, Language and Intelligence Evolved from our Primate Ancestors to Modern Humans* (Cambridge MA: 2004), especially ch. 9.
5. Iliffo, *Africans*, 13.
6. See e.g. P. Mellars and C. Stringer (eds), *The Human Revolution: Behavioural and Biological Perspectives on the Origins of Modern Humans* (Edinburgh: 1989) and its sequel volume P. Mellars et al. (eds), *Rethinking the Human Revolution* (Cambridge: 2007).

7. S. McBrearty, "Down with the Revolution," in Mellars, *Rethinking the Human Revolution*, 133–51; S. McBrearty and A.S. Brooks, "The Revolution That Wasn't: A New Interpretation of the Origin of Modern Human Behavior," *Journal of Human Evolution* 39 (2000), 453–563.
8. W.E. Wendt, "'Art Mobilier' from the Apollo 11 Cave, South West Africa's Oldest Dated Works of Art," *South African Archaeological Bulletin* 31 (1976), 5–11.
9. J. Masson, "Apollo 11 Cave in Southwest Namibia: Some Observations on the Site and Its Rock Art," *The South African Archaeological Bulletin* 61 (2006), 76–89.
10. For a comprehensive survey of issues raised by prehistoric and subsequent rock art see J. McDonald and P. Veth (eds), *A Companion to Rock Art* (Oxford: 2012).
11. See e.g. J.D. Lewis-Williams, *The Rock Art of Southern Africa* (Cambridge: 1983); J.D. Lewis-Williams and T.A. Dowson, *Images of Power: Understanding San Rock Art* (Cape Town: 2000); J.D. Lewis-Williams, "Debating Rock Art: Myth and Ritual, Theories and Facts," *The South African Archaeological Bulletin* 61 (2006), 105–14; and his contribution to McDonald and Veth, *Companion to Rock Art*. It should be noted that his work concentrates on far more recent rock art than what we have discussed here, but the findings are seen as relevant to images like those found at Apollo 11: see e.g. Masson, "Apollo 11 Cave in Southwest Namibia," 84.
12. Lewis-Williams, "Debating Rock Art," 108.
13. S. Mithen, *The Prehistory of the Mind: A Search for the Origins of Art, Religion and Science* (London: 1996).

Chapter 3

1. For Plato on Egypt, see *Phaedrus* 274c–275b. For Plutarch see *A History of Philosophy Without Any Gaps: Philosophy in the Hellenistic and Roman Worlds*, ch. 24.
2. M. Van De Mieroop, *Philosophy Before the Greeks: The Pursuit of Truth in Ancient Babylonia* (Princeton: 2016), viii. See also S.N. Kramer, *The Sumerians: Their History, Culture and Character* (Chicago: 1971), J. Bottéro, *Mesopotamia: Writing, Reasoning, and the Gods*, trans. Z. Bahrani and M. Van De Mieroop (Chicago: 1992); N. Veldhuis, *History of the Cuneiform Lexical Tradition* (Münster: 2014).
3. Van De Mieroop, *Philosophy Before the Greeks*, 51.
4. F. Rochberg, *The Heavenly Writing: Divination, Horoscopy, and Astronomy in Mesopotamian Culture* (Cambridge: 2004), 75.
5. Van De Mieroop, *Philosophy Before the Greeks*, 159.
6. Rochberg, *The Heavenly Writing*, 59.
7. Translation of the Akkadian version, from Rochberg, *The Heavenly Writing*, 70. For the structure of the cosmos in Babylonian thought see also W. Horowitz, *Mesopotamian Cosmic Geography* (Winona Lake: 1998), and for Greek ideas about the heavens as divine "writing" see *Philosophy in the Hellenistic and Roman Worlds*, ch. 28.
8. Rochberg, *The Heavenly Writing*, 256.
9. For more on the theory of signs in Mesopotamian culture see G. Manetti, *Theories of the Sign in Classical Antiquity*, trans. C. Richardson (Bloomington: 1993), part one.
10. Van De Mieroop, *Philosophy Before the Greeks*, 176.
11. Van De Mieroop, *Philosophy Before the Greeks*, 200.

12. P. Machinist, "On Self-Consciousness in Mesopotamia", in S.N. Eisenstadt (ed.), *The Origins and Diversity of Axial Age Civilizations* (Albany: 1986), 183–202, 511–18, at 200. Our thanks to Enrique Jiménez for the reference.
13. See W.G. Lambert, *Babylonian Wisdom Literature* (London: 1960), 147.
14. Lambert, *Babylonian Wisdom Literature*, 149.
15. Translated in Y. Cohen, *Wisdom from the Late Bronze Age* (Ann Arbor: 2013).
16. Cohen, *Wisdom from the Late Bronze Age*, 99.
17. Translated in W.G. Lambert, *Babylonian Wisdom Literature* (Oxford: 1960) and B. Foster, *Before the Muses: An Anthology of Akkadian Literature*, 2 vols (Bethesda: 1996). On this work see also T. Oshima, "The *Babylonian Theodicy*: An Ancient Babylonian Discourse on Human Piety and Divine Justice," *Religion Compass* 8 (2015), 483–92.
18. See S. Helle, *Enheduana: The Complete Poems of the World's First Author* (New Haven: 2023), and for further discussion K.R. Raign, "Finding Our Missing Pieces: Women Technical Writers in Ancient Mesopotamia," *Journal of Technical Writing and Composition* 49 (2019), 338–64.
19. For philosophical reflections on the Book of Job in the medieval Jewish tradition, see *A History of Philosophy Without Any Gaps: Philosophy in the Islamic World*, ch. 38.
20. We use the translation in E. Dalley (trans.), *Myths from Mesopotamia: Creation, the Flood, Gilgamesh, and Others* (Oxford: 1989). See also A.R. George, *The Babylonian Gilgamesh Epic: Introduction, Critical Edition and Cuneiform Texts* (Oxford: 2003).
21. Dalley (trans.), *Myths from Mesopotamia*, 53; see also 91 for Enkidu's beast-like upbringing.
22. On this see also B.R. Foster, "The Person in Mesopotamian Thought," in K. Radner and E. Robson (eds), *The Oxford Handbook of Cuneiform Culture* (Oxford: 2011), 117–39, at 118–19.

Chapter 4

1. For the connections between Babylonian, Egyptian, and Greek mathematics see further the classic study O. Neugebauer, *The Exact Sciences in Antiquity* (New York: 1969). See also W. Burkert, *The Orientalizing Revolution: Near Eastern Influence on Greek Culture in the Early Archaic Age* (Cambridge MA: 1992).
2. See e.g. J. Burckhardt, *History of Greek Culture* (New York: Dover, 2002, 1st ed. 1902), ch. 12.
3. For an important study of the eighteenth-century development in European historiography of the idea that "Africans and Asians had religion, but not philosophy," see P.K.J. Park, *Africa, Asia, and the History of Philosophy: Racism in the Formation of the Philosophical Canon, 1780–1830* (Albany: 2013) (quotation at 1).
4. Translation from J.P. Allen, *The Ancient Egyptian Pyramid Texts* (Atlanta: 2005), 60.
5. S.B. Morrow, *The Dawning Moon of the Mind: Unlocking the Pyramid Texts* (New York: 2015), 13.
6. Interview on the online Huffington Post, February 18, 2016.
7. See e.g. G.S. Kirk, J.E. Raven, and M. Schofield, *The Presocratic Philosophers* (Cambridge: 1983), 93.
8. Consider this grand statement by Molefi Asante on Imhotep's importance: "A discussion of Imhotep is critical to an interpretation of the ancient philosophy of the Egyptians since he was the world's first multi-dimensional personality and his achievements stand at the very dawn of reason and science in the service of human society." See M.K. Asante,

The Egyptian Philosophers: Ancient African Voices from Imhotep to Akhenaten (Chicago: 2000), 21. We will discuss Asante's own importance in the history of Africana philosophy in our second volume.

9. P.W. Brandt-Rauf and S.I. Brandt-Rauf, "History of Occupational Science: Relevance of Imhotep and the Edwin Smith Papyrus," *British Journal of Industrial Medicine* 44 (1987), 68–70.
10. See M. Lichtheim, *Ancient Egyptian Literature*, vol. 1 (Berkeley: 1973), 196, and vol. 2 (Berkeley: 1976), 177.
11. On him see E. Hornung, *Akhenaten and the Religion of Light* (Ithaca: 1999); A. Dodson, *Amarna Sunset: Nefertiti, Tutankhamun, Ay, Horemheb, and the Egyptian Counter-Reformation* (Cairo: 2009). For the theme see also J. Assmann, *The Price of Monotheism* (Stanford: 2009).
12. T. Wilkinson, *The Rise and Fall of Ancient Egypt* (London: 2011), 257.
13. Translation from W.K. Simpson, *The Literature of Ancient Egypt* (New Haven: 2003), 279.
14. Simpson, *The Literature of Ancient Egypt*, 281.
15. Simpson, *The Literature of Ancient Egypt*, 281.
16. See D. Redford, *Akhenaten: The Heretic King* (Princeton: 1984), 234.
17. A. Dodson, *Amarna Sunset: Nefertiti, Tutankhamun, Ay, Horemheb, and the Egyptian Counter-Reformation* (Cairo: 2009).
18. O. Goelet and R. Faulkner, *The Egyptian Book of the Dead: The Book of Going Forth by Day* (San Francisco: 1998).
19. Translated in Simpson, *The Literature of Ancient Egypt*.
20. M. Karenga, *The Moral Ideal in Ancient Egypt: A Study in Classical African Ethics* (New York: 2004), 135. As with Asante, whom we referenced earlier in this chapter, sustained discussion of Karenga's importance in the history of Africana philosophy will be part of our second volume on the twentieth century.

Chapter 5

1. For numerous examples see N. Strudwick, *Texts from the Pyramid Age* (Atlanta: 2005), §XVI–XVII.
2. M. Lichtheim, *Ancient Egyptian Literature*, vols 1–3 (Berkeley: 1973–80), vol. 1, 17. References in the main text in this chapter are to this volume. See also T. Wilkinson, *Writings from Ancient Egypt* (London: 2016).
3. See C. Jacq, *L'enseignement du sage égyptien Ptahhotep, le plus ancien livre du monde* (Paris: 1999); F. Hagen, *An Ancient Egyptian Literary Text in Context: The Instruction of Ptahhotep* (Leuven: 2012).
4. Lichtheim, *Ancient Egyptian Literature*, vol. 1, 6.
5. R.B. Parkinson, *The Tale of Sinuhe and Other Ancient Egyptian Poems, 1940–1640 BC* (Oxford: 1997), 246.
6. See N. Shupak, "The Instruction of Amenemope and Proverbs 22:17–24:22 from the Perspective of Contemporary Research," in R.L. Troxel et al. (eds), *Seeking Out the Wisdom of the Ancients: Essays Offered to Honor Michael V. Fox on the Occasion of His Sixty-fifth Birthday* (Winona Lake: 2005), 203–20, especially the appendix, where Shupak lays out the similar passages side by side.

7. *Instruction of Amenemope*, ch. 9; Lichtheim, *Ancient Egyptian Literature*, vol. 2, 153, has "heated"; W.K. Simpson, *The Literature of Ancient Egypt: An Anthology of Stories, Instructions, Stelae, Autobiographies, and Poetry*, 3rd ed. (New Haven: 2003), 231 has "hot-tempered."
8. D. James, "The Instruction of Any and Moral Philosophy," in A.G. Mosley (ed.), *African Philosophy: Selected Readings* (Englewood Cliffs: 1995), 147–55, and J. Maybee, "The Instruction of Any: An Ancient Egyptian Philosophical Theory of Ethics," *African Philosophy* 12 (1999), 149–74.
9. James, "*The Instruction of Any* and Moral Philosophy," 154.
10. A. Black, *A World History of Ancient Political Thought* (Oxford: 2009), 25.

Chapter 6

1. See H. Goedicke, *The Report about the Dispute of a Man and His Ba: Papyrus Berlin 3024* (Baltimore: 1970).
2. For this work see R.B. Parkinson (ed.), *The Tale of the Eloquent Peasant* (Oxford: 1991), and for commentary R.B. Parkinson, "Literary Form and the Tale of the Eloquent Peasant," *The Journal of Egyptian Archaeology* 78 (1992), 163–78; A.M. Gnirs (ed.), *Reading the Tale of the Eloquent Peasant* (Göttingen: 2000); R.B. Parkinson, *The Tale of the Eloquent Peasant: A Reader's Commentary* (Hamburg: 2012); C. Jeffers, "Embodying Justice in Ancient Egypt: *The Tale of the Eloquent Peasant* as a Classic of Political Philosophy," *British Journal for the History of Philosophy* 21 (2013), 421–42.
3. Parkinson, *A Reader's Commentary*, 1.
4. R.B. Parkinson, *The Tale of Sinuhe and Other Ancient Egyptian Poems: 1940–1640 BC* (Oxford: 1997), 55.
5. J. Assmann, *Ma'at: Gerechtigkeit und Unsterblichkeit im alten Ägypten* (Munich: 2001), 33.
6. See Parkinson, *The Tale of Sinuhe*, 212.
7. H. Goedicke, *The Report about the Dispute of a Man with his Ba: Papyrus Berlin 3024* (Baltimore: 1970). On this work see J. Assman, "A Dialogue Between Self and Soul: Papyrus Berlin 3024," in A. Baumgarten et al. (eds), *Self, Soul and Body* (Leiden: 1998), 384–403; J.P. Allen, *The Debate Between a Man and His Soul: A Masterpiece of Ancient Egyptian Literature* (Leiden: 2011).
8. We draw in what follows on O. Goelet and R. Faulkner, *The Egyptian Book of the Dead: The Book of Going Forth by Day* (San Francisco: 1998), 152, and J.P. Allen, *The Ancient Egyptian Pyramid Texts* (Atlanta: 2005), 7.
9. Allen, *The Ancient Pyramid Texts*, 7.
10. Allen, *The Debate Between a Man and His Soul*, 148.
11. Parkinson, *Tale of Sinuhe*, 161.
12. R.B. Parkinson, *Poetry and Culture in Middle Kingdom Egypt: A Dark Side to Perfection* (London: 2002), 217.

Chapter 7

1. See *A History of Philosophy Without Any Gaps: Byzantine and Renaissance Philosophy*, ch. 2. For translations in Ethiopia see e.g. A. Bausi, "Writing, Copying, Translating: Ethiopia as

a Manuscript Culture," in J. Quenzer et al. (eds), *Manuscript Cultures: Mapping the Field* (Berlin: 2014), 37–77; A. Bausi, "Translations in Late Antique Ethiopia," in F. Crevatin (ed.), *Egitto crocevia di traduzioni* (Trieste: 2018), 69–99. For Ethiopian literature more generally see the relevant chapters of S. Kelly (ed.), *A Companion to Medieval Ethiopia and Eritrea* (Leiden: 2020).

2. See A. Kitchen et al., "Bayesian Phylogenetic Analysis of Semitic Languages Identifies an Early Bronze Age Origin of Semitic in the Near East," *Proceedings of the Royal Society* 276 (2009), 2703–10. More generally see J.M. Harden, *An Introduction to Ethiopic Christian Literature* (Madras: 1926).

3. For more on Athanasius' role in the history of philosophy, see *A History of Philosophy Without Any Gaps: Philosophy in the Hellenistic and Roman Worlds*, ch. 45.

4. Cited by section number from the translations in C. Sumner, *Ethiopian Philosophy*, 5 vols (Addis Ababa: 1974–82). See on this text C. Macé and J. Gippert (eds), *The Multilingual Physiologus: Studies in the Oldest Greek Recension and its Translations* (Turnhout: 2021).

5. C. Sumner, *Classical Ethiopian Philosophy* (Addis Ababa: 1985), 17.

6. Sumner, *Ethiopian Philosophy*, vol. 5, 80–3, 86–7.

7. Since Sumner's work there have been further discoveries about Ethiopian translations from Greek. A particularly noteworthy example is the so-called *Aksumite Collection*, which includes a work called *On the One Judge*; the title refers to God. See A. Bausi, "The Treatise *On the One Judge* (CAe 6260) in the *Aksumite Collection* (CAe 1047)," *Adamantius* 27 (2021), 215–56. This text transmits Platonist ideas, such as the claim that the universe is a visible image of invisible reality (229, cf. 249) and a description of the soul as immortal and characterized by rationality (235).

8. Harden, *An Introduction to Ethiopic Christian Literature*, 20.

9. Cited by section number from E.A. Wallis Budge (trans.), *The Queen of Sheba and Her Only Son Menyelek* (*Kebra Negast*) (Cambridge ON: 2000). For recent studies see F. Battaiato et al. (eds), *La regina di Saba: un mito fra Oriente e Occidente* (Naples: 2016), 91–162.

10. The colophon is discussed in A. Bausi, "Ethiopia and the Christian Ecumene: Cultural Transmission, Translation, and Reception," in S. Kelly (ed.), *A Companion to Medieval Ethiopia and Eritrea* (Leiden: 2020), 217–51, at 237.

11. R. Pankhurst, *The Ethiopians: A History* (Malden: 1998), 55.

12. Personal communication, June 2018.

13. I. Shahid, "The *Kebra Nagast* in Light of Recent Research," *Le Muséon* 89 (1976), 133–78.

14. Shahid, "The *Kebra Nagast*," 145, n. 20.

15. M. Kebede, "The Ethiopian Conception of Time and Modernity," in C. Jeffers (ed.), *Listening to Ourselves: A Multilingual Anthology of African Philosophy* (Albany: 2013), 15–37, at 29.

16. Also translated in Sumner, *Ethiopian Philosophy*.

17. See *A History of Philosophy Without Any Gaps: Philosophy in the Islamic World*, ch. 3.

18. *Encyclopedia Aethiopica*, vol. 2, 485.

19. For the genre in Arabic see D. Gutas, "Classical Arabic Wisdom Literature: Nature and Scope," *Journal of the American Oriental Society* 101 (1981), 49–86.

20. For asceticism in ancient Christianity see *Philosophy in the Hellenistic and Roman Worlds*, ch. 45.

21. E.Z. van Donzel, *Ěnbāqom: Anqaṣa Amin (La porte de la foi)* (Leiden: 1969).

Chapter 8

1. For translations and the story of discovery see vol. 2 of C. Sumner, *Ethiopian Philosophy*, 5 vols (Addis Ababa: 1974–82). We have benefited from collaboration with members of a team preparing a collection of papers on Zera Yacob, namely Lea Cantor, Jonathan Egid, and Fasil Merawi, which is connected to the appearance of a new English translation: R. Lee with M. Worku and W.L. Belcher, *The Hatata Inquiries: Two Texts of Seventeenth-Century African Philosophy from Ethiopia about Reason, the Creator, and Our Ethical Responsibilities* (Berlin: 2023). We cite from this translation in the main text, referring to its page numbers.
2. See P. Piovanelli, "The Adventures of the Apocrypha in Ethiopia," in A. Bausi (ed.), *Languages and Cultures of Eastern Christianity: Ethiopian* (Farnham: 2012), 87–109.
3. *Encyclopedia Aethiopica*, vol. 2, 812.
4. T. Tamrat, *Church and State in Ethiopia, 1270–1527* (Oxford: 1972), 219. For one of his works see G. Haile (ed. and trans.), *The Epistle of Humanity of Emperor Zär'a Ya'əqob (Ṭomarä təsbə't)*, 2 vols (Louvain: 1991). They may be "his" in the rather loose sense that scholars at his court were commissioned to write them: see A. Bausi, "Ethiopia and the Christian Ecumene: Cultural Transmission, Translation, and Reception," in S. Kelly (ed.), *A Companion to Medieval Ethiopia and Eritrea* (Leiden: 2020), 217–51, at 241.
5. Ephraim Isaac, *A New Text-Critical Introduction to Mashafa Berhan with a Translation of Book I* (Leiden: 1973), 101. On the Stephanites see G. Haile, "The Cause of the Ǝsṭifanosites: A Fundamentalist Sect in the Church of Ethiopia," *Paideuma* 29 (1983), 93–119.
6. Isaac, *A New Text-Critical Introduction*, 120–5.
7. Isaac, *A New Text-Critical Introduction*, 129–33.
8. *Encyclopedia Aethiopica*, vol. 3, 815.
9. For Islam in Ethopia see e.g. J. Spencer Trimingham, *Islam in Ethiopia* (London: 1952); J. Cuoq, *Islam en Éthiopie: des origines au XVIe siècle* (Paris: 1981); H. Ahmed, "The Coming of Age of Islamic Studies in Ethiopia: The Present State of Research and Publication," in S. Ege et al. (eds), *Proceedings of the 16th International Conference of Ethiopian Studies*, 2 vols (Trondheim: 2009), vol. 2, 449–55.
10. See M. Salvadore, "The Jesuit Mission to Ethiopia (1555–1634) and the Death of Prester John," in A.B. Kavey (ed.), *World-Building and the Early Modern Imagination* (New York: 2010), 141–71.
11. Our thanks to Dag Herbjørnsrud for help in our research on this and the following chapter.

Chapter 9

1. As in the previous chapter, references in the main text are to the new translation by Lee et al., *The Hatata Inquiries*.
2. C. Sumner, *Ethiopian Philosophy*, 5 vols (Addis Ababa: 1974–82), vol. 2, 270.
3. Sumner, *Ethiopian Philosophy*, vol. 2, 65.
4. C. Conti Rossini, "Lo Ḥatatā Zar'a Yā'qob e il padre Giusto da Urbino," *Rendiconti della Reale Accademia dei Lincei* 29, ser. 5 (1920), 213–23.
5. E. Mittwoch, *Die amharische Version der Soirées de Carthage mit einer Einleitung: die angeblichen abessinischen Philosophen des 17. Jahrhunderts* (Berlin: 1934).

6. A. Mbodj-Pouye and A. Wion, "L'histoire d'un vrai faux traité philosophique (Ḥatatā Zar'a Yā'eqob et Ḥatatā Walda Ḥeywat)," *Afriques, Débats et lectures* [online journal], 2013.
7. G. Haile, "The *Discourse of Wärqe*, Commonly Known as *Ḥatāta zä-Zär'a Ya'əqob*," in G. Haile (ed.), *Ethiopian Studies in Honour of Amha Asfaw* (New York: 2017), 51–71, at 54.
8. Sumner, *Ethiopian Philosophy*, vol. 2, 231, 253.
9. Sumner, *Ethiopian Philosophy*, vol. 2, 176, 181.
10. As pointed out by Sumner, *Ethiopian Philosophy*, vol. 2, 131. For the points about the Sabbath and the version of the Psalms used in the works, see Haile, "The *Discourse*," 66–7.
11. For further discussion of the authenticity question see the preface to the new translation mentioned in n. 1 above. Wendy Belcher presents the pro-authenticity case with new completeness and vigor; we are, for our part, convinced.
12. This is explored at length in P. Adamson, *Don't Think for Yourself: Authority and Belief in Medieval Philosophy* (Notre Dame: 2021), the title of which inspired the title of the present chapter.
13. Haile, "The *Discourse*," 69.
14. W. Belcher and M. Kleiner (ed. and trans.), *Galawdewos: The Life and Struggles of Our Mother Walatta Petros: A Seventeenth Century African Biography of an Ethiopian Woman* (Princeton: 2015). Cited by page number in what follows.

Chapter 10

1. U. Bili, *Some Aspects of Islam in Africa* (Reading: 2008), 13–14. See further B. Hall, "The Question of 'Race' in the Pre-Colonial Southern Sahara," *Journal of North African Studies* 10 (2005), 339–67.
2. Ibn Khaldūn also believes that black people are given to excessive emotion and excitability because of the heat of their bodies, which is caused by their climate. See the fourth prefatory discussion in F. Rosenthal (trans.), *Ibn Khaldun: The Muqaddima*, 3 vols (Princeton: 1958), vol. 1; at chapter 2, section 23, he compares black people to animals and says their characteristics make them apt for slavery. The tradition of explaining differences between peoples on the basis of climate goes back to other Islamic thinkers like al-Kindī and ultimately to Greek thinkers such as Ptolemy and Hippocrates.
3. See T. Khannous, *Black-Arab Encounters in Literature and Film* (Abingdon: 2022), ch. 3.
4. See e.g. J.H. Sweet, "The Iberian Roots of American Racist Thought," *The William & Mary Quarterly* 54 (1997), 143–66.
5. See the exhibition catalogue K.B. Berzock (ed.), *Caravans of Gold, Fragments in Time: Art, Culture, and Exchange across Medieval Saharan Africa* (Princeton: 2019).
6. R. Oliver (ed.), *The Cambridge History of Africa*, vol. 3: *c.1050–c.1600* (Cambridge: 1977), 438.
7. For a taste see *A History of Philosophy Without Any Gaps: Philosophy in the Islamic World*, ch. 49.
8. J.O. Hunwick, *Sharī'a in Songhay: The Replies of al-Maghīlī to the Questions of Askia al-Ḥājj Muḥammad* (Oxford: 1985), 32. In the main text below, we quote by page number from Hunwick's translation of the advice for Askiya Muḥammad.
9. Oliver (ed.), *Cambridge History of Africa*, vol. 3, 324.
10. Oliver (ed.), *Cambridge History of Africa*, vol. 3, 391, and 417 for the number of schools. See further E. Saad, *Social History of Timbuktu: The Role of Muslim Scholars and Notables 1400–1900* (Cambridge: 1983).

11. For the treatise see B. Barbour and M. Jacobs, "The *Mi'raj*: A Legal Treatise on Slavery by Ahmad Baba," in J.R. Willis (ed.), *Slaves and Slavery in Muslim Africa* (London: 1985), and for studies see C. Gratien, "Race, Slavery and Islamic Law in the Early Modern Atlantic: Ahmad Baba al-Tinbukti's Treatise on Enslavement," *Journal of North African Studies* 18 (2013), 454–68, J.O. Hunwick, "Ahmad Baba on Slavery," *Sudanic Africa* 11 (2000), 131–9, and J. Cleaveland, "Ahmad Baba al-Timbukti and his Islamic Critique of Racial Slavery in the Maghrib," *Journal of North African Studies* 20 (2015), 42–64. For the issue in the region see J.O. Hunwick, "Islamic Law and Polemics over Race and Slavery in North and West Africa (16th–19th Century)," in S. Marmon (ed.), *Slavery in the Islamic Middle East* (Princeton: 1999), 43–68 and for slavery in Islam more generally, P. Crone, *Slaves on Horses: The Evolution of the Islamic Polity* (Cambridge: 1980); B. Lewis, *Race and Slavery in the Middle East* (Oxford: 1990); W.G. Clarence-Smits, *Islam and the Abolition of Slavery* (London: 2006); K. Ali, *Marriage and Slavery in Early Islam* (Cambridge MA: 2010); and C. El Hamel, *Black Morocco: A History of Slavery, Race, and Islam* (Cambridge: 2013).
12. Hunwick, "Islamic Law and Polemics," 51. See also the discussion in Cleaveland, "Ahmad Baba al-Timbukti."
13. Cleaveland, "Ahmad Baba al-Timbukti," 55.
14. S. Jeppie and S.B. Diagne (eds), *The Meanings of Timbuktu* (Cape Town: 2008), 140.
15. Another legal scholar worth mentioning in this regard is Ibn Ḥamdūn Jāsūs, who was killed in 1709 for his opposition to re-enslaving manumitted slaves as soldiers in Morocco. See A.A. Batran, "The 'Ulama' of Fas, M. Isma'il and the Issue of the Haratin of Fas," in J.R. Willis (ed.), *Slaves and Slavery in Muslim Africa* (London: 1985), 1–15, at 9.
16. D. van Dalen, *Doubt, Scholarship and Society in 17th-Century Central Sudanic Africa* (Leiden: 2016). We draw on this book for the following overview of his thought.
17. Van Dalen, *Doubt, Scholarship and Society*, 208.
18. Here al-Wālī was taking over, and perhaps taking further, an attitude he found in his source, since al-Sanūsī too had seen *taqlīd* as at best an inferior form of belief. For al-Sanūsī's view see *A History of Philosophy Without Any Gaps: Philosophy in the Islamic World*, ch. 58, which follows the interpretation of K. El-Rouyaheb, *Islamic Intellectual History in the Seventeenth Century: Scholarly Currents in the Ottoman Empire and the Maghreb* (Cambridge: 2015). Against El-Rouayheb, van Dalen sees al-Sanūsī as being more lenient toward *taqlīd* than al-Wālī was: see her *Doubt, Scholarship and Society*, 138.
19. C.C. Stewart, "Southern Saharan Scholarship and the *Bilad al-Sudan*," *Journal of African History* 17 (1976), 73–93, at 91.

Chapter 11

1. On him and the caliphate he founded see M. Hiskett, *The Sword of Truth: The Life and Times of the Shehu Usuman Dan Fodio* (New York: 1973), M. Last, *The Sokoto Caliphate* (London: 1977).
2. See J. Hunwick, "The Literary Tradition of Nigeria," *Research in African Literatures* 28 (1997), 210–23 and for *'ajamī* poetry, M. Hiskett, *A History of Hausa Islamic Verse* (London: 1975).
3. J. Boyd and B.B. Mack (trans.), *Collected Works of Nana Asma'u, Daughter of Usman d'an Fodio, 1793–1864* (East Lansing: 1997), 234.

4. *Collected Works*, 46.
5. A significant woman scholar from nineteenth century Mauritania, for example, was Khadījah bint al-ʿĀqil al-Daymānī, who wrote on logic and wrote a gloss on the aforementioned al-Sanūsī. Our thanks to Abdurrahman Mihirig for this information.
6. Hiskett, *The Sword of Truth*, 40.
7. U. Bili, *Some Aspects of Islam in Africa* (Reading: 2008), 52–3; Hiskett, *The Sword of Truth*, 31.
8. *Collected Works*, 12.
9. Hiskett, *The Sword of Truth*, 137–8.
10. Bili, *Some Aspects of Islam*, 84.
11. Bili, *Some Aspects of Islam*, 93 and 96.
12. Quoted at *Collected Works*, 45.
13. Hiskett, *The Sword of Truth*, 106.
14. *Collected Works*, 47, see also 49.
15. *Collected Works*, 75–6.
16. *Collected Works*, 347.
17. On this theme see also Hunwick, "The Literary Tradition of Nigeria," 217.
18. *Collected Works*, 61.
19. See *A History of Philosophy Without Any Gaps: Philosophy in the Islamic World*, ch. 2.
20. E.J. Arnett (trans.), *The Rise of Sokoto Fulani, Being a Paraphrase and in Some Parts a Translation of the Infaku'l maisuri of Sultan Mohammed Bello* (Koto: 1922); there is also a translation available online by M.S. bin Farid. Cited in the main text by section number from Arnett's translation.
21. *Collected Works*, 91.
22. W.L. Craig, *The Kalām Cosmological Argument* (London: 1979). See further H.A. Davidson, *Proofs for Eternity, Creation and the Existence of God in Medieval Islamic and Jewish Philosophy* (New York: 1987).
23. D. van Dalen, *Doubt, Scholarship and Society in 17th-Century Central Sudanic Africa* (Leiden: 2016), 143.
24. P. Naylor, *From Rulers to Rebels: Writing Legitimacy in the Early Sokoto State* (Suffolk: 2021), chs 2–3.
25. K. Kresse, *Philosophising in Mombasa: Knowledge, Islam and Intellectual Practice on the Swahili Coast* (Edinburgh: 2007), with his description of *baraza* culture at 72–80.

Chapter 12

1. On oral traditions in general see I. Okpewho, *African Oral Literature: Backgrounds, Character, and Continuity* (Bloomington: 1992); R. Finnegan, *Oral Literature in Africa* (London: 1970).
2. P.J. Hountondji, *African Philosophy: Myth and Reality* (Bloomington: 1996), 34.
3. We cite by page number from the English translation in P. Tempels, *Bantu Philosophy* (Paris: 1959). For discussion of Tempels in his missionary context see W. De Craemer, *The Jamaa Movement and the Church: A Bantu Catholic Movement in Zaire* (Oxford: 1977).
4. See G. Molnar, *Powers: A Study in Metaphysics*, ed. S. Mumford (Oxford: 2001).
5. Our thanks to Andy White for this comparison.
6. A. Kagame, *La philosophie Bantu-Rwandaise de l'être* (Brussels: 1956).

7. See C. Jeffers (ed.), *Listening to Ourselves: A Multilingual Anthology of African Philosophy* (Albany: 2013).
8. O. p'Bitek, "Fr. Tempels' Bantu Philosophy," *Transition* 13 (1964), 15–17; see further S. Imbo, "Okot p'Bitek's Critique of Western Scholarship on African Religion," in K. Wiredu (ed.), *A Companion to African Philosophy* (2004), 364–73.
9. Hountondji, *African Philosophy*, 34.

Chapter 13

1. G.J. Whitrow, *Time in History: The Evolution of Our General Awareness of Time and Temporal Perspective* (Oxford: 1988), 26–7.
2. See in the *History of Philosophy Without Any Gaps* series ch. 31 in *Classical Indian Philosophy* and ch. 10 in *Philosophy in the Hellenistic and Roman Worlds*.
3. F. Dunand and F. Zivie-Coche, *Gods and Men in Egypt: 3000 BCE to 395 CE*, trans. D. Lorton (Ithaca: 2004), 65.
4. Whitrow, *Time in History*, 25, Dunand and Zivie-Coche, *Gods and Men in Egypt*, 66.
5. J. Assmann, *Searching for God in Ancient Egypt*, trans. D. Lorton (Ithaca: 2001), 75.
6. J. Goody, *Literacy in Traditional Societies* (Cambridge: 1968), 56.
7. E.E. Evans-Pritchard, "Nuer Time-Reckoning," *Africa* 12 (1939), 189–216.
8. Evans-Pritchard, "Nuer Time-Reckoning," 208.
9. P. Bohannan, "Concepts of Time among the Tiv of Nigeria," *Southwestern Journal of Anthropology* 9 (1953), 251–62; T.O. Biedelman, "Kagaru Time Reckoning: An Aspect of the Cosmology of an East African People," *Southwestern Journal of Anthropology* 19 (1963), 9–20.
10. Bohannan, "Concepts of Time among the Tiv," 254.
11. Biedelman, "Kagaru Time Reckoning," 18.
12. Whitrow, *Time in History*, 110.
13. J.N. Kudadjie, "Aspects of Ga and Dangme Thought About Time as Contained in their Proverbs," in D. Tiemersma and H.A.F. Oosterling (eds), *Time and Temporality in Intercultural Perspective* (Amsterdam: 1996), 137–48, at 140.
14. These sayings are quoted from Kudadjie's study. For the idea of acting at the right time see also J.A.A. Ayoade, "Time in Yoruba Thought," in R.A. Wright (ed.) *African Philosophy, An Introduction* (Washington DC: 1997), 93–111, at 106.
15. G. Moore, "The Imagery of Death in African Poetry," *Africa* 38 (1968), 57–70, at 61.
16. J.S. Mbiti, *African Religions and Philosophy* (London: 1969); we quote from the second edition (London: 1990). For the religious context of his project see also his *New Testament Eschatology in an African Background* (Oxford: 1971).
17. Mbiti, *African Religions and Philosophy*, 16
18. Mbiti, *African Religions and Philosophy*, 17.
19. N.S. Booth Jr, "Time and Change in African Traditional Thought," *Journal of Religion in Africa* 7 (1975), 81–91, at 87.
20. M. Kebede, "The Ethiopian Conception of Time and Modernity," in C. Jeffers (ed.), *Listening to Ourselves: A Multilingual Anthology of African Philosophy* (Albany: 2013), 15–37, at 23 and 33.
21. Booth, "Time and Change," 81.

22. E. Beyaraza, *The African Concept of Time: A Comparative Study of Various Theories* (Kampala: 2000), 145.
23. K. Gyekye, *An Essay on African Philosophical Thought: The Akan Conceptual Scheme* (Philadelphia: 1995), 170. For more on the Akan view see K. Wiredu, "Time and African Thought," in Tiemersma and Oosterling (eds), *Time and Temporality*, 127-35.
24. Ayoade, "Time in Yoruba Thought," 105-6.
25. J. Parratt, "Time in Traditional African Thought," *Religion* 7 (1977), 117-26, at 123.
26. This point is made by D.A. Masolo, *African Philosophy in Search of Identity* (Bloomington: 1994), 114: "The absence of a tense structure through which the notion of the future is linguistically expressible cannot be taken as proof that the Akamba and Agikuyu have no concept of the future or, for that matter...that Africans in general have no concept of the future."
27. A. Kagame, "Empirical Apperception of Time and the Conception of History in Bantu Thought," in L. Gardet (ed.), *Cultures and Time* (Paris: 1976), 89-116.
28. Kagame, "Empirical Apperception of Time," 103.
29. Kagame, "Empirical Apperception of Time," 99.

Chapter 14

1. E.B. Idowu, *Olódùmarè: God in Yoruba Belief* (New York: 1973), 30 and 204.
2. E.B. Idowu, *African Traditional Religion: A Definition* (Gateshead: 1973), 78.
3. J.S. Mbiti, *Concepts of God in Africa* (London: 1970), 29.
4. O. p'Bitek, *African Religions in Western Scholarship* (Nairobi: 1970), 64. Along the same lines, D.A. Masolo, *African Philosophy in Search of Identity* (Edinburgh: 1994), 122, comments that "African scholars of African religions were convinced of the relative superiority of monotheism, and have since been eager to squeeze many African religious concepts into monotheistic conceptual frameworks." See also R. Shaw, "The Invention of 'African Traditional Religion,'" *Religion* 20 (1990), 339-53.
5. T. Lindon, "Oríkì Òrìṣà: The Yoruba Prayer of Praise," *Journal of Religion in Africa* 20 (1990), 205-24.
6. Idowu, *Olódùmarè*, 55.
7. We here follow the argument of J.S. Ukpong, "The Problem of God and Sacrifice in African Traditional Religion," *Journal of Religion in Africa* 14 (1983), 187-203.
8. Idowu, *African Traditional Religion*, 170.
9. Lindon, "Oríkì Òrìṣà," 215.
10. H. Sawyerr, *God: Ancestor or Creator? Aspects of Traditional Belief in Ghana, Nigeria, and Sierra Leone* (London: 1970).
11. J.B. Danquah, *The Akan Doctrine of God* (London: 1968), 55.
12. T.O. Biedelman, "Kaguru Time Reckoning: An Aspect of the Cosmology of an East African People," *Southwestern Journal of Anthropology* 19 (1963), 9-20, at 12.
13. M.K. Asante and A. Mazama (eds), *Encyclopedia of African Religion* (London: 2009), 287.
14. A.M. Lugira, *African Traditional Religion* (New York: 2009), 34, 36; Mbiti, *Concepts of God*, 6, 20.
15. Danquah, *The Akan Doctrine of God*, xiv; at 30-40 however, Danquah rejects this connection and suggests that the real meaning of the name *Nyame* is "shining" or "brilliant."

16. A.T. Dalfovo, "The Divinity Among the Lugbara," *Journal of Religion in Africa* 28 (1998), 468–93.
17. Mbiti, *Concepts of God*, 45.
18. The following examples are taken from Idowu, *African Traditional Religion*, 161; K. Gyekye, *An Essay on African Philosophical Thought: The Akan Conceptual Scheme* (Philadelphia: 1987), 82; Mbiti, *Concepts of God*, 38, 84.
19. As argued by Gyekye, *An Essay on African Philosophical Thought*, 78; H.K. Minkus, "Causal Theory in Akwapim Akan Philosophy," in R.A. Wright (ed.), *African Philosophy* (Lanham: 1984), 113–47, at 141–2.
20. Examples taken from J.K. Olupona, *African Religions: A Very Short Introduction* (Oxford: 2014).
21. For the following examples see Olupona, *African Religions*, 11; Asante and Mazama, *Encyclopedia of African Religion*, 288; Idowu, *African Traditional Religion*, 161–2.
22. Cited by Idowu, *African Traditional Religion*, 110.
23. Dalfovo, "The Divinity Among the Lugbara," 484.
24. See also the example of traditional Africans constantly saying "if *Onyame* wills" when undertaking any pursuit, at Gyekye, *An Essay on African Philosophical Thought*, 71.
25. Idowu, *Olódùmarè*, 100; J.A. Draper and K. Mtata, "Orality, Literature, and African Religions," in *The Wiley-Blackwell Companion to African Religions* (London: 2012), 97–111, at 100.
26. A. Gottlieb, "Babies' Baths, Babies' Remembrances: A Beng Theory of Development, History and Memory," *Africa: Journal of the International African Institute* 75 (2005), 105–18.
27. Idowu, *Olódùmarè*, 175.

Chapter 15

1. See *A History of Philosophy Without Any Gaps: Classical Indian Philosophy*, ch. 22.
2. We here agree with S. Gbadegesin, "Ènìyàn: The Yoruba Concept of a Person," in P.H. Coetzee and A.P.J. Roux (eds), *The African Philosophy Reader* (London: 2003), 192–228, at 209.
3. K. Gyekye, "Person and Community in African Thought," in K. Wiredu and K. Gyekye (eds), *Person and Community* (Washington DC: 2010), 101–52, at 115.
4. R.C. Onwuanibe, "The Human Person and Immortality in Ibo Metaphysics," in R.A. Wright (ed.), *African Philosophy: An Introduction* (Lanham: 1984), 183–97, at 193.
5. We take the phrase from the title of the classic study, K. Gyekye, *An Essay on African Philosophical Thought: The Akan Conceptual Scheme* (Philadelphia: 1987), which discusses these issues at §II.6; also Gyekye, "Person and Community," and K. Gyekye, "The Akan Concept of a Person," in Wright, *African Philosophy*, 199–212, as well as K. Wiredu, "The Akan Concept of Mind," *Ibadan Journal of Humanistic Studies* 3 (1983), 113–34, reprinted in G. Floistad (ed.), *Contemporary Philosophy, Volume 5: African Philosophy* (Netherlands: 1987).
6. J. Engmann, "Immortality and the Nature of Man in Ga Thought," in Wiredu and Gyekye, *Person and Community*, 153–89, at 178.
7. The Luo also call the departed spirit a "shadow": see D.A. Masolo, "The Concept of the Person in Luo Modes of Thought," 82–104, in Brown, *African Philosophy*, at 101.
8. For one interesting discussion of this controversy, see K.A. Appiah, *In My Father's House: Africa in the Philosophy of Culture* (New York: 1992), 96–100.
9. For which see Gbadegesin, "Ènìyàn: The Yoruba Concept," as well as L. Adeofe, "Personal Identity in African Metaphysics," in L.M. Brown (ed.), *African Philosophy: New and Traditional Perspectives* (Oxford: 2004), 69–83.

10. Indeed, widespread belief that hard work can change one's lot in life may make it better to speak of the *ori* choosing a "lot," not a destiny, given that the latter term can sometimes connote unchangeable fate. We thank Adeshina Afolayan for this point.
11. Gbadegesin, "Ènìyàn: The Yoruba Concept," 219; we've changed *okra* to *kra* in the quotation to avoid confusion.
12. Quoted by K. Labeodan in M.K. Asante and A. Mazama (eds), *Encyclopedia of African Religion* (London: 2009), 500.
13. See P. Adamson, "'Present without Being Present': Plotinus on Plato's *Daimon*," in V. Harte and R. Woolf (eds), *Rereading Ancient Philosophy: Old Chestnuts and Sacred Cows* (Cambridge: 2017), 257–75.
14. E.L. Mendosa, "The Journey of the Soul in Sisala Cosmology," *Journal of Religion in Africa* 7 (1975), 62–70.
15. T. Perman, "Awakening Spirits: The Ontology of Spirit, Self, and Society in Ndau Spirit Possession Practices in Zimbabwe," *Journal of Religion in Africa* 41 (2011), 59–92, with the quote given below at 81.
16. Quoted by Gyekye, "Person and Community," 105.
17. I. Menkiti, "Person and Community in African Traditional Thought," in Wright, *African Philosophy*, 171–81, at 172.

Chapter 16

1. J.S. Mbiti, *African Religions and Philosophy* (London: 1990), 106.
2. I. Menkiti, "Person and Community in African Traditional Thought," in R. Wright (ed.), *African Philosophy: An Introduction* (Lanham: 1984), 171–81.
3. Menkiti, "Person and Community," 172.
4. D. Tutu, *Believe: The Words and Inspiration of Desmond Tutu* (Auckland: 2007), 5. On his use of the concept see also M. Battle, *Reconciliation: The Ubuntu Theology of Desmond Tutu* (Cleveland: 1997).
5. T. Metz, "Toward an African Moral Theory," *Journal of Political Philosophy* 15 (2007), 321–41, at 334.
6. Metz, "Toward an African Moral Theory," 338.
7. K. Wiredu, "Democracy and Consensus in African Traditional Politics: Plea for a Non-party Polity," in E.C. Eze (ed.), *Postcolonial African Philosophy: A Critical Reader* (Cambridge MA: 1997).
8. K. Gyekye, *An Essay on African Philosophical Thought: The Akan Conceptual Scheme* (Philadelphia: 1995), 155, with the following quotes at 158 and 159.
9. K. Gyekye, *Tradition and Modernity: Philosophical Reflections on the African Experience* (New York: 1997), 49, also for the next quote.
10. Gyekye, *An Essay on African Philosophical Thought*, 159.
11. "What You Should Know About Contemporary African Philosophy," online on IAI News (March 2018).

Chapter 17

1. R. Thornton, "The Transmission of Knowledge in South African Traditional Healing," *Africa* 79 (2009), 17–34, remarks (at 23) that healers "believe [traditional medicine] to be

a kind of science that possesses its own standards of empirical evaluation and criticism... No two [healers] appear to believe or do precisely the same thing. The knowledge they apply is constantly in circulation, producing a diversity of regional and even personal variants."

2. R.F. Gray, "Some Structural Aspects of Mbugwe Witchcraft," in J. Middleton and E.H. Winter (eds), *Witchcraft and Sorcery in East Africa* (London: 1963), 143–73.
3. This kind of divination has been exhaustively described by W. Bascom in *Ifa Divination* (Bloomington: 1969) and *Sixteen Cowries: Yoruba Divination from Africa to the New World* (Bloomington: 1980); we draw on his reports just below. For discussions of Ifa epistemology see also O. Táíwò, "*Ifa*: An Account of a Divination System and Some Concluding Epistemological Questions," in K. Wiredu (ed.), *A Companion to African Philosophy* (Malden: 2004), 304–12, and O. Ogunnaike, *Deep Knowledge: Ways of Knowing in Sufism and Ifa, Two West African Intellectual Traditions* (Philadelphia: 2020).
4. P. Verín and N. Rajaonarimanana, "Divination in Madagascar," in P. Peek (ed.), *African Divination Systems: Ways of Knowing* (Bloomington: 1991), 53–68.
5. Bascom, *Sixteen Cowries*, 42.
6. R. Devisch, "Mediumistic Divination among the Northern Yaka of Zaire," in Peek, *African Divination Systems*, 112–32, at 117.
7. K. Graw, "Beyond Expertise: Reflections on Specialist Agency and the Autonomy of the Divinatory Process," *Africa* 79 (2009), 92–109, at 101–2.
8. S.R. Whyte, "Knowledge and Power in Nyole Divination," in Peek, *African Divination Systems*, 153–72, at 159.
9. For this example see V. Turner, *Revelation and Divination in Ndembu Ritual* (Ithaca: 1975), 219 and 225.
10. Graw, "Beyond Expertise," 96.
11. As pointed out by K.C. Myhre, "Divination and Experience: Explorations of a Chagga Epistemology," *Journal of the Royal Anthropological Institute* 12 (2006), 313–30, at 315.
12. Thornton, "The Transmission of Knowledge," 24.
13. For a good example of skeptical clients, see the discussion in E.M. Zuesse, "Divination and Deity in African Religions," *History of Religions* 15 (1975), 158–82, at 162.
14. R. Kutalek, "Divination und Diagnose bei den Bena in Südwest-Tansania," *Anthropos* 98 (2003), 59–73, at 64.
15. J. Middleton, *Lugbara Religion: Ritual and Authority among an East African People* (London: 1960), 80, and 88 for the story about the Nuer and Lugbara just below. For randomness, see also B. Epstein, "The Diviner and the Scientist: Revisiting the Question of Alternative Standards of Rationality," *Journal of the American Academy of Religion* 78 (2010), 1048–86, at 1055.
16. D. Westerlund, "Religion, Illness, and Healing," in E.K. Bongma (ed.), *The Blackwell Companion to African Religions* (London: 2012), 443–56, at 443.
17. H. Minkus, "Causal Theory in Akwapim Akan Philosophy," in R.A. Wright (ed.), *African Philosophy: An Introduction* (Washington DC: 1979), 113–47, at 121.
18. P. Pels, "The Magic of Africa: Reflections on a Western Commonplace," *African Studies Review* 41 (1998), 193–209, at 202.
19. E.H. Winter, "The Enemy Within: Amba Witchcraft and Sociological Theory," in Middleton and Winter, *Witchcraft and Sorcery*, 277–99, at 294.

20. Middleton and Winter, *Witchcraft and Sorcery*, 8.
21. A much discussed topic; see e.g. J. Comaroff and J.L. Comaroff (eds), *Modernity and Its Malcontents: Ritual and Power in Postcolonial Africa* (Chicago: 1993); P. Geschiere, *The Modernity of Witchcraft: Politics and the Occult in Postcolonial Africa* (Charlottesville: 1997); H.L. Moore and T. Sanders (eds), *Magical Interpretations, Material Realities: Modernity, Witchcraft and the Occult in Postcolonial Africa* (London: 2001).
22. T. Sanders, "Reconsidering Witchcraft: Postcolonial Africa and Analytic (Un)Certainties," *American Anthropologist* 105 (2003), 338–52.
23. For philosophical engagements with African witchcraft and magic, see e.g. P. Ikuenobe, "Cognitive Relativism, African Philosophy, and the Phenomenon of Witchcraft," *Journal of Social Philosophy* 26 (1995), 143–60; K.A. Appiah, *Cosmopolitanism: Ethics in a World of Strangers* (New York: 2006); B. Epstein, "The Diviner and the Scientist: Revisiting the Question of Alternative Standards of Rationality," *Journal of the American Academy of Religion* 78 (2010), 1048–86.
24. Appiah, *Cosmopolitanism*, 76.
25. For this contrast, see Epstein, "The Diviner and the Scientist," 1051.
26. Sanders, "Reconsidering Witchcraft," 342.
27. K. Wiredu, "How Not to Compare African Thought with Western Thought," in R.A. Wright (ed.), *African Philosophy: An Introduction* (Washington: 1977), 166–84, at 167.
28. As pointed out by Myhre, "Divination and Experience," 321.
29. Turner, *Revelation and Divination*, 235.

Chapter 18

1. English translation in C.A. Diop, *The Cultural Unity of Black Africa: The Domains of Patriarchy and of Matriarchy in Classical Antiquity* (London: 1989). Cited in the main text by page number.
2. In what follows we draw on the studies collected in S. Kent, *Gender in African Prehistory* (Walnut Creek: 1998).
3. G.P. Murdoch and C. Provost, "Factors in the Division of Labour by Sex: A Cross-Cultural Analysis," *Ethnology* 12 (1973), 203–25, at 203.
4. S. Kent, "Invisible Gender—Invisible Foragers: Southern African Hunter-Gatherer Spatial Patterning and the Archeological Record," in Kent, *Gender in African Prehistory*, 39–67, at 40.
5. D. Gifford-Gonzalez, "Gender and Early Pastoralists in East Africa," in Kent, *Gender in African Prehistory*, 115–37, at 117.
6. H.I. Schmidt, "Shaming Men, Performing Power: Female Authority in Zimbabwe and Tanzania on the Eve of Colonial Rule," in J.B. Shetler (ed.), *Gendering Ethnicity in African Women's Lives* (Madison: 2015), 265–89, at 276.
7. S.F. Miescher, "Becoming an *Opanyin*: Elders, Gender, and Masculinities in Ghana Since the Nineteenth Century," in C.M. Cole, T. Manuh, and S.F. Miescher (eds), *Africa After Gender?* (Bloomington: 2007), 253–69.
8. M. Bagwasi and J. Sunderland, "Language, Gender and Age(ism) in Setswana," in L.L. Atanga et al. (eds), *Gender and Language in Sub-Saharan Africa: Tradition, Struggle and Change* (Amsterdam: 2013), 53–78.

9. M. Kilson, "Women in African Traditional Religions," *Journal of Religion in Africa* 8 (1976), 133–43, at 135.
10. See e.g. C. Plancke, "The Spirit's Wish: Possession Trance and Female Power among the Punu of Congo-Brazzaville," *Journal of Religion in Africa* 41 (2011), 366–95.
11. O. Oyewumi, *The Invention of Women: Making an African Sense of Western Gender Discourses* (Minneapolis: 1997). Oyewumi builds on her claim that gender is a "colonial category" in her *What Gender is Motherhood? Changing Yoruba Ideals of Power, Procreation, and Identity in the Age of Modernity* (Houndmills: 2016).
12. J.D.Y. Peel, "Gender in Yoruba Religious Change," *Journal of Religion in Africa* 32 (2002), 136–66, at 139.
13. For a study of a significant and clearly female Yoruba deity, see J.M. Murphy and M.-M. Sanford (eds), *Osun Across the Waters: A Yoruba Goddess in Africa and the Americas* (Bloomington: 2001).
14. Peel, "Gender in Yoruba Religious Change," 142.
15. I. Amadiume, *Male Daughters, Female Husbands: Gender and Sex in an African Society* (London: 1987). Cited in the main text by page number.
16. C.W. Kitetu and A.N. Nioko, "Issues of Language and Gender in *Iweto* Marriage as Practised by the Kamba in Kenya," in Atanga et al. (eds), *Gender and Language*, 29–52.
17. B. Wambui, "*Kūgeria Mīario: Atumia, Ciana, Mbūri, Mīgūnda:* Conversations: Women, Children, Goats, Land," in C. Jeffers (ed.), *Listening to Ourselves: A Multilingual Anthology of African Philosophy* (Albany: 2013), 91–123.
18. On these changes see J. Pauli, "African Marriages in Transformation: Anthropological Insights," in J. Etim (ed.), *Introduction to Gender Studies in Eastern and Southern Africa* (Rotterdam: 2016), 95–113.
19. N.L. Mbah, "Matriliny, Masculinity, and Contested Gendered Definitions of Ethnic Identity and Power in Nineteenth-Century Southeastern Nigeria," in Shetler (ed.), *Gendering Ethnicity*, 233–64. On the group in question see also P. Nsugbe, *Ohaffia: A Matrilineal Ibo People* (Oxford: 1974).
20. J.B. Shetler, "Gendering the History of Social Memory in the Mara Region, Tanzania, as an Antidote to 'Tribal' History," in Shetler (ed.), *Gendering Ethnicity*, 31–56, at 33.
21. Another classic work questioning such assumptions, perhaps the most prominent by a professional philosopher, would be Nkiru Nzegwu's *Family Matters: Feminist Concepts in African Philosophy of Culture* (Albany: 2006).

Chapter 19

1. K. Wiredu, *Philosophy and an African Culture* (Cambridge: 1980), 45.
2. W. Abraham, *The Mind of Africa* (London: 1962).
3. Cited by page from the English translation in P.J. Hountondji, *African Philosophy: Myth and Reality* (Bloomington: 1996).
4. Responding to critics, Hountondji has claimed: "Though it had the formal structure of a definition, this prefatory declaration was not meant as a definition." Emphasizing its "polemical thrust," he goes on to refer to the sentence as a "counterassertion" (against "the dominant ethnological conception") and a "simple equation" ("African

philosophy equals African philosophical literature") (ix). We will not delve here into the significance of these distinctions for Hountondji, as it is sufficient for our purposes here to count the kind of stipulation of intended meaning in Hountondji's sentence as a definition, normally understood.

5. A. Césaire, *Discours sur le colonialisme* (Paris: 1955), English translation by J. Pinkham in *Discourse on Colonialism* (New York: 2001).
6. Wiredu, *Philosophy and an African Culture*, 30.
7. Cited by page number from M. Towa, *Essai sur la problematique philosophique dans l'Afrique actuelle* (Yaounde: 1971).
8. S. Imbo, *An Introduction to African Philosophy* (Lanham: 1998), 88.
9. K. Gyekye, *Essay on African Philosophical Thought: The Akan Conceptual Scheme* (Cambridge: 1986), 8. For Bondunrin see his essay "The Question of African Philosophy," in T. Serequeberhan (ed.), *African Philosophy: The Essential Readings* (New York: 1991).
10. Hountondji, *African Philosophy*, 53.
11. Towa, *Essai sur la problematique philosophique*, 55–6.
12. See the "Postscript" to Hountondji, *African Philosophy*, and 44–5 for the following quotes.
13. See H.O. Oruka, "Four Trends in African Philosophy," in A. Diemer (ed.), *Philosophy in the Present Situation of Africa* (Wiesbaden: 1981), 1–7.

Chapter 20

1. A. Graness and K. Kresse (eds), *Sagacious Reasoning: Henry Odera Oruka in Memoriam* (Nairobi: 1999), 30. In what follows we will often quote from H.O. Oruka, *Sage Philosophy: Indigenous Thinkers and Modern Debate on African Philosophy* (Leiden: 1990), which includes articles by Oruka, responses to his project, and material gathered by Oruka and his colleagues on sages in Kenya. This book is cited by page number throughout the chapter.
2. *Sagacious Reasoning*, 23.
3. *Sagacious Reasoning*, 61.
4. M. Griaule, *Conversations with Ogotemmeli: An Introduction into Dogon Religious Ideas* (Oxford: 1965). This material is summarized and discussed by D.A. Masolo, *African Philosophy in Search of Identity* (Bloomington: 1994), ch. 3.
5. A.S. Oseghare, "Sagacity and African Philosophy," *International Philosophical Quarterly* 32 (1992), 95–104, at 101.
6. These examples are actually given not by Oruka but by F. Ochieng'-Odhiambo, in *Sagacious Reasoning*, 175–6. Oddly, Rose's point about stability and change is here compared to the ideas of Parmenides (177), who actually denied the reality of change.
7. For this as a criterion alongside second-order reflectiveness, see K.M. Kalumba, "Sage Philosophy: Its Methodology, Results, Significance, and Future," in K. Wiredu (ed.), *A Companion to African Philosophy* (Oxford: 2004), 274–81, at 275.
8. For discussion of this case see F. Ochieng'-Odhiambo, *Trends and Issues in African Philosophy* (New York: 2010), 143–4.
9. For this worry see Ochieng'-Odhiambo, *Trends and Issues*, 132–3.
10. D.A. Masolo, *African Philosophy in Search of Identity* (Bloomington: 1994), 237.
11. *Sagacious Reasoning*, 159.

12. See e.g. K. Kresse, "Can Wisdom Be Taught? Kant, Sage Philosophy, and Ethnographic Reflections from the Swahili Coast," in M. Ferrari and G. Potworowski (eds), *Teaching for Wisdom* (Dordrecht: 2008), 189–204, at 192.
13. C. Neugebauer, "Ethnophilosophy in the Philosophical Discourse in Africa: A Critical Note," *Quest* 4 (1990), 43–65.
14. S. Imbo, *Oral Traditions as Philosophy: Okot p'Bitek's Legacy for African Philosophy* (Lanham: 2002). For the poems see O. p'Bitek, *Song of Lawino and Song of Okol* (Cambridge: 1985).
15. *Sagacious Reasoning*, 112.
16. *Sagacious Reasoning*, 114, see also 255.
17. Quoted in Masolo, *African Philosophy*, 198.
18. *Sagacious Reasoning*, 252.

Chapter 21

1. R.A. Wright (ed.), *African Philosophy: An Introduction* (Washington DC: 1977).
2. P. Hountondji (ed.), *Endogenous Knowledge: Research Trails* (Dakar: 1997).
3. K. Wiredu, "On Defining African Philosophy," in T. Serequeberhan (ed.), *African Philosophy: The Essential Readings* (New York: 1991), 87–110; cited by page number in what follows. This is an expanded version of a paper first presented in 1981, right around the time of the transition in his work.
4. We cite in what follows by page number from K. Gyekye, *An Essay on African Philosophical Thought: The Akan Conceptual Scheme* (Cambridge: 1987).
5. K. Wiredu, *Cultural Universals and Particulars: An African Perspective* (Bloomington: 1997); again, cited by page number.
6. K. Kresse and K. Wiredu, "Language Matters! Decolonization, Multilingualism, and African Languages in the Making of African Philosophy," published online in *Polylog: Forum for Intercultural Philosophy* 2 (1990).
7. K. Wiredu, *Philosophy and an African Culture* (Cambridge: 1980), 28.
8. Translated into English in P. Hountondji, *The Struggle for Meaning: Reflections on Philosophy, Culture, and Democracy in Africa* (Athens OH: 2002), cited by page number, with occasional modifications to the translation.
9. *Endogenous Knowledge: Research Trails*, 2, and 13–15 for the following quotes.
10. Another author associated with the professional school, whom we mentioned in Chapter 19, was Marcien Towa; he also moved toward accepting the philosophical character of many traditional African folktales, given their emphasis on using reason, acquiring knowledge, and resisting supposed intellectual superiors. See his *The Idea of a Negro African Philosophy*, published in 1979. It has also been argued that he is best understood as belonging neither to the ethnophilosophical nor the professional school but rather another strand of African philosophy dubbed the "hermeneutical school." See the introduction to T. Serequeberhan (trans.), *Marcien Towa's African Philosophy: Two Texts* (Asmara: 2012), and the categorization of texts in his introduction to T. Serequeberhan (ed.), *African Philosophy: The Essential Readings* (New York: 1991).

Chapter 22

1. For general works on the history of slavery in and beyond the Atlantic trade see D.B. Davis, *Slavery and Human Progress* (New York: 1984); B.L. Solow (ed.), *Slavery and the Rise of the Atlantic System* (Cambridge: 1991); H. Thomas, *The Slave Trade: The History of the Atlantic Slave Trade, 1440–1870* (New York: 1997); P. Manning, "Why Africans? The Rise of the Slave Trade to 1700," in G. Heuman and J. Walvin (eds), *The Slavery Reader* (London: 2003), 30–41.
2. See further E. Abbott, *Sugar: A Bittersweet History* (London: 2009).
3. E.g. in central Mexico a pre-contact population of between 10 and 25 million was reduced to about 1 million. For figures and discussion see L.A. Newson, "The Demographic Collapse of Native Peoples of the Americas, 1492–1650," *Proceedings of the British Academy* 81 (1993), 247–88.
4. Patrick Manning, "Why Africans? The Rise of the Slave Trade to 1700," in Heuman and Walvin (eds), *The Slavery Reader*, 30.
5. For a fundamental study of the question see P. Curtin, *The Atlantic Slave Trade: A Census* (Madison: 1969).
6. In what follows we draw on V.B. Spratlin, *Juan Latino, Slave and Humanist* (New York: 1938); B. Fra-Molinero, "Juan Latino and His Racial Difference," in T.F. Earle and K.J.P. Lowe (eds), *Black Africans in Renaissance Europe* (Cambridge: 2005), 326–44; H.L. Gates Jr. and M. Wolff, "An Overview of Sources on the Life and Work of Juan Latino, the 'Ethiopian Humanist'," *Research in African Literatures* 29 (1998), 14–51; E.R. Wright, *The Epic of Juan Latino: Dilemmas of Race and Religion in Renaissance Spain* (Toronto: 2016).
7. For the curious, here it is: *Ad Catholicum pariter et invictissimum Philippum dei gratia hispaniarum Regem, de foelicissima serenissimi Ferdinandi Principis navitate, epigrammatum liber. Deque Sanctissimi Pii Quinti Romanae Ecclesiae Pontificis summi, rebus, & affectibus erga Phillipum regem Christianissimum, Liber unus. Austrias Carmen, de Excellentissimi Domini D. Ioannis ab Austria, Caroli Quinti filii, ac Philippi invictissimi fratris, re benè gesta, in victoria mirabili eiusdem Philippi adversus perfidos Turcas parta, Ad Illustrissimum, pariter & Reverendissimum D. D. Petrum à Deza Praesidem, ac pro Philippo militiae praefectû. Per Magistrum Ioannem Latinum Garnatae studiosae adolescentiae moderatorem. Libri duo.*
8. Translation from Spratlin, *Juan Latino*, 190.
9. Translated in Wright, *The Epic of Juan Latino*, 188.
10. The prefatory poem uses a playful style called *versos de cabo roto* ("verses with unfinished endings"). Here is the original Spanish: "Pues al Cielo no le plu- / que saliese tan ladi- / como el negro Juan Lati- / hablar latines rehu-." M. Cervantes de Saavedra, *El ingenioso hidalgo don Quixote de la Mancha* (Madrid: 1605), 6. This translation is ours.
11. See V. Carretta, "Who Was Francis Williams?" *Early American Literature* 38 (2003), 213–37.
12. For the passage and further discussion see E.C. Eze, "Hume, Race, and Human Nature," *Journal of the History of Ideas* 61 (2000), 691–8.

Chapter 23

1. Text at B. Brentjes, *Anton Wilhelm Amo: der schwarze Philosoph in Halle* (Leipzig: 1976), 8–10.
2. As suggested by Brentjes, *Anton Wilhelm Amo*, 31. On Gannibal see H. Barnes, *Gannibal: The Moor of Petersburg* (London: 2005).

3. As pointed out by J.E.H. Smith, *Nature, Human Nature, and Human Difference* (Princeton: 2015), 208-9. For Amo's biography see also Brentjes, *Anton Wilhelm Amo*; W.E. Abraham, "The Life and Times of Anton Wilhelm Amo, the First African (Black) Philosopher in Europe," in M.K. Asanta and A.S. Abarry (eds), *African Intellectual Heritage: A Book of Sources* (Philadelphia: 1996), 424-40. Amo's biography is also presented in S. Mougnol, *Amo Afer: un Noir, professeur d'université en Allemagne au XVIIIe siècle* (Paris: 2010); O. Ette, *Anton Wilhelm Amo: philosophieren ohne festen Wohnsitz. Eine Philosophie der Aufklärung zwischen Europa und Afrika* (Berlin: 2014); J.E. Mabe, *Anton Wilhelm Amo: The Intercultural Background of His Philosophy* (Nordhausen: 2014); and Y. Somet, *Anthony William Amo: sa vie et son oeuvre* (Le Plessis-Trévise: 2016).
4. Brentjes, *Anton Wilhelm Amo*, 70, and 68-9 for the report of his return to Africa.
5. Quoted at Smith, *Nature, Human Nature*, 214.
6. For a useful discussion of the genre see the introduction to S. Menn and J.E.H. Smith (trans.), *Anton Wilhelm Amo's Philosophical Dissertations on Mind and Body* (Oxford: 2020). We are grateful to the authors for showing us a pre-publication draft of the volume. The works are cited below by Amo's (rather complicated) labels for the sections of the treatise.
7. Again, we follow here the conclusions of Menn and Smith, *Philosophical Dissertations*.
8. In addition to the English translation in Menn and Smith, *Philosophical Dissertations*, there is a French translation in Somet, *Anthony William Amo*.
9. Plotinus, *Enneads* 3.6; the Greek term for "impassivity," *apatheia*, is also used in the title of Amo's dissertation.
10. Brentjes, *Anton Wilhelm Amo*, 41; for Amo's opposition to Stahl's vitalism see also Mougnol, *Amo Afer*, 79-81, Smith, *Nature, Human Nature*, 209.
11. Here we agree with Smith, *Nature, Human Nature*, 219, in his rebuttal of Kwame Nkrumah.
12. On this idea see e.g. M.A. Kulstad, "Two Interpretations of the Pre-Established Harmony in the Philosophy of Leibniz," *Synthese* 96 (1993), 477-504.
13. Hountondji, *African Philosophy*, 129.
14. Hountondji, *African Philosophy*, 129-30.
15. K. Wiredu, "Amo's Critique of Descartes' Philosophy of Mind," in K. Wiredu (ed.), *A Companion to African Philosophy* (London: 2004), 200-6, at 204.
16. For discussion, see C. Jeffers, "Rights, Race, and the Beginnings of Modern Africana Philosophy," in P.C. Taylor, L.M. Alcoff, and L. Anderson (eds), *The Routledge Companion to Philosophy of Race* (New York: 2018), 132-4.
17. Abraham, "The Life and Times of Anton Wilhelm Amo," 430.
18. Smith, *Nature, Human Nature*, 210.
19. On whom see D.N.A. Kpobi, *Mission in Chains: The Life, Theology and Ministry of the Ex-Slave Jacobus E.J. Capitein (1717-1747) with a Translation of his Major Publications* (Zoetermeer: 1993).
20. We consulted the translation in Kpobi, *Mission in Chains*; for another translation see G. Parker (trans.), *The Agony of Asar: A Thesis on Slavery by the Former Slave Jacobus Elisa Johannes Capitein (1717-1747)* (Princeton: 1998).
21. C. Levecq, "Jacobus Capitein: Dutch Calvinist and Black Cosmopolitan," *Research in African Literatures* 44 (2013), 145-66, argues that letters sent back to Holland by Capitein in this period show him adopting a more sympathetic stance to African culture than we might expect based on the lecture on slavery.
22. Smith, *Nature, Human Nature*, 224 and 226.

Chapter 24

1. For autobiography in this period see W.L. Andrews, *To Tell a Free Story: The First Century of Afro-American Autobiography* (Urbana: 1986).
2. V. Carretta (ed.), *Unchained Voices: An Anthology of Black Authors in the English-Speaking World of the 18th Century* (Lexington: 1996), abbreviated as *UV* in this chapter.
3. H.L. Gates Jr, *The Signifying Monkey: A Theory of African-American Literary Criticism* (New York: 1988).
4. S.A. Diouf, *Servants of Allah: African Muslims Enslaved in the Americas* (New York: 1998), 48.
5. Diouf, *Servants of Allah*, 108.
6. A.D. Austin, *African Muslims in Antebellum America: Transatlantic Stories and Spiritual Struggles* (New York: 1997), 51.
7. See Diouf, *Servants of Allah*, 140–4.
8. See Y.D. Addoun and P. Lovejoy, "Muhammad Kaba Saghanughu and the Muslim Community of Jamaica," in P. Lovejoy (ed.), *Slavery on the Frontiers of Islam* (Princeton: 2003), 199–218; E.A. Dolan and A.I. Alami, "Muhammad Kabā Saghanughu's Arabic Address on the Occasion of Emancipation in Jamaica," *The William and Mary Quarterly* 76 (2019), 289–312.
9. See R. Desrochers, Jr, "'Surprizing Deliverance'?: Slavery and Freedom, Language and Identity in the Narrative of Briton Hammon," in V. Carretta and P. Gould (eds), *Genius in Bondage: Literature of the Early Black Atlantic* (Lexington: 2001), 153–74.
10. See D. Vollaro, "Sixty Indians and Twenty Canoes: Briton Hammon's Unreliable Witness to History," *Native South* (2009), 133–47.
11. For an argument that Gronniosaw is deliberately obscuring his familiarity with Islam and writing, see J. Harris, "Seeing the Light: Re-Reading James Albert Ukawsaw Gronniosaw," *English Language Notes* 42 (2005), 43–57.
12. Gates, *Signifying Monkey*, 139.
13. In what follows we cite by page number from C. May (ed.), *Jupiter Hammon: The Collected Works* (Knoxville: 2017).
14. In J. Brooks and J. Sailliant (eds), *"Face Zion Forward": First Writers of the Black Atlantic, 1785–1798* (Boston: 2002).

Chapter 25

1. The aptness of the phrase for Wheatley was already noted in the introduction to W.H. Robinson, *Critical Essays on Phillis Wheatley* (Boston: 1982), which despite the title consists mostly of historical responses to her works beginning in her own lifetime. Cited in this chapter as *Essays*, while the short title *Works* refers to J.C. Shields (ed.), *The Collected Works of Phillis Wheatley* (Oxford: 1988). See also J.D. Mason (ed.), *The Poems of Phillis Wheatley* (Chapel Hill: 1989) and for her life D. Waldstreicher, *The Odyssey of Phillis Wheatley: A Poet's Journeys Through American Slavery and Independence* (New York: 2023).
2. For more on the passage see E.D. Lamore, "Phillis Wheatley's Use of the Georgic," in J.C. Shields (ed.), *New Essays on Phillis Wheatley* (Knoxville: 2011), 111–55, at 121–2. For discussion of her geographical origin see V. Carretta, *Phillis Wheatley: Biography of a Genius in*

Bondage (Athens GA: 2011), 8; J.C. Shields, *Phillis Wheatley's Poetics of Liberation: Backgrounds and Contexts* (Knoxville: 2008), 98. Shields speculates that she may have been Fulani, like the members of the Sokoto Caliphate discussed above in Chapter 11.
3. For these quotes see the "Master's Letter" in *Works* and *Essays*, 19 and 39.
4. As documented by A. Sistrunk, "The Influence of Alexander Pope on the Writing Style of Phillis Wheatley," in *Critical Essays*, 175–88.
5. Shields, *Poetics of Liberation*, 131.
6. This connection is pointed out by Shields, *Phillis Wheatley's Poetics of Liberation*, 36.
7. Shields, *Phillis Wheatley's Poetics of Liberation*, 79.

Chapter 26

1. For his life see J. Saillant, *Black Puritan, Black Republican: The Life and Thought of Lemuel Haynes, 1753–1833* (New York: 2003). For a shorter overview see R.D. Brown, "'Not Only Extreme Poverty, but the Worst Kind of Orphanage': Lemuel Haynes and the Boundaries of Racial Tolerance on the Yankee Frontier, 1770–1820," *New England Quarterly* 61 (1988), 502–18.
2. For the New Divinity school and its relevance for Haynes see M. Valeri, *Law and Providence in Joseph Bellamy's New England: The Origins of the New Divinity in Revolutionary America* (New York: 1994); J. Saillant, "Slavery and Divine Providence in New England Calvinism: The New Divinity and a Black Protest, 1775–1805," *New England Quarterly* 68 (1995), 584–608; Saillant, *Black Puritan*, ch. 3.
3. K.P. Minkema and H.S. Stout, "The Edwardsean Tradition and the Antislavery Debate, 1740–1865," *Journal of American History* 92 (2005), 47–74.
4. Quotations taken from Minkema and Stout, "The Edwardsean Tradition," 53 and 56.
5. The quote is from his *Taxation no Tyranny* (London: 1775), 454.
6. Available online at the Evans Early American Imprint Collection. For another relevant work by Hart see S. Hopkins and J. Saillant, "'Some Thoughts on the Subject of Freeing the Negro Slaves in the Colony of Connecticut, Humbly Offered to the Consideration of All Friends to Liberty & Justice,' by Levi Hart," *New England Quarterly* 75 (2002), 107–28; here Hart suggested freeing slaves but indemnifying the slaveholders against the resulting financial loss.
7. R. Bogin, "'Liberty Further Extended': A 1776 Antislavery Manuscript by Lemuel Haynes," *William and Mary Quarterly* 40 (1983), 85–105.
8. T.M. Cooley, *Sketches of the Life and Character of the Rev. Lemuel Haynes* (New York: 1839), 63–5.
9. R. Newman (ed.), *Black Preacher to White America: The Collected Writings of Lemuel Haynes, 1774–1833* (Brooklyn: 1990), cited by page number in the main text.
10. On Washington as a slaveowner, see M. Thompson, *"The Only Unavoidable Subject of Regret": George Washington, Slavery, and the Enslaved Community at Mount Vernon* (Charlottesville: 2019).
11. For the text see P.S. Foner and R.J. Branham (eds), *Lift Every Voice: African American Oratory, 1787–1900* (Tuscaloosa: 1998), 60–5.
12. Brown, "Not Only Extreme Poverty," 503. For the episode see also J. Saillant, "'Remarkably Emancipated from Bondage, Slavery, and Death': An African American Retelling of the Puritan Captivity Narrative, 1820," *Early American Literature* 29 (1994), 122–40.
13. Brown, "Not Only Extreme Poverty," 516.

Chapter 27

1. As reported by the *Correct Copy of the Poll* from 1774, held at the Bodleian library, shelfmark Vet. A5 e.6697.
2. J. Wright, "Ignatius Sancho (1729-1780), African Composer in England," *The Black Perspective in Music* 7 (1979), 132-67.
3. For what follows we draw on the discussion in V. Carretta (ed.), *Letters of the Late Ignatius Sancho* (Peterborough: 2015). Cited below by volume and letter number. On the letters, see further M. Ellis, "Ignatius Sancho's *Letters*: Sentimental Libertinism and the Politics of Form," in V. Carretta and P. Gould (eds), *Genius in Bondage: Literature of the Early Black Atlantic* (Lexington: 2001), 199-217.
4. See Appendix B of Carretta (ed.), *Letters*.
5. See further S.S. Sandhu, "Ignatius Sancho and Laurence Sterne," *Research in African Literatures* 29 (1998), 88-105.
6. Here we rely especially on S.A. Bedini, *The Life of Benjamin Banneker: The First African-American Man of Science*, 2nd ed. (Baltimore: 1999). See also C. Cerami, *Benjamin Banneker: Surveyor, Astronomer, Publisher, Patriot* (New York: 2002).
7. Quoted in Bedini, *The Life of Benjamin Banneker*, 127. We cite this work by page number in the remainder of this chapter.
8. Cerami, *Benjamin Banneker*, 155. For the correspondence, see also W. Andrews, "Benjamin Banneker's Revision of Thomas Jefferson: Conscience vs. Science in the Early American Antislavery Debate," in Carretta and Gould, *Genius in Bondage*, 218-41; R. Newman, "'Good Communications Corrects Bad Manners': The Banneker-Jefferson Dialogue and the Project of White Uplift," in J.C. Hammond and M. Mason (eds), *Contesting Slavery: The Politics of Bondage and Freedom in the New American Nation* (Charlottesville: 2011), 69-93.
9. Bedini, *The Life of Benjamin Banneker*, xiv.

Chapter 28

1. C.S. King, *My Life, My Love, My Legacy* (New York: 2017), 134.
2. We cite from O. Equiano, *The Interesting Narrative and Other Writings*, ed. V. Carretta (London: 1995). On Equiano, see also F.A. Nussbaum, "Being a Man: Olaudah Equiano," in V. Carretta and P. Gould (eds), *Genius in Bondage: Literature of the Early Black Atlantic* (Lexington: 2001), 54-71; V. Carretta, *Equiano, the African: Biography of a Self-Made Man* (New York: 2006).
3. For different rhetorical approaches in this period, see K. Sandiford, *Measuring the Moment: Strategies of Protest in Eighteenth-Century Afro-English Writing* (Selinsgrove: 1988).
4. We cite by page number from V. Carretta (ed.), *Quobna Ottobah Cugoano: Thoughts and Sentiments on the Evil of Slavery* (New York: 1999), abbreviated as *Thoughts*. On Cugoano, see further J. Gunn, "Creating a Paradox: Quobna Ottobah Cugoano and the Slave Trade's Violation of the Principles of Christianity, Reason, and Property Ownership," *Journal of World History* 21 (2010), 629-56; M. Hoyle, *Cugoano Against Slavery* (Hertford: 2015); R. Wheeler, "'Betrayed by Some of My Own Complexion': Cugoano, Abolition, and the Language of Racialism," in Carretta and Gould, *Genius in Bondage*, 17-38.

NOTES TO PAGES 221–31

5. In *The Analytical Review* (May 1789). See further M. Ferguson, "Mary Wollstonecraft and the Problematic of Slavery," *Feminist Review* 42 (1992), 82–102.
6. Carretta, *Equiano, the African*, 319.
7. Carretta, *Equiano, the African*, 185.
8. On this famous trial, see e.g. J. Walvin, *The Zong: A Massacre, the Law and the End of Slavery* (New Haven: 2011); M. Faubert, *Granville Sharp's Uncovered Letter and the Zong Massacre* (London: 2018).

Chapter 29

1. We take this and the following figures from J.D. Popkin, *A Concise History of the Haitian Revolution* (Malden: 2012), 2. Other studies of the Revolution include L. Dubois, *Avengers of the New World: The Story of the Haitian Revolution* (Cambridge MA: 2004); L. Dubois and J.D. Garrigus (eds), *Slave Revolution in the Caribbean 1789–1804: A Brief History with Documents* (London: 2006); J.D. Popkin, *You Are All Free: The Haitian Revolution and the Abolition of Slavery* (Cambridge: 2010); J. Gonzalez, *Maroon Nation: A History of Revolutionary Haiti* (New Haven: 2019).
2. References throughout the chapter to *Black Jacobins* are to C.L.R. James, *The Black Jacobins: Toussaint L'Ouverture and the San Domingo Revolution*, 2nd ed. (New York: 1989).
3. A famous remark quoted at e.g. Popkin, *A Concise History*, 137.
4. This thesis has been followed and extended by N. Nesbitt, *Universal Emancipation: The Haitian Revolution and the Radical Enlightenment* (Charlottesville: 2008).
5. References to *Toussaint* throughout the chapter are to N. Nesbitt (ed.), *Toussaint L'Ouverture: The Haitian Revolution* (London: 2008). On him see also the overview in D. Geggus, "Toussaint L'Ouverture and the Haitain Revolution," in R.W. Weisberger (ed.), *Profiles of Revolutionaries in Atlantic History, 1750–1850* (New York: 2007), 115–35.
6. This part of his approach to Haiti was later taken up by his disciple Carolyn Fick. See her *The Making of Haiti: The Saint-Domingue Revolution from Below* (Knoxville: 1990).
7. Cited at C. Forsdick and C. Høgsbjerg (eds), *The Black Jacobins Reader* (Durham: 2017), 10.
8. For instance D.P. Geggus, *Haitian Revolutionary Studies* (Bloomington: 2002), 66–70.
9. Popkin, *A Concise History*, 49–50.
10. J.P. Marques, "Slave Revolts and the Abolition of Slavery: An Overinterpretation," trans. R. Wall in S. Drescher and P. Emmer (eds), *Who Abolished Slavery: Slave Revolts and Abolitionism* (New York: 2010), 1–89.
11. Here we broadly follow the line taken by N. Nesbitt, *Caribbean Critique: Antillean Critical Theory from Toussaint to Glissant* (Liverpool: 2014); he also compares L'Ouverture's thought to that of Robespierre, as we suggest below.
12. Geggus, *Haitian Revolutionary Studies*, 91.
13. L. Sala-Molins, *Dark Side of the Light: Slavery and the French Enlightenment*, trans. J. Conteh-Morgan (Minneapolis: 2006).
14. Sala-Molins, *Dark Side of the Light*, 53.
15. This point is made at numerous points in James' *Black Jacobins*, e.g. at 120, and more recently by R. Blackburn, "The Force of Example," in D.P. Geggus (ed.), *The Impact of the Haitian Revolution in the Atlantic World* (Columbia SC: 2001), 15–20, at 16.

16. S. Buck-Morss, "Hegel and Haiti," *Critical Inquiry* 26 (2000), 821–65.
17. On its legacy in the United States, see Geggus, *The Impact of the Haitian Revolution*, also M. Jackson, *African Americans and the Haitian Revolution: Selected Essays and Historical Documents* (New York: 2010).
18. T. Matthewson, "Jefferson and the Nonrecognition of Haiti," *Proceedings of the American Philosophical Society* 140 (1996), 22–48.
19. Quoted by D.B. Davis, "Impact of the French and Haitian Revolutions," in Geggus, *The Impact of the Haitian Revolution*, 3–9, at 3.

Chapter 30

1. Quoted by D.L. Garraway in her essay in C. Bongie (trans.), *Baron de Vastey: The Colonial System Unveiled* (Liverpool: 2016), at 213. Hereafter this volume is referred to in the main text and notes as *System*.
2. M.L. Daut, "From Classical French Poet to Militant Haitian Statesman: The Early Years and Poetry of the Baron de Vastey," *Research in African Literatures* 43 (2012), 35–57.
3. Quoted by M.L. Daut, *Baron de Vastey and the Origins of Black Atlantic Humanism* (New York: 2017), 11.
4. The original French appeared as *Le système colonial dévoilé* (Cap-Henry: 1814). We cite it from Bougie's translation in *System*.
5. *Réflexions sur une lettre de Mazères* (Cap-Henry: 1816). We cite by page number from the English translation by "W.H.M.B." (London: 1817), hereafter *Reflections*.
6. For a further response see *Vastey's Notes à M. le Baron de V.P. Malouet…Collection de mémoires sur les colonies, et particulièrement sur Saint-Domingue* (Cap-Henry: 1814).
7. Mazères, *De l'utilité des colonies, des causes intérieures de la perte de Saint Domingue et des moyens d'en recouvrer la possession* (Paris: 1814).
8. M.L. Daut, "The 'Alpha and Omega' of Haitian Literature: Baron de Vastey and the U.S. Audience of Haitian Political Writing," *Comparative Literature* 64 (2012), 49–72, at 50 and 64.
9. D. Nicholls, *From Dessalines to Duvalier: Race, Colour, and National Independence in Haiti* (Cambridge: 1979), 43; and for the label "scribe" see Bongie's introduction in *System*.
10. For Clarkson's letters with Christophe himself see E.L. Griggs and C.H. Prator (eds), *Henry Christophe and Thomas Clarkson: A Correspondence* (New York: 1968).
11. In Daut, *Baron de Vastey*.
12. *Essai sur les causes de la revolution et des guerres civiles d'Hayti* (Sans-Souci: 1819), 154.
13. *Reflexions politiques sur quelques ouvrages et journaux français concernant Hayti* (Sans-Souci: 1817), 17.
14. See D. Nicholls, "Race, couleur et indépendance en Haiti (1804–1825)," *Revue d'histoire moderne et contemporaine* 25 (1978), 177–212, at 198.
15. This point is also made by Daut and Garraway in their essays in *System*, at 190, 190, 232.
16. V. Carretta (ed.), *Olaudah Equiano: The Interesting Narrative and Other Writings* (London: 2003), 113.
17. On the general issue see D. Jenson, *Beyond the Slave Narrative: Politics, Sex, and Manuscripts in the Haitian Revolution* (Liverpool: 2011).

18. See Garraway's discussion at *System*, 222.
19. A.N. Hunt, *Haiti's Influence on Antebellum America: Slumbering Volcano in the Caribbean* (Baton Rouge: 1988); P. Wirzbicki, "'The Light of Knowledge Follows the Impulse of Revolutions': Prince Saunders, Baron de Vastey and the Haitian Influence on Antebellum Black Ideas of Elevation and Education," *Slavery and Abolition* 36 (2015), 275–97.
20. Quoted by Nicholls, "Race, couleur et indépendance," 192.
21. From her essay in *System*, 217.

Chapter 31

1. As told in Allen's autobiography, R. Allen, *The Life Experience and Gospel Labors of the Rt. Rev. Richard Allen* (New York: 1960), and recounted in R.S. Newman, *Freedom's Prophet: Bishop Richard Allen, the AME Church, and the Black Founding Fathers* (New York: 2008), 64.
2. D. Walker, *Appeal to the Coloured Citizens of the World* (Boston: 1830), 67.
3. Letter to Angelina Grimke, cited in J.O. Horton and L.E. Horton, *In Hope of Liberty: Culture, Community and Protest among Northern Free Blacks, 1700–1860* (New York: 1997), 171.
4. Cited by G.B. Nash, *The Forgotten Fifth: African Americans in the Age of Revolution* (Cambridge MA: 2006), 128.
5. Nash, *The Forgotten Fifth*, 30.
6. Horten and Horten, *In Hope of Liberty*, 188.
7. J. Sidbury, *Becoming African in America: Race and Nation in the Early Black Atlantic* (Oxford: 2007), ch. 3.
8. Newman, *Freedom's Prophet*, 48.
9. Included in D. Porter, *Early Negro Writing, 1760–1837* (Boston: 1971), which is cited in the main text as *ENW*.
10. For Hall's "Charges" see Porter, *Early Negro Writing*, 63–78, for Marrant see J. Marrant, *A Sermon Preached on the 24th Day of June...*(Boston: 1789), cited by original pagination. The sermon is available online at the Evans Early American Imprint Collection at the University of Michigan; Hall has been credited with a significant role in its authorship.
11. On this see J. Brooks, "Prince Hall, Freemasonry, and Genealogy," *African American Review* 34 (2000), 197–216. See more generally W.A. Muraskin, *Middle Class Blacks in a White Society: Prince Hall Freemasonry in America* (Berkeley: 1975).
12. See further C.V.R. George, *Segregated Sabbaths: Richard Allen and the Emergence of Independent Black Churches, 1760–1840* (New York: 1973); G.B. Nash, *Forging Freedom: The Formation of Philadelphia's Black Community, 1720–1840* (Cambridge MA: 1988); J. Winch, *Philadelphia's Black Elite: Activism, Accommodation, and the Struggle for Autonomy, 1787–1848* (Philadelphia: 1988).
13. *A Narrative of the Proceedings of the Black People, During the Late Awful Calamity in Philadelphia*, also available at the Evans Early American Imprint Collection. Cited by original pagination.
14. "Some Letters of Richard Allen and Absalom Jones to Dorothy Ripley," *The Journal of Negro History* 1 (1916), 436–43.
15. In W. Andrews, *Three Black Women's Autobiographies of the Nineteenth Century: Sisters of the Spirit* (Bloomington: 1986), following quotes at 32 and 36.

16. R.S. Newman, "'We Participate in Common': Richard Allen's Eulogy of Washington and the Challenge of Interracial Appeals," *The William and Mary Quarterly* ser. 3, 64 (2007), 117–28.
17. Nash, *Forgotten Fifth*, 62.
18. Newman, *Freedom's Prophet*, 205.
19. Cited by Brooks, "Prince Hall," 199.
20. Nash, *Forgotten Fifth*, 134, and 146–7 for the following scene at Mother Bethel.
21. See further C. Dixon, *African America and Haiti: Emigration and Black Nationalism in the Nineteenth Century* (Westport: 2000).

Chapter 32

1. Printed in R. Newman et al. (eds), *Pamphlets of Protest: An Anthology of Early African-American Protest Literature, 1790–1860* (New York: 2001), 53–65, cited by page number.
2. R.S. Newman, *Freedom's Prophet: Bishop Richard Allen, the AME Church, and the Black Founding Fathers* (New York: 2008), 176.
3. On the ACS see E. Burin, *Slavery and the Peculiar Solution: A History of the American Colonization Society* (Gainesville: 2005).
4. On this text see R.R. Thomas, "Exodus and Colonization: Charting the Journey in the Journals of Daniel Coker, a Descendant of Africa," *African American Review* 41 (2007), 507–19, with the following quote cited at 516.
5. On Cuffe see especially L.D. Thomas, *Rise to Be a People: A Biography of Paul Cuffe* (Urbana: 1986), and further S.H. Harris, *Paul Cuffe: Black America and the African Return* (New York: 1972); S. Loomis, "The Evolution of Paul Cuffe's Black Nationalism," in D.W. Wills and R. Newman (eds), *Black Apostles at Home and Abroad: Afro-Americans and the Christian Mission from the Revolution to Reconstruction* (Boston: 1982), 191–202.
6. Thomas, *Rise to Be a People*, 32–3.
7. R.C. Wiggins (ed.), *Captain Paul Cuffe's Logs and Letters, 1808–1817* (Washington DC: 1996), cited in the main text in what follows.
8. Thomas, *Rise to Be a People*, 17.
9. Thomas, *Rise to Be a People*, 51, and 91 for the following quote from the *Weekly Messenger*.
10. Thomas, *Rise to Be a People*, 111.
11. For the following quotations see J. Winston, *The Struggles of John Brown Russwurm: The Life and Writings of a Pan-Africanist Pioneer, 1799–1851* (New York: 2010), at 122, 42.
12. For the sermon see D. Porter, *Early Negro Writing, 1760–1837* (Boston: 1971), 294–302.
13. Quoted at Winston, *The Struggles of John Brown Russwurm*, 31.
14. Winston, *The Struggles of John Brown Russwurm*, 51.
15. For the critical approach see A.J. Beyan, *African American Settlements in West Africa: John Brown Russwurm and the American Civilizing Efforts* (New York: 2005), with a positive assessment in Winston, *The Struggles of John Brown Russwurm*.
16. Quotes from Winston, *The Struggles of John Brown Russwurm*, 45, 66.
17. Quoted at Winston, *The Struggles of John Brown Russwurm*, 29.
18. Thomas, *Rise to Be a People*, 104.

Chapter 33

1. We cite by page from the third edition (Boston: 1830).
2. M.J. Dinius, "Look!! Look!!! at This!!!! The Radical Typography of David Walker's *Appeal*," *PMLA* 126 (2011), 55–72, at 59.
3. See Michael P. Johnson, "Denmark Vesey and His Co-Conspirators," *William and Mary Quarterly* 58 (2001), 915–76.
4. P.P. Hinks, *To Awaken My Afflicted Brethren: David Walker and the Problem of Antebellum Slave Resistance* (University Park: 1997), 30–8.
5. The speech was published in *Freedom's Journal* and is discussed at Hinks, *To Awaken My Afflicted Brethren*, 76.
6. See M.A. Richmond, *Bid the Vassal Soar: Interpretative Essays on the Life and Poetry of Phillis Wheatley (ca. 1753–1784) and George Moses Horton (ca. 1797–1883)* (Washington DC: 1974), and for poetry in this period also M. Sandler, *The Black Romantic Revolution: Abolitionist Poets at the End of Slavery* (London: 2020).
7. W.J. Moses, *Classical Black Nationalism: From the American Revolution to Marcus Garvey* (New York: 1996), 64.
8. See also P. Thompson, "David Walker's Nationalism—and Thomas Jefferson's," *Journal of the Early Republic* 37 (2017), 47–80.

Chapter 34

1. V. Cox (trans.), *Moderate Fonte: The Worth of Women* (Chicago: 1997), 238.
2. D. Walker, *Appeal to the Coloured Citizens of the World* (Boston: 1830), 59.
3. See the documents included in M. Richardson (ed.), *Maria W. Stewart: America's First Black Woman Political Writer* (Bloomington: 1988), which is cited by page number throughout this chapter.
4. Walker, *Appeal*, 39.
5. C. Henderson, "Sympathetic Violence: Maria Stewart's Antebellum Vision of African American Resistance," *MELUS* 38 (2013), 52–75, at 54.
6. See M. Richardson, "'What If I Am a Woman?' Maria W. Stewart's Defense of Black Women's Political Activism," in D.M. Jacobs (ed.), *Courage and Conscience: Black and White Abolitionists in Boston* (Bloomington: 1993).

Chapter 35

1. L.M. Alexander and W.C. Rucker (eds), *Encyclopedia of African American History* (Santa Barbara: 2010), 569.
2. This was in Douglass' speech "Our Destiny is Largely in Our Own Hands," delivered in April of 1883.
3. Bruce Dain, *A Hideous Monster of the Mind: American Race Theory in the Early Republic* (Cambridge MA: 2002), 170.
4. We cite from G.R. Price and J. B. Stewart (eds), *To Heal the Scourge of Prejudice: The Life and Writings of Hosea Easton* (Amherst: 1999).

5. See W.C. Nell, *The Colored Patriots of the American Revolution* (Boston: 1855), 33–4.
6. D. Walker, *Appeal to the Coloured Citizens of the World* (Boston: 1830), 22.
7. M. Richardson (ed.), *Maria W. Stewart: America's First Black Woman Political Writer* (Bloomington: 1988).
8. Price and Stewart (eds), *To Heal the Scourge of Prejudice*, 38–9.
9. Nell, *The Colored Patriots*, 334.

Chapter 36

1. M.S. Lee (ed.), *The Cambridge Companion to Frederick Douglass* (Cambridge: 2009), 19.
2. The three works are collected in H. Louis Gates Jr. (ed.), *Frederick Douglass: Autobiographies* (New York: 1994), cited by page number throughout this chapter. For his writings see also J.W. Blassingame, *The Frederick Douglass Papers* (New Haven: 1979–); P.S. Foner (ed.), *The Life and Writings of Frederick Douglass*, 5 vols (New York: 1950–75); P.S. Foner (ed.), *Frederick Douglass on Women's Rights* (Westport: 1976).
3. See e.g. W.E. Martin, *The Mind of Frederick Douglass* (Chapel Hill: 1985); R.S. Levine, *The Lives of Frederick Douglass* (Cambridge MA: 2016); D. Blight, *Frederick Douglass: Prophet of Freedom* (New York: 2018).
4. Quoted at N. Roberts, *A Political Companion to Frederick Douglass* (Lexington: 2018), 173.
5. The *Salem Register*, cited in Lee, *Cambridge Companion*, 48.
6. J. Sekora, "Black Message/White Envelope: Genre, Authenticity, and Authority in the Antebellum Slave Narrative," *Callaloo* 32 (1987), 482–515.
7. G. Ganter, "'He Made Us Laugh Some': Frederick Douglass's Humor," *African American Review* 37 (2003), 535–52.
8. Cited in Lee (ed.), *Cambridge Companion*, 49.
9. Anne Weston, cited by Blight, *Prophet of Freedom*, 127.
10. R. Gooding-Williams, *In the Shadow of Du Bois: Afro-Modern Political Thought in America* (Cambridge MA: 2009), 171.
11. A. Davis, "Unfinished Lecture on Liberation—II," in L. Harris (ed.), *Philosophy Born of Struggle* (Dubuque: 1983), 130–6; the reading is further developed by B. Boxill, "The Fight with Covey," in L.R. Gordon, *Existence in Black: An Anthology of Black Existential Philosophy* (London: 1997), 273–90; L.R. Gordon, "Fighting Master Covey: Douglass as an Existential Thinker," in B.M. Lawson and F.M. Kirkland (eds), *Frederick Douglass: A Critical Reader* (Oxford: 1999), 41–61; G. Yancy, "The Existential Dimensions of Frederick Douglass's Autobiographical Narrative: A Beauvoirian Examination," *Philosophy and Social Criticism* 28 (2002), 297–320. For a critical response, on which we draw in what follows, see F.M. Kirkland, "Is an Existential Reading of the Fight with Covey Sufficient to Explain Frederick Douglass's Critique of Slavery?," *Critical Philosophy of Race* 3 (2015), 124–51.
12. Quoted at Blight, *Freedom's Prophet*, 374. For Douglass and Ireland see F. Sweeney, *Frederick Douglass and the Atlantic World* (Liverpool: 2007).
13. These two quotes taken from Lee (ed.), *Cambridge Companion*, 13 and 15.
14. See P.A. Dorsey, "Becoming the Other: The Mimesis of Metaphor in Douglass's My Bondage and My Freedom," *Proceedings of the Modern Language Association* 111 (1996), 435–50, at 443.

15. Blight, *Freedom's Prophet*, 147. On this issue see also W.J. Moses, "Writing Freely? Frederick Douglass and the Constraints of Racialized Writing," in E. Sundquist (ed.), *Frederick Douglass: New Literary and Historical Essays* (New York: 1990), 66–83.
16. B. Quarles, "The Breach between Douglass and Garrison," *The Journal of Negro History* 23 (1938), 144–54.
17. Cited by W.E. Martin, *The Mind of Frederick Douglass* (Chapel Hill: 1985), 148.
18. Martin, *The Mind of Frederick Douglass*, 138.
19. Martin, *The Mind of Frederick Douglass*, 158.
20. On which see J.R. McKivigan, "Stalwart Douglass: *Life and Times* as Political Manifesto," *Journal of African American History* 99 (2014), 46–55, with the following quote at 49.

Chapter 37

1. D. Blight, *Frederick Douglass: Prophet of Freedom* (New York: 2018), xiv.
2. On his speeches in general see D.B. Chesebrough, *Frederick Douglass: Oratory from Slavery* (Westport: 1998); S. Meer, "Douglass as Orator and Editor," in M.S. Lee (ed.), *The Cambridge Companion to Frederick Douglass* (New York: 2009), 46–59. For the Independence Day theme see J.A. Colaiaco, *Frederick Douglass and the Fourth of July* (New York: 2006).
3. See *The Life and Writings of Frederick Douglass*, vol. 2, ed. P.S. Foner (New York: 1950), 181–204, cited by page number throughout the chapter.
4. See "The Constitution and Slavery" in *The Life and Writings of Frederick Douglass*, vol. 1, ed. P.S. Foner (New York: 1950), 366. On this topic see also D.E. Schrader, "Natural Law in the Constitutional Thought of Frederick Douglass," in B.M. Lawson and F.M. Kirkland (eds), *Frederick Douglass: A Critical Reader* (Malden: 1999), 85–99.
5. C. Mills, *Blackness Visible: Essays on Philosophy and Race* (Ithaca: 1998), 167.
6. See *The Life and Writings of Frederick Douglass*, vol. 2, 426–39, cited by page number.

Chapter 38

1. A. Crummell, *Africa and America: Addresses and Discourses* (Springfield: 1891), 292–3; cited by page in what follows as *AA*. For his biography see also E.O. Hutchinson, *Let Your Motto Be Resistance: The Life and Thought of Henry Highland Garnet* (Boston: 1972); J. Schor, *Henry Highland Garnet: A Voice of Black Radicalism in the Nineteenth Century* (Westport: 1977); M.B. Pasternak, *Rise Now and Fly to Arms: The Life of Henry Highland Garnet* (New York: 1995).
2. For an insightful comparison of Garnet's "Address" to two other previous addresses to the enslaved by white abolitionists—namely, Gerrit Smith and William Lloyd Garrison—see S. Harrold, *The Rise of Aggressive Abolitionism: Addresses to the Slaves* (Lexington: 2004).
3. See H.H. Garnet, "An Address to the Slaves of the United States of America (Rejected by the National Convention, 1843)," in *Walker's Appeal, with Brief Sketch of His Life. By Henry Highland Garnet. And Also Garnet's Address to the Slaves of the United States of America* (New York: 1848), cited by page number and abbreviated *AS*.
4. Benjamin Quarles reports this story of Brown's involvement while expressing doubt that it actually happened, but notes that it is reasonable to assume Brown's familiarity with the work. This, it seems to us, suffices to make it plausible that the volume counted

as a significant source of inspiration for Brown and his raid. See B. Quarles, *Allies for Freedom: Blacks and John Brown* (New York: 1974), 67.
5. J. Jasinski, "Constituting Antebellum African American Identity: Resistance, Violence, and Masculinity in Henry Highland Garnet's (1843) 'Address to the Slaves,'" *Quarterly Journal of Speech* 93 (2007), 27–57, at 43. For the issue see also S.H. Shiffrin, "The Rhetoric of Black Violence in the Antebellum Period: Henry Highland Garnet," *Journal of Black Studies* 2 (1971), 45–56.
6. *A Memorial Discourse by Henry Highland Garnet, Delivered in the Hall of the House of Representatives, Washington, D.C., on Sabbath, February 12, 1865, with an Introduction, by James McCune Smith, M.D.* (Philadelphia: 1865), 51. For a recent and useful, though inconclusive, discussion of this textual difference, see S. Robbins, "'As Being Bound with You': Revising the Contexts of Garnet's 'Address to the Slaves of the United States of America'," *The Papers of the Bibliographical Society of America* 116 (2022), 191–213.
7. *Minutes of the National Convention of Colored Citizens; Held at Buffalo; on the 15th, 16th, 17th, 18th, and 19th of August, 1843; for the Purpose of Considering Their Moral and Political Condition as American Citizens* (New York: 1843), 13.
8. P.S. Foner (ed.), *The Life and Writings of Frederick Douglass*, 5 vols (New York: 1950–75), vol. 5, 143.
9. *North Star*, September 7, 1849, p. 3.
10. *North Star*, January 26, 1849, p. 3.
11. A.M. Duane, *Educated for Freedom: The Incredible Story of Two Fugitive Schoolboys Who Grew Up to Change a Nation* (New York: 2020), 96.
12. Pasternak, *Rise Now and Fly to Arms*, 111.

Chapter 39

1. "*tl;dr*". Congratulations for getting this far in the book nonetheless!
2. For the first speech see R.S. Levine (ed.), *Martin Delany: A Documentary Reader* (Chapel Hill: 2003), 245–79; a report of some of his remarks from the Convention is given at 280–90. This collection is cited by page number in this chapter.
3. For a detailed account of his endeavor see C.E. Griffith, *The African Dream: Martin R. Delany and the Emergence of Pan-African Thought* (University Park: 1975), ch. 5.
4. V. Ullman, *Martin R. Delany: The Beginnings of Black Nationalism* (Boston: 1971).
5. See R.S. Levine, *Martin Delany, Frederick Douglass and the Politics of Representative Identity* (Chapel Hill: 1997).
6. G.D. Crane, "The Lexicon of Rights, Power, and Community in *Blake*: Martin R. Delany's Dissent from Dred Scott," *American Literature* 68 (1996), 527–53, at 541.
7. For the phrase and its meaning in Delany see M. C. Dawson, *Black Visions: The Roots of Contemporary African-American Political Ideologies* (Chicago: 2003), 6 and 97–8.
8. See T. Adeleke, *Without Regard to Race: The Other Martin Robinson Delany* (Jackson: 2004), 44–50.
9. Cited by T. Adeleke, "Martin R. Delany's Philosophy of Education: A Neglected Aspect of African American Liberation Thought," *Journal of Negro Education* 63 (1994), 221–36.

10. See further T. Ogunleye, "Dr. Martin R. Delany, 19th Century Africana Womanist: Reflections on His Avant-Garde Politics Concerning Gender, Colorism and Nation Building," *Journal of Black Studies* 28 (1998), 628–49.
11. M. Wallace, "'Are We Men?': Prince Hall, Martin Delany, and the Masculine Ideal in Black Freemasonry, 1775–1865," *American Literary History* 9 (1997), 396–24.
12. For details, see Wallace, "Are We Men?," 410.
13. Adeleke, *Without Regard to Race*, 37.
14. J. McGann (ed.), *Martin R. Delany: Blake, or the Huts of America* (Cambridge MA: 2017).
15. As argued by Crane, "The Lexicon of Rights," P. Gilroy, *The Black Atlantic: Modernity and Double Consciousness* (Cambridge MA: 1993), 27.
16. *Blake*, 23. On this passage see R.W. Hite, "'Stand Still and See the Salvation': The Rhetorical Design of Martin Delany's *Blake*," *Journal of Black Studies* (1974), 192–202, at 195.
17. On this passage see J. A. Clymer, "Martin Delany's *Blake* and the Transnational Politics of Property," *American Literary History* 15 (2003), 709–31, at 716.
18. On this theme see R. Skidmore Biggio, "The Specter of Conspiracy in Martin Delany's *Blake*," *African American Review* 42 (2008), 439–54.
19. *Blake*, 66.
20. Adeleke, *Without Regard to Race*, 104.
21. Adeleke, *Without Regard to Race*, 118.
22. T. Shelby, "Two Conceptions of Black Nationalism: Martin Delany on the Meaning of Black Political Solidarity," *Political Theory* 31 (2003), 664–92, revised version as ch. 1 of T. Shelby, *We Who Are Dark: The Philosophical Foundations of Black Solidarity* (Cambridge MA: 2005).
23. T.J. Curry, "Doing the Right Thing: An Essay Expressing Concerns toward Tommie Shelby's Reading of Martin R. Delany as a Pragmatic Nationalist in *We Who Are Dark*," *APA Newsletter on Philosophy and the Black Experience* 9 (2009), 13–22, at 15.
24. Kahn, "The Political Ideology," 431.

Chapter 40

1. We cite by page from *Narrative of Sojourner Truth, with Book of Life and A Memorial Chapter* (New York: 2005), which prints the 1878 text of the *Narrative*. For biographies of Truth drawing on this and other sources see C. Mabee with S. Mabee Newhouse, *Sojourner Truth: Slave, Prophet, Legend* (New York: 1993), N.I. Painter, *Sojourner Truth: A Life, a Symbol* (New York: 1996), L.G. Murphy, *Sojourner Truth: A Biography* (Santa Barbara: 2011).
2. E. Stetson and L. David, *Glorying in Tribulation: The Lifework of Sojourner Truth* (East Lansing: 1994), 134, for different versions of the story.
3. Quoted at Stetson and David, *Glorying in Tribulation*, 136.
4. M. Washington, "Going 'Where They Dare Not Follow': Race, Religion, and Sojourner Truth's Early Interracial Reform," *Journal of African American History* 98 (2013), 48–71, at 52.
5. Quoted at Stetson and David, *Glorying in Tribulation*, 3.
6. N.I. Painter, "Representing Truth: Sojourner Truth's Knowing and Becoming Known," *Journal of American History* 81 (1994), 461–92, at 473.
7. Quoted at Stetson and David, *Glorying in Tribulation*, 102.

8. Quoted at Stetson and David, *Glorying in Tribulation*, 74.
9. Painter, "Representing Truth," 149.
10. See the versions in Stetson and David, *Glorying in Tribulation*, 115–16, and for discussion of the differences in these reports also T.C. Zackodnik, "'I Don't Know How You Will Feel When I Get through': Racial Difference, Woman's Rights, and Sojourner Truth," *Feminist Studies* 30 (2004), 49–73, at 52–3.
11. Quoted at Stetson and David, *Glorying in Tribulation*, 180.
12. From "Eliza Harris" (1853), quoted in M.J. Boyd, *Discarded Legacy: Politics and Poetics in the Life of Frances E.W. Harper 1825–1911* (Detroit: 1994), 60. For her works see also M. Graham (ed.), *Complete Poems of Frances E.W. Harper* (New York: 1988); F. Smith Foster (ed.), *A Brighter Coming Day: A Frances Ellen Watkins Harper Reader* (New York: 1990).
13. M. Stancliffe, *Frances Ellen Watkins Harper: African American Reform Rhetoric and the Rise of a Modern Nation State* (New York: 2011), 54.
14. Quoted at Boyd, *Discarded Legacy*, 128.
15. Quoted at Stancliffe, *Frances Ellen Watkins Harper*, 72.
16. Quoted at Boyd, *Discarded Legacy*, 124.
17. Quoted at Stancliffe, *Frances Ellen Watkins Harper*, 60.
18. Quoted at Boyd, *Discarded Legacy*, 46.
19. Quoted at Boyd, *Discarded Legacy*, 42.
20. On thematic connections between *Iola Leroy* and Harper's lectures, see H.V. Carby, *Reconstructing Womanhood: The Emergence of the Afro-American Woman Novelist* (Oxford: 1987), 86.
21. As observed by Boyd, *Discarded Legacy*, 152–3.
22. The following quotes are taken from Boyd, *Discarded Legacy*, 39 and 200, and Stancliffe, *Frances Ellen Watkins Harper*, 133.
23. Cited at Boyd, *Discarded Legacy*, 45.

Chapter 41

1. See further R.W. Winks, *The Blacks in Canada: A History*, 2nd ed. (Montreal: 1997).
2. D. Porter, *Early Negro Writing, 1760–1837* (Baltimore: 1995), 298.
3. J. Rhodes, *Mary Ann Shadd Cary: The Black Press and Protest in the Nineteenth Century* (Bloomington: 1998), 99.
4. We cite by page from the original publication (Detroit: 1852). For a modern edition see P. Antwi (ed.), *Mary Ann Shadd: A Plea for Emigration; or Notes of Canada West* (Peterborough: 2016).
5. In case you are confused because we just said that Ontario used to be called Upper Canada: the colonies of Upper Canada and Lower Canada, so-called in relation to their placement along the St. Lawrence River, were joined by an Act of Union in 1841 to form the Province of Canada. In 1867, they would be broken apart and called Ontario and Quebec, two parts of the newly formed Dominion of Canada, along with Nova Scotia and New Brunswick. This confederation is what Canadians annually celebrate as the birth of their country.
6. Rhodes, *Mary Ann Shadd Cary*, 43–4.
7. Cited by page number from S.R. Ward, *Autobiography of a Fugitive Negro* (London: 1855).

8. E. Tamarkin, *Anglophilia: Deference, Devotion, and Antebellum America* (Chicago: 2007), 201. See also her "Black Anglophilia; or, The Sociability of Antislavery," *American Literary History* 14 (2002), 444–78.
9. Cited by page from R.S. Levine (ed.), *Martin Delany: A Documentary Reader* (Chapel Hill: 2003).
10. For an interview with Adrienne Shadd and another Shadd descendant, Adrienne's daughter Marisha Mabusela, see "Mary Ann Shadd: Journalism, Activism, and the Power of Words," available online in *The Canadian Encyclopedia*.
11. For more on black Canadian literature see G.E. Clarke, *Odysseys Home: Mapping African-Canadian Literature* (Toronto: 2002), W. Siemerling, *The Black Atlantic Reconsidered: Black Canadian Writing, Cultural History, and the Presence of the Past* (Montreal: 2015).

Chapter 42

1. W.J. Moses, *Creative Conflict in African American Thought* (Cambridge: 2004), 16.
2. For his life see G.U. Rigsby, *Alexander Crummell: Pioneer in Nineteenth-Century Pan-African Thought* (New York: 1987); W.J. Moses, *Alexander Crummell: A Study of Civilization and Discontent* (Cary: 1989); J.R. Oldfield, *Alexander Crummell (1819–1898) and the Creation of an African-American Church in Liberia* (Lampeter: 1990).
3. As Crummell tells us himself; see W.J. Moses (ed.), *Alexander Crummell: Destiny and Race. Selected Writings, 1840–1898* (Amherst: 1992), 61. Cited in this chapter as *Destiny*; the tribute by Du Bois mentioned just below is at 21–8.
4. For the general context of the work of Crummell and other missionaries covered in later chapters, see W. Williams, *Black Americans and the Evangelization of Africa, 1877–1900* (Madison: 1981); S.M. Jacobs (ed.), *Black Americans and the Missionary Movement in Africa* (Westport: 1982).
5. This is how the remark is read by R. Gooding-Williams, *In the Shadow of Du Bois: Afro-Modern Political Thought in America* (Cambridge: 2009), 110. We explain this reading in what follows and take our chapter title from Gooding-Williams' mention of *Pilgrim's Progress* as a reference point for Du Bois.
6. Moses, *Alexander Crummell: A Study*, 245, 274.
7. On Green as a formative influence see P. Wirzbicki, "Alexander Crummell on Coleridge and the Politics of Abolitionist Selfhood," *Modern Intellectual History* (2019), 1–26, at 7.
8. Moses, *Creative Conflict*, 95.
9. On this see Moses, *Alexander Crummell: A Study*, 46 and 215; Wirzbicki, "Alexander Crummell on Coleridge," 3.
10. On his theories of language see S.L. Thompson, "The Grammar of Civilization: Crummell and Douglass on Doing Things with Words," in B. Lawson and F. Kirkland (eds), *Frederick Douglass: A Critical Reader* (Malden: 1999), 173–203; S.L. Thompson, "Crummell on the Metalogic of Non-Standard languages," *Philosophia Africana* 10 (2007), 77–106.
11. A. Crummell, *The Race-Problem in America* (Washington DC: 1889), cited in this chapter as *Problem*.
12. A. Crummell, *Africa and America: Addresses and Discourses* (Springfield: 1891), 40.
13. Moses, *Alexander Crummell: A Study*, 227.

Chapter 43

1. J.A.B. Horton, *Physical and Medical Climate and Meteorology of the West Coast of Africa* (London: 1867), 287.
2. See the alarming document of his medical history quoted at J. Howell, *Exploring Victorian Travel Literature* (Edinburgh: 2014), 100.
3. C. Fyfe, *Africanus Horton, 1835–1883, West African Scientist and Patriot* (New York: 1972), 86.
4. Cited by page number from J.A.B. Horton, *West African Countries and Peoples, British and Native* (London: 1868).
5. R.F. Burton, *Wanderings in West Africa from Liverpool to Fernando Po* (London: 1863).
6. He even mentions the founding of the Sokoto Caliphate by 'Uthmān Dan Fodio; see the footnote at Horton, *West African Countries*, 189.
7. Fyfe, *Africanus Horton*, 45, and 81 for the following quote.
8. Fyfe, *Africanus Horton*, 101 summarizes the proposals in Horton's 1870 *Letters on the Political Condition of the Gold Coast*.
9. See A.J. Vanderploeg, "Africanus Horton and the Idea of a University of Western Africa," *Journal of African Studies* 5.2 (1978), 188–9; A.O. Nwauwa, "Far Ahead of his Time: James Africanus Horton's Initiatives for a West African University and His Frustrations, 1862–1871," *Cahiers d'études africaines* 39 (1999), 107–21.
10. Fyfe, *Africanus Horton*, 135.
11. O. Taiwo, *How Colonialism Preempted Modernity in Africa* (Bloomington: 2010), 119.
12. N. wa Thiong'o, "Europhonism, Universities, and the Magic Fountain: The Future of African Literature and Scholarship," *Research in African Literatures* 31 (2000), 1–11, at 9.

Chapter 44

1. E.W. Blyden, *Christianity, Islam and the Negro Race*, 2nd ed. (Baltimore: 1994 [1888]), cited as *CINR*.
2. E.W. Blyden, *Liberia's Offering* (New York: 1862), E.W. Blyden, *African Life and Customs* (Baltimore: 1994), cited as *LO* and *ALC*. For collections of his writing see also H.R. Lynch (ed.), *Black Spokesman: Selected Published Writings of Edward Wilmot Blyden* (London: 1971), hereafter cited as *BS*; H.R. Lynch (ed.), *Selected Letters of Edward Wilmot Blyden* (Millwood: 1978).
3. For his changing views see C. Jeffers, "The Pitfalls of Placing the African Personality on the World Stage: Edward Blyden's Cultural Nationalism and Cosmopolitanism," *APA Newsletter on Philosophy and the Black Experience* 9 (2010), 1–5; H.N.K. Odamtten, *Edward W. Blyden's Intellectual Transformations: Afropublicanism, Pan-Africanism, Islam, and the Indigenous West African Church* (East Lansing: 2019). For a general overview of Blyden's life see H.R. Lynch, *Edward Wilmot Blyden, Pan-Negro Patriot 1832–1912* (London: 1967).
4. For Blyden's nationalism see T. Falola, *Nationalism and African Intellectuals* (Rochester: 2001), chs 1–2; T. Tibebu, *Edward Wilmot Blyden and the Racial Nationalist Imagination* (Rochester: 2012).
5. On his educational program see R. July, *The Origins of Modern African Thought: Its Development in West Africa During the Nineteenth and Twentieth Centuries* (New York: 1967), 228. Ch. 11 of this book provides a helpful overview of Blyden's ambitions in Liberia.

6. Blyden, "The African Problem," *North American Review* 161 (1895), 328.
7. Lynch, *Edward Wilmot Blyden*, 111.

Chapter 45

1. Cited from S.D. Carle, *Defining the Struggle: National Organizing for Racial Justice, 1880–1915* (Oxford: 2013), 45–6.
2. Cited from E.L. Thornbrough, *T. Thomas Fortune: Militant Journalist* (Chicago: 1972), 56, 368.
3. In this chapter *TTF* will be used as an abbreviation for S.L. Alexander (ed.), *T. Thomas Fortune the Afro-American Agitator* (Gainesville: 2008).
4. J.R. McKivigan, "Stalwart Douglass: *Life and Times* as Political Manifesto," *Journal of African American History* 99 (2014), 46–55, at 46.
5. Thornbrough, *T. Thomas Fortune*, 103.
6. In this chapter *BW* will be used as an abbreviation for T.T. Fortune, *Black and White: Land, Labor, and Politics in the South* (New York: 1884).
7. On the history of the organization see B.R. Justesen, *Broken Brotherhood: The Rise and Fall of the National Afro-American Council* (Carbondale: 2008).
8. Thornbrough, *T. Thomas Fortune*, 133.
9. Carle, *Defining the Struggle*, 47.
10. Thornbrough, *T. Thomas Fortune*, 309.
11. Thornbrough, *T. Thomas Fortune*, 48–9.
12. For one such unfortunate episode in 1901 see Justesen, *Broken Brotherhood*, 100. A year earlier he had caused outrage by declaring, "we have cringed and crawled long enough. I don't want any more 'good niggers.' I want 'bad niggers.' It is the 'bad nigger' with a Winchester that can defend his home and children and wife."
13. S.D. Carle, "Debunking the Myth of Civil Rights Liberalism: Visions of Racial Justice in the Thought of T. Thomas Fortune, 1880–1890," *Fordham Law Review* 77 (2009), 1479–533.
14. See n. 6 above.
15. On him see S.R. Fox, *The Guardian of Boston: William Monroe Trotter* (New York: 1970); K.K. Greenidge, *Black Radical: The Life and Times of William Monroe Trotter* (New York: 2020).
16. Thornbrough, *T. Thomas Fortune*, 228. See also Justesen, *Broken Brotherhood*, 112.
17. Justesen, *Broken Brotherhood*, 73.
18. T.J. Curry, "The Fortune of Wells: Ida B. Wells-Barnett's Use of T. Thomas Fortune's Philosophy of Social Agitation as a Prolegomenon to Militant Civil Rights Activism," *Transactions of the Charles S. Peirce Society* 48 (2012), 456–82, at 459.

Chapter 46

1. She tells the story in C. Fluehr-Lobban, "Anténor Firmin: Haitian Pioneer of Anthropology," *American Anthropologist* 102 (2000), 449–66. For the English translation see S. Charles (trans.), *Anténor Firmin: The Equality of the Human Races* (New York: 2000); we cite by page number from this version, with occasional modification. The original French version is A. Firmin, *De l'égalité des races humaines* (Paris: 1885).

2. For more details on racist anthropological views in France at the time, see D.W. Leonard, "Writing Against the Grain: Anténor Firmin and the Refutation of Nineteenth-Century European Race Science," in K. Radcliffe (ed.), *Anywhere But Here: Black Intellectuals in the Atlantic World and Beyond* (Jackson: 2014), 27–46; R. Bernasconi, "A Haitian in Paris: Anténor Firmin as a Philosopher against Racism," *Patterns of Prejudice* 42 (2008), 365–83.
3. Quoted by Leonard, "Writing Against the Grain," 32, and 35 for the following quote.
4. Bernasconi, "A Haitian in Paris," 383.
5. Y. Chemla, "Louis-Joseph Janvier, écrivain national," *Francofonia* 49 (2005), 7–36.
6. For Haiti during Firmin's lifetime see D. Nicholls, *Haiti in Caribbean Context: Ethnicity, Economy and Revolt* (New York: 1985); B. Plummer, *Haiti and the Great Powers, 1902–1915* (Baton Rouge: 1988).
7. G. Magloire-Danton, "Anténor Firmin and Jean Price-Mars: Revolution, Memory, Humanism," *Small Axe* 18 (2005), 150–70, at 153.
8. Leonard, "Writing Against the Grain," 29.
9. Bernasconi, "A Haitian in Paris," 367.
10. For Janvier's own use of Haiti to prove that social inequality does not imply biological inequality, see Chemla, "Louis-Joseph Janvier," 20.
11. M.J. Dash, "Nineteenth-Century Haiti and the Archipelago of the Americas: Antenor Firmin's Letters from St. Thomas," *Research in African Literatures* 35 (2004), 44–53, at 48. Lochard is also mentioned in *Equality* at 212.
12. Bernasconi, "A Haitian in Paris," 375.
13. For Delorme and other thinkers of the period in Haiti see P. Bellegarde-Smith, "Haitian Social Thought in the Nineteenth Century: Class Formation and Westernization," *Caribbean Studies* 20 (1980), 5–33.
14. Leonard, "Writing Against the Grain," 38.
15. A. Firmin, *Lettres de Saint-Thomas: études sociologiques, historiques et littéraires* (Port-au-Prince: 1910).
16. Cited from Dash, "Nineteenth-Century Haiti," 52.

Chapter 47

1. F.A. Durham, *The Lone-Star of Liberia; Being the Outcome of Reflections on Our Own People* (London: 1892), cited as *LSL*.
2. J.J. Thomas, *The Theory and Practice of Creole Grammar* (Port-of-Spain: 1869), cited as *TPCG*. On Thomas see also F.L. Smith, *Creole Recitations: John Jacob Thomas and Colonial Formation in the Late Nineteenth-Century Caribbean* (Charlottesville: 2002), and on the culture of these islands in the period, S.R. Cudjoe, *Beyond Boundaries: The Intellectual Tradition of Trinidad and Tobago in the Nineteenth Century* (Wellesley: 2003).
3. J.A. Froude, *The English in the West Indies or The Bow of Ulysses* (London: 1888), 123–4.
4. Original publication in J.J. Thomas, *Froudacity: West Indian Fables by James Anthony Froude Explained by J.J. Thomas* (London: 1889). Modern edition in J.J. Thomas, *Froudacity* (London: 1969), which we abbreviate as *Fr*.
5. Froude, *The English in the West Indies*, 121–2.

6. W. Laird-Clowes, *Black America: A Study of the Ex-Slave and His Late Master* (London: 1891), 155, and 158 for the following quote.
7. M. Sherwood, *Origins of Pan-Africanism: Henry Sylvester Williams, Africa, and the African Diaspora* (London: 2010), 278.
8. Personal correspondence.

Chapter 48

1. For the historical context see H.S. Klein and F. Vidal Luna, *Slavery in Brazil* (Cambridge: 2010).
2. Quoted by K.D. Butler, *Freedoms Given, Freedoms Won: Afro Brazilians in Post-Abolition São Paolo and Salvador* (New Brunswick: 1998), 34.
3. A.J.R. Russell-Wood, *The Black Man in Slavery and Freedom in Colonial Brazil* (New York: 1982), 25.
4. Klein and Vidal Luna, *Slavery in Brazil*, 252.
5. See R. Conrad, *The Destruction of Brazilian Slavery, 1850–1888* (Berkeley: 1972); R.B. Toplin, *The Abolition of Slavery in Brazil* (New York: 1975); R.J. Scott et al. (eds), *The Abolition of Slavery and the Aftermath of Emancipation* (Durham: 1988); C. Azevedo, *Abolitionism in the United States and Brazil* (New York: 1995); J.D. Needell, "Brazilian Abolitionism, Its Historiography, and the Uses of Political History," *Journal of Latin American Studies* 42 (2010), 231–61.
6. J.H. Kennedy, "Luiz Gama: Pioneer of Abolition in Brazil," *The Journal of Negro History* 59 (1974), 255–67, at 255.
7. Kennedy, "Luiz Gama," 255.
8. Kennedy, "Luiz Gama," 263.
9. Both this poem (*No Álbum*) and *Quem sou eu?* can be found in L. Gama, *Primeiras trovas burlescas de Getulino* (São Paulo: 1904). For another collection of his works see L. Fonseca Ferreira (ed.), *Com a palavra, Luiz Gama: poemas, artigos, cartas, máximas* (São Paulo: 2011).
10. C. Braga-Pinto, "The Honor of the Abolitionist and the Shamefulness of Slavery: Raul Pompeia, Luiz Gama, and Joaquim Nabuco," *Luso-Brazilian Review* 51 (2014), 170–99.
11. Cited by page number from R. Conrad (trans.), *Joaquim Nabuco: Abolitionism, the Brazilian Antislavery Struggle* (Urbana: 2013).
12. A.A. Isfahani-Hammond, "Joaquim Nabuco's 'Black Mandate'," *Hispania* 85 (2002), 466–75, at 466.
13. J.D. Needell, "A Liberal Embraces Monarchy: Joaquim Nabuco and Conservative Historiography," *The Americas* 48 (1991), 159–79.
14. Kennedy, "Luiz Gama," 257.
15. S. Putnam (trans.), *The Masters and the Slaves (Casa-Grande & Senzala)* (Berkeley: 1986), with the following quote at page xii. For a summary of Freyre's view and influence see also Russell-Wood, *The Black Man in Slavery*, 14–17.
16. E. de Assis Duarte, "Machado de Assis's African Descent," *Research in African Literatures* 38 (2007), 134–51, at 134.
17. Butler, *Freedoms Given*, 51.
18. On this see de Assis Duarte, "Machado de Assis's African Descent," from which the following examples are also taken.

19. R. Schwarz, *A Master on the Periphery of Capitalism: Machado de Assis*, trans. J. Gledson (Durham: 2001). For an English translation of the novel see G. Rabassa (trans.), *Machado de Assis: The Posthumous Memoirs of Brás Cubas* (Oxford: 1997), which we cite by chapter number.
20. Schwarz, *A Master on the Periphery*, 21.
21. Schwarz, *A Master on the Periphery*, 45.

Chapter 49

1. B.H. Edwards, *The Practice of Diaspora: Literature, Translation, and the Rise of Black Internationalism* (Cambridge MA: 2003), 127–8.
2. We cite from A.J. Cooper, *A Voice from the South* (Xenia: 1892), abbreviated as *VS*.
3. On her thought and career see K. Baker-Fletcher, *A Singing Something: Womanist Reflections on Anna Julia Cooper* (New York: 1994); V. May, *Anna Julia Cooper, Visionary Black Feminist: A Critical Introduction* (New York: 2007).
4. We cite from A. Crummell, *Africa and America: Addresses and Discourses* (Springfield: 1891), abbreviated as *AA*.
5. M.R. Delany, *The Condition, Elevation, Emigration and Destiny of the Colored People of the United States* (Philadelphia: 1852), 199; K.S. Belle, "Anna Julia Cooper," *Stanford Encyclopedia of Philosophy* (online, Summer 2015 edition).
6. F.A. Rollin, *The Life and Public Services of Martin R. Delany* (Boston: 1868), 19.
7. W.E.B. Du Bois, *Darkwater* (New York: 1920), 173.
8. V.D. James, "Reading Anna J. Cooper with William James: Black Feminist Visionary Pragmatism, Philosophy's Culture of Justification, and Belief," *The Pluralist* 8 (2013), 32–45.

Chapter 50

1. J. Swaine et al., "Young black men killed by US police at highest rate in year of 1,134 deaths," published Dec. 31, 2015.
2. A.M. Duster (ed.), *Crusade for Justice: The Autobiography of Ida B. Wells* (Chicago: 1970), cited here as *Autobiography*. For other biographies see M. Thompson, *Ida B. Wells-Barnett: An Exploratory Study of an American Black Woman, 1893–1930* (Brooklyn: 1990); L.O. McMurry, *Keep the Waters Troubled: The Life of Ida B. Wells* (Oxford: 1998); P.J. Giddings, *Ida, a Sword Among Lions: Ida B. Wells and the Campaign against Lynching* (New York: 2008); M. Bay, *To Tell the Truth Freely: The Life of Ida B. Wells* (New York: 2009).
3. On her appeal to British public sentiment see S.L. Silkey, *Black Woman Reformer: Ida B. Wells, Lynching, and Transatlantic Activism* (Athens GA: 2015).
4. Cited by McMurry, *Keep the Waters Troubled*, 195.
5. I.B. Wells, *Southern Horrors: Lynch Law in All Its Phases* (New York: 1892); I.B. Wells, *A Red Record: Tabulated Statistics and Alleged Causes of Lynchings in the United States* (Chicago: 1894); I.B. Wells-Barnett, *Mob Rule in New Orleans* (Chicago: 1900).
6. For the importance of Douglass' support see P.A. Schechter, *Ida B. Wells-Barnett and American Reform 1880–1930* (Chapel Hill: 2001), 97.
7. D.C. Hine, W.C. Hine, and S. Harrold, *The African-American Odyssey* (Upper Saddle River: 2003), 395.

8. Quoted at Silkey, *Black Woman Reformer*, 128.
9. Schechter, *Ida B. Wells-Barnett and American Reform*, 127; Silkey, *Black Woman Reformer*, 128.
10. Quoted at McMurry, *Keep the Waters Troubled*, 220.
11. She quotes this at *Autobiography*, 65–6, and *Southern Horrors*, ch. 1, which also includes the following response.
12. A.D. Sims, *Ethical Complications of Lynching: Ida B. Wells's Interrogation of American Terror* (New York: 2010), 59.
13. Sims, *Ethical Complications of Lynching*, 43.
14. Reproduced by Schechter, *Ida B. Wells-Barnett and American Reform*, 83.
15. From *Lynch Law in Georgia*, cited by Schechter, *Ida B. Wells-Barnett and American Reform*, 116.
16. Quoted from Sims, *Ethical Complications of Lynching*, 72.
17. McMurry, *Keep the Waters Troubled*, 307.
18. For more on their relationship see J. Curry, "The Fortune of Wells: Ida B. Wells-Barnett's Use of T. Thomas Fortune's Philosophy of Social Agitation as a Prolegomenon to Militant Civil Rights Activism," *Transactions of the Charles S. Pierce Society* 48 (2012), 456–82.
19. Cited from the *Nashville Citizen* by McMurry, *Keep the Waters Troubled*, 233.

Chapter 51

1. For the examples and the quote see G. Packer, "Turned Around: Why Do Leftists Move to the Right?" *New Yorker*, February 15, 2016 issue.
2. For a biography focusing especially on his church career, see S.W. Angell, *Bishop Henry McNeal Turner and African-American Religion in the South* (Knoxville: 1992). A more recent book on him is A.E. Johnson, *No Future in This Country: The Prophetic Pessimism of Bishop Henry McNeal Turner* (Jackson: 2020). His writings are collected in E. Redkey, *Respect Black: The Writings and Speeches of Henry McNeal Turner* (New York: 1971).
3. M.M. Ponton, *Life and Times of Henry M. Turner* (Atlanta: 1917), 146.
4. For the broader context see A.N. Owens, *Formation of the African Methodist Episcopal Church in the Nineteenth Century: Rhetoric of Identification* (New York: 2014); P.G. Foreman et al. (ed.), *The Colored Conventions Movement: Black Organizing in the Nineteenth Century* (Chapel Hill: 2021).
5. Cited at A.E. Johnson, "'I Have Had to Pass through Blood and Fire': Henry McNeal Turner and the Rhetorical Legacy of Reconstruction," in B. Greene Bond and S.E. O'Donovan (eds), *Remembering the Memphis Massacre: An American Story* (Athens GA: 2020), 178–89, at 182.
6. As argued by R.W. Leeman, "Speaking as Jeremiah: Henry McNeal Turner's 'I Claim the Rights of a Man,'" *Howard Journal of Communications* 17 (2006), 223–43, at 227.
7. T. Adeleke, *UnAfrican Americans: Nineteenth-Century Black Nationalists and the Civilizing Mission* (Lexington: 1998), 94.
8. Cited by Johnson, "I Have Had to Pass through Blood and Fire," 187.
9. Cited by Adeleke, *UnAfrican Americans*, 102.
10. For discussion see S.W. Angell, "Henry McNeal Turner: Conservative? Radical? Or Independent?" in P. Eisenstadt (ed.), *Black Conservatism: Essays in Intellectual and Political History* (New York: 1999), 25–50, at 37.
11. Cited by Angell, *Bishop Henry McNeal Turner*, 265.

12. Adeleke, *UnAfrican Americans*, ch. 5; a similar conclusion is reached by A.B. Pinn, "'Double Consciousness' in Nineteenth-Century Black Nationalism: Reflections on the Teachings of Bishop Henry McNeal Turner," *Journal of Religious Thought* 52 (1995), 15–26, at 22.
13. This and the next quote are taken from Pinn, "Double Consciousness," 20.
14. Cited at Angell, *Bishop Henry McNeal Turner*, 46.
15. Pinn, "Double Consciousness," 15.
16. Cited by A.E. Johnson, "Is the Negro Like Other People? Race, Religion and the Didactic Oratory of Henry McNeal Turner," in J. Adekunle (ed.), *Converging Identities: Blackness in the Modern African Diaspora* (Durham: 2013), 207–25, at 217.
17. Cited by A.E. Johnson, "God is a Negro: The (Rhetorical) Black Theology of Bishop Henry McNeal," *Black Theology* 13 (2015), 29–40, at 36.
18. Cited by Angell, *Bishop Henry McNeal Turner*, 261; the following quotes are taken from 260, 244, and 167.
19. C.L. Bynum, *A. Philip Randolph and the Struggle for Civil Rights* (Baltimore: 2010), 30.

Chapter 52

1. For the story of how the "immortal HeLa cell" line was cultured from the cancer of a black woman named Henrietta Lacks, a fact then withheld from her family, see R. Skloot, *The Immortal Life of Henrietta Lacks* (New York: 2010).
2. B.T. Washington, *Character Building: Being Addresses Delivered on Sunday Evenings to the Students of Tuskegee Institute* (New York: 1902), 120–1.
3. B.T. Washington, *The Future of the American Negro* (Boston: 1900), cited by chapter number with the abbreviation *Fut.*
4. L.R. Harlan, "A Black Leader in the Age of Jim Crow," in D. Cunningen, R.M. Dennis, and M.G. Glascoe (eds), *The Racial Politics of Booker T. Washington* (Amsterdam: 2006), 23–32, at 25.
5. M. Bauerlein, "Booker T. Washington and W.E.B. Du Bois: The Origins of a Bitter Intellectual Battle," *Journal of Blacks in Higher Education* 46 (2004–5), 106–14, at 113.
6. M.R. West, *The Education of Booker T. Washington: American Democracy and the Idea of Race Relations* (New York: 2006), 64, for both quotations.
7. D. Walden, "The Contemporary Opposition to the Political and Educational Ideas of Booker T. Washington," *Journal of Negro History* 45 (1960), 103–15, at 108.
8. West, *The Education*, 57.
9. W.F. Brundage (ed.), *Up from Slavery by Booker T. Washington with Related Documents* (Boston: 2003), with the speech in ch. 14. This work is also cited by chapter in what follows, and abbreviated simply as *Up*.
10. Walden, "The Contemporary Opposition," 109, 112.
11. D. Sehat, "The Civilizing Mission of Booker T. Washington," *Journal of Southern History* 73 (2007), 323–62, at 355.
12. Bauerlein, "Booker T. Washington and W.E.B. Du Bois," 107.
13. P.G. Dagbovie, "Exploring a Century of Historical Scholarship on Booker T. Washington," *Journal of African American History* 92 (2007), 239–64, at 239.
14. L.R. Harlan, *Booker T. Washington in Perspective*, ed. R. Smock (Jackson: 2006), 177.

15. See Dagbovie, "Exploring a Century."
16. Quoted in R.M. Dennis, "The Situational Politics of Booker T. Washington," in Cunningen et al. (eds), *The Racial Politics*, 3–21, at 14.
17. W.A. Drake, "Booker T. Washington: Racial Pragmatism Revisited," in Cunningen et al. (eds), *The Racial Politics*, 33–59, at 50.
18. Cited at West, *The Education*, 95.
19. D.H. Jackson Jr., *Booker T. Washington and the Struggle Against White Supremacy: The Southern Educational Tours 1908–1912* (New York: 2008), 32, 49.
20. Dennis, "The Situational Politics," 10.
21. Washington, *Character Building*, cited by page in what follows as *Char*.
22. West, *The Education*, 91.
23. Dennis, "The Situational Politics," 9.
24. On this see W.M. Marable, "Booker T. Washington and African Nationalism," *Phylon* 35 (1974), 398–406; V.J. Williams Jr., "The Myths of Africa in the Writings of Booker L Washington," in Williams, *Rethinking Race: Franz Boas and His Contemporaries* (Lexington: 1996), 54–72.
25. Cited from D.L. Lewis, *W.E.B. Du Bois: 1868–1919* (New York: 1993), 169.
26. Harlan, *Booker T. Washington in Perspective*, 84.

Chapter 53

1. Cited from H. Aptheker (ed.), *W.E.B. Du Bois: Against Racism: Unpublished Essays, Papers, Addresses, 1887–1961* (Amherst: 1985), abbreviated as *AR*.
2. We will draw here on David Levering Lewis' classic two-volume biography of Du Bois. See D.L. Lewis, *W.E.B. Du Bois: Biography of a Race, 1868–1919* (New York: 1993) and *W.E.B Du Bois: The Fight for Equality and the American Century* (New York: 2000).
3. W.E.B. Du Bois, *Dusk of Dawn: An Essay Toward an Autobiography of a Race Concept* (New York: 2007), 20.
4. Cited from W.E.B. Du Bois, *The Autobiography of W.E.B. Du Bois: A Soliloquy on Viewing My Life from the Last Decade of Its First Century* (New York: 1968), abbreviated as *Auto*.
5. W.E.B. Du Bois, *The Suppression of the African Slave-Trade to the United States of America, 1638–1870* (New York: 1896).
6. W.E.B. Du Bois, *The Philadelphia Negro: A Social Study* (Philadelphia: 1899).
7. W.E.B. Du Bois, *The Souls of Black Folk: Essays and Sketches* (Chicago: 1903), 103.
8. W.E.B. Du Bois, "The Conservation of Races," *The American Negro Academy Occasional Papers*, no. 2 (Washington DC: 1897), abbreviated as *Cons*.
9. W.E.B. Du Bois, *The Negroes of Farmville, Virginia: A Social Study* (Washington DC: 1898), 24.
10. W.E.B. Du Bois, "The Study of the Negro Problems," *Annals of the American Academy of Political and Social Science* 11 (1898), 1–23, abbreviated as *TSNP*.
11. L.K. Bright, "Du Bois' Democratic Defence of the Value Free Ideal," *Synthese* 195 (2018), 2227–45.
12. A. Appiah, "The Uncompleted Argument: Du Bois and the Illusion of Race," *Critical Inquiry* 12 (1985), 21–37. See also C. Jeffers, "The Cultural Theory of Race: Yet Another Look at Du Bois's 'The Conservation of Races'," *Ethics* 123 (2013), 403–26.

13. A.J. Cooper, *A Voice From the South* (Xenia: 1892), 152. On this theme in her work see C. Jeffers, "Anna Julia Cooper and the Black Gift Thesis," *History of Philosophy Quarterly* 33 (2016), 79–97.
14. On this concept see J.P. Pittman, "Double Consciousness," *The Stanford Encyclopedia of Philosophy* (online, Spring 2023 edition).
15. R. Gooding-Williams, *In the Shadow of Du Bois: Afro-Modern Political Thought in America* (Cambridge MA: 2009), 66–7.
16. W.E.B. Du Bois, "Strivings of the Negro People," *Atlantic Monthly* 80 (August 1897), 194–8, abbreviated as *SNP*.

FURTHER READING

Further reading is suggested here for African(a) philosophy as a whole, and then for the topics of individual chapters and sections of the book. This bibliography focuses on secondary literature. References for primary literature, and on more specific topics, can be found in the notes to the chapters.

General Overviews

L. Apostel, *African Philosophy: Myth or Reality?* (Gent: 1981).
P.O. Bodunrin (ed.), *Philosophy in Africa: Trends and Perspectives* (Ife: 1995).
L.M. Brown, *African Philosophy. New and Traditional Perspectives* (New York: 2004).
P.H. Coetzee and A.P.J. Roux, *The African Philosophy Reader* (London: 2003).
S.B. Diagne, *The Ink of the Scholars: Reflections on Philosophy in Africa* (Dakar: 2016).
G. Floistad (ed.), *African Philosophy* (Dordrecht: 1987).
D. Forde (ed.), *African Worlds: Studies in the Cosmological Ideas and Social Values of African Peoples* (Oxford: 1954).
S. Gbadegesin, *African Philosophy: Traditional Yoruba Philosophy and Contemporary African Realities* (New York: 1991).
R. Gooding-Williams, *In the Shadow of Du Bois: Afro-Modern Political Thought in America* (Cambridge MA: 2009).
L.R. Gordon, *An Introduction to Africana Philosophy* (Cambridge: 2008).
K. Gyekye, *An Essay on African Philosophical Thought: The Akan Conceptual Scheme* (Cambridge: 1987).
B. Hallen, *A Short History of African Philosophy* (Bloomington: 2002).
C.B. Hilliard (ed.), *Intellectual Traditions of Pre-Colonial Africa* (Boston: 1998).
P.J. Hountondji, *African Philosophy: Myth and Reality* (London: 1983).
S.O. Imbo, *An Introduction to African Philosophy* (Lanham: 1998).
J. Jahn, *Muntu: African Culture and the Western World*, trans. M. Grene (New York: 1961).
B.B. Janz, *Philosophy in an African Place* (Lanham: 2009).
C. Jeffers (ed.), *Listening to Ourselves: A Multilingual Anthology of African Philosophy* (Albany: 2013).
M. Kebede, *Africa's Quest for a Philosophy of Decolonization* (Amsterdam: 2004).
S. Kwame (ed.), *Readings in African Philosophy: An Akan Collection* (Lanham: 1995).
D.A. Masolo, *African Philosophy in Search of Identity* (Bloomington: 1994).
D.A. Masolo and I. Carp (eds), *African Philosophy as Cultural Inquiry* (Bloomington: 2000).
J.S. Mbiti, *African Religions and Philosophy* (London: 1969).
C.W. Mills, *Blackness Visible: Essays on Philosophy and Race* (Ithaca: 1998).
F. Ochieng'-Odhiambo, *Trends and Issues in African Philosophy* (New York: 2010).

O. Oladipo (ed.), *The Third Way in African Philosophy* (Ibadan: 2002), 215–32.
L.T. Outlaw, "African, African American, Africana Philosophy," *Philosophical Forum* 24 (1992), 63–93.
T. Serequeberhan (ed.), *African Philosophy: The Essential Readings* (New York: 1991).
T. Serequeberhan, *The Hermeneutics of African Philosophy: Horizon and Discourse* (London: 1994).
T. Shelby, *We Who Are Dark: The Philosophical Foundations of Black Solidarity* (Cambridge MA: 2005).
R.F. Thompson, *Flash of the Spirit: African and Afro-American Art and Philosophy* (New York: 1983).
K. Wiredu, *Philosophy and an African Culture* (Cambridge: 1980).
K. Wiredu, *Cultural Universals and Particulars: An African Perspective* (Bloomington: 1997).
K. Wiredu (ed.), *A Companion to African Philosophy* (Malden: 2004).
K. Wiredu and K. Gyekye, *Person and Community: Ghanaian Philosophical Studies I* (Washington DC: 1992).
R.A. Wright (ed.), *African Philosophy: An Introduction* (Washington: 1977).

Prehistoric Africa

A. Barnard, *Genesis of Symbolic Thought* (Cambridge: 2012).
J.D. Clark (ed.), *The Cambridge History of Africa, vol.1: From the Earliest Times to c.500 BC* (Cambridge: 1982).
J.D. Lewis-Williams, *The Rock Art of Southern Africa* (Cambridge: 1983).
J. McDonald and P. Veth (eds), *A Companion to Rock Art* (Oxford: 2012).
S. Mithen, *The Prehistory of the Mind: A Search for the Origins of Art, Religion and Science* (London: 1996).
C. Renfrew and I. Morley (eds), *Becoming Human: Innovation in Prehistoric Material and Spiritual Culture* (New York: 2009).

Philosophy in Ancient Mesopotamia

J. Black, G. Cunningham, E. Robson, and G. Zólyomi (eds), *The Literature of Ancient Sumer* (Oxford: 2004).
W. Burkert, "Prehistory of Presocratic Philosophy in an Orientalizing Context," in P. Curd and D.W. Graham (eds), *The Oxford Handbook of Presocratic Philosophy* (Oxford: 2009), 55–85.
C.S. Ehrlich (ed.), *From an Antique Land: An Introduction to Ancient Near Eastern Literature* (Lanham: 2009).
W.G. Lambert, *Babylonian Wisdom Literature* (Oxford: 1960).
O. Neugebauer, *The Exact Sciences in Antiquity* (New York: 1969).
K. Radner and E. Robson (ed.), *The Oxford Handbook of Cuneiform Culture* (Oxford: 2011).
F. Rochberg, *The Heavenly Writing: Divination, Horoscopy, and Astronomy in Mesopotamian Culture* (Cambridge: 2004).
M. Van De Mieroop, *Philosophy Before the Greeks: The Pursuit of Truth in Ancient Babylonia* (Princeton: 2016).

FURTHER READING

Philosophy in Ancient Egypt

J.P. Allen, *The Debate Between a Man and His Soul: A Masterpiece of Ancient Egyptian Literature* (Leiden: 2011).
M.K. Asante, *The Egyptian Philosophers: Ancient African Voices from Imhotep to Akhenaten* (Chicago: 2000).
J. Assmann, *The Mind of Egypt: History and Meaning in the Time of the Pharaohs* (Cambridge MA: 2003).
A. Dodson, *Amarna Sunset: Nefertiti, Tutankhamun, Ay, Horemheb, and the Egyptian Counter-Reformation* (Cairo: 2009).
H. Goedicke, *The Report about the Dispute of a Man with his Ba: Papyrus Berlin 3024* (Baltimore: 1970).
A.M. Gnirs (ed.), *Reading the Tale of the Eloquent Peasant* (Göttingen: 2000).
J.K. Hoffmeier, *Akhenaten and the Origins of Monotheism* (New York: 2015).
E. Hornung, *Akhenaten and the Religion of Light* (Ithaca: 1999).
C. Jeffers, "Embodying Justice in Ancient Egypt: *The Tale of the Eloquent Peasant* as a Classic of Political Philosophy," *British Journal for the History of Philosophy* 21 (2013), 421–42.
M. Karenga, *Maat: The Moral Ideal in Ancient Egypt. A Study in Classical African Ethics* (New York: 2004).
M. Lichtheim, *Ancient Egyptian Literature*, 3 vols (Berkeley: 1973–80).
S.B. Morrow, *The Dawning Moon of the Mind: Unlocking the Pyramid Texts* (New York: 2015).
T. Obenga, *African Philosophy: The Pharaonic Period, 2780–330 BC* (Popenguine: 2004).
R.B. Parkinson, *Poetry and Culture in Middle Kingdom Egypt: A Dark Side to Perfection* (London: 2002).
R.B. Parkinson, *The Tale of the Eloquent Peasant: A Reader's Commentary* (Hamburg: 2012).
L.V. Zabkar, *A Study of the Ba Concept in Ancient Egyptian Texts* (Chicago: 1968).

Early Ethiopian Philosophy

A. Bausi, "Translations in Late Antique Ethiopia," in F. Crevatin (ed.), *Egitto crocevia di traduzioni* (Trieste: 2018), 69–99.
S. Kelly (ed.), *A Companion to Medieval Ethiopia and Eritrea* (Leiden: 2020).
C. Sumner, *Ethiopian Philosophy*, 5 vols (Addis Ababa: 1974–82).
C. Sumner, *Classical Ethiopian Philosophy* (Addis Ababa: 1985).

Zera Yacob and Walda Heywat

L. Cantor, J. Egid, and F. Merawi (eds), *In Search of Zera Yacob* (Berlin: 2024).
D.W. Kidane, *The Ethics of Zär'a Ya'eqob* (Rome: 2012).
T. Kiros, *Zara Yacob: Rationality of the Human Heart* (Lawrenceville: 2005).
R. Lee with M. Worku and W.L. Belcher, *The Hatata Enquiries: Two Texts of Seventeenth-Century African Philosophy from Ethiopia about Reason, the Creator, and Our Ethical Responsibilities* (Berlin: 2023).

C. Sumner, *The Treatise of Zär'a Ya'əqob and of Wäldä Ḥəywat: Text and Authorship* (Addis Ababa: 1976).

C. Sumner, "The Light and the Shadow: Zera Yacob and Walda Heywat: Two Ethiopian Philosophers of the Seventeenth Century," in K. Wiredu (ed.), *A Companion to African Philosophy* (Malden: 2004), 172–82.

A. Wion, "The History of a Genuine Fake Philosophical Treatise (*Ḥatatā Zar'a Yā'eqob* and *Ḥatatā Walda Ḥeywat*)," in three parts on the online journal *Afriques*.

Islamic Philosophy in Africa

C. El Hamel, *La vie intellectuelle islamique dans le Sahel Ouest Africain* (Paris: 2002).

J.O. Hunwick, "The Arabic Literary Tradition of Nigeria," *Research in African Literatures* 28 (1997), 21–3.

S. Jeppie and S.B. Diagne (eds), *The Meanings of Timbuktu* (Cape Town: 2008).

O.O. Kane, *Beyond Timbuktu: An Intellectual History of Muslim West Africa* (Cambridge MA: 2006).

O.O. Kane (ed.), *Islamic Scholarship in Africa: New Directions and Global Contexts* (Woodbridge: 2021).

K. Kresse, *Philosophising in Mombasa: Knowledge, Islam and Intellectual Practice on the Swahili Coast* (Edinburgh: 2007).

M. Last, *The Sokoto Caliphate* (London: 1977).

P. Naylor, *From Rebels to Rulers: Writing Legitimacy in the Early Sokoto State* (Suffolk: 2021).

D. van Dalen, *Doubt, Scholarship and Society in 17th-Century Central Sudanic Africa* (Leiden: 2016).

Oral Philosophy in Africa

R. Finnegan, *Oral Literature in Africa* (Oxford: 1970).

K. Gyekye, *An Essay on African Philosophical Thought: The Akan Conceptual Scheme* (Philadelphia: 1987).

K. Gyekye, *Tradition and Modernity: Philosophical Reflections on the African Experience* (New York: 1997).

P.J. Hountondji, *African Philosophy: Myth and Reality* (Bloomington: 1996).

P.J. Hountondji, *The Struggle for Meaning: Reflections on Philosophy, Culture, and Democracy in Africa* (Athens OH: 2002).

S. Imbo, *Oral Traditions as Philosophy: Okot p'Bitek's Legacy for African Philosophy* (Lanham: 2002).

A. Kagame, *La philosophie Bantu-Rwandaise de l'être* (Brussels: 1956).

K. Kresse and O. Nyarwath (eds), *Rethinking Sage Philosophy: Interdisciplinary Perspectives on and beyond H. Odera Oruka* (Lanham: 2022).

D.A. Masolo, *African Philosophy in Search of Identity* (Bloomington: 1994).

J.S. Mbiti, *African Religions and Philosophy* (London: 1969).

T. Metz, "Toward an African Moral Theory," *Journal of Political Philosophy* 15 (2007), 321–41.

O. Ogunnaike, *Deep Knowledge: Ways of Knowing in Sufism and Ifa, Two West African Intellectual Traditions* (Philadelphia: 2020).

J.K. Olupona, *African Religions: A Very Short Introduction* (Oxford: 2014).

H.O. Oruka, *Sage Philosophy: Indigenous Thinkers and Modern Debate on African Philosophy* (Leiden: 1990).
G.M. Presbey, *The Life and Thought of H. Odera Oruka: Pursuing Justice in Africa* (London: 2023).
P. Tempels, *Bantu Philosophy* (Paris: 1959).
M. Towa, *Essai sur la problematique philosophique dans l'Afrique actuelle* (Yaounde: 1971).
K. Wiredu, *Conceptual Decolonization in African Philosophy* (Ibadan: 1995).
K. Wiredu, *Cultural Universals and Particulars: An African Perspective* (Bloomington: 1997).
K. Wiredu and K. Gyekye (eds), *Person and Community* (Washington: 1992).

Gender in African Tradition

I. Amadiume, *Male Daughters, Female Husbands: Gender and Sex in an African Society* (London: 1987).
I. Amadiume, *Reinventing Africa: Matriarchy, Religion and Culture* (New York: 1997).
A. Cornwall (ed.), *Readings in Gender in Africa* (Bloomington: 2005).
S. Kent, *Gender in African Prehistory* (Walnut Creek: 1998).
N. Nzegwu, *Family Matters: Feminist Concepts in African Philosophy of Culture* (Albany: 2006).
O. Oyewumi, *The Invention of Women: Making an African Sense of Western Gender Discourses* (Minneapolis: 1997).

Slavery and the Diaspora

D.D. Bruce, Jr., *The Origins of African American Literature, 1680–1865* (Charlottesville: 2001).
V. Carretta (ed.), *Unchained Voices: An Anthology of Black Authors in the English-Speaking World of the 18th Century* (Lexington: 1996).
S.R. Cudjoe, *Beyond Boundaries: The Intellectual Tradition of Trinidad and Tobago in the Nineteenth Century* (Wellesley: 2003).
O.R. Dathorne, *The Black Mind: A History of African Literature* (Minneapolis: 1974).
D.B. Davis, *The Problem of Slavery in the Age of Revolution, 1770–1823* (Ithaca: 1975).
D.B. Davis, *Slavery and Human Progress* (New York: 1984).
J. Jorati, *Slavery and Race: Philosophical Debates in the Eighteenth Century* (Oxford: 2023).
R. July, *The Origins of Modern African Thought: Its Development in West Africa During the Nineteenth and Twentieth Centuries* (New York: 1967).
G.K. Lewis, *Main Currents in Caribbean Thought: The Historical Evolution of Caribbean Society in Its Ideological Aspects, 1492–1900* (Baltimore: 1983).
W. Moses, *The Golden Age of Black Nationalism* (Hamden: 1978).
B.L. Solow (ed.), *Slavery and the Rise of the Atlantic System* (Cambridge: 1991).
S. Stuckey, *Slave Culture: Nationalist Theory and the Foundations of Black America* (New York: 1987).
E. Sundquist, *To Wake the Nations: Race in the Making of American Literature* (Cambridge MA: 1993).
O. Táíwò, *How Colonialism Preempted Modernity in Africa* (Bloomington: 2010).
A. Zamalin, *Struggle on Their Minds: The Political Thought of African American Resistance* (New York: 2017).

FURTHER READING

Anton Wilhelm Amo

B. Brentjes, *Anton Wilhelm Amo: der schwarze Philosoph in Halle* (Leipzig: 1976).
O. Ette, *Anton Wilhelm Amo: philosophieren ohne festen Wohnsitz. Eine Philosophie der Aufklärung zwischen Europa und Afrika* (Berlin: 2014).
J.E. Mabe, *Anton Wilhelm Amo: The Intercultural Background of His Philosophy* (Nordhausen: 2014).
S. Menn and J.E.H. Smith (trans.), *Anton Wilhelm Amo's Philosophical Dissertations on Mind and Body* (Oxford: 2020).
C. Meyns, "Anton Wilhelm Amo's Philosophy of Mind," *Philosophy Compass* 14 (2019), 1–13.
S. Mougnol, *Amo Afer: un Noir, professeur d'université en Allemagne au XVIIIe siècle* (Paris: 2010).
Y. Somet, *Anthony William Amo: sa vie et son ouevre* (Le Plessis-Trévise: 2016).

Early Africana Writing in English

T. Adeleke, *UnAfrican Americans: Nineteenth-Century Black Nationalists and the Civilizing Mission* (Lexington: 1998).
W.L. Andrews, *To Tell a Free Story: The First Century of Afro-American Autobiography* (Urbana: 1986).
K.C. Bassard, *Spiritual Interrogations: Culture, Gender, and Community in Early African American Women's Writing* (Princeton: 1999).
J. Brooks, *American Lazarus: Religion and the Rise of African-American and Native American Literatures* (New York: 2003).
J. Brooks and J. Sailliant (eds), *"Face Zion Forward": First Writers of the Black Atlantic, 1785–1798* (Boston: 2002).
D.D. Bruce Jr., *The Origins of African American Literature, 1680–1865* (Charlottesville: 2001).
V. Carretta and P. Gould (eds), *Genius in Bondage: Literature of the Early Black Atlantic* (Lexington: 2001).
B. Dain, *A Hideous Monster of the Mind: American Race Theory in the Early Republic* (Cambridge MA: 2002).
H.L. Gates Jr., *The Signifying Monkey: A Theory of African-American Literary Criticism* (New York: 1988).
P. Giddings, *When and Where I Enter: The Impact of Black Women on Race and Sex in America* (New York: 1984).
E.S. Glaude, *Exodus! Religion, Race, and Nation in Early Nineteenth-Century Black America* (Chicago: 2000).
S.G. Hall, *A Faithful Account of the Race: African American Historical Writing in Nineteenth-Century America* (Chapel Hill: 2009).
R. Hanley, *Beyond Slavery and Abolition: Black British Writing, c.1770–1830* (Cambridge: 2019).
S. Harrold, *The Rise of Aggressive Abolitionism: Addresses to the Slaves* (Lexington: 2004).
C. Jeffers, "Rights, Race, and the Beginnings of Modern Africana Philosophy," in P.C. Taylor, L.M. Alcoff, and L. Anderson (eds), *The Routledge Companion to the Philosophy of Race* (New York: 2017), 127–39.
B.J. Loewenberg and R. Bogin, *Black Women in Nineteenth-Century American Life* (University Park: 1976).

S.A. O'Neale, *Jupiter Hammon and the Biblical Beginnings of African American Literature* (Metuchen: 1993).
A. Potkay and S. Burr (eds), *Black Atlantic Writers of the Eighteenth Century: Living the New Exodus in England and the Americas* (New York: 1995).
K. Sandiford, *Measuring the Moment: Strategies of Protest in Eighteenth-Century Afro-English Writing* (Selinsgrove: 1988).
D. Sterling, *We Are Your Sisters: Black Women in the Nineteenth Century* (New York: 1984).
H. Woodard, *African-British Writings in the Eighteenth Century: The Politics of Race and Reason* (Westport: 1999).

Phillis Wheatley

V. Carretta, *Phillis Wheatley: Biography of a Genius in Bondage* (Athens GA: 2011).
M.A. Richmond, *Bid the Vassal Soar: Interpretative Essays on the Life and Poetry of Phillis Wheatley (ca. 1753–1784) and George Moses Horton (ca. 1797–1883)* (Washington DC: 1974).
W.H. Robinson, *Critical Essays on Phillis Wheatley* (Boston: 1982).
J.C. Shields, *Phillis Wheatley's Poetics of Liberation: Backgrounds and Contexts* (Knoxville: 2008).
J.C. Shields (ed.), *New Essays on Phillis Wheatley* (Knoxville: 2011).
D. Waldstreicher, *The Odyssey of Phillis Wheatley: A Poet's Journeys Through American Slavery and Independence* (New York: 2023).

Lemuel Haynes

K.P. Minkema and H.S. Stout, "The Edwardsean Tradition and the Antislavery Debate, 1740–1865," *Journal of American History* 92 (2005), 47–74.
R. Roberts, "Patriotism and Political Criticism: The Evolution of Political Consciousness in the Mind of a Black Revolutionary Soldier," *Eighteenth-Century Studies* 27 (1994), 569–88.
J. Saillant, "Lemuel Haynes and the Revolutionary Origins of Black Theology, 1776–1801," *Religion and American Culture* 2 (1992), 79–102.
J. Saillant, *Black Puritan, Black Republican: The Life and Thought of Lemuel Haynes, 1753–1833* (New York: 2003).

Ignatius Sancho and Benjamin Banneker

S.A. Bedini, *The Life of Benjamin Banneker: The First African-American Man of Science* (Baltimore: 1999).
C. Cerami, *Benjamin Banneker: Surveyor, Astronomer, Publisher, Patriot* (New York: 2002).
R. Newman, "'Good Communications Corrects Bad Manners': The Banneker–Jefferson Dialogue and the Project of White Uplift," in J.C. Hammond and M. Mason (eds), *Contesting Slavery: The Politics of Bondage and Freedom in the New American Nation* (Charlottesville: 2011), 69–93.
S.S. Sandhu, "Ignatius Sancho and Laurence Sterne," *Research in African Literatures* 29 (1998), 88–105.

FURTHER READING

Quobna Ottobah Cugoano and Olaudah Equiano

A. Bogues, *Black Heretics, Black Prophets: Radical Political Intellectuals* (New York: 2003), ch. 1.
V. Carretta, "Olaudah Equiano or Gustavus Vassa? New Light on an Eighteenth-Century Question of Identity," *Slavery and Abolition* 20 (1999), 96–105.
V. Carretta, *Equiano, the African: Biography of a Self-Made Man* (New York: 2006).
J. Gunn, "Creating a Paradox: Quobna Ottobah Cugoano and the Slave Trade's Violation of the Principles of Christianity, Reason, and Property Ownership," *Journal of World History* 21 (2010), 629–56.
P. Henry, "Between Hume and Cugoano: Race, Ethnicity and Philosophical Entrapment," *Journal of Speculative Philosophy* 18 (2004), 129–48.
M. Hoyle, *Cugoano Against Slavery* (Hertford: 2015).

The Haitian Revolution

S. Buck-Morss, "Hegel and Haiti," *Critical Inquiry* 26 (2000), 821–65.
L. Dubois, *Avengers of the New World: The Story of the Haitian Revolution* (Cambridge MA: 2004).
C. Forsdick and C. Høgsbjerg (eds), *The Black Jacobins Reader* (Durham: 2017).
D.P. Geggus, *Haitian Revolutionary Studies* (Bloomington: 2002).
C.L.R. James, *The Black Jacobins: Toussaint L'Ouverture and the San Domingo Revolution* (New York: 1989).
N. Nesbitt, *Universal Emancipation: The Haitian Revolution and the Radical Enlightenment* (Charlottesville: 2008).
L. Sala-Molins, *Dark Side of the Light: Slavery and the French Enlightenment*, trans. J. Conteh-Morgan (Minneapolis: 2006).
D. Scott, *Conscripts of Modernity: The Tragedy of Colonial Enlightenment* (Durham: 2004).

Baron de Vastey

M.L. Daut, *Baron de Vastey and the Origins of Black Atlantic Humanism* (New York: 2017).
D.L. Garraway, "Empire of Freedom, Kingdom of Civilization: Henry Christophe, the Baron de Vastey, and the Paradoxes of Universalism in Postrevolutionary Haiti," *Small Axe* 39 (2012), 1–21.
D. Jenson, *Beyond the Slave Narrative: Politics, Sex, and Manuscripts in the Haitian Revolution* (Liverpool: 2011).

Early Black Institutions in the US

J.O. Horton and L.E. Horton, *In Hope of Liberty: Culture, Community and Protest among Northern Free Blacks, 1700–1860* (New York: 1997).
W. Moses, *The Golden Age of Black Nationalism* (Hamden: 1978).
G.B. Nash, *The Forgotten Fifth: African Americans in the Age of Revolution* (Cambridge MA: 2006).
R.S. Newman, *Freedom's Prophet: Bishop Richard Allen, the AME Church, and the Black Founding Fathers* (New York: 2008).

J. Sidbury, *Becoming African in America: Race and Nation in the Early Black Atlantic* (Oxford: 2007).
C.H. Wesley, *Prince Hall: Life and Legacy*, 2nd ed. (Washington DC: 1983).

The Colonization Controversy

L.M. Alexander, *African or American? Black Identity and Political Activism in New York City, 1784–1861* (Urbana: 2008).
E. Burin, *Slavery and the Peculiar Solution: A History of the American Colonization Society* (Gainesville: 2005).
B.F. Stillion Southard, *Peculiar Rhetoric: Slavery, Freedom, and the African Colonization Movement* (Jackson: 2019).
A. Yarema, *The American Colonization Society: An Avenue to Freedom?* (Lanham: 2006).

David Walker

H. Aptheker, *"One Continual Cry": David Walker's Appeal to the Colored Citizens of the World (1829–1830), Its Setting and Its Meaning* (New York: 1965).
R. Burrow, *God and Human Responsibility: David Walker and Ethical Prophecy* (Macon: 2003).
P.P. Hinks, *To Awaken My Afflicted Brethren: David Walker and the Problem of Antebellum Slave Resistance* (University Park: 1997).
M.L. Rogers, "David Walker and the Political Power of the *Appeal*," *Political Theory* 43 (2015), 208–33.
D. Scriven, *A Dealer of Old Clothes: Philosophical Conversations with David Walker* (Lanham: 2007).

Maria W. Stewart

J.A. Carter, "The Insurrectionist Challenge to Pragmatism: Maria W. Stewart's Feminist Insurrectionist Ethics," *Transactions of the Charles S. Peirce Society* 49 (2013), 54–73.
V.C. Cooper, *Word, Like Fire: Maria Stewart, the Bible, and the Rights of African Americans* (Charlottesville: 2011).
C. Henderson, "Sympathetic Violence: Maria Stewart's Antebellum Vision of African American Resistance," *MELUS* 38 (2013), 52–75.
M. Richardson, "'What If I Am a Woman?' Maria W. Stewart's Defense of Black Women's Political Activism," in D.M. Jacobs (ed.), *Courage and Conscience: Black and White Abolitionists in Boston* (Bloomington: 1993).

Hosea Easton

G.R. Price, "Hosea Easton: Forgotten Abolitionist 'Giant,'" in M. Morrison (ed.), *The Human Tradition in Antebellum America* (Wilmington: 2000), 147–63.
E.S. Pryor, "The Etymology of Nigger: Resistance, Language, and the Politics of Freedom in the Antebellum North," *Journal of the Early Republic* 36 (2016), 203–45.
J.B. Stewart, *Abolitionist Politics and the Coming of the Civil War* (Amherst: 2008).

Frederick Douglass

W. Andrews (ed.), *Critical Essays on Frederick Douglass* (Boston: 1991).
D. Blight, *Frederick Douglass: Prophet of Freedom* (New York: 2018).
N. Buccola, *The Political Thought of Frederick Douglass: In Pursuit of American Liberty* (New York: 2012).
D.B. Chesebrough, *Frederick Douglass: Oratory from Slavery* (Westport: 1998).
J.A. Colaiaco, *Frederick Douglass and the Fourth of July* (New York: 2006).
M.S. Lee (ed.), *The Cambridge Companion to Frederick Douglass* (Cambridge: 2009).
R.S. Levine, *The Lives of Frederick Douglass* (Cambridge MA: 2016).
W.E. Martin, *The Mind of Frederick Douglass* (Chapel Hill: 1985).
P.C. Myers, *Frederick Douglass: Race and the Rebirth of American Liberalism* (Lawrence: 2008).
N. Roberts (ed.), *A Political Companion to Frederick Douglass* (Lexington: 2018).
E. Sundquist (ed.), *Frederick Douglass: New Literary and Historical Essays* (New York: 1990).
F. Sweeney, *Frederick Douglass and the Atlantic World* (Liverpool: 2007).

Henry Highland Garnet

E.O. Hutchinson, *Let Your Motto Be Resistance: The Life and Thought of Henry Highland Garnet* (Boston: 1972).
M.B. Pasternak, *Rise Now and Fly to Arms: The Life of Henry Highland Garnet* (New York: 1995).
J. Schor, *Henry Highland Garnet: A Voice of Black Radicalism in the Nineteenth Century* (Westport: 1977).

Martin Delany

T. Adeleke, *Without Regard to Race: The Other Martin Robinson Delany* (Jackson: 2004).
T. Adeleke, *In the Service of God and Humanity: Conscience, Reason, and the Mind of Martin R. Delany* (Columbia: 2021).
C.E. Griffith, *The African Dream: Martin R. Delany and the Emergence of Pan-African Thought* (University Park: 1975).
R.M. Kahn, "The Political Ideology of Martin Delany," *Journal of Black Studies* 14 (1984), 415–40.
R.S. Levine, *Martin Delany, Frederick Douglass, and the Politics of Representative Identity* (Chapel Hill: 1997).
D. Sterling, *The Making of an Afro-American: Martin Robinson Delany, 1812–1885* (Garden City: 1971).

Sojourner Truth

C. Mabee with S. Mabee Newhouse, *Sojourner Truth: Slave, Prophet, Legend* (New York: 1993).
N.I. Painter, *Sojourner Truth: A Life, a Symbol* (New York: 1996).
E. Stetson and L. David, *Glorying in Tribulation: The Lifework of Sojourner Truth* (East Lansing: 1994).

Frances Harper

M.J. Boyd, *Discarded Legacy: Politics and Poetics in the Life of Frances E.W. Harper 1825–1911* (Detroit: 1994).

M. Stancliffe, *Frances Ellen Watkins Harper: African American Reform Rhetoric and the Rise of a Modern Nation State* (New York: 2011).

Mary Ann Shadd and Samuel Ringgold Ward

G.E. Clarke, *Odysseys Home: Mapping African-Canadian Literature* (Toronto: 2002).

C. Jeffers, "Do We Need African Canadian Philosophy?" *Dialogue* 51 (2012), 643–66.

J. Rhodes, *Mary Ann Shadd Cary: The Black Press and Protest in the Nineteenth Century* (Bloomington: 1998).

W. Siemerling, *The Black Atlantic Reconsidered: Black Canadian Writing, Cultural History, and the Presence of the Past* (Montreal: 2015).

R.W. Winks, *The Blacks in Canada: A History* (Montreal: 1997).

Alexander Crummell

W. Moses, *Alexander Crummell: A Study of Civilization and Discontent* (Cary: 1989).

J.R. Oldfield, *Alexander Crummell (1819–1898) and the Creation of an African-American Church in Liberia* (Lampeter: 1990).

G.U. Rigsby, *Alexander Crummell: Pioneer in Nineteenth-Century Pan-African Thought* (New York: 1987).

James Africanus Beale Horton

A. Adeloye, *Doctor James Africanus Beale Horton: West African Medical Scientist of the 19th Century* (Pittsburgh: 1992).

E.A. Ayandele, "James Africanus Beale Horton, 1835–1883: Prophet of Modernization in Africa," *African Historical Studies* 4 (1971), 691–707.

C. Fyfe, *Africanus Horton, 1835–1883, West African Scientist and Patriot* (New York: 1972).

Edward Blyden

T. Falola, *Nationalism and African Intellectuals* (Rochester: 2001).

E. Holden, *Blyden of Liberia* (New York: 1966).

R. July, *The Origins of Modern African Thought: Its Development in West Africa During the Nineteenth and Twentieth Centuries* (New York: 1967).

H.R. Lynch, *Edward Wilmot Blyden: Pan-Negro Patriot, 1832–1912* (London: 1967).

H.N.K. Odamtten, *Edward W. Blyden's Intellectual Transformations: Afropublicanism, Pan-Africanism, Islam, and the Indigenous West African Church* (East Lansing: 2019).

T. Tibebu, *Edward Wilmot Blyden and the Racial Nationalist Imagination* (Rochester: 2012).

FURTHER READING

T. Thomas Fortune

T.J. Curry, "The Fortune of Wells: Ida B. Wells-Barnett's Use of T. Thomas Fortune's Philosophy of Social Agitation as a Prolegomenon to Militant Civil Rights Activism," *Transactions of the Charles S. Peirce Society* 48 (2012), 456–82.

B.R. Justesen, *Broken Brotherhood: The Rise and Fall of the National Afro-American Council* (Carbondale: 2008).

E.L. Thornbrough, *T. Thomas Fortune: Militant Journalist* (Chicago: 1972).

Anténor Firmin

R. Bernasconi, "A Haitian in Paris: Anténor Firmin as a Philosopher against Racism," *Patterns of Prejudice* 42 (2008), 365–83.

Y. Chemla, "Louis-Joseph Janvier, écrivain national," *Francofonia* 49 (2005), 7–36.

T.J. Curry, "From Rousseau's Theory of Natural Equality to Firmin's Resistance to the Historical Inequality of Races," *CLR James Journal* 15 (2009), 135–63.

C. Fluehr-Lobban, "Anténor Firmin: Haitian Pioneer of Anthropology," *American Anthropologist* 102 (2000), 449–66.

D.W. Leonard, "Writing Against the Grain: Anténor Firmin and the Refutation of Nineteenth-Century European Race Science," in K. Radcliffe (ed.) *Anywhere But Here: Black Intellectuals in the Atlantic World and Beyond* (Jackson: 2014), 27–46.

J. Price-Mars, *Joseph Anténor Firmin* (Haiti: 1964).

J.J. Thomas and F.A. Durham

S.R. Cudjoe, *Beyond Boundaries: The Intellectual Tradition of Trinidad and Tobago in the Nineteenth Century* (Wellesley: 2003).

C.L.R. James, "The West Indian Intellectual," in J.J. Thomas, *Froudacity* (London: 1969), 23–49.

R. Lewis, "J.J. Thomas and Political Thought in the Caribbean," *Caribbean Quarterly* 36 (1990), 46–58.

M. Sherwood, *Origins of Pan-Africanism: Henry Sylvester Williams, Africa, and the African Diaspora* (London: 2010).

F.L. Smith, *Creole Recitations: John Jacob Thomas and Colonial Formation in the Late Nineteenth-Century Caribbean* (Charlottesville: 2002).

Abolitionism in Brazil

C. Braga-Pinto, "The Honor of the Abolitionist and the Shamefulness of Slavery: Raul Pompeia, Luiz Gama, and Joaquim Nabuco," *Luso-Brazilian Review* 51 (2014), 170–99.

L.C. Dos Santos, *Luiz Gama* (São Paulo: 2010).

J.H. Kennedy, "Luiz Gama: Pioneer of Abolition in Brazil," *The Journal of Negro History* 59 (1974), 255–67.

H.S. Klein and F. Vidal Luna, *Slavery in Brazil* (Cambridge: 2010).

C. Nabuco, *The Life of Joaquim Nabuco*, trans. R. Hilton (Stanford: 1950).

A.J.R. Russell-Wood, *The Black Man in Slavery and Freedom in Colonial Brazil* (New York: 1982).
R. Schwarz, *A Master on the Periphery of Capitalism: Machado de Assis*, trans. J. Gledson (Durham: 2001).

Anna Julia Cooper

E. Alexander, "'We Must Be about Our Father's Business': Anna Julia Cooper and the In-Corporation of the Nineteenth-Century African-American Woman Intellectual," *Signs* 20 (1995), 336–56.
K. Baker-Fletcher, *A Singing Something: Womanist Reflections on Anna Julia Cooper* (New York: 1994).
H. Carby, *Reconstructing Womanhood: The Emergence of the Afro-American Woman Novelist* (New York: 1987).
C. Jeffers, "Anna Julia Cooper and the Black Gift Thesis," *History of Philosophy Quarterly* 33 (2016), 79–97.
V. May, *Anna Julia Cooper, Visionary Black Feminist: A Critical Introduction* (New York: 2007).

Ida B. Wells

P.J. Giddings, *Ida, a Sword Among Lions: Ida B. Wells and the Campaign against Lynching* (New York: 2008).
L.O. McMurry, *Keep the Waters Troubled: The Life of Ida B. Wells* (Oxford: 1998).
P.A. Schechter, *Ida B. Wells-Barnett and American Reform 1880–1930* (Chapel Hill: 2001).
S.L. Silkey, *Black Woman Reformer: Ida B. Wells, Lynching, and Transatlantic Activism* (Athens GA: 2015).
A.D. Sims, *Ethical Complications of Lynching: Ida B. Wells's Interrogation of American Terror* (New York: 2010).

Henry McNeal Turner

S.W. Angell, *Bishop Henry McNeal Turner and African-American Religion in the South* (Knoxville: 1992).
A.E. Johnson, *The Forgotten Prophet: Bishop Henry McNeal Turner and the African American Prophetic Tradition* (Blue Ridge Summit: 2012).
A.E. Johnson, *No Future in This Country: The Prophetic Pessimism of Bishop Henry McNeal Turner* (Jackson: 2020).
A.B. Pinn, "'Double Consciousness' in Nineteenth-Century Black Nationalism: Reflections on the Teachings of Bishop Henry McNeal Turner," *Journal of Religious Thought* 52 (1995), 15–26.

Booker T. Washington

T. Adeleke (ed.), *Booker T. Washington: Interpretive Essays* (New York: 1998).
W.F. Brundage (ed.), *Booker T. Washington and Black Progress: Up from Slavery 100 Years Later* (Gainesville: 2003).

D. Cunningen, R.M. Dennis, and M.G. Glascoe (eds), *The Racial Politics of Booker T. Washington* (Amsterdam: 2006).

L.R. Harlan, *Booker T. Washington: The Making of a Black Leader, 1856–1901* (New York: 1972).

L.R. Harlan, *Booker T. Washington: The Wizard of Tuskegee, 1901–1915* (New York: 1983).

L.R. Harlan, *Booker T. Washington in Perspective*, ed. R. Smock (Jackson: 2006).

D.H. Jackson Jr., *Booker T. Washington and the Struggle Against White Supremacy: The Southern Educational Tours 1908–1912* (New York: 2008).

D. Sehat, "The Civilizing Mission of Booker T. Washington," *Journal of Southern History* 73 (2007), 323–62.

M.R. West, *The Education of Booker T. Washington: American Democracy and the Idea of Race Relations* (New York: 2006).

W.E.B. Du Bois

A. Appiah, "The Uncompleted Argument: Du Bois and the Illusion of Race," *Critical Inquiry* 12 (1985), 21–37.

L. Balfour, *Democracy's Reconstruction: Thinking Politically with W.E.B. Du Bois* (New York: 2011).

B.W. Bell, E.R. Grosholz, and J.B. Stewart (eds), *W.E.B. Du Bois on Race and Culture: Philosophy, Politics, and Poetics* (New York: 1996).

L.K. Bright, "Du Bois' Democratic Defence of the Value Free Ideal," *Synthese* 195 (2018), 2227–45.

D.L. Lewis, *W.E.B. Du Bois: Biography of a Race, 1868–1919* (New York: 1993).

D.L. Lewis, *W.E.B Du Bois: The Fight for Equality and the American Century* (New York: 2000).

INDEX

Abyssinia: see Ethiopia
Adeleke, Tunde 314–315, 409, 412
Africa
    African Americans 9, 185, 240–248, 252, 257, 259, 262–264, 272, 276–277, 280–283, 299, 304, 308, 312–317, 324–326, 327–330, 338–339, 342, 353, 359, 360–362, 382, 401–407, 410–411, 416, 423, 427–430
    African Canadians 4, 327–335
    African Methodist Episcopal Church 242, 251, 409
    "Afro-American" 359, 362–367, 407
    Afro-Caribbean people 4, 376
    Afro-Trinidadians 225, 370, 383
    pan-Africanism 383
Africana ix–xi, 3–9, 14, 15, 56, 62, 66, 71, 79, 84–87, 91, 165–166, 174, 182, 214–216, 221, 235, 244, 256, 259, 273, 276, 300, 335, 352, 354, 357, 373, 376, 384, 393, 424, 430, 433
Aggrey, J.E.K. 423
Aḥmad Bābā 74–75, 80
Ajami 79, 443
Akan
    Language 110–111, 117, 151, 154–155, 348
    People ix, 97, 103, 108–109, 117–118, 126, 130, 143, 151, 171, 175
Akhenaten ix, 26–29, 100, 313
Aksum 48, 50, 59
Allen, Richard 241–247, 249, 253, 258, 279
Al-Wali al-Maliki, Muhammad 76–77
Almoravid Empire 72
Amadiume, Ifi 131–132, 134
American Colonization Society 251, 253, 263, 270, 280, 307, 310, 328, 352, 410
Amo, Anton Wilhelm x, 170–178, 182, 191
Anthropology 14, 22, 85, 87–88, 92, 94–96, 99, 115, 119, 120–124, 129, 133, 152, 173, 358, 368–371, 374, 375, 413, 430
    paleoanthropology 11, 15
Appiah, Kwame Anthony 125, 429
Aquinas, Thomas 147
archaeology 129

Aristotle 19, 23, 24–25, 47, 53, 55, 98, 154, 162, 177, 351, 370
Arsenal Football Club 150–151, 153, 286
asceticism 54–55, 64, 81, 394
Ashʿarite school 83
Askia Muḥammad 73–74, 76
Asmaʾu, Nana 79–83
de Assis, Machado 389, 392
Augustine 5, 9, 47, 115, 170, 177, 381, 393–394

Babylon 17–19, 21–23
Banneker, Benjamin 205, 209, 211–214, 313, 413
Bantu
    Languages 70, 90–91, 96–98, 114, 136, 341
    Peoples 89–91, 95, 99, 138, 143, 151
Bantu Philosophy 137, 152, 156
beauty 103, 190, 321, 333, 339, 417
Bello, Muhammad 79–80, 83–85
Benin 88, 136, 156
Bible 22, 34, 48–50, 59, 167, 180, 213, 222, 243, 250, 253, 272, 288, 320, 341, 348, 363, 413
Blackness 74–75, 168, 220, 413
Blyden, Edward x, 336, 350, 351–359, 363, 374, 376–377, 381–383, 414, 423, 430
Brazil 165, 385–392

Canada 4, 186, 293, 314, 326, 327–335, 353, 360, 379
Capitein, Jacobus 166, 176–178, 182
causation 88, 104, 106, 126
Christianity 45, 47–48, 54–55, 57–59, 87–88, 96, 100, 102, 105, 124, 133, 166, 177, 183, 191, 193, 198, 209, 222, 267, 287, 312, 321, 339, 341, 352, 354–355, 363, 376, 395
Consciousness 6, 14, 107, 110, 112
    Double consciousness 430–432
    racial consciousness 393
Cooper, Anna Julia 313, 340, 383, 393–400, 426, 430
Coker, Daniel 249–251, 253
colonialism 7, 69, 84, 87–88, 92, 106, 116, 142, 146, 154, 166, 235, 338
communalism 113–119, 146, 229

INDEX

Coptic 48, 50, 57
Cornish, Samuel 254, 259, 336, 360
Creole 377–378, 381
Crowther, Samuel Ajayi 339, 348, 350, 377
Crummell, Alexander x, 268, 301–303, 308–309, 336–343, 344–347, 349–350, 352–353, 365, 371–372, 397–398, 427
Cuffe, Paul 251–256, 276, 313, 328, 383
Cugoano, Quobna Ottobah 162, 165–167, 180, 215–224, 256, 353

definition 41, 171, 201–202, 241, 429
  of philosophy ix–xi, 7–9, 11, 136–137, 139, 153, 172
Delany, Martin 244, 291, 310–317, 324, 328, 334–335, 336, 338, 340, 342, 346, 383, 398–399, 414, 430
Delorme, Demesvar 374
democracy 115–117, 331, 428
Dessalines, Jean-Jacques 226–227, 230–231, 233–234
diaspora ix–x, 4, 6–8, 71, 121, 161, 166, 181, 242, 256, 311
Diop, Cheikh Anta 127
Dispute Between a Man and His Ba 38, 41–42
divination 97, 120–126, 146, 157, 171, 229
Douglass, Frederick x–xi, 232, 274, 277, 284, 285–292, 293–300, 301, 306–308, 311, 315, 318–321, 324, 326, 336–337, 343, 359–363, 366, 371, 374, 387, 398, 402, 405, 407, 410, 413–414, 417, 418–419, 421
dualism 107–108, 117, 173–175
Du Bois, W.E.B 244, 337, 340, 383, 399, 407, 419–420, 424–433
Durham, F.A. 376–377, 380–384

Easton, Hosea 274–284
education 32, 35, 74, 76, 146–147, 171, 189–190, 193, 208, 222, 244, 266–270, 273, 277, 288, 303, 313, 324, 338, 343, 350, 366, 368, 372–373, 405, 407, 416–419
  industrial 421
  Western 148, 171, 356–357
  of women 396
Egypt ix, xi, 5, 15, 16–17, 20, 24–29, 30–37, 38–44, 47, 78, 85, 128, 244, 256, 263, 373
  Ancient kingdoms 31, 35, 39
  glorification of 279–281, 313, 316, 423
  Israelites in 312, 353
  Mediaeval 48–49, 57, 59, 73
  Modern 351

religion 24–29, 86, 100
  theory of time 93–95
emancipation
  Emancipation Day 293–294, 299–300, 308
  Emancipation Proclamation 315–316, 321
  of slaves in the Caribbean 298
  of slaves in Europe 217, 230, 298
  of slaves in North America 183, 196, 246, 250–251, 260, 282, 290–291
  of women 79
Enbaqom 54–55, 58, 61
England 62, 169, 179, 181–185, 206, 211, 216–218, 222–223, 256, 295, 299, 307–308, 330, 337–338, 350, 378–380, 383, 402
epistemology 11, 19, 22, 145, 156, 171
Equiano, Olaudah 180, 185–186, 215–224, 239, 256, 286, 347
ethics 11, 29, 73, 80, 88, 115, 126, 211
Ethiopia 5, 45, 47–55, 56–62, 63–69, 71, 87, 97, 167, 211, 220, 244, 313, 316, 354, 373, 381, 382, 413
  "Ethiopia shall soon stretch out her hands unto God" 244, 354
  literature 47, 50, 54, 56
  monarchy (*see* "Solomonic dynasty")
  prehistoric 12
  Ethiopian Orthodox Church 48, 54, 59, 69
ethnophilosophy 88, 91–92, 135–137, 139–142, 146–148, 150–154, 156–157, 170
Europe x, 3, 6, 11–13, 17, 47, 68, 90, 95, 123, 127–128, 131, 141, 145, 157, 163, 166, 170–176, 184, 202, 227, 235, 238, 279, 356, 358, 385, 419, 425–429
Ezana 48

Firmin, Anténor 368–375, 376, 400, 413
Fortune, T. Thomas 359, 360–367, 402, 405, 409, 425
France 8, 10, 12–13, 62, 158, 198, 209, 213, 226–230, 234–236, 358, 374, 393, 420
freedom
  for African Americans slaves 9, 199, 243, 246, 255, 257, 327, 334
  for Africans in early modern Europe 176–177, 184, 186, 189, 222
  divine 83, 198, 321
  human 201, 207, 218, 271, 283, 292, 295, 299–300, 319, 405
  intellectual 291
  purchase of 222, 249, 260, 285, 291
  universality of 195, 232, 236

494

INDEX

Froude, James 378–381
Fulani 76, 79–80, 181

Gama, Luiz 386, 388
Gannibal, Abram Petrovich 170–171
Garrison, William Lloyd 191, 254, 268, 290–291, 294, 297, 299, 306–307, 319, 387
Garnet, Henry Highland 244, 258, 279, 300, 301–309, 328, 336, 338
Gates, Henry Louis 180
Gbadegesin, Segun 110
Ge'ez
    language 48, 50, 52, 56, 66–67
    literature 49, 50, 53–54
Getachew Haile 67–68
Ghana
    empire 72
    modern state 7, 95, 97, 104, 111, 136, 153, 171, 357
    University of 153, 156
gender 1, 61, 88, 102, 127–134, 146, 241, 246, 272, 291–292, 322–323, 373, 399, 403, 415
Giyorgis of Segla 57
Gordon, Lewis 4, 264
Grenada 161, 216, 233, 260, 378–379
Gronniosaw, James Albert Ukawsaw 179–186, 215
group agency 150–151
Gyekye, Kwame 97, 108, 117, 126, 141, 153, 378

Habesha 47
Haiti ix, 225, 225–232, 233–40, 248, 258, 285, 292, 301, 308, 311, 344, 368, 371–375, 383, 385, 420
    revolution 225–232
Hall, Prince 243–244, 247, 252, 256, 259, 270, 313
Hammon, Jupiter 184–185, 191, 259, 313
Hardjedef 31
Harper, Frances Ellen Watkins 323, 402
Hatata Zera Yacob 56–62
Hatata Walda Heywat 56, 57–62
al-Ḥarīrī 351
Hausa 78–90
Haynes, Lemuel 186, 196–204, 212, 220, 243, 247
Hegel, G.W.F. 231, 431
hijra 71
Hountondji, Paulin 88, 92, 136–141, 152, 156–157, 175
Horton, James Africanus Beale 344–350
Humanitism 391

humanity 12, 27, 115, 128, 167, 178, 207, 225, 237, 263, 283, 289, 304, 346, 368, 375, 389, 396, 399
    inhumanity 208
hygiene 65, 221

Idowu, E. Bolaji 100–101
Igbo 108, 132–133, 143, 221–222, 347–348
Imhotep 26, 214
India 3, 10, 19, 47, 86, 88, 107, 223
    Indian Ocean 165
Instruction Addressed to King Merikare 35–36, 78
Instruction of Amenemope 34
Islam x–xi, 5, 45, 87–88, 100, 103, 124, 128, 162, 181, 238, 412
    according to Blyden 352–354, 247, 376
    in early modern East Africa 54–55, 57–59, 61, 68
    in early modern West Africa 70, 72–77
    in Sokoto caliphate 80–85
Īśvarakṛṣṇa 109

James, C.L.R. 225–226, 230, 433
Janvier, Louis-Joseph 369–371
Jefferson, Thomas 190–191, 203, 209–213, 217, 231–232, 261–263, 277
Jones, Absalom 241–242, 244–245, 247
journalism 307, 359, 361, 367, 425
Judaism 54, 61, 100, 102, 222, 347
justice
    divine 18, 21, 80–81, 264
    legal 19, 39–43, 364–365, 417
    moral 185, 205, 220, 228, 250, 295–296

Kagamé, Alexis 90–91, 98–99, 136, 138–139, 341
Kamau, Chege 146
Kant, Immanuel 8, 141
Kebra Nagast 49–52, 69
Kikuyu 146
King, Jr., Martin Luther 4, 305
Kongo
    people 104, 229
kra 108–112, 175
Kush (*see* Nubia)

Latino, Juan 167–169, 182, 381
Lee, Jarena 246, 272
Liberia 251, 254–255, 263, 280, 301–302, 307, 309, 310, 320, 336–343, 344, 347, 349–351, 352–356, 358, 376–377, 380–394, 411
Life and Maxims of Secundus 47, 49

logic 72–73, 156, 171, 288, 321, 363, 412
Luo 145

ma'at 36, 40–43, 78
magic 26, 74, 79, 82, 89, 104, 119, 121–125, 229
Marrant, John 180, 186, 197, 215, 244
Marx, Karl 147, 260, 375
Masolo, D.A. 9, 146–147
Massachusetts 196–197, 204, 243–244, 247, 251, 259, 262, 276–277, 279, 319, 425
Mbiti, John 96–98, 101, 103, 113–114, 117, 128, 136, 139, 143, 146, 151–152
McDowell, John 7
medicine 24, 26, 105, 120–126, 146, 312, 323, 345
    prophetic 82
Menkiti, Ifeanyi 112, 114, 117–118
Mesopotamia xi, 5, 16–23, 25, 30, 34, 49, 342
metaphysics 7, 11, 24, 90, 145, 167, 220
Mills, Charles 297
modernity 6, 52, 92, 141, 350
    anatomical modernity 11–12
monotheism 26, 100–102, 183, 311, 313
    of Akhenaten 26–28
    diffused monotheism 128, 131, 339

Nabuco, Joaquim 387–389, 390–392
Nāgārjuna 147
nationalism 9, 57, 316–317, 414
    black nationalism 311, 316, 334
    Haitian 374
Nefer-Seshem-Re 30
Neoplatonism 55, 173
Ngugi wa Thiong'o 350
"nigger" 282, 288
Nova Scotia 186, 224, 244, 327
Nubia 27, 44–45, 47, 50
Nyame 103, 108–109

Odera Oruka, Henry 142, 143–149, 151, 153, 320, 326
Olodumare 101–102, 104, 110
Oral
    cultures 5–6, 22, 85, 151, 154, 378, 423
    philosophy x, 86–92, 103, 137–141, 145, 158
oriśa 101–102, 104, 110, 121
Osun 102
Outlaw, Jr., Lucius 4
Oyewumi, Oyeronke 131, 134

Parliament-Funkadelic 107
p'Bitek, Okot 91–92, 148

personhood ix, 88, 107–109, 112, 114, 117–118, 348
Physiologus 48–49
Plato 3, 16, 19, 35, 53, 55, 78, 82, 86–87, 102, 107–109, 111, 136, 139, 145, 147, 151, 374
    dialogues 19, 53, 107, 250
    theory of forms 53, 237
Plotinus 5, 111, 173
politics 23, 85, 142, 290, 339, 349, 356, 361–362, 363, 365, 396
    communalistic 113–119
political philosophy 4, 23, 30–37, 40, 162, 218, 258, 279, 326
polytheism 100–101
Pompeia, Raul 387, 390
Portugal 3, 58, 163
power ontology 89
Ptahhotep 31–34, 41
Pyramid Texts 25, 28, 42

Quakers 222–223, 249, 251, 276
Quran 55, 73, 81–82, 183, 351

race 59, 74–75, 178, 189, 199, 211–212, 227, 230, 255–256, 262, 281, 299, 311, 315, 322–324, 333, 338, 340, 342, 345–348, 352–359, 360–367, 370–375, 376–382, 387–389, 397–400, 401, 404–407, 408–409, 415, 416–422, 424, 429–431
    human 104, 177, 227, 235, 237, 294
    mixed 197, 250
    philosophy of 235, 275, 297
    war 227
racism 168, 236, 240, 247, 252, 258, 261–262, 270, 275–278, 286, 290–292, 312, 315, 330–333, 380, 402, 414, 417, 419, 422
Ramadan 351
rationality 19, 60, 65, 68, 116, 121, 125, 208, 210–211, 372, 396, 403, 407
    irrationality 124
reasoning (*see* rationality)
resistance 258, 268, 300, 301–309, 313, 315, 361
    violent 203, 215, 261, 263, 271–272, 278, 282, 363
Russwurm, John 254–256, 259, 308, 336, 360, 414

Sage Philosophy 118, 143–149, 153, 171, 320
Sahara 70–71, 74, 130, 165
Sahel 70–71
Sāṃkhya 107

INDEX

Sancho, Ignatius 205–214, 235, 239–240, 256, 337, 390, 413
al-Sanūsī 76
science 15, 16, 24, 121, 125–126, 140–141, 157, 211–212, 220, 256, 262, 266, 269, 272, 316, 338, 368–374, 387
self
  self-determination 255, 269
  self-government 379–383, 391, 407
  self-improvement 272, 278, 280, 282
  self-sufficiency 118, 286, 396
Shadd, Mary Ann 326, 328–335, 360
Shehu (see 'Uthmān Dan Fodio')
Sierra Leone 223–224, 237, 251–255, 337, 345–350, 355–356, 411
slaves
  narratives 179–180, 216, 239–240, 290
  owners 220, 227, 230, 232, 239, 250, 266, 287, 304
  revolt 203, 226, 233, 240, 261, 305
slavery
  Atlantic 4, 161–168, 170, 181, 200, 385
  Egyptian 19–20
  Roman 176
  Trans-Saharan 74–77, 80, 101
Smith, James McCune 299, 302, 306, 308
Smith-Ruiu, Justin (formerly Justin E.H. Smith) 10, 176, 178
sociology 427–428
Socrates 9, 10, 35, 46, 53, 86, 139, 145, 147, 237, 250, 326, 422
Sokoto caliphate ix, xi, 77, 78–85, 100, 182
Solomonic dynasty of Ethiopia 49
Soul 86, 95, 107–111, 138, 158, 168, 173, 177–178, 183, 191–194, 197, 201, 203, 213, 220, 248, 269–273, 276, 290, 295, 299, 308, 338, 344, 354, 370, 431, 432
Spain 164, 167–168, 198, 227, 377
Sterne, Laurence 206–208, 239, 390
Sumer 17
Stewart, Maria W. 265, 266–273, 274–275, 277–280, 283, 305, 312–313, 323–324, 336, 394
Swahili 70–71, 85, 96, 123

Taino 164
Taiwo, Olufemi 6, 350
Tale of the Eloquent Peasant 37, 38–39, 78
Tempels, Placide 88–92, 97, 114, 136–138, 142, 143, 152, 156, 170
Terence 170, 262

theodicy 21, 126, 183, 411–412
Thomas, John Jacob 376–384
Timbuktu 70–77, 182
time 93–98, 103, 113, 146, 348
Towa, Marcien 140, 453
translation
  into Ge'ez 49–50, 53–55
  into Yoruba 348
  of Creole 378
  of Egyptian 41, 42
Turner, Henry McNeal 359, 408–415
Turner, Nat 261, 305
Tutankhamun 28
Tutu, Desmond 115
Truth, Sojourner 284, 318–326, 337, 360, 418

Ubuntu 114–115
United States of America 259, 294, 303, 306
da Urbino, Giusto 56
'Uthmān Dan Fodio 77, 78–81, 83–84
Utilitarianism 115

de Vastey, Baron ix, 233–240
Vesey, Denmark 258, 305
virtue 33–35, 71, 81–82, 115, 201, 270, 312, 341, 357, 422

Walda Heywat 49, 56, 62, 63–69, 76
Walatta Petros 69
Walker, David 242, 244, 253, 257–265, 266, 270, 274, 300, 305, 312, 319, 323, 338
war 221, 224, 226, 280, 295, 302, 305
  American Civil 260, 268, 285, 292, 296, 308, 311, 315, 324
  American Revolutionary 276, 284, 327
  ideological 306
  Vietnam 327
Washington, Booker T. 313, 336–337, 393, 407, 416–423
Washington, George 190, 201–202, 243, 313, 394, 420
Washington DC 205, 214, 301, 306, 335, 363, 393–394, 427
Ward, Samuel Ringgold 302, 328–329, 336
Wells, Ida B. 366, 401–408, 417, 419
Wheatley, Phillis 169, 185–186, 188–195, 200, 205, 208, 210, 235, 240, 259, 313, 324
Whipper, William 312
Williams Jr., Peter 254, 256, 327
Williams, Henry Sylvester 383

Wion, Anaïs 56, 66–67
Wiredu, Kwasi 7–8, 115–117, 126, 135–136, 140–141, 151–156, 175
witchcraft 104, 110, 119, 120–126, 132, 135

X, Malcolm 7, 215–216, 220

Yoruba
　language 131, 348
　people 96, 98, 132, 143, 151, 308, 311, 314, 339, 347, 382, 386
　religious beliefs 101–102, 104–105, 108–112, 121

Zagwe dynasty 49
Zera Yacob (Philosopher) 49, 56–62, 63–69, 76, 162
Zulu
　language 114, 190
　people 91